Fodor's 2012

BOSTON

W9-BEH-435

Fodor's Travel Publications   New York, Toronto, London, Sydney, Auckland
www.fodors.com

Eugene Fodor:
The Spy Who Loved Travel

As Fodor's celebrates our 75th anniversary, we are honoring the colorful and adventurous life of Eugene Fodor, who revolutionized guidebook publishing in 1936 with his first book, *On the Continent, The Entertaining Travel Annual.*

Eugene Fodor's life seemed to leap off the pages of a great spy novel. Born in Hungary, he spoke six languages and graduated from the Sorbonne and the London School of Economics. During World War II he joined the Office of Strategic Services, the budding spy agency for the United States. He commanded the team that went behind enemy lines to liberate Prague, and recommended to Generals Eisenhower, Bradley, and Patton that Allied troops move to the capital city. After the war, Fodor worked as a spy in Austria, posing as a U.S. diplomat.

In 1949 Eugene Fodor—with the help of the CIA—established Fodor's Modern Guides. He was passionate about travel and wanted to bring his insider's knowledge of Europe to a new generation of sophisticated Americans who wanted to explore and seek out experiences beyond their borders. Among his innovations were annual updates, consulting local experts, and including cultural and historical perspectives and an emphasis on people—not just sites. As Fodor described it, "The main interest and enjoyment of foreign travel lies not only in 'the sites,' . . . but in contact with people whose customs, habits, and general outlook are different from your own."

Eugene Fodor died in 1991, but his legacy, Fodor's Travel, continues. It is now one of the world's largest and most trusted brands in travel information, covering more than 600 destinations worldwide in guidebooks, on Fodors.com, and in ebooks and iPhone apps. Technology and the accessibility of travel may be changing, but Eugene Fodor's unique storytelling skills and reporting style are behind every word of today's Fodor's guides.

Our editors and writers continue to embrace Eugene Fodor's vision of building personal relationships through travel. We invite you to join the Fodor's community at fodors.com/community and share your experiences with like-minded travelers. Tell us when we're right. Tell us when we're wrong. And share fantastic travel secrets that aren't yet in Fodor's. Together, we will continue to deepen our understanding of our world.

Happy 75th Anniversary, Fodor's! Here's to many more.

Tim Jarrell, Publisher

FODOR'S BOSTON 2012
Editor: Stephanie Butler

Writers: Bethany Cassin Beckerlegge, Amanda Knorr, Susan MacCallum-Whitcomb, Lisa Oppenheimer

Production Editor: Carrie Parker
Maps & Illustrations: Mark Stroud and Harry Colomb, Moon Street Cartography; David Lindroth, Inc.; Mapping Specialists, *cartographers;* Bob Blake, Rebecca Baer, *map editors;* William Wu, *information graphics*
Design: Fabrizio La Rocca, *creative director;* Guido Caroti, Siobhan O'Hare, *art directors;* Tina Malaney, Nora Rosansky, Chie Ushio, *designers;* Melanie Marin, *senior picture editor*
Cover Photo: (Faneuil Hall Market Place) G. Cam/eStock Photo
Production Manager: Angela L. McLean

ISBN 978–0–679–00925–2

ISSN 0882-0074

SPECIAL SALES
This book is available at special discounts for bulk purchases for sales promotions or premiums. Special editions, including personalized covers, excerpts of existing books, and corporate imprints, can be created in large quantities for special needs. For more information, write to Special Markets/Premium Sales, 1745 Broadway, MD 6-2, New York, NY 10019, or e-mail specialmarkets@randomhouse.com.

AN IMPORTANT TIP & AN INVITATION
Although all prices, opening times, and other details in this book are based on information supplied to us at press time, changes occur all the time in the travel world, and Fodor's cannot accept responsibility for facts that become outdated or for inadvertent errors or omissions. So **always confirm information when it matters,** especially if you're making a detour to visit a specific place. Your experiences—positive and negative—matter to us. If we have missed or misstated something, **please write to us.** Share your opinion instantly through our online feedback center at fodors.com/contact-us.

PRINTED IN CHINA

10 9 8 7 6 5 4 3 2 1

CONTENTS

CONTENTS

MAPS

ABOUT
THIS BOOK

Our Ratings

At Fodor's, we spend considerable time choosing the best places in a destination so you don't have to. By default, anything we recommend in this book is worth visiting. But some sights, properties, and experiences are so great that we've recognized them with additional accolades. Orange **Fodor's Choice** stars indicate our top recommendations; black stars highlight places we deem **Highly Recommended**; and **Best Bets** call attention to top properties in various categories. Disagree with any of our choices? Care to nominate a new place? Visit our feedback center at www.fodors.com/feedback.

TripAdvisor ⊙⊙

Fodor's partnership with TripAdvisor helps to ensure that our hotel selections are timely and relevant, taking into account the latest customer feedback about each property. Our team of expert writers selects what we believe will be the top choices for lodging in a destination. Then, those choices are reinforced by TripAdvisor reviews, so only the best properties make the cut.

Hotels

Hotels have private bath, phone, TV, and air-conditioning, and do not offer meals unless we specify that in the review. We always list facilities but not whether you'll be charged an extra fee to use them.

Restaurants

Unless we state otherwise, restaurants are open for lunch and dinner daily. We mention dress only when there's a specific requirement and reservations only when they're essential or not accepted—it's always best to book ahead.

Credit Cards

We assume that restaurants and hotels accept credit cards. If not, we'll note it in the review.

Budget Well

Hotel and restaurant price categories from ¢ to $$$$ are defined in the opening pages of the respective chapters. For attractions, we always give standard adult admission fees; reductions are usually available for children, students, and senior citizens.

Listings
★ Fodor's Choice
★ Highly recommended
⊠ Physical address
✛ Directions or Map coordinates
⌂ Mailing address
☎ Telephone
🖷 Fax
⊕ On the Web
✎ E-mail
☜ Admission fee
☉ Open/closed times
Ⓜ Metro stations
▭ No credit cards

Hotels & Restaurants
☷ Hotel
↱ Number of rooms
⌂ Facilities
⼁O⼁ Meal plans
✗ Restaurant
☺ Reservations
⽟ Dress code
↘ Smoking

Outdoors
🏌 Golf
⚠ Camping

Other
☾ Family-friendly
⇨ See also
⊠ Branch address
☞ Take note

Experience
Boston

BOSTON TODAY

Boston is the undisputed epicenter of American History. Much of the political ferment that spawned the nation took place here, and visitors are often awed by the dense concentration of sites. Locals, on the other hand, take them in stride. Sure, they revere Revere as much as the next guy. Yet Bostonians refuse to see their hometown as some sort of frozen-in-time memorial to the days of yore. This is a living city—not a living history museum—and, as such, it continues to evolve.

Gone Baby Gone
After 15 years and $15 billion, the Big Dig is done. Removing the elevated highway that bisected central Boston and replacing it with tunnels was a boon to motorists. The bonus for pedestrians is that the land the Central Artery formerly occupied has been transformed into a mile-long linear park. Lovely in its own right, the new Rose Fitzgerald Kennedy Greenway makes it much easier for walkers continuing past Faneuil Hall along the Freedom Trail to reach the North End. That accessibility is, in turn, bringing change to the city's oldest residential neighborhood. Red sauce still simmers in North End restaurants, just as it has since the first Italian immigrants arrived in the 1880s. *Salumerias* and Old World social clubs are further reminders that *la vita* remains *dolce*. But, encouraged by increased foot traffic, hipper new businesses are also moving in.

On the Waterfront
This city has long been defined by its harbor: after all, the first colonists were drawn here mainly because of it, and local commerce has been inextricably bound to the water ever since. Over time, development obscured the view—and what was visible wasn't always pretty. (Suffice it to say that more than British tea got dumped in it!) Massive revitalization efforts, however, are paying off. See for yourself on the ever-expanding HarborWalk. Now 39 mi long, the path allows convenient access to the New England Aquarium and other favorite harborside sites as well as picturesque piers, parks, working wharves, and even urban beaches. New attractions are popping up along it, too, like the Liberty Wharf complex, which includes four restaurants (the most noteworthy being a three-story Legal Sea Foods outlet) plus a water-view plaza and public marina, slated to open in early Spring 2011.

Hurray for Hollywood East
Lights! Camera! Action! Those words are being heard a lot lately, because a state tax credit for film producers has translated into a movie-making boom. As a result, playing "spot the star" has become a popular pastime. Big names like Leo DiCaprio, Tom Cruise, Cameron Diaz, Sandra Bullock, and Matthew McConaughey, plus emerging ones like *The Social Network*'s Jesse Eisenberg all worked here in recent years. Homegrown actors, however, still make hearts pound fastest. Cambridge-raised Ben Affleck appeared in *The Town* (though not all Charlestown residents appreciated the movie's tagline: "Welcome to the Bank Robbery Capital of America"), then returned for *The Company Men*. Dorchester native Mark Wahlberg headlined *The Fighter* with Christian Bale.

Red Sox Nation
For Bostonians, baseball isn't simply a sport. It's a religion—and Fenway Park is the place of worship. Trouble is this vintage stadium, which celebrates its centennial in 2012, doesn't have enough room for the faithful. Thanks to a multiyear

upgrading program, hundreds of additional seats and standing room spaces have been crammed into the dugout area, onto the roof, and atop the Green Monster. But getting your mitts on tickets is still notoriously difficult. Savvy spectators reserve online as soon as tickets become available. Procrastinators may get lucky at the ticket office next to Gate A, which opens at 10 am. If you strike out, a very limited number of tickets are sold at Gate E two hours before game time. Alternatively, you can sidle up to that guy holding out tickets just after the opening pitch and haggle. If all else fails, head for a neighborhood bar to watch it with other luckless members of the Red Sox Nation.

Wicked Good Food

For all the emphasis placed on traditional dishes like baked beans and cod, this area lays claim to a long line of innovative chefs: for instance, M. Sanzian (the inventor of Boston cream pie) made quite a stir in the mid-1800s, and a century later Julia Child launched a culinary revolution from her Cambridge kitchen. Today it's Todd "Iron Chef" English, Gordon Hamersley, Barbara Lynch, Ken Oringer, Michael Schlow, Lydia Shire, Ming Tsai, and Jasper White who make eating out a gastronomic adventure. These hometown talents have created a thriving independent restaurant scene; and the ideal time to taste their creations—along with those of up-and-coming competitors—is during Restaurant Week. The event, held in March and again in August, sees more than 200 eateries serving three-course *prix-fixe* dinners for as little as $33.

The Suite Life

Believing the good times would last forever, Beantown's upper-end hoteliers optimistically embarked upon a mega building and renovation spree a few years back. Some pictured minimalist decor, others opulence galore. What none could foresee, unfortunately, was the looming economic crisis. Since late 2007 11 hotels (among them the Liberty, the Renaissance Boston Waterfront, the Mandarin Oriental, the Fairmont Battery Wharf, the Ames, the W Hotel, and boutique-y Hotel Veritas) have all thrown open their doors. Needless to say, demand for luxury lodging took a nosedive during that same period. So what's the silver lining? Managers eager to fill beds are offering some great deals. Along with reduced rates, look for value-added packages that might include room upgrades, restaurant credits, or other in-house amenities.

State of the Art

Although no one refers to Boston as "The Athens of America" anymore, appreciating art seems to be as characteristic of folks here as dropping "R's" and taking the "T." That explains why the Museum of Fine Arts has expanded . . . again. A new American wing, designed by star architect Sir Norman Foster, opened in November 2010. With 53 galleries on four floors along with an auditorium, classrooms, and soaring central courtyard, the addition increases MFA's size by almost one third. Over at the Isabella Stewart Gardner Museum, Renzo Piano gets in on the act designing a glass and copper-clad wing to compliment the original Venetian-style building. Providing a new entry, performance hall, and gallery space, it is slated to open in spring 2012. Piano is also the man behind the Harvard Art Museum makeover, which should be completed in 2013.

WHAT'S WHERE

The following numbers refer to chapters in the book.

2 **Beacon Hill, Boston Common, and the Old West End.** If you follow the Freedom Trail you'll end up on Beacon Hill. The Brahmins' old stomping ground has many landmarks, including the Massachusetts State House. But sights aside, the gas-lit residential streets lined with Federalist townhouses make this a wonderful place to walk. Below Beacon Hill lies Boston Common (a popular hangout—first for cows, then for people—since 1634). The big draws in the Old West End are the Museum of Science and TD Garden, the home of Boston's pro hockey and basketball teams.

3 **Government Center and the North End.** Architecture buffs admire Government Center's Brutalist structures, but everyone else thinks they're ugly. Out-of-towners typically skip them, making a beeline for Faneuil Hall. Inside, Faneuil Hall Marketplace has boutiques, bars, and a food court; outside, street performers and souvenir vendors compete for your attention. Nearby, the North End feels like Little Italy because of the influx of Italian immigrants who have left their mark since the 19th century. But, Copp's Hill Burying Ground attests to a Puritan past, and the Paul

Lechmere

City P

CAMBRIDGE

Charles River

28

Science Park

28

OLD WEST END

Longfellow Bridge

3

Charles/MGH

2

BEACON HILL

S H

0   1200 ft

0   400 m

B

Frog Pond

Beacon Street

Boston Common

Marlborough St.

Commonwealth Ave.

Commonwealth Ave.

BACK BAY

Dartmouth Street

Clarendon Street

Berkeley St.

Arlington St.

Public Garden

Arlington

Boylston St.

28

Boylsto

THEA DISTI

Boylston St.

Copley

St. James Avenue

Stuart St.

Charles St.

Stuart St.

90

Back Bay

Arlington St.

Tufts M Cen

SOUTH END

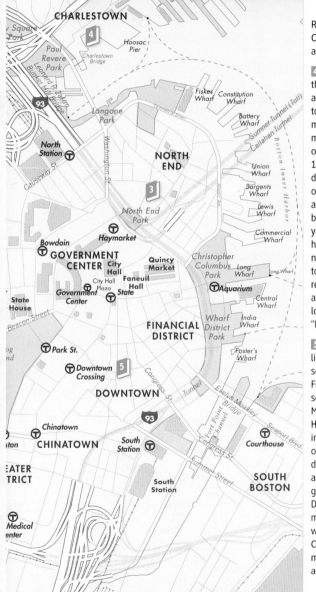

Revere House and Old North Church evoke the Revolutionary era.

4 Charlestown. Poised on the banks of Boston Harbor and the Mystic River, Charlestown's top sights can't be missed. The Bunker Hill Monument is a towering tribute to one of the pivotal battles of 1775; the USS *Constitution*, designated as America's Ship of State, is a tangle of masts and rigging. Gentrification began here more than 35 years ago, when Old Ironside's home was transformed from a naval yard into a National Historic Site. Now locals live in restored shipbuilders' houses and area restaurateurs no longer cater exclusively to the "hardtack-and-grog" crowd.

5 Downtown. This maze-like section of central Boston scores points for diversity. Freedom Trail walkers come to see sights like the Old South Meeting House and Old State House, which are wedged incongruously between office towers. Families are drawn in by the Aquarium and Children's Museum. Play goers flock to the Theater District. There is an interesting mishmash of other districts as well, among them Downtown Crossing (one of Boston's main retail zones), Chinatown, and the loft-y Leather District.

WHAT'S WHERE

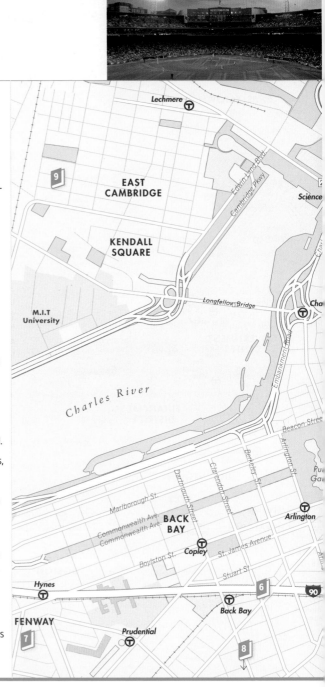

6 The Back Bay and South End. The chic Back Bay boasts the city's most impressive skyscrapers (the Prudential Center and the John Hancock Tower) and arguably its single most beautiful building, Trinity Church. It's also laid out in an orderly fashion, which makes it easy to ogle the well-dressed residents who parade through. Given the concentration of high-end stores on and around Newbury Street, emulating them is easy, if costly. More shopping opportunities await in the South End, which hugs the south side of Huntington Avenue southeast of the Back Bay. It also has enough lavishly embellished bowfront houses to earn a spot in the National Register of Historic Places and enough style to win the "hippest hood" award.

7 The Fenway. Baseball fans, art aficionados, and aspiring intellectuals meet head on in the Fens: a meandering green space that serves as the first "jewel" in Boston's Emerald Necklace. Fenway Park, a veritable shrine to the Boston Red Sox, is just northwest of the Fens. To the south sit the newly expanded Museum of Fine Arts and more intimate Isabella Stewart Gardner Museum. Academic institutions in the area include Boston University, Northeastern

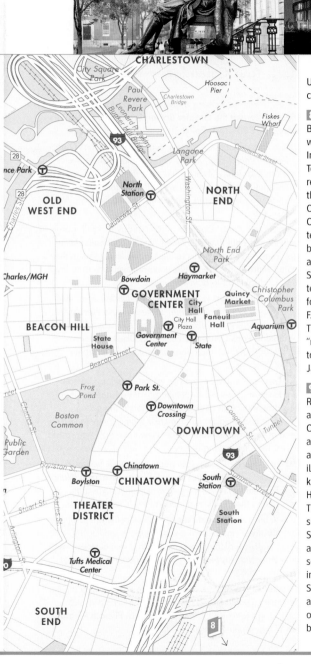

University, and Harvard Medical School.

8 Boston Outskirts. South Boston (not the South End) was a still a working-class Irish enclave a decade back. Today its Seaport District has revitalized the waterfront, thanks largely to the Boston Convention and Exhibition Center, the Institute of Contemporary Art, and the HarborWalk. South of "Southie" are the so-called Streetcar Suburbs, including Dorchester and Jamaica Plain. The former is home to the John F. Kennedy Library & Museum. The latter (described as a "mini-Cambridge") lays claim to the Arnold Arboretum and Jamaica Pond.

9 Cambridge. The "People's Republic of Cambridge," a separate city across the Charles River, has long been a haven for writers, radicals, and iconoclasts. While primarily working class, it is widely known as the location of Harvard University and M.I.T. The universities themselves support affiliated museums. Students, conversely, support an eclectic mix of stores and services. So, despite increasing gentrification in Harvard Square, the area still features a disproportionate number of quirky cafés, independent bookstores, and funky shops.

BOSTON PLANNER

When to Go

Weather-wise, late spring and fall are the optimal times to come. Aside from mild temperatures, the former offers blooming gardens throughout the city and the latter sees the surrounding countryside ablaze with brilliantly colored foliage. At both times, however, you should expect hordes of visitors.

Students must be factored into the mix as well. More than 250,000 of them flood into the area each September and then pull out again in May and June. So hotels and restaurants fill up especially fast on move-in, move-out, and graduation weekends.

The good news is that this is a four-season destination. Along with the most reliable sunshine, summer brings sailboats to Boston Harbor, concerts to the Esplanade, and café tables to sidewalks. Summer is also prime for a classic shore vacation, but advance planning is imperative.

Even winter has its pleasures. Boston gets a holiday glow, thanks to the thousands of lights strung around the Common, Public Garden, and Commonwealth Avenue Mall. During the post-Christmas lull temperatures fall, but lodging prices do, too.

Mark Your Calendar

There's *always* something happening in Boston. For a full selection, consult the **Greater Boston Convention & Visitors Bureau** (☏ 888/733–2678 ⊕ www.bostonusa.com).

Winter. Boston celebrates New Year's Eve with **First Night** (⊕ www.firstnight.org). A day of artsy, alcohol-free events peaks at midnight with fireworks over the Harbor. Oenophiles rejoice in late January when the **Boston Wine Expo** (⊕ www.wineexpoboston.com) returns to the Seaport World Trade Center.

Spring. On Patriots' Day, the third Monday in April, horsemen reenact **Paul Revere's Ride** (⊕ www.nationallancers. org) from the North End to Lexington; while runners in the **Boston Marathon** (⊕ www.bostonmarathon.org) race 26.2 mi from Hopkinton to Boylston Street.

Summer. Harborfest (⊕ www.bostonharborfest.com), Boston's six-day July 4 celebration, sponsors more than 200 events—including the USS *Constitution* Turnaround Cruise. The **Boston Pops Concert & Fireworks Display** (⊕ www. July4th.org) at the Hatch Shell caps it off on Independence Day.

Fall. Get reel in mid-September, at the weeklong **Boston Film Festival** (⊕ www.bostonfilmfestival.org). Independent films premiere, with directors and actors adding star power. In mid-October college crew teams compete in the **Head of the Charles Regatta** (⊕ www.hocr.org), the world's largest two-day rowing event.

Fall Outside the City. In late September New Bedford's commercial fishermen strut their stuff at the **Working Waterfront Festival** (⊕ www.workingwaterfrontfestival.org), showcasing their skills and loads of fresh seafood.

Essex County's **Topsfield Fair** (⊕ www.topsfieldfair.org), the nation's oldest agricultural event, happens in October, and Salem hosts candlelight tours, witch trial reenactments, and other **Haunted Happenings** (⊕ www.hauntedhappenings. com) all month.

In November, celebrate turkey day the modern way at Plymouth's **Thanksgiving Parade** (⊕ www.visit-plymouth. com), or go retro with a Pilgrim dinner at **Plimoth Plantation** (⊕ www.plimoth.org).

Getting Around

"America's Walking City," with all its historic nooks and scenic crannies, is best explored on foot. But when hoofing it around town seems too arduous, there are alternatives.

By Car. In a place where roads often evolved from cow paths and colonial lanes, driving is no simple task. A surfeit of one-way streets makes for circuitous routing. Inconsistent signage and aggressive local drivers only add to the confusion. Nevertheless, having your own car is helpful (especially if you're taking side trips), and conditions are better now that the Big Dig is done. Just keep a detailed map handy.

If you would rather leave the driving to someone else, cabs are available 24/7. They wait outside major hotels, or line up near hot spots like Harvard Square, South Station, Faneuil Hall, Long Wharf, and the Theater District. You can call a cab or hail one on the street. Rides within the city cost $2.60 for the first 1/7 mi and 40¢ for each 1/7 mi thereafter (tolls, where applicable, are extra).

By Public Transit. The "T," as the subway system is affectionately nicknamed, is the cornerstone of a far-reaching public transit network that also includes aboveground trains, buses, and ferries. Its five color-coded lines will put you within a block of almost anywhere. Subways operate from about 5:30 am to 12:30 pm, as do buses, which crisscross the city and suburbia.

A standard adult subway fare is $1.70 with a CharlieCard or $2 with a ticket or cash. For buses it's $1.25 with a CharlieCard or $1.50 with a ticket or cash (more if you are using an Inner or Outer Express bus). Commuter rail and ferry fares vary by route. For details on schedules, routes, and rates, contact the **MBTA** (☎ 617/222–3200 or 800/392–6100 ⊕ www.mbta.com).

CHARLIEPASS AND THE CHARLIECARD

Retro music fans recall the 1959 Kingston Trio hit about a fellow named Charlie, who, unable to pay his fare, "never returned" from Boston's subway system. Charlie lives on as the mascot of the MBTA's somewhat confusing ticketing scheme. There are two stored-value options: a plastic CharlieCard or paper CharlieTicket, both of which are reusable and reloadable with cash or credit or debit cards. At a station, obtain a CharlieCard from an attendant or a CharlieTicket from a machine. CharlieCards make for cheaper trips, but can't yet be used on commuter rail, commuter boats, or Inner Harbor ferries. Most visitors' best deals will be the unlimited one-day ($9) or one-week ($15) LinkPass.

Quick Forecasts

Check the coded lights atop the Berkeley Building (also known as the old John Hancock tower) overlooking Copley Square: *Steady blue means clear view; flashing blue, clouds due; steady red, rain ahead; flashing red, snow instead*... except in baseball season when red means the Sox game is canceled!

Visitor Centers

The **Greater Boston Convention & Visitors Bureau** (☎ 888/733–2678   ⊕ www.bostonusa.com) operates visitor information centers at Boston Common (✉ 148 Tremont St., Beacon Hill and Boston Common   ☎ 888/733–2678 ✆ Weekdays 8:30–5, weekends 9–5)) and the Shops at Prudential (✉ Center Court, 800 Boylston St., Back Bay ☎ 888/733–2678 ✆ Weekdays 9–5:30, weekends 10–5:30).

For specific information about Cambridge, contact the **Cambridge Tourism Office** (☎ 800/862–5678 or 617/441–2884   ⊕ www.cambridge-usa.org) or drop by the **Harvard Square Visitor Information Booth** (✉ Outside the main T entrance, Harvard Sq. ☎ 617/497–1630 ✆ Weekdays 9–5, weekends 9–1). The **Massachusetts Office of Travel and Tourism** (☎ 800/227–6277 or 617/973–8500 ⊕ www.massvacation.com) can help with Boston area side trips.

BOSTON
TOP ATTRACTIONS

USS *Constitution*

(A) The world's oldest commissioned warship (dubbed Old Ironsides thanks to her seemingly impenetrable oak hull), was launched in 1797. Even landlubbers will be impressed by the frigate's hulking masts, plentiful cannons, and cool below-deck quarters—all of which can be viewed on free tours led by active-duty sailors. Since the adjacent museum is also free, you can bone up on her back story before boarding.

Boston Public Garden

(B) The Public Garden proves landfill can look good. Built on a reclaimed marsh in the 19th century, America's first botanical garden is a striking combination of broad lawns and ornamental flower beds. At its heart is a 4-acre lagoon, which Swan Boats (floating fixtures since 1877) circle from mid-April to mid-September. Once autumn arrives, the trees here—willows, beech, oak, and maple—burst with color.

The Museum of Fine Arts

(C) In a city famous for museums, this world-class institution stands out. Its eclectic collection (including everything from Byzantine mosaics and Native American pottery to impressionist paintings and contemporary photographs) attracts almost a million visitors per year. If you join them, allot plenty of time: the MFA has about 450,000 *objets d'art* spanning 3,000 years, so ogling it all takes a while!

The New England Aquarium

(D) Though it's more than 40-years old, the New England Aquarium wears its age well. The signature exhibit—a multistory Ocean Tank containing hundreds of fish and one supersized sea turtle named Myrtle—is always entertaining. Ditto for the daily lineup of animal shows and IMAX movies. New additions like the seal pool (opened in 2009) plus a shark and ray touch tank (slated for 2011) also help keep it fresh.

Faneuil Hall Marketplace

(E) Purists swear they never come here, yet Faneuil Hall Marketplace (aka Quincy Market) is always packed. Kitschy souvenir sellers coupled with ubiquitous buskers create a Disney-esque atmosphere some disdain. But the rest of us recognize fun when we see it. Browse the 1826 complex's restored stalls; then go to the food court to sample Boston's edible holy trinity: lobster, clams, and "chowdah."

Boston Harbor Islands

(F) You can file this one under "best kept secrets." Made up of 34 islands, the National Recreation Area boasts a pre–Civil War fort, vintage lighthouses, hiking trails, swimming beaches, and picnic spots. Historical interest and outdoor opportunities aside, the islands represent one of the city's top values. May through October, the round-trip Harbor Islands Express ferry from Long Wharf to Georges Island costs just $14.

Harvard University

(G) Massachusetts reportedly has the world's highest concentration of colleges and universities. None, however, is more venerable than Harvard, a Cambridge landmark since 1636. To get a taste of the ivory tower without having to pay tuition, take a student-led campus tour. The complimentary hour-long walks are offered regularly; the university Web site has details (⊕ *www.harvard.edu*).

Longfellow National Historic Site

(H) Henry James, T. S. Eliot, and John Updike all resided in Cambridge at various points. But the writer who left the most indelible mark was Henry Wadsworth Longfellow, author of "Paul Revere's Ride." His patriotic poetry helped popularize (some would say mythologize) American history, and the Brattle Street mansion he lived in from 1837 to 1882 has been preserved as a National Historic Site.

GREAT ITINERARIES

BOSTON IN 4 DAYS

Clearly every traveler moves at a different pace. One might be content to snap a pic of the Bunker Hill Monument and push on; another might insist on climbing the obelisk's 294 spiraling steps and then studying the adjacent museum's military dioramas. Nevertheless, in four days you should be able to see the city highlights without feeling rushed. If you're lucky enough to have a few vacation days to spare, you can put them to good use exploring nearby communities.

Day 1: Hit the Trail

About 3 million visitors walk the Freedom Trail every year—and there's a good reason why: taken together, the route's 16 designated sites offer a crash course in colonial history. That makes the trail a must, so you might as well tackle it sooner rather than later. Linger wherever you like, leaving ample time for lunch amid magicians and mimes in Faneuil Hall Marketplace. Next, make tracks for the North End, where you'll find Old North Church and Paul Revere's former home (Boston's oldest house, it was constructed almost 100 years prior to his arrival). After wandering the neighborhood's narrow Italian-tinged streets, fortify yourself with a gelato and keep going across the Charlestown Bridge. You can see the USS *Constitution* and climb the Bunker Hill Monument (a breathtaking site in more ways than one) before catching the MBTA water shuttle back to Downtown.

Day 2: Head for the Hill

Named for the signal light that topped it in the 1800s, Beacon Hill originally stood a bit taller until earth was scraped off its peak and used as landfill not far away. What remains—namely gas street lamps, shady trees, brick sidewalks, and stately Brahmin brownstones—evokes old Boston. When soaking up the ambience, don't forget to take in some of Beacon Hill's "official" attractions. After all, major sites from Boston's various themed trails, including the Massachusetts State House, Boston Athenaeum, African Meeting House, and Granary Burying Ground, are here. Afterward, stroll over to the Common and the Public Garden. (Both promise greenery and great people-watching.) If shopping is more your bag, cruise for antiques along Charles Street, the thoroughfare that separates them. In the evening, feast on affordable chow mein in Chinatown or go upscale at an über trendy restaurant in the Theater District.

Day 3: Get an Overview

From the Back Bay you can cover a lot of Boston's other attractions in a single day. Start at the top (literally) by seeing 360-degree views from the Prudential Center's Skywalk Observatory. Once you understand the lay of the land, just plot a route based on your interests. Architecture aficionados can hit the ground running at the neoclassical Public Library and Romanesque Trinity Church. Shoppers, conversely, can opt for the stores of Newbury Street and Copley Place (a high-end mall anchored by Neiman Marcus). Farther west in the Fens, other choices await. Art connoisseurs might view the collection at the sprawling Museum of Fine Arts or the more manageably sized Isabella Stewart Gardner Museum. Quirky, carnival-like Fenway Park beckons baseball fans to the other side of the Fens. Depending on your taste—and the availability of tickets—cap the day with a Symphony Hall concert or a Red Sox game.

Day 4: On the Waterfront

Having spent so much time focusing on the old, why not devote a day to something new in the burgeoning Seaport District? Begin at the Institute of Contemporary Art (ICA) on Fan Pier. Boston's first new art museum in almost a century boasts a bold cantilevered design that makes the most of its waterside location. It makes the most of its art collection, too, by offering special programs that appeal even to little tykes and hard-to-please teens. Of course, keeping kids engaged may prove difficult given that the Children's Museum is close by. Check out its innovative exhibits or continue on to that old waterfront favorite, the New England Aquarium. Highlights include the Giant Ocean Tank, hands-on tidal pools, a seal-training tutorial, and scores of happy-footed penguins. Outside the facility you can sign up for a harbor cruise, whale-watching trip, or ferry ride to the Boston Harbor Islands.

BEYOND BOSTON PROPER

Day 1: Explore Cambridge

From pre-Revolutionary times, Boston was the region's commercial center and Cambridge was the 'burbs: a place more residential than mercantile, with plenty of room to build the nation's first English-style, redbrick university. Not surprisingly, the heart of the community—geographically and otherwise—is still Harvard Square. It would be easy enough to while away a day here browsing the shops, lounging at a café, then wandering over to the riverbank to watch crew teams practice. But Harvard Square is also the starting point for free student-led campus tours, as well as for strolls along Brattle Street's "Tory Row" (Longfellow lived at No. 105).

There are fine museums here, too, including the newly reconfigured Harvard Art Museum, which brings together the best of the university's vast collection, and the family-friendly Museum of Natural History. End your day in true Cantabrigian style by taking in a concert or lecture at the handsome Sanders Theatre.

Day 2: Step Back in Time

You only have to travel a short distance to visit historic places you read about in grade school. For a side trip to the 17th century, head 35 mi southeast to Plymouth. The famed rock doesn't live up to its hype, but Plimoth Plantation (an open-air museum re-creating life among Pilgrims) and *Mayflower II* are well worth the trip. A second option is to veer northwest to see Revolutionary-era sites in Lexington (now a well-to-do bedroom community). Start at the National Heritage Museum for a recap of the events that started the whole shebang; then proceed to Battle Green, where "the shot heard round the world" was fired. After stopping by Minute Man National Historic Park, continue to Concord to tour the homes of literary luminaries like Ralph Waldo Emerson, Louisa May Alcott, and Nathaniel Hawthorne. Conclude your novel excursion with a walk around Walden Pond, where Henry David Thoreau wrote one of the founding documents of the ecology movement.

Day 3: A Shore Thing

Anyone eager to taste the salt air or feel the surge of the sea should take a day trip to the North Shore towns of Salem and Gloucester. The former has a Maritime National Historic Site—complete with vintage wharves and warehouses—that proves there is more to the notorious town than just witchcraft; while the latter

(America's oldest seaport, and after *The Perfect Storm* perhaps its most identifiable one) demonstrates that men *still* go down to the sea in ships.

Prefer to just beach yourself? In summer, nature lovers flock to Crane Beach in Ipswich, about an hour north of Boston. Part of a 1,200-acre wildlife refuge, it includes 4 mi of sand rimmed by scenic dunes. For a quick sand-in-every-crevice experience, take either the MBTA's Harbor Express ferry south to Nantasket Beach in Hull or the commuter train north to Manchester-by-the-Sea's Singing Beach, where the sand has such a high silica content that it actually sings (or at least squeaks) when you walk on it.

Alternatively, get a taste of the beach-bum lifestyle with a day in Provincetown. Boston Harbor Cruises runs fast ferries to the colorful artists' hub at the tip of Cape Cod. Once there, race across nearby dunes, get back on the water and watch for whales, or soak up some rays at Race Point, a Cape Cod National Seashore beach. For a bit of culture, head to the East End's growing number of galleries or inspect the architecture along Commercial Street. Properly sunned and relaxed, return to Boston on the evening ferry or plan ahead and book a cottage for the night.

TIPS

❶ Although charming neighborhoods lend Boston a small-town vibe, it's subject to the same problems that plague other urban centers. Violent crime is rare, but residents and tourists alike sometimes fall victim to pickpockets, scam artists, or car thieves. As in any large city, use common sense and stick to well-traveled routes after dark.

❷ You can usually buy Symphony Hall concert tickets online or through your hotel concierge. But in-the-know locals get rush seats (unused subscriber tickets put on sale three hours before curtain time) Tuesday and Thursday nights and Friday afternoons. Since the Sox are in a league of their own, scoring ball tickets is trickier. If you're empty-handed, watch the action at Game On!—a two-story sports bar attached to Fenway Park.

❸ Think you need a car to venture beyond Boston? Think again. Grayline affiliate Brush Hill Tours (☎ *800/343–1328* or *781/986–6100* ⊕ *www.brushhilltours.com*) offers coach excursions for Boston-based day-trippers to Lexington, Concord, Salem, and Plymouth. In autumn, foliage-themed tours are available, too.

❹ Die-hard sightseers might consider taking a pass—a "Go Boston" Pass (☎ *800/887–9103* ⊕ *www.smartdestinations.com*). Sold in one-day to one-week increments, it's priced from $49.99 and covers dozens of attractions, tours, and excursions. CityPass (☎ *888/330–5008* ⊕ *www.citypass.com*) sells a similar product covering five key sites for $46.

CITY LIKE A LOCAL

Be a Sport

Locals mark off the seasons by checking the sports line-up. The "Boys of Summer" arrive each spring, and the Bruins come out of hibernation in the fall.

When the Red Sox play at home, being a Boston resident means braving the throngs along Yawkee Way, downing a Fenway Frank, and bellowing out "Sweet Caroline" during the seventh inning stretch. Sweet indeed.

Next stop, TD Garden. Even if you can't score tickets to watch the Bruins or Celtics, you can see their arena via the Sports Museum of New England. Come early on game day and you might catch players warming up

Football fans get a kick out of Gillette Stadium in suburban Foxborough. It is home turf for the Super Bowl–winning New England Patriots and site of an entertainment complex that houses their high-tech Hall of Fame.

Book it to the Library

Think libraries are boring? Proper Bostonians will beg to differ. Once renowned as a hotbed of writers, the city remains a haven for readers. The continuing popularity of these institutions is a case in point.

Little wonder bookworms adore the Boston Public Library, just as Ralph Waldo Emerson and his literary buddies did in the 1800s. The building is beautiful, the collection is vast, and there is no charge to browse in either.

The Mary Baker Eddy Library isn't merely full of books. It includes the **Mapparium** (a walk-in mammoth glass globe, the interior of which is spanned by a 30-foot bridge) plus a virtual fountain that spews famous quotations.

Even in an age of political cynicism, folks treasure the memory of JFK, Boston's native son. So the John F. Kennedy Library & Museum in Dorchester feels like hallowed ground. It's now undergoing a major expansion.

Join the Festivities

The Brits who founded Boston get a lot of attention. Yet they were only the first of many immigrant groups who helped shape this city. Locals applaud the others' colorful legacy through equally colorful celebrations.

Irish eyes are always smiling on the Sunday closest to March 17. That's when the St. Patrick's Day Parade passes through Southie, proving in the process that all the Boston Celtics are not basketball players.

In America's third-largest Chinatown, dragon parades and firecrackers mark Chinese New Year, while the August Moon Festival features lion dancing, lanterns, and mooncakes. Events center on Gateway Arch.

Each summer the North End hosts fun Weekend Street Fests, honoring Italy's various patron saints with processions, boisterous music, and fab food that runs the gamut from cannoli to cutting-edge pasta creations.

FAMILY FAVORITES

Costs add up when you're traveling with kids, so do your wallet a favor and download a "Family Friendly ValuePass" (⊕ *www.bostonusa.com/greatdeals*). You can use it to snag discounts for more than 75 shops, eateries, tours, and attractions.

Follow the Redbrick Road

Wannabe time travelers will have a blast on the Freedom Trail. To make the most of the walk, have your kids sign up for the free NPS Junior Ranger program, which adds treasure-hunt elements to the history lesson. Here's another tip. Most trail takers go south to north, but the reverse works best for families: this allows you to start with *Old Ironsides* and the Bunker Hill Monument (star attractions in young eyes) and end in Boston Common (an ideal place to unwind after a long trek). ⇒ *See "Follow the Redbrick Road" at the end of this chapter.*

Enjoy Fowl Play

For the quintessential Boston experience, treat your family to a Swan Boat ride around the lovely Public Garden lagoon. Afterward, check out the pair of real swans (Romeo and Juliet); then waddle over to the nearby Duckling sculpture to see Mrs. Mallard and the rest of the quacking clan from Robert McCloskey's 1941 book, *Make Way for Ducklings.*

Kid Around

Established in 1913, the Boston Children's Museum is one of oldest facilities of its kind—one of the best, too. Highlights include art studios, a full-size replica of Arthur the Aardvark's cartoon realm, and a hands-on construction zone. Some kiddies, though, may not want to leave the tempting multistory climbing structure that dominates the lobby!

Yell "Eureka"

No place does gizmos and gadgets like the Museum of Science, where almost everything is meant to be pushed, pulled, or otherwise maneuvered. Like its interactive displays, the live demos are over the top (think lightening bolts manufactured in an air-insulated Van de Graaff generator). The result is so entertaining children won't believe it's educational.

Find Nemo

The New England Aquarium features endless exhibits, including touch tanks that give children a real feel for marine life. In addition to all the no-cost activities, there are junior trainer programs and behind-the-scene tours for visitors willing to pay more. The aquarium also organizes whale-watching excursions to Stellwagen Bank April through late November.

Have a Ball

Small but mighty Fenway, the oldest Major League park, is a pilgrimage site for baseball fans of all ages, and daily 50-minute tours provide the ultimate insider's view. You'll get a first-hand look at the press box, Pesky's Pole, and (schedule permitting) the Green Monster. This is as close as anyone gets to the fabled field without being drafted into the MLB.

Tour the Town

Want your little people to get the big picture? **Boston By Foot** (☎ 617/367–2345 ⊕ *www.bostonbyfoot.org*) has guided walks aimed at the 6-to-12 crowd. **Old Town Trolley** (☎ 888/910–8687 ⊕ *www. trolleytours.com*) offers hop-on, hop-off tours for anyone who would rather ride; and **Boston Duck Tours** operates fun amphibious vehicles (☎ 617/267–3825 ⊕ *www.bostonducktours.com*).

FREE OR ALMOST FREE

Let Freebies Ring

Freedom may not be free, but the **Freedom Trail** is. So are 13 of the 16 attractions lining its route, and many of those individual sites offer informative free programs. The **Massachusetts State House**, for instance, schedules complimentary tours weekdays, 10 am to 4 pm; and the **USS Constitution** conducts tours from 10 am to 3:30 pm in winter, 10 am to 5:30 pm in summer. Mid-April through November, you're also welcome to join a free **National Park Service Tour** of the trail. The guided 90-minute walks are given on a first-come, first-served basis, and schedules vary with the seasons, so check with the Boston National Historical Park for details.

Try a Different Trail

The Freedom Trail's success has spawned other no-cost routes, including the **Black Heritage Trail** (⇨ *Box in the Beacon Hill, Boston Common, and Old West End chapter*) and the **Walk to the Sea**, which traces four centuries of civic development. The **Irish Heritage Trail** and **Boston Women's Heritage Trail** are other interesting options. The former covers sites relating to prominent Irish-Americans from John Hancock (who knew?) to John F. Kennedy, as well as the everyday folks forced from their homeland by the 1840s Potato Famine. The latter, meanwhile, pays tribute to local ladies who gained fame as patriots, suffragettes, abolitionists, and artists.

Artsy Alternatives

Symphony Hall (a Victorian showpiece with superb acoustics) and the historic **Boston Public Library** both run free tours. Moreover, the **Museum of Fine Arts** and **Institute of Contemporary Art** waive admission on Wednesday and Thursday evenings respectively. It's worth noting as well that the **Isabella Stewart Gardner Museum** is always free for those under 18—and anyone named Isabella! Penny pinchers should also watch for special events such as the Fenway Cultural District's **"Opening Our Doors Day."** Held each Columbus Day, it sponsors concerts, lectures, and tours at some of Boston's finest arts institutions.

Enjoy Free Parking

When you're ready for a rest, remember that relaxing in Boston's best-loved parks doesn't cost a dime. If you have already visited the glorious **Public Garden** and **Boston Common**, check out the **Emerald Necklace**. In 1878 renowned landscape architect Frederick Law Olmsted began work on six jewel-like parks strung together by a greenway. Connected to the Common and Public Garden by the Commonwealth Avenue Mall, the Necklace is an urban oasis that extends over 7 mi past meadows, manicured flowerbeds, and marshy ponds from Downtown to Dorchester. The American Planning Association named it one of the nation's "10 Great Public Spaces" in 2010.

Feeling Indecisive?

HarborWalk (⊕ *www.bostonharborwalk.com*) offers visitors a little of everything. Aside from scenic viewpoints (some with free pedestal-mounted binoculars), amenities range from parks, public art installations, and interpretive panels to a pocket Maritime Museum at the Fairmont Battery Wharf Hotel. HarborWalk also provides a backside glimpse at popular paid attractions like the New England Aquarium's Marine Mammal Center. Traversing the entire trail could take days. If you only have an hour, download a free audio guide from the Web site and enjoy a narrated stroll from Christopher Columbus Park to the Institute of Contemporary Art on Fan Pier.

FOLLOW THE REDBRICK ROAD

BOSTON'S FREEDOM TRAIL

by Mike Nalepa

Paul Revere

Paul Revere's ride

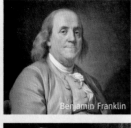
Benjamin Franklin

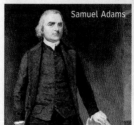
Samuel Adams

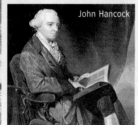
John Hancock

The Freedom Trail is more than a collection of historic sites related to the American Revolution or a suggested itinerary connecting Boston's unique neighborhoods. It's a chance to walk in the footsteps of our forefathers— literally, by following a crimson path on public sidewalks—and pay tribute to the figures all school kids know, like Paul Revere, John Hancock, and Ben Franklin. In history-proud Boston, past and present intersect before your eyes not as a re-creation but as living history accessible to all.

Boston played a key role in the dramatic events leading up to the American Revolution. Many of the founding fathers called the city home, and many of the initial meetings and actions that sparked the fight against the British took place here. In one day, you can visit Faneuil Hall—the "Cradle of Liberty"—where outraged colonial radicals met to oppose British authority; the site of the incendiary Boston Massacre; and the Old North Church, where lanterns hung to signal Paul Revere on his thrilling midnight ride. Colonists may have originally landed in Jamestown and Plymouth, but if you really want to see where America began, come to Boston.

Boston Common, Founder's Statue

⊕ www.nps.gov/bost
⊕ www.thefreedomtrail.org

☎ 617/242–5642

✉ Admission to the Freedom Trail itself is free. Several museum sites charge for admission. However, most attractions are free monuments, parks, and landmarks.

The 1729 Old South Meeting House, where many protesters gathered during the American Revolution.

PLANNING YOUR TRAIL TRIP

THE ROUTE

The 2½-mi Freedom Trail begins at Boston Common, winds through Downtown, Government Center, and the North End, and ends in Charlestown at the USS *Constitution*. The entire Freedom Trail is marked by a red line on the sidewalk; it's made of paint or brick at various points on the Trail. ⇨ *For more information on Freedom Trail sites, see listings in Neighborhood chapters.*

GETTING HERE AND BACK

The route starts near the Park Street T stop. When you've completed the Freedom Trail, head for the nearby Charlestown water shuttle, which goes directly to the downtown area. For schedules and maps, visit ⊕ *www.mbta.com.*

TIMING

If you're stopping at a few (or all) of the 16 sites, it takes a full day to complete the route comfortably. ■TIP➔ If you have children in tow, you may want to split the trail into two or more days.

VISITOR CENTERS

There are Freedom Trail information centers in Boston Common (Tremont Street), at 15 State Street (near the Old State House), and at the Charlestown Navy Yard Visitor Center (in Building 5).

TOURS

The National Park Service's free 90-minute Freedom Trail walking tours begin at the Boston National Historical Park Visitor Center at 15 State Street and cover sites from the Old South Meeting House to the Old North Church. Check online for times; it's a good idea to show up at least 30 minutes early, as the popular tours are limited to 30 people.

Half-hour tours of the USS *Constitution* are offered Tuesday through Sunday. Note that visitors to the ship must go through security screening.

FUEL UP

The trail winds through the heart of Downtown Boston, so finding a quick bite or a nice sit-down meal isn't difficult. Quincy Market, near Faneuil Hall, is packed with cafés and eateries. Another good lunch choice is one of the North End's wonderful Italian restaurants.

WHAT'S NEARBY

For a short break from revolutionary history, be sure to check out the major attractions nearby, including the Boston Public Garden, New England Aquarium, and Union Oyster House.

Above: In front of the Old State House a cobblestone circle marks the site of the Boston Massacre.

TOP SIGHTS

Benjamin Franklin Status

Boston Common

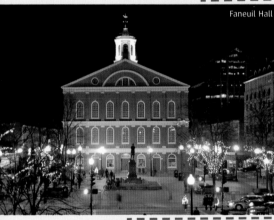
The Granary Burial Grounds

Park Street Church

Faneuil Hall

Old North Church

Bunker Hill Monument

BOSTON COMMON TO FANEUIL HALL

Old State House

Cambridge St.

0 — 100 yards
0 — 100 meters

GOVERNMENT CENTER

Clinton St.

Hancock St.

Joy St.

Bowdoin St.

Somerset St.

Court St.

Faneuil Hall

Chatham St.

BEACON HILL
Mt. Vernon St.

State House

King's Chapel and Burying Ground

School St.

Old State House

Boston Massacre Site

State St.

India S

Walnut St.

Granary Burying Ground

Old Corner Bookstore

Boston National Historic Park Visitor Center

Kilby St.

Milk St.

Broad St.

Beacon St.

Park St.

Ben Franklin Statue

Congress St.

Franklin St.

Boston Common

Park Street Church

Old South Meeting House

Devonshire St.

Arch St.

Federal St.

KEY

- - - *Freedom Trail*

Start: near the Park Street T stop.

Ⓣ PARK ST.

Boston National Historic Park Visitor Center

Washington St.

Many of the Freedom Trail sites between Boston Common and the North End are close together. Walking this 1-mile segment of the trail makes for a pleasant morning.

THE ROUTE

Begin at ★ **Boston Common,** then head for the **State House,** Boston's finest example of Federal architecture. Several blocks away is the **Park Street Church,** whose 217-foot steeple is considered to be the most beautiful in New England. The church was actually founded in 1809, and it played a key role in the movement to abolish slavery.

Reposing in the church's shadows is the ★ **Granary Burying Ground,** final resting place of Samuel Adams, John Hancock, and Paul Revere. A short stroll to Downtown brings you to **King's Chapel,** founded in 1686 by King James II for the Church of England.

Follow the trail past the **Benjamin Franklin statue** to the **Old Corner Bookstore** site, where Hawthorne, Emerson, and Longfellow were published. Nearby is the **Old South Meeting House,** where arguments in 1773 led to the Boston Tea Party. Overlooking the site of the Boston Massacre is the city's oldest public building, the **Old State House,** a Georgian beauty.

In 1770 the Boston Massacre occurred directly in front of here—look for the commemorative stone circle.

Cross the plaza to ★ **Faneuil Hall** and explore where Samuel Adams railed against "taxation without representation." ■TIP→ **A good mid-trail break is the shops and eateries of Faneuil Hall Marketplace, which includes Quincy Market.**

Old Corner Book Store Site

★ = **Fodor's**Choice   ★ = Highly Recommended   ☾ = Family Friendly

NORTH END
TO CHARLESTOWN

USS *Constitution*

Freedom Trail sites between Faneuil Hall and Charlestown are more spread out along 1½ miles. The sites here, though more difficult to reach, are certainly worth the walk.

THE ROUTE

When you depart Faneuil Hall, follow the red stripe to the North End, Boston's Little Italy.

The ○ **Paul Revere House** takes you back 200 years—here are the hero's own saddlebags, a toddy warmer, and a pine cradle made from a molasses cask. It's also air-conditioned in the summer, so try to stop here in mid-afternoon to escape the heat. Next to the Paul Revere House is one of the city's oldest brick buildings, the **Pierce-Hichborn House**.

Next, peek inside a place guaranteed to trigger a wave of patriotism: the ★ **Old North Church** of "One if by land, two if by sea" fame. Then head toward **Copp's**

Paul Revere House

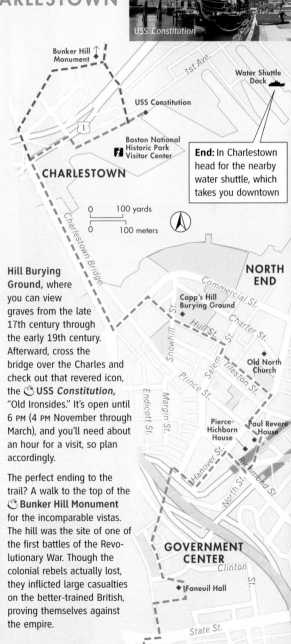

Bunker Hill
Monument

USS Constitution

Water Shuttle
Dock

1st Ave.

1

Boston National
Historic Park
Visitor Center

CHARLESTOWN

End: In Charlestown head for the nearby water shuttle, which takes you downtown

0   100 yards
0   100 meters

Charlestown Bridge

Commercial St.

Copp's Hill
Burying Ground

Hull St.

Charter St.

Snowhill St.

Old North
Church

Tileston St.

Salem St.

Prince St.

**NORTH
END**

Endicott St.

Margin St.

Pierce-
Hichborn
House

Paul Revere
House

Hanover St.

North St.

Richmond St.

**GOVERNMENT
CENTER**

Clinton

St.

◆ Faneuil Hall

State St.

Hill Burying Ground, where you can view graves from the late 17th century through the early 19th century. Afterward, cross the bridge over the Charles and check out that revered icon, the ○ **USS *Constitution*,** "Old Ironsides." It's open until 6 PM (4 PM November through March), and you'll need about an hour for a visit, so plan accordingly.

The perfect ending to the trail? A walk to the top of the ○ **Bunker Hill Monument** for the incomparable vistas. The hill was the site of one of the first battles of the Revolutionary War. Though the colonial rebels actually lost, they inflicted large casualties on the better-trained British, proving themselves against the empire.

DID YOU KNOW?

If the Freedom Trail leaves you eager to see more Revolutionary War sites, drive about 30 minutes to Lexington and Concord, where the "shot heard 'round the world" launched the first battles in 1775.

Beacon Hill, Boston Common, and the Old West End

WORD OF MOUTH

"Do the Beantown Trolley or one of the equivalents (out of town guests just did Old Town Trolley and enjoyed it) . . . These trolley things give you a good overview of the city and you should make note of what you want to return to."

—gail

GETTING ORIENTED

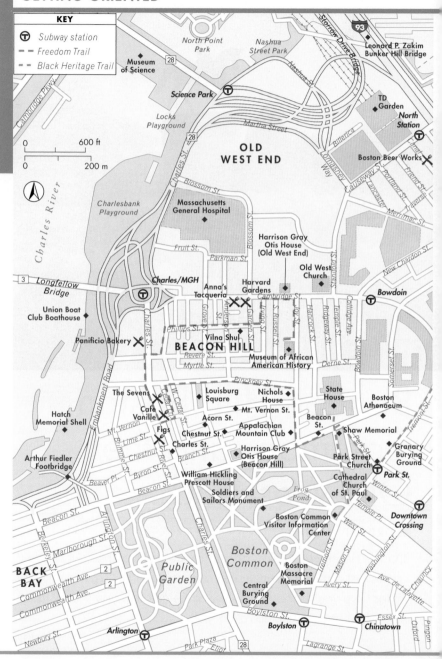

KEY

🚇 Subway station
- - Freedom Trail
- - Black Heritage Trail

GETTING HERE AND AROUND

Bounded by Cambridge Street on the north, Beacon Street on the south, the Charles River Esplanade on the west, and Bowdoin Street on the east, the small neighborhood of Beacon Hill is best experienced on foot. Take the Green Line to the Park Street stop, and walk through the Common toward Beacon Street; the Red Line to the Charles/MGH stop and stroll past the shops on Charles Street; or the Blue Line to Bowdoin Street and head toward the State House.

The Old West End is accessible by T: jump off the Red Line at the Charles/MGH stop to reach the Esplanade; get off the Green Line at Science Park for Museum of Science and a view of the Leonard P. Zakim Bunker Hill Bridge; and exit the Green Line at North Station for the Garden or for commuter trains to the northern suburbs.

TIMING AND SAFETY

Beacon Hill can be easily explored in an afternoon; add an extra few hours if you wish to linger on the Common and in the shops on Charles Street or tour the Black Heritage Trail. For the most part, the Old West End can be covered in a few hours. Extend your visit to a full day to take in the Museum of Science and an IMAX movie, check out the Sports Museum, and catch a game at the Garden.

At night, stay in well-lighted areas and avoid remote corners of the Common. Also be cautious walking late at night on Causeway Street—on nongame nights this area can be a bit deserted.

BEACON HILL QUICK BITES

Try a wood-fire grilled pizza at Todd English's **Figs** (⊠ *42 Charles St.* ✥ *Between Chestnut and Mt. Vernon Sts.*) or pub grub at The **Sevens** (⊠ *77 Charles St.* ✥ *Between Pinckney and Mt. Vernon Sts.*). Grab a cappuccino and croissant at **Cafe Vanille** (⊠ *70 Charles St.* ✥ *At Mt. Vernon St.*).

TOP REASONS TO GO

2

■ Tour the State House and experience Colonial history.

■ Discover the history of Boston's African American community on the Black Heritage Trail.

■ Explore the picture-perfect brownstones lining cobblestone streets.

■ Meander through the Common and check out the Granary Burying Ground, the final resting place of Sam Adams, John Hancock, and Paul Revere.

■ Window shop for antiques on Charles Street.

■ Enjoy the thrill of discovery at the Museum of Science.

■ Catch a glimpse of the Leonard P. Zakim Bunker Hill Bridge at night awash in blue lights.

■ Root for the home team (Celtics or Bruins) or check out the Sports Museum at the TD Garden.

FREEDOM TRAIL SIGHTS

■ Boston Common

■ The State House

■ Park Street Church

■ Granary Burying Ground

OLD WEST END QUICK BITES

In the Old West End follow the locals to **Anna's Taqueria** (⊠ *242 Cambridge St.*) for the yummiest Mexican takeout around. Sample a local microbrew and side of sour cream and chive fries at **Boston Beer Works** (⊠ *112 Canal St.*).

Sightseeing
★★★★
Dining
★★★
Lodging
★★★
Shopping
★★★★
Nightlife
★★★

Past and present home of the old-money elite, contender for the "Most Beautiful" award among the city's neighborhoods, and hallowed address for many literary lights, Beacon Hill is Boston at its most Bostonian. The redbrick elegance of its narrow streets sends you back to the 19th century just as surely as if you had stumbled into a time machine. But Beacon Hill residents would never make the social faux pas of being out of date. The neighborhood is home to hip boutiques and trendy restaurants, frequented by young, affluent professionals rather than D.A.R. matrons.

Updated
by Bethany
Cassin
Beckerlegge

Once the seat of the Commonwealth's government, Beacon Hill was called "Trimountain" and later "Tremont" by early colonists because of its three summits: Pemberton, Mt. Vernon Hill, and Beacon Hill, named for the warning light set on its peak in 1634. In 1799 settlers leveled out the ground for residences, using it to create what is now Charles Street; by the early 19th century the crests of the other two hills were also lowered.

When the fashionable families decamped for the new development of the Back Bay starting in the 1850s, enough residents remained to ensure that the south slope of the Hill never lost its Brahmin character.

By the mid-20th century, most of the multistory single-family dwellings on Beacon Hill were converted to condominiums and apartments, which are today among the most expensive in the city.

A good place to begin an exploration of Beacon Hill is at the Boston Common Visitor Information Center *(⇨ below)*, where you can buy a map or a complete guide to the Freedom Trail.

National Park Service Visitor Center. Ranger-led tours of the Freedom Trail leave from the National Park Service Visitor Center from mid-April through November. ⊠ *15 State St.* ☎ *617/242–5642* ⊕ *www.nps.gov/bost.*

Nearby, the Old West End has experienced a different sort of history. Just a few decades ago this district—separated from Beacon Hill by Cambridge Street—resembled a typical medieval city: thoroughfares that twisted and turned, maddening one-way lanes, and streets that were a veritable hive of people. Then, progress—or what passes for progress—all but eliminated the thriving Irish, Italian, Jewish, and Greek communities to make room for a mammoth project of urban renewal, designed in the 1960s by I.M. Pei.

2

BEACON HILL AND BOSTON COMMON

TOP ATTRACTIONS

★ **Acorn Street.** Surely the most photographed street in the city, Acorn is Ye Olde Colonial Boston at its best. Leave the car behind, as the cobblestone street may be Boston's roughest ride (and so narrow that only one car can squeeze through at a time). Delicate row houses line one side, and on the other are the doors to Mt. Vernon's hidden gardens. Once the homes of 19th-century artisans and tradesmen, these little jewels are now every bit as prestigious as their larger neighbors on Chestnut and Mt. Vernon streets.

Fodor'sChoice
★

Boston Common. Nothing is more central to Boston than the Common, the oldest public park in the United States and undoubtedly the largest and most famous of the town commons around which New England settlements were traditionally arranged. Dating from 1634, Boston Common started as 50 acres where the freemen of Boston could graze their cattle. (Cows were banned in 1830.) Latin names are affixed to many of the Common's trees; it was once expected that proper Boston schoolchildren be able to translate them.

On Tremont Street near Boylston stands the 1888 **Boston Massacre Memorial**; the sculpted hand of one of the victims has a distinct shine from years of sightseers' caresses. The Common's highest ground, near the park's Parkman Bandstand, was once called Flagstaff Hill. It's now surmounted by the **Soldiers and Sailors Monument,** honoring Civil War troops. The Common's only body of water is the **Frog Pond,** a tame and frog-free concrete depression used as a children's wading pool during steamy summer days and for ice-skating in winter. It marks the original site of a natural pond that inspired Edgar Allan Poe to call Bostonians "Frogpondians." In 1848 a gushing fountain of piped-in water was created to inaugurate Boston's municipal water system.

On the Beacon Street side of the Common sits the splendidly restored **Robert Gould Shaw 54th Regiment Memorial,** executed in deep-relief bronze by Augustus Saint-Gaudens in 1897. It commemorates the 54th Massachusetts Regiment, the first Civil War unit made up of free blacks, led by the young Brahmin Robert Gould Shaw. He and half of his troops died in an assault on South Carolina's Fort Wagner; their story inspired the 1989 movie *Glory*. The monument—first intended to depict only Shaw until his abolitionist family demanded it honor his regiment as well—figures in works by the poets John Berryman and Robert Lowell, both of whom lived on the north slope of Beacon Hill in the 1940s. This magnificent memorial makes a fitting first stop on the Black Heritage Trail (⇨ *The Black Heritage Trail box, below*).

Central Burying Ground. The Central Burying Ground may seem an odd feature for a public park, but remember that in 1756, when the land was set aside, this was a lonely corner of the Common. It's the final resting place of Tories and Patriots alike, as well as many British casualties of the Battle of Bunker Hill. The most famous person buried here is Gilbert Stuart, the portraitist best known for his likenesses of George and Martha Washington; he died a poor man in 1828. The Burying Ground is open daily 9–5. ⊠ *Boylston St. near Tremont, Beacon Hill* Ⓜ *Park St.* ⊠ *Bounded by Beacon, Charles, Tremont, and Park Sts., Beacon Hill* Ⓜ *Park St.*

> ### SECRET GARDENS
>
> **Hidden Gardens of Beacon Hill tour.** Strolling through Beacon Hill, you might be sorely tempted to sneak a peek into those glorious private gardens that are just barely visible behind sheltering walls and wrought-iron gates. Rather than risk arrest, time your visit for the third Thursday in May, when about a dozen of them open to the public. Or try the self-guided Hidden Gardens of Beacon Hill tour, an event that's happened annually since 1929, which costs $30 when you purchase tickets in advance. ☎ *617/227-4392* ⊕ *www.beaconhillgardenclub.org.*

Boston Common Visitor Information Center. This center, run by the Greater Boston Convention and Visitors Bureau, is on the Tremont Street side of Boston Common. It's well supplied with stacks of free pamphlets about Boston, including a useful guide to the Freedom Trail, which begins in the Common. ⊠ *147 Tremont St., Beacon Hill* ☎ *888/733-2678* ⊕ *www.bostonusa.com* ◎ *Mon.–Sat. 8:30–5, Sun. 10–6* Ⓜ *Park St.*

Fodor'sChoice ★　**Granary Burying Ground.** "It is a fine thing to die in Boston," A. C. Lyons, an essayist and old Boston wit, once remarked, alluding to the city's cemeteries, among the most picturesque and historic in America. If you found a resting place here at the Old Granary, as it's called, chances are your headstone would have been elaborately ornamented with skeletons and winged skulls. Your neighbors would have been impressive, too: among them are Samuel Adams, John Hancock, Paul Revere, and Benjamin Franklin's parents. Note the winged hourglasses carved into the stone gateway of the burial ground; they are a 19th-century addition, made more than 150 years after this small plot began receiving the earthly remains of colonial Bostonians. ⊠ *Entrance on Tremont St., Beacon Hill* ◎ *Daily 9–5* Ⓜ *Park St.*

★　**Louisburg Square.** One of Beacon Hill's most charming corners, Louisburg Square (proper Bostonians always pronounce the "s") was an 1840s model for a town-house development that was never built on the Hill because of space restrictions. Today, the grassy square, enclosed by a wrought-iron fence, belongs collectively to the owners of the houses facing it. The statue at the north end of the green is of Columbus, the one at the south end of Aristides the Just; both were donated in 1850 by a Greek merchant who lived on the square. The houses, most of which are now divided into apartments and condominiums, have seen

Several Founding Fathers rest at the Granary Burial Ground, a picturesque Freedom Trail stop.

their share of famous tenants, including author and critic William Dean Howells at Nos. 4 and 16, and the Alcotts at No. 10 (Louisa May not only lived but died here, on the day of her father's funeral). In 1852 the singer Jenny Lind was married in the parlor of No. 20. Louisburg Square is also the current home of Massachusetts Senator John Kerry.

There's a legend that Louisburg Square was the location of the Rev. William Blaxton's spring, although there's no water there today. Blaxton, or Blackstone, was one of the first Bostonians, having come to the Shawmut Peninsula in the mid-1620s. When the Puritans, who had settled in Charlestown, found their water supply inadequate, Blaxton invited them to move across the river, where he assured them they would find an "excellent spring." Just a few years later, he sold them all but 6 acres of the peninsula he had bought from the Native Americans and decamped to Rhode Island, seeking greater seclusion; a plaque at 50 Beacon Street commemorates him. ⊠ *Between Mt. Vernon and Pickney Sts., Beacon Hill* Ⓜ *Park St.*

Ⓒ
Fodor's Choice
★

Museum of African American History. Ever since runaway slave Crispus Attucks became one of the famous victims of the Boston Massacre of 1770, the African American community of Boston has played an important part in the city's history. Throughout the 19th century, abolition was the cause célèbre for Boston's intellectual elite, and during that time, blacks came to thrive in neighborhoods throughout the city. The Museum of African American History was established in 1964 to promote this history. The umbrella organization includes a trio of historic sites: the Abiel Smith School, the first public school in the nation built specifically for black children; the African Meeting House, where in 1832 the New England Anti-Slavery Society was formed under the leadership of William Lloyd Garrison; and the African Meeting House on the island of Nantucket, off the coast of Cape Cod. Park Service personnel continue to lead tours of the **Black Heritage Trail** (⇨ *The Black Heritage Trail box),* starting from the Shaw Memorial. The museum is the site of activities, including lectures, children's storytelling, and concerts focusing on black composers. ⊠ *46 Joy St., Beacon Hill* ☎ *617/725–0022* ⊕ *www.afroammuseum.org* ⊠ *$5* ⊗ *Mon.– Sat. 10–4* Ⓜ *Charles/MGH.*

HISTORIC BY LAW

The classic face of Beacon Hill comes from its brick row houses, nearly all built between 1800 and 1850. Even the sidewalks are brick, and will remain so by public fiat; in the 1940s, residents staged an uncharacteristic sit-in to prevent conventional paving. Since then, public law, the Beacon Hill Civic Association, and the Beacon Hill Architectural Commission have maintained tight control over everything from the gas lamps to the colors of front doors.

WORTH NOTING

Appalachian Mountain Club. The bowfront mansion that serves as the headquarters of one of New England's oldest environmental institutions draws nature lovers from all over the world. The club is a reliable source of useful information on outdoor recreation throughout the region, including cross-country skiing and hiking. (You don't have to be a member to use its resources.) Architecturally, the building is notable for its carved cornices and oriel window decorated with vines and gargoyles. ⊠ *5 Joy St., Beacon Hill* ☎ *617/523–0636* ⊕ *www.outdoors.org* ⊗ *Weekdays 9–5* Ⓜ *Park St.*

Beacon Street. Some New Englanders believe that wealth is a burden to be borne with a minimum of display. Happily, the early residents of Beacon Street were not among them. They erected many fine architectural statements, from the magnificent State House to grand patrician mansions. Here are some of the most important buildings of Charles Bulfinch, the ultimate designer of the Federal style in America: dozens of bowfront row houses, the Somerset Club, and the glorious Harrison Gray Otis House. ⇨ *"Touring Beacon Street" box for a walking tour of the area.*

Boston Athenaeum. It was William Tudor, one of the cofounders of the Boston Athenaeum, who first compared Boston with Athens because of its many cultural and educational institutions; Bostonians now jealously guard the title "Athens of America." One of the oldest libraries in the country, the Athenaeum was founded in 1807 from the seeds sown by the Anthology Club (headed by Ralph Waldo Emerson's father) and moved to its present imposing quarters—modeled after Palladio's Palazzo da Porta Festa in Vicenza, Italy—in 1849. Only 1,049 proprietary shares exist for membership in this cathedral of scholarship, and most have been passed down for generations; the Athenaeum is, however, open for use by qualified scholars, and yearly memberships are open to all by application.

TOURING BEACON STREET

After the **Boston Athenaeum**, Beacon Street highlights begin at No. 34, originally the Cabot family residence and until 1996 the headquarters of Little, Brown and Company, once a mainstay of Boston's publishing trade. At 33 Beacon Street is the **George Parkman House**, its gracious facade hiding more than a few secrets. One of the first sensational "trials of the century" involved the murder of Dr. George Parkman, a wealthy landlord and Harvard benefactor. He was bludgeoned to death in 1849 by Dr. John Webster, a Harvard medical professor and neighborhood acquaintance who allegedly became enraged by Parkman's demands that he repay a personal loan. At the conclusion of the trial, the professor was hanged; he's buried in an unmarked grave on Copp's Hill in the North End. Parkman's son lived in seclusion in this house overlooking the Common until he died in 1908. The building is now used for civic functions.

Notice the windows of the twin **Appleton-Parker Houses**, built by the pioneering textile merchant Nathan Appleton and a partner at Nos. 39 and 40. These are the celebrated purple panes of Beacon Hill; only a few buildings have them, and they are incredibly valuable. Their amethystine mauve color was the result of the action of the sun's ultraviolet light on the imperfections in a shipment of glass sent to Boston around 1820. The mansions aren't open to the public.

The quintessential snob has always been a Bostonian—and the **Somerset Club**, at 42 Beacon Street, has always been the inner sanctum of blue-nose Cabots, Lowells, and Lodges. The mansion is a rare intrusion of the granite Greek Revival style into Beacon Hill. The older of its two buildings was erected in 1819 by David Sears and designed by Alexander Parris, the architect of Quincy Market. A few doors down is the grandest of the three houses Harrison Gray Otis built for himself during Boston's golden age.

The first floor is open to the public and houses an art gallery with rotating exhibits, marble busts, porcelain vases, lush oil paintings, and books. The children's room is also open for the public to browse or read a story in secluded nooks overlooking the Granary Burying Ground. Take the guided tour to spy one of the most marvelous sights in the world of Boston academe, the fifth-floor Reading Room. With two levels of antique books, comfortable reading chairs, high windows, and assorted art, the room appears straight out of a period movie, rather than a modern scholarly institution. ■TIP→ Only eight people can fit in the tiny elevator to the fifth floor, so call at least 24 hours in advance to reserve your spot on the tour. Among the Athenaeum's holdings are most of George Washington's private library and the King's Chapel Library, sent from England by William III in 1698. With a nod to the Information Age, an online catalog contains records for more than 600,000 volumes. The Athenaeum extends into 14 Beacon Street. ✉ *10½ Beacon St., Beacon Hill* ☎ *617/227–0270* ⊕ *www.bostonathenaeum.org* ▨ *Free* ☉ *Mon. and Wed. 9–8, Tues., Thurs., and Fri. 9–5:30, Sat. 9–4 (excluding summer when closed). Tours Tues. and Thurs. at 3* Ⓜ *Park St.*

Cathedral Church of St. Paul. Though it looks a bit like a bank, St. Paul's is actually the first Boston structure built in the Greek Revival style (1820). It was established by a group of wealthy and influential patriots who wanted a wholly American Episcopal parish—the two existing Episcopal churches, Christ Church (Old North) and Trinity, were both founded before the Revolution—that would contrast with the existing colonial and "gothick" structures around town. The building was to be topped with an entablature showing St. Paul preaching to the Corinthians—but the pediment remains uncarved, as Bishop Henry Sherrill instead used the money to start the clergy pension program for the national Episcopal church. ✉ *138 Tremont St., Beacon Hill* ☎ *617/482–5800* ⊕ *www.stpaulboston.org* ☯ *Weekdays 9–5. Services Sun. at 8 am, 10 am, and 12:30 (in Cantonese), Mon. at 1, and Fri. at 1 (Ju'mah, the Muslim Friday Prayers). Luncheon concerts Oct.–May, Wed. at 12:15* Ⓜ *Park St.*

Charles Street. Chockablock with antiques shops, clothing boutiques, small restaurants, and flower shops, Charles Street more than makes up for the general lack of commercial development on Beacon Hill. You won't see any glaring neon; in keeping with the historic character of the area, even the 7-Eleven has been made to conform to the prevailing aesthetic standards. Notice the old-fashioned signs hanging from storefronts—the bakery's loaf of bread, the florist's topiary, the tailor's spool of thread, and the chiropractor's human spine. Once the home of Oliver Wendell Holmes and the publisher James T. Fields (of the famed Bostonian firm of Ticknor and Fields), Charles Street sparkles at dusk from gas-fueled lamps, making it a romantic place for an evening stroll.

Chestnut Street. Delicacy and grace characterize virtually every structure on this street, from the fanlights above the entryways to the wrought-iron boot scrapers on the steps. Author and explorer Francis Parkman lived here, as did the lawyer Richard Henry Dana (who wrote *Two Years Before the Mast*), and 19th-century actor Edwin Booth, brother of John Wilkes Booth. Edwin Booth's sometime residence, 29A, dates from 1800, and is the oldest house on the south slope of the hill. Also note the **Swan Houses,** at Nos. 13, 15, and 17, commissioned from Charles Bulfinch by Hepzibah Swan as dowry gifts for her three daughters. Complete with Adam-style entrances, marble columns, and recessed arches, they are Chestnut Street at its most beautiful.

Harrison Gray Otis House. Harrison Gray Otis, a U.S. senator, Boston's third mayor, and one of the Mt. Vernon Proprietors (a group of prosperous Boston investors), built in rapid succession three of the city's most splendidly ostentatious Federal-era houses, all designed by Charles Bulfinch and all still standing. This, the third Harrison Gray Otis House, was the grandest. Now the headquarters of the American Meteorological Society, the house was once freestanding and surrounded by English-style gardens. The second Otis house, built in 1800 at 85 Mt. Vernon Street, is now a private home. The first Otis house, built in 1796 on Cambridge Street, is the only one open to the public (⇨ *Old West End*).

The Black Heritage Trail

Until the end of the 19th century the north side of opulent Beacon Hill contained a vibrant community of free blacks—more than 8,000 at its peak—who built houses, schools, and churches that stand to this day. In the African Meeting House, once called the Black Faneuil Hall, orators rallied against slavery. The streets were lined with black-owned businesses. The black community has since shifted to other parts of Boston, but visitors can rediscover this 19th-century legacy on the Black Heritage Trail.

Established in the late 1960s, the self-guiding trail stitches together 14 sites in a 1½-mi walk. Park rangers give tours daily Memorial Day through Labor Day at 10 am, noon, and 2 pm, and from Labor Day to Memorial Day at 2 pm, starting from the Shaw Memorial in Boston Common. To tour on your own, pick up brochures from the **Museum of African American History** (✉ 46 Joy St., Beacon Hill) or the **National Park Service Visitor Center** (✉ 15 State St., Beacon Hill).

Start at the stirring **Robert Gould Shaw 54th Regiment Memorial** in Boston Common. Shaw, a young white officer from a prominent Boston abolitionist family, led the first black regiment to be recruited in the North during the Civil War. From here, walk up Joy Street to 5–7 Pinckney Street to see the 1797 **George Middleton House,** Beacon Hill's oldest existing home built by blacks. Nearby, the **Phillips School** at Anderson and Pinckney streets was one of Boston's first integrated schools. The **John J. Smith House,** at 86 Pinckney, was a rendezvous point for abolitionists and escaping slaves, and the **Charles Street Meeting House,** at Mt. Vernon and Charles streets, was

once a white Baptist church and later a black church and community center. In 1876 the building became the site of the **African Methodist Episcopal Church,** which was the last black institution to leave Beacon Hill, in 1939. The **Lewis and Harriet Hayden House** at 66 Phillips Street, the home of freed slaves turned abolitionists, was a stop on the Underground Railroad. Harriet Beecher Stowe, author of *Uncle Tom's Cabin,* visited here in 1853 for her first glimpse of fugitive slaves. The Haydens reportedly kept a barrel of gunpowder under the front step, saying they'd blow up the house before they'd surrender a single slave. At **2 Phillips Street,** John Coburn, cofounder of a black military company, ran a gaming house, described as a "private place for gentlemen."

The five residences on **Smith Court** are typical of African-American Bostonian homes of the 1800s, including No. 3, the 1799 clapboard house where William C. Nell, America's first published black historian and a crusader for school integration, boarded from 1851 to 1865. At the corner of Joy Street and Smith Court is the **Abiel Smith School,** the city's first public school for black children. The school's exhibits interpret the ongoing struggle started in the 1830s for equal school rights. Next door is the venerable **African Meeting House,** which was the community's center of social, educational, and political activity. The ground level houses a gallery; in the airy upstairs, you can imagine the fiery sermons that once rattled the upper pews.

Otis moved into 45 Beacon Street in 1805, and stayed until his death in 1848. His tenure thus extended from the first days of Beacon Hill's residential development almost to the time when many of the Hill's prominent families decamped for the Back Bay, which was just beginning to be filled at the time of Otis's death. ✉ *45 Beacon St., Beacon Hill.*

Mt. Vernon Street. Mt. Vernon Street, along with Chestnut Street, has some of Beacon Hill's most distin-

> **DID YOU KNOW?**
>
> Beacon Hill's north slope played a key part in African-American history. A community of free blacks lived here in the 1800s; many worshipped at the African Meeting House, established in 1805 and still standing. It came to be known as the "Black Faneuil Hall" for the fervent antislavery activism that started within its walls.

guished addresses. Mt. Vernon is the grander of the two, however, with houses set back farther and rising taller; it even has a freestanding mansion, the second Harrison Gray Otis House, at No. 85. Henry James once wrote that Mt. Vernon Street was "the only respectable street in America," and he must have known, as he lived with his brother William at No. 131 in the 1860s. He was just one of many literary luminaries who resided here, including Julia Ward Howe, who composed "The Battle Hymn of the Republic" and lived at No. 32, and the poet Robert Frost, who lived at No. 88.

Nichols House. The only Mt. Vernon Street home open to the public, the Nichols House was built in 1804 and is attributed to Charles Bulfinch. It became the lifelong home of Rose Standish Nichols (1872–1960), Beacon Hill eccentric, philanthropist, peace advocate, and one of the first female landscape designers. Although Miss Nichols inherited the Victorian furnishings, she added a number of colonial-style pieces to the mix, such as an American Empire rosewood sideboard and a bonnet-top Chippendale highboy. The result is a delightful mélange of styles. Nichols made arrangements in her will for the house to become a museum, and knowledgeable volunteers from the neighborhood have been playing host since then. To see the house, you must take a tour (included in the price of admission). ✉ *55 Mt. Vernon St., Beacon Hill* ☎ *617/227–6993* ⊕ *www.nicholshousemuseum.org* ▣ *$7* ☉ *Apr.–Oct., Tues.–Sat. 11–4; Nov.–Mar., Thurs.–Sat. 11–4. First tour at 11, tours on ½ hr thereafter; last tour starts at 4* Ⓜ *Park St.*

Park Street Church. If this Congregationalist church at the corner of Tremont and Park streets could sing, what joyful noise it would be. Samuel Smith's hymn "America" was first sung inside the church, which was designed by Peter Banner and erected in 1809–10, on July 4, 1831. The country's oldest musical organization, the Handel & Haydn Society, was founded here in 1815; in 1829 William Lloyd Garrison began his long public campaign for the abolition of slavery here. The distinguished steeple is considered by many critics to be the most beautiful in New England. Just outside the church, at the intersection of Park and Tremont streets (and the main subway crossroads of the city) is **Brimstone Corner.** Whether the name refers to the fervent thunder of the church's preachers, the gunpowder that was once stored in the church's crypt, or the burning sulfur that preachers once scattered on the pavement to attract potential churchgoers, we'll never know—historians simply can't agree. ⊠ *1 Park St., Beacon Hill* ☎ *617/523–3383* ⊕ *www. parkstreet.org* ☉ *Tours mid-June–Aug., Tues.–Fri. 9–4, Sat. 9–3. Sun. services at 8:30, 11, 4, and 6:30* Ⓜ *Park St.*

Park Street Station. One of the first four stops on the first subway in America, Park Street Station was part of the line that originally ran only as far as the present-day Boylston stop. It was opened for service in 1897, against the warnings of those convinced it would make buildings along Tremont Street collapse. The copper-roof kiosks are National Historic Landmarks—outside them cluster flower vendors, street musicians, and partisans of causes and beliefs ranging from Irish nationalism to Krishna Consciousness. The station is the center of Boston's subway system; "inbound" trains are always traveling toward Park Street. ⊠ *Park and Tremont Sts., Beacon Hill.*

NEED A BREAK?

Panificio Bakery. While window-shopping on Charles Street, stop in at the Panificio Bakery, a cozy neighborhood hangout and old-fashioned Italian café. Soups and pizzas are made on the premises; for quick fortification, go for one of the Mediterranean sandwiches, or satisfy your sweet tooth with a raspberry turnover with a cappuccino. ⊠ *144 Charles St., Beacon Hill* ☎ *617/227–4340* ⊕ *www.panificioboston.com.*

State House. On July 4, 1795, the surviving fathers of the Revolution were on hand to enshrine the ideals of their new Commonwealth in a graceful seat of government designed by Charles Bulfinch. Governor Samuel Adams and Paul Revere laid the cornerstone; Revere would later roll the copper sheathing for the dome.

Bulfinch's neoclassical design is poised between Georgian and Federal; its finest features are the delicate Corinthian columns of the portico, the graceful pediment and window arches, and the vast yet visually weightless golden dome (gilded in 1874 and again in 1997). During World War II the dome was painted gray so that it would not reflect moonlight during blackouts and thereby offer a target to anticipated Axis bombers. It's capped with a pinecone, a symbol of the importance of pinewood, which was integral to the construction of Boston's early houses and churches—as well as the State House itself.

Inside the building are Doric Hall, with its statuary and portraits; the Hall of Flags, where an exhibit shows the battle flags from all the wars in which Massachusetts regiments have participated; the Great Hall, an open space used for state functions that houses 351 flags from the cities and towns of Massachusetts; the governor's office; and the chambers of the House and Senate. The Great Hall contains a giant, modernistic clock designed by New York artist R. M. Fischer. Its installation in 1986 at a cost of $100,000 was roundly slammed as a symbol of legislative extravagance. There's also a wealth of statuary, including figures of Horace Mann, Daniel Webster, and a youthful-looking President John F. Kennedy in full stride. Just outside Doric Hall is *Hear Us,* a series of six bronze busts honoring the contributions of women to public life in Massachusetts. But perhaps the best-known piece of artwork in the building is the carved wooden *Sacred Cod*, mounted in the Old State House in 1784 as a symbol of the commonwealth's maritime wealth. It was moved, with much fanfare, to Bulfinch's structure in 1798. By 1895, when it was hung in the new House chambers, the representatives had begun to consider the Cod their unofficial mascot—so much so that when *Harvard Lampoon* wags "codnapped" it in 1933, the House refused to meet in session until the fish was returned, three days later. ⊠ *Beacon St. between Hancock and Bowdoin Sts., Beacon Hill* ☎ *617/727–3676* ⊕ *www.state. ma.us/sec/trs/trsidx.htm* 🎟 *Free* ☉ *Weekdays 9–5. Tours 10–4; call ahead to schedule* Ⓜ *Park St.*

Vilna Shul. As the oldest synagogue in Boston, this historic treasure is the focus of both renovation and research. The two-story brick building was completed in 1919 by Jews from Vilna (or Vilnius), in what is now Lithuania. Modeled after the medieval synagogues of Europe, it's the last remaining immigrant era synagogue in Boston. The building, abandoned in 1985 after the congregation dropped to a single member, was bought by the Boston Center for Jewish Heritage, which is overseeing its ongoing restoration. Above the doorway gleams renewed gilded Hebrew lettering; the hand-carved ark and the stained-glass Star of David are worth a peek; and murals depicting traditional themes are being uncovered from beneath seven layers of paint. Three skylights flood it with natural light. ⊠ *14–18 Phillips St., Beacon Hill* ☎ *617/523–2324* ⊕ *www.vilnashul.org* 🎟 *Donations accepted* ☉ *Wed., Thurs., and Fri. 11–5, Sun. 1–5* Ⓜ *Charles/MGH.*

William Hickling Prescott House. A modest but engaging house museum has been installed in this 1808 Federal structure designed by Asher Benjamin. Now the headquarters for the Massachusetts Society of Colonial Dames of America, the house was the home of noted historian William Hickling Prescott from 1845 to 1859. Some rooms are furnished with period furniture, including the former study with Prescott's desk and "noctograph," which helped the nearly blind scholar write. (He was blinded in one eye by a flying crust of bread during a food fight at Harvard.) Ask about Prescott's secret staircase, which allowed him to escape into his study from boring guests in the parlor. The house also has a fine costume collection. ⊠ *55 Beacon St., Beacon Hill* ☎ *617/742–3190* ⊕ *www.nscda. org/ma/william_hickling_prescott_house.htm* 🎟 *$5* ☉ *Tours May–Oct., Wed., Thurs., and Sat. noon–4* Ⓜ *Park St., Charles/MGH.*

THE OLD WEST END

Just a few decades ago this district—separated from Beacon Hill by Cambridge Street—resembled a typical medieval city: thoroughfares that twisted and turned, maddening one-way lanes, and streets that were a veritable hive of people. Then, progress—or what passes for progress—all but eliminated the thriving Irish, Italian, Jewish, and Greek communities to make room for a mammoth project of urban renewal, designed in the 1960s by I.M. Pei.

Today little remains of the Old West End except for a few brick tenements and a handful of monuments, including the first house built for Harrison Gray Otis. The biggest surviving structures in the Old West End with any real history are two public institutions, Massachusetts General Hospital and the former Suffolk County Jail, which dates from 1849 and was designed by Gridley Bryant. The onetime prison is now part of the luxurious, and wryly named, Liberty Hotel.

Behind Massachusetts General and the sprawling Charles River Park apartment complex (famous among Storrow Drive commuters as the place with signs reading "If you lived here, you'd be home now") is a small grid of streets recalling an older Boston. Here are furniture and electric-supply stores, a discount camping-supply house (Hilton's Tent City), and many of the city's most popular watering holes. The main drag here is Causeway Street. North Station and the area around it, on Causeway between Haverhill and Canal streets, provide service to commuters from the northern suburbs and cheap brews to local barflies, and can be jammed when there's a game at the TD Garden, the home of the Bruins and Celtics.

In addition to the Garden, the innovative Museum of Science is one of the more modern attractions of the Old West End. The newest addition to the area's skyline is the Leonard P. Zakim Bunker Hill Bridge, which spans the Charles River just across from the TD Garden.

TOP ATTRACTIONS

Museum of Science.

Fodor's Choice   *See highlighted listing in this chapter.*
★

WORTH NOTING

Harrison Gray Otis House. If the name sounds familiar, it's because a Beacon Hill home bears the same name. This is the first of three houses built for Harrison Gray Otis, Boston's third mayor and a prominent citizen and developer. It's now the headquarters for the Society for the Preservation of New England Antiquities (SPNEA), an organization that owns and maintains dozens of properties throughout the region. The society restored the 1796 house; two of the floors are open as a museum. The furnishings, textiles, wall coverings, and even the interior paint, specially mixed to match old samples, are faithful to the Federal period, circa 1790–1810. You may be surprised to see the bright and vivid colors favored in those days. Otis lived here only four years before

MUSEUM OF SCIENCE

✉ *Science Park at Charles River Dam, Old West End* ☎ *617/723-2500* ⊕ *www. mos.org* 💲 *$21* ⊙ *July 5– Labor Day, Sat.–Thurs. 9–7, Fri. 9–9; after Labor Day–July 4, Sat.–Thurs. 9–5, Fri. 9–9* Ⓜ *Science Park.*

TIPS

■ The planetarium shows are best for children older than five.

■ After touring the museum, refuel the family at one of the six eateries located in the Riverview Cafe located in the Red Wing on the first level.

■ From April through November you can catch a Duck Tour from the first level of the museum. You'll need a reservation, so plan ahead. You might be in the mood to sit and tour the city after spending a morning on your feet walking through the exhibit halls.

■ Combine your admission with tickets to either the planetarium or Omni Theater and save $5 overall.

With 15-foot lightning bolts in the Theater of Electricity and a 20-foot-long Tyrannosaurus rex model, this is just the place to ignite any child's scientific curiosity. Occupying a compound of buildings north of Massachusetts General Hospital, the museum sits astride the Charles River Dam. More than 550 exhibits cover astronomy, astrophysics, anthropology, medical progress, computers, the organic and inorganic earth sciences, and much more. The emphasis is on hands-on education.

HIGHLIGHTS

At the "Investigate!" exhibit, there are no wrong answers, only discoveries. Children explore such scientific principles as gravity by balancing objects. They learn the physics behind everyday play activities such as swinging and bumping up and down on a teeter-totter in the "Science in the Park" exhibit. Other displays include "Light House," where you can experiment with color and light, and the perennial favorite,"Dinosaurs: Modeling the Mesozoic," which lets kids become paleontologists and examine dinosaur bones, fossils, and tracks.

The Charles Hayden Planetarium (☎ *617/723–2500*), with its sophisticated multimedia system based on a Zeiss planetarium projector, produces exciting programs on astronomical discoveries. Laser light shows, with laser graphics and computer animation, are scheduled Thursday through Sunday evenings. The museum also includes the Mugar Omni Theater (☎ *617/723–2500*), a five-story dome screen. The theater's state-of-the-art sound system provides extra-sharp acoustics, and the huge projection allows the audience to practically experience the action on-screen. Try to get tickets in advance online or over the phone; call or check the museum's Web site for show times.

moving to more sumptuous digs, designed by Charles Bulfinch, on Beacon Hill. A second-floor room brings to life the home's days as a late-19th-century boardinghouse, and a hallway display describes the "champoo baths" of former resident Mrs. Mott. Thought a quack in her time, she actually promoted the first aromatherapy saunas. From May through October Historic New England, which manages the property, runs the "Magnificent and Modest" walking tour from the house. It highlights the two sides of Beacon Hill, taking visitors past grandious mansions and more modest townhomes. Along the way, you'll pass the African Meeting House, Louisburg Square and the Boston Common. The $12 price includes admission to the Otis house. ⊠ *141 Cambridge St., Old West End* ☎ *617/994–5920* ⊕ *www.historicnewengland.org* ☛ *$8* ☉ *Tours on hr and ½ hr Wed.–Sun. 11–4:30* Ⓜ *Charles/MGH, Bowdoin.*

DUCK TOURS

With its colorful duck vehicles, Boston Duck Tours is a Boston fixture, taking more than half a million people a year on unique amphibious tours of the city: Boylston Street, Tremont Street, and the River Charles, all in one 80-minute trip. Tours depart from the Prudential Center and the Museum of Science, and run seven days a week, rain or shine, from late March to late November (all ducks are heated). Tickets are $31 for adults and $21 for ages 3–11. They sell out fast, so reserve early (☎ *617/267–3825* ⊕ *www. bostonducktours.com*).

NEED A BREAK?

Harvard Gardens. Harvard Gardens, a Beacon Hill legend, was the first bar in the city to get its liquor license after the repeal of Prohibition. It opened in 1930, and was owned by the same family until the 1990s. Once considered a dive bar, it's become much more upscale, with a menu of gourmet pizzas and sandwiches and scrumptious brunch fare, including a spectacular Bloody Mary. The tuna melt on tandoori bread provides a solid start to a day's exploring. The place is often packed with doctors and nurses enjoying post-shift drinks. ⊠ *316 Cambridge St., Beacon Hill* ☎ *617/523–2727.*

Leonard P. Zakim Bunker Hill Bridge. The crown jewel of the "Big Dig" construction project, the 1,432-foot-long Zakim Bridge, designed by Swiss bridge architect Christian Menn, is one of the widest cable-stayed hybrid bridges ever built, and the first to use an asymmetrical design. The towers evoke the Bunker Hill Monument, and the distinctive fan shape of the cables gives the bridge a modern flair. The bridge was named after Lenny Zakim, a local civil-rights activist who headed the New England Region of the Anti-Defamation League and died of cancer in 1999, and the Battle of Bunker Hill, a defining moment in U.S. history. One of the best spots to view the bridge is from the Charlestown waterfront across the river. The best viewing is at night, when the illuminated bridge glows blue. ⊕ *www.leonardpzakimbunkerhillbridge.org.*

Massachusetts General Hospital (MGH). Incorporated in 1811, MGH has traditionally been regarded as the nation's premier general hospital. The domed, granite **Bulfinch Pavilion** was designed in 1818 by Boston's leading architect, Charles Bulfinch. Harvard Medical School was once on the grounds of Massachusetts General, and today the hospital is the school's oldest teaching affiliate. **Amphitheater.** It was in the hospital's amphitheater that, on October 16, 1846, Dr. John Collins Warren performed the first operation on a patient anesthetized by ether; the place was promptly nicknamed the "Ether Dome." You may visit the amphitheater today when it's not in use (admission free; open daily 9–5) and see the fourth-floor display describing the procedure that made modern surgery possible. ⊠ *Main entrance on N. Grove St.; turn right after coffee shop,* ⊠ *55 Fruit St., Old West End* ☎ *617/726–2000* ⊕ *www.mgh. harvard.edu* Ⓜ *Charles/MGH.*

Old West Church. Built in 1806 to a design of the builder and architect Asher Benjamin, this imposing United Methodist church stands, along with the Harrison Gray Otis House next door, as a reminder of the area's more fashionable days. The church was a stop on the Underground Railroad, and it was the first integrated congregation in the country, giving open seating to blacks and whites alike just before 1820. In the early 1960s, when the church served as a public library and polling place, Congressman John F. Kennedy voted here. Free organ concerts are held here Tuesday at 8 pm in June, July, and August. ⊠ *131 Cambridge St., Old West End* ☎ *617/227–5088* ⊕ *www.oldwestchurch. org* ☉ *Tues.–Fri. 10–3. Sun. services at 11 am* Ⓜ *Bowdoin, Government Center.*

� **TD Garden.** Diehards still moan about the loss of the old Boston Garden, a much more intimate venue than this mammoth facility, which opened in 1995. A decade after it opened as the FleetCenter, the home of the Celtics (basketball) and Bruins (hockey) is once again known as the good old "Gah-den," and its air-conditioning, comfier seats, improved food selection, 1,200-vehicle parking garage, and nearly double number of bathrooms, has won grudging acceptance. The Garden occasionally offers public-skating sessions in the winter months; call ahead for hours and prices. **Sports Museum of New England.** The fifth and sixth levels of the TD Garden house the Sports Museum of New England, where displays of memorabilia and photographs showcase local sports history and legends. Take a tour of locker and interview rooms (off-season only), test your sports knowledge with interactive games, or see how you stand up to life-size statues of heroes Carl Yastrzemski and Larry Bird. The museum is open daily 10–4, with admission allowed only on the hour. Last entrance is at 3 pm on most days, 2 pm on game days; admission is $10. ⊠ *Use west premium seating entrance,* ☎ *617/624–1234* ⊕ *www.sportsmuseum.org* 🎫 *$10* ⊠ *Causeway St. at Canal St., Old West End* ☎ *617/624–1000* ⊕ *www.tdbanknorthgarden. com* Ⓜ *North Station.*

Government Center
and the North End

WORD OF MOUTH

"I visited Paul Revere House earlier this week; it's quite interesting
and worth a visit. Old North Church is just round the corner."

—yk

"Don't forget to do a cannoli tasting—try them at Mike's, Modern,
and Maria's (all in the North End) and see which you like best!"

—sf7307

GETTING ORIENTED

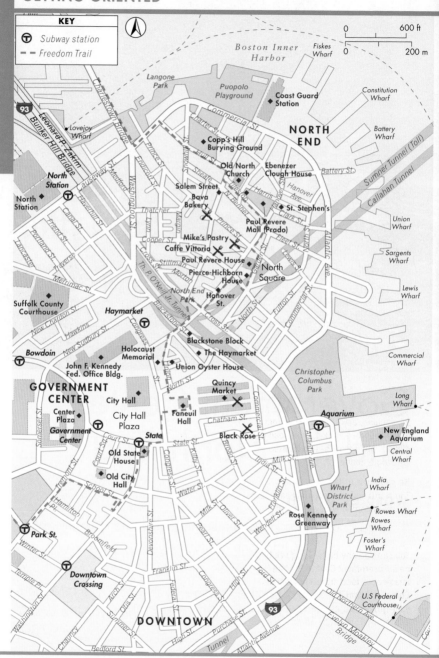

KEY
🅣 Subway station
- - Freedom Trail

0 _____ 600 ft
0 _____ 200 m

Boston Inner Harbor

Fiskes Wharf

Langone Park

Puopolo Playground

Coast Guard Station

Constitution Wharf

93

Leonard P. Zakim Bunker Hill Bridge

Charlestown Bridge

Commercial St.

NORTH END

Battery Wharf

Lovejoy Wharf

Charter St.

Copp's Hill Burying Ground

Old North Church

Ebenezer Clough House

Battery St.

Sumner Tunnel (Toll)

Callahan Tunnel

North Station

North Station

Causeway St.

Medford St.

Washington St.

Prince St.

Snelling

Salem Street

Bava Bakery

N. Bennet

Harris St.

Hanover Ave.

St. Stephen's

Clark St.

Union Wharf

Thatcher

Lynn

Margin

Cooper St.

Mike's Pastry

Caffe Vittoria

Fleet St.

Paul Revere Mall (Prado)

Sargents Wharf

Friend St.

Canal St.

Portland St.

Travers

Lancaster

Merrimac St.

Cross St.

Stillman

Morton

Paul Revere House

Pierce-Hichborn House

North Square

Lewis Wharf

Suffolk County Courthouse

New Chardon St.

North End Park

Hanover St.

North St.

Fulton St.

Commercial St.

T.P. O'Neill Jr. Tunnel

Haymarket

🅣

Blackstone St.

Cross St.

Christopher Columbus Park

Commercial Wharf

Hawkins

New Sudbury St.

Congress St.

Blackstone Block

The Haymarket

Bowdoin

🅣

Holocaust Memorial

John F. Kennedy Fed. Office Bldg.

Union Oyster House

Long Wharf

GOVERNMENT CENTER

Center Plaza

Government Center

🅣

City Hall

City Hall Plaza

Faneuil Hall

Quincy Market

Aquarium

🅣

North St.

Chatham St.

Commercial St.

Atlantic Ave.

New England Aquarium

Somerset

Court St.

State

🅣

Old State House

Old City Hall

State St.

Congress St.

Arch St.

Broad St.

India St.

Milk St.

Central Wharf

Tremont St.

Hamilton

School St.

Water St.

Devonshire St.

Milk St.

Oliver St.

Wharf District Park

India Wharf

Rowes Wharf

Rowes Wharf

Foster's Wharf

🅣 **Park St.**

Winter St.

Temple Pl.

Downtown Crossing

🅣

Bromfield

Franklin St.

Congress St.

High St.

Federal St.

Ford St.

Rose Kennedy Greenway

Old Northern Ave.

U.S Federal Courthouse

Washington St.

Otis St.

Temple St.

Summer St.

Arch St.

Chauncy

DOWNTOWN

High St.

Purchase St.

Atlantic Avenue

Evelyn Moakley Bridge

Tunnel

Bedford St.

GETTING HERE AND AROUND

Government Center is perfect for walking. If you arrive via the T, jump off the Green Line at Government Center, the Blue Line at State Street, or the Orange Line at Haymarket to explore. The T is your best bet for accessing the North End. Get off the Orange Line at Haymarket and walk southeast to Hanover Street; take a left there to enter the North End. Alternatively, jump off the Blue Line at Aquarium and walk northeast on Atlantic Avenue, past Christopher Columbus Park to access the North End.

TIMING AND SAFETY

You can easily spend several hours hitting the stores, boutiques, and historic sites of the Faneuil Hall and Quincy Market complex. On Friday and Saturday join crowds at the Haymarket farmers' market (wear good walking shoes, as the cobblestones get slippery with trampled produce).

Allow two hours for a walk through the North End, longer if you plan on dawdling in a café. This part of town is made for strolling, day or night. Many people like to spend part of a day at Quincy Market, then head over to the North End for dinner—the district has an impressive selection of traditional and contemporary Italian restaurants.

Be cautious in the Government Center area late at night. The North End is a relatively safe neighborhood; you'll have plenty of company day or night!

GOVERNMENT CENTER QUICK BITES

You can't do any better for quick bites than **Quincy Market** near Government Center. The hall is filled with stalls of every imaginable food from chowder and lobster rolls to pizza, Chinese, Indian, Italian pastries, ice cream, and candy. Grab your grub to go and enjoy a meal outside on the benches between the North or South Markets.

TOP REASONS TO GO

■ Shop 'till you drop at the North and South markets of Quincy Marketplace.

■ Imagine the debates of old during a tour of historic Faneuil Hall.

■ Grab a slice of Pizzeria Regina's cheesy best on the way through Quincy Market.

■ Enjoy a pint with a side of live Irish music at the Black Rose.

■ Come hungry, leave happy! Enjoy the delicious Italian fare in Boston's Little Italy.

■ Visit Old North Church and relive the night of Paul Revere's Ride.

■ Visit Paul Revere's house, the oldest standing home in Boston, to experience colonial life in Boston.

FREEDOM TRAIL SIGHTS

■ Faneuil Hall

■ The Old State House

■ Boston Massacre Site

■ Copp's Hill Burying Ground

■ Old North Church

■ Paul Revere House

NORTH END QUICK BITES

For a quick bite and a classic North End experience, head to **Mike's Pastry** (✉ *300 Hanover St.*) for cappuccino, cannoli, and people-watching in their bustling café.

3

Sightseeing
★★★★
Dining
★★★★★
Lodging
★★★★
Shopping
★★★★
Nightlife
★★★★★

Government Center is a section of town Bostonians love to hate. Not only does it house what they can't fight—City Hall—but it also contains some of the bleakest architecture since the advent of poured concrete. But though the stark, treeless plain surrounding City Hall has been roundly jeered for its user-unfriendly aura, the expanse is enlivened by feisty political rallies, free summer concerts, and the occasional festival. On the corner of Tremont and Court streets the landmark Steaming Kettle, a gilded kettle cast in 1873 that once boiled around the clock, lightens the mood a bit. (It now marks a Starbucks.) More historic buildings are just a little farther on: 18th-century Faneuil Hall and the frenzied Quincy Market.

Updated
by Bethany
Cassin
Beckerlegge

The curving six-story Center Plaza building, across from the Government Center T stop and the broad brick desert of City Hall Plaza, echoes the much older Sears Crescent, a curved commercial block next to the Government Center T stop. The Center Plaza building separates Tremont Street from Pemberton Square and the old and "new" courthouses to the west.

The warren of small streets on the northeast side of Government Center is the North End, Boston's Little Italy. In the 17th century the North End *was* Boston, as much of the rest of the peninsula was still under water or had yet to be cleared. Here the town bustled and grew rich for a century and a half before the birth of American independence. Now visitors can get a glimpse into Revolutionary times while filling up on some of the most scrumptious pastries and pastas to be found in modern Boston.

3

A GOOD WALK

The modern, stark expanse of Boston's **City Hall** and the twin towers of the **John F. Kennedy Federal Office Building** are an introduction to Boston in its urban-renewal stage. But just across Congress Street is **Faneuil Hall**, a site of political speech making since Revolutionary times, and just beyond that is **Quincy Market**, where you can shop (and eat) until you drop. For more Bostonian fare, walk back toward Congress Street to the **Blackstone Block** and the city's oldest restaurant, the **Union Oyster House**.

(Fashionable ladies take note: The cobblestones are treacherous if you're wearing heels.) Near the restaurant is the **Holocaust Memorial**, a six-tower construction of glass and steel. Follow Marshall Street north and turn right onto Blackstone Street to pass The **Haymarket**, a flurry of activity on Friday and Saturday, with open-air stalls selling produce and other foodstuffs. To sample Italian goodies, make your way to the North End via the pedestrian walkways that lead to Salem and Hanover streets.

Today's North End is almost entirely a creation of the late 19th century, when brick tenements began to fill up with European immigrants—first the Irish, then Central European Jews, then the Portuguese, and finally the Italians. For more than 60 years the North End attracted an Italian population base, so much so that one wonders whether wandering Puritan shades might scowl at the concentration of Mediterranean verve, volubility, and Roman Catholicism here. This is Boston's haven not only for Italian restaurants but also for Italian groceries, bakeries, boccie courts, churches, social clubs, cafés, and street-corner debates over home-team soccer games. ■TIP→ July and August are highlighted by a series of street festivals, or *feste*, honoring various saints, and by local community events that draw people from all over the city. A statue of St. Agrippina di Mineo—which is covered with money when it's paraded through the streets—is a crowd favorite.

Although hordes of visitors follow the redbrick ribbon of the Freedom Trail through the North End, the jumbled streets retain a neighborhood feeling, from the grandmothers gossiping on fire escapes to the laundry strung on back porches. Gentrification diluted the quarter's ethnic character some, but linger for a moment along Salem or Hanover streets and you can still hear people speaking with Abruzzese accents. If you wish to study up on this fascinating district, head for the North End branch of the Boston Public Library on Parmenter Street, where a bust of Dante acknowledges local cultural pride.

GOVERNMENT CENTER

TOP ATTRACTIONS

Blackstone Block. Between North and Hanover streets, near the Haymarket, lies the Blackstone Block, now visited mostly for its culinary landmark the **Union Oyster House.** Named for one of Boston's first settlers,

William Blaxton, or Blackstone, it's the city's oldest commercial block, for decades dominated by the butcher trade. As a tiny remnant of Old Boston, the Blackstone Block remains the city's "family attic"—to use the winning metaphor of critic Donlyn Lyndon: more than three centuries of architecture are on view, ranging from the 18th-century Capen House to the modern Bostonian Hotel. A colonial-period warren of winding lanes surrounds the block.

Facing the Blackstone Block, in tiny **Union Park,** framed by Congress Street and Dock Square, are two bronze figures, one seated on a bench and the other standing eye to eye with passersby. Both represent James Michael Curley, the quintessential Boston pol and a questionable role model for urban bosses. It's just as well that he has no pedestal. Also known as "the Rascal King" or "the Mayor of the Poor," and dramatized by Spencer Tracy in *The Last Hurrah* (1958), the charismatic Curley was beloved by the city's dominant working-class Irish for bringing them libraries, hospitals, bathhouses, and other public-works projects. His career got off to a promising start in 1903, when he ran—and won—a campaign for alderman from the Charles Street Jail, where he was serving time for taking someone else's civil-service exam. Over the next 50 years he dominated Boston politics, serving four nonconsecutive terms as mayor, one term as governor, and four terms as congressman. No one seemed to mind the slight glitch created when his office moved, in 1946, to the federal penitentiary, where he served five months of a 6- to 18-month sentence for mail fraud: he was pardoned by President Truman and returned to his people a hero.

★ **Faneuil Hall.** The single building facing Congress Street is the real Faneuil Hall, though locals often give that name to all five buildings in this shopping complex. Bostonians pronounce it *Fan*-yoo'uhl or *Fan*-yuhl. Like other Boston landmarks, Faneuil Hall has evolved over many years. It was erected in 1742, the gift of wealthy merchant Peter Faneuil, who wanted the hall to serve as both a place for town meetings and a public market. It burned in 1761 and was immediately reconstructed according to the original plan of its designer, the Scottish portrait painter John Smibert (who lies in the Granary Burying Ground). In 1763 the political leader James Otis helped inaugurate the era that culminated in American independence when he dedicated the rebuilt hall to the cause of liberty.

In 1772 Samuel Adams stood here and first suggested that Massachusetts and the other colonies organize a Committee of Correspondence to maintain semiclandestine lines of communication in the face of hardening British repression. In later years the hall again lived up to Otis's dedication when the abolitionists Wendell Phillips and Charles Sumner pleaded for support from its podium. The tradition continues to this day: in presidential-election years the hall is the site of debates between contenders in the Massachusetts primary.

Faneuil Hall was substantially enlarged and remodeled in 1805 according to a Greek Revival design of the noted architect Charles Bulfinch; this is the building you see today. Its purposes remain the same: the balconied Great Hall is available to citizens' groups on presentation

Imagine Samuel Adams stoking the fires of revolution at Faneuil Hall.

of a request signed by a required number of responsible parties; it also plays host to regular concerts.

Inside Faneuil Hall are dozens of paintings of famous Americans, including the mural *Webster's Reply to Hayne*, Gilbert Stuart's portrait of Washington at Dorchester Heights. Park rangers give informational talks about the history and importance of Faneuil Hall on the hour and half-hour. The rangers are a good resource, as interpretive plaques are few. Brochures about Faneuil Hall's history, distributed by the National Park Service, make lighthearted references to the ongoing commercialism nearby by reprinting a 1958 ditty by Francis Hatch: "Here orators in ages past / Have mounted their attacks / Undaunted by proximity / Of sausage on the racks." Faneuil Hall has always sat in the middle of Boston's main marketplace: when such men as Andrew Jackson and Daniel Webster debated the future of the Republic here, the fragrances of bacon and snuff—sold by merchants in **Quincy Market** across the road—greeted their noses. Today the aroma of coffee wafts through the hall from a snack bar. The shops at ground level sell New England bric-a-brac. **Ancient & Honorable Artillery Company of Massachusetts.** On the building's top floors are the headquarters and museum of the Ancient & Honorable Artillery Company of Massachusetts. Founded in 1638, it's the oldest militia in the Western Hemisphere, and the third oldest in the world, after the Swiss Guard and the Honorable Artillery Company of London. Its status is now strictly ceremonial, but it's justly proud of the arms, uniforms, and other artifacts on display. Admission is free. The museum is open weekdays 9 to 3:30. ☎ *617/227–1638* ✉ *Faneuil Hall Sq., Government Center* ☎ *617/523–1300* ⊕ *www.*

The haunting Holocaust Memorial sits at the north end of Union Park.

cityofboston.gov/freedomtrail/faneuilhall.asp ✉ *Free* ⊙ *Great Hall daily 9–5; informational talks every ½ hr. Shops Mon.–Sat. 10 am–9 pm, Sun. noon–6 pm* Ⓜ *Government Center, Aquarium, State.*

Fodor's Choice
★

Holocaust Memorial. At night its six 50-foot-high glass-and-steel towers glow like ghosts. During the day the monument seems at odds with the 18th-century streetscape of Blackstone Square behind it. Shoehorned into the north end of Union Park, the Holocaust Memorial is the work of Stanley Saitowitz, whose design was selected through an international competition; the finished memorial was dedicated in 1995. Recollections by Holocaust survivors are set into the glass-and-granite walls; the upper levels of the towers are etched with 6 million numbers in random sequence, symbolizing the Jewish victims of the Nazi horror. Manufactured steam from grates in the granite base makes for a particularly haunting scene after dark. ✉ *Union St. near Hanover St., Government Center.*

Quincy Market. Not everyone likes Quincy Market, also known as Faneuil Hall Marketplace; some people prefer grit to polish, and disdain the shiny cafés and boutiques. But there's no denying that this pioneer effort at urban recycling set the tone for many similar projects throughout the country, and that it has brought tremendous vitality to a once-tired corner of Boston. Quincy Market continues to attract huge crowds of tourists and locals throughout the year. In the early '70s, demolition was a distinct possibility for the decrepit buildings. Fortunately, with the participation of the Boston Redevelopment Authority, architect Benjamin Thompson planned a renovation of Quincy Market, and the Rouse Corporation of Baltimore undertook its restoration, which was completed in 1976. Try to look beyond the shop windows to the grand design of the market buildings themselves; they represent a vision of the market as urban centerpiece, an idea whose time has certainly come again.

The market consists of three block-long annexes: **Quincy Market, North Market,** and **South Market,** each 535 feet long and across a plaza from Faneuil Hall. The structures were designed in 1826 by Alexander Parris as part of a public-works project instituted by Boston's second mayor, Josiah Quincy, to alleviate the cramped conditions of Faneuil Hall and clean up the refuse that collected in Town Dock, the pond behind it. The central structure, made of granite, with

> **PAHK YOUR CAH**
>
> Government Center and the North End are best seen on foot, but if you must bring a car here are some tips. There is parking near Government Center at 75 State Street. Be sure to ask for the $3 off parking coupon when purchasing anything at Quincy Market
>
> The North End barely has enough parking for residents let alone visitors. The closest parking garages to Hanover Street (the North End's main thoroughfare) are the Dock Square Garage (✉ 20 Clinton St.) and Parcel 7 Garage (✉ 136 Blackstone St.).

a Doric colonnade at either end and topped by a classical dome and rotunda, has kept its traditional market-stall layout, but the stalls now purvey international and specialty foods: sushi, frozen yogurt, bagels, calzones, sausage-on-a-stick, Chinese noodles, barbecue, and baklava, plus all the boutique chocolate-chip cookies your heart desires. This is perhaps Boston's best locale for grazing.

Along the arcades on either side of the Central Market are vendors selling sweatshirts, photographs of Boston, and arts and crafts—some schlocky, some not—along with a couple of patioed bars and restaurants. The North and South markets house a mixture of chain stores and specialty boutiques. Quintessential Boston remains here only in Durgin Park, opened in 1826 and known for its plain interior, brassy waitresses, and large portions of traditional New England fare.

A greenhouse flower market on the north side of Faneuil Hall provides a splash of color; at Christmastime trees along the cobblestone walks are strung with thousands of sparkling lights. In summer up to 50,000 people a day descend on the market; the outdoor cafés are an excellent spot to watch the hordes if you can find a seat. Year-round the pedestrian walkways draw street performers, and rings of strollers form around magicians and musicians. ✉ *Bordered by Clinton, Commercial, and Chatham Sts., Government Center* ☎ *617/523–1300* ⊕ *www.faneuilhallmarketplace.com* ☯ *Mon.–Sat. 10–9, Sun. noon–6. Restaurants and bars generally open daily 11 am–2 am; food stalls open earlier* Ⓜ *Government Center, Aquarium, State.*

Union Oyster House. Billed as the oldest restaurant in continuous service in the United States, the Union Oyster House first opened its doors as the Atwood & Bacon Oyster House in 1826. Charles Forster of Maine was the first American to use the curious invention of the toothpick on these premises. And John F. Kennedy was also among its patrons; his favorite booth has been dedicated to his memory. The charming facade is constructed of Flemish bond brick and adorned with Victorian-style signage. With its scallop, clam, and lobster dishes—as well as the de rigueur oyster—the menu hasn't changed much since the restaurant's early days (though the prices have). ⊠ *41 Union St., Government Center* ☎ *617/227-2750* ⊕ *www.unionoysterhouse.com* ☾ *Sun.–Thurs. 11–9:30, Fri. and Sat. 11–10; bar open until midnight* Ⓜ *Haymarket.*

NEED A BREAK?

Black Rose. If all that snacking has you craving something more substantial, you might want to sample the cuisine of Boston's Irish at the Black Rose; take a right at the far end of the South Market. The bar-restaurant features traditional Irish fare and live music seven nights a week. ⊠ *160 State St., Government Center* ☎ *617/742-2286* ⊕ *www.irishconnection. com/blackrose.html.*

WORTH NOTING

City Hall. Over the years, various plans—involving gardens, restaurants, music, and hotels—have been floated to make this a more people-friendly site. Possibly the only thing that would ameliorate Bostonians' collective distaste for the chilly Government Center is tearing it down. But for the moment, City Hall, an upside-down ziggurat design on a brutalist redbrick plaza remains in commission. The design, by Kallman, McKinnell, and Knowles, confines administrative functions to the upper floors and places offices that deal with the public at street level. ⊠ *Congress St. at North St., Government Center* Ⓜ *Government Center.*

The Haymarket. Loud, self-promoting vendors pack this exuberant maze of a marketplace at Marshall and Blackstone streets on Friday and Saturday from 7 am until mid-afternoon (all vendors will likely be gone by 5). Pushcart vendors hawk fruits and vegetables against a backdrop of fish, meat, and cheese shops. The accumulation of debris left every evening has been celebrated in a whimsical 1976 public-arts project—Mags Harries's *Asaroton*, a Greek word meaning "unswept floors"—consisting of bronze fruit peels and other detritus smashed into pavement. Another Harries piece, a bronze depiction of a gathering of stray gloves, tumbles down between the escalators in the Porter Square T station in Cambridge. At Creek Square, near the Haymarket, is the **Boston Stone.** Set into the brick wall of the gift shop of the same name, this was a marker long used as milepost zero in measuring distances from Boston. ⊠ *Marshall and Blackstone Sts., Government Center* ☾ *Fri. and Sat. 7 am–mid-afternoon* Ⓜ *Government Center.*

John F. Kennedy Federal Office Building. Looming at the northwest edge of City Hall Plaza, these twin towers are noted structures for architecture aficionados: they were designed by the founder of the Bauhaus movement, Walter Gropius, who taught at Harvard toward the end of his illustrious career. Gropius's house, designed by him in textbook Bauhaus style, is in nearby suburban Lincoln.

TWO WAYS TO EXPLORE THE NORTH END

LA DOLCE VITA

Known as Boston's Little Italy, the North End has, in addition to an abundance of top-notch Italian eateries, many deliciously authentic Italian bakeries and cafés. Take a stroll down **Hanover Street,** the main thoroughfare, and you'll find all the cannoli and cappuccinos your heart could desire. On this street alone you'll find Caffe Paradiso at 255, Caffe Pompei at 278, and Caffe Vittoria at 290. Have a seat in any of these to relax, have a small snack, and take in the scene. Hanover Street is almost always crowded on weekend afternoons and nights, so it's an excellent place to people-watch. If you're looking to take a piece of the North End home with you in a little cardboard box tied up with string, visit one of Hanover's excellent bakeries: Modern Pastry Shop at 257, Mike's Pastry at 300, or Bova's Bakery at 134 Salem Street. Bova's claim to fame is that they are open 24 hours a day, so they are at your service no matter when the sweet tooth strikes.

RELIVE REVOLUTIONARY HISTORY

Since the North End was Boston at the time of the Revolution, some of the city's most historic buildings reside here. Visit the **Paul Revere House,** the oldest home in Boston, and learn how this legendary patriot made his historic midnight ride to warn of the oncoming British troops. The **Pierce-Hitchborn house** next door was owned by some of Revere's relatives and provides a peek into 18th-century middle-class life. Also in the North End is **Old North Church,** where Paul Revere hung two lanterns to signal that the British troops would depart by sea. Finally, stroll the **Prado,** or Paul Revere Mall to see the bronze statue that commemorates Revere's famous ride.

THE NORTH END

TOP ATTRACTIONS

Copp's Hill Burying Ground. An ancient and melancholy air hovers like a fine mist over this colonial-era burial ground. The North End graveyard incorporates four cemeteries established between 1660 and 1819. Near the Charter Street gate is the tomb of the Mather family, the dynasty of church divines (Cotton and Increase were the most famous sons) who held sway in Boston during the heyday of the old theocracy. Also buried here is Robert Newman, who crept into the steeple of the Old North Church to hang the lanterns warning of the British attack the night of Paul Revere's ride. Look for the tombstone of Captain Daniel Malcolm; it's pockmarked with musket-ball fire from British soldiers, who used the stones for target practice. Across the street at 44 Hull is the **narrowest house in Boston**—it's a mere 10 feet across. ⊠ *Intersection of Hull and Snowhill Sts., North End* ☉ *Daily 9–5* Ⓜ *North Station.*

Hanover Street. This is the North End's main thoroughfare, along with the smaller and narrower Salem Street. It was named for the ruling dynasty of 18th- and 19th-century England; the label was retained after the Revolution, despite a flurry of patriotic renaming (King Street became State Street, for example). Hanover's business center is thick with restaurants, pastry shops, and Italian cafés; on weekends Italian immigrants who have moved to the suburbs return to share an espresso with old friends and maybe catch a

> **DID YOU KNOW?**
>
> Longfellow's poem aside, the Old North Church lanterns were not a signal *to* Paul Revere but *from* him to Charlestown across the harbor.

soccer game broadcast via satellite. Hanover is one of Boston's oldest public roads, once the site of the residences of the Rev. Cotton Mather and the colonial-era patriot Dr. Joseph Warren, as well as a small dry-goods store run by Eben D. Jordan—who went on to launch the Jordan Marsh department stores.

NEED A BREAK?

Caffe Vittoria. Caffe Vittoria is rightfully known as Boston's most traditional Italian café. Gleaming brass, marble tabletops, and one of the city's best selections of grappa keep the place packed with locals. ⊠ *290–296 Hanover St., North End* ☎ *617/227-7606.*

Fodor's Choice
★

Old North Church. Standing at one end of the **Paul Revere Mall** is a church famous not only for being the oldest one in Boston (built in 1723) but for housing the two lanterns that glimmered from its steeple on the night of April 18, 1775. This is Christ, or Old North, Church, where Paul Revere and the young sexton Robert Newman managed that night to signal the departure by water of the British regulars to Lexington and Concord.

Although William Price designed the structure after studying Christopher Wren's London churches, Old North—which still has an active Episcopal congregation (including descendants of the Reveres)—is an impressive building in its own right. Inside, note the gallery and the graceful arrangement of pews; the bust of George Washington, pronounced by the Marquis de Lafayette to be the truest likeness of the general he ever saw; the brass chandeliers, made in Amsterdam in 1700 and installed here in 1724; and the clock, the oldest still running in an American public building. The pews—No. 54 belonged to the Revere family—are the highest in the United States because of the little charcoal-burning foot warmers. Try to visit when changes are rung on the bells, after the 11 am Sunday service; they bear the inscription, "We are the first ring of bells cast for the British Empire in North America." On the Sunday closest to April 18, descendants of the patriots reenact the raising of the lanterns in the church belfry during a special evening service.

Behind the church is the **Washington Memorial Garden,** where volunteers cultivate a plot devoted to plants and flowers favored in the 18th century. The garden is studded with several unusual commemorative plaques, including one for the Rev. George Burrough, who was hanged in the Salem witch trials in 1692; Robert Newman was his great-grandson. In another niche hangs the "Third Lantern," dedicated in 1976 to mark the country's bicentennial celebration. ⊠ *193 Salem St., North End* ☎ *617/523–6676* ⊕ *www.oldnorth.com* ☉ *Jan. and Feb.,*

The statue of Paul Revere outside the Old North Church commemorates his famous ride.

Tues.–Sun. 10–4; Mar.–May, daily 9–5; June–Oct., daily 9–6; Nov. and Dec., daily 9:30–4:30. Sun. services at 9 and 11 am Ⓜ *Haymarket, North Station.*

WORTH NOTING

Ebenezer Clough House. Built in 1712, this house is now the only local survivor of its era aside from Old North Church, which stands nearby. Picture the streets lined with houses such as this, with an occasional grander Georgian mansion and some modest wooden-frame survivors of old Boston's many fires—this is what the North End looked like when Paul Revere was young. During the summer, free tours of the home are available. ⊠ *21 Unity St., North End* ⊘ *July and Aug., Wed. 10–2.*

Ⓒ **Paul Revere House.** Originally on the site was the parsonage of the Second Church of Boston, home to the Rev. Increase Mather, the Second Church's minister. Mather's house burned in the great fire of 1676, and the house that Revere was to occupy was built on its location about four years later, nearly a hundred years before Revere's 1775 midnight ride through Middlesex County. Revere owned it from 1770 until 1800, although he lived there for only 10 years and rented it out for the next two decades. Pre-1900 photographs show it as a shabby warren of storefronts and apartments. The clapboard sheathing is a replacement, but 90% of the framework is original; note the Elizabethan-style overhang and leaded windowpanes. A few Revere furnishings are on display here, and just gazing at his silverwork—much more of which is displayed at the Museum of Fine Arts—brings the man alive.

Paul Revere's Ride

Test: Paul Revere was (1) a patriot whose midnight ride helped ignite the American Revolution; (2) a part-time dentist; (3) a silversmith who crafted tea services; (4) a printer who engraved the first Massachusetts state currency; or (5) a talented metallurgist who cast cannons and bells. The only correct response is "all of the above." But there's much more to this outsize Revolutionary hero—bell ringer for the Old North Church, founder of the copper mills that still bear his name, and father of 16 children.

Although his life spanned eight decades (1734–1818), Revere is most famous for that one night, April 18, 1775, when he became America's most celebrated Pony Express rider. *"Listen, my children, and you shall hear / Of the midnight ride of Paul Revere"* are the opening lines of Henry Wadsworth Longfellow's poem, which placed the event at the center of American folklore. Longfellow may have been an effective evangelist for Revere, but he was an indifferent historian.

Revere wasn't the only midnight rider. As part of the system set in motion by Revere and William Dawes Jr., also dispatched from Boston, there were at least several dozen riders, so that the capture of any one of them wouldn't keep the alarm from being sounded. It's also known that Revere never looked for the lantern signal from Charlestown. He told Robert Newman to hang two lanterns from Old North's belfry since the Redcoats were on the move by water, but by that time Revere was already being rowed across the Charles River to begin his famous ride.

Revere and Dawes set out on separate routes, but had the same mission: to warn patriot leaders Samuel Adams and John Hancock that British regular troops were marching to arrest them, and alarm the countryside along the way. The riders didn't risk capture by shouting the news through the streets—and they never uttered the famous cry "The British are coming!," since Bostonians still considered themselves British. When Revere arrived in Lexington a few minutes past midnight and approached the house where Adams and Hancock were lodged, a sentry challenged him, requesting that he not make so much noise. "Noise!" Revere replied. "You'll have noise enough before long."

Despite Longfellow's assertion, Revere never raised the alarm in Concord, because he was captured en route. He was held and questioned by the British patrol, and eventually released, without his horse, to walk back to Lexington in time to witness part of the battle on Lexington Green.

Poetic license aside, this tale has become part of the collective American spirit. Americans dote on hearing that Revere forgot his spurs, only to retrieve them by tying a note to his dog's collar, then awaiting its return with the spurs attached. The resourcefulness he showed in using a lady's petticoat to muffle the sounds of his oars while crossing the Charles is greatly appreciated. Little wonder that these tales resonate in the hearts and imagination of America's citizenry, as well as in Boston's streets on the third Monday of every April, Patriots' Day, when Revere's ride is reenacted—in daylight—to the cheers of thousands of onlookers.

■ TIP→ Special events are scheduled throughout the year, many designed with children in mind.

The immediate neighborhood also has Revere associations. The little park in North Square is named after Rachel Revere, his second wife, and the adjacent brick **Pierce-Hichborn House** once belonged to relatives of Revere. The garden connecting the Revere house and the Pierce-Hichborn House is planted with flowers and medicinal herbs favored in Revere's day. ⊠ *19 North Sq., North End* ☎ *617/523–2338* ⊕ *www.paulreverehouse.org* ✍ *$3.50, $5.50 with Pierce-Hichborn House* ⊗ *Jan.–Mar., Tues.–Sun. 9:30–4:15; Nov. and Dec. and 1st 2 wks of Apr., daily 9:30–4:15; mid-Apr.–Oct., daily 9:30–5:15* Ⓜ *Haymarket, Aquarium, Government Center.*

A STICKY SUBJECT

Boston has had its share of grim historic events, from massacres to stranglers, but on the sheer weirdness scale, nothing beats the Great Molasses Flood. In 1919 a steel container of molasses exploded on the Boston Harbor waterfront, killing 21 people and 20 horses. More than 2.3 million gallons of goo oozed onto unsuspecting citizenry, a veritable tsunami of sweet stuff. Some say you can still smell molasses on the waterfront during steamy weather. Smells to us like urban myth!

Paul Revere Mall (*Prado*). This makes a perfect time-out spot from the Freedom Trail. Bookended by two landmark churches—Old North and St. Stephen's—the mall is flanked by brick walls lined with bronze plaques bearing the stories of famous North Enders. An appropriate centerpiece for this enchanting cityscape is Cyrus Dallin's equestrian **statue of Paul Revere.** Despite his depictions in such statues as this, the gentle Revere was stocky and of medium height—whatever manly dash he possessed must have been in his eyes rather than his physique. That physique served him well enough, however, for he lived to be 83 and saw nearly all of his Revolutionary comrades buried. ⊠ *Bordered by Tileston, Hanover, and Unity Sts., North End* Ⓜ *Haymarket, Aquarium, Government Center.*

Pierce-Hichborn House. One of the city's oldest brick buildings, this structure, just to the left of the Paul Revere House, was once owned by Nathaniel Hichborn, a boatbuilder and Revere's cousin on his mother's side. Built about 1711 for a window maker named Moses Pierce, the Pierce-Hichborn House is an excellent example of early Georgian architecture. The home's symmetrical style was a radical change from the wood-frame Tudor buildings, such as the Revere House, then common. Its four rooms are furnished with modest 18th-century furniture, providing a peek into typical middle-class life. ⊠ *29 North Sq., North End* ☎ *617/523–2338* ✍ *$2, $5.50 with Paul Revere House* ⊗ *Guided tours only; call to schedule* Ⓜ *Haymarket, Aquarium, Government Center.*

Rose Kennedy Greenway. The Rose Kennedy Greenway, a winding series of parks that marks the path the highway once took through the city, adds much needed flora and fauna to the area. The park's Web site has a map of its 15 acres; a pleasant stroll through all of them will take you from the North End to Chinatown. ⇨ *See the Sports and Outdoors chapter for more information.* ⊕ *www.rosekennedygreenway.org.*

St. Stephen's. Rose Kennedy, matriarch of the Kennedy clan, was christened here; 104 years later, St. Stephen's held mourners at her 1995 funeral. This is the only Charles Bulfinch church still standing in Boston, and a stunning example of the Federal style to boot. Built in 1804, it was first used as a Unitarian Church; since 1862 it has served a Roman Catholic parish. When the belfry was stripped during a major 1960s renovation, the original dome was found beneath a false cap; it was covered with sheet copper and held together with hand-wrought nails, and later authenticated as being the work of Paul Revere. ⊠ *401 Hanover St., North End* ☎ *617/523–1230* ⊗ *Daily 7:30–4:30. Sun. Mass at 11, Sat. at 4:30, Tues.–Fri. at 7:30 am* Ⓜ *Haymarket, Aquarium, Government Center.*

Salem Street. This ancient and constricted thoroughfare, one of the two main North End streets, cuts through the heart of the neighborhood and runs parallel to and one block west of Hanover. Between Cross and Prince streets, Salem Street contains numerous restaurants and shops. One of the best is Shake the Tree, one of the North End's trendiest boutiques, selling stylish clothing, gifts, and jewelry. The rest of Salem Street is mostly residential, but makes a nice walk to the Copp's Hill Burying Ground.

NEED A BREAK?

Bova's Bakery. The allure of Bova's Bakery, a neighborhood institution, lies not only in its takeaway Italian breads, calzones, and pastries, but also in its hours: 24 a day (the deli closes at 1 am, however). ⊠ *134 Salem St., North End* ☎ *617/523–5601* ⊕ *bovabakeryboston.com.*

Charlestown

WORD OF MOUTH

"Climb to the top of the Bunker Hill Monument—be prepared for very wobbly legs when you get back down to the bottom. Then walk through Charlestown."

—sf7307

GETTING ORIENTED

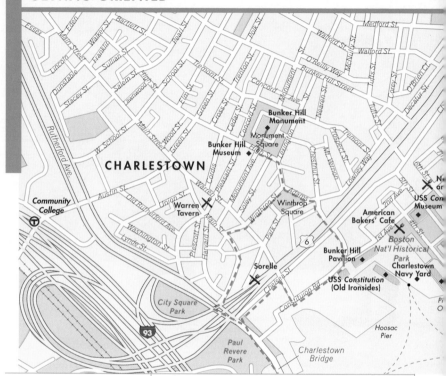

QUICK BITES

Navy Yard Bistro and Wine Bar. Enjoy a cozy dinner at Navy Yard Bistro and Wine Bar. Housed in a National Historic Site in the heart of the Charlestown Navy Yard, this restaurant offers French bistro fare at reasonable prices, with outdoor dining in summer. ✉ *6th St., on corner of 1st Ave.* ⊕ *www. navyyardbistro.com.*

American Bakers' Cafe. For coffee, pastries, or panini at lunchtime, try American Bakers' Cafe also in the Navy Yard. ✉ *39 1st Ave.*

TIMING AND SAFETY

Give yourself two to three hours for a Charlestown walk; the lengthy Charlestown Bridge calls for endurance in cold weather. You may want to save Charlestown's stretch of the Freedom Trail, which adds considerably to its length, for a second-day outing. You can always save time backtracking from the route by taking the MBTA water shuttle, which ferries back and forth between Charlestown's Navy Yard and downtown Boston's Long Wharf.

The Charlestown Navy Yard is generally a safe area, but as always use common sense, as Boston is a big city. Stick to well-lighted streets at night and avoid walking alone.

KEY

🇹 *Subway station*

– – *Freedom Trail*

0		600 ft
0		200 m

Barry Playground

CHARLESTOWN NAVY YARD

Navy Yard Bistro and Wine Bar

Constitution

Shipyard Park

Tavern on the Water

USS *Cassin Young*

Pier One

Paul Revere Mall

EAST BOSTON

Mystic River

Lopresti Park

Boston Inner Harbor

4

TOP REASONS TO GO

■ Climb the 294 steps to the top of the Bunker Hill Monument, and enjoy the views of the city while reliving the battles of the past.

■ Tour the USS *Constitution,* and discover why the oldest commissioned warship still afloat in the world is nicknamed "Old Ironsides."

FREEDOM TRAIL SIGHTS

■ Bunker Hill Monument

■ USS *Constitution*

GETTING HERE AND AROUND

The closest subway stop to the Charlestown Navy Yard is North Station (accessible by the Green and Orange lines), about a 15-minute walk. Take Causeway Street northeast and make a left to walk over the Charlestown Bridge. Take a right on Chelsea Street and right again on Warren Street. Constitution Road will be your next left, and from here you can enter the Navy Yard. From Downtown Crossing, take the 92 or 93 bus, which will drop you directly at the Navy Yard. If you are coming from downtown, try the water shuttle from Long Wharf near the Aquarium. Boats run daily on the hour and half-hour, and the ride is 10 minutes long.

Sightseeing
★ ★ ★
Dining
★ ★ ★
Lodging
★
Shopping
★
Nightlife
★ ★

Boston started here. Charlestown was a thriving settlement a year before colonials headed across the Charles River at William Blaxton's invitation to found the city proper. Today the district's attractions include two of the most visible—and vertical—monuments in Boston: the Bunker Hill Monument, which commemorates the grisly battle that became a symbol of patriotic resistance against the British, and the USS *Constitution,* whose masts continue to tower over the waterfront where she was built more than 200 years ago.

Updated
by Bethany
Cassin
Beckerlegge

The blocks around the Bunker Hill Monument are a good illustration of how gentrification is changing the neighborhoods. Along streets lined with gas lamps are impeccably restored Federal and mid-19th-century town houses; cheek by jowl are working-class quarters of similar vintage but more modest recent pasts. Near the Navy Yard along Main Street is City Square, the beginning of Charlestown's main commercial district, which includes City Square Park, with brick paths and bronze fish sculptures. On Phipps Street is the grave marker of John Harvard, a young minister who in 1638 bequeathed his small library to the fledgling Cambridge College, thereafter renamed in his honor. The precise location of the grave is uncertain, but a monument of 1828 marks its approximate site.

To get to Charlestown, you can walk across the Charlestown Bridge from the North End, or take Bus 93 from the Haymarket T station; it stops three blocks from the Navy Yard entrance. A more interesting and speedy way to get here is to take the MBTA water shuttle from Long Wharf in downtown Boston, which runs every 15 or 30 minutes year-round.

TOP ATTRACTIONS

Fodor'sChoice
★

Bunker Hill Monument. Three misunderstandings surround this famous monument. First, the Battle of Bunker Hill was actually fought on Breed's Hill, which is where the monument sits today. (The real Bunker Hill is about ½ mi to the north of the monument; it's slightly taller

than Breed's Hill.) Bunker was the original planned locale for the battle, and for that reason its name stuck. Second, although the battle is generally considered a colonial success, the Americans lost. It was a Pyrrhic victory for the British Redcoats, who sacrificed nearly half of their 2,200 men; American casualties numbered 400–600. And third: the famous war cry "Don't fire until you see the whites of their eyes" may never have been uttered by American Colonel William Prescott or General Israel Putnam, but if either one did shout it, he was quoting an old Prussian command made necessary by the notorious inaccuracy of the musket. No matter. The Americans did employ a deadly delayed-action strategy on June 17, 1775, and conclusively proved themselves worthy fighters, capable of defeating the forces of the British Empire.

Among the dead were the brilliant young American doctor and political activist Joseph Warren, recently commissioned as a major general but fighting as a private, and the British Major John Pitcairn, who two months before had led the Redcoats into Lexington. Pitcairn is believed to be buried in the crypt of Old North Church.

In 1823 the committee formed to construct a monument on the site of the battle chose the form of an Egyptian obelisk. Architect Solomon Willard designed a 221-foot-tall granite obelisk, a tremendous feat of engineering for its day. The Marquis de Lafayette laid the cornerstone of the monument in 1825, but because of a nagging lack of funds, it wasn't dedicated until 1843. Daniel Webster's stirring words at the ceremony commemorating the laying of its cornerstone have gone down in history: "Let it rise! Let it rise, till it meets the sun in his coming. Let the earliest light of the morning gild it, and parting day linger and play upon its summit."

The monument's zenith is reached by a flight of 294 steps. There's no elevator, but the views from the observatory are worth the effort of the arduous climb. A statue of Colonel Prescott stands guard at the base. In the Bunker Hill Museum across the street, artifacts and exhibits tell the story of the battle, while a detailed diorama shows the action in miniature. ☎ 617/242–5641 ⊕ www.nps.gov/bost/historyculture/bhm.htm. ✉ Free ⊙ Museum daily 9–5, monument daily 9–4:30 Ⓜ Community College.

USS Constitution. Better known as "Old Ironsides," the USS Constitution rides proudly at anchor in her berth at the Charlestown Navy Yard. The oldest commissioned ship in the U.S. fleet is a battlewagon of the old school, of the days of "wooden ships and iron men"—when she and her crew of 200 succeeded at the perilous task of asserting the sovereignty of an improbable new nation. Every July 4 and on certain other occasions

Fodor'sChoice
★

she's towed out for a turnabout in Boston Harbor, the very place her keel was laid in 1797.

The venerable craft has narrowly escaped the scrap heap several times in her long history. She was launched on October 21, 1797, as part of the nation's fledgling navy. Her hull was made of live oak, the toughest wood grown in North America; her bottom was sheathed in copper, provided by Paul Revere at a nominal cost. Her principal service was during Thomas Jefferson's campaign against the Barbary pirates, off the coast of North Africa, and in the War of 1812. In 42 engagements her record was 42–0.

The nickname "Old Ironsides" was acquired during the War of 1812, when shots from the British war-

> ### A GOOD WALK
>
> If you choose to hoof it to Charlestown, follow Hull Street from Copp's Hill Burying Ground to Commercial Street; turn left on Commercial and, two blocks later, right onto the bridge. The entrance to the **Charlestown Navy Yard** is on your right after crossing the bridge. Just ahead is the Charlestown Navy Yard Visitors Information Center; inside the park gate are the **USS** *Constitution* and the associated **USS** *Constitution* **Museum**. From here, the red line of the Freedom Trail takes you to the **Bunker Hill Monument**.

ship *Guerrière* appeared to bounce off her hull. Talk of scrapping the ship began as early as 1830, but she was saved by a public campaign sparked by Oliver Wendell Holmes's poem "Old Ironsides." She underwent a major restoration in the early 1990s, and only about 8%–10% of her original wood remains in place, including the keel, the heart of the ship. Today she continues, the oldest commissioned warship afloat in the world, to be a part of the U.S. Navy.

The men and women who look after the *Constitution*, regular navy personnel, maintain a 24-hour watch. Sailors show visitors around the ship, guiding them to her top, or spar, deck, and the gun deck below. Another treat when visiting the ship is the spectacular view of Boston across Boston Harbor. ■ TIP→ Instead of taking the T, you can get closer to the ship by taking MBTA Bus 92 to Charlestown City Square or Bus 93 to Chelsea Street from Haymarket. Or you can take the Boston Harbor Cruise water shuttle from Long Wharf to Pier 4. ⊠ *Charlestown Navy Yard, 55 Constitution Rd., Charlestown* ☎ *617/242–7511* ⊕ *www.history.navy.mil/USSconstitution/index. html* 🖭 *Free* ☉ *Apr. 1–Oct., Tues.–Sun. 10–6; Nov.–Mar. 31, Thurs.–Sun. 10–4; last tour at 3:30* Ⓜ *North Station.*

NEED A BREAK?

Warren Tavern. After a blustery walk at the Navy Yard, get a seat by the fireplace and warm yourself with a hearty chowder and Sam Adams draft at the Warren Tavern. Built in 1780, this restored colonial neighborhood pub was once frequented by George Washington and Paul Revere. It was one of the first buildings reconstructed after the Battle of Bunker Hill, which leveled Charlestown. ⊠ *2 Pleasant St., Charlestown* ☎ *617/241–8142* ⊕ *www. warrentavern.com.*

Tavern on the Water. For a meal on the waterfront, try the Tavern on the Water in the Charlestown Navy Yard. It's a neighborhood hangout with outstanding harbor views and the requisite New England seafood dishes. ⊠ *1 8th St., Pier 6, Charlestown* ☎ *617/242–8040* ⊕ *www.tavernonthewater.com.*

WORTH NOTING

Charlestown Navy Yard. A National Park Service Historic Site since it was decommissioned in 1974, the Charlestown Navy Yard was one of six established to build warships. For 174 years, as wooden hulls and muzzle-loading cannons gave way to steel ships and sophisticated electronics, the yard evolved to meet the Navy's changing needs. Here are early-19th-century barracks, workshops, and officers' quarters; a rope-walk (an elongated building for making rope, not open to the public), designed in 1834 by the Greek Revival architect Alexander Parris and used by the Navy to turn out cordage for more than 125 years; and one of the oldest operational naval dry docks in the United States. The USS *Constitution* was the first to use this dry dock, in 1833. In addition to the ship itself, check out the *Constitution* Museum, the collections of the Boston Marine Society, and the USS *Cassin Young*, a World War II destroyer typical of the ships built here during that era. At the entrance of the Navy Yard is the **Charlestown Navy Yard Visitors Information Center.** ⊠ *55 Constitution Rd., Charlestown* ☎ *617/242–5601* ⊕ *www.nps.gov/bost/historyculture/cny.htm* ⊙ *Visitors Information Center daily 9–5* Ⓜ *North Station; MBTA Bus 92 to Charlestown City Sq. or Bus 93 to Chelsea St. from Haymarket; or Boston Harbor Cruise water shuttle from Long Wharf to Pier 4.*

USS Cassin Young. From a later date than the *Constitution*, this destroyer saw action in Asian waters during World War II. She served the Navy until 1960. ⊠ *Charlestown Navy Yard, 55 Constitution Rd., Charlestown* ☎ *617/242–5601* ⊕ *www.nps.gov/bost/historyculture/usscassinyoung.htm* 🎟 *Free* ⊙ *July and Aug., daily 10–5; Sept.–June, daily noon–3; tours at 11 and 2* Ⓜ *North Station; MBTA Bus 92 to Charlestown City Sq. or Bus 93 to Chelsea St. from Haymarket; or Boston Harbor Cruise water shuttle from Long Wharf to Pier 4.*

USS Constitution Museum. Artifacts and hands-on exhibits pertaining to the USS *Constitution* are on display—firearms, logs, and instruments. One section takes you step-by-step through the ship's most important battles. Old meets new in a video-game battle "fought" at the helm of a ship. ⊠ *Adjacent to USS Constitution, Charlestown Navy Yard, Charlestown* ☎ *617/426–1812* ⊕ *www.ussconstitutionmuseum.org* 🎟 *Donations accepted* ⊙ *Apr.–Oct., daily 9–6; Nov.–Mar., daily 10–5* Ⓜ *North Station; MBTA Bus 92 to Charlestown City Sq. or Bus 93 to Chelsea St. from Haymarket; or Boston Harbor Cruise water shuttle from Long Wharf to Pier 4.*

NEED A BREAK?

Sorelle. Walking the Freedom Trail is exhausting. Whether Charlestown is your stopping or ending point, take a breather at Sorelle, a hot little bakery with two locations, delicious sandwiches, and refreshing iced coffees. ⊠ *100 City Sq., Charlestown* ☎ *617/242–5980.*

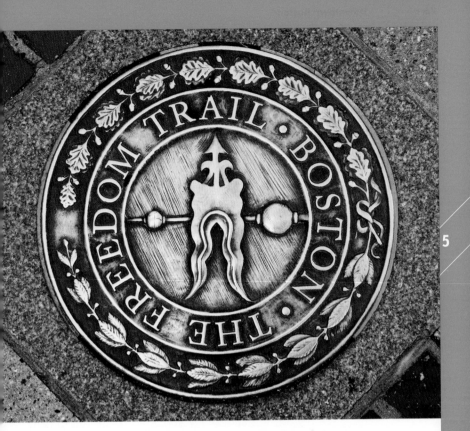

Downtown Boston

WORD OF MOUTH

"The Freedom Trail is very interesting if you are a history buff . . .
There are guided tours—some done in period character . . . I love
the New England Aquarium on the harbor. The Aquarium, the historic sights of the Freedom Trail, the architecture, the harbor are all
part of what make Boston unique."

—ktmc

GETTING ORIENTED

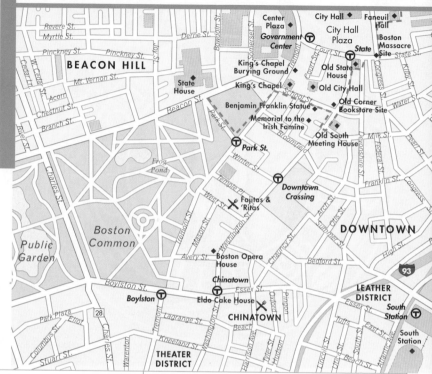

GETTING HERE AND AROUND

Downtown Boston is easily accessible by T; take the Orange Line to Downtown Crossing, the Blue Line to Aquarium, or the Red Line to South Station or Downtown Crossing. If you are in a car, a garage is your best bet; the **Interpark Garage** (⊠ 270 Atlantic Ave.) is near the New England Aquarium. The Children's Museum is a bit farther away: either walk from South Station or park nearby at the **Stanhope Garage** (⊠ 338 Congress St.).

TIMING AND SAFETY

This section of Boston has a generous share of attractions, so it's wise to save a full day, spending the bulk of it at either the New England Aquarium or the Children's Museum. There are optimum times to catch some sights: the only tours to the top of the U.S. Custom House are at 10 and 4 on sunny days, and a stroll along the waterfront at Rowes Wharf is most romantic at dusk. No need to visit the aquarium at a special hour to catch feeding time—there are five of them throughout the day.

Downtown Boston is a safe area, but the Financial District empties out after 6, so choose well-lighted streets when walking alone at night.

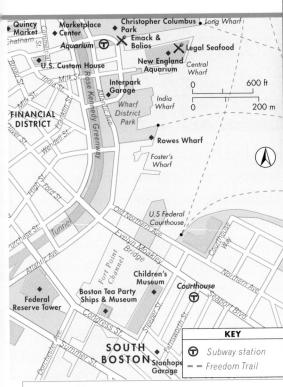

Quincy Market • Chatham St. • Marketplace Center • Christopher Columbus Park • Long Wharf
Commercial St. • Aquarium Ⓣ • Emack & Bolios • Legal Seafood
Broad St. • U.S. Custom House • New England Aquarium • Central Wharf
India St. • Milk St.
Rose Kennedy Greenway • Atlantic Ave.
FINANCIAL DISTRICT
Milk St. • Wendell St. • High St. • Ford St.
Interpark Garage
Wharf District Park • India Wharf
Rowes Wharf
Foster's Wharf

0 ——— 600 ft
0 ——— 200 m

Purchase St. • Tunnel • Atlantic Ave.
Old Northern Ave.
Evelyn Moakley Bridge
Fort Point Channel
U.S Federal Courthouse
Courthouse Way • Northern Ave.

Children's Museum
Boston Tea Party Ships & Museum
Courthouse Ⓣ
Seaport Blvd • Sleeper St.
Federal Reserve Tower
Congress St.
Dorchester Ave. • Summer St.
SOUTH BOSTON
Farnsworth St.
Stanhope Garage

KEY
Ⓣ Subway station
- - Freedom Trail

TOP REASONS TO GO

■ Walk like a penguin and watch the seals play at the New England Aquarium.

■ Set the kids free in the two-story climbing maze at the Children's Museum.

■ Explore the stores of Downtown Crossing, an outdoor pedestrian mall.

■ Visit the 26th-floor observation deck at the U.S. Custom House for a bird's-eye view of Downtown.

FREEDOM TRAIL SIGHTS

■ Benjamin Franklin Statue/Boston Latin School

■ Old Corner Bookstore Site

■ Old South Meeting House

■ King's Chapel and Burying Ground

■ First Public School Site

■ Park Street Church

QUICK BITES

The quintessential Boston fish haunt, **Legal Sea Foods** (✉ *255 State St.*) is at Long Wharf, steps from the New England Aquarium and other Downtown attractions. Stop in for a bowl of their famous clam chowder—just the thing to take the chill off a cool fall day. For dessert, step right around the corner to **Emack & Bolios** (✉ *255 State St.*) for homemade ice cream with a rock-and-roll vibe.

DID YOU KNOW?

The Boston Tea Party occurred on Atlantic Avenue near Congress Street. The area was once a wharf—further evidence of Boston's relentless expansion into the harbor. There isn't much to see here now; a commercial building with a plaque marking the site has been torn down.

Boston's commercial and financial districts—the area commonly called Downtown—are concentrated in a maze of streets that seem to have been laid out with little logic; they are, after all, only village lanes that happen to be lined with modern 40-story office towers. Just as the Great Fire of 1872 swept the old Financial District clear, the Downtown construction in more-recent times has obliterated many of the buildings where 19th-century Boston businessmen sat in front of their rolltop desks. Yet many historic sites remain tucked among the skyscrapers; a number of them have been linked together to make up a fascinating section of the Freedom Trail.

Updated
by Bethany
Cassin
Beckerlegge

The area is bordered by State Street on the north and by South Station and Chinatown on the south. Tremont Street and the Common form the west boundary, and the harbor wharves the eastern edge. Locals may be able to navigate the tangle of thoroughfares in between, but very few of them manage to give intelligible directions when consulted, so you're better off carrying a map.

Washington Street (aka Downtown Crossing) is the main commercial thoroughfare of downtown Boston. It's a pedestrian street once marked by two venerable anchors of Boston's mercantile district, Filene's Basement (now closed, though some of the facade remains, for the moment) and Jordan Marsh (now Macy's). The block reeks of history—and sausage carts. Street vendors, flower sellers, and gaggles of teenagers, businesspeople, and shoppers throng the pedestrian mall.

Downtown is also the place for some of Boston's most idiosyncratic neighborhoods. The Leather District directly abuts Chinatown, which is also bordered by the Theater District (and the buildings of Tufts Medical Center) farther west, and to the south, the red light of the

Kids are entertained and educated at the Children's Museum.

once-brazen Combat Zone flickers weakly in a pair of adjacent strip clubs. The Massachusetts Turnpike and its junction with the Southeast Expressway cut a wide swath through the area, isolating Chinatown from the South End.

TOP ATTRACTIONS

Children's Museum. Most children have so much fun here that they don't realize they're actually learning something. Creative hands-on exhibits demonstrate scientific laws, cultural diversity, and problem solving. After completing a massive 23,000 square-foot expansion in 2007, the museum has updated a lot of its old exhibitions and added new ones. Some of the most popular stops are also the simplest, like the bubble-making machinery and the two-story climbing maze. At the Japanese House you're invited to take off your shoes and step inside a two-story silk merchant's home from Kyoto. The "Boston Black" exhibit stimulates dialogue about ethnicity and community while children play in a Cape Verdean restaurant and the African Queen Beauty Salon. In the toddler PlaySpace, children under three can run free in a safe environment. There's also a full schedule of special exhibits, festivals, and performances. ⊠ *300 Congress St., Downtown* ☎ *617/426–6500* ⊕ *www.bostonkids.org* ✉ *$12, Fri. 5–9 $1* ⏱ *Sat.–Thurs. 10–5, Fri. 10–9* Ⓜ *South Station.*

Fodor'sChoice
★

New England Aquarium.

Fodor'sChoice
★

See highlighted listing in this chapter.

WORTH NOTING

Benjamin Franklin Statue/Boston Latin School. This stop on the Freedom Trail commemorates the famous revolutionary and inventor. His likeness also marks the original location of Boston Latin School, the country's oldest public school, which still molds young minds, albeit from the Fenway neighborhood, today. Franklin attended Boston Latin with three other signers of the Declaration of Independence—Samuel Adams, John Hancock, and Robert Treat Paine—but he has the dubious distinction of being the only one of the four not to graduate. ⊠ *School St. at City Hall Ave., Downtown* ☎ *617/357–8300* ⊕ *www.thefreedomtrail. org/visitor/boston-latin.html* Ⓜ *Park.*

Boston Massacre Site. Directly in front of the **Old State House** a circle of cobblestones (on a traffic island) marks the site of the Boston Massacre. It was on the snowy evening of March 5, 1770, that nine British regular soldiers fired in panic upon a taunting mob of more than 75 Bostonians. Five townsmen died. In the legal action that followed, the defense of the accused soldiers was undertaken by John Adams and Josiah Quincy, both of whom vehemently opposed British oppression but were devoted to the principle of fair trial. All but two of the nine regulars charged were acquitted; the others were branded on the hand for the crime of manslaughter. Paul Revere lost little time in capturing the "massacre" in a dramatic engraving that soon became one of the Revolution's most potent images of propaganda. ⊠ *Congress and Court Sts., Downtown* Ⓜ *State.*

Boston Opera House. Originally the B.F. Keith Memorial Theatre in the days of vaudeville, this venue was designed in beaux arts style by Thomas Lamb and modeled after the Paris Opera House. The theater shut its doors in 1991, but a multimillion-dollar restoration completed in 2004 has brought theater and dance performances back to the Opera House. ⊠ *539 Washington St., Downtown* ☎ *617/259–3400* ⊕ *bostonoperahouseonline.com/* Ⓜ *Boylston.*

Ⓒ **Boston Tea Party Ships & Museum.** After a lengthy renovation, the museum is, as of this writing, scheduled to reopen in the summer of 2011 (though the opening date has been extended more than once). The *Beaver II*, a reproduction of one of the ships forcibly boarded and unloaded the night Boston Harbor became a teapot, is supposed to return to the Fort Point Channel at the Congress Street Bridge and be joined by two tall ships, the *Dartmouth* and the *Eleanor.* Visitors are promised a chance to explore the ships and museum exhibits, meet reenactors, or drink a cup of tea in a new Tea Room. ⊠ *Fort Point Channel at Congress St. Bridge, Downtown* ⊕ *www.bostonteapartyship.com* ⊘ *Check Web site for updated information* Ⓜ *South Station.*

Chinatown. Boston's Chinatown may seem small, but it's said to be the third-largest in the United States, after those in San Francisco and Manhattan. Beginning in the 1870s, Chinese immigrants started to trickle in, many setting up tents in a strip they called Ping On Alley. The trickle increased to a wave when immigration restrictions were lifted in 1968. As in most other American Chinatowns, the restaurants are a big draw; on Sunday many Bostonians head to Chinatown for

NEW ENGLAND AQUARIUM

✉ *Central Wharf between Central and Milk Sts., 1 Central Wharf, Downtown* ☎ *617/973–5200* ⊕ *www. neaq.org* 🎟 *$21.95, IMAX $9.95* 🕐 *July–early Sept., Sun.–Thurs. 9–6, Fri. and Sat. 9–7; early Sept.–June, weekdays 9–5, weekends 9–6* Ⓜ *Aquarium, State.*

TIPS

■ If you are planning to see an IMAX show as well as check out the aquarium, buy a combo ticket; you'll save $3.95 for the adult ticket.

■ Also, buy the combo ticket if you'd like to do the whale watch and the Aquarium, you'll save $7.95 over purchasing them separately.

■ Save yourself the torture of waiting in long weekend lines, and purchase your tickets ahead of time online at www. neaq.org. You can skip ahead of the crowd and pick up your tickets at the will call window, or print them out at home.

■ Want to make your day at the aquarium really special for the kids? Call ahead for a reservation to play with the seals! For $45, kids 9 and up can go behind the scenes and help feed and entertain the seals. Call Central Reservations at 617/973–5206 for more information.

This aquarium challenges you to really imagine life under and around the sea. Seals bark outside the West Wing, its glass-and-steel exterior constructed to mimic fish scales. Inside the main facility you can see penguins, sea otters, sharks, and other exotic sea creatures—more than 2,000 species in all.

HIGHLIGHTS

In the semi-enclosed outdoor space of the New Balance Foundation Marine Mammal Center visitors enjoy the antics of northern fur seals while gazing at a stunning view of Boston Harbor.

One of the aquarium's exhibits, Amazing Jellies, features thousands of jellyfish, many of which were grown in the museum's labs.

Some of the aquarium's 2,000 sea creatures make their home in the four-story, 200,000-gallon ocean-reef tank, one of the largest of its kind in the world. Ramps winding around the tank lead to the top level and allow you to view the inhabitants from many vantage points. Don't miss the five-times-a-day feedings; each lasts nearly an hour and takes divers 24 feet into the tank.

From outside the glassed-off Aquarium Medical Center you can watch veterinarians treat sick animals—here's where you can see an eel in a "hospital bed." At the Edge of the Sea exhibit children can gingerly pick up starfish and other creatures, while the Curious George Discovery Corner is a fun spot for younger kids. Whale-watch cruises leave from the aquarium's dock from April to October, and cost $39.95. Across the plaza is the aquarium's Education Center; it, too, has changing exhibits. The 6½-story-high IMAX theater takes you on virtual journeys from the bottom of the sea to the depths of outer space with its 3-D films.

5

TWO WAYS TO EXPLORE DOWNTOWN

FOR KIDS

Two of the best museums in Boston for children are in the Downtown area: the Children's Museum and the New England Aquarium. Let the kiddies run wild in the two-story climbing maze at the Children's Museum and then get up close and personal with their favorite marine animals, like seals and penguins, at the aquarium. Both venues are great for rainy day entertainment (a likely event in Boston). There's even an Emack and Bolio's ice-cream shop across from the aquarium; end this kid-tastic day there with a cherry on top.

FOR GROWN-UPS

Stop by the King's Chapel to immerse yourself in history and music during one of the regular Tuesday concerts at 12:15. You could easily spend a couple of hours perusing the bargains in Downtown Crossing or taking a leisurely walk along the harbor front at Rowes Wharf. While you're there, sample one of the more than 40 different scotches at the Rowes Wharf Bar in the Boston Harbor Hotel. Need an idea for date night? Why not take in a show at the Opera House and savor a late night dinner for two in Chinatown.

dim sum. Today the many Chinese establishments—most found along Beach and Tyler streets and Harrison Avenue—are interspersed with Vietnamese, Korean, Japanese, Thai, and Malaysian eateries. A three-story pagoda-style arch at the end of Beach Street welcomes you to the district. ⊠ *Bounded (roughly) by Essex, Washington, Marginal, and Hudson* Ⓜ *Chinatown.*

NEED A BREAK?

Eldo Cake House. Never considered bean paste for dessert or eaten a Chinese-style pork bun? Expand your horizons at Eldo Cake House, which has both sweet and savory pastries. ⊠ *36 Harrison Ave., Downtown* ☎ *617/350–7977* ⊕ *eldocakehouse.bzlnk.com.*

Christopher Columbus Park (*Waterfront Park*). It's a short stroll from the Financial District to a view of Boston Harbor. Once a national symbol of rampant pollution, the harbor is making a gradual comeback. This green space bordering the harbor and several of Boston's restored wharves is a pleasant oasis with benches and an arborlike shelter. Lewis Wharf and Commercial Wharf (north of the park), which long lay nearly derelict, had by the mid-1970s been transformed into condominiums, offices, restaurants, and upscale shops. Long Wharf's Marriott hotel was designed to blend in with the old seaside warehouses. In September the park is home to the Boston Arts Festival. ⊠ *Bordered by Atlantic Ave., Commercial Wharf, and Long Wharf, Downtown* Ⓜ *Aquarium.*

Federal Reserve Tower. On Atlantic Avenue, across from South Station, is this striking aluminum-clad building, designed in 1976 by Hugh Stubbins and Associates. The tower is mainly used for offices, and is not open to the public. ⊠ *600 Atlantic Ave., Downtown* Ⓜ *South Station.*

King's Chapel. Both somber and dramatic, King's Chapel looms over the corner of Tremont and School streets. Its distinctive shape wasn't

King's Chapel is missing a steeple, which was never built due to lack of funds.

achieved entirely by design; for lack of funds, it was never topped with the steeple that architect Peter Harrison had planned. The first chapel on this site was erected in 1688, when Sir Edmund Andros, the royal governor whose authority temporarily replaced the original colonial charter, appropriated the land for the establishment of an Anglican place of worship. This rankled the Puritans, who had left England to escape Anglicanism and had until then succeeded in keeping it out of the colony.

It took five years to build the solid Quincy-granite structure. As construction proceeded, the old church continued to stand within the rising walls of the new, the plan being to remove and carry it away piece by piece when the outer stone chapel was completed. The builders then went to work on the interior, which remains essentially as they finished it in 1754; it's a masterpiece of proportion and Georgian calm (in fact, its acoustics make the use of a microphone unnecessary for Sunday sermons). The pulpit, built in 1717 by Peter Vintoneau, is the oldest pulpit in continuous use on the same site in the United States. To the right of the main entrance is a special pew once reserved for condemned prisoners, who were trotted in to hear a sermon before being hanged on the Common. The chapel's bell is Paul Revere's largest and, in his judgment, his sweetest sounding. ⊠ *Tremont St. at School St., Downtown* ☎ *617/227–2155* ⊕ *www.kings-chapel.org* ☉ *Labor Day–Memorial Day, Sat. 10–4, Sun. 1:30–4; Memorial Day–Labor Day, Mon., Thurs.–Sat., 10–4, Sun. 1:30–4, Tues. and Wed., 10–11:15 and 1:30–4. Year-round music program Tues. 12:15–1; services Sun. at 11, Wed. at 12:15* Ⓜ *Park St., Government Center.*

King's Chapel Burying Ground. Legends linger in this oldest of the city's cemeteries. Glance at the handy map of famous grave sites (posted a short walk down the left path) and then take the path to the right from the entrance and then left by the chapel to the gravestone (1704) of Elizabeth Pain, the model for Hester Prynne in Nathaniel Hawthorne's *The Scarlet Letter.* Note the winged death's head on her stone. Also buried here is William Dawes Jr., who, with Dr. Samuel Prescott, rode out to warn of the British invasion the night of Paul Revere's famous ride. Other Boston worthies entombed here—including the first Massachusetts governor, John Winthrop, and several generations of his descendants—were famous for more conventional reasons. The prominent slate monument between the cemetery and the chapel tells (in French) the story of the Chevalier de Saint-Sauveur, a young officer who was part of the first French contingent that arrived to help the rebel Americans in 1778. He was killed in a riot that began when hungry Bostonians were told they couldn't buy the bread the French were baking for their men, using the Bostonians' own wheat—an awkward situation only aggravated by the language barrier. The chevalier's interment here was probably the occasion for the first Roman Catholic Mass in what has since become a city with a substantial Catholic population. ⊠ *Tremont St. at School St., Downtown* ☎ *617/227–2155* ⊕ *www.cityofboston. gov/freedomtrail/kingschapel.asp* ☉ *Late spring–early fall, Mon. and Thurs.–Sat. 10–4; winter, Sat. 10–4* Ⓜ *Park St., Government Center.*

NEED A BREAK? **Fajitas & 'Ritas.** Fajitas & 'Ritas, is a fun stop for a quick dose of Tex-Mex or a liter of frozen margaritas. Service is quick, prices are low, and you can select your nacho toppings. ⊠ *25 West St., Downtown* ☎ *617/426–1222* ⊕ *www.fajitasandritas.com/.*

Leather District. Opposite South Station and inside the angle formed by Kneeland Street and Atlantic Avenue is a corner of Downtown that has been relatively untouched by high-rise development: the old Leather District. It's probably the best place in downtown Boston to get an idea of what the city's business center looked like in the late 19th century. This was the wholesale supply area for raw materials in the days when the shoe industry was a regional economic mainstay; a few leather firms are still here, but most warehouses now contain expensive loft apartments. ⊠ *Bordered by Kneeland St., Atlantic Ave., and Lincoln St.* Ⓜ *South Station.*

Memorial to the Irish Famine. A reminder of the rich immigrant past of this most Irish of American cities consists of two sculptures by artist Robert Shure, one depicting an anguished family on the shores of Ireland, the other a determined and hopeful Irish family stepping ashore in Boston. ⊠ *Plaza outside Borders, Washington St. near School St., opposite Old South Meeting House* Ⓜ *State, Downtown Crossing.*

Old City Hall. Just outside this site sits Richard S. Greenough's bronze statue (1855) of Benjamin Franklin, Boston's first portrait sculpture. Franklin was born in 1706 just a few blocks from here, on Milk Street, and attended the Boston Latin School, founded in 1635 near the City Hall site. (The school has long since moved to Louis Pasteur Avenue,

Boston's Old City Hall is surrounded by modern buildings.

near the Fenway.) As a young man, Franklin emigrated to Philadelphia, where he lived most of his long life. Boston's municipal government settled into the new City Hall in 1969, and the old Second Empire building now houses business offices, not to mention the luxurious Ruth's Chris Steakhouse. ✉ *41–45 School St., Downtown* ⊕ *www.oldcityhall. com* Ⓜ *State.*

Old Corner Bookstore Site. Through these doors, between 1845 and 1865, passed some of the century's literary lights: Henry David Thoreau, Ralph Waldo Emerson, and Henry Wadsworth Longfellow—even Charles Dickens paid a visit. Many of their works were published here by James T. "Jamie" Fields, who in 1830 had founded the influential firm Ticknor and Fields. In the 19th century the graceful, gambrel-roof early-Georgian structure—built in 1718 on land once owned by religious rebel Anne Hutchinson—also housed the city's leading bookstore. Today the building is occupied by a jewelry store. ✉ *1 School St., Downtown* ⊕ *www.thefreedomtrail.org/visitor/old-corner.html* Ⓜ *State.*

Old South Meeting House. This is the second-oldest church building in Boston, and were it not for Longfellow's celebration of the Old North in "Paul Revere's Ride," it might well be the most famous. Some of the fieriest of the town meetings that led to the Revolution were held here, culminating in the gathering of December 16, 1773, which was called by Samuel Adams to confront the crisis of three ships, laden with dutiable tea, anchored at Griffin's Wharf. The activists wanted the tea returned to England, the governor would not permit it—and the rest is history. To cries of "Boston Harbor a teapot tonight!" and John Hancock's "Let every man do what is right in his own eyes," the protesters poured out of the Old South, headed to the wharf with their waiting comrades, and dumped 18,000 pounds' worth of tea into the water.

One of the earliest members of the congregation was an African slave named Phillis Wheatley, who had been educated by her owners. In 1773 a book of her poems was printed (by a London publisher), making her the first published African-American poet. She later traveled to London, where she was received as a celebrity, but was again overtaken by poverty and died in obscurity at age 31.

The church suffered no small amount of indignity in the Revo-

lution: its pews were ripped out by occupying British troops, and the interior was used for riding exercises by General John Burgoyne's light dragoons. A century later it escaped destruction in the Great Fire of 1872, only to be threatened with demolition by developers. Aside from the windows and doors, the only original interior features surviving today are the tiered galleries above the main floor. The pulpit is a reproduction of the one used by Puritan divines and secular firebrands. Public contributions saved the church.

The exhibition "Voices of Protest" highlights Old South as a forum for free speech from Revolutionary days to the present, and the 20-minute audio program "If These Walls Could Speak" offers a reenactment of the major events that occurred here. ⊠ *310 Washington St., Downtown* ☎ *617/482–6439* ⊕ *www.oldsouthmeetinghouse.org* 🖾 *$6* ⊙ *Apr.–Oct., daily 9:30–5; Nov.–Mar., daily 10–4* Ⓜ *State, Downtown Crossing.*

Old State House. This colonial-era landmark has one of the most recognizable facades in Boston, with its State Street gable adorned by a brightly gilded lion and unicorn, symbols of British imperial power. The original figures were pulled down in 1776. For proof that bygones are bygones, consider not only the restoration of the sculptures in 1880 but also that Queen Elizabeth II was greeted by cheering crowds on July 4, 1976, when she stood on the Old State House balcony (from which the Declaration of Independence was first read in public in Boston and which overlooks the site of the Boston Massacre).

This was the seat of the colonial government from 1713 until the Revolution, and after the evacuation of the British from Boston in 1776 it served the independent Commonwealth until its replacement on Beacon Hill was completed in 1798. John Hancock was inaugurated here as the first governor under the new state constitution.

Like many other colonial-era landmarks, it fared poorly in the years that followed. Nineteenth-century photos show the old building with

Tours Worth Trying

Boston Movie Tours. Boston Movie Tours takes you to Boston's television and movie hot spots like the South Boston of *The Departed*, the *Ally McBeal* building, the tavern from *Good Will Hunting*, the *Cheers* bar, and Fenway Park, home of the Red Sox and location for movies like *Field of Dreams* and *Fever Pitch*. Guides share filming secrets and trivia from movies like *Legally Blonde* and *Mystic River* along with the best celeb spots in town. The "theater-on-wheels" bus tour takes 2–3 hours, depending on traffic ($37). ☎ 866/668–4345 ⊕ www.bostonmovietours.net.

Boston Women's Heritage Trail. Boston Women's Heritage Trail has nine self-guided walks that highlight remarkable women who played an integral role in shaping the history of Boston and the nation as patriots, intellectuals, abolitionists, suffragists, artists, and writers. ☎ 617/776–1809 ⊕ www.bwht.org.

5

a mansard roof and signs in the windows advertising assorted businesses. In the 1830s the Old State House served as Boston's City Hall. When demolition was threatened in 1880 because the real estate was so valuable, the Bostonian Society organized a restoration, after which the Old State House reopened with a permanent collection that traces Boston's Revolutionary War history and, on the second floor, exhibits that change every few years.

Immediately outside the Old State House, at 15 State Street, is a **visitor center** run by the National Park Service; it offers free brochures and has restrooms. ⊠ *206 Washington St., at State St., Downtown* ☎ *617/720–1713* ⊕ *www.bostonhistory.org* ⊠ *$7.50* ⊙ *Sept.–Dec. and Feb.–June, daily 9–5; Jan., daily 9–4; July and Aug., daily 9–6* Ⓜ *State.*

Rowes Wharf. Take a Beacon Hill redbrick town house, blow it up to the *n*th power, and you get this 15-story Skidmore, Owings & Merrill extravaganza from 1987, one of the more welcome additions to the Boston Harbor skyline. From under the complex's gateway six-story arch, you can get great views of Boston Harbor and the yachts docked at the marina. Water shuttles pull up here from Logan Airport—the most intriguing way to enter the city. A windswept stroll along the HarborWalk waterfront promenade at dusk makes for an unforgettable sunset on clear days. ⊠ *Atlantic Ave. south of India Wharf* Ⓜ *Aquarium.*

South Station. The colonnaded granite structure is the terminal for all Amtrak trains in and out of Boston as well as commuter trains originating from the west and south of the city. Next door on Atlantic Avenue is the terminal for Greyhound, Peter Pan, and other bus lines. Behind the station's grand 1900s facade a major renovation project has created an airy, modern transit center. Thanks to its eateries, coffee bars, newsstand, flower stand, and other shops, waiting for a train here can actually be a pleasant experience. ⊠ *Atlantic Ave. and Summer St., Downtown* Ⓜ *South Station.*

State Street. During the 19th century State Street was headquarters for banks, brokerages, and insurance firms; although these businesses have spread throughout the Downtown District, "State Street" still connotes much the same thing as "Wall Street" does in New York. The early commercial hegemony of State Street was symbolized by Long Wharf, built in 1710 and extending some 1,700 feet into the harbor. If today's Long Wharf doesn't appear to be that long, it's not because it has been shortened but because the land has crept out toward its end. State Street once met the water at the base of the Custom House; landfill operations were pursued relentlessly through the years, and the old coastline is now as much a memory as such colonial State Street landmarks as Governor Winthrop's 1630 house and the Revolutionary-era Bunch of Grapes Tavern, where Bostonians met to drink and wax indignant at their treatment by King George.

U.S. Custom House. This 1847 structure resembles a Greek Revival temple that appears to have sprouted a tower. It's just that. This is the work of architects Ammi Young and Isaiah Rogers—at least, the bottom part is. The tower was added in 1915, at which time the Custom House became Boston's tallest building. It remains one of the most visible and best loved structures in the city's skyline. To appreciate the grafting job, go inside and look at the domed rotunda. The outer surface of that dome was once the roof of the building, but now the dome is embedded in the base of the tower.

The federal government moved out of the Custom House in 1987 and sold it to the city of Boston, which, in turn, sold it to the Marriott Corporation, which has converted the building into hotel space and luxury time-share units, a move that disturbed some historical purists. You can now sip a cocktail in the hotel's Counting Room Lounge, or visit the 26th-floor observation deck. The magnificent Rotunda Room sports maritime prints and antique artifacts, courtesy of the Peabody Essex Museum in Salem. ⊠ *3 McKinley Sq., Downtown* ☎ *617/310–6300* Ⓜ *State, Aquarium.*

Back Bay and the South End

WORD OF MOUTH

"Walk on Newbury Street to window shop and/or dine. Everything from H&M to high-end designer stores. I also love to walk the quieter Commonwealth Avenue, which runs parallel to Newbury. It is a gorgeous tree-lined park, with lovely townhomes on both sides. My fave."

—PeaceOut

GETTING ORIENTED

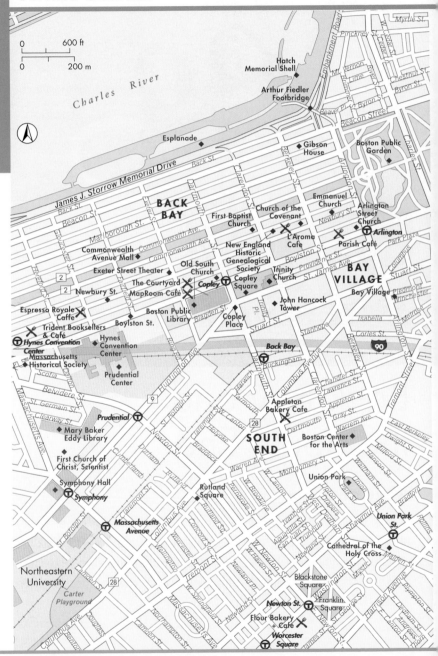

0 ___ 600 ft
0 ___ 200 m

Charles River

Hatch Memorial Shell

Arthur Fiedler Footbridge

Esplanade

Gibson House

Boston Public Garden

James J. Storrow Memorial Drive

Back St.

BACK BAY

Marlborough St.

Commonwealth Ave.

Emmanuel Church

Arlington Street Church

Church of the Covenant

First Baptist Church

L'Aroma Cafe

Parish Cafe

Arlington

Commonwealth Avenue Mall

New England Historic Genealogical Society

Boylston St.

Providence St.

St. James Ave.

BAY VILLAGE

Exeter Street Theater

Old South Church

Trinity Church

Copley

The Courtyard

Copley Square

Bay Village

Newbury St.

MapRoom Cafe

John Hancock Tower

Espresso Royale Caffe

Boston Public Library

Copley Place

Stuart St.

Trident Booksellers & Café

Boylston St.

Blagden St.

Stanhope

Hynes Convention Center

Hynes Convention Center

Back Bay

90

Massachusetts Historical Society

Buckingham

Prudential Center

Huntington Ave.

9

Appleton Bakery Cafe

28

Prudential

SOUTH END

Boston Center for the Arts

Mary Baker Eddy Library

Warren Ave.

First Church of Christ, Scientist

Montgomery St.

Union Park

Symphony Hall

Symphony

Rutland Square

Union Park St.

Massachusetts Avenue

Cathedral of the Holy Cross

Northeastern University

Blackstone Square

Washington St.

Carter Playground

28

Franklin Square

Newton St.

Flour Bakery + Café

Worcester Square

GETTING HERE AND AROUND

There are myriad parking garages in Back Bay. Take the Orange Line to the Back Bay station or the Green Line to Copley for the heart of the shopping areas. The Arlington stop on the Green Line is the most convenient to the Public Garden.

The South End is easily accessible by T; take the Orange Line to Back Bay and head south on Dartmouth Street to Columbus Avenue, or jump off the Silver Line at Union Park Street or East Berkley Street to access the neighborhood.

TIMING

If you're not looking to max out your credit cards, then you can hurry past the boutiques and cover the Back Bay in about two hours. Allow at least half a day for a leisurely walk with frequent stops on Newbury Street and the shops at Copley Place and the Prudential Center. The reflecting pool at the Christian Science Church is a great time-out spot. Around the third week of April, magnolia time arrives, and nowhere do the flowers bloom more magnificently than along Commonwealth Avenue. In May the Public Garden bursts with color, thanks to its flowering dogwood trees and thousands of tulips. To stay oriented, remember that the north–south streets are arranged in alphabetical order, from Arlington to Hereford.

A few hours is perfect for exploring the South End; add a few hours for a show at the Boston Center of the Arts or to dine at one of the many excellent restaurants in the area.

NEWBURY QUICK BITES

L'Aroma Cafe. Shopping on Newbury can really wear you (and your wallet) out, so stop in at L'Aroma Cafe for a steaming latte, grilled panini, fresh salad, or plate of quiche. For its designer address, the prices are reasonable, and the Italian pastries to die for. ⊠ *85 Newbury, between Berkley and Clarondon* ☎ *617/412–4001.*

TOP REASONS TO GO

■ Join the throngs of students, locals, and visitors window shopping on Newbury Street.

■ Admire the architecture, revel in the artistry, and even enjoy an excellent lunch at the Boston Public Library—all without taking out a single book.

■ Visit the Public Garden on a sunny, late-spring day and take in the scenery from your seat on the Swan Boats. Don't forget to check out the bronzed statues of the ducklings from Robert McCloskey's Boston classic *Make Way for Ducklings.*

■ Enjoy a play, concert, or art installation at the "people's" art-and-culture complex, the Boston Center for the Arts.

■ Shop Columbus Avenue and Tremont Street for the perfect additions to your home decor.

■ Walk the streets around Rutland Square, Union Park, and Bay Village. Architecture buffs will love the Victorian and Italianate row houses harking back to the neighborhood's 19th-century roots.

SOUTH END QUICK BITES

■ **Appleton Bakery Cafe.** After a morning of gallery hopping in the South End, stop in to Appleton Bakery Cafe. All the bakery goods are made fresh every day, and the meat loaf sandwich for lunch has many fans. ⊠ *123 Appleton St., at Dartmouth St.* ⊕ *appletonbakery.com.*

6

Sightseeing
★★★★
Dining
★★★★
Lodging
★★★★
Shopping
★★★★★
Nightlife
★★★★★

In the folklore of American neighborhoods, the Back Bay stands with New York's Park Avenue and San Francisco's Nob Hill as a symbol of propriety and high social standing. Before the 1850s it really was a bay, a tidal flat that formed the south bank of a distended Charles River. The filling in of land along the isthmus that joined Boston to the mainland (the Neck) began in 1850, and resulted in the creation of the South End. To the north a narrow causeway called the Mill Dam (later Beacon Street) was built in 1814 to separate the Back Bay from the Charles. By the late 1800s Bostonians had filled in the shallows to as far as the marshland known as the Fenway, and the original 783-acre peninsula had been expanded by about 450 acres. Thus the waters of Back Bay became the neighborhood of Back Bay.

Updated
by Bethany
Cassin
Beckerlegge

Heavily influenced by the then-recent rebuilding of Paris according to the plans of Baron Georges-Eugène Haussmann, the Back Bay planners created thoroughfares that resemble Parisian boulevards. The thorough planning included service alleys behind the main streets to allow provisioning wagons to drive up to basement kitchens. (Now they're used for waste pickup and parking.)

Today the area retains its posh spirit, but mansions are no longer the main draw. Locals and tourists alike flock to the commercial streets of Boylston and Newbury to shop at boutiques, galleries, and the usual mall stores. Many of the bars and restaurants have patio seating and bay windows, making the area the perfect spot to see and be seen while indulging in ethnic delicacies or an invigorating coffee. The Boston Public Library, Symphony Hall, and numerous churches ensure that high culture is not lost amid the frenzy of consumerism.

The nearby South End lost many residents to the Back Bay in the late 19th century, but in the late 1970s, middle-class professionals began snapping up town houses at bargain prices and restoring them. Solidly back in fashion now, the South End's redbrick row houses in various states of refurbished splendor now house a mix of ethnic groups, the city's largest gay community, and some excellent shops.

Today a large African-American community resides along Columbus Avenue and Mass Ave., which marks the beginning of the predominantly black neighborhood of Roxbury. Boston's gay community also has a strong presence in the South End, with most of the gay-oriented restaurants and businesses on Columbus Avenue and Tremont Street between East Berkeley Street and Mass Ave. If you like to shop, you'll have a blast in this area, which focuses on home furnishings and accessories, with a heavy accent on the unique and handmade. At the northern tip of the South End, where Harrison Avenue and Washington Street lead to Chinatown, are several Chinese supermarkets, and south of Washington Street is the burgeoning "SoWa" District, home to a growing number of art galleries, many of which have relocated here from pricey Newbury Street.

THE BACK BAY

TOP ATTRACTIONS

    ♻   **Boston Public Garden.** Although the Boston Public Garden is often lumped
Fodor's Choice together with Boston Common, the two are separate entities with dif-
    ★   ferent histories and purposes and a distinct boundary between them at Charles Street. The Common has been public land since Boston was founded in 1630, whereas the Public Garden belongs to a newer Boston, occupying what had been salt marshes on the edge of the Common. By 1837 the tract was covered with an abundance of ornamental plantings donated by a group of private citizens. The area was defined in 1856 by the building of Arlington Street, and in 1860 the architect George Meacham was commissioned to plan the park.

The central feature of the Public Garden is its irregularly shaped pond, intended to appear, from any vantage point along its banks, much larger than its nearly 4 acres. Near the Swan Boat dock is what has been described as the world's smallest suspension bridge, designed in 1867 to cross the pond at its narrowest point.

The Public Garden is America's oldest botanical garden, and has the finest formal plantings in central Boston. The beds along the main walkways are replanted for spring and summer. The tulips during the first two weeks of May are especially colorful, and there's a sampling of native and European tree species.

The dominant work among the park's statuary is Thomas Ball's equestrian **George Washington** (1869), which faces the head of Commonwealth Avenue at the Arlington Street gate. This is Washington in a triumphant pose as liberator, surveying a scene that, from where he stood with his cannons at Dorchester Heights, would have included an immense stretch of blue water. Several dozen yards to the north of Washington (to the right if you're facing Commonwealth Avenue) is the granite-and-red-marble **Ether Monument,** donated in 1866 by Thomas Lee to commemorate the advent of anesthesia 20 years earlier at nearby Massachusetts General Hospital. Other Public Garden monuments include statues of the Unitarian preacher and transcendentalist William Ellery Channing, at the corner opposite his Arlington Street Church; Edward Everett Hale, the author (*The Man Without a Country*) and philanthropist, at the Charles Street Gate; and the abolitionist senator Charles Sumner and the Civil War hero Colonel Thomas Cass, along Boylston Street.

The park contains a special delight for the young at heart; follow the children quack-quacking along the pathway between the pond and the park entrance at Charles and Beacon streets to the *Make Way for Ducklings* bronzes sculpted by Nancy Schön, a tribute to the 1941 classic children's story by Robert McCloskey. **Swan Boats**. The pond has been famous since 1877 for its foot-pedal-powered (by a captain) Swan Boats, which make leisurely cruises during warm months. The pond is favored by ducks and swans, and for the modest price of a few boat rides you can amuse children here for an hour or more. ☎ *617/522–1966* ⊕ *www.swanboats.com* ⊠ *Swan Boats $2.75* ☯ *Swan Boats mid-Apr.–June 20, daily 10–4; June 21–Labor Day, daily 10–5; day after Labor Day–mid-Sept., weekdays noon–4, weekends 10–4* ⊠ *Bounded by Arlington, Boylston, Charles, and Beacon Sts., Back Bay* Ⓜ *Arlington.*

★ **Boston Public Library.** This venerable institution is a handsome temple to literature and a valuable research library. The Renaissance Revival building was opened in 1895; a 1972 addition emulates the mass and proportion of the original, though not its extraordinary detail; this skylighted annex houses the library's circulating collections.

You don't need a library card to enjoy the magnificent art. The murals at the head of the staircase, depicting the nine muses, are the work of the French artist Puvis de Chavannes; those in the book-request processing room to the right are Edwin Abbey's interpretations of the Holy Grail legend. Upstairs, in the public areas leading to the fine-arts, music, and rare-books collections, is John Singer Sargent's mural series on the *Triumph of Religion*, shining with renewed color after its cleaning and restoration in 2003. The corridor leading from the annex opens onto the Renaissance-style **courtyard**—an exact copy of the one in Rome's Palazzo della Cancelleria—around which the original library is built. A covered arcade furnished with chairs rings a fountain; you can bring books or lunch into the courtyard, which is open all the hours the library is open, and escape the bustle of the city. Beyond the courtyard is the main entrance hall of the 1895 building, with its immense stone lions by Louis St. Gaudens, vaulted ceiling, and marble staircase. The corridor at the top of the stairs leads to **Bates Hall,** one of Boston's most sumptuous interior spaces. This is the main reference reading room, 218 feet long with a barrel-arch ceiling 50 feet high. ⊠ *700 Boylston St., at Copley Sq., Back Bay* ☎ *617/536–5400* ⊕ *www.bpl.org* ☯ *Mon.–Thurs. 9–9, Fri. and Sat. 9–5; also Sun. 1–5 (Oct.–May only). Free guided art*

The Boston Public Library is a stunning cathedral of books.

and architecture tours Mon. at 2:30, Tues. and Thurs. at 6, Fri. and Sat. at 11, Sun. at 2 (Oct.–May only) Ⓜ *Copley.*

NEED A BREAK?

Courtyard. You can take a lunch break at the Courtyard or the **MapRoom Café**, adjoining restaurants in the Boston Public Library. Breakfast and lunch are served in the 1895 map room, and the main restaurant, which overlooks the courtyard, is open for lunch and afternoon tea. The Courtyard is open weekdays 11:30–4, and the MapRoom Café is open Monday–Saturday 9–5. ✉ *700 Boylston St., at Copley Sq., Back Bay* ☎ *617/859–2251* ⊕ *www.thecateredaffair.com/bpl/index.html.*

★ **Trinity Church.** In his 1877 masterpiece, architect Henry Hobson Richardson brought his Romanesque Revival style to maturity; all the aesthetic elements for which he was famous come together magnificently—bold polychromatic masonry, careful arrangement of masses, sumptuously carved interior woodwork—in this crowning centerpiece of Copley Square. A full appreciation of its architecture requires an understanding of the logistical problems of building it here. The Back Bay is a reclaimed wetland with a high water table. Bedrock, or at least stable glacial till, lies far beneath wet clay. Like all older Back Bay buildings, Trinity Church sits on submerged wooden pilings. But its central tower weighs 9,500 tons, and most of the 4,500 pilings beneath the building are under that tremendous central mass. The pilings are checked regularly for sinkage by means of a hatch in the basement.

Richardson engaged some of the best artists of his day—John LaFarge, William Morris, and Edward Burne-Jones among them—to execute the

TWO WAYS TO EXPLORE BACK BAY

ART AND ARCHITECTURE

Art and architecture buffs should first stop at the Boston Public Library. Constructed in the Renaissance Revival style, it houses murals by John Singer Sargent; sculpture by Louis St. Gaudens; and immense bronze doors by Daniel Chester French, sculptor of the Lincoln Memorial; and a book or two. Next, take in Trinity Church, a Romanesque Revival gem designed by Henry Hobson Richardson, complete with paintings by William Morris and John LaFarge. Visit the Church of the Covenant to view the largest collection of liturgical stained-glass windows by Louis Comfort Tiffany. The First Church of Christ, Scientist melds the 19th and 20th centuries with a Renaissance Revival basilica next to an office building by I.M. Pei. Complete your tour with a stop at the modern John Hancock Tower, also by I.M. Pei, which at 790 feet is the tallest building in New England.

SHOPPER'S PARADISE

Between Copley Place and Prudential Center, Boylston Street and Newbury Street, there's a store for every shopper. Visit Newbury Street for high-end designer boutiques (think Chanel, Burberry, and Marc Jacobs) and streetside cafés for watching the other conspicuous consumers. Boylston Street is home to more modest retailers like Crate and Barrel and Apple, as well as numerous bars and restaurants. The Prudential Center mall fronts on Boylston and is anchored by Saks Fifth Avenue, Lord & Taylor, and, luckily for neighborhood residents, a Shaw's supermarket. You can walk through the Prudential Center to reach Copley Place, another chichi mall home to the likes of Neiman Marcus, Louis Vuitton, and Tiffany; there's a Gap, too, for those who must have some new jeans. If you haven't found what you're looking after an afternoon here, it just might not exist.

6

paintings and stained glass that make this a monument to everything that was right about the pre-Raphaelite spirit and the nascent aesthetic of Morris's Arts and Crafts movement. LaFarge's intricate paintings and ornamented ceilings received a much-needed overhaul during the extensive renovations that wrapped up in 2005. Along the north side of the church, note the Augustus Saint-Gaudens statue of Phillips Brooks—the most charismatic rector in New England, who almost single-handedly got Trinity built and furnished. Shining light of Harvard's religious community and lyricist of "O Little Town of Bethlehem," Brooks is shown here with Christ touching his shoulder in approval. For a nice respite, try to catch one of the Friday organ concerts beginning at 12:15. ■TIP➔ The 11:15 Sunday service is followed by a free guided tour. ⊠ 206 Clarendon St., Back Bay ☎ 617/536–0944 ⊕ www.trinityboston.org ⊠ Church free, guided and self-guided tours $6 ☉ Mon.–Sat. 9–5, Sun. 1–5; services Sun. at 7:45, 9, and 11:15 am and 6 pm. Tours take place several times daily; call to confirm times Ⓜ Copley.

WORTH NOTING

Arlington Street Church. Opposite the Park Square corner of the Public Garden, this church was erected in 1861—the first to be built in the Back Bay. Though a classical portico is a keynote and its model was London's St. Martin-in-the-Fields, Arlington Street Church is less picturesque and more Georgian in character. Note the Tiffany stained-glass windows. During the year preceding the Civil War the church was a hotbed of abolitionist fervor. Later, during the Vietnam War, this Unitarian-Universalist congregation became famous as a center of peace activism. ⊠ *351 Boylston St., Back Bay* ☎ *617/536–7050* ⊕ *www.ascboston.org* ☉ *Call to arrange sanctuary tours. Services Sun. at 11* Ⓜ *Arlington.*

> ### NAME CHANGE
>
> One of Back Bay's main thoroughfares, Huntington Avenue, which stretches from Copley Square past the Museum of Fine Arts, has technically been renamed the Avenue of the Arts. However, old habits die hard, particularly with Bostonians; everyone still calls it Huntington.

Back Bay Mansions. If you like nothing better than to imagine how the other half lives, you'll suffer no shortage of old homes to sigh over in Boston's Back Bay. Most, unfortunately, are off-limits to visitors, but there's no law against gawking from the outside. Stroll Commonwealth, Beacon and Marlborough streets for the best views.

Two Back Bay mansions are now used by organizations that promote foreign language and culture: The French Library and Cultural Center and the German-oriented Goethe Institute. See the free, biweekly Improper Bostonian, or the *Boston Globe*'s "Calendar" section on Thursday or the weekly listings in the *Boston Phoenix* for details on lectures, films, and other events held in these respected institutions.

Boylston Street. Less posh than Newbury Street, this broad thoroughfare is the southern commercial spine of the Back Bay, lined with interesting restaurants and shops.

Church of the Covenant. This 1867 Gothic Revival church at the corner of Newbury and Berkeley streets has one of the largest collections of liturgical windows by Louis Comfort Tiffany in the country. It's crowned by a 236-foot-tall steeple—the tallest in Boston—that Oliver Wendell Holmes called "absolutely perfect." Inside, a 14-foot-high Tiffany lantern hangs from a breathtaking 100-foot ceiling. The church is now Presbyterian and United Church of Christ. ⊠ *67 Newbury St., enter at church office, Back Bay* ☎ *617/266–7480* ⊕ *www.churchofthecovenant.org* ☉ *Call for hrs; Sun. service at 10:30* Ⓜ *Arlington.*

Commonwealth Avenue Mall. The mall that extends down the middle of the Back Bay's Commonwealth Avenue is studded with statuary. One of the most interesting memorials, at the Exeter Street intersection, is a portrayal of naval historian and author Samuel Eliot Morison seated on a rock as if he were peering out to sea. The most recent addition was the **Boston Women's Memorial** in 2003 by Meredith Bergmann, between Fairfield and Gloucester streets. Statues of Abigail Adams,

The Houses of the Back Bay

The Back Bay remains a living museum of urban Victorian–residential architecture. The earliest specimens are nearest to the Public Garden (there are exceptions where showier turn-of-the-20th-century mansions replaced 1860s town houses), and the newer examples are out around the Massachusetts Avenue and Fenway extremes of the district. The height of Back Bay residences and their distance from the street are essentially uniform, as are the interior layouts, chosen to accord with lot width. Yet there's a distinct progression of facades, beginning with French academic and Italianate designs and moving through the various "revivals" of the 19th century. By the time of World War I, when development of the Back Bay was virtually complete, architects and their patrons had come full circle to a revival of the Federal period, which had been out of fashion for only 30 years when the building began. If the Back Bay architects had not run out of land, they might have gotten around to a Greek Revival revival.

The Great Depression brought an end to the Back Bay style of living, and today only a few of the houses are single-family residences. Most have been cut up into apartments, then expensive condominiums; during the boom years of the late 1990s some were returned to their original town-house status. Interior details have experienced a mixed fate: they suffered during the years when Victorian fashions were held in low regard, and are undergoing careful restoration now that the aesthetic pendulum has reversed itself and moneyed condo buyers are demanding period authenticity. The original facades have survived on all but Newbury and Boylston streets, so the public face of the Back Bay retains much of the original charm and grandeur.

An outstanding guide to the architecture and history of the Back Bay is Bainbridge Bunting's *Houses of Boston's Back Bay* (Harvard, 1967). A few homes are open to the public.

Lucy Stone, and Phillis Wheatley celebrate the progressive ideas of these three women and their contributions to Boston's history.

A dramatic and personal memorial was added to the mall in 1997 near Dartmouth Street: the **Vendome Monument,** dedicated to the nine firemen who died in a 1972 blaze at the Back Bay's Vendome Hotel, which, now office space, is across the street. The curved black-granite block, 29 feet long and waist high, is etched with the names of the dead. A bronze cast of a fireman's coat and hat are draped over the granite. ⊠ *Commonwealth Ave. between Arlington St. and Massachusetts Ave.* Ⓜ *Arlington, Copley.*

Copley Place. Two bold intruders dominate Copley Square—the **John Hancock Tower** off the southeast corner and the even more assertive Copley Place skyscraper on the southwest. An upscale, glass-and-brass urban mall built between 1980 and 1984, Copley Place includes two major hotels: the high-rise Westin and the Marriott Copley Place. Dozens of shops, restaurants, and offices are attractively grouped on several levels, surrounding bright, open indoor spaces. ⊠ *100 Huntington Ave., Back Bay* ☉ *Shopping galleries Mon.–Sat. 10–8, Sun. noon–6* Ⓜ *Copley.*

Copley Square. Every April thousands find a glimpse of Copley Square the most wonderful sight in the world: this is where the runners of the Boston Marathon end their 26-mi race. A square now favored by skateboarders (much to the chagrin of city officials), the civic space is defined by three monumental older buildings. One is the stately, bow-front 1912 **Fairmont Copley Plaza Hotel,** which faces the square on St. James Avenue and serves as a dignified foil to its companions, two of the most important works of architecture in the United States: Trinity Church—Henry Hobson Richardson's masterwork of 1877—and the Boston Public Library, by McKim, Mead & White. The John Hancock Tower looms in the background. To honor the runners who stagger over the marathon's finish line, bronze statues of the Tortoise and the Hare engaged in their mythical race were cast by Nancy Schön, who also did the much-loved *Make Way for Ducklings* group in the Boston Public Garden. ⊠ *Bounded by Dartmouth, Boylston, and Clarendon Sts. and St. James Ave., Back Bay* Ⓜ *Copley.*

Emmanuel Church. Built in 1860, this Back Bay brownstone Gothic Epis-copal church is popular among classical music lovers—every Sunday at 10 am from September to May, as part of the liturgy, a Bach cantata is performed; guest conductors have included Christopher Hogwood and Seiji Ozawa. ⊠ *15 Newbury St., Back Bay* ☎ *617/536–3355* ⊕ *www. emmanuel-boston.org* ☉ *Services Sun. at 10 am* Ⓜ *Arlington.*

Esplanade. Near the corner of Beacon and Arlington streets, the Arthur Fiedler Footbridge crosses Storrow Drive to the Esplanade and the **Hatch Memorial Shell.** The free concerts here in summer include the Boston Pops' immensely popular televised Fourth of July performance. For shows like this, Bostonians haul lawn chairs and blankets to the lawn in front of the shell; bring a take-out lunch from a nearby res-taurant, find an empty spot—no mean feat, so come early—and you'll feel right at home. An impressive stone bust of the late maestro Arthur Fiedler watches over the walkers, joggers, picnickers, and sunbathers who fill the Esplanade's paths on pleasant days. Here, too, is the turn-of-the-20th-century **Union Boat Club Boathouse,** headquarters for the country's oldest private rowing club.

Exeter Street Theater. This massive Romanesque structure was built in 1884 as a temple for the Working Union of Progressive Spiritualists. Beginning in 1914, it enjoyed a long run as a movie theater; as the *AIA Guide to Boston* points out, "it was the only movie theater a proper Boston woman would enter, probably because of its spiritual overtones." ⊠ *26 Exeter St., at Newbury St., Back Bay* ⊕ *www.fst.org/ exeter.htm* Ⓜ *Copley.*

First Baptist Church. This 1872 structure, at the corner of Clarendon Street and Commonwealth Avenue, was architect Henry Hobson Richard-son's first foray into Romanesque Revival. It was originally erected for the Brattle Square Unitarian Society, but Richardson ran over budget and the church went bankrupt and dissolved; in 1882 the building was bought by the Baptists. The figures on each side of its soaring tower were sculpted by Frédéric Auguste Bartholdi, the sculptor who designed the Statue of Liberty. The friezes represent four points at which God enters an individual's life: baptism, communion, marriage, and death. The trumpeting angels at each corner have earned First Baptist its nickname, "Church of the Holy Bean Blowers." If you phone ahead for an appointment on a weekday, you may be given an informal tour. ⊠ *110 Commonwealth Ave., Back Bay* ☎ *617/267–3148* ⊕ *www.firstbaptistchurchofboston.org* ⊠ *Free* ☉ *Tues., Thurs., and Fri. 11–2; services Sun. at 11 am* Ⓜ *Copley.*

NEED A BREAK?
Espresso Royale Caffe. Espresso Royale Caffe is a basement spot with solid coffee and espresso drinks, snacks, and Wi-Fi access. ⊠ *286 Newbury St., Back Bay* ☎ *617/859–9515* Ⓜ *Hynes.*

Parish Café. To try the creations of some of the best local chefs without paying four-star restaurant prices, stop by Parish Café. For $10 to $15 you can get a sandwich designed by the top culinary minds in Boston. The bar is open until 2 am daily, with food service until 1 am. ⊠ *361 Boylston St., Back Bay* ☎ *617/247–4777* ⊕ *www.parishcafe.com* Ⓜ *Arlington.*

First Church of Christ, Scientist. The world headquarters of the Christian Science faith mixes the traditional with the modern—marrying Bernini to Le Corbusier by combining an Old World basilica with a sleek office complex designed by I. M. Pei. Mary Baker Eddy's original granite First Church of Christ, Scientist (1894) has since been enveloped by a domed Renaissance Revival basilica, added to the site in 1906, and both church buildings are now surrounded by the offices of the Christian Science Publishing Society, where the *Christian Science Monitor* is produced, and by Pei's complex of church-administration structures completed in 1973. You can hear all 13,290 pipes of the church's famed Aeolian-Skinner organ during services. ⊠ *175 Huntington Ave., Back Bay* ☎ *617/450–2000* ⊕ *www.tfccs.com* ⊠ *Free* ☉ *Services Sept.–June, Sun. at 10 am and 5 pm; July and Aug., Sun. at 10 am, Wed. at noon and 7:30 pm* Ⓜ *Hynes, Symphony.*

Gibson House. Through the foresight of an eccentric bon vivant, this house provides an authentic glimpse into daily life in Boston's Victorian era. One of the first Back Bay residences (1859), the Gibson House is relatively modest in comparison with some of the grand mansions built during the decades that followed; yet its furnishings, from its circa-1790 Willard clock to the raised and gilded wallpaper to the multipiece faux-bamboo bedroom set, seem sumptuous to modern eyes. Unlike other Back Bay houses, the Gibson family home has been preserved with all its Victorian fixtures and furniture intact. The house serves as the meeting place for the New England chapter of the Victorian Society in America; it was also used as an interior for the 1984 Merchant-Ivory film *The Bostonians.* ■ TIP→ Though the sign out front instructs visitors not to ring the bell until the stroke of the hour, you will have better luck catching the beginning of the tour if you arrive a few minutes early and ring forcefully. ⊠ *137 Beacon St., Back Bay* ☎ *617/267–6338* ⊕ *www.*

thegibsonhouse.org ☞ *$9* ⊙ *Tours Wed.–Sun. at 1, 2, and 3 and by appointment* Ⓜ *Arlington.*

John Hancock Tower. In the early 1970s, the tallest building in New England became notorious as the monolith that rained glass from time to time. Windows were improperly seated in the sills of the blue rhomboid tower, designed by I. M. Pei. Once the building's 13 acres of glass were replaced and the central core stiffened, the problem was corrected. Bostonians originally feared the Hancock's stark modernism would overwhelm nearby Trinity Church, but its shimmering sides reflect the older structure's image, actually enlarging its presence. The Tower is closed to the public. ⊠ *200 Clarendon St., Back Bay* Ⓜ *Copley.*

Mary Baker Eddy Library for the Betterment of Humanity. One of the largest single collections by and about an American woman is housed at this library within Christian Science Plaza, along with two floors of exhibits celebrating the power of ideas and highlighting the link between spirituality and health. The library is home to the fascinating **Mapparium,** a huge stained-glass globe whose 30-foot interior can be traversed on a footbridge. You can experience a sound-and-light show in the Mapparium and learn about the production of the *Christian Science Monitor* in the Monitor Gallery. The Quest Gallery explores Mary Baker Eddy's life and encourages others to think about their own personal quests, and the Hall of Ideas showcases the ideas of the world's greatest thinkers in a virtual fountain. ⊠ *200 Massachusetts Ave., Back Bay* ☎ *888/222–3711* ⊕ *www.marybakereddylibrary.org* ☞ *Hall of Ideas and 3rd-fl. library free, exhibits $6* ⊙ *Tues.–Sun. 10–4* Ⓜ *Prudential.*

Massachusetts Historical Society. The oldest historical society in the United States (founded in 1791) has paintings, a library, and a 10-million-piece manuscript collection from 17th-century New England to the present. Among these manuscripts are the Adams Papers, which comprise more than 300,000 pages from the letters and diaries of generations of the Adams family, including papers from John Adams and John Quincy Adams. Casual visitors are welcome, but if you'd like to examine the papers in depth, call ahead. ⊠ *1154 Boylston St., Back Bay* ☎ *617/536–1608* ⊕ *www.masshist.org* ☞ *Free* ⊙ *Weekdays 9–4:45 (Thurs. until 7:45 pm), Sat. 9–4* Ⓜ *Hynes.*

Newbury Street. Eight-block-long Newbury Street has been compared to New York's 5th Avenue, and certainly this is the city's poshest shopping area, with branches of Chanel, Brooks Brothers, Armani, Burberry, and other top names in fashion. But here the pricey boutiques are more intimate than grand, and people live above the trendy restaurants and hair salons, giving the place a neighborhood feel. Toward the Mass Ave. end cafés proliferate and the stores get funkier, ending with Newbury Comics, Urban Outfitters, and Best Buy. Ⓜ *Hynes, Copley.*

New England Historic Genealogical Society. Are you related to Miles Standish or Priscilla Alden? The answer may lie here. If your ancestors were pedigreed New Englanders—or if you're just interested in genealogical research of any kind—you can trace your family tree with the help of the society's collections. The society dates from 1845, and is the oldest genealogical organization in the country. ⊠ *101 Newbury St.,*

6

Shoppers take a break at a Newbury Street café.

Back Bay ☎ *888/296–3447* ⊕ *www.newenglandancestors.org* ✉ *$15 fee to use facility* ⊘ *Tues. and Thurs.–Sat. 9–5, Wed. 9–9* Ⓜ *Copley.*

NEED A BREAK?

Trident Booksellers & Café. Folks gather at the Trident Booksellers & Café to review literary best sellers, thumb through the superb magazine selection, and munch on homemade desserts, sandwiches, and soups. It's open until midnight daily. ✉ **338 Newbury St., Back Bay** ☎ **617/267-8688** ⊕ **tridentbookscafe.com** Ⓜ **Hynes.**

Old South Church. Members of the Old South Meeting House, of Tea Party fame, decamped to this new parish in 1875, a move not without controversy for the congregation. In an Italian Gothic style inspired by the sociologist John Ruskin and an interior decorated with Venetian mosaics and stained-glass windows, the "new" structure could hardly be more different from the original plain meetinghouse. ✉ *645 Boylston St., Back Bay* ☎ *617/536–1970* ⊕ *www.oldsouth.org* ⊘ *Services Sun. at 9 and 11 am, jazz services Thurs. at 6* Ⓜ *Copley.*

Prudential Center. The only rival to the John Hancock's claim on Boston's upper skyline is the 52-story Prudential Tower, built in the early 1960s when the scale of monumental urban redevelopment projects had yet to be challenged. The Prudential Center, which replaced the railway yards that blocked off the South End, now dominates the acreage between Boylston Street and Huntington Avenue. Its enclosed shopping mall is connected by a glass bridge to the more upscale Copley Place. As for the Prudential Tower itself, the architectural historian Bainbridge Bunting made an acute observation when he called it "an apparition so vast in size that it appears to float above the surrounding district without being related to it." Later modifications to the Boylston Street frontage of the Prudential Center effected a better union of the complex with the urban space around it, but the tower itself floats on, vast as ever. **Prudential Center Skywalk**, a 50th-floor observatory atop the Prudential Tower, offers panoramic vistas of Boston, Cambridge, and the suburbs to the west and south—on clear days, you can even see Cape Cod. **Hynes Convention Center**. The Hynes Convention Center is connected to the Prudential Center; there's also a branch of the Greater Boston Visitors Bureau here, in the center court of the mall. ☎ 617/954–2000 ⊠ 800 Boylston St., Back Bay ☎ 617/236–3100, 617/859–0648 for Skywalk ⊕ www.prudentialcenter.com ▧ Skywalk $12 ☉ Mon.–Sat. 10–9, Sun. 11–6; Skywalk Nov.–Feb. daily 10–8, Mar.–Oct. daily 10–10 Ⓜ Hynes.

Symphony Hall. Acoustics rather than aesthetics make this hall, the home of the Boston Symphony Orchestra and the Boston Pops, special for performers and concertgoers. Although acoustical science was a brand-new field of research when Professor Wallace Sabine planned the interior, not one of the 2,500 seats is a bad one—the secret is the box-within-a-box design. ⊠ 301 Massachusetts Ave., Back Bay ☎ 888/266–1200 box office, 617/638–9390 tours ☉ Free walk-up tours Oct.–May, Wed. at 4 and 2nd Sat. of month at 2 Ⓜ Symphony.

THE SOUTH END

TOP ATTRACTIONS

Rutland Square. Reflecting a time when the South End was the most prestigious Boston address, this slice of a park is framed by lovely Italianate bowfront houses. ⊠ Rutland Sq. between Columbus Ave. and Tremont St.

Union Park. Cast-iron fences, Victorian-era town houses, and a grassy area all add up to one of Boston's most charming mini-escapes. ⊠ Union Park St. between Shawmut Ave. and Tremont St.

WORTH NOTING

Bay Village. This pocket of early-19th-century brick row houses, near Arlington and Piedmont streets, is a fine, mellow neighborhood (Edgar Allan Poe was born here). Its window boxes and short, narrow streets make the area seem a toylike reproduction of Beacon Hill. Note that, owing to the street pattern, it's nearly impossible to drive to Bay Village, and it's easy to miss on foot. ⊠ Bounded (roughly) by Arlington, Stuart, Charles, and Marginal Sts.

Boston Center for the Arts. Of Boston's multiple arts organizations, this city-sponsored arts-and-culture complex is the one that is closest to "the people." Here you can see the work of budding playwrights, view exhibits on Haitian folk art, or walk through an installation commemorating World AIDS Day. The BCA houses four theaters, a community music center, the Mills Art Gallery, and studio space for some 40 Boston-based contemporary artists. ⊠ 539 Tremont St., South End ☎ 617/426–5000

CLOSE UP

Prestige Lost

Not long after its conception in the mid-1800s, the South End, somewhat unfairly, lost its elite status to the Back Bay. The literature of the time documents this exodus: the title character in William Dean Howells's *The Rise of Silas Lapham* abandoned the South End to build a house on the waterside of Beacon as material proof of his arrival in Boston society. In *The Late George Apley*, John P. Marquand's Brahmin hero tells how his father decided, in the early 1870s, to move the family from his South End bowfront to the Back Bay—a consequence of his walking out on the front steps one morning and seeing a man in his shirtsleeves on the porch opposite. Regardless of whether Marquand exaggerated Victorian notions of propriety (if that was possible), the fact is that people such as the Apleys did decamp for the Back Bay, leaving the South End to become what a 1913 guidebook called a "faded quarter."

⊕ *www.bcaonline.org* ⊠ *Free* ⊙ *Weekdays 9–5; Mills Gallery Wed. and Sun. noon–5, Thurs.–Sat. noon–9* Ⓜ *Back Bay/South End.*

Cathedral of the Holy Cross. This enormous 1875 Gothic cathedral dominates the corner of Washington and Union Park streets. The main church of the Archdiocese of Boston and therefore the seat of Archbishop Seán Patrick O'Malley, Holy Cross is also New England's largest Catholic church. ⊠ *1400 Washington St., South End* ☎ *617/542–5682* ⊕ *www.holycrossboston.com* ⊙ *Mass Sun. at 8 am and 11:30 am, Mon.–Sat. at 9 am; in Spanish Sun. at 9:30 am, Tues. and Thurs. at 7 pm* Ⓜ *Chinatown, then Bus 49 to Cathedral.*

NEED A
BREAK?

Flour Bakery and Café. A good spot to refuel on a budget is Flour Bakery and Café, a perennial candidate for Boston's best sandwiches and stuffed bread. Also superb are the fresh pizzas, dinner specials, and delicious pastries. ⊠ *1595 Washington St., South End* ☎ *617/267–4300* ⊕ *www. flourbakery.com* Ⓜ *Back Bay/South End.*

The Fenway

WORD OF MOUTH

"Sure, it's an old park. Sure, the seats are uncomfortable. Sure, it may be cold in April. But, in spite of all that, it's still a great experience! Tear down Fenway Park? That's sacrilege! Definitely take the tour of the stadium."

—HowardR

GETTING ORIENTED

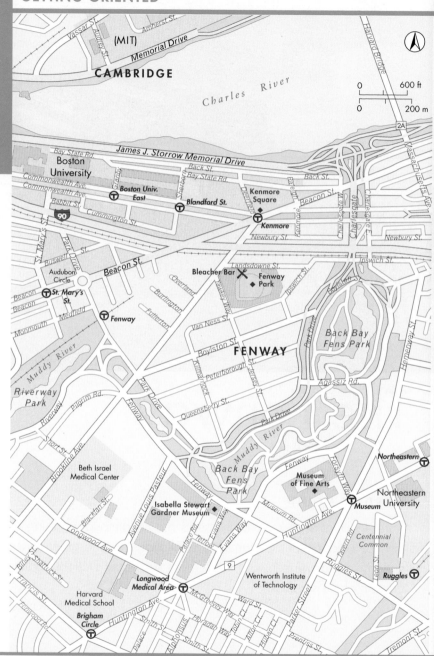

GETTING HERE AND AROUND

The Green Line is the way to go when it comes to getting to the Fenway; get off at the Kenmore or Fenway stops for a short walk to the ballpark. It is possible to drive around this part of town; on-street parking can usually be found with a little hunting on nongame days, and there are many lots and garages within reasonable walking distance of Fenway Park.

TIMING AND SAFETY

Although this area can be walked through in a couple of hours, art lovers could spend a week here, thanks to the glories of the MFA and the Isabella Stewart Gardner Museum. (If you want to do a museum blowout, avoid Monday, when the Gardner is closed.) To cap off a day of culture, plan for dinner in the area and then a concert at nearby Symphony Hall. Another option, if you're visiting between spring and early fall, is to take a tour of Fenway Park—or better yet, catch a game.

The Fenway and Kenmore Square area is generally safe, and is home to thousands of college students attending Boston University, Wheelock, Simmons, and Emmanuel, to name only a few of the nearby institutions. While the main streets Beacon, Commonwealth, and Brookline Avenues can be choked with pedestrians during game day, the marshy area of the Fens is quiet and poorly lit: avoid walking there alone at night.

QUICK BITES

Nothing beats a dog and a beer at Fenway when you're enjoying the game on a warm summer's night. But even if you don't have a ticket, you can enjoy the same vibe at **Bleacher Bar** (⊠ *82A Landsdowne St.*) a hidden-away bar in Fenway Park with a view into center field, and enough historical Red Sox memorabilia to open its own museum.

TOP REASONS TO GO

■ Root for the home team (the *only* team in the eyes of Red Sox Nation) at Fenway Park.

■ Immerse yourself in the artistic masterpieces collected at the Museum of Fine Arts and the Isabella Stuart Gardiner museum.

■ Relish the perfect acoustics of a concert at Symphony Hall.

WORD OF MOUTH

The musical instruments room [at the Museum of Fine Arts] alone is incredible. I could have spent the entire day at this museum but wanted to see the Isabella Gardner Museum, too, so I stayed until 3, having arrived at 10.

—AnnMarie_C

FENWAY PARK TOURS

If you can't score a ticket to see the Sox while you're in town, you can still see the Green Monster up close by going on a tour of the park. The 50-minute walking tours Fenway run year round, and the last tour of the day on a home game day offers access to batting practice. Tours run hourly from 9 am to 3 pm and cost $12. ☎ *617/226–6666* ✐ *tours@redsox.com.*

DID YOU KNOW?

Yawkey Way is named for the late Tom Yawkey, who bought the Red Sox in 1933 as a 30th-birthday present for himself and spent the next 43 years pursuing his elusive grail.

7

Sightseeing
★★★★
Dining
★★★
Lodging
★★★
Shopping
★★
Nightlife
★★★★

The marshland known as the Back Bay Fens gave this section of Boston its name, but two quirky institutions give it its character: Fenway Park, which in 2004 saw the triumphant reversal of an 86-year drought for Boston's beloved Red Sox, and the Isabella Stewart Gardner Museum, the legacy of a high-living Brahmin who attended a concert at Symphony Hall in 1912 wearing a headband that read, "Oh, You Red Sox." Not far from the Gardner is another major cultural magnet: the Museum of Fine Arts. Kenmore Square, a favorite haunt for Boston University students, adds a bit of funky flavor to the mix.

Updated
by Bethany
Cassin
Beckerlegge

After the outsize job of filling in the bay had been completed, it would have been small trouble to obliterate the Fens with gravel and march row houses straight through to Brookline. But the planners, deciding that enough pavement had been laid between here and the Public Garden, hired vaunted landscape architect Frederick Law Olmsted to turn the Fens into a park. Olmsted applied his genius for heightening natural effects while subtly manicuring their surroundings; today the Fens park consists of irregularly shaped reed-bound pools surrounded by broad meadows, trees, and flower gardens.

The Fens marks the beginning of Boston's Emerald Necklace, a loosely connected chain of parks designed by Olmsted that extends along the Fenway, Riverway, and Jamaicaway to Jamaica Pond, the Arnold Arboretum, and Franklin Park. Farther off, at the Boston–Milton line, the Blue Hills Reservation offers some of the Boston area's best hiking, scenic views, and even a ski lift.

The Daughters of Edward Darley Boit (1882) by John Singer Sargent is just one of the Museum of Fine Arts' 450,000 works of art.

TOP ATTRACTIONS

Fodor's Choice ★ **Fenway Park.** For 86 years, the Boston Red Sox suffered a World Series dry spell, a streak of bad luck that fans attributed to the "Curse of the Bambino," which, stories have it, struck the team in 1920 when they sold Babe Ruth (the "Bambino") to the New York Yankees. All that changed in 2004, when a maverick squad broke the curse in a thrilling seven-game series against the team's nemesis in the Series semifinals. This win against the Yankees was followed by a four-game sweep of St. Louis in the finals. Boston, and its citizens' ingrained sense of pessimism, hasn't been the same since. The repeat World Series win in 2007 has just cemented Bostonians' sense that the universe is finally working correctly and made Red Sox caps the residents' semiofficial uniform. ⇨ *See the Fenway Park spotlight in the Sports and the Outdoors chapter for more information.* ⊠ *4 Yawkey Way, between Van Ness and Lansdowne Sts., The Fenway* ☎ *877/733–7699 box office, 617/226–6666 tours* ⊕ *www.redsox.com* 🎫 *Tours $12* ⊙ *Tours Mon.–Sat. 9–4, Sun. 9–3; on game days, last tour is 3 hrs before game time* Ⓜ *Kenmore.*

Fodor's Choice ★ **Isabella Stewart Gardner Museum.**
See highlighted listing in this chapter.

Fodor's Choice ★ **Museum of Fine Arts.**
See highlighted listing in this chapter.

ISABELLA STEWART GARDNER MUSEUM

✉ *280 The Fenway, The Fenway* ☎ *617/566–1401, 617/566–1088 café* ⊕ *www.gardnermuseum.org* 🎟 *$12* ⊗ *Museum Tues.–Sun. 11–5, open some holidays; café Tues.–Fri. 11:30–4, weekends 11–4* Ⓜ *Museum.*

TIPS

■ If you've visited the MFA in the past two days, there's a $2 discount to the admission fee.

■ A charming quirk of the museum's admission policy waives entrance fees to anyone named Isabella.

■ Allot about two hours to tour the museum properly, and note that the collections generally appeal to a "grown-up" audience. There isn't much for young children here.

■ If you're looking for a light lunch after your tour, visit the Gardiner Cafe near the gift shop. The restaurant serves up quiches, soup, salads, and more, and features award winning desserts.

A spirited young society woman, Isabella Stewart had come in 1860 from New York—where ladies were more commonly seen and heard than in Boston—to marry John Lowell Gardner, one of Boston's leading citizens. "Mrs. Jack" promptly set about becoming the most un-Bostonian of the Proper Bostonians. She decided to build the Venetian palazzo to hold her collected arts in an isolated corner of Boston's newest neighborhood. Her will stipulated that the building remain exactly as she left it—paintings, furniture, and the smallest object in a hall cabinet—and that is as it has remained. Today, it's probably America's most idiosyncratic treasure house.

HIGHLIGHTS

Gardner's palazzo contains a trove of amazing paintings—including such masterpieces as Titian's *Europa,* Giotto's *Presentation of Christ in the Temple,* Piero della Francesca's *Hercules,* and John Singer Sargent's *El Jaleo.* Spanish leather panels, Renaissance hooded fireplaces, and Gothic tapestries accent salons; eight balconies adorn the majestic Venetian courtyard. There's a Raphael Room, Spanish Cloister, Gothic Room, Chinese Loggia, and a magnificent Tapestry Room for concerts, where Gardner entertained Henry James and Edith Wharton. An adjacent gallery houses the works of participants in museum's artist-in-residence program.

There are some conspicuously bare spots on the walls. On March 18, 1990, the Gardner was the target of a sensational art heist. Thieves disguised as police officers stole 12 works, including Vermeer's *The Concert.* To date, none of the art has been recovered, despite a $5 million reward. Because Mrs. Gardner's will prohibited substituting other works for any stolen art, empty expanses of wall identify spots where the paintings once hung.

7

MUSEUM OF FINE ARTS

✉ *465 Huntington Ave., The Fenway* ☎ *617/267–9300* ⊕ *www.mfa.org* 🖼 *$20; by donation Wed. 4–9:45* ⊘ *Sat.–Tues. 10–4:45, Wed.–Fri. 10–9:45. 1-hr tours daily; call for scheduled times* Ⓜ *Museum.*

TIPS

■ From October to April, tea is served 2:30–4 in the second-floor Upper Rotunda. Take a much-needed break from the art viewing and enjoy.

■ The year-round cocktail party "MFA Fridays," from 5:30 to 9:30—held weekly in summer and monthly at other times—has become quite the social event. Stop by to admire the art in a festive atmosphere.

■ Be aware that the museum will require you to check any bag larger than 11"x15", even if it's your purse. Save that oversized "it" bag for another day and bring along only the essentials.

■ With such extensive collections, you could easily spend a whole afternoon perusing the galleries, but if you only have an hour, head to the second floor and take in the Monets.

Count on staying a while if you have any hope of seeing what's here. Eclecticism and thoroughness, often an incompatible pair, have coexisted agreeably at the MFA since its earliest days. From Renaissance and baroque masters to impressionist marvels to African masks to sublime samples of Native American pottery and contemporary crafts, the collections are happily shorn of both cultural snobbery and shortsighted trendiness.

HIGHLIGHTS

The MFA's collection of approximately 450,000 objects was built from a core of paintings and sculpture from the Boston Athenaeum, historical portraits from the city of Boston, and donations by area universities. The MFA has more than 60 works by John Singleton Copley; major paintings by Winslow Homer, John Singer Sargent, Fitz Hugh Lane, and Edward Hopper; and a wealth of American works ranging from native New England folk art and colonial portraiture to New York abstract expressionism of the 1950s and 1960s. Also of particular note are the John Singer Sargent paintings adorning the Rotunda. They were specially commissioned for the museum in 1921, and make for a dazzling first impression on visitors coming through the Huntington Street entrance.

American decorative arts are also liberally represented, particularly those of New England in the years before the Civil War. Native son Paul Revere, much more than a sounder of alarms, is amply represented as well, with superb silver teapots, sauceboats, and other tableware.

The museum also owns one of the world's most extensive collections of Asian art under one roof. Its Japanese art collection is the finest outside Japan, and Chinese porcelains of the Tang Dynasty are especially well represented. The Egyptian rooms display statuary, furniture, and exquisite gold jewelry; a special funerary-arts gallery exhibits coffins, mummies, and burial treasures.

Founded in 1870, the MFA first resided on the upper floors of the Boston Athenaeum, then in a Gothic structure on the site where the Copley Plaza Hotel now stands. As the museum was beginning to outgrow that space, the Fenway area was becoming fashionable, and in 1909 the move was made to Guy Lowell's somewhat severe beaux arts building, to which the West Wing, designed by I.M. Pei, was added in 1981. The move helped cap the half-century of expansion of the Back Bay area.

French impressionists abound, and are perhaps more comprehensively displayed here than at any other New World museum aside from the Art Institute of Chicago; many of the 38 Monets (the largest collection of his work outside France) vibrate with color. There are canvases by Renoir, Pissarro, Manet, and the American painters Mary Cassatt and Childe Hassam.

Three important galleries explore the art of Africa, Oceania, and the Ancient Americas, expanding the MFA's emphasis on civilizations outside the Western tradition. The museum also has strong collections of textiles, costumes, and prints dating from the 15th century, including many works by Dürer and Goya, and its collection of antique musical instruments is among the finest in the world.

Fifteen second-floor galleries contain the MFA's European painting and sculpture collection, dating from the 11th century to the 20th. Among the standouts are Donatello's marble relief *The Madonna of the Clouds* and J.M.W. Turner's powerful work *The Slave Ship*. Most striking, however, is the William I. Koch Gallery, a former tapestry room whose 40-foot-high marble walls are now hung, nearly floor to ceiling, with 53 dramatic Renaissance and baroque paintings by El Greco, Claude Lorraine, Poussin, Rubens, Tintoretto, Titian, Van Dyck, Velázquez, Veronese, and other masters.

The West Wing, an airy, well-lighted space, is used primarily to mount special exhibitions, temporary shows drawn from the museum's holdings, and lively contemporary-art and photography exhibits. It also has the Bravo Restaurant, a cafeteria, and a café serving light snacks.

In 2005 the museum broke ground on a massive construction project that the trustees hope will keep it in America's cultural vanguard for the next 100 years. A new East Wing has been built to house the Art of the Americas collection, expanding the current gallery space by 50%. Other aspects of the 133-year-old building's enormous face-lift include a new glass-enclosed courtyard, the reopening of the Fenway entrance, and a "crystal spine" to run the full length of the museum. The construction is now complete and the new American Wing opened in November 2010 to much fanfare; the wing houses more than 5,000 works from North, Central, and South American in its 53 brand new galleries.

7

A GOOD WALK

With Boston's two major art museums on this itinerary, a case of museum fatigue could set in. Happily, both the Museum of Fine Arts and the Isabella Stewart Gardner Museum are surrounded by the sylvan glades of the Fenway—a perfect oasis and time-out location when you're suffering from gallery gout. From the intersection of Massachusetts and Huntington avenues, with the front entrance of Symphony Hall on your right, walk down Huntington Avenue. On your left is the New England Conservatory of Music and, on Gainsborough Street, its recital center, Jordan Hall. Between Huntington Avenue and the Fenway is the **Museum of Fine Arts (MFA)** and, just around the corner, the **Isabella Stewart Gardner Museum**. If you prefer to pay homage to the Red Sox: from Symphony Hall, go north on Mass Ave., turn left on Commonwealth Avenue, and continue until you reach **Kenmore Square**; from here it's a 10-minute walk down Brookline Avenue to Yawkey Way and **Fenway Park**.

WORTH NOTING

Kenmore Square. Two blocks north of Fenway Park is Kenmore Square, where you'll find fast-food joints, record stores, and an enormous sign advertising Citgo gasoline. The red, white, and blue neon sign from 1965 is so thoroughly identified with the area that historic preservationists fought, successfully, to save it—proof that Bostonians are an open-minded lot who don't insist that their landmarks be identified with the American Revolution. The old Kenmore Square punk clubs have given way to a block-long development of chain stores and pricey restaurants, as well as brick sidewalks, gaslight-style street lamps, and tree plantings. In the shadow of Fenway Park between Brookline and Ipswich is **Lansdowne Street,** a nightlife magnet for the young and trendy who have their pick of can't-hear-yourself-think dance clubs and pre-game bars. The urban campus of Boston University begins farther west on Commonwealth Avenue, in blocks thick with dorms, shops, and restaurants. ⊠ *Convergence of Beacon St., Commonwealth Ave., and Brookline Ave.* Ⓜ *Kenmore.*

8

Boston Outskirts

GETTING ORIENTED

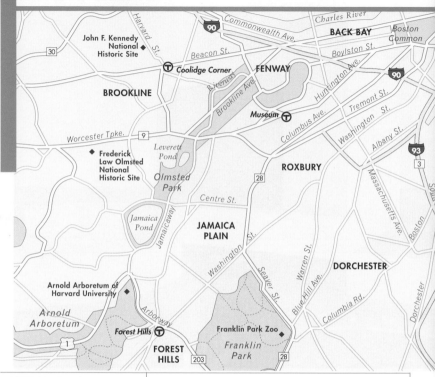

GETTING HERE AND AROUND	TOP REASONS TO GO
While driving to these suburbs is relatively painless, they're not called the "streetcar suburbs" for nothing. To get to South Boston, hop off the Red Line at Broadway. To reach the Arnold Arboretum in Jamaica Plain, take the Orange Line to the end at Forest Hills. Brookline is accessible via the C and D lines of the Green Line.	■ Marvel at the architectural wonder cantilevered over Boston Harbor that houses the Institute of Contemporary Art. ■ Relive the history of Camelot with a visit to the John F. Kennedy Library and Museum. ■ Tour the Samuel Adams Brewery, home to Boston's own award-winning beers. Free samples at the end are the highlight of the tour.

TIMING AND SAFETY

Timing all depends on which areas you decide to explore. Each neighborhood merits a half-day, especially in factoring travel time from Boston proper and a leisurely lunch or dinner.

Generally, most of these neighborhoods are safe, particularly in the areas where these attractions reside. But use common sense: stick to well-lighted areas and avoid walking alone late at night.

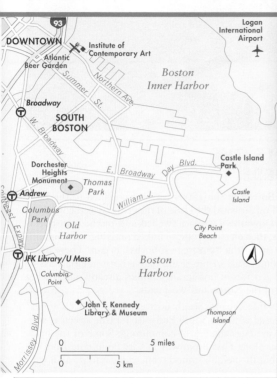

WORD OF MOUTH

"Sam Adams Brewery: highly recommended. They ask for $2 donation. I had read Friday and Saturdays are the busiest, so we timed to make the second tour on a Friday. It appeared to be filling up as we left. The 60 minute tour [came with a] cute souvenir glass and three tastings. I thought my parents would yell at me for taking them to a brewery at 10:30 in the morning, but they enjoyed themselves, so I think they forgot."

—absolutkz

"The new Institute of Contemporary Art is also good but depends on the exhibit because they don't have much of a permanent collection... the museum is brand new and designed to be very family friendly."

—Sally30

QUICK BITES

Atlantic Beer Garden. If you happen to be visiting the ICA, take a break at the Atlantic Beer Garden. Just steps from the museum, the bar and restaurant has a million flat screens to catch every game, and gorgeous views of the ICA and the harbor from their deck, where you can dine alfresco in summer. ⊠ *146 Seaport Blvd.* ☎ *617/357–8000* ⊕ *www. atlanticbeergarden.com.*

A GOOD WALK

A stroll down Brookline's Harvard Street is a great way to spend a few hours if you're in the neighborhood. Browse the bookshelves at **Brookline Booksmith** (⊠ *279 Harvard St.*), an excellent local bookstore; or take in an independent film at the **Coolidge Corner Theater** (⊠ *290 Harvard St.*). After window shopping, treat yourself to a few scoops at **J. P. Licks** (⊠ *311 Harvard St.*), arguably some of the Boston area's best ice cream.

BOSTON OUTSKIRTS (THE "STREETCAR SUBURBS")

Sightseeing
★★★

Dining
★★

Lodging
★★

Shopping
★★★

Nightlife
★★

Updated
by Bethany
Cassin
Beckerlegge

The expansion of Boston in the 1800s was not confined to the Back Bay and the South End. Toward the close of the century, as the working population of the Downtown district swelled and public transportation (first horsecars, then electric trolleys) linked outlying suburbs with the city, development of the "streetcar suburbs" began. These areas answered the housing needs of the rising native-born middle class as well as the second-generation immigrant families already outgrowing the narrow streets of the North and West ends.

The landfill project that became South Boston—known as "Southie" and not to be confused with the South End—isn't a true streetcar suburb; its expansion predates the era of commuting. Some of the brick bowfront residences along East Broadway in City Point date from the 1840s and 1850s, but the neighborhood really came into its own with the influx of Irish around 1900, and Irish-Americans still hold sway here. Southie is a Celtic enclave, as the raucous annual St. Patrick's Day parade attests.

Among the streetcar suburbs are Dorchester and Jamaica Plain (now part of Boston proper)—rural retreats barely more than a century ago that are now thick with tenements and Boston's distinctive three- and six-family triple-decker apartment houses. Dorchester is almost exclusively residential, tricky to navigate by car, and accessible by the T only if you know exactly where you're going. Jamaica Plain is a hip, young neighborhood with a strong lesbian and ecofriendly population; brunch and a wander through the neighborhood's quirky stores or through the Arnold Arboretum makes for a relaxing weekend excursion. Both towns border Franklin Park, an Olmsted creation of more than 500 acres, noted for its zoo. Farther west, Brookline is composed of a mixture of the affluent and students.

SOUTH BOSTON

Castle Island Park. South Boston projects farther into the harbor than any other part of Boston except Logan Airport, and the views of the Harbor Islands from along Day Boulevard or Castle Island are expansive. At L Street and Day Boulevard is the L Street Beach, where an intrepid group called the L Street Brownies swims year-round, including a celebratory dip in the icy Atlantic every New Year's Day. Castle Island Park is no longer on an island, but **Fort Independence,** when it was built here in 1801, was separated from the mainland by water. The circular walk from the fort around Pleasure Bay, delightful on a warm summer day, has a stunning view of the city's skyline late at night. To get here by the T, take the Red Line to Broadway Station. Just outside the station, catch Bus 9 or 11 going east on Broadway, which takes you to within a block of the waterfront. From the waterfront park you can walk the loop, via piers, around the island. ⊠ *Off William J. Day Blvd., South Boston* ☎ *617/727–5290* ⊕ *www.mass.gov/dcr/parks/metroboston/castle.htm* ⊗ *Tours Memorial Day–Labor Day, call for specific tour times.*

Fodor's Choice ★ **Institute of Contemporary Art.** Housed in a breathtaking cantilevered edifice that juts out over the Boston waterfront, the ICA moved to this site in 2006 as part of a massive reinvention that's seeing the museum grow into one of Boston's most exciting attractions. Since its foundation in 1936, the institute has cultivated its cutting-edge status: it's played host to works by Edvard Munch, Egon Schiele, and Oskar Kokoschka. Andy Warhol, Robert Rauschenberg, and Roy Lichtenstein each mounted pivotal exhibitions here early in their careers. Now the ICA is building a major permanent collection for the first time in its history, while continuing to showcase innovative paintings, videos, installations, and multimedia shows. The performing arts get their due in the museum's new theater, and the Water Café features cuisine from Wolfgang Puck. ⊠ *100 Northern Ave., South Boston* ☎ *617/478–3100* ⊕ *www.icaboston.org* ⊠ *$15, free Thurs. 5–9, free for families last Sat. of every month* ⊗ *Tues. and Wed. 10–5, Thurs. and Fri. 10–9, weekends 10–5. Tours on select weekends at 2 and select Thurs. at 6* Ⓜ *Courthouse.*

8

DORCHESTER

Dorchester Heights Monument and National Historic Site. In 1776 Dorchester Heights hill commanded a clear view of central Boston, where the British had been under siege since the preceding year. Here George Washington set up the cannons that Henry Knox, a Boston bookseller turned soldier, and later secretary of war, had hauled through the wilderness after their capture at Fort Ticonderoga. The artillery did its job of intimidation, and the British troops left Boston, never to return. The view of Boston from the site is magnificent, particularly if you go during the hours the graceful white tower is staffed. Climb its 93 steps and you'll be rewarded with vistas from the Blue Hills to the Harbor Islands, although the lovely park grounds are a destination on their own on a warm day. ⊠ *Thomas Park off Telegraph St., near G St., Dorchester* ☎ *617/242–5642* ⊠ *Free* ⊗ *Grounds daily. Monument call for schedule* Ⓜ *Broadway, then City Point Bus (9 or 11) to G St.*

Ↄ **Franklin Park Zoo.** Lion and tiger habitats, the Giraffe Savannah, and a 4-acre mixed-species area called the Serengeti Crossing that showcases zebras, ostriches, ibex, and wildebeests keep this zoo roaring. The Tropical Forest, with its renovated Western Lowland Gorilla environment, is a big draw, and wallabies, emus, and kangaroos populate

Arnold Arboretum of Harvard University is an urban oasis just 6 miles from downtown.

the Australian Outback Trail. From May to September butterflies flit and flutter at Butterfly Landing, where docents are on hand to answer questions and give advice on attracting the colorful insects to your own garden. The Children's Zoo entices with sheep, goats, and other beasts. In winter, call in advance to find out which animals are braving the cold. The park, 4 mi from Downtown, is reached by Bus 16 from the Forest Hills (Orange Line) or Andrew (Red Line) T stops; there's plenty of parking. ⊠ *1 Franklin Park Rd., Dorchester* ☎ *617/541–5466* ⊕ *www.zoonewengland.com* ✉ *$14* ☉ *Oct.–Mar., daily 10–4; Apr.–Sept., weekdays 10–5, weekends 10–6.*

★   **John F. Kennedy Library & Museum.** Chronicling a time now passing from memory to history, the library-museum is both a center for serious scholarship and a focus for Boston's nostalgia for her native son. The stark, white, prowlike building (another modernist monument designed by I. M. Pei) at this harbor-enclosed site pays homage to the life and presidency of John F. Kennedy and to members of his family, including his wife, Jacqueline, and brother Robert.

The Kennedy Library is the official repository of his presidential papers; the museum displays a trove of Kennedy memorabilia, including re-creations of his desk in the Oval Office and of the television studio in which he debated Richard M. Nixon in the 1960 election. At the entrance, high and dry during the summer months, is the president's 26-foot sailboat; inside, two theaters show a film about his life. The museum exhibits, ranging from the Cuban missile crisis to his assassination, include 20 video presentations. There's also a permanent display on the late Jacqueline Kennedy Onassis, including some samples of her distinctive wardrobe and such personal mementos as a first edition of *One Special Summer,* the book she and her sister wrote and illustrated shortly after a 1951 trip to Paris. A re-creation of the office Robert Kennedy occupied as attorney general from 1961 to 1964 complements "legacy" videos of John's idealistic younger brother. As a somber note in an otherwise gung-ho museum, continuous videos of the first news bulletin of the assassination and the funeral are shown in a darkened hall. Fourth-floor research facilities are open only to serious scholars. The Steven M. Smith Wing provides space for meetings and events; the facility also includes a store and a small café. ⊠ *Columbia Point, Dorchester* ☎ *617/514–1600* ⊕ *www. jfklibrary.org* ⊒ *$12* ⊙ *Daily 9–5* Ⓜ *JFK/UMass, then free shuttle bus every 20 mins.*

BEER HERE

Before Prohibition, Jamaica Plain was home to a thriving beer industry, the remnants of which today can be seen in the neighborhood's many 19th-century brick breweries, long since converted to offices and lofts.

Samuel Adams Brewery. The Samuel Adams Brewery is the only hint that the area was once awash in hops, malt, and happy tipplers. Complimentary tastings are the highlight of the brewery's tours. ⇨ *See the Hometown Brew box in the Nightlife chapter for more information.* ⊠ *30 Germania St., Jamaica Plain* ☎ *617/368–5080.*

JAMAICA PLAIN

FodorsChoice
★

Arnold Arboretum of Harvard University. This 265-acre living laboratory is incongruously set in a dense urban area. Established in 1872 in accordance with the terms of a bequest from New Bedford merchant James Arnold, it contains more than 4,000 kinds of woody plants, most from the hardy north temperate zone. The rhododendrons, azaleas, lilacs, magnolias, and fruit trees are eye-popping when in bloom, and something is always in season from early April through September. In October the park puts on a display in blazing colors. Peters Hill has a grand view of the Boston skyline and local surroundings. The Larz Anderson bonsai collection, with individual specimens imported from Japan that are more than 200 years old, includes a 3½-acre Leventritt Shrub and Vine Collection. In the visitor center is a 40-to-1 scale model of the arboretum (with 4,000 tiny trees), plus an exhibit on "Science in the Pleasure Ground," a kind of "green" history of the landscape. If you visit during May, Lilac Sunday is an annual celebration of blooming trees, Morris dancing, and picnicking. The arboretum, 6 mi from downtown Boston, is accessible by the MBTA Orange Line or Bus 39 from Copley Square to Forest Hills; then follow the signs at the T station. ⊠ *125 Arborway, at Centre St., Jamaica Plain* ☎ *617/524–1718* ⊕ *www. arboretum.harvard.edu* ⊒ *Free* ⊙ *Grounds daily dawn–dusk; visitor center weekdays 9–4, Sat. 10–4, Sun. noon–4. Tours Sat. at 10:30, Sun. at 1, Wed. at 12:15, and Fri. at 6; call to confirm* Ⓜ *Forest Hills.*

8

BROOKLINE

John F. Kennedy National Historic Site. This was the home of the 35th president from his birth on May 29, 1917, until 1921, when the family moved to nearby Naples and Abbottsford streets. Rose Kennedy provided the furnishings for the restored 2½-story, wood-frame structure. You can pick up a brochure for a walking tour of young Kennedy's school, church, and neighborhood. To get here, take the MBTA Green Line to Coolidge Corner and walk north on Harvard Street four blocks. ✉ *83 Beals St.* ☎ *617/566–7937* ⊕ *www.nps.gov/jofi* ✉ *$3, tours free* ⊙ *Mid-May–Nov., Wed.–Sun. 10–4:30, call for tour schedule* Ⓜ *Coolidge Corner.*

Cambridge

WORD OF MOUTH

"I do want to draw people's attention to Cambridge. Nowhere else in the world can you find such a high concentration of Modernist architecture designed by famous architects . . . My husband and I took a 5-hr walking tour (organized by Historic New England & Gropius House) of the Harvard and MIT area . . . The tour covered 20+ buildings, and architects included Walter Gropius, Josep Lluis Sert, Le Corbusier, Eero Saarinen, I.M. Pei, just to name a few."

—yk

GETTING ORIENTED

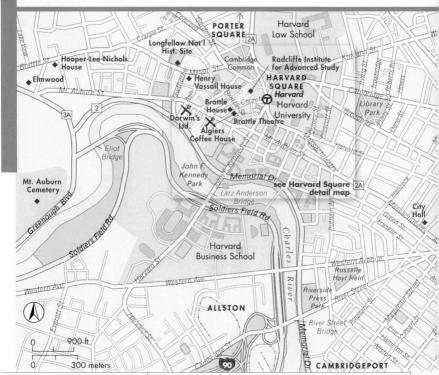

TIMING	GETTING HERE AND AROUND
Harvard Square is worth an afternoon; be sure to take a tour. Most visitors don't go beyond Harvard Square and Harvard Yard, but this is a unique town filled with funky restaurants, independent shops, unique art installations, important historic sites, and a large concentration of independent bookstores. If you plan to explore Harvard's natural-history or art museums or explore other Cambridge neighborhoods, give yourself a day or two here. ⇨ *See It's Hip to Be Square, below, for ideas on where to go.*	Just minutes from Boston, Cambridge is easily reached by taking the Red Line train (otherwise known as the T) outbound to any stop past Charles/MGH station. There are stops at MIT (Kendall Square), Central Square, Harvard Square, Porter Square, Davis Square (actually in Somerville), and Alewife. Harvard Square is the best place to begin any visit to Cambridge, but driving (and parking) here is a small nightmare. Do yourself a favor and take the T. If you insist on driving, suck it up and park in a garage. (Street parking is usually limited to two hours, and most spots are reserved for Cambridge residents.) Driving is less of a pain in other parts of Cambridge, but you're still better off getting around via the T. Try to spend as much time as possible exploring on foot. This is a walking town, and you'll miss a lot of Cambridge's quirkiness if you're moving too fast.

TOP REASONS TO GO

■ Browse the new- and used-book stores, trawl the artsy boutiques, and people-watch in Harvard Square. Take a break at one of the local coffee shops.

■ Do the museum circuit: The Harvard Museums for art; the Semitic Museum; the Peabody and the Natural History Museum for artifacts and culture.

■ Visit MIT to wander the halls, visit its museum, and see Frank Gehry's Seuss-like Stata Center.

■ Breathe the rarefied air of Harvard on an official tour (or an irreverent unofficial one), then return to real life with a burger from Mr. Bartley's Burger Cottage.

■ Amble down Brattle Street, visiting the 1700s era homes of Tory Row (Washington really did sleep here), and have a treat at Hi-Rise bakery in the original Blacksmith House of Longfellow's poem.

MOBILE TOUR

The Cambridge Office for Tourism offers walking tour for your mobile device ($4.99) on its Web site ⊕ *www.cambridge-usa.org.*

VISITOR INFORMATION

Cambridge Visitor Information Booth. A good place to start is the Cambridge Visitor Information Booth, outside the T station in Harvard Square. Free maps, brochures, historical walking tours, an excellent list of bookstores in the area, and a guide to seasonal events are available. ⊠ *Harvard Sq., near MBTA station entrance* ☎ *617/497–1630* ⊕ *www.cambridge-usa.org* ⊙ *Weekdays 9–5, weekends 9–1* Ⓜ *Harvard.*

QUICK BITES

You won't have a hard time finding food in Cambridge; all of the major squares are surrounded by interesting independent restaurants. Near Harvard Square try **Mr. Bartley's Burger Cottage** (⊠ *1246 Massachusetts Ave.*), a Harvard institution with an extensive (and hilarious) menu that includes dozens of riffs on the humble burger. Casual cafés abound on Brattle Street; good bets include **Tory Row** (⊠ *3 Brattle St.*) and **Cardullo's Gourmet Shop** (⊠ *6 Brattle St.*), which makes great sandwiches.

Sightseeing
★★★★
Dining
★★★★★
Lodging
★★
Shopping
★★★★
Nightlife
★★★★★

Updated
by Bethany
Cassin
Beckerlegge

The city of Cambridge takes a lot of hits, most of them thrown across the Charles River by jealous Bostonians. But Boston's Left Bank—an überliberal academic enclave—is a must-visit if you're spending more than a day or two in the Boston area.

The city is punctuated at one end by the funky tech-noids of MIT and at the other by the grand academic fortress that is Harvard University. Civic life connects the two camps into an urban stew of 100,000 residents who represent nearly every nationality in the world, work at every kind of job from tenured professor to taxi driver, and are passionate about living on this side of the river.

The Charles River is the Cantabrigians' backyard, and there's virtually no place in Cambridge more than a 10-minute walk from its banks. Strolling, running, or biking here is one of the great pleasures of Cambridge, and your views will include graceful bridges, the distant Boston skyline, crew teams rowing through the calm water, and the elegant spires of Harvard soaring into the sky. The relaxed atmosphere here is the polar opposite of the intellectual buzz you'll feel at the city's great universities.

No visit to Cambridge is complete without an afternoon (at least) in Harvard Square. It's a hub, a hot spot, and home to every variation of the human condition; Nobel laureates, homeless buskers, trust-fund babies, and working-class Joes all mill around the same piece of real estate. A walk down Brattle Street past Henry Wadsworth Longfellow's house is a joy. Farther along Massachusetts Avenue is Central Square, an ethnic melting pot of people and restaurants. Ten minutes more brings you to MIT, with its eclectic architecture from postwar pedestrian to Frank Gehry's futuristic fantasyland. In addition to providing a stellar view, the Mass Ave. Bridge, spanning the Charles from Cambridge to Boston, is also notorious in MIT lore for its Smoot measurements (⇨ *see "Campus Pranksters" under Massachusetts Institute of Technology*).

HARVARD SQUARE

In Cambridge all streets point toward Harvard Square. In addition to being the gateway to Harvard University and its various attractions, Harvard Square is home to the tiny yet venerable folk-music club Passim (Bob Dylan played here, and Bonnie Raitt was a regular during her time at Harvard), first-run and vintage movie theaters, concert and lecture venues, and a tempting collection of eclectic, independent shops. Harvard Square is a multicultural microcosm. On a warm day street musicians coax exotic tones from their Andean pan flutes and Chinese erhus, while cranks and local pessimists pass out pamphlets warning against all sorts of end-of-the-world scenarios. You will hear people speaking dozens of languages. In the small plaza atop the main entrance to the Harvard T station known as "the Pit," skaters and punk rockers strut and pose while fresh-faced students impress each other and/or their dates, and quiet clusters study the moves and strategy of the chess players seated outside Au Bon Pain. It's a wonderful circus of humanity.

TOP ATTRACTIONS

Harvard Art Museums. The artistic treasures of the ancient Greeks, Egyptians, and Romans are a major draw here. Make a beeline for the Ancient and Asian art galleries, the permanent installations on the fourth floor, which include Chinese bronzes, Buddhist sculptures, Greek friezes, and Roman marbles. Currently, the Sackler is the only one of the University's art museums open to the public. The Busch-Reisinger and Fogg museums closed in 2008. At present, visitors to the Sackler will enjoy a sampling of works culled from both. In 2013 the combined collections of all three museums will be represented under one roof under the umbrella name Harvard Art Museum. Works include Picasso, Klee, Toulouse-Lautrec, and Manet. ⊠ *485 Broadway* ☎ *617/495–9400* ⊕ *www.artmuseums.harvard.edu/collection/sackler* 🖘 *$9* ⊙ *Mon.–Sat. 10–5, Sun. 1–5* Ⓜ *Harvard.*

NEED A BREAK? **Broadway Marketplace.** The Broadway Marketplace is just around the corner from Harvard Yard. Besides the excellent fresh produce, there's a selection of sandwiches and prepared meals; choose one to be heated up and then grab a seat for a quick, delicious (if pricey) bite. ⊠ *468 Broadway* ☎ *617/547–2334* ⊕ *www.broadwaymarketplace.com.*

Ⓒ **Fodor's Choice** ★ **Harvard Museum of Natural History.** Many museums promise something for every member of the family; the vast Harvard Museum complex actually delivers. Swiss naturalist Louis Agassiz, who founded the zoology museum, envisioned a museum that would bring under one roof the study of all kinds of life: plants, animals, and humankind. The result is three distinct museums, all accessible for one admission fee.

The **Museum of Comparative Zoology** traces the evolution of animals and humans. You literally can't miss the 42-foot-long skeleton of the underwater *Kronosaurus*. Dinosaur fossils and a zoo of stuffed exotic animals can occupy young minds for hours. The museum is old-fashioned. You can almost feel the brush of the whiskers of the ardent explorers and the naturalists who combed the world for these treasures.

9

It's also the right size for kids—not jazzy and busy, a good place to ask and answer quiet questions. ■TIP→ Check the Web site for children's events and special engagements, which occur throughout the year.

Oversize garnets and crystals sparkle at the **Mineralogical and Geological Museum,** founded in 1784. The museum also contains an extensive collection of meteorites.

Perhaps the most famous exhibits of the museum complex are the glass flowers in the **Harvard University Herbaria (Botanical Museum),** created as teaching tools that would never wither and die. This unique collection holds 3,000 models of 847 plant species. Each one is a masterpiece, meticulously created in glass by a father and son in Dresden, Germany, who worked continuously from 1887 to 1936. Even more amazing than the colorful flower petals are the delicate roots of some plants; numerous signs assure the viewer that everything is, indeed, of glass. ⊠ *26 Oxford St.* ☏ *617/495–3045* ⊕ *www.hmnh.harvard.edu* ◁ *$9; free for Massachusetts residents Sun. 9–noon year-round and Wed. 3–5 Sept.–May* ☉ *Daily 9–5* Ⓜ *Harvard.*

☾ **Harvard Square.** Tides of students, tourists, political-cause proponents,
Fodor'sChoice and bizarre street creatures are all part of the nonstop pedestrian flow
★ at this most celebrated of Cambridge crossroads.

Harvard Square is where Mass Ave., coming from Boston, turns and widens into a triangle broad enough to accommodate a brick peninsula (above the T station). The restored 1928 kiosk in the center of the square once served as the entrance to the MBTA station (it's now Out of Town News, a fantastic newsstand). Harvard Yard, with its lecture halls, residential houses, libraries, and museums, is one long border of the square; the other three are comprised of clusters of banks and a wide variety of restaurants and shops.

On an average afternoon you'll hear earnest conversations in dozens of foreign languages; see every kind of youthful uniform from Goth to impeccable prep; wander by street musicians playing Andean flutes, singing opera, and doing excellent Stevie Wonder or Edith Piaf imitations; and lean in on a tense outdoor game of pickup chess between a street-tough kid and an older gent wearing a beard and a beret, while you slurp a cappuccino or an ice-cream cone (the two major food groups here). An afternoon in the square is people-watching raised to a high art; the parade of quirkiness never quits.

As entertaining as the locals are, the historic buildings are worth noting. Even if you're only a visitor (as opposed to a prospective student), it's still a thrill to walk though the big brick-and-wrought-iron gates to Harvard Yard, past the residence halls and statues, on up to Widener Library.

Across Garden Street, through an ornamental arch, is **Cambridge Common,** decreed a public pasture in 1631. It's said that under a large tree that once stood in this meadow George Washington took command of the Continental Army on July 3, 1775. A stone memorial now marks the site of the "Washington Elm." Also on the Common is the Irish Famine Memorial by Derry artist Maurice Herron, unveiled in 1997 to coincide with the 150th anniversary of "Black '47," the deadliest year of the potato famine. It depicts a desperate Irish mother sending her child off

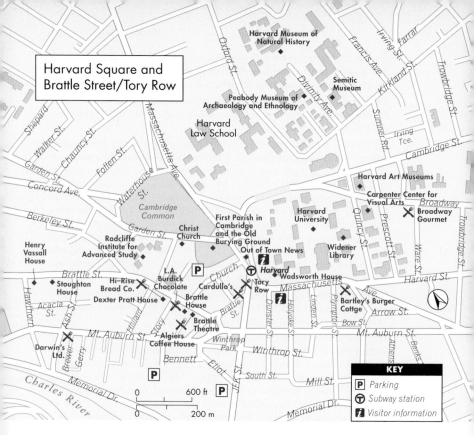

Harvard Square and
Brattle Street/Tory Row

to America. At the center of the Common a large memorial commemorates the Union soldiers and sailors who lost their lives in the Civil War. On the far side of the Common (on Waterhouse St. between Garden St. and Massachusetts Ave.) is a fantastic park. ⊕ *www.harvardsquare. com* Ⓜ *Harvard*.

★ **Harvard University.** The tree-studded, shady, and redbrick expanse of **Harvard Yard**—the very center of Harvard University—has weathered the footsteps of Harvard students for more than 300 years. In 1636 the Great and General Court of the Massachusetts Bay Colony voted funds to establish the colony's first college, and a year later chose Cambridge as the site. Named in 1639 for John Harvard, a young Charlestown clergyman who died in 1638 and left the college his entire library and half his estate, Harvard remained the only college in the New World until 1693, by which time it was firmly established as a respected center of learning. Local wags refer to Harvard as WGU—World's Greatest University—and it's certainly the oldest and most famous American university. It boasts numerous schools or "faculties," including the Faculty of Arts and Sciences, the Medical School, the Law School, the Business School, and the John F. Kennedy School of Government.

Although the college dates from the 17th century, the oldest buildings in Harvard Yard are from the 18th century (though you'll sometimes see

A young academic ponders his studies at Harvard University.

archaeologists digging here for evidence of older structures). Together the buildings chronicle American architecture from the colonial era to the present. **Holden Chapel,** completed in 1744, is a Georgian gem. The graceful **University Hall** was designed in 1815 by Charles Bulfinch. An 1884 statue of John Harvard by Daniel Chester French stands outside; ironically for a school with the motto of "Veritas" ("Truth"), the model for the statue was a member of the class of 1882, as there is no known contemporary likeness of Harvard himself. **Sever Hall,** completed in 1880 and designed by Henry Hobson Richardson, represents the Romanesque revival that was followed by the neoclassical (note the pillared facade of Widener Library) and the neo-Georgian, represented by the sumptuous brick houses along the Charles River, many of which are now undergraduate residences. **Memorial Church,** a graceful steepled edifice of modified Colonial Revival design, was dedicated in 1932. Just north of the Yard is **Memorial Hall,** completed in 1878 as a memorial to Harvard men who died in the Union cause; it's High Victorian both inside and out. It also contains the 1,166-seat Sanders Theatre, which serves as the university's largest lecture hall, site of year-round concerts by students and professionals, and the venue for the festive Christmas Revels.

Many of Harvard's cultural and scholarly facilities are important sights in themselves, including the **Harvard Museum of Natural History,** the **Peabody Museum of Archaeology & Ethnology,** and the **Widener Library.** Of the three much-loved art museums (the Fogg, the Busch-Reisinger, and the Arthur M. Sackler), only the latter remains. The two former are currently closed for extensive renovations and will reopen in

TWO WAYS TO EXPLORE HARVARD SQUARE

HISTORY 101

If you want to revisit the city's Tory beginnings, walk past the **Wadsworth House**, a clapboard house on Mass Ave. that dates from 1726, and enter the dignified hush of the Yard at **Harvard University**. Admire the exterior of **Widener Library** (only students and their guests are allowed inside); it houses one of the largest collections of books, historical materials, and journals in the academic world. Then circle back through the yard, crossing Mass Ave. to view the **First Parish in Cambridge and the Old Burying Ground** on the corner of Church Street. Through the iron railing of the cemetery you can make out a number of tombstones. Buried here are the remains of 17th- and 18th-century Tory landowners, slaves, and soldiers. Continue up Garden Street to **Christ Church**, designed in 1761 and still an active parish. The Cambridge Common, across Garden Street, has a terrific playground in the back corner away from the university (see below); this is a good spot to take a rest.

Retrace your steps along Mass Ave. and cross the street near the First Parish Church. Cut through Harvard Yard, bearing to your left, pass the modern Science Center (a good place for a bathroom break; restrooms are in the basement), and look for the striking Victorian architecture of Memorial Hall. Spend some time milling around the Yard and getting in touch with your inner undergrad.

ARTS ELECTIVES

If you're inclined toward art, the **Harvard Art Museums** (currently housed in the Arthur M. Sackler Museum space), will show you visions of the ancient world, while the **Carpenter Center for the Visual Arts** on Quincy Street offers a strictly contemporary perspective on film and graphic arts. Alas, those coming to ogle the fine wares of the Fogg and Busch-Reisinger museums will have to wait. At this writing, both are shut down for a lengthy renovation that will last until 2013 when they reopen under one roof as the Harvard Art Museum (along with the Sackler). Happily, some of the collections will be displayed during this time at the Sackler.
■TIP➜ Film lovers: Visit the film archive section on the Harvard Web site to find film screenings that coincide with your visit. When you've had your fill of culture, head back to one of the Harvard Square cafés for a snack and serious people-watching.

2010 as the Harvard Art Museums (which will also include the Sackler Museum). Be aware that most campus buildings, other than museums and concert halls, are off-limits to the general public.

Harvard University Events & Information Center. Harvard University Events & Information Center, run by students, includes a small library, a video-viewing area, computer terminals, and an exhibit space. It also distributes maps of the university area and has free student-led tours of Harvard Yard. The tour doesn't include visits to museums, and it doesn't take you into campus buildings, but it provides a fine orientation. The information center is open year-round (except during spring recess and other semester breaks), Monday through Saturday

9–5. Tours are offered September–May, weekdays at 10 and 2 and Saturday at 2 (except during university breaks). From the end of June through August, guides offer four tours Monday–Saturday at 10, 11:15, 2, and 3:15. Groups of 20 or more can schedule their tours ahead. ⊠ *Holyoke Center, 1350 Massachusetts Ave.* ☎ *617/495–1573* ⊕ *www.harvard. edu* ⊠ *Bounded by Massachusetts Ave. and Mt. Auburn, Holyoke, and Dunster Sts.* ☎ *617/495–1000* ⊕ *www.harvard.edu* Ⓜ *Harvard.*

> ### DID YOU KNOW?
>
> If you have $1,100, you too can get a Harvard Education! The surprisingly affordable Harvard Extension School, part of the university's Faculty of Arts and Sciences, offers a wide range of continuing education courses (some online), taught by honest-to-goodness members of the Harvard faculty. Check the Web site for details (⊕ *www.extension. harvard.edu*).

Peabody Museum of Archaeology & Ethnology. With one of the world's outstanding anthropological collections, the Peabody focuses on Native American and Central and South American cultures; there are also interesting displays on Africa. The Hall of the North American Indian is particularly outstanding, with art, textiles, and models of traditional dwellings from across the continent. The Mesoamerican room juxtaposes ancient relief carvings and weavings with contemporary works from the Maya and other peoples. ⊠ *11 Divinity Ave.* ☎ *617/496–1027* ⊕ *www.peabody.harvard.edu* ✉ *$9, includes admission to Harvard Museum of Natural History, accessible through the museum; free for Massachusetts residents only Sun. 9–noon year-round and Wed. 3–5 Sept.–May* ⊙ *Daily 9–5* Ⓜ *Harvard.*

WORTH NOTING

Carpenter Center for the Visual Arts. This gravity-defying mass of concrete and glass, built in 1963 to contrast with the now-defunct and more traditional Fogg Art Museum next door, is the only building in North America designed by the French architect Le Corbusier. The open floor plan provides students with five stories of flexible workspace, and the large, outward-facing windows ensure that the creative process is always visible and public. The center regularly holds free lectures and receptions with artists on Thursday evenings. At the top of the ramp, the **Sert Gallery** plays host to changing exhibits of contemporary works and has a café. The Main Gallery on the ground floor often showcases work by students and faculty. The **Harvard Film Archive** downstairs screens films nightly, often accompanied by discussions with the filmmakers. ⊠ *24 Quincy St.* ☎ *617/495–3251* ⊕ *www.ves.fas.harvard.edu/ccva. html* ✉ *Galleries free, film screenings $8* ⊙ *Main Gallery Mon.–Sat. 10 am–11 pm, Sun. 1 pm–11 pm; Sert Gallery Tues.–Sun. 1–5* Ⓜ *Harvard.*

Christ Church. This modest, yet beautiful gray clapboard structure was designed in 1761 by Peter Harrison, the first architect of note in the colonies. During the Revolution, members of its mostly Tory congregation fled for their lives. The organ was melted down for bullets and the building was used as a barracks during the Siege of Boston. (Step into the vestibule to look for the bullet hole left during the skirmish.) Martha Washington requested that the church reopen for services on New

Year's Eve in 1775. The church's historical significance extends to the 20th century: Teddy Roosevelt was a Sunday-school teacher here, and Martin Luther King Jr. spoke from the pulpit to announce his opposition to the Vietnam War. ⊠ *Zero Garden St.* ☎ *617/876–0200* ⊕ *www.cccambridge.org* ☉ *Visit building any day 8–4. Sun. services at 7:45 and 10:15, with choral evensong at 4; Wed. services at 12:10* Ⓜ *Harvard.*

NEED A BREAK?

Out of Town News. Need a news fix? Out of Town News has got you covered. Browse the world at this fascinating international news seller. Peruse the racks at this fabled landmark for international publications in languages from around the world. It's definitely worth a browse. ☎ *617/354–1441.*

★ **First Parish in Cambridge and the Old Burying Ground.** Next to the imposing church on the corner of Church Street and Mass Ave., a spooky-looking colonial graveyard houses 17th- and 18th-century tombstones of ministers, early Harvard presidents, and Revolutionary War soldiers. The wooden Gothic Revival church, known locally as "First Church" or "First Parish," was built in 1833 by Isaiah Rogers. The congregation dates to two centuries earlier, and has been linked to Harvard since the founding of the college. **Cambridge Forum.** The church sponsors this popular lecture series, which features well-known authors and academics. ☎ *617/495–2727* ⊕ *www.cambridgeforum.org* ⊠ *3 Church St.* ☎ *617/876–7772* ⊕ *www.firstparishcambridge.org* ☉ *Church weekdays 8–4, Sun. 8–1, service at 10:30. Burying ground daily dawn–dusk* Ⓜ *Harvard.*

Semitic Museum. An almost unknown gem, this Harvard institution serves as an exhibit space for Egyptian, Mesopotamian, and ancient Near East artifacts and as a center for archaeological exploration. Who knew that the Sphinx may have had curls? The museum's extensive collection rotates, and there are temporary exhibits; you never know what you might see here! The building also houses the Department of Near Eastern Languages and Civilization, with offices tucked among the artifacts. Note that there are no elevators. ⊠ *6 Divinity Ave.* ☎ *617/495–4631* ⊕ *www.fas.harvard.edu/~semitic* ▦ *Free; donations appreciated* ☉ *Weekdays 10–4, Sun. 1–4* Ⓜ *Harvard.*

Wadsworth House. On the Harvard University side of Harvard Square stands the Wadsworth House, a yellow clapboard structure built in 1726 as a home for Harvard presidents. It served as the first headquarters for George Washington, who arrived on July 2, 1775, to take command of the Continental Army, which he did the following day. The house, closed to the public, now houses general Harvard offices. ⊠ *1341 Massachusetts Ave.* ⊕ *www.harvard.edu* Ⓜ *Harvard.*

Old School

Cambridge dates from 1630, when the Puritan leader John Winthrop chose this meadowland as the site of a carefully planned village he named Newtowne. The Massachusetts Bay Colony chose Newtowne as the site for the country's first college in 1636. Two years later, John Harvard bequeathed half his estate and his private library to the fledgling school, and the college was named in his honor. The town elders changed the name to Cambridge, emulating the university in England where most of the Puritan leaders had been educated.

When Cambridge was incorporated as a city in 1846, the boundaries were drawn to include the university area (today's Harvard Square and Tory Row), and the more industrial communities of Cambridgeport and East Cambridge. By 1900 the population of these urban industrial and working-class communities, made up of Irish, Polish, Italian, Portuguese, and French Canadian residents, dwarfed the Harvard end of town. Today's city is much more a multiethnic urban community than an academic village. Visitors in search of any kind of ethnic food or music will find it in Cambridge—the local high school educates students who speak more than 40 different languages at home.

When MIT, originally Boston Tech, moved to Cambridge in 1916, it was the first educational institution that aimed to be more than a trade school, training engineers but also grounding them in the humanities and liberal arts. Many of MIT's postwar graduates remained in the area, and went on to form hundreds of technology-based firms engaged in camera manufacturing, electronics, and space research. By the 1990s manufacturing had moved to the burbs, and software developers, venture capitalists, and robotics and biotech companies claimed the former industrial spaces. This area around Kendall Square is now nicknamed "Intelligence Alley."

9

Widener Library. Harvard University's Harry Elkins Widener Library was named for a young book lover who went down with the *Titanic*. Holding more than 15 million volumes in more than 90 libraries around the world, the Harvard University Library system is second in size in the United States only to the Library of Congress, and Widener Library itself is one of the world's largest individual book repositories. Sixty-five miles of bookshelves snake around six stories above and four stories below ground. Two additional levels are attached by underground tunnel. The imposing neoclassical structure was designed by one of the nation's first major African-American architects, Julian Abele. In the center of the building stands the private collection of Mr. Widener himself (including his Gutenberg Bible and Shakespeare First Folio) in a circular room featuring his original desk. It was his mother's express wish that fresh flowers be placed on the desk each day, a tradition that continues to this day. The library isn't open to the public; people with a "scholarly need" can apply for admission at the privileges office inside. ⊠ *Harvard Yard* ☎ *617/495–2413* ⊕ *hcl.harvard.edu/libraries/widener* Ⓜ *Harvard*.

BRATTLE STREET/TORY ROW

Brattle Street remains one of New England's most elegant thorough-fares. Elaborate mansions line both sides from where it meets JFK Street to Fresh Pond Parkway. Brattle Street was once dubbed Tory Row, because during the 1770s its seven mansions, on lands that stretched to the river, were owned by staunch supporters of King George. These properties were appropriated by the patriots when they took over Cambridge in the summer of 1775. Many of the historic houses are marked with blue signs, and although only two (the Hooper-Lee-Nichols House and the Longfellow National Historic Site) are fully open to the public, it's easy to imagine yourself back in the days of Ralph Waldo Emerson and Henry David Thoreau as you stroll the brick sidewalks. Mt. Auburn Cemetery, an exquisitely landscaped garden cemetery is less than 2 mi down Brattle Street from Harvard Square.

TOP ATTRACTIONS

Brattle House. This 18th-century, gambrel-roof Colonial once belonged to the Loyalist William Brattle. He moved to Boston in 1774 to escape the patriots' anger, then left in 1776 with the British troops. From 1831 to 1833 the house was the residence of Margaret Fuller, feminist author and editor of *The Dial.* Today it's the office of the Cambridge Center for Adult Education, and is listed on the National Register of Historic Places. ⊠ *42 Brattle St.* ☎ *617/547–6789* ⊕ *www.ccae.org* ☯ *Mon.– Thurs. 9–9, Fri. 9–7, Sat. 9–2. Summer hrs vary* Ⓜ *Harvard.*

NEED A BREAK?

Algiers Coffee House. Algiers Coffee House, upstairs from the Brattle Theatre, is a favorite evening hangout for young actors and artists. Linger over mint tea or plate of hummus, and don't expect rapid service. ⊠ *40 Brattle St.* ☎ *617/492–1557.*

Brattle Theatre. Occupying a squat, barnlike building from 1890, the Brattle Theatre is set improbably between a modern shopping center and a colonial mansion. The resident repertory company gained notoriety in the 1950s when it made a practice of hiring actors blacklisted as Communists by the U.S. government. For the last half-century it has served as the square's independent movie house, screening indie, foreign, obscure, and classic films, from nouveau to noir; check the Web site for current offerings and events. ⊠ *40 Brattle St.* ☎ *617/876–6837* ⊕ *www.brattlefilm.org* Ⓜ *Harvard.*

★ **Longfellow National Historic Site.** Henry Wadsworth Longfellow, the poet whose stirring tales of the Village Blacksmith, Evangeline, Hiawatha, and Paul Revere's midnight ride thrilled 19th-century America, once lived in this elegant mansion. If there's one historic house to visit in Cambridge, this is it. The house was built in 1759

WORD OF MOUTH

"I live in Cambridgeport between Harvard and MIT and walk to Harvard Square all the time. It's a lovely walk by the river. Eat outdoors or in at Henrietta's Kitchen at the Charles Hotel or at Legal Seafoods, or Rialto, all top dining spots. Upstairs on the Square is good also, as is Sandrine's on Holyoke St."   —cigalechanta by John Vassall Jr., and is one of several original Tory Row homes on Brattle Street; George Washington lived here during the Siege of Boston from July 1775 to April 1776. Longfellow first boarded here in 1837, and later received the house as a gift from his father-in-law on his marriage to Frances Appleton, who burned to death here in an accident in 1861. For 45 years Longfellow wrote his famous verses here and filled the house with the exuberant spirit of his own work and that of his literary circle, which included Ralph Waldo Emerson, Nathaniel Hawthorne, and Charles Sumner, an abolitionist senator. Longfellow died in 1882; but the splendor of the house remains—from the Longfellow family furniture to the wallpaper to the books on the shelves (many the poet's own)—all preserved for future generations by the National Park Service, which currently runs it. ■TIP→ Longfellow Park, across the street, is the place to stand to take photos of the house. The park was created to preserve the view immortalized in the poet's "To the River Charles." ⊠ *105 Brattle St.* ☎ *617/876–4491* ⊕ *www.nps.gov/ long* ☎ *$3* ⊙ *Check Web site for seasonal tour schedules* Ⓜ *Harvard.*

Mt. Auburn Cemetery. A cemetery might not strike you as a first choice for a visit, but this one is a pleasure. Opened in 1831, it was the country's first garden cemetery, and more than 90,000 people have been buried here—among them Henry Wadsworth Longfellow, Mary Baker Eddy, Winslow Homer, Amy Lowell, Isabella Stewart Gardner, and architect Charles Bullfinch. The grave of engineer Buckminster Fuller bears an engraved geodesic dome. In spring local nature lovers and bird-watchers come out of the woodwork to see the warbler migrations and the glorious blossoms. Brochures, maps, and audio tours are at the entrance. ⊠ *580 Mt. Auburn St.* ☎ *617/547–7105* ⊕ *www.mountauburn.org* ⊙ *May–Aug., daily 8–7; Sept.–Apr., daily 8–5* Ⓜ *Harvard; then Watertown (71) or Waverly (73) bus to cemetery.*

Radcliffe Institute for Advanced Study. The famed women's college, situated around a serene yard, was founded in 1879 and wedded to Harvard University in 1977. It was subsumed under Harvard in 1999, when its name officially changed from Radcliffe College. **Schlesinger Library**. The Schlesinger Library, in Radcliffe Yard, houses more than 50,000 volumes on the history of women in America, including the papers of Harriet Beecher Stowe, Julia Child, Betty Friedan, and other notables. The library is also known for its extensive culinary collections, which contain cookbooks from the 16th century to the present. The library is open to the public, but materials do not circulate. ☎ *617/495–8540* ⊠ *10 Garden St.* ☎ *617/495–8601* ⊕ *www.radcliffe.edu* Ⓜ *Harvard.*

9

NEED A BREAK?

Darwin's Ltd. Once beyond the vicinity of Harvard Square, Brattle Street lacks eateries, so before your walk consider stocking up at Darwin's Ltd., which carries delectable, Cambridge-inspired sandwiches and other "comestibles and spirituous provisions." ⊠ *148 Mt. Auburn St.* ☎ *617/354–5233* ⊕ *www.darwinsltd.com.*

ALL IN GOOD FUN

Harvard's Hasty Pudding Club is well known for its theatricals—its pun-filled burlesque shows and its annual Man and Woman of the Year spectacles have elicited groans from audiences for more than a century. The similarly irreverent *Harvard Lampoon* has been influencing American comedy since the club's inception; early members wrote for the *New Yorker*, while more recently it has proven fertile ground for television comics and writers: the *National Lampoon*, *Saturday Night Live*, and *The Simpsons* were all spawned by its alumni. The Lampoon Castle (simultaneously located at 44 Bow Street, 14 Linden Street, 17 Plympton Street, and 57 Mt. Auburn Street), replete with hidden doors and secret passages, was built for the club in 1909 by William Randolph Hearst and Boston socialite Isabella Stewart Gardner. The copper ibis on top is reputedly electrified to ward off pranksters from the daily *Harvard Crimson* newspaper, who at the height of the Cold War cut it down and formally presented it to the Soviet Union as a "gift from the students of America." Connections at the State Department had to be called in to retrieve the purloined bird.

WORTH NOTING

Dexter Pratt House. Also known as the "Blacksmith House," this yellow Colonial is now owned by the Cambridge Center for Adult Education. The tree itself is long gone, but this spot inspired Longfellow's lines: "Under a spreading chestnut tree, the village smithy stands." The blacksmith's shop, today commemorated by a granite marker, was next door, at the corner of Story Street. ⊠ *56 Brattle St.* Ⓜ *Harvard.*

NEED A BREAK?

Hi-Rise Bread Company in the Blacksmith House. The Hi-Rise Bread Company in the Blacksmith House, on the first floor of the Dexter Pratt House, is the perfect stop for a pick-me-up coffee, fresh-baked treat, or fantastic sandwich on homemade bread. Snag an outdoor table; it's a choice spot for people-watching. And the espresso is excellent. ☎ *617/492–3003.*

L. A. Burdick Chocolates. Chocolate lovers may be seduced by the aromas emanating from L. A. Burdick Chocolates; rich confections or elegant, life-changing hot cocoa may be just the things to restore flagging spirits. ⊠ *52 Brattle St.* ☎ *617/491–4340* ⊕ *www.burdickchocolate.com.*

Elmwood. Shortly after its construction in 1767, this three-story Georgian house was abandoned by its owner, colonial governor Thomas Oliver. Elmwood House was home to the accomplished Lowell family for two centuries. Elmwood is now the Harvard University president's residence, ever since student riots in the 1960s drove President Nathan Pusey from his house in Harvard Yard. ⊠ *33 Elmwood Ave.* Ⓜ *Harvard.*

Henry Vassall House. Brattle Street's seven Tory houses were once occupied by wealthy families linked by friendship, if not blood. This one may have been built as early as 1636. In 1737 it was purchased by John Vassall Sr.; four years later he sold it to his younger brother Henry. It

CLOSE UP

It's Hip to Be Square

In Cambridge any commercial area where three or more streets meet in a jumble of traffic and noise has been dubbed a "square." (There are literally hundreds, though most are just simple intersections.) Harvard Square draws the most visitors, but several other neighborhood squares exude their own charms. These are a few of our favorites; if you want to see where real Cambridgians hang out, head here.

Impossibly hip **Inman Square,** at the intersection of Cambridge and Hampshire streets, has a great cluster of restaurants, cafés, bars, and shops. This place is just plain cool. Some highlights include Christina's (⊠ 1255 Cambridge St.), where you can enjoy some wildly inventive ice cream, and Punjabi Dhaba (⊠ 225 Hampshire St.), a perfect stop for cheap-but-good late-night Indian food and outstanding people-watching. Sadly, there's no T service to Inman, but you can get here from Harvard Square or Central Square on foot; it's near the intersection of Hampshire and Cambridge streets.

Central Square, at Massachusetts Avenue (known by locals as "Mass. Ave."), Prospect Street, and Western Avenue, has Irish pubs, ethnic eats, music clubs, and a row of furniture stores. Cambridge's city government is located here, and Ben Affleck and Matt Damon live in the neighborhood. For good eats, check out the Baraka Café (⊠ 80 Pearl St.) or Green Street (⊠ 280 Green St.). The Central Square T stop is on the Red Line.

Porter Square, about a mile northwest of Harvard Square on Mass. Ave., has several shopping centers and, within the nearby Porter Exchange,

Japanese noodle and food shops. As you walk north (away from Harvard) past the heart of Porter Square, you'll pass pretty much every ethnic eatery imaginable, many of them excellent and far cheaper than Harvard Square restaurants. Standouts include the Cambodian-French fusion Elephant Walk (⊠ 2067 Massachusetts Ave.) and Greek Corner (⊠ 2366 Massachusetts Ave.), but you'll also find Indian, Chinese, Thai, Bangladeshi, Vietnamese, and Himalayan. There are also quite a few unique shops along the way. The Porter Square T stop is on the Red Line.

Somerville's **Davis Square** is just over the border from northwest Cambridge and easily accessible on the Red Line. This funky neighborhood near Tufts University is packed with great eateries, lively bars, and candlepin bowling. Harvard Square can sometimes feel a little tired after midnight, but there's still a lot of energy here late at night. At the Somerville Theater (⊠ 55 Davis Sq.) you can enjoy cheap first-run movies ($8), excellent popcorn, and even beer and wine with your feature. The Davis Square T stop is on the Red Line.

At **Kendall Square,** near the Massachusetts Institute of Technology (MIT) and the heart of the city's thriving biotech industry, an art-house multiplex shows first-run films. The square is also a stone's throw from the Charles and a short walk from riverside restaurant Dante (⊠ 40 Edwin H. Land Blvd.). The Kendall Square/MIT T stop is on the Red Line.

9

MIT's Stata Center was designed by Frank Gehry.

was used as a hospital during the Revolution, and the traitor Dr. Benjamin Church was held here as a prisoner. The house was remodeled during the 19th century. It's now a private residence. ⊠ *94 Brattle St.* Ⓜ *Harvard.*

Hooper-Lee-Nichols House. Now headquarters of the Cambridge Historical Society, this is one of two Tory-era homes on Brattle Street fully open to the public. The Emerson family gave it to the society in 1957. Built between 1685 and 1690, the house has been remodeled at least six times, but has maintained much of the original structure. The downstairs is elegantly, although sparsely, appointed with period books, portraits, and wallpaper. An upstairs bedroom has been furnished with period antiques, some belonging to the original residents. Visits are by tour only, and run about one hour. A virtual tour of the house is available on the Cambridge Historical Society's Web site. ⊠ *159 Brattle St.* ☎ *617/547–4252* ⊕ *www.cambridgehistory.org* ⊴ *$5* ☉ *Mon. and Wed., 1–5* Ⓜ *Harvard.*

KENDALL SQUARE/MIT

Harvard Square may be the center of the "People's Republic of Cambridge," but the Kendall Square neighborhood is the city's hard-driving capitalist core. Gritty industrial buildings share space with sleek office blocks and the sprawling Massachusetts Institute of Technology. Although the MIT campus may lack the ivied elegance of Harvard Yard, major modern architects, including Alvar Aalto, Frank Gehry, I.M. Pei, and Eero Saarinen, created signature buildings here. To reach MIT, take the Red Line T to Kendall station; if you're headed for the MIT Museum on the western edge of the campus, the Central Square station is more convenient.

TOP ATTRACTIONS

List Visual Arts Center. Local Boston-area artists and art students consider the List Gallery to be the most interesting gallery in town. Founded by Albert and Vera List, pioneer collectors of modern art, this MIT center has three galleries showcasing exhibitions of cutting-edge art and mixed media. Works from the center's collection of contemporary art, such as Thomas Hart Benton's painting *Fluid Catalytic Crackers* and Harry Bertoia's altarpiece for the MIT Chapel, are on view here and around campus. The center's Web site includes a map indicating the locations of more than 25 of these works. ✉ *20 Ames St., Bldg. E 15* ☎ *617/253–4680* ⊕ *listart.mit.edu* ✉ *Free* ⊙ *Tues., Wed., and Fri.–Sun. noon–6, Thurs. noon–8* Ⓜ *Kendall/MIT.*

CAMPUS PRANKSTERS

A popular recurring exhibit at the MIT Museum is the "Hall of Hacks," a look at the pranks MIT students have played over the years. Most notable here is a rare photo of Oliver Reed Smoot Jr., a 1958 MIT Lambda Chi Alpha pledge. Smoot's future fraternity brothers used the diminutive freshman to measure the distance of the nearby Harvard Bridge. Every 5 feet and 6 inches became "one Smoot." The markings on the bridge are repainted by the frat every two years, and Boston police actually use them to indicate locations when filing accident reports. All told, the bridge is "364.4 Smoots plus 1 ear" long.

Massachusetts Institute of Technology. Celebrated for both its brains and its cerebral sense of humor, this once-tidy engineering school at right angles to the Charles River is growing like a sprawling adolescent, consuming old industrial buildings and city blocks with every passing year. Once dissed as "the factory," particularly by its Ivy League neighbor, MIT mints graduates that are the sharp blades on the edge of the information revolution. It's perennially in the top five of U.S. News and World Report's college rankings.

Founded in 1861, MIT moved to Cambridge from Copley Square in the Back Bay in 1916. It has long since fulfilled the predictions of its founder, the geologist William Barton Rogers, that it would surpass "the universities of the land in the accuracy and the extent of its teachings in all branches of positive science." Its emphasis shifted in the 1930s from practical engineering and mechanics to the outer limits of scientific fields.

Architecture is important at MIT. Although the original buildings were obviously designed by and for scientists, many represent pioneering designs of their times. The **Kresge Auditorium,** designed by Eero Saarinen, with a curving roof and unusual thrust, rests on three, instead of four, points. The nondenominational **MIT Chapel,** a circular Saarinen design, is lighted primarily by a roof oculus that focuses natural light on the altar and by reflections from the water in a small surrounding moat; it's topped by an aluminum sculpture by Theodore Roszak. The serpentine **Baker House,** now a dormitory, was designed in 1947 by the Finnish architect Alvar Aalto in such a way as to provide every room with a view of the Charles River. Sculptures by Henry Moore and other notable artists dot the campus. The latest addition is the newly minted Green Center, punctuated by the splash of color that is Sol Lewitt's 5,500-square-foot mosaic floor mural.

The East Campus, which has grown around the university's original neoclassical buildings of 1916, also has outstanding modern architecture and sculpture, including the stark high-rise **Green Building** by I. M. Pei, housing the Earth Science Center. Just outside is Alexander Calder's giant stabile (a stationary mobile) *The Big Sail.* Another Pei work on the East Campus is the **Wiesner Building,** designed in 1985, which houses the **List Visual Arts Center.** Architect Frank Gehry made his mark on the campus with the cockeyed, improbable **Ray & Maria Stata Center,** a complex of buildings on Vassar Street. The center houses computer, artificial intelligence, and information systems laboratories, and is reputedly as confusing to navigate on the inside as it is to follow on the outside. East Campus's **Great Dome,** which looms over neoclassical Killian Court, has often been the target of student "hacks," and has at various times supported a telephone booth with a ringing phone, a life-size statue of a cow, and a campus police cruiser. Nearby, the domed **Rogers Building** has earned unusual notoriety as the center of a series of hallways and tunnels dubbed "the infinite corridor." Twice each winter the sun's path lines up perfectly with the corridor's axis, and at dusk students line the third-floor hallway to watch the sun set through the westernmost window. The phenomenon is known as "MIT-henge."

MIT maintains an information center in the Rogers Building, and offers free tours of the campus weekdays at 11 and 3. Check the schedule, as the tours are often suspended during school holidays. General hours for the information center are weekdays 9–5. ⊠ *77 Massachusetts Ave.* ☎ *617/253–4795* ⊕ *web.mit.edu* Ⓜ *Kendall/MIT.*

NEED A BREAK?

Toscanini's Ice Cream. Toscanini's Ice Cream is a well-loved local spot, specializing in all sorts of creative flavors. Also a good place for coffee, the shop frequently has small art exhibits. From the MIT Museum it's two blocks up Mass Ave. toward Central Square; look for it on the right. ⊠ *899 Main St.* ☎ *617/491–5877* ⊕ *www.tosci.com.*

WORTH NOTING

Ⓒ **MIT Museum.** A place where art and science meet, the MIT Museum displays photos, paintings, and scientific instruments and memorabilia in a dynamic, hands-on setting. The world's largest collection of holograms is downright eye-popping, though young kids may prefer the moving gestural sculptures of Arthur Ganson. The robot room shows off inventions of MIT's renowned robotics lab and an extensive exhibit on artificial intelligence. Allow an hour or two for a visit. ⊠ *265 Massachusetts Ave.* ☎ *617/253–5927* ⊕ *web.mit.edu/museum* 🎫 *$7.50* ☉ *Daily 10–5* Ⓜ *Kendall/MIT.*

Where to Eat

WORD OF MOUTH

"My favorite in the North End is Antico Forno. I've been going there for years and it has remained reliably consistent and affordable. Their oven-baked ziti is to die for."

—amyb

Updated
by Lisa
Oppenheimer

In a city synonymous with tradition, Boston chefs have spent recent years rewriting culinary history. The stuffy, wood-paneled formality is gone; the endless renditions of chowdah, lobster, and cod have retired; and the assumption that true foodies better hop the next Amtrak to New York is also—thankfully—a thing of the past.

In their place, a crop of young chefs have ascended, opening small, upscale neighborhood spots that use local New England ingredients to delicious effect. Traditional eats can still be found (Durgin Park remains the best place to get baked beans), but many diners now gravitate toward innovative food in understated environs. Whether you're looking for casual French, down-home Southern cooking, some of the best sushi in the country, or Vietnamese banh mi sandwiches, Boston restaurants are ready to deliver. Eclectic Japanese spot O Ya and iconic French restaurant L'Espalier have garnered widespread attention, while a coterie of star chefs like Barbara Lynch, Lydia Shire, and Ken Oringer have built mini-empires and thrust the city to the forefront of the national dining scene.

The fish and shellfish brought in from nearby shores continue to inform the regional cuisine: expect to see several seafood options on local menus, but don't expect them to be boiled or dumped into the lobster stew that JFK loved. Instead, you might be offered swordfish with salsa verde, cornmeal-crusted scallops, or lobster cassoulet with black truffles. In many ways, though, Boston remains solidly skeptical of trends. To wit: the cupcake craze hit only recently, and without the furor that overtook other cities; the frozen yogurt movement is also behind the times. And over in the university culture of Cambridge, places like East Coast Grill, Oleana, and Rendezvous espoused the locovore and slow-food movements before they became buzzwords.

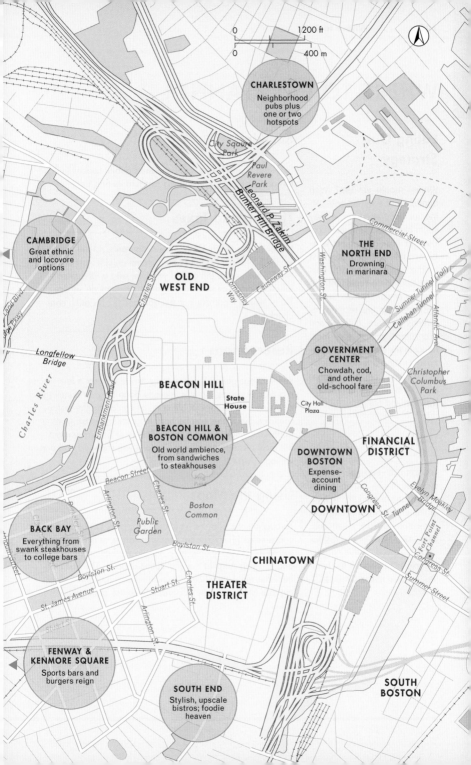

CHARLESTOWN
Neighborhood pubs plus one or two hotspots

City Sqoare Park

Paul Revere Park

Leonard P. Zakim Bunker Hill Bridge

CAMBRIDGE
Great ethnic and locovore options

Causeway St.

Washington St.

THE NORTH END
Drowning in marinara

Commercial Street

OLD WEST END

Charles St.

Lomasney Way

Sumner Tunnel (Toll)

Callahan Tunnel

Atlantic Ave.

Longfellow Bridge

Charles River

Embankment Road

BEACON HILL

State House

GOVERNMENT CENTER
Chowdah, cod, and other old-school fare

Christopher Columbus Park

City Hall Plaza

FINANCIAL DISTRICT

BEACON HILL & BOSTON COMMON
Old world ambience, from sandwiches to steakhouses

DOWNTOWN BOSTON
Expense-account dining

Evelyn Moakley Bridge

Congress St.

Congress St. Tunnel

Fort Point Channel

Congress St.

DOWNTOWN

Beacon Street

Arlington St.

Public Garden

Boston Common

BACK BAY
Everything from swank steakhouses to college bars

Boylston St.

Boylston St.

CHINATOWN

Summer Street

St. James Avenue

Charles St.

Stuart St.

THEATER DISTRICT

Arlington St.

SOUTH BOSTON

FENWAY & KENMORE SQUARE
Sports bars and burgers reign

SOUTH END
Stylish, upscale bistros; foodie heaven

0   1200 ft
0   400 m

WHERE TO EAT PLANNER

Eating Out Strategy

Where should we eat? With hundreds of eateries competing for your attention, it may seem like a daunting question. But fret not—our expert writers and editors have done most of the legwork. The 100-plus selections here represent the best the city has to offer. Search Best Bets for top recommendations by price, cuisine, and experience, and sample local flavor in the neighborhood features. Or find a review quickly in the listings, organized alphabetically within neighborhoods. Delve in and enjoy!

With Kids

Though it's unusual to see children in the dining rooms of Boston's most elite restaurants, dining with youngsters does not have to mean culinary exile. Many of the restaurants reviewed *in this chapter* are excellent choices for families, and are marked with a ☾ symbol

Smoking

Smoking is prohibited in all enclosed public spaces in Boston and Cambridge, including restaurants and bars.

Tipping and Taxes

Never tip the maître d'. In most restaurants, tip the waiter at least 15%–20%. (To figure the amount quickly, just double the 7% tax on the bill and, if you like, add a little more.) Bills for parties of six or more sometimes include service. Tip at least $1 per drink at the bar, and $1 for each coat checked.

Reservations

Reservations generally need to be made at least a few nights in advance, but this is easily done by your concierge or online at www.opentable.com, or by calling the restaurant directly. Tables can be hard to come by if you want to dine between 7 and 9, or on Friday or Saturday night. But most restaurants will get you in if you show up and are willing to wait.

Using the Maps

Throughout the chapter, you'll see mapping symbols and coordinates (✛ 3:F2) after property names or reviews. To locate the property on a map, turn to the Boston Dining and Lodging Atlas at the end of this chapter. The first number after the ✛ symbol indicates the map number. Following that is the property's coordinate on the map grid.

What to Wear

Boston is a notch or two more reserved in its fashion than New York or Los Angeles. Its dining dress code normally hovers at the level of casual chic. Few of the city's most formal restaurants require jackets, and even at some of the most expensive places jeans are acceptable as long as they're paired with a dressy top and posh shoes. Shorts are appropriate only in the most casual spots. When in doubt, call and ask.

Mealtimes

Boston's restaurants close relatively early; most shut their doors by 10 or 11 pm, and a few have bars that stay open until 1 am. Restaurants that serve breakfast often do so until 11 am or noon, at which point they start serving lunch. Unless otherwise noted, the restaurants listed in this guide are open daily for lunch and dinner.

Prices

Entrée prices fluctuate with the state of the economy. Top-tier restaurants remain impervious to market changes, but more restaurants are accommodating every price range with small or half portions at a lower price. Some restaurants are marked with a price range ($$–$$$, for example). This indicates one of two things: either the average cost straddles two categories, or if you order strategically, you can get out for less than most diners spend.

Credit cards are widely accepted, but some restaurants accept only cash. If you plan to use a credit card it's a good idea to double-check when making reservations or before sitting down to eat.

WHAT IT COSTS

	¢	$	$$	$$$	$$$$
Restaurant	under $10	$10–$17	$18–$24	$25–$35	over $35

Price per person for a median main course or equivalent combination of smaller dishes.

In This Chapter

10

RESTAURANT REVIEWS

Listed alphabetically within neighborhoods.

BOSTON

BEACON HILL AND BOSTON COMMON

$

MIDDLE EASTERN

✕ **Lala Rokh**. Persian miniatures and medieval maps cover the walls of this beautifully detailed fantasy of food and art. The focus is on the Azerbaijanian corner of what is now northwest Iran, including exotically flavored specialties and dishes such as familiar (and superb here) eggplant puree, pilaf, kebabs, *fesanjoon* (the classic pomegranate-walnut sauce), and lamb stews. The staff obviously enjoys explaining the menu, and the wine list is well selected for foods that often defy wine matches. ⊠ *97 Mt. Vernon St., Beacon Hill* ☎ *617/720–5511* ⊕ *www.lalarokh.com* ⊟ *AE, DC, MC, V* ⊘ *No lunch weekends* Ⓜ *Charles/MGH* ✛ *1:D6.*

$$–$$$

SEAFOOD

♻

✕ **Legal Sea Foods**. What began as a tiny restaurant upstairs over a Cambridge fish market has grown to important regional status, with more than 30 East Coast locations, plus a handful of national ones. The hallmark is the freshest possible seafood, whether you have it wood-grilled, in New England chowder, or doused with an Asia-inspired sauce. The smoked-bluefish pâté is delectable, and the clam chowder is so good it has become a menu staple at presidential inaugurations. This location has private dining inside its beautiful, bottle-lined wine cellar. ⊠ *26 Park Sq., Theater District* ☎ *617/426–4444* ⊕ *www.legalseafoods.com* ⊟ *AE, D, DC, MC, V* Ⓜ *Arlington* ✛ *1:H6.*

$$$$

STEAKHOUSE

✕ **Mooo**. Inside the swanky XV Beacon hotel, Mooo opened in 2007, offering a luxurious, refined dining space that remains civilized despite the restaurant's somewhat goofy name. Chef David Hutton's menu strays toward steak-house fare (hence the title), with dishes driven by local ingredients; look for a well-rounded list of raw-bar items, iceberg-lettuce salads, dry-aged sirloins, and a smattering of seafood selections. Portions are as exaggerated as the prices, so it's a worthwhile visit, and the wine list, with more than 500 entries, including a few century-old bottles, is an impressive but expensive proposition. ⊠ *15 Beacon St., XV Beacon Hotel, Beacon Hill* ☎ *617/670–2515* ⊕ *www.mooorestaurant. com* ⊟ *AE, D, DC, MC, V* Ⓜ *Park St.* ✛ *1:G5.*

$$$$

CONTINENTAL

Fodor'sChoice

★

✕ **No. 9 Park**. The stellar cuisine at Chef Barbara Lynch's first restaurant continues to draw plenty of well-deserved attention from its place in the shadow of the State House's golden dome. Settle into the plush but unpretentious dining room and indulge in pumpkin risotto with rare lamb or the memorably rich prune-stuffed gnocchi drizzled with bits of foie gras, the latter of which is always offered even if you don't see it on the menu. The wine list bobs and weaves into new territory, but is always well chosen, and the savvy bartenders are of the classic ilk, so you'll find plenty of classics and very few cloying, dessert-like sips here. ⊠ *9 Park St., Beacon Hill* ☎ *617/742–9991* ⊕ *www.no9park.com* ⊟ *AE, D, DC, MC, V* Ⓜ *Park St.* ✛ *1:E6.*

BEST BETS FOR BOSTON DINING

With hundreds of restaurants to choose from, how will you decide where to eat? Fodor's writers and editors have selected their favorite restaurants by price, cuisine, and experience in the Best Bets lists below. In the first column, Fodor's Choice properties represent the "best of the best" in every price category. Find specific details about a restaurant in the full reviews, listed alphabetically within neighborhoods.

10

$$$$ ✕ **Pigalle.** A quaint, 20-table spot, Pigalle is a romantic destination to
FRENCH hit before taking in a show in the neighboring Theater District. Chef
Fodor'sChoice Marc Orfaly spices up basic French fare by throwing in the occasional
★ Asian-inspired special. He plays around with global flavors, so don't
be alarmed to find spicy tempura tuna roll or grilled squid with paella
stuffing on the menu next to the steak frites and cassoulet. For a delicious, cozy meal, this spot consistently has some of the best service
in town. A jazz pianist adds a musical note Sunday evenings. ✉ 75
Charles St. S, Theater District ☎ *617/423–4944* ⊕ *www.pigalleboston.
com* ⌕ *Reservations essential* ▭ *AE, DC MC, V* ⊘ *Closed Mon. No
lunch* Ⓜ *Boylston* ✛ *2:D2.*

$$$ ✕ **Scampo.** In the revamped Liberty Hotel—the former site of the infa-
ITALIAN mous Charles Street Jail—this Beacon Hill hot spot has a prison-chic
vibe, complete with barred windows and a sign on the wall reminding
patrons that "crime doesn't pay." The restaurant's Italian fare, however,
is anything but institutional: the house-made mozzarella bar, crusty
pizzas, handmade pastas, and Maine crab risotto are all exceptional.
Chef Lydia Shire's creative menu is complemented by a sleek orange
bar, curved white-leather booths, and one of the city's most beauti-
ful crowds. ✉ *215 Charles St., Beacon Hill* ☎ *617/536–2100* ⊕ *www.
scampoboston.com* ▭ *AE, DC, MC, V* Ⓜ *Charles/MGH* ✛ *1:D5.*

GOVERNMENT CENTER AND THE NORTH END
GOVERNMENT CENTER
Government Center is home to Faneuil Hall, a tourist magnet, packed
with fast-food concessions as well as some more serious alternatives. If
you're not on a schedule, and if you've seen enough of Faneuil Hall and
want a change of scene, you shouldn't rule out a walk to the North End.

$$ ✕ **Durgin Park Market Dining Room.** You should be hungry enough to cope
AMERICAN with enormous portions, yet not so hungry you can't tolerate a long
wait (or sharing a table with others). Durgin Park was serving its same
hearty New England fare (Indian pudding, baked beans, corned beef
and cabbage, and a prime rib that hangs over the edge of the plate) back
when Faneuil Hall was a working market instead of a tourist attraction.
The service is as brusque as it was when fishmongers and boat captains
dined here, but that's just part of its charm. ✉ *340 Faneuil Hall Market
Pl., North Market Bldg.* ☎ *617/227–2038* ⊕ *www.arkrestaurants.com/
durgin_park.html* ▭ *AE, D, DC, MC, V* Ⓜ *Government Center* ✛ *1:G5.*

$$$ ✕ **Union Oyster House.** Established in 1826, this is Boston's oldest con-
SEAFOOD tinuing restaurant, and almost every tourist considers it a must-see. If
you like, you can have what Daniel Webster had—oysters on the half
shell at the ground-floor raw bar, which is the oldest part of the restau-
rant and still the best. The rooms at the top of the narrow staircase are
dark and have low ceilings—very Ye Olde New England—and plenty of
nonrestaurant history. The small tables and chairs (as well as the end-
less lines and kitschy nostalgia) are as much a part of the charm as the
simple and decent (albeit pricey) food. Weekends, especially in summer,
make reservations a few days ahead or risk enduring waits of historic
proportions. There is valet parking after 5:30 pm Monday through
Saturday. One cautionary note: Locals hardly ever eat here. ✉ *41 Union*

St., Government Center ☎ *617/227–2750* ⊕ *www.unionoysterhouse. com* ▬ *AE, D, DC, MC, V* Ⓜ *Haymarket* ✛ *1:F5.*

THE NORTH END

$ ✕ **Antico Forno.** Many of the menu choices here come from the eponymous
ITALIAN wood-burning brick oven, which turns out surprisingly delicate pizzas
Fodor's Choice simply topped with tomato and fresh buffalo mozzarella. But though its
★ pizzas receive top billing, Antico excels at a variety of Italian country dishes. Don't overlook the hearty baked dishes and handmade pastas; the specialty, gnocchi, is rich and creamy but light. The terra-cotta–walled room is cramped and noisy, but also homey and comfortable—which means that your meal will resemble a raucous dinner with an adopted Italian family. ✉ *93 Salem St., North End* ☎ *617/723–6733* ⊕ *www. anticofornoboston.com* ▬ *AE, D, MC, V* Ⓜ *Haymarket* ✛ *1:F5.*

$$$ ✕ **Bricco.** A sophisticated but unpretentious enclave of nouveau Italian,
ITALIAN Bricco has carved out quite a following. And no wonder: the handmade pastas alone are argument for a reservation. Simple but well-balanced main courses such as roast chicken marinated in seven spices and a brimming *brodetto* (fish stew) with half a lobster and a pile of seafood may linger in your memory. You're likely to want to linger in the warm room, too, gazing through the floor-to-ceiling windows while sipping a glass of Sangiovese from the all-Italian wine list. ✉ *241 Hanover St., North End* ☎ *617/248–6800* ⊕ *www.bricco.com* ⚓ *Reservations essential* ▬ *AE, D, DC, MC, V* ☺ *No lunch* Ⓜ *Haymarket* ✛ *1:G5.*

$$$ ✕ **Carmen.** Here's the kind of undeniably friendly, downright cute hole-
ITALIAN in-the-wall that keeps the neighborhood real. With seating for 40, Carmen keeps its capacity crowds happy with glasses of wine and small tapas-style plates of roasted red pepper and olives at the up-front bar. At tables, meanwhile, diners tuck into clean-flavored specials such as creamy homemade pappardelle with mushroom ragu. Desserts and coffee, however, aren't on the menu. ✉ *33 North Sq., North End* ☎ *617/742–6421* ⊕ *www.carmenboston.com* ⚓ *Reservations essential* ▬ *AE, MC, V* ☺ *Closed Mon. No lunch Sun.–Thurs.* Ⓜ *Haymarket* ✛ *1:G4.*

$ ✕ **Daily Catch.** You've just got to love this place—for the noise, the
SEAFOOD intimacy, the complete absence of pretense, and, above all, the food. Shoulder-crowdingly small and always brightly lighted, the storefront restaurant, a local staple for more than 30 years, specializes in calamari dishes, black-squid-ink pastas, and linguine with clam sauce. There's something about a big skillet of linguine and calamari that would seem less perfect if served on fine white china. ✉ *323 Hanover St., North End* ☎ *617/523–8567* ⊕ *www.dailycatch.com* ⚓ *Reservations not accepted* ▬ *No credit cards* Ⓜ *Haymarket* ✛ *1:G4.*

$$$ ✕ **Mamma Maria.** Don't let the clichéd name fool you: Mamma Maria is far
ITALIAN from a typical red-sauce joint, although some locals find the service lacking. From the handmade wild-mushroom ravioli to the authentic sauces and entrées to some of the best desserts in the North End, you can't go wrong here. The view, meanwhile, is lovely; gaze out onto cobblestone-lined North Square as you finish your pappardelle layered with braised rabbit and a finale of *limoncello* (an Italian lemon-flavored liquor). ✉ *3 North Sq., North End* ☎ *617/523–0077* ⊕ *www.mammamaria.com* ▬ *AE, D, DC, MC, V* ☺ *No lunch* Ⓜ *Haymarket* ✛ *1:G4.*

10

THE NORTH END

As the city's oldest residential area, the North End contains some remarkable Revolutionary history (including Paul Revere's home)—and some really remarkable Italian food.

(above) Shop for Italian groceries in the North End. (lower right) Italian bakery Modern Pastry is a mainstay in the North End neighborhood. (upper right) Pistachio gelato and a cup of espresso at Caffé Vittoria

Though it's been the center of Italian culture in Boston since the early 20th century, the North End was cut off from the rest of Boston for more than five decades by the construction of an unsightly elevated highway. With the completion of the Big Dig project in 2007, the highway was torn down, and the young professionals who work in the nearby Financial District raced to move into the neighborhood.

Today the North End remains largely residential, an interesting mix of twentysomethings and Italian grandpas. The narrow streets can be eerily quiet during the day, but transform into vibrant meeting places come evening, as couples take advantage of the romantic opportunities afforded by the neighborhood's small, rustic restaurants. On summer evenings there's a good chance you'll encounter a street fair celebrating a saint's feast day, filled with food booths selling cannoli, fried dough, and sausage sandwiches.

NORTH TOUR

To eat like an Italian, you've got to know your sfogliatelle from your amaretti. **North End Market Tours** (⊠ *6 Charter St.* ☎ *617/523–6032*), by local foodie Michele Topor, school visitors on the "right" kind of olive oil and the primo places to buy Italian pastries during three-hour tours that get off the beaten Hanover Street path. The $50 tour includes a few sample noshes.

A NORTH END "COURSE CRAWL"

The neighborhood is so densely packed with authentic Italian eateries (there are more than 85 lining just a few blocks) that it's nearly impossible to suggest only one. Instead, we recommend embarking on an evening-long "course crawl" to enjoy a variety of the North End's flavors while severely challenging your stomach capacity.

During the summer, start with a drink at **Ristorante Fiore** (⊠ *250 Hanover St.* ☎ *617/371–1176* ✛ *1:G4*), which has one of the city's best roof decks and a similarly impressive wine list heavy on the Tuscan varietals. Then swing by **Neptune Oyster** (⊠ *63 Salem St.* ☎ *617/742–3474* ✛ *1:G5*) for a batch of its namesake crispy oysters served with pistachio aioli as a starter, before crossing the street to **Terramia** (⊠ *98 Salem St.* ☎ *617/523–3112* ✛ *1:G4*), where the huge sea-scallop ravioli come dressed in a lobster mascarpone cream and the gnocchi is accented by white truffle oil.

True Italians make room for *secondi*, or a second, meat-based course. You can't go wrong with **Prezza**'s (⊠ *24 Fleet St.* ☎ *617/227–1577* ✛ *1:G4*) wood-grilled venison with pumpkin risotto, braised greens, and a red-wine bacon glaze, or try the seared salmon fillet at the broom closet–sized **Pomodoro** (⊠ *319 Hanover St.* ☎ *617/367–4348* ✛ *1:G4*).

Before you can succumb to a carbohydrate-stuffed stupor, you need dessert—but most North End restaurants don't serve it. That's because everyone buys cannolis at local bakeries instead. Stop by **Modern Pastry** (⊠ *257 Hanover St.* ☎ *617/523–3783* ✛ *1:G4*) and **Mike's Pastry** (⊠ *300 Hanover St.* ☎ *617/742–3050* ✛ *1:G4*), the two main North End dessert shops, to conduct your own cannoli taste test. Located across Hanover Street from each other, both shops have around-the-clock lines snaking out the door. Modern's cannoli are smaller, more delicate, and flakier than Mike's counterparts, but as for the preference? It's up to you. If you're ricotta-averse, the two bakeries also serve whipped-cream versions, as well as lots of other treats, from gelato to biscotti and marzipan.

COFFEE TALK

Café culture is alive and well in the North End. **Caffe Vittoria** (⊠ *290–296 Hanover St.* ☎ *617/227–7606* ✛ *1:G4*), established in 1929, is Boston's oldest Italian café. With four levels of seating, three bars that serve aperitifs, and one massive, ancient espresso maker, this old-fashioned café will make you want to lose your iPhone. At **Caffé Paradiso** (⊠ *255 Hanover St.* ☎ *617/742–1768* ✛ *1:G5*) soccer pennants hang from the rafters and the TV plays only European *futbol* matches—two sure signs of authenticity. The nearby **Caffe dello Sport** (⊠ *308 Hanover St.* ☎ *617/523–5063* ✛ *1:G4*) is an Italianate version of a sports bar, with two wide screens transmitting live soccer while patrons order espressos, cordials, and gelato. If you're not able to kill a whole afternoon sipping cappuccino, stop by **Polcari's Coffee** (⊠ *105 Salem St.* ☎ *617/227–0786* ✛ *1:G4*), a dried-goods mecca that has coffees, teas, herbs, and spices displayed in antique brass bins and sold by the pound.

10

MODERN PASTRY SHOP

$$$ ✗**Marco**. The second-story dining room is meant to evoke a charm-
ITALIAN ing Italian bistro, a cozy nook to dig into any one of a long list of
antipasti, pastas (handmade tagliatelle with Bolognese is a must), and
grilled meats. Sunday, dinner is served family style. Plates are meant to
be shared and grazed over while enjoying a bottle or two from the all-
Italian wine list. This is an unpretentious spot where candlelight and
laughter usually fill the room. ✉ *253 Hanover St., 2nd fl., North End*
☎ *617/742–1276* ⊕ *www.marcoboston.com* ⊟ *AE, D, MC, V* ⊙ *Closed
Mon.* Ⓜ *Haymarket* ✛ *1:G5.*

$$$ ✗**Mare**. Anchoring an out-of-the-way corner on Richmond Street, this
ITALIAN organic Italian seafood restaurant has stepped out of tradition and
moved into nouveau Italian. Ignore the distraction of the color-changing
walls and scope out the menu: the chefs here prefer the simplicity of
grilling and poaching seafood and meat dishes rather than dousing
them in seasonings, which makes the place a simple but delicious option
among its red-sauce-heavy neighbors. Go for a plate of wild boar pappardelle. And don't miss the mixed grill—a selection of fresh-caught
fish prepared with a touch of seasoning. ✉ *135 Richmond St., North
End* ☎ *617/723–6273* ⊕ *www.marenatural.com* ⊟ *AE, D, DC, MC, V*
⊙ *Closed Mon. in winter. No lunch* Ⓜ *Haymarket* ✛ *1:G4.*

$$ ✗**Neptune Oyster**. This tiny oyster bar, the first of its kind in the neigh-
SEAFOOD borhood, has only 20 chairs, but the long marble bar has extra seating
for about 20 more patrons, and mirrors hang over the bar with hand-
written menus. From there, watch the oyster shuckers as they deftly
undo handfuls of bivalves. The *plateau di frutti di mare* is a gleaming
tower of oysters and other raw-bar items piled over ice that you can
order from the slip of paper they pass out listing each day's crustacean
options. Dishes change seasonally, but a couple of favorites to count
on year round include the signature North End Cioppino (fish stew)
and the lobster roll that, hot or cold, overflows with meat. Service is
prompt even when it gets busy (as it is most of the time). Go early to
avoid a long wait. ✉ *63 Salem St., North End* ☎ *617/742–3474* ⊕ *www.
neptuneoyster.com* ⌂ *Reservations not accepted* ⊟ *AE, D, DC, MC, V*
Ⓜ *Haymarket* ✛ *1:G5.*

$$ ✗**Pomodoro**. This teeny trattoria—just eight tables—is worth the wait,
ITALIAN with excellent country Italian favorites such as rigatoni with white
beans and arugula, a sweet veal scaloppini with balsamic glaze, and a
light-but-filling zuppa di pesce. The best choice could well be the clam-
and-tomato stew with herbed flat bread, accompanied by a bottle of
Vernaccia. Pomodoro doesn't serve dessert, but it's easy to find great
espresso and pastries in the cafés on Hanover Street. ✉ *319 Hanover St.,
North End* ☎ *617/367–4348* ⊕ *www.pomodoroboston.com* ⌂ *Reservations essential* ⊟ *No credit cards* ⊙ *No lunch weekdays* Ⓜ *Haymarket* ✛ *1:G4.*

$$$ ✗**Ristorante Euno**. Tiny and friendly, Euno is the North End's culinary
ITALIAN mouse that roars. The rustic, two-story space used to be a butcher shop,
and meat hooks still stud the wall, doubling as coat hangers. Everything
from start (a bowl of the buttery olives) to middle (handmade pastas
and risottos) to finish (porcini-dusted tuna with roasted vegetables)
explains why this postage-stamp gem is a neighborhood favorite. It's

usually full on weekends, but those wise enough to make reservations might snag a table in the romantic downstairs dining room. ✉ *119 Salem St., North End* ☎ *617/573–9406* ⊕ *www.eunoboston.com* 🖃 *AE, D, DC, MC, V* ☺ *No lunch* Ⓜ *Haymarket* ✛ *1:G4.*

$$$
FRENCH

✕ **Sensing.** Though it is a younger sister to Michelin Chef Guy Martin's Sensing in Paris, the Fairmont Battery Wharf restaurant retains a distinct New England flavor. That's hardly surprising, since it prides itself on using locally sourced seasonal ingredients. From artful appetizers to the generously portioned desserts, the food is elegant without being fussy. Ditto for the decor in the minimalist main dining room. An open kitchen means you can see entrées like cod steamed in lemongrass or lobster linguine Bolognese being prepared. But foodies will want to go for the Thursday night Chef's Counter to watch chef Gerard Barbin whip up a four-course tasting menu ($50 per person). Reenvisioned breakfast classics (such as eggs Benedict with truffle salsa) also make this an excellent choice for a morning meal. ✉ *Fairmont Battery Wharf, 3 Battery Wharf, North End* ☎ *617/994–9001* ⊕ *www. sensingrestaurant.com* 🖃 *AE, D, DC, MC, V* Ⓜ *Haymarket* ✛ *1:H4.*

$$$
ITALIAN

✕ **Terramia Ristorante.** Nearly everything this little autumnal-color restaurant kicks out tastes home-cooked and authentic. The simple, largely southern Italian cuisine includes rich, freshly homemade pastas tossed with equally fresh ingredients and risottos that come perfectly cooked and powerfully flavored. Dessert and coffee aren't on the menu, but you can walk off the large portions while searching the neighborhood looking for cannoli. Lines can get long on weekends. ✉ *98 Salem St., North End* ☎ *617/523–3112* ⊕ *www.terramiaristorante.com* 🖃 *AE, D, MC, V* ☺ *No lunch* Ⓜ *Haymarket* ✛ *1:G4.*

CHARLESTOWN

This little neighborhood across Boston Harbor contains the Bunker Hill Monument, the USS *Constitution*, and one culinary landmark, the famous Olives, a standout among the local taverns.

$$$
MEDITERRANEAN

✕ **Olives.** ⚠ After 21 years as a beloved Boston staple, Todd English's flagship (and original) gustatory emporium shuttered in 2010 for a face-lift. As of this writing, the reopening is scheduled for spring 2011. Check with the restaurant before planning a visit. The new look is under wraps, but you can count on the retooled version to be worth a visit, with English's wood-fire brick oven, not to mention his signature Olives tart with carmelized onion and goat cheese. You may not see chef Todd English tending the wood-fire brick oven here—these days he's splitting his time between his many restaurants in New York and elsewhere. But don't worry, English's recipes are in good hands. Witness smart offerings such as a number of wood-grilled fish and meat dishes. A view into the open kitchen and noisy dining room only adds to the excitement. If you can't secure a reservation, come early or late or be prepared for an extended wait. ✉ *10 City Sq., Charlestown* ☎ *617/242–1999* ⊕ *www. toddenglish.com* ⌨ *Reservations essential* 🖃 *AE, D, DC, MC, V* ☺ *No lunch* Ⓜ *Community College* ✛ *1:E2.*

10

$$
MOROCCAN

✕ **Tangierino.** Chef Samad Naamad draws visitors into his enchanting Moroccan fantasy with hearty, spice-driven food, fragrant cocktails, and belly-dancing shows (Wednesday through Sunday). Indulge in small plates like calamari rubbed with *ras al hanout*; then enjoy a drawn-out meal of entrées cooked in a tagine (a clay pot used for slow cooking). Tangierino bills itself as the first Moroccan chophouse, meaning those with a taste for the slightly less exotic can partake of meat-and-potato offerings, albeit with Moroccan flair. The downstairs hookah bar, Koullshi, is owned by Tangierino. ✉ *83 Main St., Charlestown* ☎ *617/242–6009* ⊕ *www.tangierino.com* ▭ *AE, D, MC, V* ⊗ *No lunch* Ⓜ *Community College* ✛ *1:E2.*

DOWNTOWN BOSTON

Boston's Downtown scene revs up at lunchtime, but the streets get quiet after 5 pm, when everyone goes back to the suburbs. The city center is great for after-hours dining, though, especially in the hideaway restaurants around the former Leather District.

$$$
FRENCH

✕ **Les Zygomates.** *Les zygomates* is the French expression for the muscles on the human face that make you smile—and this combination wine bar–bistro inarguably lives up to its name, with quintessential French bistro fare that is both simple (made with a number of New England sourced ingredients) and simply delicious. The lunch and dinner prix-fixe menus beautifully match the ever-changing wine list, with all wines served by the 2-ounce taste, 6-ounce glass, or bottle. An oyster bar has recently been added, and there is live jazz five nights a week. ✉ *129 South St., Downtown* ☎ *617/542–5108* ⊕ *www.winebar.com* ⚴ *Reservations essential* ▭ *AE, D, DC, MC, V* ⊗ *Closed Sun. No lunch Sat.* Ⓜ *South Station* ✛ *2:F2.*

$$$–$$$$
CONTINENTAL

✕ **Locke-Ober.** Chef-owner Lydia Shire gave this old Boston spot a much-needed update when she took the reins in 2001. The ornate woodwork gleams again, and the once-stodgy kitchen is turning out classics with flair—and a slightly lighter touch. Traditionalists needn't worry, though; many favorites remain on the menu, including Shire's signature JFK lobster stew, broiled Boston scrod with hot crab, and clams casino. There is valet parking after 6 pm. ✉ *3 Winter Pl., Downtown* ☎ *617/542–1340* ⊕ *www.lockeober.com* ⚴ *Reservations essential* ▭ *AE, D, MC, V* ⊗ *Closed Sun. No lunch* Ⓜ *Downtown Crossing* ✛ *2:F1.*

$$$$
FRENCH

✕ **Menton.** Foodies have been plotzing over Barbara Lynch's newest eatery, an Italian-meets-French (it's named for the French town near Italy's border), prix-fixe–only establishment that has brought critics and food aficionados to the brink of euphoria. Located in the forever up-and-coming Fort Point neighborhood, Menton has elicited sighs of "incredible" and "perfection" for the four-course meal (there's also a seven-course chef's-tasting menu) that might begin with a chestnut bisque, peak with a perfectly prepared venison, and end with a cranberry-walnut crepe. Menus change regularly to reflect the season's ingredients, and meals can be complemented with expertly chosen wine pairings by request. Jackets are recommended but not required. ✉ *354 Congress St., Fort Point Channel, Downtown* ☎ *617/737–0099* ⊕ *www.mentonboston.com* ⚴ *Reservations essential* ▭ *AE, D, DC, MC, V* ⊗ *No lunch* Ⓜ *South Station.*

$$$$
JAPANESE
Fodor's Choice
★

✕ **O Ya.** Despite its side-street location and hidden door, O Ya isn't exactly a secret: dining critics from the *New York Times, Bon Appetit,* and *Food & Wine* have all named this tiny, improvisational sushi

CLOSE UP

Kid-Friendly Restaurants

The vast majority of restaurants in Boston are happy to accommodate kids with simplified dishes and an out-of-the-way booth. Here are some particularly family-friendly options.

Charley's Saloon. Saloons may be no place for kids, but this is no real saloon. Charley's doles out American classics (cheeseburgers, steaks, and apple pies) in a fun retro setting. The chain fare is dependable and above average, and the kids get to color and people-watch. ⊠ *284 Newbury St., Back Bay* ☎ *617/266–3000* ✛ *2:A2.*

Full Moon. Kids will delight in the play kitchen and dollhouse, and parents can cheer that they get to tuck into lovelies such as grilled salmon with sautéed spinach. Meanwhile there's plenty of macaroni and cheese or quesadillas for the young ones. ⊠ *344 Huron Ave., Cambridge* ☎ *617/354–6699* ✛ *4:A1.*

Joe's American Bar & Grill. Even with a classy Newbury Street address, Joe's offers oversize burgers and a slice of apple pie alongside a frenzied July 4-style decor. The clam chowder is almost always a hit with all generations. ⊠ *181 Newbury St., Back Bay* ☎ *617/536–4200* ✛ *2:B2.*

Kingfish Hall. Parents can dig into Todd English's fare from the fresh raw bar, and juniors can sup on clam chowder while watching the grill in the open kitchen. ⊠ *188 Faneuil Hall Market Pl., South Market Bldg.* ☎ *617/523–8860* ✛ *1:G5.*

Mr. Bartley's Burger Cottage. Maybe it's the frappés (thick milk shakes), silly cartoons all over the walls, or just the fun, high-energy vibe. Whatever it is, Bartley's is a hit with kids. Closed Sunday. ⊠ *1246 Massachusetts Ave., Cambridge* ☎ *617/354–6559* ✛ *4:B3.*

Pizzeria Regina. This North End favorite offers kid-pleasing thin-crust slices that just might be the best pie in town. ⊠ *11-1/2 Thatcher Ct., North End* ☎ *617/227–0765.*

Stephanie's on Newbury. Here's comfort food at its best—sophisticated enough for parents, simple enough for kids. The place is pretty but homey, and has plenty of booths for spreading out in. ⊠ *190 Newbury St., Back Bay* ☎ *617/236–0990* ✛ *2:B2.*

Summer Shack. Boston überchef Jasper White has given New England seafood an urban tweak in his laidback, loud, and fun spot next to the Prudential Center. The colors are bright, and the entire affair is like one big indoor clambake. ⊠ *50 Dalton St., Back Bay* ☎ *617/867–9955* ✛ *3:H3.*

Sweet Cupcakes. This old-fashioned, pink-and-brown Back Bay shop serving cupcakes topped with buttercream frosting is an 8-year-old girl's dream; frazzled parents can get a much-needed sugar jolt from the cappuccino and dark chocolate cake flavors. Check out the other outposts on Newbury Street and Harvard Square. ⊠ *49 Massachusetts Ave., Back Bay* ☎ *617/247–2253* ⊠ *Zero Brattle St., Harvard Square* ☎ *617/547–2253* ⊠ *225 Newbury St., Back Bay* ☎ *617/267–2253* ✛ *3:H2.*

Zaftigs. Fill up on huge plates of deli fixings such as matzo-ball soup, first-rate knishes, and heaping plates of grilled chicken, thick-cut onion rings, and three-cheese macaroni. Families cram the place regularly, so servers are used to kids' requests. ⊠ *335 Harvard St., Brookline* ☎ *617/975–0075* ✛ *3:A4.*

10

spot among the best in the country. Chef Tim Cushman's nigiri menu features squid-ink bubbles, homemade potato chips—even foie gras. Other dishes offer a nod to New England, such as the braised pork with Boston baked beans and grilled lobster with a light shiso tempura. Cushman's wife Nancy oversees an extensive sake list that includes sparkling and aged varieties. ⊠ *9 East St., Leather District* 🕾 *617/654–9900* ⊕ *www.oyarestaurantboston.com* ⊟ *AE, MC, V* ⊘ *Closed Sun. and Mon. No lunch* Ⓜ *South Station* ✛ *2:G2.*

$$$
FRENCH
FodorśChoice
★

✕ **Radius.** Acclaimed chef Michael Schlow's notable contemporary French cooking lures scores of designer- and suit-clad diners to the Financial District. The decor and menu are minimalist at first glance, but closer inspection reveals equal shares of luxury, complexity, and whimsy. Peruse the menu in the dining room for choices such as ginger-poached duck, a selection of ceviches, buttery Scottish salmon, or huckleberry-and-goat-cheese cheesecake for dessert. At the bar they serve a phenomenal (and award-winning) burger. Either way, it's a meal made for special occasions and business dinners alike. ⊠ *8 High St., Downtown* 🕾 *617/426–1234* ⊕ *www.radiusrestaurant.com* ⚞ *Reservations essential* ⊟ *AE, D, DC, MC, V* ⊘ *Closed Sun. No lunch Sat.* Ⓜ *South Station* ✛ *2:G1.*

$–$$
AMERICAN

✕ **Silvertone.** Devotees of this hip basement restaurant swear by the no-fuss options such as a truly addictive macaroni and cheese, meat loaf, and steak tips. Among the more interesting offerings are the appetizers, such as the Caesar salad with honey-chili chicken, and the fish of the day, which might be trout amandine or locally caught bluefish. The wine list is compact but varied, and retains one of the lowest mark-ups in the city. ⊠ *69 Bromfield St., Downtown* 🕾 *617/338–7887* ⊕ *www. silvertonedowntown.com* ⚞ *Reservations not accepted* ⊟ *AE, D, DC, MC, V* ⊘ *Closed Sun. No lunch Sat.* Ⓜ *Park St.* ✛ *1:F6.*

$$
ITALIAN

✕ **Sportello.** Barbara Lynch, the queen of Boston's dining scene, recently added a casual lunch-counter restaurant to her impressive roster (see also: No. 9 Park, B&G Oysters, the Butcher Shop). By the waterfront and South Station in the city's burgeoning Fort Point Channel neighborhood, Sportello is modeled after a diner—but its fare, like eggplant-stuffed calamari and goat-cheese ravioli, is far from standard. An impressive weekend brunch menu and delicious bakery selection, including excellent lemon-cornmeal cookies and splurge-worthy carrot cake, makes Sportello a must-visit. Be sure to grab an after-dinner cocktail at Drink, Lynch's next-door bar, where you can watch bartenders create custom-made libations. ⊠ *348 Congress St., Fort Point Channel, Downtown* 🕾 *617/737–1234* ⊕ *www.sportelloboston.com* ⊟ *AE, D, DC, MC, V* Ⓜ *South Station* ✛ *2:H2.*

$$
AMERICAN

✕ **Woodward.** The beautiful people found this urban chic tavern in a hurry after it opened in 2009, if not just for its food, then for the scene and the other beautiful people that go with it. Diners sip from martini glasses while noshing on signatures like the Duck confit, goat cheese and dried cranberry flatbreads, or heartier fare like monkfish with sweet-potato hash. The noise level in the minimalist downstairs can get quite loud, and the cozy upstairs gets less cozy on weekends when the fire-placed nook houses a DJ. A tasty brunch (try the lobster and sweet potato hash) is a decidedly quieter way to enjoy the place. Either way, make sure to belly up to the bar, as the groovy and creative cocktails— "No Means No," "Model Behavior"—are a signature. ⊠ *Ames Hotel, 1 Court St., Downtown Boston* ☏ *617/979–8200* ⊕ *woodwardatames. com* ▭ *AE, D, DC, MC, V* Ⓜ *State St.*

CHINATOWN

Boston's Chinatown is the focal point of Asian cuisines of all types, from authentic Cantonese and Vietnamese to Malaysian, Japanese, and Mandarin. Many places are open after midnight, while the rest of the city sleeps or lurks. It's definitely worth the trek, especially if you're tracking down live-tank seafood prepared in Hong Kong or Chiu Chow style.

$$–$$$ ✕ **Chau Chow City**. Spread across three floors, this is the largest, glitziest,
CHINESE and most versatile production yet of the Chau Chow dynasty, with dim sum by day and live-tank seafood by night. Overwhelmed? At lunch, head to the third floor for dim sum. Or sit on the main floor and order the clams in black-bean sauce, the sautéed pea-pod stems with garlic, or the honey-glazed shrimp with walnuts. Chau Chow is one of the area's only restaurants that keeps serving well into the wee hours, making it a staple for late night diners. ⊠ *83 Essex St., Chinatown* ☏ *617/338–8158* ▭ *AE, D, MC, V* Ⓜ *Chinatown* ✛ *2:F1.*

WATERFRONT

Tourists flock to Faneuil Hall and the Marketplace almost year-round, so tried-and-true cuisine tends to dominate there. However, some of Boston's most famous seafood restaurants are on the waterfront.

$$ ✕ **Barking Crab Restaurant**. It is, believe it or not, a seaside clam shack
SEAFOOD plunk in the middle of Boston, with a stunning view of the Downtown
Ⓒ skyscrapers. An outdoor lobster tent in summer, in winter it retreats indoors to a warmhearted version of a waterfront dive, with chestnuts roasting on a cozy woodstove. Look for the classic New England clambake—chowder, lobster, steamed clams, corn on the cob—or the spicier crab boil. ⊠ *88 Sleeper St., Northern Ave. Bridge, Waterfront* ☏ *617/426–2722* ⊕ *www.barkingcrab.com* ▭ *AE, MC, V* Ⓜ *South Station* ✛ *2:H1.*

$$ ✕ **Legal Sea Foods**. What better place than the waterfront to build one
SEAFOOD of the snazziest branches of the local Legal Sea Foods chain? The
Ⓒ classic and contemporary seafood preparations mirror those of the other locations, but this one's dining room is full of colorful tiles and sea-inspired sculpture. ⊠ *255 State St., Waterfront* ☏ *617/227–3115* ⊕ *www.legalseafoods.com* ▭ *AE, D, DC, MC, V* Ⓜ *Aquarium* ✛ *2:D2.*

$$$ ✕ **Meritage**. Set inside the stately Boston Harbor Hotel, Meritage stays
CONTINENTAL focused with its astounding wine list. Chef Daniel Bruce creates scintillating menus to match the cellar's treasures (arranged, appropriately, like a wine list, with headings like "full bodied" and "sparklers"). All menu items are available as small or large plates, and priced at $16 or $32 respectively. With the stunning Rowes Wharf as its backdrop, Meritage has, perhaps, the city's finest waterfront view. ⊠ *Boston Harbor Hotel at Rowes Wharf, 70 Rowes Wharf, Waterfront* ☏ *617/439–3995* ⊕ *www.meritagetherestaurant.com* ▭ *AE, D, DC, MC, V* ☉ *Closed Sun. and Mon. No lunch* Ⓜ *Aquarium* ✛ *1:H6.*

10

$ ✕ **No Name Restaurant**. Famous for
SEAFOOD not being famous, the No Name has been serving fresh seafood, simply broiled or fried, since 1917. Once you find it, tucked off New Northern Avenue (as opposed to Old Northern Avenue) between the World Trade Center and the Bank of America Pavilion, you can close your eyes and pretend you're in a

little fishing village—it's not much of a stretch. Free Parking? That's just a bonus. ⊠ *15½ Fish Pier, off Northern Ave., Waterfront* ☎ *617/338– 7539* ═ *AE, D, DC, MC, V* Ⓜ *Courthouse* ✣ *2:H1.*

$$$ ✕ **Sel de la Terre**. Sitting between the waterfront and what used to be the
FRENCH Central Artery, this is a hot spot to hit before the theater, after sightseeing, or for a simple lunch Downtown. The rustic, country-French menu features items like steak frites with red wine–shallot reduction. Stop by the *boulangerie* (bread shop) to take home fresh, homemade loaves, which are some of the best in the city. ⊠ *255 State St., Waterfront* ☎ *617/720–1300* ⊕ *www.seldelaterre.com* ⌂ *Reservations essential* ═ *AE, D, DC, MC, V* Ⓜ *Aquarium* ✣ *2:H6.*

BACK BAY AND THE SOUTH END
BACK BAY

$$$$ ✕ **Abe & Louie's**. Go ahead: live the fantasy of the robber baron feasting
STEAKHOUSE in a setting of cavernous fireplaces and deep-textured, plush mahogany booths. Abe & Louie's may be a tad Disney-esque in its decor, but its menu lives up to the promise with gorgeous, two-tiered raw platters and juicy rib-eye steaks under velvety hollandaise. Even the linen napkins have little buttonholes for the perfect collar hold. ⊠ *793 Boylston St., Back Bay* ☎ *617/536–6300* ⊕ *www.abeandlouies.com* ═ *AE, D, DC, MC, V* Ⓜ *Copley* ✣ *2:A2.*

¢ ✕ **Boloco**. This unassuming eatery near the Berklee College of Music
ECLECTIC started a chain reaction when it opened in 1997. Today Boloco (short
ↄ for Boston Local Company) has more than a dozen area outposts. All offer "inspired burritos" that extend far beyond the standard Mexican variety. Fillings, for instance, can include Buffalo chicken with blue cheese, braised pork in Thai peanut sauce, or organic tofu topped with hummus and feta. The resulting wraps are easy on both your wallet and the environment. Thanks to ecofriendly initiatives—like using naturally raised meats and biodegradable cups—Boloco is certified by the Green Restaurant Association. ⊠ *1080 Boylston St., Back Bay* ☎ *617/369–9087* ⊠ *71 Mt. Auburn St., Harvard Square* ☎ *617/354– 5838* ⊕ *www.boloco.com* ⌂ *Reservations not accepted* ═ *AE, D, DC, MC, V* Ⓜ *Hynes* ✣ *3:H3.*

$$$$ ✕ **Capital Grille**. A carnivore's utopia awaits within these clubby, dark-
STEAKHOUSE wood walls. Steak-house staples such as lobster and crab cakes and a massive shellfish platter start things nicely, followed by succulent meats such as the 24-ounce dry-aged porterhouse. The crowd-watching is as tasty as the food: VIPs in striped suits make deals over dessert, and wives in Manolo Blahnik heels sip martinis. ⊠ *359 Newbury St., Back*

A smoked salmon amuse bouche served at L'Espalier.

Bay ☎ 617/262–8900 ⊕ www.thecapitalgrille.com ▭ AE, D, DC, MC, V ⊗ No lunch Ⓜ Hynes ⊹ 3:H2.

$$$$
FRENCH
Fodor's Choice
★

✕**Clio**. Years ago, when Ken Oringer opened his snazzy leopard skin–lined hot spot in the tasteful boutique Eliot Hotel, the hordes were fighting over reservations. Things have quieted down since then, but the food hasn't. Luxury offerings including foie gras, Maine lobster, and Kobe sirloin share menu space with fail-safe crispy chicken and Scottish salmon. A magnet for romantics and foodies alike, the place continues to serve some of the city's most decadent and well-crafted meals. ⊠ *Eliot Hotel, 370 Commonwealth Ave., Back Bay* ☎ 617/536–7200 ⊕ www. cliorestaurant.com ⟑ Reservations essential ▭ AE, D, MC, V ⊗ No lunch Ⓜ Hynes ⊹ 3:H2.

$$$
ITALIAN

✕**Davio's**. Eating here is like sitting at the grown-ups' table for the first time. Comfy armchairs and a grand, high-ceilinged dining room give diners a sense of self-importance. Come at lunch, like the rest of the city's power elite, for great pastas (half portions are available) and over-size salads. For dinner, patrons rushing off to the theater grab a quick bite at the bar—others are in for a lengthy meal, since the kitchen's focus on sophisticated Italian cuisine makes every meal a special occasion. Those lucky enough to snag Pats' tickets can enjoy Davio's food at the new Patriots Place outpost, right next to Gilette Stadium, on game day. ⊠ *75 Arlington St., Back Bay* ☎ 617/357–4810 ⊕ www.davios. com ▭ AE, D, DC, MC, V ⊗ No lunch weekends Ⓜ Arlington ⊹ 2:D2.

$$$
STEAKHOUSE

✕**Grill 23 & Bar**. Pinstriped suits, dark paneling, Persian rugs, and waiters in white jackets give this steak house a posh demeanor. The food is anything but predictable, with dishes such as prime steak tartar with a shallot marmalade and weekly cuts of beef like the 14-ounce dry-aged

New York sirloin. Seafood specialties such as scallops with caramelized apples give beef sales a run for their money. Chef Jay Murray uses prime, all-natural Brandt beef exclusively. Desserts, such as the wonderfully decadent French-toast bread pudding, are far above those of the average steak house. Make sure to leave room. ⊠ *161 Berkeley St., Back Bay* ☎ *617/542–2255* ⊕ *www.grill23.com* ▤ *AE, D, DC, MC, V* ☽ *No lunch* Ⓜ *Back Bay/South End* ⊹ *2:C2.*

$$$$
FRENCH
Fodor'sChoice
★

✕ **L'Espalier.** In late 2008 L'Espalier left its longtime home in a Back Bay town house, reopening beside the Mandarin Oriental Hotel. The new locale, with its floor-to-ceiling windows and modern decor, looks decidedly different. But chef-owner Frank McClelland's dishes—from caviar and roasted foie gras to venison with escargots de Bourgogne—are as elegant as ever. In the evening, three-course prix-fixe and seasonal degustation menus tempt discriminating diners. A budget-minded, Power lunch as well as à la carte options are available weekday afternoons. Finger sandwiches and sublime sweets are served for weekend tea. ⊠ *774 Boylston St., Back Bay* ☎ *617/262–3023* ⊕ *www.lespalier. com* ⌁ *Reservations essential* ▤ *AE, D, DC, MC, V* ☽ *Closed Sun. No lunch weekends* Ⓜ *Copley* ⊹ *2:A2.*

$$
AMERICAN

✕ **Post 390.** This "urban tavern" established itself quickly in 2009, with a buzzy opening fete and an upscale twist on unfussy bar fare like duck-hot-wing potstickers, sea scallops with succotash, and cherry pie à la mode. Mac and cheese and one of the world's biggest hot dogs (the veggie topped "Dragged through the Garden" version adds a semblance of health to the dish) draw comfort-food seekers. More than 200 wines, twelve beers on tap, and a host of craft cocktails give tipplers good reason to make frequent visits. The open kitchen, four-sided fireplace, and reasonable prices are inviting enough to turn everyone else into regulars, too. ⊠ *406 Stuart St., Back Bay* ☎ *617/399–0015* ⊕ *www. post390restaurant.com* ▤ *AE, D, DC, MC, V* Ⓜ *Back Bay* ⊹ *2:C2.*

$$–$$$
AMERICAN

✕ **Sonsie.** Café society blossoms along Newbury Street, particularly at Sonsie, where a well-heeled crowd sips coffee up front or angles for places at the bar. Lunch and dinner dishes, such as charcoal duck breast and leg with brown rice and five-spice turnips, are basic bistro fare with an American twist. The restaurant is a terrific place for weekend brunch, when the light pours through the long windows, and is at its most vibrant in warm weather, when the open doors make for colorful people-watching. A downstairs wine room meanwhile offers more intimacy. The late-night menu (nightly until 12:30 am) is perfect for those after-hours cravings. ⊠ *327 Newbury St., Back Bay* ☎ *617/351–2500* ⊕ *www.sonsieboston.com* ▤ *AE, MC, V* Ⓜ *Hynes* ⊹ *3:H2.*

$$$
ITALIAN

✕ **Sorellina.** Everything about this upscale Italian spot is oversized: its space near Copley Square, its portions, and unfortunately, its prices. The sexy, all-white dining room is filled with well-heeled locals (some live in the gorgeous apartment building above it) who come for the modern twist on basic Italian dishes. Crudo, various versions of carpaccio, and the signature tuna tartare dot the list of starters, while handmade ravioli with toasted chestnuts and *maccheroncelli* (fat, tubular noodles) with Kobe beef meatballs take the spotlight. Just save room for dessert: it's always a highlight here. ⊠ *1 Huntington Ave., Back Bay*

☎ *617/412–4600* ⊕ *www.sorellinaboston.com* 🖃 *AE, DC, MC, V* ⊗ *No lunch* Ⓜ *Copley, Back Bay* ✛ *2:2.*

$$$$ ✕ **Troquet.** Despite boasting what might well be Boston's longest wine
FRENCH FUSION list, with nearly 500 vintages (more than 45 of which are available by the glass), plus an unobstructed view of the Common, this French fusion spot flies somewhat under the radar. Still, locals know that Troquet offers all the ingredients for a lovely evening: a quietly elegant dining room, decadent dishes like crispy duck confit and sticky-toffee pudding, and a knowledgeable yet unpretentious staff. Better yet, the menu includes by-the-glass wine recommendations after each entrée, so you're sure to sip something delicious and appropriate. ✉ *140 Boylston St., Back Bay* ☎ *617/695–9463* ⊕ *www.troquetboston.com* 🖃 *AE, D, DC, MC, V* ⊗ *Closed Sun. and Mon. No lunch* Ⓜ *Boylston* ✛ *2:E1.*

$$$ ✕ **Turner Fisheries.** On the first floor of the Westin hotel in Copley Square,
SEAFOOD Turner Fisheries is second only to Legal Sea Foods in its traditional appeal. Turner broils, grills, bakes, fries, and steams everything in the ocean, but also prepares classic and modern sauces, vegetables, and pastas with panache. Any meal should begin with the creamy chowder—the restaurant has won Boston's yearly Chowderfest so many times to contend any more. Round it out with one of the city's best-looking lobster rolls. ✉ *Westin Copley Place Boston, 10 Huntington Ave., Back Bay* ☎ *617/424–7425* ⊕ *www.turnersboston.com* ⌕ *Reservations essential* 🖃 *AE, D, DC, MC, V* Ⓜ *Copley* ✛ *2:B2.*

$$$$ ✕ **Uni.** Seven years after he opened his small Back Bay sashimi bar inside
JAPANESE the swanky Eliot Hotel, Ken Oringer has added several other acclaimed restaurants to his stable of properties, but Uni remains consistently superb. From tuna tataki with foie gras to sea urchin, the creations change daily depending on what's fresh. There are also a handful of options for the less adventurous, including Kobe beef teriyaki and halibut tacos. Regardless of your menu decisions, the strong shiso mojitos and a sleekly intimate space (with just 21 seats) make Uni a great date destination. ✉ *370A Commonwealth Ave. (in the Eliot Hotel), Back Bay* ☎ *617/536–7200* ⊕ *www.unisashimibar.com* 🖃 *AE, DC, MC, V* ⊗ *No lunch* Ⓜ *Hynes* ✛ *3:H2.*

$$ ✕ **Via Matta.** The city's most stylish Italian spot is paradoxically one of
ITALIAN its simplest on the culinary front. The kitchen's emphasis is on fresh, intensely flavored ingredients in traditional dishes like pappardelle with rabbit, chestnuts, dates, and olives, and Sicilian tuna salad mixed with white beans and grilled zucchini. Even frequent visitors can enjoy an oft-changing menu, the result of the chef's penchant for seasonal ingredients. The abutting *enoteca* (café)—all mosaic tile and dim lighting—serves daily pizzas, and is the perfect spot for a rendezvous or a nightcap. ✉ *79 Park Plaza, Back Bay* ☎ *617/422–0008* ⊕ *www. viamattarestaurant.com* ⌕ *Reservations essential* 🖃 *AE, D, DC, MC, V* Ⓜ *Arlington* ✛ *2:D2.*

THE SOUTH END

$–$$ ✕ **B&G Oysters, Ltd.** Chef Barbara Lynch (of No. 9 Park, the Butcher
SEAFOOD Shop, and Sportello fame) has made yet another fabulous mark on
Fodor's Choice Boston with a style-conscious seafood restaurant that updates New
★ England's traditional bounty with flair. Designed to imitate the inside

10

of an oyster shell, the iridescent bar glows with silvery, candlelit tiles and a sophisticated crowd. They're in for the lobster roll, no doubt—an expensive proposition at $27, but worth every cent for its decadent chunks of meat in a perfectly textured dressing. If you're sans reservation, be prepared to wait: the line for a seat can be epic. ⊠ *550 Tremont St., South End* ☎ *617/423–0550* ⊕ *www.bandgoysters.com* ⌂ *Reservations essential* ⊟ *AE, D, DC, MC, V* Ⓜ *Back Bay/South End* ⊹ *2:D4.*

$$ ✕ **The Butcher Shop.** Chef Barbara Lynch has remade the classic meat
AMERICAN   market as a polished wine bar–cum–hangout, and it's just the kind of high-quality, low-pretense spot every neighborhood could use. Stop in for a glass of wine, chat with any of the friendly but cosmopolitan clientele, and grab a casual, quick snack of homemade prosciutto and salami, daily pasta and sandwich specials, or a plate of artisanal cheeses. Reservations are accepted for parties of six or more. ⊠ *552 Tremont St., South End* ☎ *617/423–4800* ⊕ *www.thebutchershopboston.com* ⊟ *AE, D, DC, MC, V* Ⓜ *Back Bay/South End* ⊹ *2:D4.*

$$ ✕ **Estragon.** The urbane 1930s decor makes this South End Spanish res-
SPANISH   taurant feel high-class, but the tapas plates and easy-to-share *raciones* (entrées) make dining here an entirely casual experience. A selection of traditional tapas, such as grilled baby leeks and sizzling shrimp in garlic and oil, can easily fill up two people when coupled with entrées like paella or the lamb empanadas. Adventurous diners might go for the seared pork belly instead. Nonmeat eaters can go for the vegetarian paella. Look for a seat on the couches in the back lounge for a more social dining experience. A semiprivate dining area in the front is candlelit and more intimate. ⊠ *700 Harrison Ave., South End* ☎ *617/266–0443* ⊕ *www.estragontapas.com* ⊟ *AE, D, DC, MC, V* ⊘ *Closed Sun. No lunch* Ⓜ *East Newton* ⊹ *2:D5.*

¢–$ ✕ **Flour Bakery + Café.** When the neighbors need coffee, or a sandwich,
AMERICAN   or a muffin, or just a place to sit and chat, they come here. A communal
Ⓒ   table in the middle acts as a gathering spot, around which diners enjoy classic sandwiches and a few specialties, like the grilled chicken with Brie and arugula, or the BLT with applewood-smoked bacon. Take-out dinner specials range from pecan-encrusted chicken to garlic-herb meat loaf with goat-cheese mashed potatoes. Flour has proved so popular that owner Joanne Chang opened a second location in the up-and-coming Fort Point Channel neighborhood. ⊠ *1595 Washington St., South End* ☎ *617/267–4300* Ⓜ *Massachusetts Ave.* ⊠ *12 Farnsworth St., Fort Point Channel* ☎ *617/338–4333* ⊕ *www.flourbakery.com* ⌂ *Reservations not accepted* ⊟ *AE, D, DC, MC, V* Ⓜ *South Station* ⊹ *2:C5.*

$$ ✕ **Franklin Café.** This place has jumped to the head of the class by keep-
AMERICAN   ing things simple yet effective. (The litmus test: Local chefs gather here to wind down after work.) Try the excellent southern-fried pork chop or pork dumplings, or opt for tempting items from vegetarian and gluten-free menus. The vibe is generally more that of a bar than a restaurant (hence the many bartender awards), so be forewarned: it can get loud. Waits for tables can be downright impossible on week-end nights, and desserts are not served. On the upside, food is served till 1 am. ⊠ *278 Shawmut Ave., South End* ☎ *617/350–0010* ⊹ *www.*

franklincafe.com ⟰ *Reservations not accepted* ▭ *AE, D, DC, MC, V* Ⓜ *South End* ✛ *2:D4.*

$$$

FRENCH

✕ **Hamersley's Bistro.** Gordon Hamersley has earned a national reputation, thanks to signature dishes such as the roast chicken, spicy halibut, and souffléed lemon custard. He's one of Boston's great chefs, and is famous for wearing a Red Sox cap instead of his white chef's hat. His place has a full bar, a café area with 10 tables for walk-ins, and a larger dining room that's a little more formal and decorative than the bar and café, though nowhere near as stuffy as it looks. Brunch is served Sunday. ⊠ *553 Tremont St., South End* ☏ *617/423–2700* ⊕ *www. hamersleysbistro.com* ▭ *AE, D, DC, MC, V* ☾ *No lunch* Ⓜ *Back Bay/ South End* ✛ *2:C4.*

$$$

FRENCH

✕ **Mistral.** Attentive service, upscale yet unpretentious dishes (try the beef-tenderloin pizza topped with mashed potatoes and white-truffle oil), and Provence-theme decor make Mistral a perennial South End hot spot. Grab a table by the arched, floor-to-ceiling windows or a seat at the always-buzzing bar—either way, there'll be plenty to see. Boston's fashionable set has been coming here for more than a decade, which speaks to chef Jamie Mammano's consistently excellent French-Mediterranean cuisine. The menu, packed with fail-safe favorites like grilled sirloin au poivre and French Dover sole, rarely changes—but no one's complaining. Unlike many trendy restaurants, Mistral sticks to what it does best. ⊠ *223 Columbus Ave., South End* ☏ *617/867–9300* ⊕ *www.mistralbistro.com* ▭ *AE, D, DC, MC, V* ☾ *No lunch* ✛ *2:C3.*

$–$$

CHINESE

✕ **Myers + Chang.** Pink and orange dragon decals cover the windows of this all-day Chinese café, where Joanne Chang (of Flour fame) has returned to her familial cooking roots. Sharable platters of dumplings, wok-charred udon noodles, and stir-fries are packed with fresh ingredients and flavors. The staff is young and hip, and the crowd generally follows suit. ⊠ *1145 Washington St., South End* ☏ *617/542–5200* ⊕ *www. myersandchang.com* ▭ *AE, MC, V* Ⓜ *Back Bay/South End* ✛ *2:E4.*

$$

ITALIAN

✕ **Rocca.** Long-time local restaurateur Michela Larson and partner Gary Sullivan designed this colorful, spacious South End spot based on inspirations from Liguria, Italy. The food—simple, with a focus on seafood and fresh pasta—carries that same theme with highlights like handmade pesto and whole-roasted fish. The patio, one of only a few in the neighborhood, is shaded with bright yellow umbrellas and gets crowded in the summer. The Sunday brunch menu skews Italian with offerings like pizzetas and ricotta griddle cakes. ⊠ *500 Harrison Ave., South End* ☏ *617/451–5151* ⊕ *www.roccaboston.com* ▭ *AE, MC, V* ☾ *No lunch* Ⓜ *Back Bay/South End* ✛ *2:E4.*

$$$

SPANISH

Fodor's Choice

★

✕ **Toro.** The buzz from chef Ken Oringer's tapas joint still hasn't quieted down—for good reason. Small plates of garlic shrimp and crusty bread smothered in tomato paste are hefty enough to make a meal out of many, or share the regular or vegetarian paella with a group. An all-Spanish wine list complements the plates. Crowds have been known to wait it out for more than an hour. ⊠ *1704 Washington St., South End* ☏ *617/536–4300* ⊕ *www.toro-restaurant.com* ⟰ *Reservations not accepted* ▭ *AE, MC, V* Ⓜ *Massachusetts Ave.* ✛ *2:B6.*

10

THE SOUTH END

Home to lovely Victorian brownstones, art galleries, and the city's most diverse crowd, the South End is Boston's cultural engine.

(above) Tasty tapas at Ken Oringer's Toro. (upper right) Ahi tuna tartare from Stephi's on Tremont. (lower right) Tapas with a twist at Masa.

It's also ground zero for local foodies, who flood the scores of resto-bars that morph from neighborhood bistros into packed hot spots as the evening progresses. Some of the city's most popular restaurants are clustered here in the small square between Berkeley Street and Massachusetts Avenue to the west, Harrison Avenue and Columbus Avenue to the north. French brasseries predominate, but the neighborhood also offers up everything from modern American (Union Bar & Grille; Franklin Café) to Italian and Indian. Don't miss the well-executed Spanish tapas at Toro on Washington Street.

A five-minute walk from Back Bay, the South End is also a popular shopping destination, with bakeries and cafés sprinkled alongside emerging jewelry designers and cool boutiques. It's easy to wander the entire length of the neighborhood in an afternoon, but beware: Many South End spots stop serving lunch at 2 and don't reopen til 5.

TORO LUNCH

At night, chef Ken Oringer's tapas bar is a buzzy, standing-room-only collection of Boston's young and fabulous. But on weekdays from noon til 2 **Toro** (⊠ *1704 Washington St.* ☎ *617/536-4300* ✛ *2:B6*) hosts a lesser-known (and cheaper) lunch, minus the evening wait and parking hassles. Try the tortilla Española or the selection of artisanal cheeses. But plan the remainder of your afternoon accordingly: you'll probably need a Barcelona-style siesta.

SWEET SPOTS

These places make a South End stroll dangerous to your waistline.

Flour (✉ *1595 Washington St.* ☎ *617/267–4300* ✛ *2:C5*) is the consummate neighborhood bakery. Owner Joanne Chang stocks a rotating selection of decadent homemade oreos, Belgian chocolate brownies, and meringue clouds, plus thick sandwiches and a great cup of joe.

Neighborhood denizens swear by the oatmeal cookies and carrot-cake cupcakes, but the biggest buzz is saved for the back-room bistro at **South End Buttery** (✉ *314 Shawmut Ave.* ☎ *617/482–1015* ✛ *2:D4*). The rear room—easy to miss from the front of the café—boasts a fireplace, wine list, and down-to-earth dinner options like pan-roasted halibut and pesto capellini.

Some of the city's best muffins—including the best-selling morning-glory variety (a carrot-raisin-little-bit-of-everything muffin)—are baked fresh at the **Appleton Bakery** (✉ *123 Appleton St.* ☎ *617/859–8222* ✛ *2:C3*). Simple and unpretentious, this spot often lacks the morning lines that form at Flour and the Buttery.

BRUNCH STEALS

Come Sunday, it seems like every single person in the South End is enjoying a leisurely late-morning meal. Luckily, the neighborhood's favorite pastime doesn't need to be a pricey habit: popular eateries offer prix-fixe weekend brunches with single-digit price tags. At **Union Bar and Grill** (✉ *1357 Washington St.* ☎ *617/423–0555* ✛ *2:D4*) $9.95 gets you a veritable smorgasbord: crumb cake, a salmon egg scramble, homefries, toast, coffee, and fresh-squeezed juice. While Southwestern-flavored **Masa** (✉ *439 Tremont St.* ☎ *617/338–8884* ✛ *2:D3*) offers tapas dishes like carmelized plantain empanadas for about $4, and huevos rancheros with all the fixings for less than $10.

SISTER SISTER

Boston's a small city, so it's no wonder that the same names are repeated…and repeated…and repeated again in the dining world. Particularly in the South End, a handful of hip restaurateurs are opening multiple properties with similar atmospheres—so if you like one, maybe you'll like them all. After enjoying **Toro**'s success, Ken Oringer recently welcomed sister property **Coppa** (✉ *253 Shawmut Ave.* ☎ *617/391–0902*), an Italian wine bar with a small-plates menu just a few blocks away. Meanwhile, local entrepreneur Seth Woods is behind **Aquitaine**, **Metropolis Café** (✉ *584 Tremont St.* ☎ *617/247–2931* ✛ *2:C4*), **Union Bar and Grill**, and **Gaslight**—all of which have upscale brasserie vibes. Finally, neighborhood newcomer Stephanie Sokolov of **Stephanie's on Newbury** fame opened a second, smaller outpost, **Stephi's on Tremont** (✉ *571 Tremont St.* ☎ *617/236–2063* ✛ *2:C4*), which borrows a few popular entrées (like the mac 'n' cheese and heaping salads) from its big sib.

10

Trendsetters nosh on upscale American classics at Union Bar and Grill.

$$$ ✕ **Union Bar and Grille**. There's rarely a quiet night at Union, where the
AMERICAN bar buzzes with the neighborhood's coolest residents and couples on
dates fill the darkly lighted dining room's leather banquettes. Despite
all the show, the menu keeps things relatively down to earth, with
tender-as-can-be beef tenderloin and smoked red onion rings. Brunch
is served weekends. ✉ *1357 Washington St., South End* ☎ *617/423–
0555* ⊕ *www.unionrestaurant.com* ▭ *AE, D, DC, MC, V* ☉ *No lunch*
Ⓜ *South End* ✛ *2:D4.*

THE FENWAY AND KENMORE SQUARE

$$ ✕ **Eastern Standard Kitchen and Drinks**. A vivid red awning beckons
AMERICAN patrons of this spacious brasse-
Fodor'sChoice rie-style restaurant. The bar area
★ and red banquettes are filled most
nights with Boston's power players
(members of the Red Sox manage-
ment are known to stop in), thirtysomethings, and students from
the nearby universities all noshing
on raw-bar specialties and comfort

> ### WORD OF MOUTH
>
> "I really like Eastern Standard
> in Kenmore Square; very lively,
> pretty space with great food and
> cocktails."   —wyatt92

dishes such as lamb-sausage rigatoni, rib eye, and burgers. It's a Sunday
brunch hot spot, especially on game days (the Big Green Monster is a
very short walk away). The cocktail list is one of the best in town, filled
with old classics and new concoctions. A covered, heated patio offers
alfresco dining much of the year. ✉ *528 Commonwealth Ave., Kenmore Sq.* ☎ *617/532–9100* ⊕ *www.easternstandardboston.com* ▭ *AE,
D, MC, V* Ⓜ *Kenmore* ✛ *3:F2.*

BOSTON OUTSKIRTS

ALLSTON

More or less northwest of Downtown, this densely packed little enclave of grunge mixes twentysomething college students with immigrants from four continents. In general, the restaurants are homey and cheap, but the best offer a culinary world tour. A number of places allow low-key BYOB (Blanchard's and Marty's on Harvard Avenue are both great wine stores). For cheap eats and a young vibe, the neighborhood can't be beat.

$ ✕ **Café Brazil**. Terrific sizzling entrées from Brazil's Minas Gerais region
BRAZILIAN   fill the menu, including a fine mixed grill, and a couple of fish stews are borrowed from the neighboring province of Bahia. This little place, run by a friendly staff that speaks mostly Portuguese, also turns out a great version of the fried yucca appetizer called *mandioca*. Thankfully, the decor has been recently updated, the outdated travel posters replaced by beach paintings that almost transport you to Brazil. Live Brazilian music adds further ambience on weekends. ⊠ *421 Cambridge St., Allston* ☎ *617/789–5980* ⊕ *www.cafebrazilrestaurant.com* ▭ *AE, D, MC, V* Ⓜ *Harvard* ✛ *3:A1.*

¢–$ ✕ **Soul Fire Barbecue**. What this neighborhood needed most took a long
SOUTHERN   time to get here, but there's finally a quick stop for barbecue, complete with a range of sauces and styles. The pit resides in the kitchen, but the enticing, smoky aroma fills the whole high-ceiling space. Everything from pulled pork to spare- and baby-back ribs to hickory-roasted chicken can be smothered in the sauce of your choice. There is also a bar to sit at that's covered with old soul and blues album covers. ⊠ *182 Harvard Ave., Allston* ☎ *617/787–3003* ⊕ *www.soulfirebbq.com* ▭ *AE, MC, V* Ⓜ *Harvard* ✛ *3:A1.*

BROOKLINE

Going to Brookline is a nice way to get out of the city without really leaving town. Although it's surrounded by Boston on three sides, Brookline has its own suburban flavor, seasoned with a multitude of historic—and expensive—houses and garnished with a diverse ethnic population that supports a string of sushi bars and a small list of kosher restaurants. Most Brookline eateries are clustered in the town's commercial centers: Brookline Village, Washington Square, Longwood, and bustling Coolidge Corner.

10

¢   ✕ **Clear Flour Bread**. Finding this bakery on a small Brookline side street
BAKERY   can be tough—if you don't have a GPS, follow the online directions carefully—and then finding parking is tougher still. But Clear Flour rewards the persistent with delicious croissants both sweet (chocolate) and savory (Gruyère), brioches, and European-style crusty breads like a Gorgonzola-walnut fougasse. While strictly a bakery (there are no sit-down meals or sandwiches), Clear Flour is a perfect weekend option for decadent, Euro-style goodies. You'll come for the scones and sticky buns, and leave with a couple of loaves of pesto foccacia and polenta bread to get you through the week. ⊠ *178 Thorndike St., Coolidge Corner* ☎ *617/739–0060* ⊕ *www.clearflourbread.com* ▭ *D, MC, V* Ⓜ *Packard's Corner* ✛ *3:A2.*

The bustling dining room at Eastern Standard Kitchen and Drinks.

$
CAMBODIAN/
FRENCH

✕ **Elephant Walk.** Technically, this outpost of Elephant Walk (there are two others in Cambridge and Waltham) is in Boston, but psychologically it's the gateway to Brookline. The French-Cambodian menu is separated by region, so you get the best of both worlds. Tease your palate with an exotic assortment of dumpling appetizers, spring rolls that you wrap in fresh lettuce leaves, and mouthwatering coq au vin. Many (or even most) dishes can be made meat-free for the veggie set. The airy atmosphere evokes a British Colonial hotel; the food reminds you of why Phnom Penh was "the Paris of Asia." The desserts, though, are pure Paris. ⊠ *900 Beacon St., Brookline* ☎ *617/247–1500* ⊕ *www.elephantwalk.com* ⊟ *AE, D, DC, MC, V* Ⓜ *St. Mary's* ✛ *3:D3.*

$$
JAPANESE

✕ **Fugakyu.** The name sounds vaguely offensive in English, but in Japanese it means "house of elegance." The interior hits the mark, with tatami mats, rice-paper partitions, and wooden ships circling a moat around the sushi bar. The menu is both elegant and novel, with Boston's first live-tank sashimi, the rare Japanese *matsutake* mushrooms in a vegetarian stir-fry, and appetizers such as marinated scallops served in a martini glass. Bento boxes are available at lunch only. ⊠ *1280 Beacon St., Brookline* ☎ *617/734–1268* ⊕ *www.fugakyu.net* ⊟ *AE, D, DC, MC, V* Ⓜ *Coolidge Corner* ✛ *3:A4.*

$$
JAPANESE

✕ **Ginza.** The sole remaining Ginza (its sister restaurant in Chinatown closed in 2009 to the dismay of local sushi lovers) gains extra points for its broad selection of sake. Avant-sushi these days includes hot spices, fried morsels, boozy marinades, and presentations with props, such as a martini glass. There are lots of good appetizers and hot dinners as well, including teriyaki, tempura, and *nabemono* (one-pot meals). To boot, the warm aesthetic is long on Zen. ⊠ *1002 Beacon St., Brookline*

Boston Classics

Not for nothing did Boston become known as the home of the bean and the cod: simple Yankee specialties—many of them of English origin—and traditional seafood abound.

Boston baked beans are a thick, syrupy mixture of navy beans, salt pork, and molasses cooked for hours. They were originally made by Puritan women on Saturday, so that the left-overs could be eaten on Sunday without breaking the Sabbath by cooking.

You may also want to keep an eye out for Parker House rolls, yeast-bread dinner rolls first concocted at the Parker House Hotel in the 1870s.

Boston cream pie is an addictive simple yellow vanilla cake filled with a creamy custard and iced with chocolate frosting. Many traditional New England eateries (and some steak houses and hotel restaurants) serve a house version. Occasionally you'll find a modernized version, with some creative new element added at trendier restaurants.

The city's beer-drinking enthusiasm is older than the Declaration of Independence—which, incidentally, was signed by Samuel Adams, an instigator of the Boston Tea Party and the man whose name graces the bottles of the country's best-selling craft-brew beer.

☎ 617/566–9688 ⊕ www.ginzabrookline.com ⊟ AE, D, DC, MC, V Ⓜ Brookline ✛ 3:D3.

$$
SEAFOOD
✕ **Lineage.** Downtown is saturated with decent seafood options, but few hit the mark on inventive fare quite like Lineage. Chef-owner Jeremy Sewall puts the restaurant's central wood-burning stove to good use, and roasts everything from halibut to pork chops. His cousin Mark is a lobsterman, and provides a fresh catch now and then. A number of seats at the bar, along with ample dining room space, allow diners the option of a casual meal or a comfortable fine-dining experience. ✉ 242 Harvard St., Brookline ☎ 617/232–0065 ⊕ www.lineagerestaurant.com ⊟ AE, D, MC, V ☉ No lunch Ⓜ Coolidge Corner ✛ 3:A4.

$
IRISH
✕ **Matt Murphy's Pub.** Boston has dozens of Irish pubs, but very few are notable for food—this being a welcome exception. Even with a hefty renovation in 2010, the place maintained its heart, making real poetry out of thick slabs of bread and butter served on wooden boards, giant servings of soup, fish-and-chips presented in a twist of newspaper, and shepherd's pie. Don't miss the house-made ketchup with your French fries. ✉ 14 Harvard St., Brookline ☎ 617/232–0188 ⊟ No credit cards Ⓜ Brookline Village ✛ 3:A6.

$–$$
AMERICAN
✕ **The Publick House.** What started as a simple neighborhood beer bar has reached cultlike status for Brookline-ites and beyond. Serving more than 175 out-of-the-ordinary and artisanal beers, the bar also offers tasty sandwiches, smaller entrées, and main dishes, many of which have beer incorporated into them. A Smuttynose grilled-chicken sandwich, for example, is marinated in IPA, and fried shrimp are battered with Japanese breadcrumbs and Whale's Tale pale ale, and there are beer recommendations to match. An adjacent taproom—the Monk's Cell—specializes in Belgian brews. Weekend nights find long lines, but one taste of

10

"Off the Chain" Chains

If you're on the go, you might want to try a local chain restaurant, where you can stop for a quick bite or get some takeout. The places listed here are fairly priced, committed to quality, and use decent, fresh ingredients.

Au Bon Pain. The locally based chain whips up quick salads and sandwiches, fresh-daily croissants and muffins, and has plenty of fruit and juices. It's recently added some appealing snack options, including an apple, blue cheese, and cranberry combo.

B.Good. This chainlet's avocado- and salsa-topped veggie burgers, baked sweet-potato fries, and sesame-ginger chicken salad are redefining fast food in Boston.

Bertucci's. Thin-crust pizzas fly fast from the brick ovens here, along with pastas and a decent tiramisu.

BoLoCo. For quick, cheap, healthful, and high-quality wraps and burritos, this is easily the city's most dependable (and also locally based) chain. BoLoCo's menu also includes smoothies and breakfast options, and its hours are some of the longest in this notoriously early-to-bed city.

Finagle A Bagel. Find fresh, doughy bagels in flavors from jalapeño cheddar to triple chocolate, plus sandwiches and salads. Service is swift and efficient.

UBurger. Better-than-average burgers with toppings that lean toward the gourmet (sautéed mushrooms, blue cheese) and a great chocolate frappe (Boston-ese for milk shake) make this spot the East Coast's answer to California's much-loved In-n-Out.

the city's only "cuisine à la bier" is absolutely worth it. ⊠ *1648 Beacon St., Brookline* ☎ *617/277–2880* ⊕ *www.eatgoodfooddrinkbetterbeer. com* ▭ *MC, V* ⊙ *No lunch* Ⓜ *Washington Sq.* ✛ *3:A4.*

$ ✕ **Rani.** One of Brookline's more unusual restaurants serves excellent
INDIAN Indian cuisine in the Hyderabadi style, which incorporates northern and southern flavors. Dishes are complex, rich, and layered with sweet and salty. *Murg musalam,* a roasted chicken in a fragrant brown sauce, is tender and juicy, and any of the tandoori dishes (meats cooked in a clay oven) are designed for beginners. The variety of specialty breads is impressive, and the sleek interior fills up nightly with locals looking for a change of pace from Downtown's more casual Indian buffet. During the day, explore the menu via the daily lunch buffet. ⊠ *1353 Beacon St., Brookline* ☎ *617/734–0400* ⊕ *www.ranibistro.com* ▭ *AE, D, MC, V* Ⓜ *Coolidge Corner* ✛ *3:A4.*

$ ✕ **Rubin's.** The last kosher Jewish delicatessen in the Boston area is
DELI award-winning, and serves a hand-cut pastrami sandwich any New Yorker can respect. There are *kasha varnishkes* (buckwheat with bow-tie noodles), hot brisket, and many other high-cholesterol classics, but, of course, no real cream for your coffee or dairy desserts. ⊠ *500 Harvard St., Brookline* ☎ *617/731–8787* ⊕ *www.rubinskosher.com* ▭ *AE, DC, MC, V* ⊙ *Closed Sat. No dinner Fri.* Ⓜ *Coolidge Corner* ✛ *3:A4.*

$$ ✕ **Taberna de Haro.** Although Bostonians have already fallen for tapas,
SPANISH this is the first tapas bar to fully capture authentic Spanish cuisine.

At dinner, along with a few entrées, you have a choice of about 40 tapas, including such classics as a tortilla Española, jamón Serrano, and garlic shrimp. A well-planned and inexpensive all-Spanish wine list is hand-selected by the owners, and an outdoor patio fills up throughout the summer. ⊠ *999 Beacon St., Brookline* ☎ *617/277–8272* ⊕ *www. tabernaboston.com* ▤ *DC, MC, V* ☉ *Closed Sun. No lunch* Ⓜ *Coolidge Corner* ✥ *3:D3.*

$$$ ╳ **Village Smokehouse.** This stalwart Brookline Village BBQ joint has
SOUTHERN been literally luring customers in by the nose (you can practically smell it from the Brookline Village T stop) since it set up shop 23 years ago. In recent years the vintage plastic checkered tablecloths have been replaced by wooden tables (albeit with red-checkered tops) and more upscale decor. But, the ambience is still a tribute to sauce-drippin' BBQ chicken and ribs, right down to the plastic bibs. Bottom line: expect to get messy. And enjoy. ⊠ *1 Harvard St., Brookline* ☎ *617/566–3782* ⊕ *villagesmokehouse.com* ⌦ *No reservations* ▤ *AE, MC, V* ☉ *No lunch Sun.–Thurs.* Ⓜ *Brookline Village.*

$ ╳ **Zaftigs.** Here's something different: a contemporary version of a Jew-
AMERICAN ish delicatessen. How refreshing to have genuinely lean corned beef, a
☺ modest slice of cheesecake, low-sugar homemade borscht, and a lovely whitefish-salad sandwich? Believe breakfast is the most important meal? It's served all day. Weekend brunch time can bring hour-long waits for a plate of the area's best pancakes. Just make sure to leave room for one of the goodies (cupcakes, Conga bars) in the bakery case. ⊠ *335 Harvard St., Brookline* ☎ *617/975–0075* ⊕ *www.zaftigs.com* ▤ *AE, D, MC, V* Ⓜ *Coolidge Corner* ✥ *3:A4.*

JAMAICA PLAIN

This neighborhood is a kind of a mini-Cambridge: multiethnic and filled with cutting-edge artists, graduate students, political idealists, and yuppie families. Recently, the area, known for its affordable and unusual ethnic spots, has seen a swell of a more gentrified—but no less creative—sort.

$–$$ ╳ **Bella Luna.** After being priced out of its former Jamaica Plain digs,
ITALIAN this 15-year-old restaurant-cum-candlepin bowling alley-cum nightclub
☺ moved to a new spot nearby. Not much has changed: sci-fi jokes are still sprinkled across this spot's spaced-out menu of eccentric pizzas, calzones, and Italian standards. Menu favorites remain, including the "Pizza Menino" (named for the city's mayor), topped with pepperoni, sausage, mushrooms, and peppers, and the "Diedre Delux," which mixes dried cranberries, caramelized onions, and Gorgonzola cheese. Works by local artists lines the walls, and local musicians provide the music in its lounge, the Milky Way. (The weekly schedule ranges from jazz to salsa.) The only reason to mourn Luna's old location? The new space has no room for a bowling alley. ⊠ *284 Amory St., Sam Adams Brewery complex, Jamaica Plain* ☎ *617/524–3740* ⊕ *www.milkywayjp. com* ▤ *AE, D, DC MC, V* Ⓜ *Stony Brook* ✥ *3:C6.*

$–$$ ╳ **Bukhara.** The menu here covers the cuisines of several Indian regions,
INDIAN so the daily midday buffet essentially lets you eat your way around the country. The heavenly aroma and the condiments alone could keep you satiated, but check out the dosas, curries, and anything from the

10

CLOSE UP

Cold Comforts

Bostonians eat more ice cream per capita than anyone else in the U.S., according to an oft-repeated—though difficult to verify—factoid. Whether it's actually true, there are a remarkable number of independent, premium ice cream and gelato shops in town, and business remains brisk even on the most bone-chilling January days.

Inman Square dessert mecca **Christina's** (⊠ 1255 Cambridge St., Inman Square ☎ 617/492–7021 ⊕ www. christinasicecream.com ✛ 4:F2) dishes up more than 45 creative flavors, from Wild Turkey and walnut, to cinnamon rice pudding, and an amazingly addictive chocolate mousse.

Dieting meets decadence at **Emack & Bolio's** (⊠ 255 State St., Waterfront ☎ 617/367–0220 ✛ 2:A2 ⊠ 290 Newbury St., Back Bay ☎ 617/536–7127 ✛ 1:H6 ⊕ www.emackandbolios.com), a half juice/smoothie bar, half ice-cream parlor with several tourist-friendly locations. The flavors here aren't as extreme as the offerings at some competitors, but you'll find rock-solid renditions of favorites like cookie dough, butter pecan, and pistachio nut.

Simple but sublime cones have addicted many to the fun and funky likes of **J.P. Licks** (⊠ 352 Newbury St., Back Bay ☎ 617/236–1666 ⊕ www. jplicks.com ✛ 3:H2). In addition to a stable of reliable favorites, this locally grown mini-chain mixes up the flavors each month with offerings like gingersnap molasses and s'mores. Don't miss their ice-cream floats—they're equal parts cream and fizz.

If you're looking for serious ice cream, look no further than **Toscanini's** (⊠ 899 Main St., Central Square ☎ 617/491–5877 ⊕ www.tosci. com ✛ 4:F5). With flavors such as

cardamom, mango ginger, bourbon black pepper, and burnt caramel, this MIT establishment has few equals.

Lizzy's Ice Cream (⊠ 29 Church St., Harvard Square ☎ 617/354–2911 ⊕ www.lizzysicecream.com ✛ 4:A2) is a relative newcomer to Harvard Square, but sure to get more traffic now that the legendary Herrell's has closed. Lizzy's offers flavor options like orange pineapple and Charles River Crunch (a dark-chocolate ice cream with almond toffee nuggets). However, we suggest you stick to the basics: the sundaes here are unrivaled.

With a name that's short for Pizza and Ice Cream Company, **Picco** (⊠ 513 Tremont St., South End ☎ 617/927–0066 ⊕ www.piccorestaurant.com ✛ 2:D3) is perfect for both kids and kids at heart. This South End spot combines an upscale, trendy feel with an old-fashioned soda fountain and homemade ice-cream flavors including coconut chocolate chip, honey, and Vietnamese cinnamon.

Most gelato contains 8% milk fat (as compared to about 12% to 15% in ice cream); not **Caffe Paradiso's** (⊠ 255 Hanover St., North End ☎ 617/742–1768 ⊕ www.caffeparadiso.com ✛ 1:G5). This North End café's version, made on-site daily, weighs in at a hefty 14% fat and tastes accordingly decadent. Try the traditional *nocciola* (hazelnut).

Whether it's quantity or a good cause that you're after, nothing beats the **Scooper Bowl** (☎ 800/525–4669 ⊕ www.scooperbowl.org), an annual all-you-can-eat extravaganza held in early June at City Hall Plaza. Organizers serve up 10 tons of brand-name ice cream. Proceeds benefit the Dana-Farber Cancer Institute.

Gelato, a favorite sweet treat in Boston.

tandoor oven. The spice quotient varies from mild to incendiary. ⊠ *701 Centre St., Jamaica Plain* ☎ *617/522–2195* ⊕ *www.oneworldcuisine. com* ⊟ *AE, D, DC, MC, V* Ⓜ *Forest Hills* ✛ *3:C6.*

$
AMERICAN
✕ **Centre Street Café.** It's impossible not to love JP's funky and fun hangout, where neighborhood residents pack the limited number of tables and local artwork fills the walls. The eclectic menu veers from ethnic inspirations like Asian-inspired Shrimp Nirvana to super-fresh salads brimming with local produce to the favorite "Slacker's Breakfast," fittingly served until 3 pm. Lines snake around the block every Saturday and Sunday for the spectacular (and spectacularly filling) brunch. ⊠ *669A Centre St., Jamaica Plain* ☎ *617/524–9217* ⊕ *www.centrestcafe.com* ☝ *Reservations not accepted* ⊟ *MC, V* Ⓜ *Green St.* ✛ *3:C6.*

¢–$
CUBAN
✕ **El Oriental de Cuba.** This small haven, which was refurbished into a bigger, better space after a fire, serves a large variety of excellent Cuban food, including a restorative chicken soup, a classic Cuban sub, superb rice and beans (opt for the red beans over the black), and sweet "tropical shakes." The *tostones* (twice-fried plantains) are beloved during cold New England winters by the city's many Cuban transplants. Breakfast is also served. ⊠ *416 Centre St., Jamaica Plain* ☎ *617/524–6464* ⊕ *www. elorientaldecuba.com* ⊟ *AE, D, MC, V* Ⓜ *Stony Brook* ✛ *3:C6.*

$
MEXICAN
✕ **Tacos El Charro.** Drag naysayers who claim that "Boston has no *real* Mexican restaurants" to this authentic hole-in-the-wall. Order them one of the delectable soft tacos crammed with chicken or pineapple-flavored pork, or tempt them with a rich enchilada or savory goat stew. Wash it all down with a thickly blended *horchata* (a cold, frappé-like drink made with rice, milk, and ground almonds). Soon the guilty offenders will be thanking you while eating their words—along with

An oversized sandwich from All Star Sandwich Bar.

everything else. Odds are they won't even comment on the cute but perfunctory decor. ⊠ *349 Centre St., Jamaica Plain* ☏ *617/983–9275* ⌂ *Reservations not accepted* ☰ *AE, D, DC, MC, V* ☾ *Closed Tues.* Ⓜ *Jackson Sq.* ⊹ *3:C6.*

$$ ✕ **Ten Tables.** Jamaica Plain's postage-stamp-size, candlelit boîte (there's
FRENCH a sister restaurant in Cambridge) is an enchanting mix of Gallic elegance and chummy neighborhood revelry. So, too, the food. Simple but high-quality dishes such as Moroccan-spiced swordfish and Sicilian-style fish stew—followed by a carefully chosen "one perfect cheese" plate—seamlessly seal the deal. The $40 tasting menu ($30 if you're a vegetarian) makes ordering easy. Just be prepared to wait it out for a table, or reserve weeks in advance. Make your reservation online, as phones are generally staffed by recording. ⊠ *597 Centre St., Jamaica Plain* ☏ *617/524–8810* ⊕ *www.tentables.net* ⌂ *Reservations essential* ☰ *MC, V* ☾ *No lunch* Ⓜ *Stony Brook* ⊹ *3:C6.*

WELLESLEY

Wellesley, a western suburb of Boston, is about a 35-minute drive from the city. Or you could jump on the commuter rail's Framingham/ Worcester line, which runs between Wellesley and Boston's Back Bay and South Station depots, with trains leaving nearly every hour during the week and every two hours on Saturday.

$$$ ✕ **Blue Ginger.** Chef Ming Tsai's nimble maneuvers in the kitchen have
ASIAN caught the nation's eye via a public TV cooking program, *Simply Ming,* and his many cookbooks, including the first, *Blue Ginger: East Meets West Cooking with Ming Tsai* (1999). Plan ahead (and make sure Tsai is there) to savor his Occident-meets-Asian cuisine. Top choices include his

CLOSE UP

Top Chef Travels: Ming Tsai's Boston

Ming Tsai has made a name for himself as the premier chef of East-West cuisine. As the owner and chef of popular Blue Ginger restaurant in Wellesley, Massachusetts, and host/executive producer of the cooking show Simply Ming, Ming Tsai showcases the fusion of Eastern and Western flavors, dishes, and culinary techniques.

Q: Where are some of your favorite places to eat in Boston?
A: In Porter Square there's a place called **Sapporo Ramen** (⊠ *1815 Massachusetts Ave.* ☎ *617/876–4805* ⊹ *4:B1*). They make the best miso udon noodles. It's just unimaginable that you can finish this bowl of noodles, and I finish it every time. It's like $8.50 or 9 bucks and it's so good. The only other claim to fame at Porter Square is **Japonaise Bakery** (⊠ *1815 Massachusetts Ave.* ☎ *617/547–5531* ⊹ *4:B1*). They make these great little sandwiches and this adzuki bean puree with a whipped-cream doughnut. It is off the charts. I don't care how many calories it is, it's delicious. I will run 6 miles to have one of those.

Q: Are there any other restaurants in Boston that you like?
A: Yeah, Uni and Clio. When Clio opened, it really took Boston by storm, and it's really one of the top places in Boston. Clio is fine dining, with white tablecloths and the whole nine yards. If my parents were in town and it was a holiday, I'd go to Clio. But [Uni] is very unconventional. There's no sushi rice, so it's a sashimi bar. Almost 90% of the menu is raw. There are a couple of hot things that come from the Clio kitchen, but most is raw. [Ken Oringer] gets pristine fish from Japan, and obviously uni, sea urchin, is one of his signature products.

Q: Are there any bars that you really like?
A: I love the Eastern Standard in the Hotel Commonwealth. It's a very Old French bistro-style bar—good burgers, good fries. We tend to go there for beers before a Fenway game.

Q: Are there any other places you like to go for a bite on the day of the game?
A: Jasper White's **Summer Shack** (⊠ *50 Dalton St.* ☎ *617/867–9955* ⊹ *3:H3*) is great for Rhode Island calamari, roasted lobster, fried clams. [It's] the best raw bar. He always has the best oysters and clams. And as a fun thing, if it happens to rain and you don't go to the game, you can go downstairs to **King's Bowling Alley** (⊠ *50 Dalton St.* ☎ *617/266–2695*), where there is fluorescent or neon bowling. That's always a good place to burn an afternoon during crappy weather.

Q: Tell us about Blue Ginger. What can people expect when dining there?
A: It's very casual. I mean we have people who come in tuxes and people who come in shorts. It's an open kitchen—the entertainment, action, the feel, the smells are all in the restaurant.

10

mother's recipe for three-vinegar roasted shrimp and the flavor-packed garlic and black-pepper lobster served with the shell as part of the presentation. On evenings and Saturdays the last-minute set can drop into the lounge for the chef's Ming's Bings (Blue-Ginger style burgers) and Asian tapas. Blue Ginger Noodle Bar offers weekday quick lunches (pad Thai, Ramen noodles) that can be eaten in the lounge or taken out. While the restaurant is but a 15-minute jaunt west on the Massachusetts Turnpike to Route 16/Washington St., public transportation is a schlep. Commuter Rail travelers can easily walk from the Wellesley Square stop, but will have to contend with maddeningly infrequent trains, especially on weekends. The T runs more frequently, but the nearest stops (Riverside or Woodland on the Green Line D) are a 10-minute cab ride. All that said, local connoisseurs swear that a culinary tour of Boston is incomplete without a visit. And Ming never disappoints. ⊠ *583 Washington St., Wellesley* ☎ *781/283–5790* ⊕ *www.ming.com* ▭ *AE, MC, V* ☺ *No lunch Sun.* ✛ *3:A1.*

CAMBRIDGE

Among other collegiate enthusiasms, Cambridge has a long-standing fascination with ethnic restaurants. A certain kind of great restaurant has also evolved here, mixing world-class cooking with a studied informality. Famous chefs, attired in flannel shirts, cook with wood fires and borrow flavors from every continent. For more posh tastes and the annual celebrations that come with college life (or the end of it), Cambridge also has its share of linen-cloth tables.

¢ ✕ **All Star Sandwich Bar**. This place has a strict definition of what makes
AMERICAN   a sandwich: no wraps. It has put together a list of classics, like crispy,
Fodor's Choice   overstuffed Reubens and beef on weck, which are served quickly from
★   an open kitchen. The only nonsandwich option on the board is a hot dog. With bright colors and the personality of a beloved sandwich joint, the place has about a dozen tables that fill up at lunchtime. At dinner, burgers are also served, along with a small selection of beer and wine. ⊠ *1245 Cambridge St., Cambridge* ☎ *617/868–3065* ⊕ *www. allstarsandwichbar.com* ⌦ *Reservations not accepted* ▭ *MC, V* Ⓜ *Central/Inman* ✛ *4:F2.*

$ ✕ **Baraka Café**. Tiny Baraka may be atmospherically challenged, but
MEDITERRANEAN   after a few bites you won't care. Chef-owner Alia Rejeb was born in France and raised in Tunisia—a fact reflected sharply in her menu. Imagine a smoky, creamy dish of peppers awakened with mint, oregano, and cheese (*mechouia*), or a spice-laden deep-chocolate cake, redolent of star anise. Make a meal from the selection of small plates or try an entrée of couscous or marinated vegetables. No alcohol is served. ⊠ *80½ Pearl St., Cambridge* ☎ *617/868–3951* ⊕ *www.barakacafe.com* ⌦ *Reservations essential* ▭ *No credit cards* ☺ *Closed Mon. No lunch Sun.* Ⓜ *Central* ✛ *4:E5.*

$$$ ✕ **The Blue Room**. Totally hip, funky, and Cambridge, the Blue Room
AMERICAN   blends a host of cuisines from Moroccan to Mediterranean with fresh, local ingredients. Brightly colored furnishings, counters where you can meet others while you eat, and a friendly staff add up to a good-time

place that's serious about food. Try the wood-grilled lamb rack, or perhaps the local chicken roasted in Moroccan spices. An extraordinary buffet brunch with grilled meats and vegetables, as well as regular breakfast fare and a gorgeous array of desserts, is served on Sunday. ⊠ *1 Kendall Sq., Cambridge* ☎ *617/494–9034* ⊕ *www.theblueroom.net* ⊜ *AE, D, DC, MC, V* ⊘ *No lunch* Ⓜ *Kendall/MIT* ✛ *4:H4.*

$$$ ✕ **Casablanca.** Long before *The Rocky Horror Picture Show,* Harvard
MEDITERRANEAN and Radcliffe types would put on trench coats and head to the Brattle Theatre to see *Casablanca,* rising to recite the Bogart and Bergman lines in unison. Then it was on to this restaurant, where the walls are painted with scenes from the film, for more of the same. The path to this local institution is still well worn, thanks to deep-flavored wild-mushroom tart and slow-roasted lamb with charred tomatoes. The bar still attracts a worldly graduate-student crowd with its range of local beers and classic cocktails. ⊠ *40 Brattle St., Cambridge* ☎ *617/876–0999* ⊕ *www. casablanca-restaurant.com* ⊜ *AE, DC, MC, V* Ⓜ *Harvard* ✛ *4:A2.*

$$$ ✕ **Chez Henri.** French with a Cuban twist—odd bedfellows, but it works
ECLECTIC for this restaurant. The dinner menu gets serious, with succulent grilled
Fodor's Choice lamb sharing space with a Latin-spiced bouillabaisse and sinfully sweet
★ desserts like the chocolate bread pudding with Mexican chocolate sauce. At the cozy bar you can sample spiced fries, clam fritters, and the best grilled three-pork Cuban sandwich in Boston. The place fills quickly with Cantabrigian locals—an interesting mix of students, professors, and sundry intelligentsia. The closest T stop (Harvard Square) is about a mile away. ⊠ *1 Shepard St., Cambridge* ☎ *617/354–8980* ⊕ *www. chezhenri.com* ⊜ *AE, DC, MC, V* ⊘ *No lunch* Ⓜ *Harvard* ✛ *4:B1.*

$$$ ✕ **Craigie on Main.** Late in 2008 Chef Tony Maws shuttered the popu-
FRENCH lar Craigie Street Bistrot, reopening in this new eatery a few blocks away in Central Square. Though the premises are larger (with room for a full bar!), the space retains its charm, and Maws's passion for all things fresh, local, and organic hasn't wavered. He is in the kitchen every morning, prepping ingredients that most likely came from the Harvard Square farmers' market or another local purveyor. The menu changes daily, so options can range from a Spanish-style octopus to tender beef short ribs to pork done three ways. Sunday is Chef's Whim Night, meaning that after 9 pm you'll eat (and likely love) four to six courses of whatever Maws feels like cooking for a discounted price ($40 to $55). Brunch is served Sunday. ⊠ *853 Main. St., Cambridge* ☎ *617/497–5511* ⊕ *www.craigieonmain.com* ⊜ *AE, MC, V* ⊘ *Closed Mon.* Ⓜ *Central* ✛ *4:F5.*

$$ ✕ **Dante.** With one of the best patio views of the Charles River, Dante
MEDITERRANEAN almost resembles a seaside café on the Amalfi coast. Almost. Chef-owner Dante DeMagistris culls flavors from that region, and a few others, to present a seafood- and pasta-heavy menu with entrées that focus on hearty portions of protein like porcini-basted scallops and basil-roasted guinea hen. Try the chef's tasting menu for seven to nine courses that might include a number of specialties not on the daily menu. ⊠ *Royal Sonesta Hotel, 40 Edwin H. Land Blvd., Cambridge* ☎ *617/497–4200* ⊕ *www.restaurantdante.com* ⊜ *AE, D, MC, V* Ⓜ *Lechmere* ✛ *1:B3.*

10

CLOSE UP

Brain Food

As you wander through Cambridge it's safe to assume that almost every other person on the street attends a nearby institute of higher learning. (Forty percent of the city's population is between the ages of 18 and 29.) Luckily, although soaring Harvard Square rents have been the death knell for many quirky diners and coffee shops, a handful of places that cater to poor grad students continue to persevere.

Pinnochio's Pizza and Subs (⊠ 74 Winthrop St. ☎ 617/876–4897 ⊕ www.pinocchiospizza.net ✛ 4:A3) is a hole-in-the-wall that's been serving late-night pies to Harvard students for three decades. "Noch's" offers thick, Sicilian-style pizza for little more than two bucks a slice.

LA Burdick's (⊠ 52–D Brattle St. ☎ 617/491–4340 ⊕ www. burdickchocolate.com ✛ 4:A2), a Harvard Square chocolatier, is known for its unbelievably decadent hot chocolate and bite-size gourmet chocolate in the shape of mice (complete with almond ears). Founder Larry Burdick, a Boston native, spent years in France and Switzerland before founding his shop—and as you sit at one of the

small tables nibbling a macaroon or Linzer torte while watching the bustle along Harvard Square's cobblestone streets, you might forget what country you're in.

The funky and casual **Miracle of Science** (⊠ 321 Massachusetts Ave. ☎ 617/868–2866 ⊕ www. miracleofscience.us ✛ 4:F5) is a Central Square restaurant and bar that is chock-full of MIT neuroscientists and PhD students at leisure. And no wonder: If anything could drag them away from the lab, it's the Periodic Table of Elements–theme menu with chipotle-tinged turkey chili and several local beers on tap.

A self-described "shabby-chic deli and café," **Darwin's** (⊠ 148 Mt. Auburn St. ☎ 617/354–5233 ⊠ 1629 Cambridge St. ☎ 617/491–2999 ⊕ www. darwinsltd.com ✛ 3:H2) symbolizes both the bohemian Harvard Square of yore and its newer, more gentrified persona. With nearly 20 sandwiches that cost less than $8 (try the Longfellow, a delicious ham-apple-cheddar combo) plus very good coffee, locally baked breads, and free Wi-Fi, Darwin's is many a student's second home.

$
AMERICAN

✕**East Coast Grill and Raw Bar.** Owner-chef-author Chris Schlesinger built his national reputation on grilled foods and red-hot condiments. The Jamaican jerk and North Carolina pulled pork are still here, but this restaurant has made an extraordinary play to establish itself in the front ranks of fish restaurants. Spices and condiments are more restrained, and Schlesinger has compiled a wine list bold and flavorful enough to match the highly spiced food. The dining space is completely informal. A killer brunch (complete with cornbread-crusted French toast and a do-it-yourself Bloody Mary bar) is served on Sunday. ⊠ 1271 Cambridge St., Cambridge ☎ 617/491–6568 ⊕ www.eastcoastgrill.net ⊟ AE, D, MC, V ☉ No lunch Ⓜ Central ✛ 4:F2.

$
CAMBODIAN/
FRENCH

✕**Elephant Walk.** The chef of this popular Cambodian-French fusion house, Longtaine de Monteiro, learned to manage a Cambodian kitchen as the wife of a diplomat, and for a time ran a restaurant in Provence. Her daughter Nadsa now runs the kitchen. The common element in both cuisines (which are listed separately on the menu) is garlic, from appetizers such as *moules* (mussels) swimming in garlic-infused butter to superb Cambodian spring rolls, delicate salads, and a red curry of surpassingly fresh flavor. Vegetarians and diners suffering food allergies are easily accommodated. Equally important in this parking-challenged city: the restaurant has a large parking lot in the back (park anywhere at night; use "Elephant Walk" spaces during weekday lunch). ⊠ *2067 Massachusetts Ave., Cambridge* ☎ *617/492–6900* ⊕ *www.elephantwalk.com* ⊟ *AE, D, DC, MC, V* Ⓜ *Porter* ✢ *4:B1.*

$ ✕ **Full Moon.** Here's a happy reminder that dinner with children doesn't
AMERICAN have to mean hamburgers. Choices include child pleasers like home-
ⓒ made mac and cheese as well as grown-up entrées that include grilled sirloin with blue-cheese butter. Youngsters can spread out with plenty of designated play space and juice-filled sippy cups, while parents weigh the substantial menu and a well-paired wine list. Not that you have to bring a tot. Folks visiting sans child can ask for one of the grownups tables in the quiet, screened-off area near the front. ⊠ *344 Huron Ave., Cambridge* ☎ *617/354–6699* ⊕ *www.fullmoonrestaurant.com* ⌂ *Reservations not accepted* ⊟ *MC, V* Ⓜ *Harvard* ✢ *4:A1.*

$$ ✕ **Green Street.** The tables are small and the service is casual, but the
AMERICAN relatively inexpensive New England menu speaks to the young, artistic community that now claims the neighborhood. Locally caught bluefish with a tomato-basil vinaigrette is a highlight from the menu, which mostly features modern comfort fare. An emphasis on microbrews and cocktails (the latest owner is a whiz of a bartender) gives this restaurant a relaxed and neighborly bar-scene air. ⊠ *280 Green St., Cambridge* ☎ *617/876–1655* ⊕ *www.greenstreetgrill.com* ⊟ *AE, MC, V* ⊘ *No lunch* Ⓜ *Central* ✢ *4:E5.*

$$$ ✕ **Harvest.** The New England–inspired menu of up-to-date dishes by
AMERICAN Chef Mary Dumont (cooking-show enthusiasts will recognized her from *Iron Chef*) is hedged with traditional regional favorites made with locally sourced ingredients. Starters include the seasonal mussel soup laced with saffron; Pennsylvania duck breast and Berkshire pork loin are among the recommended main plates. The open kitchen makes some noise, but customers at the ever-popular bar don't seem to mind. Outdoor heaters and fireplaces beat back the elements and keep the lush outdoor patio warm and inviting for a surprisingly long stretch of the year. Brunch is served on Sunday. ⊠ *44 Brattle St., on walkway, Cambridge* ☎ *617/868–2255* ⊕ *www.harvestcambridge.com* ⊟ *AE, D, DC, MC, V* Ⓜ *Harvard* ✢ *4:A2.*

$ ✕ **The Helmand.** The area's first Afghan restaurant is named after
AFGHAN an Afghanistan province south of Kabul, but the fresh flowers and wood-burning oven make this Kendall Square spot seem more homey than exotic. Standouts include terrific *aushak* (ravioli stuffed with leeks), spiced tenderloin chapendaz, and the vegetarian baked pumpkin platter. ⊠ *143 1st St., Cambridge* ☎ *617/492–4646* ⊕ *www.helmandrestaurantcambridge.com* ⌂ *Reservations essential* ⊟ *AE, MC, V* ⊘ *No lunch* Ⓜ *Lechmere* ✢ *1:B4.*

10

¢–$ ✕ **Hi-Rise Bread Company.** The best
AMERICAN   sandwiches start with stellar bread.
☺   Here a range of breads are made
on-site, and sandwiches are given
odd names like Bill's Seoul Show
(chicken, bacon, and tarragon
mayo on corn bread). The service matches the noontime rush:
brusque and slightly harried. But
once you get through the line with
your daily soup and a Mahatma

Gloves (curried-chicken salad with cashews), you can join the neighborhood regulars at communal wooden tables and take in a noisy but
comforting slice of Cambridge life. ⊠ *208 Concord Ave., Cambridge*
☎ *617/876–8766* ⌂ *Reservations not accepted* ▭ *MC, V* Ⓜ *Harvard*
⊹ *4:A1.*

$$ ✕ **Hungry Mother.** You'll forget you're well above the Mason-Dixon line
SOUTHERN   when you enter this Kendall Square gem, where Virginia-born chef
Fodor'sChoice Barry Maiden whips up Southern comfort food with a hint of French
★   sophistication—and New England ingredients. From fried green toma-
toes to cornbread with sorghum butter, from Berkshire pork loin to
apple bread pudding, this cozy two-story bistro serves up decidedly
soul-warming fare. (And if you need an extra shot of warmth, the expert
bartenders create excellent house-mixed drinks, such as the No. 58, a
gin-grapefruit-Grand Marnier concoction.) ⊠ *233 Cardinal Medeiros
Ave., Kendall Square* ☎ *617/499–0090* ▭ *AE, MC, V* ☺ *Closed Mon.
No lunch* Ⓜ *Kendall/MIT* ⊹ *4:H4.*

$$–$$$ ✕ **Legal Sea Foods.** All the regional seafood classics, from famed New
SEAFOOD   England chowder to a sumptuous raw bar, can be found here in the
☺   Cambridge outpost of the Legal chain. Just as worthwhile are the more
modern takes: seafood stew with Indian spices, for example, and grilled
swordfish with mango salsa. ⊠ *5 Cambridge Center, Kendall Square*
☎ *617/864–3400* ⊕ *www.legalseafoods.com* ▭ *AE, D, DC, MC, V*
Ⓜ *Kendall/MIT* ⊹ *4:H5.*

¢–$ ✕ **Le's.** Vietnamese noodle soup called *pho* is the name of the game in
VIETNAMESE this quick-and-casual eatery (it's set inside the Garage, a small mall in
Harvard Square). At less than $10, it's a meal unto itself. Get it filled
with chicken, shrimp, or beef, steaming hot in a big bowl. Fresh salads
and stir-fries are offered as well. It's all notably fresh fare, and, even
better, it's healthy, without gloppy sauces, and many of the dishes are
steamed. Those approaching from JFK Street can access the restau-
rant through the main Garage entrance; just head all the way through
toward the Dunster Street side at the back. ⊠ *35 Dunster St., Cam-
bridge* ☎ *617/864–4100* ⊕ *www.lescambridge.com* ▭ *AE, MC, V*
Ⓜ *Harvard* ⊹ *4:B2.*

¢ ✕ **Mr. Bartley's Burger Cottage.** It may be perfect cuisine for the student
AMERICAN   metabolism: a huge variety of variously garnished thick burgers, deli-
☺   ciously crispy french fries (regular and sweet-potato), and onion rings.
There's also a competent veggie burger. The nonalcoholic "raspberry
lime rickey," made with fresh limes, raspberry juice, sweetener, and

soda water, is the must-try classic drink. Tiny tables in a crowded space make eavesdropping unavoidable. ⊠ *1246 Massachusetts Ave., Cambridge* ☎ *617/354–6559* ⊕ *www.bartleysburgers.com* ♤ *Reservations not accepted* ⊟ *No credit cards* ☉ *Closed Sun.* Ⓜ *Harvard* ♦ *4:B3.*

$$
MEDITERRANEAN
Fodor's Choice
★

✕ **Oleana.** Chef-owner Ana Sortun is one of the city's culinary treasures—and so is Oleana. Here flavors from all over the Eastern Mediterranean sing loud and clear, in the hot, crispy fried mussels starter and in the smoky eggplant puree beside tamarind-glazed beef. Lamb gets jacked up with Turkish spices, while the rabbit is accented by Moroccan-spiced almonds. In warm weather the back patio is a hidden piece of utopia—a homey garden that hits the perfect note of casual refinement. ⊠ *134 Hampshire St., Cambridge* ☎ *617/661–0505* ⊕ *www. oleanarestaurant.com* ♤ *Reservations essential* ⊟ *AE, MC, V* ☉ *No lunch* Ⓜ *Central* ♦ *4:F3.*

$$
MEDITERRANEAN

✕ **Rendezvous.** In 2005 chef Steve Johnson commandeered a defunct Burger King in Central Square and turned it into a Mediterranean spot that is seriously committed to locally grown ingredients. (Try the crispy roast chicken with sautéed farmers'-market veggies and herbs from his own rooftop garden.) This locovorism, along with a wine list that's updated weekly and specialty cocktails like the Nehru (saffron gin, lemon, and cardamom), makes Rendezvous appear always fresh and new. Exposed brick and a glass ceiling (which provides a great view of the garden above) add sophistication to the cheery yellow and orange interior. Sundays, the chef assembles a well-priced $38 three-course prix fixe menu. ⊠ *502 Massachusetts Ave., Central Square* ☎ *617/576–1900* ⊕ *www.rendezvouscentralsquare.com* ⊟ *AE, DC, MC, V* ☉ *No lunch* Ⓜ *Central Sq.* ♦ *4:E5.*

$$$-$$$$
ITALIAN

✕ **Rialto.** The posh dining room and its bar have drifted back to their Italian beginnings, with a few signature New England favorites, such as grilled local clams and fisherman's soup still among items to order. An updated menu encourages ordering the salads, pastas, and meats as appetizer, midcourse, and entrée, with each dish layered with deeper and richer flavors. Or try the no-fail favorites like Tuscan-style sirloin steak with portobello-and-arugula salad from chef Jody Adams, one of Boston's most admired kitchen wizards. ⊠ *Charles Hotel, 1 Bennett St., Harvard Sq., Cambridge* ☎ *617/661–5050* ⊕ *www.rialto-restaurant. com* ⊟ *AE, DC, MC, V* ☉ *No lunch* Ⓜ *Harvard* ♦ *4:A2.*

$-$$
INDIAN

✕ **Tamarind Bay.** This tiny, subterranean space is brick-lined and filled with enticing aromas—a cozy place to try dishes from all over India. The owners, longtime residents, decided to open a restaurant that truly represented their homeland cuisine, hence scallops marinated in yogurt and spices. Lamb chops *bhunna* masala are a sweet, spicy trio of chops served on a crescent-shape plate. A small selection of Indian wines is also available. ⊠ *75 Winthrop St., Cambridge* ☎ *617/491–4552* ⊕ *www.tamarind-bay.com* ⊟ *AE, D, MC, V* Ⓜ *Harvard* ♦ *4:B2.*

$
INDIAN

✕ **Tanjore.** The menu at this fully regional restaurant reaches from Sindh to Bengal, with some strength in the western provincial foods (Gujarat, Bombay) and their interesting sweet-hot flavors. The *Baigan Bhurta* is a platter of grilled, mashed eggplant; the rice dishes, chais, and breads are all excellent, and the lunchtime buffet is usually a quick in-and-out

10

affair. The spicing starts mild, so don't be afraid to order "medium." ⊠ *18 Eliot St., Cambridge* ☎ *617/868–1900* ⊕ *www.tanjoreharvardsq. com* ⊟ *AE, D, MC, V* Ⓜ *Harvard* ✛ *4:A3.*

$$$
CONTINENTAL

✕ **Upstairs on the Square.** In the middle of Harvard Square, this restaurant strikes just the right balance between funky and urbane, with pink linens and fringes tempering the dining room's old-boy look. The Monday Club Bar offers a more casual, yet still chic, spot to nosh. Entrées aren't too straitlaced either; you might try a lobster bouillabaisse or salmon with a divine mustard sauce. A thoughtfully chosen tasting menu includes a vegetarian option. Finish with the chocolate truffle parfait or vanilla fritters. ⊠ *91 Winthrop St., Cambridge* ☎ *617/864–1933* ⊕ *www.upstairsonthesquare.com* ⊟ *AE, DC, MC, V* Ⓜ *Harvard* ✛ *4:A2.*

$
AMERICAN

✕ **West Side Lounge.** "*Understated*" is the buzzword at this relaxed but suave bistro, where the food is as comfortable as the setting. A homey, rotating menu complements the room's earthy tones and cushy banquette seating. The crispy seasoned fries are a justified hit—they all but fly out of the kitchen—and the black-pepper mussels release an aromatic cloud of steam when they arrive. Couples on first dates and groups of regulars gather nightly for the well-priced specials and signature cocktails that change with the seasons. Brunch is served Sunday. ⊠ *1680 Massachusetts Ave., Cambridge* ☎ *617/441–5566* ⊕ *www. westsidelounge.com* ⊟ *AE, D, DC, MC, V* ☉ *No lunch* Ⓜ *Porter or Harvard* ✛ *4:B1.*

Boston Dining and Lodging Atlas

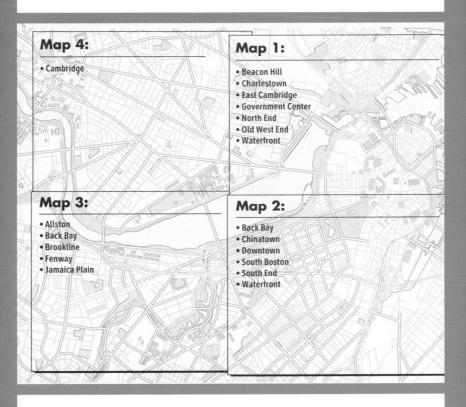

Map 4:
- Cambridge

Map 1:
- Beacon Hill
- Charlestown
- East Cambridge
- Government Center
- North End
- Old West End
- Waterfront

Map 3:
- Allston
- Back Bay
- Brookline
- Fenway
- Jamaica Plain

Map 2:
- Back Bay
- Chinatown
- Downtown
- South Boston
- South End
- Waterfront

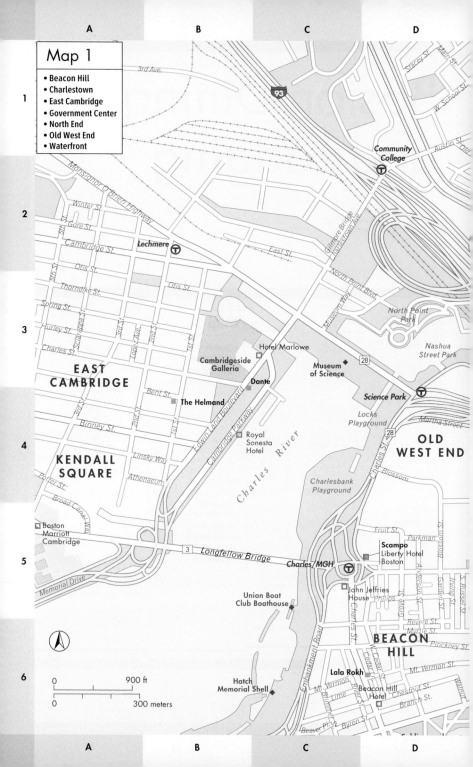

Map 1

- Beacon Hill
- Charlestown
- East Cambridge
- Government Center
- North End
- Old West End
- Waterfront

3rd Ave.

Monsignor O'Brien Highway

Winter St.

Gore St.

Cambridge St.

Otis St.

Thorndike St.

Spring St.

Hurley St.

Charles St.

Lechmere Ⓣ

East St.

Gilmore Bridge

Charlestown Ave.

Community College Ⓣ

Stacey St.

Main St.

W. School St.

Austin St.

North Point Blvd.

Museum Mall

North Point Park

Nashua Street Park

EAST CAMBRIDGE

Bent St.

Binney St.

KENDALL SQUARE

Linsky Way

Athenaeum

Porter St.

Broad Canal Way

Hotel Marlowe 🔲

Cambridgeside Galleria

Dante 🔲

The Helmand ■

Royal Sonesta Hotel 🔲

Cambridge Parkway

Land Boulevard

Museum of Science ◆

28

Science Park Ⓣ

Locks Playground

Martha Street

OLD WEST END

Charles St.

Blossom

Charlesbank Playground

28

Charles River

🔲 Boston Marriott Cambridge

Memorial Drive

3 Longfellow Bridge

Charles/MGH Ⓣ

Union Boat Club Boathouse 🔲

Fruit St.

Parkman

Scampo 🔲
Liberty Hotel Boston

John Jeffries House 🔲

Phillips

Anderson St.

Blossom St.

Irving St.

Garden St.

Russell St.

Revere St.

Myrtle St.

Pinckney St.

BEACON HILL

Lala Rokh ■

W. Cedar St.

Cedar

Mt. Vernon

Beacon Hill Hotel

Mt. Vernon St.

Chestnut St.

Branch St.

Lime

Embankment Road

Hatch Memorial Shell ◆

Beaver Pl.

Byron St.

🧭

0   900 ft
0   300 meters

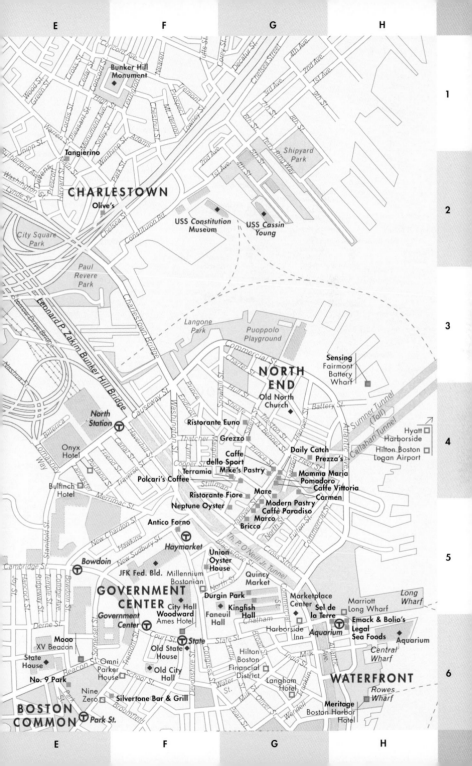

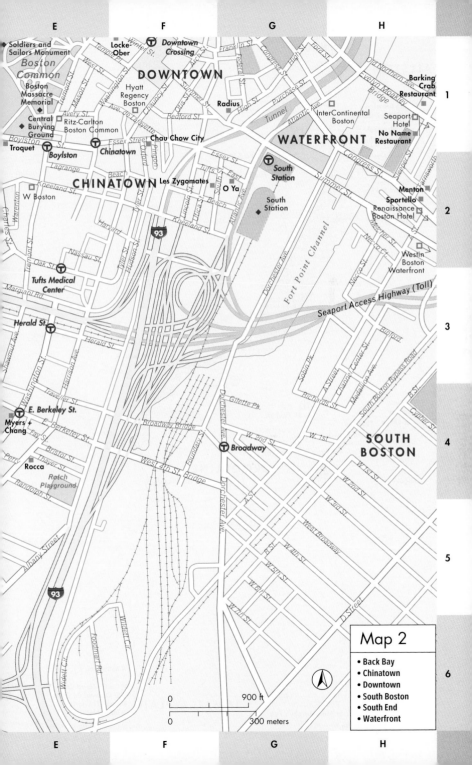

Map 2

- Back Bay
- Chinatown
- Downtown
- South Boston
- South End
- Waterfront

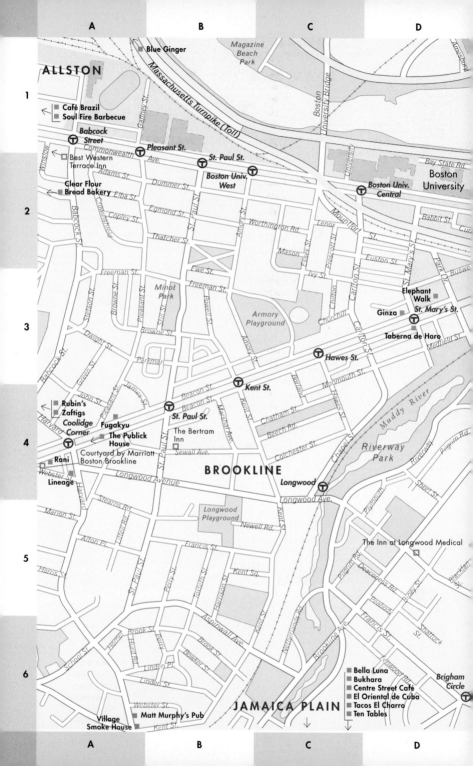

A · B · C · D

1
ALLSTON
Blue Ginger
Magazine Beach Park
Boston University Bridge
Café Brazil
Soul Fire Barbecue
Babcock Street
Commonwealth Ave.
Pleasant St.
St. Paul St.
Best Western Terrace Inn
Adams St.
Dummer St.
Boston Univ. West
University
Bay State Rd.
Boston University

2
Clear Flour Bread Bakery
Elba St.
Egmont St.
Copley St.
Thatcher St.
Amory St.
Worthington Rd.
Mason
Lenox
Ivy St.
Mountfort
St.
Euston St.
Prescott St.
Carlton St.
Boston Univ. Central
Babbit St.
Park Dr.
Buswell
Crowninshield
Pleasant St.

3
Freeman St.
Minot Park
Freeman St.
Powell St.
Armory Playground
Chilton
Churchill
Carlton St.
Elephant Walk
Ginza
St. Mary's St.
Taberna de Haro
Medfield St.
Stetson St.
Browne St.
Dwight St.
Browne St.
Parkman
Amory St.
Hawes St.
Monmouth St.

4
Rubin's
Zaftigs
Coolidge Corner
Fugakyu
The Publick House
Courtyard by Marriott Boston Brookline
Rani
Lineage
Webster St.
John St.
James St.
Green St.
Beacon St.
St. Paul St.
Beacon St.
Kent St.
Marshal Ave.
The Bertram Inn
Sewall Ave.
Chatham St.
Beech Rd.
Colchester St.
Chapel St.
Riverway Park
Muddy River
Pilgrim Rd.
Riverway
Longwood Avenue
BROOKLINE
Longwood
Longwood Ave.

5
Marion St.
Stearns Rd.
Alton Pl.
Harris St.
Francis St.
Longwood Playground
Newell Rd.
Kent Sq.
Kent St.
Plymouth
Pilgrim Rd.
Deaconess Rd.
Francis St.
Short St.
The Inn at Longwood Medical
Blackfan

6
School St.
Flower St.
Brook St.
Linden Pl.
Linden St.
Aspinwall Ave.
Bowker St.
Brook St.
Kent St.
Netherlands Rd.
Brookline Ave.
Peabody
Pearl
Shattuck
Village Smoke House
Matt Murphy's Pub
Webster St.
Kent St.
JAMAICA PLAIN
Bella Luna
Bukhara
Centre Street Café
El Oriental de Cuba
Tacos El Charro
Ten Tables
Brigham Circle
Francis St.
Tremont

A · B · C · D

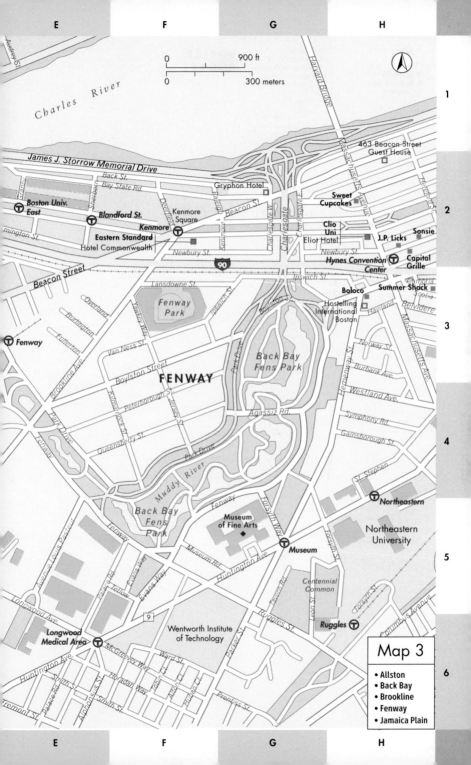

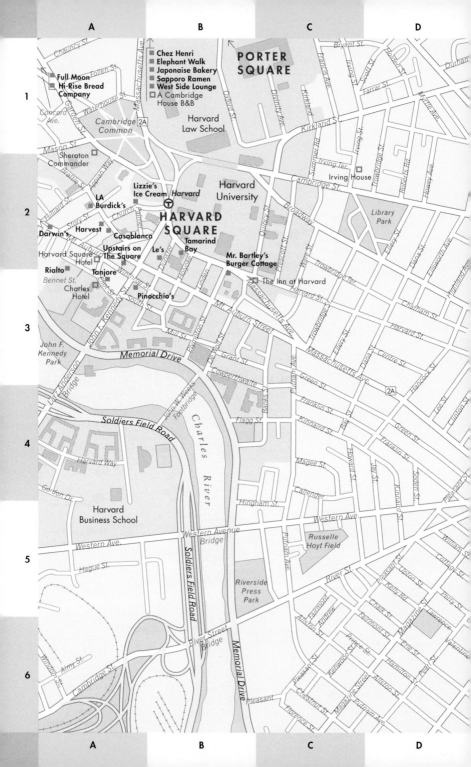

A   **B**   **C**   **D**

Chauncy St.

Full Moon
Hi-Rise Bread
Company

■ Chez Henri
■ Elephant Walk
■ Japonaise Bakery
■ Sapporo Ramen
■ West Side Lounge
□ A Cambridge
   House B&B

PORTER
SQUARE

Bryant St.

Follen St.

Massachusetts Ave.

Concord Ave.

Garden St.

Waterhouse St.

1

Cambridge
Common

2A

Harvard
Law School

Oxford St.

Kirkland St.

Francis Ave.

Scott St.

Museum

Farrar St.

Irving St.

Durham

Mason St.

Sheraton
Commander

Appian Way

Irving Ter.

Irving House

Roberts Rd.

Lowey Rd.

Myrtle Ave.

2

Brattle St.

LA
Burdick's

Lizzie's
Ice Cream

Harvard

Harvard
University

Cambridge St.

Broadway

Library
Park

Story St.

Harvest

Church St.

HARVARD
SQUARE

Darwin's

Casablanca

Harvard Square
Hotel

Upstairs on
The Square

Le's

Tamarind
Bay

Dunster St.

Holyoke

Mt. Auburn Street

Mr. Bartley's
Burger Cottage

Massachusetts Ave.

Trowbridge St.

Dana St.

Ellsworth Ave.

Rialto

Tanjore

Bennet St.

Charles
Hotel

Pinocchio's

John F. Kennedy St.

Linden

Mill St.

Grant St.

The Inn at Harvard

Harvard St.

Hilliard St.

Dana St.

Centre St.

Chatham St.

Harvard St.

Highland Ave.

3

John F.
Kennedy
Park

Memorial Drive

Cowperthwaite

Banks St.

Massachusetts Ave.

Green St.

2A

Hancock St.

Lee St.

Clinton St.

Pleasant St.

Lef Anderson Bridge

Soldiers Field Road

John W. Weeks Footbridge

Flagg St.

Franklin St.

Kinnaird St.

Green St.

Franklin St.

Howard St.

Jay St.

Soden St.

Kinnaird St.

4

Harvard Way

Charles River

Magee St.

Callender

Western Ave.

William

Gordon Dr.

Harvard
Business School

Western Ave.

Western Avenue
Bridge

Hingham St.

Putnam Ave.

Russelle
Hoyt Field

Cottage St.

Percy St.

5

Hague St.

Soldiers Field Road

River St.

Riverside
Press Park

River St.

Fairmont St.

Andrew

Pleasant St.

Upton St.

Kelly Rd.

Chalk St.

Magazine St.

Lawrence

Erie St.

Valentine

Almy St.

Cambridge St.

River Street
Bridge

Memorial Drive

Pleasant St.

Auburn St.

Fairmont St.

Kenwood St.

Pierce St.

Hamilton St.

Chestnut St.

Florence St.

Magazine Street

Putnam Ave.

Pearl

6

A   **B**   **C**   **D**

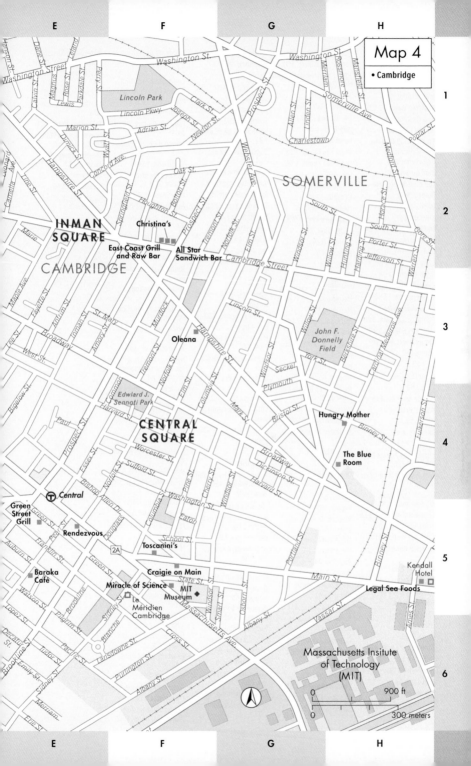

Map 4

• Cambridge

E   F   G   H

Washington Street

Washington St.

Washington St.

Lincoln Park

Lincoln Pkwy.

Clark St.

1

Lewis

Rose St.

Paradise R.

Perry St.

Joseph St.

Newton St.

Marion St.

Adrian St.

Charlestown

SOMERVILLE

2

Hampshire St.

Concord Ave.

Oak St.

Houghton St.

Webster Ave.

Prospect St.

INMAN
SQUARE

Christina's

CAMBRIDGE

East Coast Grill
and Raw Bar

All Star
Sandwich Bar

Tremont St.

Cambridge Street

South St.

Porter St.

Jefferson St.

3

Broadway

St. Mary

Murdock St.

Oleana

Hampshire St.

Lincoln St.

Windsor St.

Secket

Plymouth

John F.
Donnelly
Field

York St.

Berkshire St.

4

Edward J.
Sennott Park

Harvard St.

CENTRAL
SQUARE

Worcester St.

Suffold St.

Pine St.

Cherry St.

Windsor St.

Harvard St.

Broadway

Dickinson St.

Bristol St.

Hungry Mother

The Blue
Room

Binney St.

5

Green
Street
Grill

Central

Rendezvous

2A

Toscanini's

Craigie on Main

Miracle of Science

Baraka
Café

Le
Méridien
Cambridge

Bishop Allen Dr.

Washington St.

Columbia St.

Eaton

School St.

Portland St.

MIT
Museum

Main St.

Kendall
Hotel

Legal Sea Foods

6

Massachusetts Insitute
of Technology
(MIT)

Albany St.

Vassar St.

0   900 ft

0   300 meters

E   F   G   H

Where to Stay

WORD OF MOUTH

"I spent 4 days last April, and got a great hotel, Nine Zero. If I were to go back to Boston, I would pay for the location at this hotel. It was a great central location for all things Boston. The Freedom trail ran right outside, and it was 1½ blocks to the subway station and Boston Common."

—SEW

Updated
by Bethany
Cassin
Beckerlegge

At one time, great lodging was scarce in Boston. If you were a persnickety blueblood in town to visit relatives, you checked into the Charles or the old Ritz on Newbury. If you were a parent in town to see your kid graduate from one of the city's many universities, you suffered through a stay at a run-down chain. And if you were a young couple in town for a little romance, well, you could just forget it. A dearth of suitable rooms practically defined us. Oh, how things have changed.

About five years ago Boston finally got wise to modernization, and a rush of new construction took the local hotel scene by storm. Sleek, boutique accommodations began inviting guests to Cambridge and Downtown, areas once relegated to alumni and business traveler sets. New, mega-luxury lodgings like the Mandarin Oriental and the Taj (the latter, in that old Ritz spot) infiltrated posh Back Bay, while high-end, hipster-friendly spots like the W and Ames are drawing visitors to up-and-coming 'hoods. Even mostly residential areas like the South End now draw discerning boarders, thanks to the revamped Chandler and the nearby Inn@St. Botolph.

Speaking of revamped, it seems that nearly every hotel in town just got a face-lift. From spruced up decor (good-bye, grandma's bedspread; hello, puffy white duvets) to hopping restaurant-bars to new spas and fitness centers, Boston's lodgings are feeling the competitive heat and acting accordingly. You don't just get a room anymore—you get an experience.

Of course, as in any industry, the recession hit a plethora of new and old properties hard. While business is picking up, many lodgings have slashed their rates—and introduced stellar weekend deals—so don't be afraid to aim four-star if you think you can only afford three.

WHERE SHOULD I STAY?

	Neighborhood Vibe	Pros	Cons
Beacon Hill and Boston Common	Old brick and stone buildings host luxe boutique hotels and B&Bs on the hill or along busy, preppy Charles Street; some skyscraper lodging right on Boston Common.	Safe, quaint area with lamp-lit streets; chain-free upscale shopping and dining; outdoor fun abounds in the park; good T access.	Street parking is extremely hard to come by; not budget friendly; close to noisy hospital; hills can be steep.
Downtown Boston	The city's financial center hums with activity and busy hotels during the week; new boutique lodging is moving in to compete with the big-box chains.	Excellent area for business travelers; frequent low weekend rates; good T and bus access; walking distance to Theater District and some museums.	All but dead at night; expensive garage parking during the day; Downtown Crossing is mobbed at lunchtime and on weekends; poorly marked streets.
The Back Bay	High-priced hotels in the city's poshest neighborhood, home to shops, restaurants, bars, spas, and salons. Commonwealth Avenue is lined with historic mansions.	Easy, central location; safe, beautiful area to walk around at night; ample T access; excellent people-watching.	Rooms, shopping, and eating can be ridiculously expensive; Newbury Street is overcrowded with tourists on weekends.
The South End	Small, funky lodgings in a hip and happening (and gay-friendly) area packed with awesome independent restaurants and shops.	The city's best dining scene; easy T and bus access; myriad parks; walking distance from the Back Bay and Downtown; safe along the main avenues at night.	Some bordering blocks turn seedy after dusk; difficult street parking (and few garages); only a handful of hotel options.
The Fenway and Kenmore Square	A sampling of large and small hotels and inns, plus two hostels; the area is a mix of students, young professionals, and die-hard Sox fans.	Close to Fenway Park (home of the Red Sox); up-and-coming dining scene; less expensive than most 'hoods; accessible by T.	Impossible street parking on game days (and pricey garages); expect big crowds for concerts and sporting events; some bars are loud and tacky.
Boston Outskirts	Mostly mid-size chain hotels in student neighborhoods full of coffee shops, convenience stores, and rowdy college bars; except for sweet inns in lovely Brookline.	Serviceable airport lodging near Logan; cheap rates on rooms in Brighton and parts of Brookline; easier driving than downtown.	No overnight street parking in Brookline; far from Boston center, museums, shopping, and the river; some areas get dicey at night; T rides into the city proper can take an hour.
Cambridge	A mix of grand and small hotels pepper the hip, multi-university neighborhood; expect loads of young freethinkers and efficient (if laid-back) service.	Hallowed academia; verdant squares; good low- and high-cost eating and lodging; excellent neighborhood restaurants; few chain anythings.	Spotty T access; less of a city feel; a few areas can be quiet and slightly dodgy at night; lots of one-way streets make driving difficult.

WHERE TO STAY PLANNER

Lodging Strategy

Where should we stay? With so many new and improved Boston hotels, it may seem like a daunting question. But fret not—our expert writers and editors have done most of the legwork. The selections here represent the best this city has to offer—from the best affordable picks to the sleekest designer hotels. Scan "Best Bets" on the following pages for top recommendations by price and experience. Or find a review quickly in the listings—search by neighborhood, then alphabetically. Happy hunting!

In This Chapter

Need a Reservation?

Commencement weekends in May and June book months in advance; prices can be triple the off-season rate, with minimum stays of two to four nights. Leaf-peepers arrive in early October, and fall conventions bring waves of business travelers, especially in the Seaport District.

Using the Maps

Throughout the chapter, you'll see mapping symbols and coordinates (⊕ 3:F2) after property names or reviews. To locate the property on a map, turn to the Boston Dining and Lodging Atlas at the end of the Where to Eat chapter. The first number after the ⊕ symbol indicates the map number. Following that is the property's coordinate on the map grid.

Prices and Price Chart

The new hotel tax in Boston will add 14.95% to your bill; some hotels also tack on energy, service, or occupancy surcharges. Though it's not an absolute necessity, many visitors prefer to bring a car, and parking is another expense to consider. Almost all lodgings have parking, and most charge for the privilege—anywhere from $15 per day for self-garaging to $35 for valet. When looking for a hotel, don't write off the pricier establishments immediately. Price categories are determined by "rack rates"—the list price of a hotel room, which is usually discounted. Specials abound, particularly downtown on weekends. With so many new rooms in Boston, pricing is very competitive, so always check out the hotel Web site in advance for current special offers.

WHAT IT COSTS FOR HOTELS					
	¢	$	$$	$$$	$$$$
Hotel	under $100	$100–$199	$200–$299	$300–$399	over $400

Prices are for two people in a standard double room in high season, excluding 14.45% tax and service charges.

HOTEL REVIEWS

Listed alphabetically within neighborhoods.

11

BOSTON

BEACON HILL AND BOSTON COMMON

$$$ **Beacon Hill Hotel & Bistro.** Looking for a home away from home? Or, rather, a full-service version of home where you hardly have to lift a finger (unless it's to dial room service)? Housed in two meticulously renovated 19th-century brick town houses, this intimate Charles Street hotel is within walking distance of the Public Garden, Back Bay, Government Center, and the river Esplanade. Minimalist-style rooms are individually decorated with soft neutral colors and plush bed linens; each has plenty of natural light thanks to large windows overlooking city streets. There's a petite rooftop deck for lounging and a popular street-side bistro that's open for breakfast, lunch, and dinner. **Pros:** free Wi-Fi; many nearby shops and restaurants; chef Matt Molloy's decadent Sunday brunch at the ground-floor bistro. **Cons:** neighborhood parking is nonexistent; the rooms are somewhat small. **TripAdvisor:** "perfect retreat," "great location," "cozy, quaint." ✉ *25 Charles St., Beacon Hill* ☎ *617/723–7575* ⊕ *www.beaconhillhotel.com* ↪ *12 rooms, 1 suite* ⚭ *In-room: Wi-Fi. In-hotel: restaurant, bar* ⚭ *Breakfast* Ⓜ *Arlington, Charles/MGH* ✛ *1:D6.*

$$ **John Jeffries House.** If there's one thing all Bostonians can agree on, it's that driving in the city should be avoided at all costs. So savvy travelers should know to find lodging near the T, Boston's metro system. Right next to the Charles/MGH stop, the John Jeffries isn't only easily accessible, it's affordable—a veritable home run in this city. The turn-of-the-20th-century building, across from Massachusetts General Hospital, was once a housing facility for nurses. Now it's a four-story inn with a Federal-style double parlor that serves afternoon tea or coffee. Rooms are full of handsome upholstered pieces; nearly all have kitchenettes. Triple-glazed windows block noise from the busy Charles Circle, and many rooms have river views. Nearby Charles Street is home to lovely cafés, specialty stores, and antiques shops. **Pros:** great Beacon Hill location; free Wi-Fi; good value. **Cons:** the busy (and noisy) hospital across the street; no spa or gym facilities. **TripAdvisor:** "great value," "helpful staff," "very comfortable." ✉ *14 David G. Mugar Way, Beacon Hill* ☎ *617/367–1866* ⊟ *617/742-0313* ⊕ *www.johnjeffrieshouse.com* ↪ *23 rooms, 23 suites* ⚭ *In-room: kitchen, Wi-Fi. In-hotel: parking* ⚭ *Breakfast* Ⓜ *Charles/MGH* ✛ *1:C5.*

$$$$ **Liberty Hotel Boston.** When it opened in late 2007, the buzz around the Liberty was deafening. Bankers, tech geeks, foreign playboys, and fashionistas all scrambled to call it their own, and after a few months the hotel felt more like a nightclub than a retreat. A few years later, the hype has thankfully died down. Yes, scenesters still hit the reborn Charles Street Jail's cheekily named bar and restaurant, Alibi and Clink, and its outstanding Italian-Mediterranean restaurant, Scampo, but the focus is more or less on guests. Rooms are either in the original granite building or an adjacent 16-story modern tower; both sets carry a jailhouse chic aesthetic, albeit one with luxe linens, Wi-Fi, and views of the Charles River. Some Fodorites complain that quarters in the old

Fodor's Choice
★

BEST BETS FOR BOSTON LODGING

Fodor's offers a selective listing of quality lodging experiences in every price range, from the city's best budget beds to its most sophisticated luxury hotels. Here we've compiled our top recommendations by price and experience. The very best properties—in other words, those that provide a particularly remarkable experience in their price range—are designated in the listings with the Fodor's Choice logo.

Fodor's Choice ★

Boston Harbor Hotel at Rowes Wharf, p. 205
Charles Hotel, p. 229
Charlesmark Hotel, p. 214
Eliot Hotel, p. 217
Fairmont Copley Plaza, p. 217
Hotel Commonwealth, p. 224
Inn@St. Botolph, p. 220
Liberty Hotel Boston, p. 201
Nine Zero, p. 209

By Price

¢

463 Beacon Street Guest House, p. 213
Best Western Terrace Inn, p. 227

$

Chandler Inn, p. 222

Charlesmark Hotel, p. 214
Gryphon House, p. 223
John Jeffries House, p. 201

$$

Copley Square Hotel, p. 215
Encore, p. 223
Inn @ St. Botolph, p. 220
Renaissance Boston Waterfront Hotel, p. 210

$$$

Charles Hotel, p. 229
Eliot Hotel, p. 217
Fairmont Copley Plaza, p. 217
Hotel Commonwealth, p. 224
Le Meridien Cambridge, p. 231
Liberty Hotel Boston, p. 201
Seaport Hotel, p. 211

$$$$

Boston Harbor Hotel at Rowes Wharf, p. 205
Colonnade Hotel, p. 215
Mandarin Oriental Boston, p. 220
Nine Zero, p. 209
XV Beacon, p. 204

By Experience

BEST GYM

InterContinental, p. 207
Ritz-Carlton Boston Common, p. 211
Seaport Hotel, p. 211

BEST HOTEL BAR

Charles Hotel, p. 229
Copley Square Hotel, p. 215
Hotel Commonwealth, p. 224
InterContinental, p. 207
Langham Hotel, p. 208
Liberty Hotel, p. 201

BEST SERVICE

Boston Harbor Hotel, p. 205
Boston Park Plaza Hotel, p. 214
Four Seasons, p. 218
Mandarin Oriental Boston, p. 220

BEST HIP HOTELS

Ames Hotel, p. 204
Charlesmark Hotel, p. 214
Colonnade Hotel, p. 215
Copley Square Hotel, p. 215
Hotel Marlowe, p. 230
Inn@St. Botolph, p. 220
Nine Zero, p. 209
W Boston, p. 212

BEST GRAND DAMES

Boston Harbor Hotel at Rowes Wharf, p. 205
Fairmont Copley Plaza, p. 217
Omni Parker House, p. 210
Park Plaza Hotel & Towers, p. 214
Taj Boston Hotel, p. 222

BEST DESIGN

Ames Hotel, p. 204
Eliot Hotel, p. 217
Le Meridien Cambridge, p. 231
Liberty Hotel, p. 201
W Boston, p. 212

The Liberty Hotel Boston

Boston Harbor Hotel at Rowes Wharf

section reverberate with noise from Alibi well into the night, but others know that the lively environs are just part of the experience. All parties agree that few places in town can rival the hotel's soaring lobby—ringed by several layers of revamped metal catwalks—for a glass of bubbly on plush leather couches. **Pros:** Scampo's mouthwatering house-made mozzarella bar; bustling nightlife; proximity to the river and Beacon Hill. **Cons:** loud in-house nightlife; long waits at bars and restaurants. **TripAdvisor:** "view of the Charles and the Back Bay is spectacular," "bathroom was huge with a separate tub and walk-in shower," "easy access to the T." ⊠ *215 Charles St., Beacon Hill* ☎ *617/224–4000* 🖨 *617/224–4001* ⊕ *www.libertyhotel.com* ⤵ *290 rooms, 10 suites* ⚴ *In-room: safe, Wi-Fi. In-hotel: restaurant, bar, gym, parking, some pets allowed* ⦾ *No meals* Ⓜ *Charles/MGH* ✛ *1:D5.*

$$$$ ⛫ **XV Beacon.** Though its 1903 beaux arts exterior remains the same—a study in understated class and elegance—one of the city's first small luxury hotels just got an internal face-lift. The much-needed renovation ushered in new carpeting, paint, and 42-inch TVs in all guest rooms, as well as a completely revamped fitness center (think state-of-the-art cardio machines and free weights). The tiny lobby is all black mahogany with bold splashes of red, brightened with recessed lighting and abstract art. The refreshed rooms are done up in soothing, neutral shades of espresso, taupe, and cream, and each has a gas fireplace and surround-sound stereo. ■ **TIP➜ If your stay coincides with the July 4 Harborfest celebration, make your way to the hotel's roof deck (open from Memorial Day through Labor Day) for unparalleled fireworks viewing.** **Pros:** in-room massages; chef Jamie Mammano's steak house, Mooo; for a fee, pets get their own pampering and sitting programs. **Cons:** some rooms are very small; mattresses are just average; can be very expensive on weekends during peak months (May, June, September, October). **TripAdvisor:** "bathrobes are thick and soft," "customer service is the best," "great workout room, which overlooks the roof deck." ⊠ *15 Beacon St., Beacon Hill* ☎ *617/670–1500, 877/982–3226* ⊕ *www.xvbeacon.com* ⤵ *62 rooms* ⚴ *In-room: safe, Wi-Fi. In-hotel: restaurant, bar, gym, parking, some pets allowed* ⦾ *No meals* Ⓜ *Government Center, Park St.* ✛ *1:E6.*

DOWNTOWN BOSTON

$$$ ⛫ **Ames Hotel.** The newest player on the Boston scene, the Ames opened to quiet fanfare in November 2009. Run by the hip Morgans Hotel Group (think the Delano and Shore Club in Miami), the 114-room downtown spot is all New England modernity. Sound like an oxymoron? It's not: forgoing the region's typical brocade and earth-tone interiors for something a bit more sleek, über-designer David Rockwell infused the rooms with sink-into white bedding, white marble, and light oak floors, iPod docks, and rain showerheads. Don't worry purists, he also nodded to the 19th-century building's past with a sprinkling of Federal-style furniture. There are Korres products in the bathroom (perched on a white sink, natch) and plasma HDTVs in the bedrooms; and for the visiting family, a one-bedroom apartment on the ninth floor. Downstairs are a fitness center and Woodward, the property's "modern-day tavern." **Pros:** very cool design; cushy beds; limo service. **Cons:** far from South End and Back Bay shopping. **TripAdvisor:** "excellent

customer service," "beautiful lobby and fitness center," "super comfy beds." ✉ *1 Court St., Downtown* ☎ *617/979–8100, 800/697–1791* ⊕ *www.ameshotel.com* ➳ *114 rooms* ♿ *In-room: Wi-Fi. In-hotel: restaurant, bar, laundry facilities, parking* ❘◯❘ *No meals* Ⓜ *State St.* ✛ *1:F6.*

$$$$ 🏨 **Boston Harbor Hotel at Rowes Wharf.** Boston has plenty of iconic land-
Fodor's Choice marks—the "salt and pepper" bridge, Fenway Park, the Public Garden
★ ducklings. But none are as synonymous with über-hospitality as the Boston Harbor Hotel's 80-foot-tall outdoor archway and rotunda. The splurge-worthiness continues inside, thanks to smaller marble arches, framed antique maps, and an ample placement of fresh flowers. Marble bathrooms, custom-made desks, Frette linens, flat-panel TVs, and laptop-size safes give the guestrooms a leg up on other city lodgings. And amenities abound—there are even complimentary daily shoe shines. The hotel's older, well-heeled clientele has been coming here for ages, and the city and Boston harbor views just keep getting better. The excellent on-site restaurant, Meritage, offers a unique menu that pairs small plates with appropriate vintages, all under light fixtures that mimic a starry sky. Eat up and worry about working it off later—the health club will lend you athletic gear if you forget yours. **Pros:** high-quality Meritage and Sea Grille restaurants; easy walk to Faneuil Hall; water shuttle to Logan Airport. **Cons:** pricey; the spa gets booked up early; less convenient to the Back Bay and South End. **TripAdvisor:** "spacious well-appointed room," "staff are very attentive, friendly," "beautiful views." ✉ *70 Rowes Wharf, Downtown/Waterfront* ☎ *617/439–7000, 800/752–7077* ⊕ *www.bhh.com* ➳ *204 rooms, 26 suites* ♿ *In-room: safe, Wi-Fi. In-hotel: restaurant, bar, pool, gym, spa, parking, some pets allowed* ❘◯❘ *No meals* Ⓜ *Aquarium, South Station* ✛ *1:H6.*

$$ 🏨 **Bulfinch Hotel.** The crisp, contemporary look of this boutique hotel is modern simplicity at its best. Steps from the TD Garden (forever known as the Boston Garden) and an easy walk from Government Center, Faneuil Hall, and the North End, the nine-floor, 79-room property is a great value—if you don't mind tiny accommodations. The miniature, minimalist yellow-and-white rooms have walnut furnishings, gunmetal light fixtures, marble-tiled baths, and high-end mattresses, plus flat-screen TVs, CD players, and work desks. Cramped or not, the Bulfinch is a welcome oasis away from the cacophony of concert- and sporting-event crowds. **Pros:** great group rates; free Internet; close to North Station and the T. **Cons:** small rooms and lobby; staff can be indifferent; past guests have complained about spotty cleaning. **TripAdvisor:** "front desk staff was helpful, friendly and efficient," "rooms are small," "easy walking distance to the wharf, downtown, Little Italy." ✉ *107 Merrimac St., Downtown* ☎ *617/624–0202, 877/267–1776* 🖷 *617/624-0211* ⊕ *www.bulfinchhotel.com* ➳ *71 rooms, 8 suites* ♿ *In-room: Internet. In-hotel: restaurant, bar, gym, parking, some pets allowed* ❘◯❘ *No meals* Ⓜ *North Station* ✛ *1:E4.*

$$$$ 🏨 **Fairmont Battery Wharf.** One of the growing number of lodgings
� clustered along Boston's ever-expanding Harborwalk—a pretty pedestrian path that runs from Charlestown to Dorchester—this Fairmont looks more like a gated community than a chain hotel. The four guest and residence buildings are accessible by water taxi ($10 from Logan

Airport); inside, savvy decorators resisted the obvious nautical theme and went for a "manly modern" look. That means lots of polished nickel, maple, and granite, with sparkling contemporary glass sculpture by artist Nikolas Weinstein. Rooms offer all the good stuff you'd expect at this price point, including marble baths, flat-screen TVs, ergonomic chairs, and high-tech coffeemakers. The fine-dining restaurant, Sensing, is run by Michelin-starred chef Guy Martin. Sensing's outdoor patio has the potential to morph into a summertime hot spot, something badly needed on the waterfront dining scene. Exhale, an upscale spa, opened a 13,000-square-foot facility directly adjacent to the hotel in 2011. **Pros:** great water views; access to Harborwalk; close to the North End. **Cons:** far from Newbury Street and South End shopping; development lacks neighborhood feel; some "unobstructed" water views are in fact partially obstructed; 15–20 minute walk to nearest T stations. **TripAdvisor:** "room service was brilliant and reasonable," "location was great, close to the huge number of Italian restaurants," "comfortable bed, nice desk area." ⊠ *3 Battery Wharf, Downtown* ☎ *617/994–9000, 800/257–7544* 🖷 *617/994–9092* ⊕ *www.fairmont. com/batterywharf* 🛏 *120 rooms, 30 suites* ♿ *In-room: safe, Wi-Fi. In-hotel: restaurant, bar, gym, parking, some pets allowed* Ⓜ *Haymarket, North Station* ✦ *1:H4.*

$$$ 🖼 **Harborside Inn.** Not quite as hip as its sister property the Charlesmark, the Harborside nonetheless carries a certain charm. And by charm, we mean rates considerably lower than most Waterfront hotels. That's welcome news to business travelers and budget-conscious thirtysomethings who parade through the modern marine-minimalist lobby and rooms decorated with shipwreck prints, exposed brick walls, hardwood floors, Federal-style furnishings, and teak accents. Many of the snug, variously shaped rooms (no two are alike) have windows overlooking the small, open lobby, which extends eight stories up to the roof. Amenities include flat-screen TVs and complimentary Wi-Fi; Faneuil Hall, Quincy Market, and the North End are all short walks away. ■ **TIP→** For a great view, request a room overlooking the city; for a quieter stay, book a room that faces the interior atrium. **Pros:** free Wi-Fi; rare value for the location; close to Quincy Market and the New England Aquarium; nearby water taxi. **Cons:** neighboring nightclubs can be noisy; the area might be too touristy for some leisure travelers. **TripAdvisor:** "rooms were small but clean," "minimum of natural light," "subway stop at your front door." ⊠ *185 State St., Downtown/Waterfront* ☎ *617/723–7500, 888/723–7565* 🖷 ⊕ *www.harborsideinnboston.com* 🛏 *98 rooms, 2 suites* ♿ *In-room: safe, Wi-Fi* ❙◯❙ *No meals* Ⓜ *Aquarium* ✦ *1:G6.*

$$$ 🖼 **Hilton Boston Financial District.** If you're looking for comfortable downtown lodging, you'll find it at this upscale business hotel. A 2008, $10-million renovation refreshed the inside of the 1928 building, the first art deco structure and first skyscraper in the city. Inside, the lobby's mahogany paneling and soft gold lighting give the whole outfit an old-school Mad Men vibe. The guest rooms are relatively spacious, with high ceilings and crown moldings; some overlook the waterfront. (For extra legroom, ask for a room at the end of the hallway.) Comforting touches include terrycloth robes and feather pillows. Night owls can

take advantage of the 24-hour health club and business center. Readers praise the efficient, professional staff. **Pros:** well maintained; clean and quiet; ideal for business travelers with work downtown. **Cons:** $15 daily Wi-Fi fee; a somewhat corporate vibe. **TripAdvisor:** "would recommend to friends and family," "bed was extremely comfortable," "room and facilities were very clean and well maintained." ⊠ *89 Broad St., Downtown* ☎ *617/556–0006* 🖷 *617/556–0053* ⊕ *www.hilton.com* ↩ *362 rooms, 66 suites* ♿ *In-room: safe, Wi-Fi. In-hotel: restaurant, bar, gym, parking, some pets allowed* 🍽 *No meals* Ⓜ *State* ✛ *1:G6.*

$$$ 🖵 **Hyatt Regency Boston.** Picturesque, Downtown Crossing is not. Packed with every conceivable kind of discount store and street vendor, the area hums with low- and high-end activity all week. In the midst of all the action is the 22-story Hyatt Regency Boston. Walk out of the crowds and into the cool marble lobby decorated with dark-wood furnishing and geometric-pattern rugs. Take an elevator ride upstairs to a guest room equipped with an iPod dock, Nintendo 64, pillowtop mattress, and understated earth-colored furnishings. Or sweat the day away in the 24-hour fitness center. Smart travelers call ahead for good deals on theater or shopping packages. Bonus: the hotel is fairly green— among other things, it composts leftover food and uses energy-efficient lighting, including motion-detector light switches. **Pros:** good package deals; saunas and whirlpools; good for business travelers. **Cons:** views of office buildings from guest rooms; few chairs around indoor pool; thin walls. **TripAdvisor:** "hotel was clean and elegant," "rooms were comfortable, if small," "smart, good service." ⊠ *1 Ave. de Lafayette, Downtown Crossing/Chinatown* ☎ *617/912–1234, 800/233–1234* ⊕ *www.regencyboston.hyatt.com* ↩ *498 rooms, 26 suites* ♿ *In-room: safe, Wi-Fi. In-hotel: restaurant, bar, pool, gym, spa, parking, some pets allowed* 🍽 *No meals* Ⓜ *Chinatown, Downtown Crossing* ✛ *2:F1.*

$$$$ 🖵 **InterContinental Boston.** Call it the anti-boutique hotel. The 424-room InterContinental, facing both the harbor and the Rose Kennedy Greenway, consists of two opulent, 22-story towers wrapped in blue glass. In a nod to the city's history, the skyscrapers are the height of old ships' masts (and are curved like sails), and the pewter bar at in-house boite RumBa would surely delight metalsmith Paul Revere. The lobby gleams with Italian marble and leather, and hallways are lined with Texan limestone, lending the large space a sleek, upscale aesthetic. Upstairs, guest rooms are wired with the latest technology, and have flat-screen TVs and spacious bathrooms done in mosaic tile and granite, with separate tubs and showers. Other draws are the 6,600-square-foot spa and health club and a pool that overlooks Atlantic Avenue and the Greenway. Sushi-Teq, the hotel's strange-but-good sushi-tequila restaurant, regularly draws lively crowds, while movers and shakers from Financial District banking, real estate, and law firms make merry after work at the aforementioned RumBa. The hotel's brasserie, Miel, serves organic Provençal cuisine. **Pros:** upper-floor rooms have great views; cool bathrooms; close to Financial District and South Station. **Cons:** huge function rooms mean lots of conventioneers; far from Newbury Street and South End shopping; guests say the soundproofing could be better. **TripAdvisor:** "wonderful dining in lobby area," "concierge was friendly

and helpful with advice," "fabulous staff and services." ✉ *510 Atlantic Ave., Downtown/Waterfront* ☎ *617/747–1000, 866/493–6495* ⊕ *www.intercontinentalboston. com* ⏎ *424 rooms, 38 suites & In-room: safe, Wi-Fi. In-hotel: restaurant, bar, pool, gym, spa, children's programs, parking, some pets allowed* ¶○¶ *No meals* Ⓜ *South Station* ⊹ *2:H1.*

WORD OF MOUTH

"We've stayed at the Long Wharf Marriott and loved it—very pretty harbor views and right next to a nice park. We were able to walk or take the T everywhere we wanted; there's a stop right in front. Make sure you request a room with a harbor view—not all the rooms have them. There's a Legal Sea Foods close by that's good."   —volcanogirl

$$$$ ⌂ **Langham Hotel.** The red awnings of this 1922 Renaissance Revival landmark (the former Federal Reserve Building) announce a well-appointed red- and gold-accented marble lobby, a stark contrast to the ubiquitous gray-suited Financial District types who gather here. Crystal chandeliers light the hallways, and jewel-tone fabrics swath just-updated guest rooms—the decor isn't exactly daring, but it works. While the Post Office Square spot is all business during the week (including the who's-who power breakfast and lunch crowds at Café Fleuri), families and couples drop in on weekends for much lower room rates and special deals at the Chuan Body + Soul spa. Bond, the Langham's in-house restaurant-bar, attracts dressed-to-the-nines partygoers. The contrast between bumping nightclub and stately old hotel is obvious, and at first quite puzzling. But the hotel has deftly merged the young and venerable and the hip and refined, and has ended up being a place with a little something for everyone. ■TIP➔ Use a nearby public parking lot, where rates are cheaper on weekends. **Pros:** ideal spot for business travelers; fabulous Sunday brunch at Café Fleuri; bustling scene at Bond. **Cons:** the downtown location feels remote on weekends; pricey during the week; expensive valet parking. **TripAdvisor:** "awesome workout equipment," "plush comfortable bed with high-quality linens," "easy walking distance to Faneuil Hall." ✉ *250 Franklin St., Downtown* ☎ *617/451–1900, 800/543–4300* ⎙ *617/423–2844* ⊕ *www.boston. langhamhotels.com* ⏎ *318 rooms, 17 suites & In-room: safe, Wi-Fi. In-hotel: restaurant, bar, pool, gym, spa, children's programs, parking, some pets allowed* ¶○¶ *No meals* Ⓜ *South Station* ⊹ *1:G6.*

$$$ ⌂ **Marriott Long Wharf.** Families favor this spot that looks like a big brick ship docked in Boston Harbor. It's close to great group outing locales like the New England Aquarium and the shops and restaurants of Quincy Market. Even the North End isn't far, if you're willing to walk a bit. Manicured Christopher Columbus Park is right outside the door, with myriad walkways and wisteria-covered archways. And then there's the Marriott's great swimming pool, overlooking the harbor, plus a huge gym and an itty-bitty game room. Most of the rooms, renovated in 2008 and decorated in cream-and-gold brocade with pillow-top mattresses, open onto a five-story atrium. Some rooms have views of the park or the aquarium. Clean-freak alert: plush feather duvets on the beds are changed every night. ■TIP➔ For more dining options,

head to Quincy Market instead of eating on-site, even for breakfast. **Pros:** next door Tia's bar is a must for outdoor happy hour; good weekend rates (check the Web for deals); great location for first-time visitors. **Cons:** restaurant is pricey; feels like a chain hotel. **TripAdvisor:** "staff was friendly and accomodating," "rooms were clean," "design somewhat dated." ⊠ *296 State St., Downtown/Waterfront* ☎ *617/227–0800* 🖷 *617/227–2867* ⊕ *www.marriott.com/boslw* 🖙 *397 rooms, 15 suites* ♿ *In-room: safe, Wi-Fi. In-hotel: restaurant, bar, pool, gym, parking* ⍾◯ *No meals* Ⓜ *Aquarium* ✛ *1:H5.*

$$$$ 🏨 **Millennium Bostonian Hotel.** Once a Boston great, the Millennium spent the last decade sinking into downtown hotel anonymity . . . until it emerged fresh from a $25-million transformation. Local interior-design firm Jinnie Kim (See: the St. Regis and Plaza hotels in New York City) spruced up the joint with cove lighting, red leather decor accents, gas fireplaces, and, in the rooms, Frette linens, pillowtop mattresses, and the obligatory mammoth TVs. Though the place seems brand-new, a few former amenities like guest-room balconies remain intact. And the entire building is now online with Wi-Fi—albeit, sadly, for a fee. Its New American restaurant, North 26, is a steak-and-eggs-meets-fresh-fruit-smoothie hot spot. Bonus: outdoor seating aplenty. **Pros:** extensive renovation; North 26's strong cocktails; updated fitness center. **Cons:** some rooms still get street noise; Faneuil Hall can get clogged with tourists. **TripAdvisor:** "staff couldn't have been nicer," "best rate in the city for a well reviewed hotel," "best thing about this hotel is the location." ⊠ *Faneuil Hall Marketplace, 26 North St., Downtown* ☎ *617/523–3600, 866/866–8086* 🖷 *617/523–2454* ⊕ *www.millenniumhotels.com* 🖙 *187 rooms, 14 suites* ♿ *In-room: safe, Wi-Fi. In-hotel: restaurant, bar, gym, spa, parking* ⍾◯ *No meals* Ⓜ *Government Center, Haymarket* ✛ *1:F5.*

$$$$ 🏨 **Nine Zero.** Nine Zero knows that hotel rooms can get a little lonely.
Fodor's Choice That's why the Downtown spot instated its "guppy love" program;
★ yes, that's right, you get a pet fish on loan. Feeling tight? Turn on the TV and tune into the in-house yoga channel. (Forgot your mat? They'll lend you that, too.) It's touches like these that set this Kimpton property apart from other up-and-coming boutique hotels. Style-wise, the place is sleek, sleek, sleek; all smooth lines with sudden bursts of vibrant color. Request corner rooms (ending in 05) for the best city and river views. Then, partake of the hotel's personal-shopper-for-hire program and dress to join the young, hip crowds at in-house modern steak house KO Prime, run by celeb chef Ken Oringer. **Pros:** pet-friendly; kid-friendly; lobby wine-tasting every evening (from 5 to 6); Mario Russo bath products. **Cons:** smallish rooms; high parking fees. **TripAdvisor:** "good sized rooms and spacious bathrooms," "stunning views," "hotel's food is a little expensive." ⊠ *90 Tremont St., Downtown* ☎ *617/772–5800,*

866/906–9090 ⌨ 617/772–5810 ⊕ *www.ninezero.com* ⟿ *185 rooms, 5 suites* ☆ *In-room: safe, Internet. In-hotel: restaurant, bar, gym, children's programs, parking, some pets allowed* �‖ *No meals* Ⓜ *Park St., Government Center* ✛ *1:E6.*

$$$$ 🖼 **Omni Parker House.** In 2008 America's oldest continuously operating
Ⓒ   hotel got a $30-million makeover, so you can still steep yourself in Boston history . . . while watching a flat-screen TV. As at many city lodgings, the guestrooms are a tad small, but here they're nicely turned out with updated cherry-wood furniture, red-and-gold Roman shades, ivory wall coverings, and cushy mattress covers. The lobby and restaurants were also invigorated with new decor and menu items. Longtimers, rest easy: The Omni's famous Boston Cream Pie is still on hand (even for breakfast); but now you can work it off in a new in-house gym packed with cardio and weight equipment. If any hotel really says "Boston," it's this one, where JFK proposed to Jackie, and Charles Dickens gave his first reading of "A Christmas Carol." In fact, you may well see a Dickens impersonator in the lobby, since history tours always include the Parker House on their routes. **Pros:** historic property; near Downtown Crossing on the Freedom Trail. **Cons:** small rooms, some quite dark; thin-walled rooms can be noisy. **TripAdvisor:** "the walls are very thin," "excellent service," "valet parking was costly." ✉ *60 School St., Downtown* ☎ *617/227–8600, 800/843–6664* ⌨ *617/742–5729* ⊕ *www. omniparkerhouse.com* ⟿ *551 rooms, 21 suites* ☆ *In-room: safe, Internet. In-hotel: restaurant, bar, gym, children's programs, parking, some pets allowed* �‖ *Breakfast* Ⓜ *Government Center, Park St.* ✛ *1:F6.*

$$$ 🖼 **Onyx Hotel.** Sexy, supper-club atmosphere oozes from this five-year-old contemporary Kimpton Group hotel a block from North Station, making it a favorite of hipsters and hoopsters alike. Sip an ice-cold martini and nibble some tapas in the intimate Ruby Room; if there's a concert going on at the nearby TD Garden, you might party with rock stars. If the Celtics or the Bruins are in town, you'll get a lively, sports-loving crowd. Later, head upstairs to slip into your leopard-print bathrobe and cushy socks. Rooms are done in black and taupe with funky checkerboard carpeting and colorful accents, including red suede chairs. All have plush linens, flat-screen TVs, and Soames bath products. **Pros:** good location for catching a sporting event or concert at the Garden; near North Station commuter rail and T stop; near several inexpensive restaurants and bars. **Cons:** smallish rooms and bathrooms; small gym; neighborhood can get noisy at night. **TripAdvisor:** "wine reception every evening was a nice touch," "extremely comfortable bed," "awesome customer service." ✉ *155 Portland St., Downtown* ☎ *617/557– 9955, 866/660–6699* ⊕ *www.onyxhotel.com* ⟿ *110 rooms, 2 suites* ☆ *In-room: safe, Wi-Fi. In-hotel: restaurant, bar, gym, parking, some pets allowed* �‖ *No meals* Ⓜ *North Station* ✛ *1:E4.*

$$ 🖼 **Renaissance Boston Waterfront Hotel.** Set along the working wharves of Boston Harbor, near the must-visit Institute of Contemporary Art, the Renaissance plays to a watery theme. In the modern lobby, blue-and-green glass orbs complement a suspended glass lighting fixture and spiral staircase created to look like a nautilus shell. The building is flooded with light, and most guest rooms have water views. It all adds up to a clean, cool ambience, completely different from the dark woods and colonial style you might encounter at the city's older hotels. The pool is a lap pool, not designed for lingering. If that feels a bit no-nonsense, that's just fine with the spot's business clientele, who love the proximity to the Seaport World Trade Center. The mood changes on weekends, when package deals lure weekenders and family travelers. **Pros:** sleek new lobby Capiz Bar and Lounge; close to the Silver Line (airport transportation) and convention center. **Cons:** some guest-room harbor views are more industrial than scenic; hordes of conventioneers; far from major city attractions. **TripAdvisor:** "rooms are extremely comfortable, airy, and clean," "bit of a walk to the main downtown areas," "nice and quiet in this hotel." ⊠ *606 Congress St., Downtown/Seaport District* ☎ *617/338–4111, 888/796–4664* ⊕ *www. renaissanceboston.com* ⤴ *450 rooms, 21 suites* ♿ *In-room: safe, Wi-Fi. In-hotel: restaurant, bar, pool, gym, spa, children's programs, parking* ⵐ *No meals* Ⓜ *World Trade Center* ✢ *2:H2.*

$$$$ 🏨 **Ritz-Carlton Boston Common.** The Sports Club/LA, the Ritz's mega–fit-
🌣 ness center, is the go-to gym for visiting celebs and poptarts, so you might feel a bit more fabulous—or a whole lot fatter—simply by hanging out here. While traditionalists often compare the very modern hotel unfavorably to other Ritz-Carltons, it's only fair to judge it for what it is: a sleek, contemporary spot that speaks more to rock stars than royalty. Plus, thanks to the shuttering of the Newbury Street Ritz-Carlton (known to locals as the "old Ritz") and an $11 million remodeling, this location is getting all the attention. Warm wood walls and trim complement an extensive art collection in the lobby lounge, where furnishings are draped in velvet and silk, and lamps are made of hand-blown Venetian glass. Guest rooms are dressed in apricot, yellow, and blue, with hardwood armoires and separate marble showers and deep tubs. Some rooms have spectacular views of Boston Common. A short walk will get you to Downtown Crossing's shopping zone, the Theater District, and Newbury Street. Besides the gym, the hotel complex houses a movie theater and a couple of fine-dining restaurants. **Pros:** the Sports Club's über-social blu eatery has a great post-gym scene; central location. **Cons:** some complain that guest rooms are too dark and lack "wow" factor; food service is "brutally expensive." **TripAdvisor:** "elegant and calm," "beyond expectations," "very spacious." ⊠ *10 Avery St., Downtown* ☎ *617/574–7100, 800/241–3333* 🖷 *617/574–7200* ⊕ *www.ritzcarlton.com* ⤴ *150 rooms, 43 suites* ♿ *In-room: safe, Wi-Fi. In-hotel: restaurant, bar, pool, gym, spa, children's programs, parking, some pets allowed* ⵐ *No meals* Ⓜ *Boylston St.* ✢ *2:E1.*

$$$$ 🏨 **Seaport Hotel.** Chances are, if you've ever been to Boston on business,
🌣 you've already stayed at the Seaport. The 428-room hotel is an ocean of badge-wearing, convention-going suits, most of whom scurry back and forth between the lobby and the adjacent World Trade Center, land of a thousand conference rooms. Wait a minute! Keep reading—just because it's all business doesn't mean it's not nice. Case in point: the full-service health club, complete with a lap pool, spa, and cardio and weight equipment. Guest rooms are among the biggest in the city, and are outfitted with lime-green and red furnishings, marble bathrooms, Bose radios, laptop safes, and, of course, complimentary daily *Wall*

Street Journals. Currying favor with all kinds of clientele, the Seaport prides itself on being ecofriendly and having hypoallergenic rooms. **Pros:** the Wave Health & Fitness Club; a no-tipping policy; close to water taxi; free Wi-Fi. **Cons:** far from city center; limited nearby dining options; pricey room service. **TripAdvisor:** "room service was prompt with good food," "overall high value," "big bathroom with best mirror lighting." ⊠ *World Trade Center, 1 Seaport La., Downtown/Seaport District* ☎ *617/385–4000, 800/440–3318* ⊕ *www.seaportboston.com* ↻ *428 rooms* ⚷ *In-room: safe, Wi-Fi. In-hotel: restaurant, bar, pool, gym, spa, parking, some pets allowed* ⏹ *No meals* Ⓜ *World Trade Center* ⊹ *2:H1.*

$$$$ ⛏ **W Boston.** After a lengthy (and loud) construction, this 235-room glass tower is finally open. The metal-and-glass "awning" is outfitted with soft, color-changing neon lights that cast a cheeky glow on passersby. Inside, the nature-inspired decor is modern through and through, with typical W brand touches like a sleek, sceney lobby lounge (complete with falling water display and open fireplace) and a host of room categories such as the standard Wonderful and expanded Wow lodgings. Decor is a mix of deep blues, browns, and sheer glass (don't worry, shower doors are frosted), and the views from the higher-level floor-to-ceiling windows are breathtaking. Hint: Look for low introductory rates and weekend theater packages. **Pros:** Bliss spa on-site; free Wi-Fi in public areas; signature W feather-top beds; fashion scene. **Cons:** fee for Wi-Fi in rooms; area theater and bar crowds can be loud; expensive parking. **TripAdvisor:** "level of service provided is top notch," "right in the theater district," "street noise can be heard within some rooms." ⊠ *100 Stuart St., Downtown/Theater District* ☎ *617/261–8700* ⊕ *www.whotels.com/boston* ↻ *235 rooms* ⚷ *In-room: kitchen, Wi-Fi. In-hotel: restaurant, bar, gym, spa, parking, some pets allowed* ⏹ *No meals* Ⓜ *Boylston, Tufts Medical Center* ⊹ *2:E2.*

$$$ ⛏ **Westin Boston Waterfront.** Opened in June 2006, the 17-story glass-and-steel tower has already been updated to include a 25,000-square-foot exhibit hall and two in-house restaurants. (One of the latter, Sauciety, is slavishly devoted to the most au courante condiments.) The South Boston property is connected to the enormous Boston Convention & Exhibition Center, a magnet for men and women wearing suits and badges. Guest rooms are handsome, with a neutral palette of whites, tans, and pastels punctuated with cherry-wood furnishings; most have water or skyline views. When you're not in meetings, work out kinks at the state-of-the-art fitness center, complete with a slew of up-to-date machines, an indoor pool, and steam and sauna rooms. **Pros:** close to the stellar Institute of Contemporary Art; lobby stations with wireless check-in; Silver Line to Logan Airport; Westin's signature "heavenly" beds. **Cons:** clusters of meeting-goers; a businesslike chain hotel feel. **TripAdvisor:** "heavenly beds are awesome," "front desk staff very helpful," "large lobby with plenty of seating." ⊠ *425 Summer St., Downtown/Seaport District* ☎ *617/532–4600* ⊕ *www.starwoodhotels.com* ↻ *761 rooms, 32 suites* ⚷ *In-room: safe, Wi-Fi. In-hotel: restaurant, bar, pool, gym, children's programs, parking, some pets allowed* ⏹ *No meals* Ⓜ *South Station* ⊹ *2:H2.*

CLOSE UP

Kid-Friendly Hotels

Almost every Boston hotel allows kids, but a few go out of their way to make little ones feel welcome. The **Fairmont Copley Plaza**'s resident Labrador retriever, Catie Copley, is extra sweet and family-friendly; she's also available on loan for long walks in the park. The **Inn@St. Botolph**'s "Inn-formational" packages are fun for all ages—bring the kids along to cooking classes (including gelato making and, of course, eating) or ultracool glass-blowing lessons. A stuffed animal is waiting for every child at the **Lenox Hotel**, where the staff puts together myriad kid-focused trips to the Children's Museum and New England Aquarium. At the **Four Seasons** the VIK (Very Important Kids) lineup includes a complimentary toy wagon, ice-cream surprise, backpack stuffed with games and kiddy toiletries, and scavenger hunts galore. If

all that sounds exhausting, you could just drop your tot at the **Taj Boston**'s Children's Suite, or partake of a pre-planned "Family Connection" package at the **Colonnade Hotel**.

If you're looking for a place for kids to splash around, **the Seaport Hotel** and the **Colonnade** have two of the best pools in the city (Note: The latter becomes a bit of a scene on weekends, so your best bet is an early weekday.)

Greater Boston Convention & Visitors Bureau. Request a "Kids Love Boston" brochure from the Greater Boston Convention & Visitors Bureau. The Web site lists a variety of family-friendly packages that include such extras as complimentary use of strollers and discounts to city attractions. ☎ 617/536–4100, 888/733–2678 ⊕ www.bostonusa.com.

THE BACK BAY AND THE SOUTH END
THE BACK BAY

$ 🖼 **463 Beacon Street Guest House.** Though there's no sign on the door of this handsome brownstone, international visitors and college students have discovered the rooming house—and quickly warmed to its slightly quirky, old-auntie charm. Check out the old black-and-white photos of Boston in the hallways as you head to your room (each is slightly different, as befits a historic house). The antiques-filled common area functions as a guest room in summertime, and it's the best one in the house. All other digs are tidy but basic, with hardwood floors; those on the fifth floor are loft-style. This is not the place for anyone looking for an all-inclusive, private getaway: there's no restaurant at 463 Beacon, and a few rooms share a bath. **Pros:** Newbury Street is three blocks away; the Charles River and Esplanade are one block in the other direction. **Cons:** some rooms have a two-person occupancy limit, and because of the layout, the house isn't appropriate for children under seven. **TripAdvisor:** "great value," "friendly service," "wonderful stay." ⊠ 463 Beacon St., Back Bay ☎ 617/536–1302 ⊕ www.463beacon.com ⇨ 20 rooms, 17 with bath ⚇ In-room: no a/c, kitchen, Wi-Fi. In-hotel: laundry facilities, parking ⦿ No meals Ⓜ Kenmore ✚ 3:H2.

$$$ 🖼 **The Back Bay Hotel.** "Great staff." "Great bar." "Great vibe." See a pattern yet? Travelers rave about the renamed Jurys Boston, one of the few hotels in the city where you can nip into the bar for a beverage and actually chat with a friendly local or two. Part of the Doyle Collection,

a Dublin-based chain, the Back Bay Hotel may remind you more of Iceland than Ireland; its fire-and-ice decor, from the bed of icy glass shards in the lobby's igloo-like gas fireplace to the puffs of steam coming from the main staircase's waterfall, is eye-catching. Blown-glass chandeliers and edgy statues only add to the cool appeal. The hotel gets the small touches right, such as free bottled water in the guest-room fridges, toasty down comforters, and heated towel racks. Readers praise the pub grub at on-site Cuff's Bar, a great place for a post-work cocktail. **Pros:** lively bar; laptop safes; Korres toiletries; friendly staff. **Cons:** very small gym; the bar scene can get loud. **TripAdvisor:** "room service was excellent," "bathroom was small but had everything needed," "pricey but you can find package deal." ⊠ *350 Stuart St., Back Bay* ☎ *617/266–7200* ⊕ *www.doylecollection.com* ⇆ *222 rooms, 3 suites* ♿ *In-room: Wi-Fi. In-hotel: restaurant, bar, parking* ⦿ *No meals* Ⓜ *Back Bay* ✛ *2:C2.*

$$$ ▦ **Boston Park Plaza Hotel & Towers.** To keep up with the incoming rush of ultracool, ultramodern hotels, the Park Plaza rooms include pillow-top mattresses and plasma TVs. There's also a trendy rooftop organic herb garden and an energy-efficient infrastructure (that cost more than $500,000). But make no mistake—it didn't sell its soul. The old-school, antique-laden 1927 building is just as historically grand as ever, as evidenced in its gilded, chandelier-lit lobby and classically decorated lodging. As at most vintage city hotels, the rooms are rather diminutive; the bathrooms, even more so (except on the 15th floor concierge level). But travelers looking for an all-inclusive stay would be wise to book the Park Plaza—the property houses a handful of restaurants and bars. Hint: Don't miss decadent dessert shop Finale. **Pros:** Old World charm; one of Boston's best locations; helpful concierge; adjacent to an Exhale spa. **Cons:** rooms are cramped; bathrooms are small; not for hip modernists. **TripAdvisor:** "very reasonable price," "location is fantastic," "have to pay for internet service." ⊠ *64 Arlington St., Back Bay* ☎ *617/426–2000, 800/225–2008* ⊕ *www.bostonparkplaza.com* ⇆ *941 rooms, 39 suites* ♿ *In-room: Internet. In-hotel: restaurant, bar, gym, parking, some pets allowed* ⦿ *No meals* Ⓜ *Arlington* ✛ *2:D2.*

$$$
Fodor's Choice
★

▦ **Charlesmark Hotel.** Hipsters and romantics who'd rather spend their cash on a great meal than a hotel bill have put this skinny little place on the map. Formally just another Boylston Street office building, the 40-room spot has rooms that go for as low as $119 in the off-season, an almost unheard of price for Back Bay lodging. The funky, eclectic design is just zany enough, and attracts guests who want to relax on the outdoor patio and check out passersby—or the Boston Marathon (the hotel sits on the finish line). Smallish guest rooms have contemporary custom-made oak furnishings, plus surround-sound stereo and free wireless Internet. You can order Thai food in the cocktail lounge, but would be better off walking to one of some 40 nearby restaurants. The Charlesmark doubles as a gallery, with the work of local artists lining its winding brick corridors. **Pros:** fantastic price for the location; free Wi-Fi and water bottles. **Cons:** hot-air heating system is noisy; not much storage space; rooms at the front of the house can be noisy. **TripAdvisor:** "FREE help-yourself continental breakfast," "rooms are small but comfortable," "would definitely stay here again." ⊠ *655 Boylston*

St., Back Bay ☎ *617/247–1212* ⊕ *www.thecharlesmarkhotel.com* ⤴ *40 rooms* ⅏ *In-room: Wi-Fi. In-hotel: bar* ⍾ *Breakfast* Ⓜ *Copley* ✢ *2:B2.*

$$$$ ⌂ **Colonnade Hotel.** The Colonnade's $25-million makeover—a spruced-
☾ up facade, new windows, updated room decor—was a hit. The hotel went from an '80s brass-and-mahogany showcase to a clean, modern environs injected with hues of khaki, chocolate, and chrome. Guest-friendly touches now include flat-panel TVs, DVD players, and alarm clock/MP3 players, plus extendable reading lights and high-tech coffeemakers. The look is slightly masculine but quite comfy and clean, with pillow-top mattresses, high-thread-count sheets, and round tables perfect for both eating and working. The floor-to-ceiling windows (that, eureka!, actually open) are triple glazed to keep out the traffic noise of Huntington Avenue. In summer the roof-deck pool is the place to be, and draws a mix of local glitterati and lithe European vacationers. As an added perk, the hotel lends out its mini fleet of cute, if not quite convenient, Smart cars. For your gastronomic needs, Brasserie Jo is an authentic French brasserie with fantastic salads (hint: get the niçoise). **Pros:** roof-deck pool; across from Prudential Center shopping; good Red Sox packages. **Cons:** Huntington Avenue can get clogged with rush-hour traffic; on summer days the pool is packed by 11 am. **TripAdvisor:** "everyone was so friendly and helpful," "efficient, quiet air-conditioning," "handsomely decorated rooms." ⊠ *120 Huntington Ave., Back Bay* ☎ *617/424–7000, 800/962–3030* ⊕ *www.colonnadehotel. com* ⤴ *276 rooms, 9 suites* ⅏ *In-room: safe, Wi-Fi. In-hotel: restaurant, bar, pool, gym, children's programs, parking, some pets allowed* ⍾ *No meals* Ⓜ *Prudential Center* ✢ *2:B3.*

$$$$ ⌂ **Copley Square Hotel.** Thanks to an $18-million renovation, the Copley Square Hotel has hurtled into the present with high-tech registration pods, fully stocked workstations, cushy mattresses, and in-room iPod docks. Not too shabby for a place that opened in 1891 and has provided respite to a century of celebrities like Babe Ruth, Ella Fitzgerald, and Billie Holiday. The mod rooms are so clean and streamlined that you just might overlook the fact that they're teeny. Nevertheless, the old-meets-new vibe is fun, and the neighborhood couldn't be livelier; the hotel itself is home to minibar, the city's social spot du jour. If its all-white banquette seating is filled or reserved, order some Kobe sliders and hang at the bar until nextdoor nightclub Saint starts hopping. To maximize your Zs, get a room in the back of the hotel, preferably high up, where traffic noise—and the rowdy partying—isn't so audible. **Pros:** free Wi-Fi; free nightly wine tastings; cool bar and club scene. **Cons:** small rooms; those facing Huntington Avenue can be very noisy; not ideal for older couples seeking peace and quiet. **TripAdvisor:** "staff was extremely courteous," "good location and amenities," "rooms are small." ⊠ *47 Huntington Ave., Back Bay* ☎ *617/536–9000* ⊕ *www.copleysquarehotel.com* ⤴ *143 rooms* ⅏ *In-room: safe, Wi-Fi. In-hotel: restaurant, bar, gym, parking, some pets allowed* ⍾ *No meals* Ⓜ *Copley* ✢ *2:B2.*

$$$$ ⌂ **Courtyard by Marriott Boston Copley Square.** The hotel makes no bones about its mission to appeal to business travelers. No matter, some guests consider it the best Courtyard Marriott they've seen, and praise its

The Charlesmark Hotel

Eliot Hotel

modern, upscale, and large-for-Boston rooms. They don't mind that the lobby isn't grand, there's no doorman, and room service consists of a handful of menus to nearby eateries. Small niceties include cookies and fruit in the lobby and make-up mirrors in the bathrooms. The best thing about this spot, though, is its location smack in the middle of all the central Boston action. **Pros:** good-size modern rooms (nicer than the "big" Marriott, some say); great location; free Internet. **Cons:** restaurant is fairly lame; no room service. **TripAdvisor:** "would highly recommend as a nice place to stay," "very convenient to shopping, restaurants, bars," "comfortable bed." ⊠ *88 Exeter St., Back Bay* ☎ *617/437–9300, 800/321–2211* ⊕ *www.courtyardboston.com* ⤳ *77 rooms, 4 suites* ♿ *In-hotel: restaurant, gym* ⎮○⎮ *No meals* Ⓜ *Copley* ✛ *2:B2.*

$$$$ 🖼 **Eliot Hotel.** Ever imagine that you live on posh Commonwealth Avenue, modeled after Paris's epic Champs Élysées? You probably can't swing the real thing, but you can indulge in a weekend away at the Eliot. One of the city's best small hotels expertly merges the old blue-blood Boston aesthetic with modern flair (See: zebra-print rugs mingling with crystal chandeliers), and everyone from well-heeled Sox fans to traveling CEOs to tony college parents has noticed. The smallish rooms are smart, not stuffy, and feel a bit French country and a bit Soho chic. And there's good news for those naysayers who gripe about the timeworn bathrooms: each one got a redo in 2009. The majority of rooms are one- or two-bedroom suites; all have marble-topped bar areas and flat-panel TVs. ■**TIP→ Rooms ending in 02 have views of Commonwealth Avenue; those ending in 04 and 08 are larger corner rooms.** Downstairs, the fine-dining Clio, helmed by chef Ken Oringer, garners raves for its contemporary French-American cuisine. Not to be outdone, Oringer's next-door sashimi bar, also in the hotel, regularly plays host to Boston's gliterratti. **Pros:** super location; top-notch restaurants; pet-friendly; beautiful rooms. **Cons:** very expensive; some complain of elevator noise. **TripAdvisor:** "staff bent over backwards to help us," "rooms are comfortable and elegant," "clean and well-stocked with towels and toiletries." ⊠ *370 Commonwealth Ave., Back Bay* ☎ *617/267–1607, 800/443–5468* ⊕ *www.eliothotel.com* ⤳ *16 rooms, 79 suites* ♿ *In-room: Wi-Fi. In-hotel: restaurant, bar, parking, some pets allowed* ⎮○⎮ *No meals* Ⓜ *Hynes* ✛ *3:H2.*

Fodor'sChoice
★

$$$$ 🖼 **Fairmont Copley Plaza.** Too much of a good thing is just fine by the Fairmont's loyal clientele. Past guests, including one Judy Garland, felt at home in the decadent, unabashedly romantic hotel. Present guests feel much the same way, thanks to the meticulous preservation of the 1912 stallwart. Those who really love pampering should book the Fairmont Gold floor (worth the extra cost, readers say), an ultradeluxe club level offering a dedicated staff, free breakfast and tea-time snacks, and a library. Shopping fanatics adore the close proximity to Newbury Street, the Prudential Center, and Copley Place. The hotel's venerable Oak Room restaurant is worth a meal; the equally stately—and tryst-worthy—Oak Bar has live music and one of the longest martini menus in town. If you're missing your dog (or just have a hard-to-please kid), borrow Catie Copley, the in-house Labrador retriever, for a walk around the 'hood. **Pros:** very elegant; famous cozy bar. **Cons:** tiny bathrooms

☾
Fodor'sChoice
★

with scratchy towels; charge for Internet access (no charge on Fairmont Gold level); small fitness center. **TripAdvisor:** "can't say enough about the customer service," "rooms were comfortable with great attention to detail," "we walked to Fenway, Quincy Market, Boston Common . . . great location." ⊠ *138 St. James Ave., Back Bay* ☎ *617/267–5300, 866/540–4417* ⊕ *www.fairmont.com/copleyplaza* ⟿ *366 rooms, 17 suites* ♿ *In-room: safe, Wi-Fi. In-hotel: restaurant, bar, gym, parking, some pets allowed* ⍾ *No meals* Ⓜ *Copley, Back Bay/South End* ✛ *2:B2.*

$$$$ 🏨 **Four Seasons.** The Four Seasons keeps a surprisingly low profile in
☯ Boston. And that's OK by the jeans-clad millionaires and assorted business types who cluster in the glossy lobby. Facing more and more competition from incoming luxury brands (Mandarin Oriental, Taj), the Public Garden-facing spot is holding its own. Upper-crust types nosh on excellent breakfast in the Bristol lounge (try the pancakes), and visiting celebs are still whisked to the 3,000-square-foot, $6,900-per-night Presidential Suite. Lovely guest rooms boast black-and-cream toile decor with gold and lemon accents, large bay windows, and oversize work areas. Luxury amenities include DVD players, 42-inch plasma TVs, and L'Occitane toiletries. (Even those celebrities steal the soaps, we're told.) If you spring for a basic city-view room, you can still enjoy views of the park from the pool and whirlpool on the eighth floor. The new 24/7 "e Center" off the lobby has touch-screen computers, printers, faxes, and a copy machine. ∎**TIP**➔ Check the Web for fantastic winter-weekend deals. **Pros:** overlooks the Public Garden; a short walk from Newbury; signature Four Seasons service; Mercedes courtesy car. **Cons:** pricey during peak times; valet service can be slow. **TripAdvisor:** "great gym and pool," "great service—first class all the way," "quiet and spacious." ⊠ *200 Boylston St., Back Bay* ☎ *617/338–4400, 800/819–5053* ⊕ *www.fourseasons.com/boston* ⟿ *199 rooms, 74 suites* ♿ *In-room: safe, Wi-Fi. In-hotel: restaurant, bar, pool, gym, spa, children's programs, parking, some pets allowed* ⍾ *No meals* Ⓜ *Arlington* ✛ *2:D1.*

$$$$ 🏨 **Hilton Boston Back Bay.** Fresh from a $15-million renovation, the Back Bay Hilton is as spruced up as a slightly anonymous chain hotel can get. The rooms are relatively spacious, with plush "Serenity" bedding, premium cable channels, Lavazza coffee, and La Source amenities. All of that sounds even better if you snagged one of the frequent online deals. The 26-story hotel sits in a quiet pocket between the Prudential Center and the pretty Christian Science Church complex; rooms above the ninth floor have great views of Back Bay, Fenway Park, and Boston's famous Citgo sign. **Pros:** oversize showers; good roof-level fitness center; free Wi-Fi in the lobby. **Cons:** fee for Internet in guest rooms; expensive breakfast ("go elsewhere," readers advise). **TripAdvisor:** "clean quiet hotel," "comfortable beds and well equipped (if a little small) bathroom," "free internet computers in lobby with a printer." ⊠ *40 Dalton St., Back Bay* ☎ *617/236–1100, 800/874–0663* ⊕ *www. hilton.com* ⟿ *385 rooms, 5 suites* ♿ *In-room: Internet. In-hotel: restaurant, bar, pool, gym, parking, some pets allowed* ⍾ *No meals* Ⓜ *Hynes* ✛ *2:A3.*

The Fairmont Copley Plaza

The Inn @ St. Botolph

$$$$ 🛏 **Inn@St. Botolph.** Like its sister
☺   property, XV Beacon, the 16-room
Fodor's Choice inn packs plenty of style. Unlike XV
★   Beacon, it follows a groundbreak-
      ing new hotel model: There's no
      front desk, no restaurant, and no
      valet. Guests book and pay online,
      eliminating the need for agoniz-
      ingly slow check-ins or long lines.
      Each room feels like the chicest city
      apartment you never had, deco-
      rated in black, white, and chocolate

tones by local design luminaries. The four-poster beds are heavenly, so
is the deep leather seating. Every room also comes with a full kitchen,
a fireplace, Frette robes, and a gigantic flat-screen TV. Set on a quiet
residential street lined with flowering trees and brownstones, the inn
is a short walk from the South End and Back Bay. Best of all, for all
the at-home-style luxury you get, you'll pay half of what you would at
a nearby hotel. Just remember to book early. The St. Botolph fills up
fast with fashionable clients who know how to spot a hot deal. **Pros:**
affordable style; great location; posh yet homey; free satellite TV and
Wi-Fi; "preferred" pricing at and free transit to top area restaurants.
Cons: DIY parking; for those who need hand-holding, there's no front
desk. **TripAdvisor:** "bed was heavenly," "room was spacious, clean and
well-equiped," "designed with excellent taste." ✉ *99 St. Botolph St.,
Back Bay* ☎ *617/236–8099* ⊕ *www.innatstbotolph.com* ⤶ *16 rooms*
⚒ *In-room: safe, kitchen, Wi-Fi. In-hotel: gym, laundry facilities, busi-
ness center* ⦿ *Breakfast* Ⓜ *Prudential* ✛ *2:A3.*

$$$$ 🛏 **Lenox Hotel.** A good alternative to chain-owned, big-box Back Bay
☺   hotels, the family-owned Lenox nearly sparkles after a $30-million
      makeover. Ongoing top-notch service continues to please a well-
      groomed clientele (or maybe it's the handsome doormen). A T stop
      is right across the street, making the hotel a good launching pad for
      exploring the city sans car. Readers appreciate the Lenox's sweet, small
      touches, like cookies and bottled water at turndown service, and give
      kudos to the friendly staff. Standard guest rooms have custom-made
      furnishings, marble baths, and flat-screen TVs (suites have mirror TVs
      in their bathrooms). Of the 24 more spacious corner rooms, 12 come
      with working fireplaces. **Pros:** free Wi-Fi; fantastic Copley Square loca-
      tion; historic/architectural charm; City Table eatery. **Cons:** bathrooms
      are small; no minibar; costly parking. **TripAdvisor:** "room was very
      comfortable and spacious," "great base from which to explore the city,"
      "hotel was spotlessly clean." ✉ *61 Exeter St., Back Bay* ☎ *617/536–
      5300, 800/225–7676* ⊕ *www.lenoxhotel.com* ⤶ *187 rooms, 27 suites*
      ⚒ *In-room: Wi-Fi. In-hotel: restaurant, bar, gym, children's programs,
      parking, some pets allowed* ⦿ *No meals* Ⓜ *Copley* ✛ *2:B2.*

$$$$ 🛏 **Mandarin Oriental Boston.** A relative newcomer to Boston's luxury
☺   hotel scene, the Mandarin took the city by storm—after, that is, a seem-
      ingly endless construction. The 148-room hotel has helped redefine lux-
      ury in town (pay attention, Ritz and Four Seasons), and offers services

many guests are calling "out of this world." Need your pants hemmed in 30 minutes? No problem. Feel like a pot of green tea at check-in? It's complimentary. Forgot your Gucci sunglasses? The store's next door. The hotel's Asian decor does feel a tad out of place in Boston, but locals love visiting for a touch of the exotic. The limestone and marble lobby offers direct access to the Prudential Center and Copley Place, and other gallery-like public areas are adorned with art on loan from the Peabody Essex Museum. Large guest rooms—for the city, anyway—are outfitted with contemporary Asian design, soaking tubs, rain shower heads, and 400-thread-count Frette linens. Even if you don't drink, pop into M Bar for a look at the cool glass-topped, illuminated bar. And don't miss a visit to the quartz-crystal steam room at the outstanding spa, especially if you've overindulged on mandarin martinis. **Pros:** amazing service; very quiet; good-size rooms; too many amenities to list. **Cons:** small fitness center; exorbitantly expensive; average views. **TripAdvisor:** "well appointed," "most attentive staff," "spa was incredible." ⊠ 776 *Boylston St., Back Bay* ☎ *617/535–8888* ⊕ *www.mandarinoriental. com/boston* ↝ *136 rooms, 12 suites* ⌂ *In-room: safe, Wi-Fi. In-hotel: restaurant, bar, gym, spa, children's programs, parking, some pets allowed* ⏃ *No meals* Ⓜ *Prudential, Copley* ⊹ *2:A2.*

$$$ 🏨 **Marriott Hotel at Copley Place.** It's busy-busy, with throngs of tourists and their offspring, but you can't beat the location of this 38-story megahotel. It may be just another Marriott, but it's a nice one, thanks to a just-finished $22-million renovation that freshened up the health club, pool, sports restaurant-bar, and on-site Starbucks, and debuted the tech-heavy Connexion Lounge. The mammoth spot has three entrances—a street-level door, a glass sky bridge from the Prudential Center, and a walk-in from the Copley mall—ensuring that you rarely have to go outside to shop or eat. Rooms have the quintessential Marriott flavor with flat-screen TVs; the best ones overlook Boston Harbor or the Charles River. **Pros:** good service; comfortable beds; great location; new look. **Cons:** crowded pool area; chaotic lobby; housekeeping not always up to par. **TripAdvisor:** "hotel staff was very accomodating," "easy indoor access to the Prudential Center, Hynes Convention Center, Copley Place shopping," "location is ideal for pedestrians." ⊠ *110 Huntington Ave., Back Bay* ☎ *617/236–5800, 800/228–9290* ⊕ *www. marriott.com* ↝ *1,101 rooms, 47 suites* ⌂ *In-room: safe, Internet. In-hotel: restaurant, bar, pool, gym, spa, parking* ⏃ *No meals* Ⓜ *Copley, Back Bay/South End.*

$$ 🏨 **Newbury Guest House.** Shopping enthusiasts have designated this elegant brownstone the "center of the universe." On Boston's most fashionable shopping street, the 1882 row house looks the part, with natural pine flooring, Victorian furnishings, and prints from the Museum of Fine Arts. Guests can order room service from the tiny French bistro, La Voile, downstairs. Some rooms have bay windows; others have decorative fireplaces. Limited parking is available. **Pros:** cozy; homey; great location. **Cons:** dated rooms; small bathrooms; street noise. **TripAdvisor:** "perfect price," "wonderful experience," "great location." ⊠ *261 Newbury St., Back Bay* ☎ *617/670–6100, 800/437–7668* ⊕ *www. newburyguesthouse.com* ↝ *32 rooms* ⌂ *In-room: Wi-Fi. In-hotel: parking* ⏃ *Breakfast* Ⓜ *Hynes, Copley* ⊹ *2:A2.*

$$$$ [icon] **Taj Boston Hotel.** Old-school elegance reigns at the Taj, formerly the [icon] landmark Ritz-Carlton Boston. (Don't worry, former fans, the Ritz Boston Common is still across the park.) Standing guard at the corner of fashionable Newbury Street and the Public Garden, the Taj is doing its best to win over the old Ritz fans, as well as woo new guests, with discounted weekend rates and a soft renovation. Thanks to that effort, it's the most affordable luxury hotel in town, with standard room rates starting at $299. Changes include plush new robes and towels in guest rooms, Molton Brown bath amenities, and vibrant floral displays in the lobby. Happily, some of the best features of the old Ritz remain, including wood-burning fireplaces (and fireplace butlers), Boston's best afternoon tea, and glorious views. Readers warn: Avoid rooms on the 16th floor, under the roof-deck party space. **Pros:** white-glove service; great views; proximity to shopping, dining, and the park. **Cons:** occasionally snobby staff; frequently barren restaurant. **TripAdvisor:** "pleasant stay with good value for money," "helpful staff," "rooms are spacious and comfortable." ⊠ *15 Arlington St., Back Bay* ☎ *617/536–5700* ⊕ *www. tajhotels.com* ⤳ *273 rooms, 45 suites* ⌂ *In-room: safe, Wi-Fi. In-hotel: restaurant, bar, gym, children's programs, parking, some pets allowed* ⊚*No meals* Ⓜ *Arlington* ✛ *2:C1.*

$$$$ [icon] **Westin Copley Place Boston.** If the idea of sleeping in an upscale mall appeals to you, meet your new favorite hotel. The Westin has its own pod of retail shops and is connected by a covered skywalk to Copley Place (more high-end shopping) and the Hynes Convention Center. The top-floor rooms of this contemporary 36-story hotel have some of the best views in Boston—of the Charles River, Copley Square, the South End, Back Bay, and Boston skylines (especially gorgeous when a-twinkle at night). No surprise that business travelers and visiting families love this place, especially when you factor in the pool and fitness center. Guest rooms are awash in beiges, dark greens, and blues, with wildly comfortable beds and plush linens. **Pros:** great location; wide views; clean, spacious rooms; Heavenly beds. **Cons:** big and busy-feeling; pool area is nothing special; some say it's overpriced. **TripAdvisor:** "maid service was first class," "what a great location," "room was clean, spacious and comfortable." ⊠ *10 Huntington Ave., Back Bay* ☎ *617/262–9600, 800/937–8461* ⊕ *www.westin.com/copleyplace* ⤳ *753 rooms, 50 suites* ⌂ *In-room: safe, Wi-Fi. In-hotel: restaurant, bar, pool, gym, spa, some pets allowed* Ⓜ *Copley, Back Bay/South End* ✛ *2:B2.*

THE SOUTH END

$$ [icon] **Chandler Inn.** There's big news at the Chandler. Namely, it's almost all new. Big-shot local designers Dennis Duffy and Eric Roseff took to the place and redid 40 of the 55 guest rooms in a fresh, contemporary style. Then, the owners updated the amenities to include iPod docks, plasma TVs, and marble bathrooms with walk-in glass showers. Next up: a central air system. The gay-friendly inn sits on one of the South End's prettiest streets, and is easy walking distance from shops, restaurants, the T, and Back Bay Station. As far as South End lodging goes, this may be your best hotel bet, despite slightly cramped quarters. ■ TIP➡ Try to snag a sun-lit corner room with a number ending in 08. Fritz, the in-house bar, moonlights as a brunch spot on weekends. **Pros:**

can't beat the price; friendly staff; lively gay scene. **Cons:** area parking is brutally hard to find or expensive; rooms can be noisy. **TripAdvisor:** "rooms were small but clean," "will definitely stay here again," "in a quiet area close to the heart of the city." ✉ *26 Chandler St., South End* ☎ *617/482–3450, 800/842–3450* ⊕ *www.chandlerinn.com* ⌨ *55 rooms* ♿ *In-room: Wi-Fi. In-hotel: restaurant, bar, some pets allowed* Ⓜ *Back Bay* ✚ *2:D3.*

$$$$ ⊡ **Clarendon Square Inn.** In the heart of the residential South End, this hip property is for travelers who appreciate the intimacy of a B&B and the style and sophistication of an upscale hotel. Renovations have blended original 1860 Victorian touches, including hardwood floors, marble fireplaces, and decorative moldings, with modern art and up-to-date amenities. All rooms have queen-size beds and baths with limestone floors, tile walls, and whirlpools or two-person showers; some even have skylights. The fifth floor has a roof deck and hot tub with a view of the Boston skyline. **Pros:** free Wi-Fi; feels more boutique hotel than B&B. **Cons:** just three rooms means reservations are hard to come by; no elevator; once-free parking now costs $25. **TripAdvisor:** "innkeepers are all friendly and extremely helpful," "very comfortable bed," "hot tub on the roof terrace with views over Boston." ✉ *198 W. Brookline St., South End* ☎ *617/536–2229* ⊕ *www.clarendonsquare.com* ⌨ *3 rooms* ♿ *In-room: Wi-Fi. In-hotel: parking* ⏀ *Breakfast* Ⓜ *Back Bay/ South End* ✚ *2:B4.*

$$$ ⊡ **Encore.** Innkeepers Reinhold Mahler and David Miller know a thing or two about ambience. An architect and creative set designer, respectively, they've pooled their creative energies into Encore, a gem of a South End lodging (trust us, they're hard to come by). The stylish converted 19th-century townhouse boasts sun-filled rooms named for famous gay men in the arts (Sondheim, Albee, Bernstein) that are spacious and spotless, and bedecked with modern Italian furnishings, brushed-steel and chrome touches, and brick accent walls. The Albee room has a private deck; all rooms have ultramodern baths with glossy tiles and steel sinks. **Pros:** trendy South End location; free Wi-Fi; Bang & Olufson sound systems; David and Reinhold are gracious hosts. **Cons:** small breakfast nook; frequent two-night minimums; no elevator. **TripAdvisor:** "free coffee downstairs," "excellent restaurant in the hotel," "having and indoor pool and hot tub is a definite plus." ✉ *116 W. Newton St., South End* ☎ *617/247–3425* ⊕ *www.encorebandb.com* ⌨ *3 rooms* ♿ *In-room: Wi-Fi. In-hotel: parking* ⏀ *Breakfast* Ⓜ *Back Bay, Mass. Ave* ✚ *2:B4.*

THE FENWAY AND KENMORE SQUARE

$$$ ⊡ **Gryphon House.** The suites in this four-story 19th-century brownstone are thematically decorated: one evokes rustic Italy; another is inspired by neo-Gothic art. Among the many amenities—including gas fireplaces, wet bars, DVD and CD players, and private voice mail—the enormous bathrooms with oversize tubs and separate showers are the most appealing. Even the staircase is extraordinary: a wallpaper mural, *El Dorado*, wraps along the walls. Trompe-l'oeil paintings and murals by local artist Michael Ernest Kirk decorate the common spaces. **Pros:** awesome value; free Wi-Fi; elegant suites are lush and spacious;

gas fireplaces in all rooms; helpful, friendly staff. **Cons:** closed from Christmas to New Year's Eve; may be too fussy for some; there's no elevator or handicapped access. ⊠ *9 Bay State Rd., Kenmore Sq.* ☎ *617/375–9003, 877/375–9003* ⊕ *www.innboston.com* ↘ *8 suites* ⚫ *In-room: kitchen, Wi-Fi. In-hotel: laundry facilities, parking* ▯ *Breakfast* Ⓜ *Kenmore* ✛ *3:G2.*

¢ ▯ **Hostelling International Boston.** The bare-bones, low-cost option near the Museum of Fine Arts is ideal if you don't mind sharing one of the six-person dormitory rooms with a slew of backpacking, college-age travelers. (Private rooms are available for a higher price.) Bright purple paint enlivens the rather drab decor, but everything is ultraclean. Linens are provided (no sleeping bags allowed), and there's a full kitchen and TV room. Discounted tickets are often available to cultural events, and continental breakfast is included. The lodging does not require membership, but does suggest reservations. If this one's booked solid, try the sister Fenway location (summers only). Travelers under 18 must be accompanied by parent or guardian. **Pros:** free Wi-Fi; clean and professional; open 24 hours a day; unbeatable price. **Cons:** not for hotel snobs; little privacy; noisy during peak times. ⊠ *12 Hemenway St., Kenmore Square* ☎ *617/536–9455* ⊕ *www.bostonhostel.org* ↘ *52 rooms (100 rooms, Fenway)* ⚫ *In-room: no a/c, no TV. In-hotel: restaurant, laundry facilities* ▯ *Breakfast* Ⓜ *MFA* ✛ *3:H3.*

$$$ ▯ **Hotel Commonwealth.** Rumor has it that Bono and the Boss have
☾ walked the hallways of the Hotel Commonwealth. So have a host of
Fodor's Choice local celebs and visitors intent on branching out of the downtown Bos-
★ ton hospitality scene. Luxury and service without pretense makes the hip spot a solid choice. Rich color schemes enhance the elegant lodgings, and king- or queen-size beds are piled with down pillows and Italian linens. All rooms have marble baths, floor-to-ceiling windows, separate work areas, and flat-screen TVs. The wildy accommodating staff and chauffeur are added bonuses. In-house Eastern Standard serves up some of the best old-school cocktails in the city. **Pros:** free Wi-Fi; down bedding; perfect locale for Red Sox fans; happening bar scene at Eastern Standard. **Cons:** area is mobbed during Sox games; small gym. **TripAdvisor:** "staff is uniformly gracious, friendly, and helpful," "very comfortable beds," "close to many great restaurants as well as Fenway Park." ⊠ *500 Commonwealth Ave., Kenmore Square* ☎ *617/933–5000, 866/784–4000* ⊕ *www.hotelcommonwealth.com* ↘ *149 rooms, 1 suite* ⚫ *In-room: safe, Wi-Fi. In-hotel: restaurant, bar, gym, children's programs, parking, some pets allowed* ▯ *No meals* Ⓜ *Kenmore* ✛ *3:F2.*

CLOSE UP

Lodging Alternatives

11

Hotels are an obvious lodging choice, but they aren't your only option; there are plenty of other ways to stay in Boston, some with much more affordable rates than your average double room. Bed-and-breakfasts often get a bad rap for being too cloying, cutesy, or dusty, but many in the Boston area are updated, clean, and modern, and well worth a look. If you don't happen to have a friend with an extra bed- and bathroom, and you don't mind doing a bit of legwork, you can look into short-term sublets or apartment rentals or swaps. Or, if you decide there's no need for fancy service or, really, any amenities, plan to stay in the simplest lodging possible: a hostel.

APARTMENT RENTALS

If you want a home base that's roomy enough for a family and comes with cooking facilities, consider a furnished rental. Home-exchange directories sometimes list rentals as well as exchanges, and many of the B&B agencies *below* also handle apartment, cottage, and house rentals.

BED-AND-BREAKFASTS

Bed & Breakfast Agency of Boston ☎ *617/720–3540, 800/248–9262* ⊕ *www.boston-bnbagency.com.* **Bed & Breakfast Associates** ☎ *781/449–5302, 888/486–6018* ⊕ *www. bnbboston.com.* **Bed and Breakfast Reservations: North Shore/Greater Boston/Cape Cod** ☎ *617/964–1606, 978/281–9505* ⊕ *www.bbreserve.com.* **Greater Boston Hospitality Bed & Breakfast Service** ☎ *617/393–1548* ⊕ *www.bostonbedandbreakfast.com.* **Host Homes of Boston** ☎ *617/244–1308, 800/600–1308* ⊕ *www. hosthomesofboston.com.*

HOME EXCHANGES

A home-exchange organization will send you its updated listings of available exchanges via either email or printed brochure. It's up to you to make specific arrangements.

HomeLink International ☎ *954/566–2687, 800/638–3841* ⊕ *www.homelink. org.* **Intervac U.S.** ☎ *800/756–4663* ⊕ *www.intervacus.com.*

HOSTELS

Hostelling International (HI), the umbrella group for a number of national youth-hostel associations, offers single-sex, dorm-style beds and, at many hostels, rooms for couples and family accommodations. Membership in any HI national hostel association, open to travelers of all ages, allows you to stay in HI-affiliated hostels at member rates; one-year U.S. membership is about $28 for adults; hostels charge about $10–$45 per night. Members have priority if the hostel is full; they're also eligible for discounts around the world, even on rail and bus travel in some countries.

Eastern New England Council of Hostelling International–American Youth Hostels. Eastern New England Council of Hostelling International–American Youth Hostels provides information on membership and on hostels in the Boston area. ☎ *617/718–7990* ⊕ *www.usahostels.org.* **Hostelling International Australia** ⊕ *www.yha. com.au.* **Hostelling International Canada** ☎ *613/237–7884, 800/663–5777* ⊕ *www.hihostels.ca.* **Hostelling International New Zealand** ☎ *03/379–9970, 0/800/278–299* ⊕ *www.yha.co.nz.* **Hostelling International UK** ☎ *0800/0191700* ⊕ *www. yha.org.uk.* **Hostelling International US** ☎ *301/495–1240* ⊕ *www.hiusa.org.*

Hotel Commonwealth

The Charles Hotel

BOSTON OUTSKIRTS

BRIGHTON

11

$$$ **Best Western Terrace Inn.** In a residential neighborhood between Boston University and Boston College, this motel is well priced, if unremarkable. Thanks to a recent renovation, guest rooms are spiffed up in a modern taupe palette. All rooms have refrigerators and microwave ovens; suites have kitchenettes. There's a Whole Foods supermarket just a block away. The T is nearby, but the ride to downtown Boston and major attractions can take up to an hour. **Pros:** free Wi-Fi; economical option for parents visiting BU or BC students; free parking. **Cons:** no elevator; drab decor; college-kid neighborhood; slow T ride to downtown. **TripAdvisor:** "staff was very pleasant and helpful," "basic but clean," "best deal at this proximity to town." ✉ *1650 Commonwealth Ave., Brighton* 🕾 *617/566–6260, 800/780–7234* ⊕ *www.bostonbw. com* 🛏 *68 rooms, 6 suites* ⬙ *In-room: kitchen, Wi-Fi. In-hotel: parking* 🍽 *Breakfast* Ⓜ *Washington St.* ✛ *3:A2.*

BROOKLINE

$$ **Bertram Inn.** Quiet and old-fashioned is the Bertram's m.o. The antiques-laden inn, in walking distance from Cleveland Circle, was built in 1907 as a wedding present for a wealthy merchant's daughter. The Victorian-style building still has wood floors, paneled walls, and marble fireplaces. Each room is unique—one has hummingbird wallpaper, another, a high canopy bed with steps. The one off the large living room is a favorite, with a four-poster bed, Oriental rug, cherry paneling, and working fireplace. Sound ho-hum? Hear this: Some rooms have ultra-deluxe (and super-expensive) Duxiana mattresses, worth the trip alone. **Pros:** fresh fruit, pastries, and drinks available all day; relaxing living room; hushed vibe. **Cons:** no elevator; could be tidier; far from downtown Boston. **TripAdvisor:** "great location," "charming," "lovely B&B." ✉ *92 Sewall Ave., Brookline* 🕾 *617/566–2234, 800/295–3822* ⊕ *www.bertraminn.com* 🛏 *14 rooms* ⬙ *In-room: Wi-Fi. In-hotel: parking, some pets allowed* 🍽 *Breakfast* Ⓜ *St. Paul St.* ✛ *3:B4.*

$$$ **Courtyard by Marriott Boston Brookline.** If you don't mind the anonymity and predictability of a chain hotel—and don't mind staying outside of Boston proper—this is a decent choice. Five colleges sit less than 5 mi from the Marriott, making it popular with visiting families. The just-renovated guest rooms are pleasant and clean, and the property has an indoor pool, hot tub, and small gym. The T is right outside the door, as are ample neighborhood restaurants. (An on-site eatery is open for breakfast and dinner.) **Pros:** kid-friendly with adjoining rooms; 1 mi from Fenway Park; roomy bathrooms; free Wi-Fi. **Cons:** staff can be indifferent; dull decor. **TripAdvisor:** "more than accomodating," "great gem," "enjoyed our stay." ✉ *40 Webster St., Brookline* 🕾 *617/734–1393, 866/296–2296* ⊕ *www.marriott.com/bosbl* 🛏 *188 rooms* ⬙ *In-room: Wi-Fi. In-hotel: restaurant, bar, pool, gym, parking* 🍽 *No meals* Ⓜ *Beacon St.* ✛ *3:A4.*

$$$ **Inn at Longwood Medical.** If close proximity to Harvard Medical School or any of its partner hospitals is your top priority, book a room at this Best Western affiliate. Many hotel guests are patients or relatives of patients (there's a discounted medical rate, even on the busiest weekends). In summer, expect baseball fans to crowd the halls and

lobby, as the hotel is also close to Fenway Park. For the most part, rooms are cookie-cutter, but nicely appointed with desks and updated linens. **Pros:** helpful staff; medical rate packages, attached to Long-wood Galleria Mall and food court. **Cons:** subdued vibe; nothing-special decor; expensive area parking.

TripAdvisor: "staff was very friendly and helpful," "have always had a great experience," "comfortable quiet room." ⊠ *342 Longwood Ave., Brookline* ☎ *617/731–4700, 800/468–2378* ⊕ *www.innatlongwood. com* ⊊ *140 rooms, 15 suites* ⚲ *In-room: kitchen, Wi-Fi. In-hotel: restaurant, bar, parking* ¡○¡ *No meals* Ⓜ *Longwood* ✛ *3:D5.*

LOGAN AIRPORT (EAST BOSTON)

$$$ 🏨 **Hilton Boston Logan Airport.** Quiet rooms, competitive prices, and an on-airport location make this modern Hilton a good choice for in-and-out visitors to Boston. The 600-room hotel is attached to a skywalk to Logan terminals A and E; it also runs a free shuttle bus to the airport. Rooms have been updated with granite countertops and desks with ergonomic chairs. There's an unremarkable restaurant, Berkshires, and a casual, publike eatery on the premises, plus a health club with a steam room. **Pros:** easy access to Logan Airport; competitive prices. **Cons:** Internet and parking can add up; far from downtown Boston. **TripAdvisor:** "exceptionally quiet with a comfortable bed," "fitness center is great," "perfect for an overnight stay to catch an early flight." ⊠ *1 Hotel Dr., East Boston* ☎ *617/568–6700, 800/445-8667* ⊕ *www. hiltonfamilyboston.com* ⊊ *599 rooms, 5 suites* ⚲ *In-room: Wi-Fi. In-hotel: restaurant, bar, pool, gym, parking, some pets allowed* ¡○¡ *No meals* Ⓜ *Airport* ✛ *1:H4.*

$$$ 🏨 **Hyatt Harborside at Boston Logan International Airport.** Half the rooms at the airport Hyatt have sweeping views of either the city skyline or the ocean; the others overlook planes taking off and landing. As a major convenience, the hotel operates its own 24-hour shuttle to all Logan Airport terminals and the airport T stop. Rooms, done up in soothing taupes and beiges, are soundproof. **Pros:** close to airport; pool area has skyline views; competent, can-do staff. **Cons:** close to airport; over-priced restaurant (skip it); airport shuttle is frustratingly slow. **TripAdvisor:** "room service food was excellent," "indoor pool and fitness rooms have great views," "attractive room and a nice bed." ⊠ *101 Harborside Dr., East Boston* ☎ *617/568–1234, 800/233–1234* ⊕ *www.harborside. hyatt.com* ⊊ *270 rooms* ⚲ *In-room: Wi-Fi. In-hotel: restaurant, bar, pool, gym, parking, some pets allowed* ¡○¡ *No meals* Ⓜ *Airport* ✛ *1:H4.*

CAMBRIDGE

$$ 🏨 **A Cambridge House Inn.** Recently, this sweet Cambridge spot bought and renovated the adjacent building, adding 18 rooms and a new look to its Victorian aesthetic. Now guests can choose between old-school B&B charm and modernized hospitality. The original property,

a restored 1892 National Register of Historic Places house, has richly carved cherry paneling, a grand fireplace, elegant antiques, and polished wood floors overlaid with Oriental rugs. Its antiques-filled guest rooms come with fabric-covered walls, four-poster canopy beds, and the standard New England doily decor. Rooms in the new part are decidedly less frilly, and outfitted with single-color paints and furnishings. Harvard Square isn't terribly close, but public transportation is available nearby. **Pros:** cozy fireplace lounges; free parking and Wi-Fi; complimentary coffee, tea, and hot chocolate. **Cons:** not for modernists; very quiet area; no elevators. ⊠ *2218 Massachusetts Ave., Cambridge* ☎ *617/491–6300, 800/232–9989* ⊕ *www.acambridgehouse.com* ⤴ *33 rooms* ⌂ *In-room: Wi-Fi. In-hotel: parking* ⊙| *Breakfast* Ⓜ *Davis Sq* ✛ *4:B1.*

$$$$ ⊡ **Boston Marriott Cambridge.** Traveling businesspeople and families like the modern look and efficiency of this 26-story, high-rise hotel in Kendall Square, just steps from the subway and MIT. The rooms are decorated in soothing creams and reds, and the Revive beds feature crisp white duvets and fluffier pillows. Book a room on one of the two concierge floors and score complimentary breakfast, hors d'oeuvres, and desserts in the lounge. **Pros:** top-floor rooms have stunning views; comfy bed linens; decent cost-saving packages on weekends. **Cons:** zero original charm; tiny pool. **TripAdvisor:** "gorgeous view of the Boston skyline," "room service was good," "very reasonable price." ⊠ *2 Cambridge Center, 50 Broadway* ☎ *617/494–6600, 800/228–9290* ⊕ *www. marriotthotels.com/boscb* ⤴ *433 rooms, 11 suites* ⌂ *In-room: Wi-Fi. In-hotel: restaurant, bar, pool, gym, parking* ⊙| *No meals* Ⓜ *Kendall/ MIT* ✛ *1:A5.*

$$$$ ⊡ **Charles Hotel.** It used to be that the Charles was *the* place to stay in ⟳ Cambridge. Other luxury hotels have since arrived to give it a little **Fodor's Choice** healthy competition, but this Harvard Square staple is standing strong. ★ A recent lobby and public space renovation refreshed the lower floors with Le Corbusier furniture, sketches by JFK himself, and work by various local artists. Gracious service and top-notch room amenities like terrycloth robes, handmade quilts, and LCD mirror-TVs also keep the hotel in high demand. Relax in the lobby library, chock-full of titles, some autographed by authors who happen to be frequent guests. Sign up for an art tour of the property or pick up a self-guided map of Cambridge. For a partial river or skyline view, ask for something above the seventh floor. In-house restaurants Rialto and Henrietta's Table are excellent; the latter especially for weekend brunch. ■TIP→ For the best rate, call the hotel directly. **Pros:** free Wi-Fi; free domestic calls; kid-friendly; on-site jazz club and hip Noir bar; outdoor skating rink in winter. **Cons:** luxury comes at a price; less convenient for downtown Boston trips. **TripAdvisor:** "staff was incredibly friendly," "restaurants are both very good," "rooms are more than comfortable with plenty of space." ⊠ *1 Bennett St., Cambridge* ☎ *617/864–1200, 800/882–1818* ⊕ *www.charleshotel.com* ⤴ *294 rooms, 45 suites* ⌂ *In-room: safe, Wi-Fi. In-hotel: restaurant, bar, pool, children's programs, parking, some pets allowed* Ⓜ *Harvard* ✛ *4:A3.*

$$ ⊡ **Harvard Square Hotel.** Don't feel like shelling out a week's salary to stay at the venerable Charles? Check in to the next-door Harvard

Square Hotel, where you'll get the location and convenience for half the cost. The lodging is basic, some say nondescript, but it's just steps from the square's plethora of shops, eateries, and bars. Rooms are simple but clean, with refrigerators and Internet access. Thankfully, the bathrooms—always a sore point here—have been modernized, and in-room flat-screen TVs were added as well. The desk clerks are particularly helpful, assisting with everything from sending faxes to securing dinner reservations. **Pros:** awesome location; some windows open for fresh air. **Cons:** unexciting decor; Wi-Fi, in-lobby computer use, and parking cost extra. **TripAdvisor:** "minimal amenities," "friendly staff," "overpriced." ⊠ *110 Mt. Auburn St., Cambridge* ☎ *617/864–5200, 800/458–5886* ⊕ *www.harvardsquarehotel.com* ➷ *73 rooms* ♿ *In-room: Wi-Fi. In-hotel: parking* ❙○❙ *No meals* Ⓜ *Harvard* ✛ *4:A2.*

$$$$ 🖥 **Hotel Marlowe.** If Alice in Wonderland dreamt up a hotel, it might look a bit like the Marlowe. Vivid stripes, swirls, and other geometric patterns lend the decor a wild, lively aesthetic. The unique, slightly over-the-top spot manages to be both luxe and wacky, with guest-room accessories like Frette linens, Aveda toiletries, leopard-print pillows, and fake-fur throws. Many of the generously sized rooms overlook the Charles River, and the property proffers complimentary wine receptions each evening and free use of bikes and kayaks in summer. Book readings and other literary events are often held in the lobby. **Pros:** family- and pet-friendly; fun, eclectic atmosphere, free wine tastings. **Cons:** unless you're a Kimpton program member, Wi-Fi comes at a charge; a cab or T ride or walk from central Boston; not for formal decor purists. **TripAdvisor:** "enjoyed their pet friendly atmosphere," "staff could not have been nicer," "nice extras such as a wine reception and free bikes." ⊠ *25 Edwin H. Land Blvd., Cambridge* ☎ *617/868–8000, 800/825–7140* ⊕ *www.hotelmarlowe.com* ➷ *222 rooms, 14 suites* ♿ *In-room: safe, Wi-Fi. In-hotel: restaurant, bar, gym, business center, parking, some pets allowed* ❙○❙ *No meals* Ⓜ *Lechmere* ✛ *1:C3.*

$$$$ 🖥 **Inn at Harvard.** You don't have to be an alumnus to enjoy the handsome, hushed elegance of this hotel, which borders Harvard Yard and has a Georgian-style brick exterior that mirrors many of those on campus. The updated guest rooms have classic furnishings in black, brown, and neutral fabrics, and spiffed up bathrooms with new fixtures, tubs, and showers. Oversize windows frame views of Harvard Square or Harvard Yard and help give rooms a bright, cheerful feel. The skylit atrium lobby is studded with sculptures and fine woodwork. The comfy, albeit a tad stuffy, meeting space is a hangout for Harvard executives and visiting parents. **Pros:** excellent Harvard Square location; flat-screen TVs; potential for meeting visiting movers and shakers. **Cons:** smallish rooms; prices can soar during graduation week. **TripAdvisor:** "excellent stay," "great location," "service above and beyond." ⊠ *1201 Massachusetts Ave.* ☎ *617/491–2222, 800/458–5886* ⊕ *www.theinnatharvard.com* ➷ *109 rooms, 4 suites* ♿ *In-room: Wi-Fi. In-hotel: restaurant, gym, parking* ❙○❙ *No meals* Ⓜ *Harvard* ✛ *4:B3.*

$$$ 🖥 **Irving House.** On a residential street three blocks from Harvard Square, this four-story gray clapboard B&B is a bargain. It has two small porches, hardwood floors, and Oriental carpets, making it homier than a hotel, and there's a real sense of conviviality among guests, mostly Europeans

and visiting parents or professors. The small, super-clean rooms are being refurbished one by one with new paint and furnishings (ask for a finished one when you book). The limited off-street parking is a real coup in car-clogged Cambridge. So is the green and guilt-free solar thermal water-heating system. As a nice added touch, the Irving House will mail postcards anywhere free of charge. **Pros:** free Wi-Fi; good location and price; coffee, tea, and pastries are available until 10 pm. **Cons:** parking spaces are first-come, first-served; some rooms with shared baths. **TripAdvisor:** "courteous service," "breakfasts are extraordinary," "lovely place." ✉ *24 Irving St., Cambridge* ☎ *617/547–4600, 877/547–4600* ⊕ *www. cambridgeinns.com/irving* ↝ *44 rooms, 29 with bath* ♿ *In-room: Wi-Fi. In-hotel: laundry facilities, parking* ⦿ *Breakfast* Ⓜ *Harvard* ✛ *4:C2.*

$$$$ ⊡ **Kendall Hotel.** You might think a place in such a high-tech neighborhood would be all stainless steel and chrome. Think again. The Kendall Hotel is homey and ultrafriendly, bright-hue and lively. Based in the former Engine House 7 fire station, it is stuffed with related memorabilia. Owner Charlotte Forsythe loves all collectibles, so an antique Chinese checkerboard, a ceramic Dalmatian, and a whimsical grandfather clock contribute to the mishmash decor. Rooms are done up in Easter-egg hues, and a seven-story addition includes an enclosed rooftop lounge, eight deluxe rooms, and four suites with kitchens perfect for families. On Monday through Thursday evenings the hotel hosts a wine hour on its seventh floor. Bonus for workout buffs: free guest passes to nearby gym, Fitcorp. **Pros:** free Wi-Fi; accommodating staff; included hot buffet breakfast; quiet rooms. **Cons:** tchotchkes aplenty; far from Downtown and the Back Bay. **TripAdvisor:** "service was wonderful," "great boutique hotel feel," "Black Sheep is so cozy and romantic." ✉ *350 Main St., Cambridge* ☎ *617/566–1300, 866/566–1300* ⊕ *www. kendallhotel.com* ↝ *73 room, 4 suites* ♿ *In-room: kitchen, Internet. In-hotel: restaurant, bar, parking* ⦿ *Breakfast* Ⓜ *Kendall/MIT* ✛ *4:H5.*

$$$ ⊡ **Le Meridien Cambridge.** When the Meridien chain took over the cult favorite geek-chic Hotel at MIT, some fans worried the Cambridge spot would lose its charm. But the new owners only amped up the offerings—and added some luxe touches—by displaying cool interactive lobby art from MIT and refurbishing the guest rooms with platform beds, puffy white duvets, flat-screen TVs, and ergonomically designed furniture. In the lobby and the large, open-kitchen restaurant, Sidney's Grille, cool metal decor is mixed with burnished maple, redwood, and oak. Not surprisingly, the hotel is a hub for techie business travelers. It can also be a bargain for weekend vacationers. **Pros:** free Wi-Fi; tech-savvy rooms and surroundings; 24-hour fitness center; great off-season rates. **Cons:** a 10-minute walk to the T; pricey high-season rates; good area dining hard to come by. **TripAdvisor:** "full of light and stylishly decorated," "comfortable and convenient," "great location near MIT." ✉ *20 Sidney St., Cambridge* ☎ *617/577–0200, 800/222–8733* ⊕ *www. lemeridien.com/cambridge* ↝ *196 rooms, 14 suites* ♿ *In-room: safe, Wi-Fi. In-hotel: restaurant, bar, gym, parking, some pets allowed* ⦿ *No meals* Ⓜ *Central, Kendall/MIT* ✛ *4:F5.*

$$$$ ⊡ **Royal Sonesta Hotel.** Right next to the Charles River, the Sonesta has one of the best sunset views in Boston. Diners at in-house Italian restaurant can sip a glass of prosecco while watching dusk fall on the boats

sailing by. Inside, modern art lines the hotel's hallways, and a friendly, professional staff make this just-renovated Cambridge riverfront property a bit of a surprise. Also great: an attractive indoor-outdoor pool. Guest rooms are done in neutral earth tones, with modern amenities such as flat-screen TVs, gaming consoles, Wi-Fi, and CD clock radios. Note to parents: Kids 12 and under eat and stay for free if you book via the hotel's Web site. **Pros:** free Wi-Fi; nice pool; certified green hotel. **Cons:** a bit sterile; close to the Museum of Science but a far walk from the Back Bay and South End. **TripAdvisor:** "nice room (good size and clean)," "water pressure in the shower wasn't great," "great view on Charles River." ⊠ *40 Edwin Land Blvd., off Memorial Dr., Cambridge* ☎ *617/806–4200, 800/766–3782* ⊕ *www.sonesta.com/boston* ⤴ *379 rooms, 21 suites* ⬧ *In-room: safe, Wi-Fi. In-hotel: restaurant, bar, pool, gym, spa, business center, parking* ⎸❍⎹ *No meals* Ⓜ *Lechmere* ✢ *1:B4.*

$$$$ 📺 **Sheraton Commander.** The beloved, 1927 Harvard Square landmark has finally gotten a face-lift. Its signature bright red neon sign still towers overhead, but, inside, the rooms have been updated with classic furnishings; handsome, jewel colored accents; wireless Internet; and cushy leather lounge chairs. In the lobby and common spaces lovely architectural touches like grand arches and a bi-level ballroom with a carved ceiling and gilt mirrors delight the Sheraton's mature clientele. ■TIP→ If you need to get online, visit the lobby-level Link@Sheraton lounge for computer stations with free Wi-Fi and complementary magazines. **Pros:** historic landmark; helpful, knowledgeable staff; old-school Sunday brunch. **Cons:** small bathrooms; some rooms have views of the parking lot. **TripAdvisor:** "kind staff," "thoroughly impressed," "excellent location." ⊠ *16 Garden St., Cambridge* ☎ *617/547–4800* ⊕ *www. starwoodhotels.com* ⤴ *176 rooms* ⬧ *In-room: Internet. In-hotel: restaurant, bar, gym, business center, parking, some pets allowed* ⎸❍⎹ *No meals* Ⓜ *Harvard* ✢ *4:A1.*

Nightlife and the Arts

WORD OF MOUTH

"The Nutcracker is an institution here in Boston [and] the Boston Pops Holiday concerts are wonderful . . . book a table on the floor and enjoy hot cocoa and champagne!"

—bennnie

NIGHTLIFE AND THE ARTS PLANNER

Covers

Cover charges for local acts and club bands generally run $8–$20; big-name acts can be double that. Dance clubs usually charge a cover of $5–$10. Nearly all nightlife spots accept major credit cards; cash-only places are noted.

Last Call

Because Boston retains some vestiges of its puritanical blue laws, the only places open after the official 2 am closing time for bars and clubs are a few restaurants in Chinatown (at some you can ask for "cold tea" and still get a beer) and a few all-night diners, which won't serve alcohol. Bars may also close up shop early if business is slow or the weather is bad. Blue laws also prohibit bars from offering happy-hour drink specials, although happy-hour food specials abound.

Smoking

Boston and Cambridge's tough anti-cigarette laws ban smoking in all bars and restaurants.

Getting Informed

The best source of arts and nightlife information is the *Boston Globe*'s "Arts & Entertainment" section, available in the paper and online (⊕ *www.boston.com/thingstodo*). Also worth checking out are the Thursday "Calendar" section of the *Boston Globe;* the Friday "Scene" section of the *Boston Herald;* and the calendar listings in the many free magazines in drop boxes around town, especially the *Dig* (⊕ *www.weeklydig.com*), *Stuff@Night, Boston Phoenix* (⊕ *www.thephoenix.com*), and the *Improper Bostonian.* In addition to the *Globe*'s online listings, the *Dig* and *Boston Phoenix* also provide up-to-the-minute information online.

Getting Tickets

Boston's supporters of the arts are an avid group; tickets often sell out well in advance, so buy tickets when you make your hotel reservations if possible.

BosTix. BosTix is a full-price Ticketmaster outlet with two locations that sell half-price tickets for same-day performances and for select advance shows online. Only cash and traveler's checks are accepted in person; credit cards are accepted online. On Friday, Saturday, or Sunday, show up at least a half-hour before the booth opens. Booths are located in Quincy Market and Copley Square. ⊕ *www.bostix.org* ☉ *Tues.–Sat. 10–6, Sun. 11–4.*

Broadway Across America—Boston. This organization brings Broadway shows to Boston in pre- and post-Broadway runs. ☎ 866/523–7469 ⊕ *www.broadwayacrossamerica.com.*

Live Nation. Live Nation, a Boston-based outlet, handles tickets for shows at the House of Blues, Bank of America Pavilion, Orpheum Theatre, Paradise Rock Club, and other nightclubs. All transactions are conducted online. ☎ 800/745–3000 ⊕ *www.livenation.com.*

Ticketmaster. Ticketmaster allows phone charges, with no refunds or exchanges. It also has outlets in local stores; check online for locations. ☎ 800/653–8000, 800/745–3000 ⊕ *www.ticketmaster.com.*

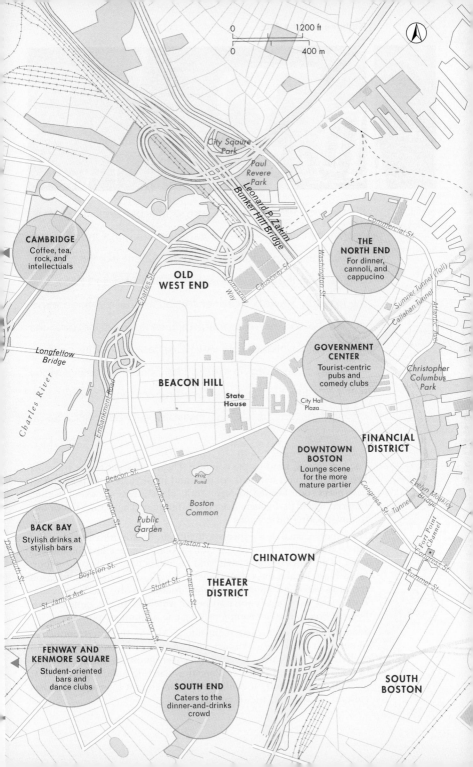

0   1200 ft
0   400 m

City Sqaure Park

Paul
Revere
Park

Leonard P. Zakim
Bunker Hill Bridge

CAMBRIDGE
Coffee, tea,
rock, and
intellectuals

**THE
NORTH END**
For dinner,
cannoli, and
cappucino

**OLD
WEST END**

Commercial St.

Washington St.

Causeway St.

*Lomasney
Way*

Sumner Tunnel (Toll)

Callahan Tunnel

Atlantic Ave.

*Longfellow
Bridge*

**GOVERNMENT
CENTER**
Tourist-centric
pubs and
comedy clubs

*Christopher
Columbus
Park*

Charles St.

Embankment Road

BEACON HILL

State
House

City Hall
Plaza

**FINANCIAL
DISTRICT**

Charles River

**DOWNTOWN
BOSTON**
Lounge scene
for the more
mature partier

*Evelyn Moakley
Bridge*

*Fort Point
Channel*

Beacon St.

*Frog
Pond*

Congress St. Tunnel

Arlington St.

Charles St.

*Boston
Common*

*Boston
Public
Garden*

BACK BAY
Stylish drinks at
stylish bars

Congress St.

Boylston St.

Summer St.

CHINATOWN

Dartmouth St.

Boylston St.

St. James Ave.

Stuart St.

Charles St.

Arlington St.

**THEATER
DISTRICT**

**SOUTH
BOSTON**

Stuart St.

**FENWAY AND
KENMORE SQUARE**
Student-oriented
bars and
dance clubs

SOUTH END
Caters to the
dinner-and-drinks
crowd

Updated by Bethany Cassin Beckerlegge

Boston's cultural attractions are a mix between Old World aesthetics and New World experimentation. On the classical side of the spectrum, revered institutions like the Museum of Fine Arts, the Boston Symphony Orchestra and Pops, and the Isabella Stewart Gardner Museum offer a refined experience. For a less reverential attitude toward the arts, the Institute of Contemporary Art (ICA) features exhibitions by multimedia and graffiti artists like Shepard Fairey. Many museums, like the MFA, the Gardner Museum, and the ICA also put on unique shows, festivals, and performances in their spaces.

For live shows, head to the compact Theater District to see traveling Broadway revues, national comedy and music acts, and previews of new plays soon headed to New York. Have a fancy cocktail in Bina Osteria, where performers from the Paramount Theater next door like to unwind after their shows.

For a more casual, less expensive night out, Boston provides plenty of alternatives. Indie rock and jazz clubs abound, dance clubs and lounges cater to all types of night owls, and countless bars in every neighborhood blare local games. Good luck, though, during baseball season trying to catch any sports game that doesn't involve the home team. Bostonians have been known to prefer watching an old game of their beloved Sox to even a championship game of another sport.

Scan the crowd over a late-night bite at Miel in the InterContinental Hotel or at the House of Blues on Lansdowne Street for both local and visiting celebrities. Whether it's cheering on the Bruins, Revolution (soccer), Sox, Celtics, or Pats at a watering hole, rocking out at an underground club, or chilling out at an elegant lounge, Boston has cultural amusements for all moods.

NIGHTLIFE

First and foremost, Boston is a Cinderella city. With public transportation shutting down each night between midnight and 1 am, most nightspots follow accordingly, with last call typically around 2 am. While true night owls may be disappointed by the meager late-night options, there are plenty of possibilities for visitors open to stepping out on the earlier side. The martini crowd may want to stroll Newbury and Boylston streets in the Back Bay, selecting from the neighborhood's swank restaurants, lounges, and clubs. Coffee and tea drinkers can find numerous cafés in Cambridge and Somerville, particularly Harvard and Davis squares. And beer swillers—well, there's pretty much an option on every corner. If you're having trouble finding a place to down a pint, you must have wandered out of Boston. For dancing, Lansdowne Street near Fenway Park has a mix of student-oriented clubs, sports bars, and techno clubs. There's also a thriving "lounge" scene in Downtown's coolest hybrid bar-restaurant-clubs providing a mellower, more mature alternative to the student-focused club scene. Tourists crowd Faneuil Hall for its pubs, comedy club, and dance spots. The South and North ends, as well as Cambridge and Somerville, cater to the "dinner-and-drinks" set, while those seeking great rock clubs should look no further than Allston, Jamaica Plain, and Cambridge, especially Central Square.

BARS

BOSTON

ALLSTON

Sunset Grill & Tap. It's a bit off the beaten path and looks, at first glance, like any other regular neighborhood hangout. But venture inside, and you'll be greeted by 500 varieties of beer, 112 of them on tap. Forget about pale domestic brews; try something unpronounceable from a faraway country—and if you're really thirsty, get a yard of it. ⊠ 130 *Brighton Ave., Allston* ☎ *617/254–1331* ⊕ *www.allstonsfinest.com* Ⓜ *Harvard.*

BACK BAY/BEACON HILL

★ **Alley.** Several watering holes, packed onto one cozy street just off Boston Common, serve those wanting a late night out without having to crisscross the city. **Liquor Store.** With a mechanical bull and loud music, the Liquor Store is a place to check your inhibitions at the door. ⊠ *25 Boylston Pl.* ☎ *617/357–6800* ⊕ *www.liquorstoreboston.com* **Sweetwater Tavern.** Sweetwater Tavern has a booming sound system and plenty of drink options. After a night of carousing, patrons appreciate its $1 oysters and locally sourced food. ⊠ *3 Boylston Pl.* ☎ *617/351–2515* ⊕ *www.sweetwatercafeboston.com* ⊠ *Boylston Pl. off Boylston St., Theater District* Ⓜ *Boylston.*

Bond Restaurant and Lounge. One of the hottest bars in the city this is a stylish and modern spot, belying its location in the conservative, tony Langham Boston Hotel. Thirty types of whiskey top the extensive menu; come expecting top shelf liquor and top shelf prices. ⊠ *250 Franklin St., Back Bay* ☎ *617/956–8765* ⊕ *www.bondboston.com* Ⓜ *State.*

Bukowski Tavern. This narrow barroom has a literary flair and more than 100 beers on the menu. It's cash-only policy tends to dissuade travelers, but locals love the place. The burgers are cheap (if you're daring, try the peanut-butter burger), the draft selection is original, and the sound track is loud and very cool. ⊠ *50 Dalton St., Back Bay* ☎ *617/437–9999* ⊟ *No credit cards* Ⓜ *Hynes.*

Cactus Club. One of the few places in Boston that make a decent margarita, the Cactus Club has a popular outdoor patio for kicking back, sipping frozen drinks, and watching the stylish Back Bay crowds pass by. ⊠ *939 Boylston St., Back Bay* ☎ *617/236–0200* ⊕ *www.bestmargaritas. com* Ⓜ *Hynes.*

> ### THE REAL CHEERS
>
> TV's *Cheers* may have ended in 1993, but that doesn't stop die-hard fans from paying their respects at the "real" Cheers bar on Beacon Street (or its second location in Faneuil Hall). Although the inspiration for the TV show doesn't quite look like its fictional double, the same atmosphere of good spirits persists. You can find your own kind of notoriety here by devouring the double-decker "Giant Norm burger" and adding your name to the Hall of Fame.

Champions Sports Bar. Calling all sports fans—the more rabid, the better. Thanks to its more than 30 TVs, you'll be sure to get a good view at this bar. Visiting-team fans may be welcome, but expect to be drowned out by cheers for the home team. ⊠ *Boston Marriott Copley Place, Copley Place Mall, 2nd level, 110 Huntington Ave., Back Bay* ☎ *617/927–5304* ⊕ *www.championsboston.com* Ⓜ *Prudential Center.*

Cheers. Formerly known as the Bull & Finch Pub, Cheers was dismantled in England, shipped to Boston, and reassembled here. Though it was the inspiration for the TV series of the same name, it doesn't look anything like the bar in the show. Addressing that complaint, however, a branch in Faneuil Hall that opened in 2001 is an exact reproduction of the TV set. ⊠ *Hampshire House, 84 Beacon St., Beacon Hill* ☎ *617/227–9605* ⊕ *www.cheersboston.com* Ⓜ *Park St., Charles/MGH.*

District Restaurant & Lounge. This lounge evokes a sleek, 1960s-era bachelor loft and draws equally stylish twenty- and thirtysomethings who lounge at the white banquettes sipping cocktails until the 2 am closing time. ⊠ *180 Lincoln St., Leather District* ☎ *617/426–0180* ⊕ *www. districtboston.com* Ⓜ *South Station.*

Fodor'sChoice ★ **Gypsy Bar.** Prowl on over to party with scantily clad, well-imbibed club cats. It's a great option for singles who want to dance the night away. ⊠ *116 Boylston St., Theater District* ☎ *617/482–7799* ⊕ *www. gypsybarboston.com* Ⓜ *Boylston.*

Oak Bar. This bar, inside the historic Fairmont Copley Plaza hotel, boasts an elegant backdrop of whirring ceiling fans, marble, and (of course) oak evoking cricket matches under the Bombay sun and duels fought over illicit love affairs. The Old World atmosphere is perfect for perusing a generous menu of signature martinis, single malts, and desserts. ⊠ *Fairmont Copley Plaza hotel, 138 St. James Ave., Back Bay* ☎ *617/267–5300* ⊕ *www.fairmont.com/copleyplaza/* Ⓜ *Copley.*

Poe's Kitchen @ The Rattlesnake. A few blocks off the Public Garden, the restaurant–bar has pool tables, televised sports, and (in-season) an open-air rooftop patio that lure in Back Bay shoppers and the after-work crowd. ⊠ *384 Boylston St., Back Bay* ☎ *617/859–7772* ⊕ *www. rattlesnakebar.com* Ⓜ *Arlington.*

TOP SPORTS BARS

- **Bukowski Tavern,** Back Bay
- **Champions,** Back Bay
- **The Fours,** Old West End
- **Fritz Lounge,** South End

12

Fodor's Choice
★

Saint. Saint, despite its name, draws patrons who are anything but. The spacious underground lounge consists of two rooms: an airy main space is decorated in blue and silver, with long couches to lounge on over appetizers while making eyes across the room. A more devilish "bordello room" is all plush red velvet and tasseled light fixtures, and offers private alcoves for intimate conversations. ⊠ *90 Exeter St., Back Bay* ☎ *617/236–1134* ⊕ *www. saintboston.com* Ⓜ *Copley.*

Sevens. There's nothing stuffy or pretentious at this laid-back alternative to the tony atmosphere of Beacon Hill, just good pints and old-fashioned mixed drinks, plus darts and the televised game of the night. ⊠ *77 Charles St., Beacon Hill* ☎ *617/523–9074* Ⓜ *Charles/MGH.*

Sonsie. The bar crowd, which spills through the French doors onto a sidewalk café in warm weather, is full of young, trendy, cosmopolitan types, professionals—and on some nights—local sports celebrities. The stereo volume stays at a manageable level for those wanting to chat while people-watching. ⊠ *327 Newbury St., Back Bay* ☎ *617/351–2500* ⊕ *www.sonsieboston.com* Ⓜ *Hynes.*

Splash Ultra Lounge & Burger Bar. Inspired by the watery atmosphere of clubs in Las Vegas, Splash features a pool fountain (no swimming allowed, unfortunately) on its roofdeck flanked by cabanas. It attracts well-dressed locals and suburbanites 25 years and older with its drink menu (try the strawberry-basil martini) and dozen or so hamburgers, which can also be ordered as sliders. ⊠ *150 Kneeland St., Leather District* ☎ *617/426–6397* ⊕ *www.splash150kneeland.com* Ⓜ *South Station.*

Top of the Hub. This fancy lounge has an incomparable view over the city; that and the hip jazz help to ease the sting of pricey drinks. ⊠ *Prudential Tower, 800 Boylston St., 52nd fl., Back Bay* ☎ *617/536–1775* ⊕ *www. topofthehub.net* Ⓜ *Prudential Center, Hynes.*

21st Amendment. Named after the amendment that ended Prohibition, this convivial pub, across from the State House, draws state legislators and lobbyists as well as neighborhood regulars. Gossip and insider info are traded at notched wooden tables over beer and barbecued-chicken salad. Or come for lively trivia (with discounted wings) on Sunday nights. ⊠ *150 Bowdoin St., Beacon Hill* ☎ *617/227–7100* ⊕ *21stboston.com* Ⓜ *Park St.*

CHARLESTOWN

Warren Tavern. Massachusetts' oldest watering hole is more than 200 years old, and was once frequented by Paul Revere. Today it caters mostly to tourists and Charlestown professionals. It's an easy stop for a pint en route to the Bunker Hill Monument or historic Navy Yard. Ask for the house-made potato chips with your ale of choice. ⊠ *2 Pleasant St., Charlestown* ☎ *617/241–8142* ⊕ *www. warrentavern.com* Ⓜ *Community College.*

DOWNTOWN

Beantown Pub. Right on the Freedom Trail, this is the only pub in Boston where you can enjoy a Sam Adams lager while overlooking the grave of Adams himself. It's a great place to watch the game, play pool, or get a snapshot of the passing throngs of tourists, professionals, and students. The menu—also available until 1 am—includes burgers, sandwiches, and other traditional pub fare. ⊠ *100 Tremont St., Downtown* ☎ *617/426–0111* ⊕ *www. beantownpub.com* Ⓜ *Park St., Downtown Crossing.*

Felt. Dress to impress; once past the velvet ropes, you will encounter four floors full of dressed-up, made-up clubgoers, and you may even spot a celebrity at a pool table, on the dance floor, or just enjoying a cocktail. ⊠ *533 Washington St., Downtown* ☎ *617/350–5555* ⊕ *feltclubboston. com* Ⓜ *Chinatown, Downtown Crossing, Boylston, Park.*

Good Life. This creative martini bar boasts exotic varieties such as cucumber, strawberry-basil, and caramel macchiato. On the basement level is the Afterlife Lounge, with more than 150 frozen vodka options on the menu. Rotating DJs draw a crowd ready for a boisterous night. ⊠ *28 Kingston St., Downtown* ☎ *617/451–2622* ⊕ *www.goodlifebar. com* Ⓜ *Downtown Crossing.*

J.J. Foley's Bar & Grill. This is another Irish pub that's worth a visit. Blue-collar workers down their Guinness pints along with neighboring Financial District suits; shoppers from Downtown Crossing take a break with a cider or ale. The atmosphere is no-frills, no-fuss. ⊠ *21 Kingston St., Downtown* ☎ *617/695–2529* ⊕ *jjfoleysbarandgrill.com* Ⓜ *Downtown Crossing.*

Kinsale. By day crowds of Government Center business people come for lunch and a pint. By night, the pub fills with revelers from nearby Faneuil Hall. It was reassembled here, piece by piece, after being constructed in Ireland, and has live music several nights a week. To share your vocal talents, come by on Thursday for karaoke. ⊠ *2 Center Plaza, Downtown* ☎ *617/742–5577* ⊕ *www.classicirish.com* Ⓜ *Government Center.*

Last Hurrah. The mahogany club chairs and silver-tray service might make you feel like a Brahmin, even if it's just for a martini or two. The historic setting and location inside the Omni Parker House right on the Freedom Trail make it an easy stop for those hitting the main sites Downtown. ⊠ *60 School St., Downtown* ☎ *617/227–8600* Ⓜ *Downtown Crossing, Park.*

MAKE IT A DATE

■ **Bristol Lounge** (for dessert), Back Bay

■ **Casablanca,** Cambridge

■ **Oak Bar,** Back Bay

■ **Sonsie,** Back Bay

■ **Top of the Hub,** Back Bay

Limelight Stage + Studios. Bold patrons can belt out their favorite tunes to the audience, and shy types can rent a "studio" room with friends at this karaoke bar. Linger around the main room to perhaps catch a local celebrity—American Idol contestant Ayla Brown, Mayor Menino, and other familiar faces have graced the stage in the past. Expect theatrics and a lively crowd. ✉ *204 Tremont St., Downtown/ Theater District* ☎ *617/423–0785,*

12

> **MOST HISTORIC PUBS**
>
> ■ **Bell in Hand Tavern,** Faneuil Hall
>
> ■ **Doyle's,** Jamaica Plain
>
> ■ **Green Dragon Tavern,** Faneuil Hall
>
> ■ **The Last Hurrah,** Downtown
>
> ■ **Warren Tavern,** Charlestown

877/557–8271 ⊕ *www.limelightboston.com* ✉ *Main stage: $5 before 10 pm, $10 after 10 pm; private studios: $10 per person per hr* ☉ *Thurs. 8 pm–1 am, Fri. and Sat. 7 pm–1 am* Ⓜ *Bolston, Park St.*

Revolution Rock Club. Fans of rock and roll should head to Revolution Rock Club: there's live music three nights a week, and DJs on the other evenings. Expect to hear alternative, classic rock, and punk on the dance floor. There are two floors for mixing and mingling. ✉ *200 High St., Downtown/Financial District* ☎ *617/261–4200* ⊕ *www. revolutionrockbar.com* ☉ *Weekdays 11:30 am–2 am, Sat. 5 pm–2 am* Ⓜ *Aquarium.*

RumBa. In the InterContinental hotel RumBa highlights two distinctive spirits: rum (more than 70 varieties) and champagne. Check out the hidden champagne lounge area behind sliding mahogany doors for quieter, more secluded celebrations—make sure to book in advance ✉ *510 Atlantic Ave., Downtown* ☎ *617/747–1000* ⊕ *www. intercontinentalboston.com/dining* Ⓜ *South Station, Aquarium.*

FANEUIL HALL

★ **Bell in Hand Tavern.** The country's oldest continuously operating pub is named after the occupation of its original owner, a town crier. It's on the perimeter of Faneuil Hall and has live music every night of the week. If you're brave, you can join the Tuesday-night karaoke. ✉ *45–55 Union St., Faneuil Hall* ☎ *617/227–2098* ⊕ *www.bellinhand. com* Ⓜ *Haymarket.*

Black Rose. The Black Rose is decorated with family crests, pictures of Ireland, and portraits of the likes of Samuel Beckett, Lady Gregory, and James Joyce—just like a Dublin pub. Its Faneuil Hall location draws as many tourists as locals, but nightly shows by traditional Irish and contemporary performers make it worth braving the crowds. ✉ *160 State St., Faneuil Hall* ☎ *617/742–2286* ⊕ *www.irishconnection.com/ blackrose.html* Ⓜ *Aquarium, State.*

Cheers. This outpost in Faneuil Hall was established by popular demand. The owners of the former Bull & Finch in Beacon Hill, which was the inspiration for the show, created an exact reproduction of the TV set, complete with Sam's Red Sox jacket and the photo of the Native-American chief behind the bar. Despite overpriced burgers and seafood, tourists and students are frequent customers. ✉ *Faneuil Hall Marketplace,*

Government Center ☎ 617/227–0150 ⊕ *www.cheersboston.com* Ⓜ *Government Center, Haymarket.*

Green Dragon Tavern. Less rowdy pub than its Faneuil Hall neighbors, this bar claims to be where local silversmith Paul Revere overheard the plans for a British assault on Lexington and Concord, prompting his famous ride. Today it's known more for having cover bands a few nights a week, regular lunch specials, and very friendly waitstaff. ✉ *11 Marshall St., Faneuil Hall* ☎ 617/367–0055 ⊕ *www.somerspubs.com* Ⓜ *Haymarket, Government Center.*

Hennessy's. Owned by the same group as the Green Dragon Tavern, Hennessy's claims to be the best Irish pub in town, although it has plenty of competition in that category, not least from its neighboring watering holes in Faneuil Hall. Expect a rowdy crowd on weekends and a quieter scene during the workweek. ✉ *25 Union St., Faneuil Hall* ☎ 617/742–2121 ⊕ *www.somerspubs.com* Ⓜ *Haymarket, Government Center.*

Hong Kong. This is a contender for Faneuil Hall's rowdiest bar. A caricature version of its Harvard Square location, the space is packed with bachelorette parties, fraternity boys hungry for a famous Scorpion Bowl, and revelers ready to hit the dance floor. It's often a first or last stop on a bar crawl. ✉ *65 Chatham St., Faneuil Hall* ☎ 617/227–2226 ⊕ *www.hongkongboston.com* Ⓜ *Aquarium, State, Government Center.*

Jose McIntyre's. Satisfy your double craving for a margarita and a Guinness—each expertly poured—at this Irish-Mexican bar. The eclecticism continues with a dance floor, several big-screen TVs, and a pool table. ✉ *160 Milk St., Faneuil Hall* ☎ 617/451–9460 ⊕ *www.irishconnection. com/joses.html* Ⓜ *Aquarium.*

Kitty O'Shea's. On the outskirts of Faneuil Hall in the Financial District is a sister pub to the original in Dublin. The bar, the fireplace, the stained-glass windows, and even some of the staffers have been imported from the Emerald Isle, giving the impression of a dyed-in-the-wool Irish establishment. ✉ *131 State St., Downtown* ☎ 617/725–0100 ⊕ *www.kittyosheas.com* Ⓜ *Aquarium, State.*

Living Room. The Living Room, on the outskirts of the North End, has killer martinis and tasty appetizers in an upscale setting modeled after its name—feel free to stretch out on the lounge's many elegant love seats and armchairs, or pull up a seat at the bar. On weeknights the bar is quieter, with friends enjoying the half-priced appetizers 4–7, meeting for drinks, or watching the game; on weekends, expect a packed house, a DJ, and dancing. ✉ *101 Atlantic Ave., Waterfront* ☎ 617/723–5101 ⊕ *www.thelivingroomboston.com* Ⓜ *Haymarket, Aquarium.*

Purple Shamrock. The Purple Shamrock is a tourist favorite. Just off Faneuil Hall, the bar has live music (including karaoke some nights), standard pub grub, and a chance to mingle with your fellow travelers. Be prepared to wait in line on weekends. ✉ *1 Union St., Faneuil Hall* ☎ 617/227–2060 ⊕ *www.irishconnection.com/shamrock.html* Ⓜ *Haymarket, Government Center.*

THE FENS

Boston Beer Works. This is a "naked brewery," with all the works exposed—the tanks, pipes, and gleaming stainless-steel and copper kettles used in producing beer. Seasonal brews, in addition to 16 microbrews on tap, draw students, young adults, and tourists alike to the original location (its sibling by the TD Garden is popular, too). The atmosphere is too crowded and noisy for intimate chats, and good luck trying to get in when there's a home game. ⊠ *61 Brookline Ave.* ☎ *617/536–2337* ⊕ *beerworks.net* Ⓜ *Kenmore.*

> **BOSTON'S BEST IRISH PUBS**
>
> ■ **The Burren,** Somerville
> ■ **Doyle's,** Jamaica Plain
> ■ **The Druid,** Cambridge
> ■ **The Kinsale,** Downtown
> ■ **Kitty O'Shea's,** Downtown

12

Jillian's Boston. This sprawling nightspot with multiple bars, pool tables, a bowling alley, and a nightclub, is like Chuck E. Cheese for adults. The first floor is Tequila Rain, a nightclub that bills itself as a year-round spring-break destination; the second is Jillian's proper, where you can drink, play pool, or just kick back; and the third is Lucky Strike, where you should expect to wait for a lane if you want to bowl. ⊠ *145 Ipswich St.* ☎ *617/437–0300* ⊕ *www.jilliansboston.com* Ⓜ *Kenmore.*

JAMAICA PLAIN

Fodor's Choice
★

Doyle's Cafe. Doyle's Cafe, truly an institution, is a friendly, crowded, neighborhood Irish pub that opened in 1882 and has been a Boston political landmark ever since. Candidates for everything from Boston City Council to the U.S. Senate drop by to eat corned beef and cabbage, sample one of the 21 brews on tap or 60 single-malt Scotches, and, of course, make speeches and shake hands. ⊠ *3484 Washington St., Jamaica Plain* ☎ *617/524–2345* ⊕ *www.doylescafeboston.com* ▭ *No credit cards* Ⓜ *Green St., Forest Hills.*

OLD WEST END

Boston Beer Works. Located near the TD Garden, this bar is nearly identical to its sister spot outside Fenway Park, but this one is naturally frequented by more Celtics and Bruins fans. ⊠ *112 Canal St., Old West End* ☎ *617/896–2337* ⊕ *beerworks.net* Ⓜ *North Station.*

Fours. The Fours is all about sports. Just outside the TD Garden, it's packed with fans on game and concert nights. Visit during lunch on a weekday for a quieter atmosphere. ⊠ *166 Canal St., Old West End* ☎ *617/720–4455* ⊕ *www.thefours.com* Ⓜ *North Station.*

Harp. Find a crowded, rollicking atmosphere just outside North Station and the TD Garden. Although technically an Irish pub, the Harp is a three-story megabar that serves postgame or concert crowds, sports fans, and ticketless night owls wanting to be close to the action. ⊠ *85 Causeway St., Old West End* ☎ *617/742–1010* ⊕ *www.harpboston. com* Ⓜ *North Station.*

Ruby Room. This spot in the Onyx Hotel is true to its name, with every shade of red imaginable. It's a sexy and comfortable spot to sip a designer cocktail and nosh on appetizers. Try the apricotti martini or the chocolate-cinnamon bread pudding. ⊠ *Onyx Hotel, 155 Portland St., Old West End* ☎ *617/557–9950* ⊕ *www.rubyroomboston.com* Ⓜ *North Station.*

SOUTH BOSTON

Drink. Perhaps the most exciting cocktail lounge to open in recent years, Drink is housed in a brick warehouse in the Fort Point Channel area. There's no cocktail menu, so patrons are expected to rely on the knowledgeable bartenders, who concoct libations on the spot according to drinkers' preferences. The space has an underground, modern speakeasy feel. If he's there, chat with bar manager John Gertsen, a pioneer of the local mixology scene, and ask him for a Fort Point. ⊠ *348 Congress St., Fort Point, South Boston* ☎ *617/695–1806* ⊕ *www.drinkfortpoint. com* Ⓜ *South Station.*

Franklin Café. This is the second location of the popular South End gastropub. Like its sibling, it's known equally for its great drinks and its upscale pub food, like the killer roast chicken. Serving dinner until 1:30 and drinks until 2 daily, the restaurant's a welcome addition to the quickly gentrifying neighborhood. ⊠ *152 Dorchester Ave., South Boston* ☎ *617/269–1003* ⊕ *www.franklincafe.com* Ⓜ *Broadway.*

Lucky's Lounge. Lucky's Lounge is a subterranean spot with live jazz on weekends, perfect martinis, and a mixed yuppie–artist crowd. The Rat Pack vibe is a lot of fun, and the salads, pizzas, and homemade meat loaf are first-rate. ⊠ *355 Congress St., Fort Point, South Boston* ☎ *617/357–5825* ⊕ *www.luckyslounge.com* Ⓜ *South Station.*

SOUTH END

★ **Clery's.** Depending on the patron's mood, Clery's can be a neighborhood bar, an Irish pub, a dance hall, or a karaoke bar, as all are offered here. Lines can get long on weekend nights, so plan ahead. ⊠ *113 Dartmouth St., Back Bay/South End* ☎ *617/262–9874* ⊕ *www.irishconnection. com/clerys.html* ☽ *11 am–1:30 am* Ⓜ *Copley.*

Club Café. This is among the smartest spots in town for gay men and lesbians—even when they're dining or partying with their straight friends. Behind stylish restaurant 209, the two-room "video lounge" is a relaxed place to dance to current and classic music videos, watch cult movies and TV shows, or bust out with weekly karaoke. There's never a cover charge. ⊠ *209 Columbus Ave., South End* ☎ *617/536–0966* ⊕ *www. clubcafe.com* Ⓜ *Back Bay/South End.*

Delux Café & Lounge. Mix with hipsters and young professionals or to grab affordable comfort food; the grilled-cheese sandwich is worth trying. Yellowing posters and postcards on the wall and relatively cheap drinks (for this area) give the place a retro vibe. The quesadillas are generally worth the wait for a table. ⊠ *100 Chandler St., South End* ☎ *617/338–5258* ⊟ *No credit cards* Ⓜ *Back Bay/South End.*

Franklin Café. This neighborhood institution is known for great martinis, microbrews on tap, and upscale pub food. There's no placard bearing its name; just look for the martini sign (or the crowd waiting for a dinner table) to know you're there. ⊠ *278 Shawmut Ave., South End* ☎ *617/350–0010* ⊕ *www.franklincafe.com* Ⓜ *Back Bay/South End.*

CLOSE UP

Blue-Law Blues

Why do Boston bars close so early? Something of the old Puritan ethic of the Massachusetts Bay Colony lingers in the so-called "blue laws" that prohibit sales of alcoholic drinks at bars and restaurants after 1 am on weekdays and 2 am on weekends. The state remains of two minds when it comes to social leniency. The first state to legalize gay marriage was also one of the last to allow liquor sales on Sunday. (Both became legal in 2004.)

Historians surmise that the name "blue laws" goes back to colonial times, when special laws were actually written on blue paper. In 17th-century Boston it was forbidden to walk the street on Sunday, or to sing, dance, fiddle, pipe, or use a musical instrument at night. Most

of these laws have been repealed (though it's still technically illegal to sit on the grass on Boston Common without a proclamation from the mayor). But periodic attempts to push back closing time still meet with heavy opposition from conservative neighborhood groups.

Late-night revelers party on in other ways. Asking for "cold tea" at certain Chinatown restaurants might get you a beer, and at certain Irish bars around town the lights are off but somebody's home. A modern trend has been to form "private clubs" such as Rise, on Stuart Street, where members pay yearly fees for the privilege of partying (although not drinking) all night. Thankfully, it's no longer illegal to dance until dawn.

CAMBRIDGE AND SOMERVILLE

Fodor's Choice
★ **Burren.** The Burren pulls in a devoted local, mostly student, crowd. It's got all the elements of a great Irish bar—expertly poured Guinness on tap, comfort food such as fish-and-chips, bangers and mash, and shepherd's pie, and live Irish music nightly—all in a warm, friendly environment. ⊠ *247 Elm St.Somerville* ☎ *617/776–6896* ⊕ *www.burren. com* Ⓜ *Davis.*

Cambridge Brewing Company. This cheerful, collegial, cavernous microbrewery is a favorite among MIT students and techies. Try a pint of the company's Cambridge Amber or Charles River Porter. If you've got a group, order a "tower" (83 ounces). In warm weather, come early for a coveted table outside on the patio, the perfect spot for people-watching. ⊠ *1 Kendall Sq., Bldg. 100, at Hampshire St. and BroadwayCambridge* ☎ *617/494–1994* ⊕ *www.cambridgebrewing.com* Ⓜ *Kendall/MIT.*

Casablanca. Casablanca has a Moroccan interior replete with wicker chairs and ceiling fans. The bar serves fantastic martinis and rich North African–influenced appetizers. It's the cool place to be, especially with a date: rattan love seats and Bogey's aura make it an ideal spot for two. ⊠ *40 Brattle St.Cambridge* ☎ *617/876–0999* ⊕ *www.casablanca-restaurant.com* Ⓜ *Harvard.*

★ **Chez Henri.** Enjoy a hip after-work scene at this French-Cuban restaurant equidistant from Harvard and Porter squares. There you'll find the best Cuban sandwiches north of Miami, and mojitos *muy fuertes*

BIG-PICTURE BOSTON

Hollywood has turned Boston into celluloid gold. Its ethnic enclaves, crooked cops, and notorious love for the Red Sox have all featured prominently in recent movies, many of which met with critical and box office success. Here are a few of the films in which Boston has starred:

Gone Baby Gone (2007): Ben Affleck's directorial debut follows the case of a missing girl in Dorchester with plenty of South Boston, Dorchester, and Chelsea scenes, as well as the historic Mount Auburn Cemetery in Cambridge.

The Departed (2006): Hometown boys Matt Damon and Mark Wahlberg star in this thriller of lies and betrayal between the Irish mob and state police. Visit Chinatown to see where Matt Damon leads Leonardo DiCaprio on a good chase, mimic Martin Sheen with a ride on the Red Line between South Station and Park Street, or conduct your own clandestine meeting (just like Wahlberg and DiCaprio) under Dorchester's Neponset Bridge.

Fever Pitch (2005): Drew Barrymore falls for Jimmy Fallon, a die-hard Sox fan. Show your team spirit by visiting the North End (where Fallon's character lives), Boston Common (where Fallon confesses his love for the Sox to Barrymore), and, of course, Fenway Park.

Mystic River (2003): Based on the book by local author Dennis Lehane (who also penned *Gone Baby Gone*), this murder mystery takes place in South Boston, although much of the movie was actually filmed in Eastie (East Boston). Drive across the Tobin Bridge, a prominent backdrop in many scenes, or down a pint at

Doyle's, the famous pub in Jamaica Plain where a despondent Tim Robbins gets drunk.

Legally Blonde (2001): The movie that made Reese Witherspoon an A-list star takes place at Harvard Law School, where her character Elle Woods takes on the academic establishment. See aerial shots of Cambridge and close-ups of Harvard Yard.

Next Stop Wonderland (1998): A nurse (Hope Davis) and a plumber (Alan Gelfant) are slowly drawn to one another in this romantic comedy that includes great scenes of everyday Boston. Have a pint at the Burren in Davis Square, where Davis hangs out with friends; tour the New England Aquarium, where Gelfant volunteers; or take the Blue Line out to Revere Beach, where the lovebirds finally connect.

Good Will Hunting (1997): Matt Damon is a "Southie"-born genius janitor at MIT. Harvard Square features prominently in scenes where Damon woos Minnie Driver's character; relax at the Boston Public Garden, where Damon and Robin Williams have a heart-to-heart. South Boston (particularly the L Street Tavern) is also well represented.

Governor Deval Patrick has been instrumental in bringing film crews to the city, so expect to see more celebrities in Boston. For a movie-themed afternoon, consider a guided walking or bus tour with **Boston Movie Tours** (☎ 866/MOVIE45). Movie locations include those from *The Departed, Fever Pitch, Good Will Hunting,* and more.

with which to wash them down. ✉ *1 Shepard St., midway between Harvard and Porter Sqs. Cambridge* ☏ *617/354–8980* ⊕ *www.chezhenri.com* Ⓜ *Harvard, Porter.*

Dante. The Royal Sonesta hotel's Dante features a sleek bar and lounge for both real and aspiring jet-setters. In addition to creative cocktails and an expertly created wine list, Dante offers a variety of parties, including football tailgating, barbecue get-togethers, and other festive events that also showcase the latest creations from executive chef Dante de Magistris. In warmer months head outside to the patio for glorious views of the Boston skyline and sailboats along the Charles River. ✉ *40 Edwin Land Blvd., Royal Sonesta Hotel, East Cambridge* ☏ *617/497–4200* ⊕ *www.restaurantdante.com* ⊗ *Mon.–Thurs. 5:30 pm–10 pm, Fri. and Sat. 5:30–11 pm* Ⓜ *Lechmere, Kendall Square.*

Druid. The Druid makes you feel like you're in Dublin, with well-poured pints, a dusky atmosphere, and black-and-white pudding on the menu. Its location in vibrant Inman Square gives you a chance to get to know the locals, a mix of Portuguese- and Italian-Americans, Harvard and MIT students, and young families. ✉ *1357 Cambridge St. Cambridge* ☏ *617/497–0965* ⊕ *www.druidpub.com* Ⓜ *Central, Harvard.*

★ **Enormous Room.** This somewhat whimsically named establishment is tucked into a tiny space above a restaurant in Central Square. Cambridge hipsters line up on weekends in front of the door, which is coolly unmarked. Inside, they nosh on Middle Eastern appetizers, including the "enormous platter" full of chicken skewers, olives, pita wedges, and other bites perfect for sharing. Good thing the food and music are stellar, because the bar stops serving at 11. Instead of tables or booths, you'll find luxurious rugs and oversized throw pillows for stretching out, drinking, and people-watching. ✉ *569 Massachusetts Ave. Cambridge* ☏ *617/491–5550* ⊕ *www.enormous.tv* Ⓜ *Central.*

Grendel's Den. This quintessential grad-student hangout is low-lighted and brick-walled. During happy hour (5–7:30 daily and 9–11:30 Sunday through Thursday), spinach, artichoke, clam dip, littleneck clams, and other tasty entrées go for half price with a $3-per-person drink purchase. ✉ *89 Winthrop St. Cambridge* ☏ *617/491–1160* ⊕ *www.grendelsden.com* Ⓜ *Harvard.*

Independent. The Independent, in Somerville's Union Square, offers a hip place for a pint, a martini, or even a hot toddy. Try the Moscow Mule, a cocktail featuring organic vodka, fresh limes, and ginger beer. ✉ *75 Union Sq., Union Sq.* ☏ *617/440–6022* ⊕ *www.theindo.com* ⊗ *Sun.–Thurs. 4:30 pm–1 am, Fri. and Sat. 4 pm–2 am* Ⓜ *Bus 86, 87, 91, CT2.*

John Harvard's Brew House. John Harvard's Brew House, a convivial gathering place for the Ivy Leaguers next door, dispenses ales, lagers, pilsners, and stouts brewed on the premises. It even smells

---

TOP LOUNGES

- **The Enormous Room,** Cambridge
- **The Good Life,** Downtown
- **The Living Room,** Waterfront
- **Lucky's Lounge,** South Boston
- **West Side Lounge,** Cambridge

12

like a real English pub. The food is no-frills and hearty. On Monday, college students get selected appetizers at half price. ⊠ *33 Dunster St.Cambridge* ☎ *617/868–3585* ⊕ *www.johnharvards.com* Ⓜ *Harvard.*

Middlesex Lounge. The minimalist design of a New York lounge combined with the laid-back friendliness of a Cambridge pub has created one of the hottest scenes on this side of the river. Rolling settees lend themselves to a variety of seating configurations, or they can be cleared at night for dancing to crowd-pleasing electronic and indie music. ⊠ *315 Massachusetts Ave.Cambridge* ☎ *617/868–6739* ⊕ *www. middlesexlounge.us* Ⓜ *Central.*

★ **Noir.** Noir is a sexy nightspot in the Charles Hotel where Cary Grant and Katharine Hepburn would feel right at home. Sink into a wraparound black-leather couch, order a martini (try the strawberry-basil), and perfect your best air of mystery. ⊠ *Charles Hotel, 1 Bennett St.Cambridge* ☎ *617/661–8010* ⊕ *www.noir-bar.com* Ⓜ *Harvard.*

Orleans. Orleans brings a cool Back Bay vibe to Somerville's Davis Square. It has live music on Friday nights, a lounge full of comfy couches and settees, and a large-projector screen playing the night's game. Try the bar's mango mojito or peach martini for a sweet buzz. ⊠ *65 Holland St.Somerville* ☎ *617/591–2100* ⊕ *www.orleansrestaurant.com* Ⓜ *Davis.*

Plough & Stars. This Irish pub that's also a bohemian oasis has Guinness and Bass on tap and rock, Irish, or country music nightly. Narrow and cozy, it's a comfortable, noisy place popular with students but also a fine place to have lunch alone. The cover charge varies. Fun fact: This is where the literary magazine *Ploughshares* was founded. ⊠ *912 Massachusetts Ave.Cambridge* ☎ *617/576–0032* ⊕ *www.ploughandstars. com* Ⓜ *Central, Harvard.*

River Gods. This eclectic bar emphasizes pagan Celtic lore in its decor and is situated just outside Central Square. True to the name, it's cluttered with frequently changing decorations of the pub's namesake gods on every surface. It's also known for a variety of great meals (Irish, Thai, American, and more) done on the cheap, as well as a rotating roster of DJs, including regulars from MIT's alternative-music station, 88.1 WMBR. ⊠ *125 River St.Cambridge* ☎ *617/576–1881* ⊕ *www. rivergodsonline.com* Ⓜ *Central.*

Temple Bar. The chef here emphasizes house-made everything (including condiments). It's a great place to enjoy a cocktail after a long day's exploring, with signature drinks including espresso and chocolate martinis. If you're hungry, be prepared to be impressed by the kobe beef sliders. ⊠ *1688 Massachusetts Ave.Cambridge* ☎ *617/547–5055* ⊕ *www. templebarcambridge.com* Ⓜ *Porter, Harvard.*

SAMUEL ADAMS
A better glass of beer

MUEL ADAMS BREWHOUSE

HOMETOWN BREW

A fun way to get to know a town is to get to know its hometown drinks. And there are few places as closely affiliated with their town of origin as the Samuel Adams Brewery is to Boston.

Samuel Adams beer might seem like it's everywhere, but its producer, the Boston Beer Company is still considered a craft brewer, with an annual production of less than 2 million barrels per year.

It was in 1984 when founder, Jim Koch, unhappy with the low quality of industrially produced beers at the time, decided to try his hand at the family business and introduce a new way of brewing and selling beer based on traditional methods and high-quality ingredients. He decided to name his new beer after another man who had revolutionary ideas— early Bostonian Samuel Adams.

(Interestingly enough, generations of Adams' family had produced the malt used for beer.)

Boston Beer Company's Jamaica Plain facility. You can tour the Boston Beer Company's Jamaica Plain facility, where its research and development into new products is conducted (the bulk of Samuel Adams production is done elsewhere). The entertaining hour-long tour is free, and, naturally, includes a tasting. You will get to smell and taste the various elements of brewing: hops, malt, and barley; get a good look at the flavoring process, and hear about and perhaps even see new beers in development. On fair-weather weekends, there can be a wait, so get there early to avoid standing around. Tours run continuously throughout the day. ⊠ *30 Germania St.* ☎ *617/368–5080* ⊙ *Mon.–Thurs. 10–3, Fri. 10–5:30, Sat. 10–3.*

West Side Lounge. Cool cats and hipsters come for delicious comfort food, a comprehensive list of martinis and cocktails, and late-night lounging. Try the white-ginger cosmo or prickly-pear margarita. ⊠ *1680 Massachusetts Ave. Cambridge* ☎ *617/441–5566* ⊕ *www.westsidelounge. com* Ⓜ *Porter, Harvard.*

BOWLING ALLEYS AND POOL HALLS

Pool halls in Boston make a popular winter refuge for teens and university students. Forget Paul Newman and smoky interiors: Boston likes its billiards halls swanky and well lighted, with plenty of polished brass and dark wood. Many of them do double duty as bowling alleys. Be forewarned, however, that in New England bowling is often "candlepin," with smaller balls and different rules. Some pool halls have age requirements (over either 18 or 21); call for details.

Felt. Felt is decked out so stylishly with chrome furnishings, cushy lounge chairs, and space-age light fixtures that it's easy to forget it's a pool hall. Sports stars and other minor celebrities mingle among young professionals and businesspeople on a night out to impress. Upstairs are 16 billiards tables covered with dark-blue felt, and a fourth-floor dance club. ⊠ *533 Washington St., Downtown* ☎ *617/350–5555* ⊕ *www.*

CLOSE UP

Candlepin Bowling

It was back in 1880 that Justin White adjusted the size of his pins at his Worcester, Mass., bowling hall, giving birth to candlepin bowling, a highly popular pint-size version of 10-pin bowling. Now played almost exclusively in northern New England and in the Canadian Maritime Provinces, candlepin bowling is a game of power and accuracy.

Paradoxically, candlepin bowling is both much easier and far more difficult than regular bowling. The balls are significantly smaller, weighing less than 3 pounds. There are no finger holes, and players of all ages and abilities can whip the ball down the alley. But because both the ball and the pins are lighter, it is far more difficult to bowl strikes and spares. Players are allowed three throws per frame, and bowlers may hit fallen pins (called wood) to knock down other pins. There has never been a perfect "300" score. The top score is 245. Good players will score around 100 to 110, and novice players should be content with a score of 90.

There are a handful of alleys in and around Boston, and many of them maintain their own quirky charm and history.

Boston Bowl. Boston Bowl attracts a more adult crowd, and is open 24 hours a day. It has both ten-pin and candlestick bowling as well as pool tables and a game room. ⊠ *820 Morrissey Blvd., Dorchester* ☎ *617/825–3800* ⊕ *www.bostonbowl.com.*

Bowlaway. One of the area's oldest bowling alleys, this tiny place has eight cramped lanes in a tucked-away facility down a flight of stairs. Fans say Bowlaway is like bowling in your own basement. ⊠ *16 Chestnut St., Needham* ☎ *781/444–9614* ⊕ *www.needhambowlaway.com.*

Sacco's Bowl Haven. Sacco's Bowl Haven is proud that its '50s decor "makes bowling the way it was, the way it is." Run by the fourth generation of the Sacco family, the alley was recently renovated to include a Flatbread pizza restaurant. ⊠ *45 Day St., Somerville* ☎ *617/776–0552.*

12

---

feltclubboston.com Ⓜ *Chinatown, Downtown Crossing, Boylston, Park St.*

Flat Top Johnny's. Flat Top Johnny's, in a mixed commercial and high-tech business park in Kendall Square, wears its hipster cred on its sleeve. Alternative rock, chosen by the tattooed and pierced staff, blares from behind the bar. Artwork by local painters hangs on the exposed-brick walls; the tables are covered in crimson instead of green. Bartenders pour one of the best selections of draft beers in the city. Members of Boston's cooler local bands often hang out here on their nights off. ⊠ *1 Kendall Sq., Bldg. 200Cambridge* ☎ *617/494–9565* ⊕ *www.flattopjohnnys. com* Ⓜ *Kendall/MIT.*

Jillian's Boston. Often called the city's best playground for grown-ups this multistory and multisensory complex on the corner of club-hopping Lansdowne Street has more than 30 pool tables, and each floor has a lively bar. On the third level, Lucky Strike Lanes has 16 bowling lanes and an 80-foot video wall blasting sports and music videos, and the ground floor is home to Tequila Rain, "where it's Spring Break 52 weeks a year." Everything's open until 2 am. ⊠ *145 Ipswich St.* ☎ *617/437–0300* ⊕ *www.jilliansboston.com* Ⓜ *Kenmore.*

Milky Way Lounge & Lanes. Milky Way Lounge & Lanes has Wii bowling, dancing, live music, DJ acts, cabaret shows, or karaoke. Particularly popular is Tuesday night "live karaoke," where you can live out your rock-and-roll fantasies in front of your own backup band. It draws a hip urban crowd of twenty- and thirtysomethings, as well as families with children. Upstairs, Bella Luna, its culinary sibling, offers upgraded American comfort food and pizzas. ⊠ *284 Armory St., Jamaica Plain* ☎ *617/524–3740* ⊕ *www.milkywayjp.com* Ⓜ *Stony Brook.*

CAFÉS AND COFFEEHOUSES

Boston has a great nighttime coffeehouse scene. If you just want a cup of coffee, you can find plenty of Starbucks cafés and Dunkin' Donuts. But beyond the cookie-cutter establishments, a more interesting set of independent cafés pumps out espresso. A few of them feel like true old-fashioned coffeehouses, complete with live folk music. Others are perfect for recaffeinating your spirits during a busy day of sightseeing. To eavesdrop on the liveliest conversations—some in Italian—head to one of the many espresso bars on Hanover Street in the North End.

BOSTON

Boston Common Coffee Company. Boston Common Coffee Company, with locations in the North End, Financial District, and Downtown Crossing, is an independent that's more Starbucks than Italian café. It has comfy couches, a roaring fireplace in winter, free wireless Internet, and a host of soups, sandwiches, and baked goods for sampling. It's one of the few cafés in the neighborhood where you can get a nonespresso cup of joe. ⊠ *97 Salem St., North End* ☎ *617/725–0040* ⊕ *www.bostoncommoncoffee.com* Ⓜ *Haymarket* ⊠ *10 High St., Financial District* ☎ *617/695–9700* ⊕ *www.bostoncommoncoffee.com* Ⓜ *South Station* ⊠ *515 Washington St., Downtown Crossing* ☎ *617/542–0595* ⊕ *bostoncommoncoffee.com* Ⓜ *Downtown Crossing.*

Fodor'sChoice ★ **Caffe Vittoria.** This is the biggest of the cafés in the North End, with gleaming espresso machines going nonstop. Skip the lines at Mike's Pastry down the street and head here to indulge in dessert—think tiramisu, cannoli, and gelati—and coffee after a meal in one of the nearby restaurants. ⊠ *290–296 Hanover St., North End* ☎ *617/227–7606* ⊕ *www.vittoriacaffe.com* Ⓜ *Haymarket.*

★ **Trident Booksellers & Café.** Trident Booksellers & Café stocks esoteric books and magazines, and serves coffee and teas. This is a nice spot for a light meal with a date, solo journal writing or reading, or surfing the Web with the free wireless access. The windows facing Newbury Street are great for people-watching. It's open daily until midnight. ⊠ *338 Newbury St., Back Bay* ☎ *617/267–8688* ⊕ *www.tridentbookscafe.com* Ⓜ *Hynes.*

SWEET NIGHTSPOTS

12

Bristol Lounge. The Viennese Dessert Buffet at the Four Seasons' Bristol Lounge is a scrumptious array of pastries, dessert crepes, and chocolates, accompanied by live jazz 9 to midnight Friday and Saturday. The drinks menu includes chai tea and a pomegranate martini. ⊠ *200 Boylston St., Back Bay* ☎ *617/338-4400* ⊕ *www.fourseasons.com/boston/dining/the_bristol_lounge.html* Ⓜ *Arlington, Boylston.*

Finale. With the creative ingredients and immaculate presentations of Finale's desserts, it's hard to pick just one. Possibilities include a molten chocolate cake, an updated Boston cream pie, and crème brûlée. Tasting plates for sharing and sampling make decisions easy. ⊠ *1 Columbus Ave., Theater District* ☎ *617/423-3184* ⊕ *www.finaledesserts.com* Ⓜ *Arlington* ⊠ *30 Dunster St.* ☎ *617/441-9797* Ⓜ *Harvard* ⊠ *1306 Beacon St.* ☎ *617/232-3233* Ⓜ *Coolidge Corner.*

CAMBRIDGE AND SOMERVILLE

Café Algiers. This genuine Middle Eastern café serving pita-bread lunches, teas, and strong coffee. Small, tightly clustered tables fill both floors. Upstairs you can peer at the soaring, wood-panel cathedral ceiling. Service is sluggish; visit when in the mood to linger over conversation or a novel. ⊠ *40 Brattle St. Cambridge* ☎ *617/492-1557* Ⓜ *Harvard.*

Café Luna. This is the Cambridge coffeeshop version of the South End's hip club the Beehive. Both are favorite spots for talented Berklee musicians, up-and-coming rock stars, and classical music performers who flock there to play Wednesday through Sunday. Serving beer, wine, and delicious meals (there's even a gelato bar), Café Luna is an urbane oasis for music and food lovers alike. ⊠ *403 Massachusetts Ave. Cambridge* ☎ *617/576-3400* ⊕ *cafeluna-centralsq.com* Ⓜ *Central.*

★ **Club Passim.** Joan Baez, Bob Dylan, Suzanne Vega, and many other folkies have passed through Club Passim on their way up. It's one of the country's first and most famous venues for live folk music. In the basement room, where the seating is pressed close together, there's table service and a counter where you can buy prepared food—Middle Eastern vegetarian items are especially good. If you travel with your guitar, call about one of the club's many open-mike nights. ⊠ *47 Palmer St. Cambridge* ☎ *617/492-5300, 617/492-7679 box office* ⊕ *www.clubpassim.org* Ⓜ *Harvard.*

Dado Tea. Dado Tea has a new-age feel, with an extensive listing of teas, multigrain meals, and a few sweet options, too. The Harvard Square location is a bit roomier than other cafés in the area, and if it's not too crowded, you can linger without interruption. ⊠ *50 Church St. Cambridge* ☎ *617/547-0950* ⊕ *www.dadotea.com* Ⓜ *Harvard* ⊠ *955 Massachusetts Ave.* ☎ *617/497-9061* Ⓜ *Harvard, Central.*

★ **Diesel Cafe.** This is a bright and sunny spot with bold local artwork and spacious booths. In addition to drawing Davis Square hipsters and Tufts students, it's a favorite hangout for lesbians and their friends, who congregate around the pool tables in back. Wireless is available for $5 an hour. ✉ *257 Elm St.Somerville* ☎ *617/629–8717* ⊕ *www.diesel-cafe. com* Ⓜ *Davis.*

Tealuxe. A "tea bar" with Bombay flair, Tealuxe more than 70 different herbal and traditional blends, an assortment of teatime snacks—and no coffee. It's a favorite hangout for students, who huddle over textbooks as they savor a cup of Earl Grey or ginseng chai at one of the copper-top tables. ✉ *0 Brattle St.Cambridge* ☎ *617/441–0077* ⊕ *www. tealuxe.com* Ⓜ *Harvard.*

1369 Coffeehouse. Quirky characters rub elbows with book-writing professors and stressed out students at this Cambridge institution devoted to espresso. Although the original Inman Square location and its Central Square sibling pride themselves on pouring the perfect latte, locals are also devoted to the cold-brewed coffee in the summer and spiced apple cider in the cooler months. With pastries galore and a selection of pre-made sandwiches and salads, the cafés are packed until 10 most nights. ✉ *1369 Cambridge St.Cambridge* ☎ *617/576–1369* ⊕ *www.1369coffeehouse.com* Ⓜ *Bus 69, 83, or 91* ✉ *757 Massachusetts Ave.* ☎ *617/576–4600* Ⓜ *Central.*

COMEDY CLUBS

Comedy Connection. Comedy Connection, now residing at the Wilbur Theatre, has a mix of local and nationally known acts such as Tracy Morgan, Aziz Ansari, and Wayne Brady. ✉ *246 Tremont St., in Wilbur Theatre* ☎ *617/931–2000* ⊕ *www.thewilburtheatre.com* Ⓜ *Boylston.*

Comedy Studio. The Comedy Studio, upstairs at the Hong Kong in Harvard Square, schedules a smorgasbord of silly offerings. A host of local and touring comedians make stops here; there's also a popular magic show every Tuesday night. ✉ *1238 Massachusetts Ave., Harvard Sq.Cambridge* ☎ *617/661–6507* ⊕ *www.thecomedystudio.com* ⌑ *$8–$10* ⊙ *All shows start at 8 pm, Tues.–Sun.* Ⓜ *Harvard.*

★ **ImprovAsylum.** ImprovAsylum features comedians who weave audience suggestions into seven weekly shows blending topical sketches with improv in shows such as "Lost in Boston" and "New Kids on the Blog." Tickets are $20; students can get a two-for-one deal for $10 apiece. ✉ *216 Hanover St., North End* ☎ *617/263–6887* ⊕ *www. improvasylum.com* Ⓜ *Haymarket, North Station.*

ImprovBoston. ImprovBoston in Central Square turns audience suggestions into a situation comedy, complete with theme song and commercials. Be careful when you go to the restroom; you might be pulled onstage. On some nights performers face off in improv competitions judged by audiences. Shows, which run Wednesday through Sunday, are $7 to $16. There's a beer and wine bar. ✉ *40 Prospect St.Cambridge* ☎ *617/576–1253* ⊕ *www.improvboston.com* Ⓜ *Central.*

Nick's Comedy Stop. Nick's Comedy Stop presents local comics Thursday through Saturday night. Well-known comedians occasionally pop in. Local boy Jay Leno reportedly got his start here. Reservations are advised on weekends, and cover charges vary. ✉ *100 Warrenton*

St., Theater District ☎617/438–1068 ⊕ www.nickscomedystop.com Ⓜ Boylston.

DANCE CLUBS

SWINGING SINGLES SCENES

■ **Felt,** Downtown

■ **Gypsy Bar,** Theater District

■ **Harp,** Old West End

■ **The Hong Kong,** Faneuil Hall

■ **Museum of Fine Arts** (first Friday), The Fens

12

Gypsy Bar. Gypsy Bar calls to mind the decadence of a dark European castle, with its rich red velvet and crystal chandeliers. Rows of video screens broadcast the Fashion Network, adding a sexier, more modern touch. Thirtysomething revelers and European students snack on lime-and-ginger-marinated tiger shrimp and sip "See You in Church" martinis (vodka with fresh marmalade) while the trendy dance floor throbs to Top 40 and house music. ⊠ 116 Boylston St., Theater District ☎ 617/482–7799 ⊕ www.gypsybarboston.com Ⓜ Boylston.

Rumor. Come to Rumor ready to dance, dance, dance, with all types of DJs spinning throughout the week. Options include house on Tuesday, hip-hop and house on Friday, and house, hip-hop, Latin, and Latin house on weekends. ⊠ 100 Warrenton St., Theater District ☎ 617/422–0045 ⊕ www.rumorboston.com ☕ Varies by DJ/night, expect a $10 minimum Ⓜ NE Medical Center.

Umbria. This Financial District establishment a mature, upscale crowd that ranges from mid-twenties to over-forties. Dress accordingly: no sneakers or caps. Wander among the five floors for formal Italian or informal dining, an "ultralounge," and a nightclub featuring R&B, techno, and international tunes. ⊠ 295 Franklin St., Downtown ☎ 617/338–1000 ⊕ www.umbriaristorante.com Ⓜ South Station.

Venu. Miami's South Beach comes to Boston, minus the 80-degree weather. A warm energy distinguishes this club from the city's other dark, techno-industrial spots. The crowd is diverse—stylish international students mix with young downtown suits cutting loose on their off-hours. Local DJs spin Top 40 and international tunes. Friday offers house, Latin, and hip-hop DJs, and Saturday features Top 40, rock, and mashups. ⊠ 100 Warrenton St., Theater District ☎ 617/338–8061 ⊕ www.venuboston.com Ⓜ Boylston, Arlington.

GAY AND LESBIAN

Estate. The Estate, part of the Alley entertainment complex, offers guest DJs from around the globe the occasional live act, belly dancers, and a celebrity (e.g., Paris Hilton) or two. Suite Boston, the property's "subterranean den," often hosts special events such as fashion shows and parties with guest DJs. ⊠ 1 Boylston Pl., Downtown/Theater District ☎ 617/351–7000 ⊕ www.theestateboston.com ☕ $15–$25 ⊙ Thurs.–Sun. 9 pm–2 am.

Fritz Lounge. Fritz Lounge is a gay sports bar popular with the local after-work crowd. Casually dressed older gentlemen drop in for the large beer list and steak and eggs during the hopping weekend brunch. ✉ *26 Chandler St., South End* ☎ *617/482–4428* ⊕ *www.fritzboston. com* ▭ *No credit cards* Ⓜ *Back Bay/South End.*

Jacque's Cabaret. There's nothing traditional about Jacque's Cabaret, an institution for more than 60 years. Nightly female-impersonator shows draw everyone from drag queens to bachelorette parties to watch while swilling cocktails from paper cups. Downstairs, Jacque's Underground features indie-rock bands on Friday and Saturday, while cabaret acts perform upstairs every night except Tuesday. Because of a longrunning licensing dispute, the whole carnival shuts down nightly at midnight. ✉ *79 Broadway, Theater District* ☎ *617/426–8902* ⊕ *www. jacquescabaret.com* ▭ *No credit cards* Ⓜ *Arlington.*

Midway Café. This Jamaica Plain café books a mix of live rock bands, DJs, and noise artists for an eclectic set any night of the week. There's also a lesbian dance party and "queeraoke" each Thursday night. Cover varies nightly. ✉ *3496 Washington St., Jamaica Plain* ☎ *617/524–9038* ⊕ *www.midwaycafe.com* Ⓜ *Green St., Forest Hills.*

MUSIC CLUBS

BLUES AND R&B CLUBS

★ **Cantab Lounge/Third Rail.** The Cantab Lounge/Third Rail hums every night with live Motown, rhythm and blues, folk, or bluegrass. The Third Rail bar, downstairs, holds poetry slams, open-mike readings and bohemia nights. It's friendly and informal, with a diverse under-forty crowd. ✉ *738 Massachusetts Ave. Cambridge* ☎ *617/354–2685* ⊕ *www. cantab-lounge.com* ▭ *No credit cards* Ⓜ *Central.*

Johnny D's Uptown. Johnny D's Uptown is a restaurant–cum–music hall where every seat is a good seat. It lines up Cajun, country, Latin, jazz, blues, and more. Come early for Southern and Mediterranean bistro food. On weekends it hosts a popular jazz brunch. ✉ *17 Holland St. Somerville* ☎ *617/776–9667 recorded info, 617/776–2004* ⊕ *www. johnnyds.com* Ⓜ *Davis.*

JAZZ CLUBS

Clubs often alternate jazz with other kinds of music; always call ahead for program information and times.

Beehive. This is a jazz-lover's dream, where both professional and up-and-coming acts light up the cavernous brick space with their music. Diners can enjoy seasonal cocktails by well-trained staff and delicious plates including a delightful Mediterranean platter and hearty comfort entrées. The club regularly books talented faculty and students from Berklee College of Music. ✉ *541 Tremont St., Back Bay/South End* ☎ *617/423–0069* Ⓜ *Back Bay.*

Regattabar. Regattabar is host to some of the top names in jazz, including Sonny Rollins and Herbie Hancock. Tickets for shows are $15–$35. Even when there's no entertainment, the large, low-ceiling club is a pleasant (if expensive) place for a drink. ✉ *Charles Hotel, 1 Bennett St. Cambridge* ☎ *617/661–5000, 617/395–7757* ⊕ *www.regattabarjazz. com* Ⓜ *Harvard.*

The first club in the U.S. to host U2, Paradise Rock Club has offered big names in an intimate venue since 1977.

★ **Ryles Jazz Club.** Soft lights, mirrors, and greenery set the mood for first-rate jazz. The first-floor stage is one of the best places for new music and musicians. Upstairs is a dance hall staging regular tango, salsa, and merengue nights, often with lessons before the dancing starts. Ryles also holds occasional open-mike poetry slams and a Sunday jazz brunch (call for reservations). It's open nightly, with a cover charge. ✉ *212 Hampshire St.Cambridge* ☎ *617/876–9330* ⊕ *www.ryles.com* Ⓜ *Bus 69, 83, or 91.*

Scullers Jazz Club. Well-known acts such as Wynton Marsalis, Diana Krall, and Tony Bennett pass through Scullers Jazz Club. Shows are Tuesday through Sunday nights; tickets are $18–$50 per show, more with dinner included; advance tickets are advised. ✉ *Doubletree Guest Suites hotel, 400 Soldiers Field Rd., Allston* ☎ *617/562–4111* ⊕ *www. scullersjazz.com* Ⓜ *BU West, Bus 47, or CT2.*

Fodor'sChoice
★ **Wally's Café.** Wally's Café is a rare gem for blues and jazz fans. Founded in 1947, the club continues to play host to big names such as Branford Marsalis and Chick Corea, but is still best known for performances by local bands. Wally's has a more diverse crowd than most other Boston clubs, and brings in both South End and Roxbury locals and lots of college students, especially students from Berklee College of Music. It's open every night of the year and there's no cover. ■ **TIP→ Get here early if you want a seat.** ✉ *427 Massachusetts Ave., South End* ☎ *617/424–1408* ⊕ *www.wallyscafe.com* Ⓜ *Massachusetts Ave.*

BEHIND THE MUSIC SCENE

Unlike showier music towns, Boston quietly goes about nurturing young musicians across genres, and the list of Boston acts that made it big is long and impressive. From rock legend Aerosmith and the Cars, to punk gods the Pixies and Mission of Burma, to wildly successful boy bands New Kids on the Block and New Edition, to classical cellist Yo Yo Ma, the city's youthful energy, bars and clubs provide fertile ground for developing musical talent. It also means that a night out could be a night spent listing to the "next big thing" in an intimate setting and without the blockbuster ticket prices.

The venerable Berklee College of Music deserves credit for drawing hardworking hopefuls to Boston. Many of the school's former students have become stars, including singer/songwriter John Mayer, punk rocker Johnny Ramone, producer Quincy Jones and jazz musician Branford Marsalis. The Beehive in the South End taps into the deep talent well by booking jazz shows downstairs in its club space. For intimate folk performances by up-and-comers, connoisseurs head to Harvard Square's Club Passim, where Joan Baez and Joni Mitchell played in their salad days when it was called Club 47.

Putting on eclectic shows that might feature a five-person rock band followed by a string quartet, Central Square's Café Luna is a small coffeeshop with a big love of music, nurturing the next generation of artists, whom you might find earnestly playing inches away from diners. It's located across the street from the Middle East, a favorite venue of ska-core pioneers the Mighty Mighty Bosstones and the location of the annual WBCN Rock 'N' Roll Rumble, an often sold-out battle of unsigned local bands held in April.

With no shortage of talent, supportive venues, and college students eager to either be or to hear the next great group, Boston's music scenes don't disappoint.

ROCK CLUBS

Great Scott. Great Scott books an impressive lineup of local and visiting indie rock bands, with live music from bands like Passion Pit and Echo and the Bunnymen nearly every night of the week. Check out Friday night's Brit-pop indie-dance night. The crowd typically consists of Allston hipsters, and locals from the area. ⊠ *1222 Commonwealth Ave., Allston* ☎ *617/566–9014* ⊕ *www.greatscottboston.com* Ⓜ *Harvard Ave.*

Hard Rock Cafe. Rock shows, private parties, and an an extensive bar and restaurant draw music fans to this fairly large space. Expect to see a cover band or two during an evening here, particularly on weekend nights. ⊠ *22–24 Clinton St., Faneuil Hall* ☎ *617/424–7625* ⊕ *www.hardrock.com/boston* ⊠ *No cover for drinks/dinner; shows will vary* ⊙ *Sun.–Thurs. 11 am–1 am, Fri. and Sat. 11 am–2 am* Ⓜ *Haymarket, Government Center.*

Lizard Lounge. Lizard Lounge is a low-key nightspot that often features more experimental and local cult bands. Seven nights a week, see folk, rock, acid jazz, and pop, sometimes mixed with cabaret, burlesque shows, or poetry readings. Martinis are a house specialty; upstairs, the Cambridge Common restaurant serves excellent burgers and comfort food (sweet-potato fries, basket of tater tots). ⊠ *1667 Massachusetts Ave., between Harvard and Porter Sqs.Cambridge* ☎ *617/547–0759* ⊕ *www.lizardloungeclub.com* Ⓜ *Harvard, Porter.*

★ **Middle East Restaurant & Nightclub.** The Middle East Restaurant & Nightclub manages to be both a Middle Eastern restaurant and one of the area's most eclectic rock clubs, with three rooms showcasing live local and national acts. Local phenoms the Mighty Mighty Bosstones got their start here. Music-world celebs often drop in when they're in town. There's also belly dancing, folk, jazz, and even the occasional country-tinged rock band. ⊠ *472–480 Massachusetts Ave.Cambridge* ☎ *617/497–0576, 617/864–3278* ⊕ *www.mideastclub.com* Ⓜ *Central.*

Fodor'sChoice **Paradise Rock Club.** This small place is known for hosting big-name talent
★ like U2, Coldplay, and local stars such as the Dresden Dolls. Two tiers of booths provide good sight lines anywhere in the club, as well as some intimate and out-of-the-way corners, and four bars quench the crowd's thirst. The 18-plus crowd varies with the shows. The newer Paradise Lounge, next door, is a more intimate space to experience local, often acoustic songsters, as well as literary readings and other artistic events. It serves dinner. ⊠ *967–969 Commonwealth Ave., Allston* ✛ *Near Boston University* ☎ *617/562–8800* ⊕ *www.thedise.com* Ⓜ *Pleasant St.*

T.T. the Bear's Place. The nightly live rock schedule showcases the hottest local bands and on-the-rise alternative bands such as Dear Leader and the Rudds. Separate rooms make it easy to concentrate on the music, chat around the bar, or relax over a game of pool. Monday night is usually acoustic night. It closes at 1 am. ⊠ *10 Brookline St.Cambridge* ☎ *617/492–2327* ⊕ *www.ttthebears.com* Ⓜ *Central.*

SALSA CLUBS

An Tua Nua. An Tua Nua is an Irish pub that, however improbably, hosts one of the city's most popular salsa nights each Wednesday. Arrive early for a lesson with local experts, then put your new moves to the test on the packed dance floor. ⊠ *835 Beacon St., Boston University* ☎ *617/262–2121* ⊕ *www.antuanuabar.com* Ⓜ *Fenway, Kenmore, St. Mary St.*

Havana Club. Havana Club at the Greek American Political Club in Central Square has a 5,400-square-foot ballroom dance floor, a rotating cast of DJs and live bands, and (usually) free food such as burritos or nachos. Typically, 300 people show up to dance, creating a lively scene for dancers at any level. The club is open for salsa on Friday and Saturday (open for private functions other nights), with lessons at 9; the party gets going around 10. ⊠ *288 Green St.Cambridge* ☎ *617/312–5550* ⊕ *www.havanaclubsalsa.com* Ⓜ *Central.*

Ryles. Ryles is home to one of the city's friendliest salsa scenes, **Temporada Latina.** It's held Tuesday through Thursday and Sunday nights with newcomers and experts dancing the night away (often together). Dancing starts at 9:30; arrive at 8 for the lesson. ⊠ *212 Hampshire*

St.Cambridge ☎ *617/876–9330* ⊕ *www.ryles.com/dancing.cfm* Ⓜ *Bus 68 or 69.*

THE ARTS

DANCE

Boston Dance Alliance. Boston Dance Alliance serves as a clearinghouse for local dance information. Visit its Web site for upcoming performances and details about Boston dance companies and venues. ⊠ *19 Clarendon St., South End* ☎ *617/456–6295* ⊕ *www.bostondancealliance.org* Ⓜ *Back Bay.*

BALLET

★ **Boston Ballet.** The city's premier dance company performs at the Boston Opera House. In addition to a world-class repertory of classical and high-spirited modern works, it presents an elaborate signature *Nutcracker* during the holidays. ⊠ *19 Clarendon St., South End* ☎ *617/695–6950* ⊕ *www.bostonballet.org* Ⓜ *Back Bay.*

José Mateo's Ballet Theatre. José Mateo's Ballet Theatre is a troupe building an exciting, contemporary repertory under Cuban-born José Mateo, the resident artistic director-choreographer. The troupe's performances include an original *Nutcracker,* and take place October through April at the **Sanctuary Theatre,** a beautifully converted former church at Massachusetts Avenue and Harvard Street in Harvard Square. ⊠ *400 Harvard St.Cambridge* ☎ *617/354–7467* ⊕ *www.ballettheatre.org* Ⓜ *Harvard.*

CONTEMPORARY

Dance Complex. Dance Complex presents varied dance styles by local and visiting choreographers at Odd Fellows Hall, an intimate space that draws a multicultural crowd. Works range from classical ballet to contemporary and world dance. Recent performances have included video and spoken word elements. ⊠ *536 Massachusetts Ave., Central Sq.Cambridge* ☎ *617/547–9363* ⊕ *www.dancecomplex.org* Ⓜ *Central.*

FOLK/MULTICULTURAL

★ **Art of Black Dance and Music.** Art of Black Dance and Music performs the music and dance of Africa, the Caribbean, and the Americas at venues including the **Strand Theatre,** at Columbia Road and Stoughton Street in Dorchester, and local area universities. ☎ *617/666–1859* ⊕ *www.abdm.net* Ⓜ *Andrew, then 16 or 17 bus; Ruggles, then 15 bus.*

Cambridge Multicultural Arts Center. Cambridge Multicultural Arts Center presents local and visiting arts programs, ethnic music, and dance performances. Two galleries showcase the visual arts. ⊠ *41 2nd St.Cambridge* ☎ *617/577–1400* ⊕ *www.cmacusa.org* Ⓜ *Lechmere.*

Folk Arts Center of New England. Folk Arts Center of New England promotes participatory international folk dancing and music for adults and children, as well as traditional New England contra dancing at locations throughout the greater Boston area. ⊠ *10 Franklin St.Stoneham* ☎ *781/438–4389 recorded info, 781/438–4387* ⊕ *www.facone.org* Ⓜ *No stop; Venues vary.*

12

World Music. World Music presents the biggest names in traditional dance and music from around the globe; regular performers include Africa's Ladysmith Black Mambazo and Ireland's Mary Black, and its annual Boston Flamenco Festival has become a winter highlight. Its CRASHArts series offers more daring, contemporary fare. Performances take place at the Somerville Theatre in Davis Square, Berklee Performance Center, and other venues around Boston. ✉ *720 Massachusetts Ave.Cambridge* ☎ *617/876–4275* ⊕ *www.worldmusic.org* Ⓜ *Central.*

FILM

With its large population of academics and intellectuals, Boston has its share of discerning moviegoers and movie houses, especially in Cambridge. Theaters at suburban malls, downtown, and at Fenway have better screens, if less adventurous fare. The *Boston Globe* has daily listings in the "Living/Arts" and "Sidekick" sections, and both the *Boston Herald* Friday "Scene" section and the *Boston Phoenix* "Arts" section list films for the week. Movies cost $9–$11. Many theaters have half-price matinees, but theaters sometimes suspend bargain admissions during the first week or two of a major film opening.

★ **Boston Public Library.** Boston Public Library regularly screens free family, foreign, classic, and documentary films in the Rabb Lecture Hall. ✉ *700 Boylston St., Copley Sq., Back Bay* ☎ *617/536–5400* ⊕ *www. bpl.org* Ⓜ *Copley.*

Brattle Theatre. Brattle Theatre shows classic movies, new foreign and independent films, themed series, and directors' cuts. Tickets sell out every year for its acclaimed Bogart festival, scheduled around Harvard's exam period; the Bugs Bunny Film Festival in February; and *Trailer Treats,* an annual fund-raiser featuring an hour or two of classic and modern movie previews in July. It also has holiday screenings such as *It's a Wonderful Life* at Christmas. ✉ *40 Brattle St., Harvard Sq.Cambridge* ☎ *617/876–6837* ⊕ *www.brattlefilm.org* Ⓜ *Harvard.*

Coolidge Corner Theatre. The Coolidge Corner Theatre has an eclectic and frequently updated bill of art films, foreign films, animation festivals, and classics, as well as an intimate 45-seat video-screening room for more experimental offerings. It also holds book readings, concerts, and popular midnight cult movies. ✉ *290 Harvard St.Brookline* ☎ *617/734–2501, 617/734–2500 recorded info* ⊕ *www.coolidge.org* Ⓜ *Coolidge Corner.*

Harvard Film Archive. Harvard Film Archive screens works from its vast collection of classics and foreign films that are not usually shown at commercial cinemas. Actors and directors frequently appear to introduce newer work. The theater was created for student and faculty use, but the general public may attend regular screenings for $9 per person. ✉ *Carpenter Center for the Visual Arts, 24 Quincy St.Cambridge* ☎ *617/495–4700* ⊕ *hcl.harvard.edu/hfa/* Ⓜ *Harvard.*

Institute of Contemporary Art, Boston. The Institute of Contemporary Art, Boston screens art films, foreign-film award winners, experimental movies, and documentaries, and it offers the opportunity to take in its modern design and waterfront location, which are reason enough to visit.

✉ *100 Northern Ave., Waterfront* ☎ *617/478–3100* ⊕ *www.icaboston. org/programs/film/* Ⓜ *South Station, Courthouse, World Trade Center.*

Kendall Square Cinema. Kendall Square Cinema is devoted to first-run independent and foreign films. There are nine screens and a concession stand with choices such as cappuccino and homemade cookies. Note that 1 Kendall Square stands where Hampshire runs into Broadway, not near the Kendall Square T stop. Although the free Galleria Mall shuttle runs directly from the T stop to the theater every 20 minutes, Monday–Saturday 9–7, and Sunday noon–7, the theater is a 10-minute walk away. ✉ *1 Kendall Sq.Cambridge* ☎ *617/499–1996* ⊕ *www. landmarktheatres.com* Ⓜ *Kendall/MIT.*

Museum of Fine Arts. Screenings of international and avant-garde films, works by local filmmakers, and movies connected to museum exhibitions take place in Remis Auditorium. The refined setting, eclectic topics, and educated audience make the MFA a fitting setting for serious annual film festivals like the Boston Jewish Film Festival. Although tickets usually run around $10, special screenings, which might include guest speakers can boost prices up to $20–$25. ✉ *465 Huntington Ave.* ☎ *800/440–6975 box office* ⊕ *www.mfa.org/film* Ⓜ *Museum of Fine Arts, Ruggles.*

MUSIC

For its size, Boston has a great diversity and variety of live music choices. (➪ *See also Music Clubs in Nightlife, above.)* Supplementing appearances by nationally known artists are performers from the area's many colleges and conservatories, which also provide music series, performing spaces, and audiences.

Classical music aficionados love the Boston Symphony Orchestra, which performs at Symphony Hall October through early May and at Tanglewood Music Center in Lenox, Massachusetts, from late June through and August. A favorite of TV audiences, the Boston Pops presents concerts of "lighter music" from May to July and during December.

Boston also has emerged as the nation's capital of early-music performance. Dozens of small groups, often made up of performers who have one foot in the university and another on the concert stage, play pre-18th-century music on period instruments, often in small churches where the acoustics resemble the venues in which some of this music was first performed.

Boston Early Music Festival. If you're a die-hard early-music devotee, plan to visit Boston in odd-number years, when the biennial Boston Early Music Festival takes over the city for a week in June. ☎ *617/661–1812* ⊕ *www.bemf.org.*

Cambridge Society for Early Music. The Cambridge Society for Early Music helps promote early-music performances and deserves much of the credit for early music's preeminence in Boston's musical scene. ☎ *617/489–2062* ⊕ *www.csem.org.*

CONCERT HALLS

Bank of America Pavilion. Bank of America Pavilion gathers up to 5,000 people on the city's waterfront for summertime concerts. National pop, folk, and country acts play the tentlike pavilion from about mid-June to mid-September. ⊠ *290 Northern Ave., South Boston* ☎ *617/728–1600* Ⓜ *South Station.*

Berklee Performance Center. Associated with Berklee College of Music, Berklee Performance Center is best known for its jazz programs, but it's also host to folk performers such as Joan Baez and pop and rock stars such as Andrew Bird, Aimee Mann, and Henry Rollins. ⊠ *136 Massachusetts Ave., Back Bay* ☎ *617/747–2261 box office* ⊕ *www. berkleebpc.com* Ⓜ *Hynes.*

Boston Opera House. The Boston Opera House hosts plays, musicals, and traveling Broadway shows, but also has booked diverse performers such as David Copperfield, B.B. King, and Pat Metheny. The occasional children's production may schedule a run here as well. ⊠ *539 Washington St., Downtown* ☎ *617/259–3400* ⊕ *bostonoperahouseonline.com* Ⓜ *Boylston, Chinatown, Downtown Crossing, Park St.*

★ **Hatch Memorial Shell.** On the bank of the Charles River, this wonderful acoustic shell is where the Boston Pops perform their famous free summer concerts (including their traditional Fourth of July show, broadcast live nationwide on TV). Local radio stations also put on music shows and festivals here April through October. ⊠ *Off Storrow Dr. at embankment, Beacon Hill* ☎ *617/626–4970* ⊕ *www.mass.gov/dcr/ hatch_events.htm* Ⓜ *Charles/MGH, Arlington.*

Institute of Contemporary Art, Boston. The Institute of Contemporary Art, Boston hosts experimental musicians, with some performances in partnership with World Music/CRASHArts. Expect the unexpected—concerts here could contain a mix of disparate instruments, fusions of melody and spoken word, or electronica mashups. ⊠ *100 Northern Ave., Waterfront* ☎ *617/478–3100* ⊕ *www.icaboston.org/programs/ performance* Ⓜ *South Station, Courthouse, World Trade Center.*

Fodor's Choice
★ **Isabella Stewart Gardner Museum.** The beautiful Tapestry Room hosts concerts. Young artist showcases and chamber music are presented every Sunday, and an "after hours" series runs the third Thursday of each month. The "composer portrait series" highlights the work of a particular composer. The charge ($23) includes museum admission. ⊠ *280 The Fenway* ☎ *617/278–5156 box office, 617/566–1401 recorded info* ⊕ *www.gardnermuseum.org* Ⓜ *Museum of Fine Arts.*

Museum of Fine Arts. The Museum of Fine Arts has jazz, blues, and folk concerts in its outdoor courtyard every Wednesday evening from late June through August (bring a blanket and a picnic). During the rest of the year, the action moves inside to the Remis Auditorium on various nights of the week. ⊠ *465 Huntington Ave.* ☎ *800/440–6975* ⊕ *www. mfa.org/programs/music* Ⓜ *Museum of Fine Arts.*

★ **New England Conservatory's Jordan Hall.** New England Conservatory's Jordan Hall, one of the world's acoustic treasures, is ideal for chamber music yet large enough to accommodate a full orchestra. The Boston Philharmonic and the Boston Baroque ensemble often perform at

Renowned Symphony Hall is the home to the Boston Symphony Orchestra and Boston Pops.

the relatively intimate 1,000-seat hall. ✉ *30 Gainsborough St., Back Bay* ☎ *617/585–1260 box office* ⊕ *necmusic.edu/calendar_event* Ⓜ *Symphony.*

Orpheum Theatre. The Orpheum Theatre is cramped and occasionally overheated, but is nonetheless a beloved forum for local and national performers such as Van Morrison, Paul Simon, and the Strokes. ✉ *1 Hamilton Pl., off Tremont St., Downtown* ☎ *617/482-0106 box office* Ⓜ *Park St.*

Sanders Theatre. This jewel box of a stage plays host local and visiting classical, folk, and world-music performers. "The Christmas Revels," a traditional, participatory Yule celebration, delights families here each December. ✉ *Harvard University, 45 Quincy St. Cambridge* ☎ *617/496–2222* ⊕ *www.fas.harvard.edu/tickets* Ⓜ *Harvard.*

Symphony Hall. One of the world's best acoustical settings—if not *the* best—is home to the Boston Symphony Orchestra (BSO) and the Boston Pops. The BSO is led by the incomparable James Levine, who's known for commissioning special works by contemporary composers, as well as for presenting innovative programs such as his two-year Beethoven/Schoenberg series. The Pops concerts, led by conductor Keith Lockhart, take place in May and June and around the winter holidays. The hall is also used by visiting orchestras, chamber groups, soloists, and many local performers. Rehearsals are sometimes open to the public, with tickets sold at a discount. ✉ *301 Massachusetts Ave., Back Bay* ☎ *617/266–1492* ⊕ *www.bostonsymphonyhall.org* Ⓜ *Symphony.*

TD Garden. TD Garden hosts concerts by big-name artists from Celine Dion to U2, ice shows, and, of course, Bruins and Celtics games. ✉ *100*

Legends Way, Old West End ☎ *617/624–1000 event info line* ⊕ *www.tdbanknorthgarden.com* Ⓜ *North Station.*

Tsai Performance Center. Tsai Performance Center, associated with Boston University, presents many free classical concerts by both student and professional groups. The New England Philharmonic and Boston Musica Viva are regular guests in the 500-seat theater. ✉ *685 Commonwealth Ave.* ☎ *617/353–6467, 617/353–8725 box office* ⊕ *www.bu.edu/tsai* Ⓜ *Boston University East.*

12

CHORAL GROUPS

It's hard to imagine another city with more active choral groups than Boston. Many outstanding choruses are associated with Boston schools and churches.

Boston Cecilia. The Boston Cecilia, which dates from 1876, holds regular concerts at Jordan Hall and other venues, and is especially noted for its period-instrument performances of Handel. ☎ *617/232–4540* ⊕ *www.bostoncecilia.org.*

Boston Gay Men's Chorus. Boston Gay Men's Chorus seeks to "create a more tolerant society through the power of music." Their repertoire ranges from holiday favorites to show tunes, chamber selections to pop hits. They perform at Symphony Hall, Jordan Hall, the Cutler Majestic Theatre, and other venues around town. ☎ *617/542–7464* ⊕ *www.bgmc.org.*

Boston Secession. This professional vocal ensemble is trying to modernize the choral experience with both virtuoso singing and creative, thematic programs such as "Handel in the Strand" and the annual anti-Valentine "(un)Lucky in Love." ☎ *617/499–4860* ⊕ *www.bostonsecession.org.*

Cantata Singers. Cantata Singers perform music dating from the 17th century to the present at various venues in Boston. ☎ *617/868–5885* ⊕ *www.cantatasingers.org.*

CHURCH CONCERTS

Boston's churches have outstanding music programs. The Saturday *Boston Globe* and the Friday *Boston Herald* list performance schedules.

★ **Emmanuel Music.** Emmanuel Music holds concerts at Emmanuel Church, known as "the Bach church" for its Holy Eucharist services on Sunday at 10 am. The concert series, which is performed by a professional chamber orchestra and chorus, is one of Boston's hidden gems, and runs weekly from September to May. ✉ *15 Newbury St., Back Bay* ☎ *617/536–3356* ⊕ *www.emmanuelmusic.org* Ⓜ *Arlington.*

Trinity Boston. Trinity Boston presents a free half-hour organ or choir recital Friday at 12:15 pm, as well as seasonal choral concerts, in the vaulted neo-Romanesque interior of Copley Square's Trinity Church. ✉ *Trinity Church, 206 Clarendon St., Copley Sq., Back Bay* ☎ *617/536–0944* ⊕ *www.trinityboston.org* Ⓜ *Back Bay/South End, Copley.*

CONCERT SERIES

Bank of America Celebrity Series. The Bank of America Celebrity Series presents about 50 events annually—renowned orchestras, chamber groups, recitalists, vocalists, and dance companies—often at Symphony Hall or Jordan Hall. Regulars include Yo-Yo Ma and the Alvin Ailey

CLOSE UP

Frugal Fun

The nightlife and arts options we list are worth their weight in gold. Yet if you're feeling the pinch, you can be entertained without dropping a dime.

Nosh on gratis appetizers at the **Fritz Lounge** during happy hour on weekdays.

See a film at the **Boston Public Library.**

Go baroque—not broke—with select classical concerts performed by the Boston University Symphony Orchestra or College of Fine Arts faculty members at the **Tsai Performance Center.**

Head to **Trinity Church** for free Friday organ or choir recitals at 12:15 pm.

Get down to blues and jazz at **Wally's Café** jazz club, the **Beehive,** or **Café Luna** (in Cambridge), where talented students from the Berklee College of Music perform.

Buy a coffee or smoothie, and surf wireless Internet for free at **Trident Booksellers & Café.**

See art in the making: check out one of the weekend **Boston Open Studios** (⊕ *www.cityofboston.gov/arts/ visual/openstudios.asp*) in neighborhoods throughout the city. Summer brings even more free activities:

Boston Pops. Bop along with the Boston Pops and other free concerts at the Hatch Memorial Shell June through August. ☎ *617/266–1200, 888/266–1200* ⊕ *www.bso.org.*

Shakespeare in the Park. In July and August the Commonwealth Shakespeare Company brings you Shakespeare in the Park in Boston Common. ☎ *617/426–0863* ⊕ *commshakes.org.*

Esplanade Summer Events. From April through September the Hatch Shell on the Esplanade is abuzz with free concerts, movie showings, and more, all part of the Esplanade Summer Events. Perennial favorites include the Boston Pops' Fourth of July concert and "Free Friday Flicks" outdoor movie screenings. ☎ *617/626–4970* ⊕ *www.mass.gov/dcr/hatch_events. htm.*

Summer in the City Series. Cinephiles can catch "Movies by Moonlight," classic films shown waterside as part of the Boston Harbor Hotel's outdoor Summer in the City Series. Other weekly offerings include swing dancing, soul singing, and blues concerts staged on a barge anchored behind the hotel. ☎ *617/439–7000* ⊕ *www.bhh.com.*

American Dance Theater. ✉ *20 Park Plaza, Suite 1032, Downtown* ☎ *617/482–2595, 617/482–6661 box office* ⊕ *www.celebrityseries.org.*

EARLY-MUSIC GROUPS

Boston Baroque. Boston Baroque has been headed by founder-conductor Martin Pearlman for more than 30 years, and showcases soloists and guest musicians in period-instrument performances of works by Bach, Handel, Vivaldi, and others. Their yearly *Messiah* performance for the holidays is a stunner; the recorded version was nominated for a Grammy in 1992. Performances are held at NEC's Jordan Hall, Sanders Theatre in Cambridge, and other venues. ☎ *617/484–9200* ⊕ *www. bostonbaroque.org.*

The Boston Opera stages four shows a year.

Boston Camerata. Founded in 1954, Boston Camerata has become a worldwide favorite thanks to its popular recordings. It performs a series of medieval, Renaissance, and baroque concerts at various venues. ☎ 617/262–2092 ⊕ *www.bostoncamerata.org.*

Boston Early Music Festival. Boston Early Music Festival focuses on medieval, baroque, and Renaissance music. Throughout the year, concerts, master classes, and lectures take place at churches and concert halls throughout Boston. Every other year in June, a fully staged opera is performed. Past productions have included Conradi's *Ariadne* (1691) and Mattheson's 1710 opera *Boris Goudenow.* ☎ 617/661–1812 ⊕ *www. bemf.org.*

★ **Handel & Haydn Society.** America's oldest music organization has a history of performances that dates from 1815. It presents instrumental and choral performances at Symphony Hall. The group's holiday-season performances of Handel's *Messiah* draw many music lovers. ☎ 617/266–3605 *box office*, 617/262–1815 ⊕ *www.handelandhaydn.org.*

ORCHESTRAS

★ **Boston Philharmonic.** Boston Philharmonic is headed by the charismatic Benjamin Zander, whose informal preconcert talks help audiences better understand what they're about to hear. Most performances take place at Harvard's Sanders Theatre or the New England Conservatory's Jordan Hall. ☎ 617/236–0999 ⊕ *www.bostonphil.org.*

Boston Pops. Boston Pops perform a mix of American standards, movie themes, and contemporary vocal numbers during May and June at Symphony Hall, followed by outdoor concerts at the Hatch Memorial Shell throughout July. The popular outdoor concerts are free; make sure to bring a blanket or foldable chairs for a memorable picnic. ☏ *617/266–1492, 888/266–1200 box office* ⊕ *www.bostonpops.org.*

Boston Symphony Orchestra. The season at Symphony Hall runs from October to early May. In July and August the activity shifts to the orchestra's beautiful summer home at the Tanglewood Music Center in Lenox, Massachusetts. All in all Boston Symphony Orchestra presents more than 250 concerts annually. ☏ *617/266–1492, 888/266–1200 box office* ⊕ *www.bso.org* Ⓜ *Symphony.*

OPERA

Boston Lyric Opera. Boston Lyric Opera stages four full productions each season at Citi Performing Arts Center, which usually include one 20th-century work. Recent highlights have included Bizet's *Carmen* and Britten's *A Midsummer Night's Dream.* ☏ *617/542–4912, 617/542–6772 audience services office* ⊕ *www.blo.org* Ⓜ *Boylston.*

Opera Boston. Opera Boston draws a connoisseur crowd for its fully staged performances of little-known or rarely seen works such as Handel's *Semele* or Verdi's *Ernani.* Shows are at the Cutler Majestic Theatre at Emerson College. ☏ *617/451–3388* ⊕ *www.operaboston.org* Ⓜ *Boylston.*

THEATER

In the 1930s Boston had no fewer than 50 performing-arts theaters; by the 1980s the city's downtown Theater District had all but vanished. Happily, in the late 1990s several historic theaters saw major restoration, opening to host pre-Broadway shows, visiting artists, and local troupes. More recently, the glorious renovation of the Opera House in 2004 has added new light to the district. Meanwhile, established companies such as the Huntington Theatre Company, near Northeastern University, and the American Repertory Theatre, in Cambridge, continue to offer premieres of works by major writers, including David Mamet, August Wilson, and Don DeLillo.

MAJOR THEATERS

★ **Boston Opera House.** The Boston Opera House features lavish musical productions such as *The Lion King* and Boston Ballet's *The Nutcracker.* The meticulously renovated 2,500-seat, beaux arts building has $35 million worth of gold leaf, lush carpeting, and rococo ornamentation. ✉ *539 Washington St., Downtown Crossing/Chinatown* ☏ *617/259–3400* ⊕ *bostonoperahouseonline.com/* Ⓜ *Boylston, Chinatown, Downtown Crossing, Park St.*

Charles Playhouse. The Charles Playhouse was formerly a church, a YWCA, a Prohibition-era speakeasy, and a nightclub. These days it plays host to the *Blue Man Group,* a loud, messy, exhilarating trio of playful performance artists painted vivid cobalt. (Warning: Don't dress up, especially if you're sitting close to the stage.) ✉ *74 Warrenton St., Theater District* ☏ *800/982–2787 Blue Man Group* Ⓜ *Boylston.*

Citi Performing Arts Center. Citi Performing Arts Center, formerly the Wang Center for the Performing Arts and the Shubert Theatre, is a performance space complex dedicated to both large-scale productions (at the former Wang) and more intimate shows (at the former Shubert). Expect names such as *Alvin Ailey American Dance Theater* and other nationally touring Broadway shows, popular comedians, and the occasional ballet. ✉ *270 Tremont St., Theater District* ☎ *617/482–9393, 866/348–9738* ⊕ *www.citicenter.org* Ⓜ *Boylston*.

Colonial Theatre. Ornate red wallpaper, intricately carved balconies, and stately marble columns evoke turn-of-the-20th-century glamour. Visiting stars from W. C. Fields to Fanny Brice to Katharine Hepburn have trod the theater's boards. More recently, the theater welcomed Broadway productions *Mamma Mia* and *Jersey Boys*. ✉ *106 Boylston St., Back Bay* ☎ *617/426–9366* ⊕ *www.bostoncolonialtheatre.com* Ⓜ *Boylston*.

Huntington Theatre Company. Boston's largest resident theater company consistently performs a high-quality mix of 20th-century plays, new works, and classics under the leadership of artistic director Peter DuBois, and commissions artists to produce original dramas. The Huntington performs at two locations: at the Boston University Theatre and a the Calderwood Theatre Pavilion in the South End. ✉ *Boston University Theatre, 264 Huntington Ave., Back Bay* ☎ *617/266–0800 box office* ⊕ *www.huntingtontheatre.org* Ⓜ *Symphony* ✉ *Calderwood Theatre Pavilion, Boston Center for the Arts, 527 Tremont St., South End* ☎ *617/426–5000* ⊕ *www.bcaonline.org* Ⓜ *Back Bay/South End, Copley*.

SMALL THEATERS AND COMPANIES

★ **American Repertory Theater.** American Repertory Theaterstages experimental, classic, and contemporary plays, often with unusual lighting, stage design, or multimedia effects. With new director Diane Paulus bringing in immersive theatre performances, like *The Donkey Show* and *Sleep No More* (where audience and actors interact), the A.R.T. is selling out shows at its multiple venues. Its home at the Loeb Drama Center has two theaters; the smaller also holds productions by the Harvard-Radcliffe Drama Club. A modern theater space down the street, called berone, has a more flexible stage design for electrifying contemporary productions. ✉ *64 Brattle St., Harvard Sq.Cambridge* ☎ *617/547–8300* ⊕ *www.amrep.org* Ⓜ *Harvard*.

★ **Boston Center for the Arts.** Boston Center for the Arts houses more than a dozen quirky, low-budget troupes in six performance areas, including the 300-seat Stanford Calderwood Pavilion, two black-box theaters, and the massive Cyclorama, built to hold a 360-degree mural of the

---

BEST ALFRESCO ARTS EVENTS

■ The Boston Pops at the Hatch Memorial Shell

■ Summer rock shows at the Bank of America Pavilion

■ Shakespeare in the Park on the Boston Common

■ Summer concerts at the Museum of Fine Arts' Calderwood Courtyard

■ Live music on summer evenings in Copley Square

12

Battle of Gettysburg (the painting is now in a building at the battlefield). The multiracial Company One, gay/lesbian Theatre Offensive, and contemporary SpeakEasy Stage Company put on shows here year-round. ✉ *539 Tremont St., South End* ☎ *617/426–5000* ⊕ *www.bcaonline.org* Ⓜ *Back Bay/South End, Copley.*

Harvard's Hasty Pudding Theatricals. Harvard's Hasty Pudding Theatricals at Harvard University calls itself the "oldest collegiate theatrical company in the United States" and is an all-male troupe. It produces one show annually, which plays in Boston in February and March and then goes on tour. The troupe also honors a famous actor and actress each year with an awards ceremony, and the actress participates in a parade (surrounded by Hasty Pudding members in drag) through Cambridge. Recent honorees include Justin Timberlake and Anne Hathaway. Performances are scattered around Cambridge and Harvard Square. ✉ *Harvard Sq., Cambridge* ☎ *617/495–5205* ⊕ *www.hastypudding. org* Ⓜ *Harvard.*

Lyric Stage Company Boston. The Lyric Stage Company Boston mounts a mix of classic and new, musical and nonmusical productions. The 2010–11 season included the musical *The 25th Annual Putnam County Spelling Bee.* ✉ *YWCA, 140 Clarendon St., 2nd fl., Back Bay* ☎ *617/585–5678* ⊕ *www.lyricstage.com* Ⓜ *Arlington.*

Sports and the Outdoors

WORD OF MOUTH

"Walk, walk, walk. Walk the Harbor path, the Gardens, Commonwealth Ave, the Rose Kennedy Greenway, and up and down the Charles river crossing the Salt and Pepper and Mass Ave. bridges."

—Kealalani

FENWAY PARK

For baseball fans of any age a trip to Fenway Park is a religious pilgrimage to see the home of former baseball greats such as Ted Williams and Carl Yastrzemski. The Boston Red Sox have played here since 1912. The oldest Major League ballpark is one of the last of its kind, a place where the scoreboard is hand operated and fans endure uncomfortable seats.

(above) Take yourself out to a ballgame at legendary Fenway Park. (lower right) Iconic sox mark the park walls. (upper right) Flags adorn the epicenter of Red Sox Nation.

For much of the ballpark's history Babe Ruth's specter loomed large. The team won five titles by 1918 but endured an 86-year title drought after trading away the Sultan of Swat. It wasn't enough to lose; the team vexed generations of loyal fans with colossal late-season collapses and post-season bungles. The Sox "reversed the curse" in 2004, defeating the rival Yanks in the American League Championship Series after being down 3–0 in the series (an unheard of comeback in baseball) and sweeping the St. Louis Cardinals in the World Series. The Red Sox won it all again in 2007, completely exorcising the curse.

FUN FACT

A lone red seat in the right-field bleachers marks the spot where Ted Williams's 502-foot shot—the longest measurable home run hit inside Fenway Park—landed on June 9, 1946.

THE SPORTS GUY

For an in-depth view of the psyche of a die-hard Red Sox fan read Bill Simmons' book *Now I Can Die in Peace.*

THE NATION

The Red Sox have the most rabid fans in baseball. Knowledgeable and dedicated, they follow the team with religiouslike intensity. Red Sox Nation has grown in recent years, much to the chagrin of "die-hards." You may hear the term "pink hat" used to derisively tag someone who is a bandwagon fan (i.e., anyone who didn't suffer with the rest of the Nation during the title drought).

THE MONSTER

Fenway's most dominant feature is the 37-foot-high "Green Monster," the wall that looms over left field. It's just over 300 feet from home plate and in the field of play, so deep fly balls that would have been outs in other parks sometimes become home runs. The Monster also stops line drives that would have been over the walls of other stadiums, but runners can often leg these hits out into doubles (since balls are difficult to field after they ricochet off the wall).

THE MUSIC

Fans sing "Take Me Out to the Ballgame" during the 7th-inning stretch in every ballpark...but at Fenway, they also sing Neil Diamond's "Sweet Caroline" in the middle of the 8th. If the Sox win, the Standell's "Dirty Water" blasts over the loudspeakers at the end of the game.

THE CURSE

In 1920 the Red Sox traded pitcher Babe Ruth to the Yankees, where he became a home-run-hitting baseball legend. Some fans—most famously *Boston Globe* columnist Dan Shaughnessy, who wrote a book called *The Curse of the Bambino*—blamed this move for the team's 86-year title drought, but others will claim that "The Curse" was just a media-driven storyline used to explain the team's past woes. Still fans who watched a ground ball roll between Bill Buckner's legs in the 1986 World Series or saw Aaron Boone's winning home run in the 2003 American League Division Series swear the curse was real.

VISIT THE NATION **13**

Not lucky enough to nab tickets ahead of time? Try your luck at Gate E two hours before the game, when a handful of tickets are sold. There's a one-ticket limit, so everyone in your party must be in line. If that doesn't yield results, you can still experience the Nation. Head down to the park and hang out on Yawkey Way, which borders the stadium. On game days it's closed to cars and filled with vendors, creating a street-fair atmosphere. Duck into a nearby sports bar and enjoy the game with other fans who weren't fortunate enough to secure seats. A favorite is the **Cask'n Flagon,** at Brookline Avenue and Lansdowne Street, across the street from Fenway. The closest you can get to Fenway without buying a ticket is the **Bleacher Bar** (✉ *82A Lansdowne St.*), which actually has a huge window in the center field wall overlooking the field. If you want to see a game from this unique vantage point, get here early—it starts filling up a few hours before game time.

Updated
by Bethany
Cassin
Beckerlegge

Everything you've heard about the zeal of Boston fans is true; here you root for the home team. You cheer, and you pray, and you root some more. "Red Sox Nation" witnessed a miracle in 2004, with the reverse of the curse and the team's first World Series victory since 1918.

Then in 2007 they proved it wasn't just a fluke with another Series win. In 2008 the Celtics ended their 18-year NBA championship drought with a thrilling victory over longtime rivals the LA Lakers. And despite the sting of their first Super Bowl loss (in recent memory) earlier in 2008, the three-time champion New England Patriots are still a remarkable force to be reckoned with.

Bostonians' long-standing fervor for sports is equally evident in their leisure-time activities. Harsh winters keep locals wrapped up for months, only to emerge at the earliest sign of oncoming spring, striving to push back the February blues through feverish exercise. Once the mercury tops freezing and the snows begin to melt, Boston's extensive parks, paths, woods, and waterways teem with sun worshippers and athletes—until the bitter winds bite again in November, and that energy becomes redirected once again toward white slopes, frozen rinks, and sheltered gyms and pools.

Department of Conservation & Recreation (*DCR*). Most public recreational facilities, including skating rinks and tennis courts, are operated by the Department of Conservation & Recreation. The DCR provides information about recreational activities in its facilities and promotes the conservation of Massachusetts parks and wilderness areas. ✉ *251 Causeway St., Suite 600, North End* ☎ *617/626–1250* ⊕ *www.mass. gov/dcr.*

Appalachian Mountain Club. This is a helpful first stop for anyone with questions about the great outdoors. Its bookstore has maps and guides about hiking and other active pursuits in the Northeast and Mid-Atlantic. The club also runs workshops and organized hiking, paddling, biking, and skiing trips throughout New England. Programs fill up fast, so advance reservations are essential. Fees are higher for non-members. A one-year individual membership starts at $50; discounted family, youth, and senior memberships are available. The club is open weekdays 9–5. ⊠ *5 Joy St., Beacon Hill* ☎ *617/523–0655* ⊕ *www.outdoors.org* Ⓜ *Park St.*

BEACHES

Although nearly 20 years of massive cleanup efforts have made the water in Boston Harbor safe for swimming, many locals and visitors still find city beaches unappealing, since much better beaches are a short drive or train ride away. If you're using public transportation to get around, you have several choices.

Revere Beach. Just north of the city, Revere Beach, the oldest public beach in America, has faded somewhat since its glory days in the early 20th century when it was a Coney Island–type playground, but it still remains a good spot to people-watch and catch some rays. The sand and water are less than pristine, but on hot summer days the waterfront is still packed with colorful local characters and Bostonians looking for an easy city escape. Most of the beach's former amusements are gone, but you can still catch concerts at the bandstand in summer. ⊠ *Revere Beach Blvd., Revere* ☎ *781/289–3020* ⊕ *www.mass.gov/dcr/parks/metroboston/revere.htm* Ⓜ *Revere Beach, Wonderland.*

TOP 5

■ Taking in a Red Sox game at Fenway Park.

■ Running, walking, or biking along the Charles River or, better yet, sailing on it with Community Boating.

■ Seeing magnificent whales and their young close-up on a whale-watch boat tour.

■ Exploring the quiet, awe-inspiring trails and shorelines of the Boston Harbor Islands.

■ Strolling through the parks and gardens of the Emerald Necklace (including the Boston Common and Public Garden).

'WHICH WAY TO THE BEACH

Kelly's Roast Beef. The huge, juicy roast-beef sandwiches served at Kelly's Roast Beef, a local institution since 1951, are the sole reason some Bostonians make the trek to Revere. Other menu favorites include the fried clams and hand-breaded onion rings. It's open from 5 am to 2:30 am Sunday through Thursday, and until 3 am Friday and Saturday. ⊠ *410 Revere Beach Blvd., Revere* ☎ *781/284–9129* ⊕ *wwww.kellysroastbeef.com.*

Singing Beach. Singing Beach, 32 mi north of Boston in a quiet Cape Ann town, gets its name from the musical squeaking sound its gold-color sand makes when you step on it. The beach is popular with both locals and out-of-towners in summer. It's also worth a visit in fall, when the crowds have gone home and you'll have the splendid shores all to yourself. There's a snack bar at the beach, but it's worth taking a 10-minute stroll up Beach Street into town to get a cone at Captain Dusty's Ice Cream (⊠ *60 Beach St.* ☉ *Mar.–Oct.*). Because there's no public parking at the beach in season (May–September), the easiest way to get here is by MBTA's Newburyport/Rockport commuter rail line from Boston's North Station to the Manchester stop, which is a 15-minute walk from the beach. From downtown Boston the train takes 45 minutes and

Sunbathers soak up the rays at Revere Beach.

costs $6.75 each way. ✉ *Beach St., Manchester-by-the-Sea* ☎ *978/526–2019* ⊕ *www.manchester.ma.us/Pages/ManchesterMA_Recreation/singingbeach.*

If you have access to a car, many more wonderful beaches are within an hour or two of Boston.

The rocky North Shore—about an hour away—is studded with New England beach towns, each with its favorite swimming spot.

Crane Beach on the Crane Estate. The 1,200-acre Crane Beach on the Crane Estate, an hour's drive to the north of Boston in the 17th-century village of Ipswich, has 4 mi of sparkling white sand that serve as a nesting ground for the threatened piping plover. From Route 128 North (toward Gloucester), follow signs for Route 1A North, 8 mi to Ipswich. Admission fees range from $2 to $25, depending on the time of year and whether you arrive on foot or by car. ✉ *Argilla Rd., Ipswich* ☎ *978/356–4354* ⊕ *www.thetrustees.org/places-to-visit/northeast-ma/crane-beach-on-the-crane.html.*

Plum Island. The well-groomed beaches of Plum Island are worth the effort to find a parking space. The water is clear and blue, but quite cold. From I–95 follow Route 113 East (becomes Route 1A South) 3½ mi to Newbury. Then, take a left on Rolfe's Lane and a right on to the Plum Island Turnpike. ✉ *Plum Island Blvd., Newburyport* ☎ *978/465–5753 parking info* ⊕ *www.newburyportchamber.org/plum_island.shtml.*

⇨ *For more information on North Shore beaches, see Chapter 15, Side Trips.*

Nantasket Beach. Nantasket Beach, a 45-minute drive from downtown Boston, has cleaner sand and warmer water than most local beaches. Take Route 3A South to Washington Boulevard, Hingham, and follow signs to Nantasket Avenue. ⊠ *Rte. 3A, Hull* ☎ *617/727–5290* ⊕ *www.mass.gov/dcr/parks/metroboston/nantask.htm.*

13

If the traffic isn't too awful (and during the summer, that's a big if), you can reach the southern tip of Cape Cod in about an hour. For more information on the many amazing beaches on the Cape and the nearby islands of Martha's Vineyard and Nantucket (which are reachable by ferry from Boston and several towns on the Cape), pick up a copy of *Fodor's New England* or *Fodor's Cape Cod, Nantucket, and Martha's Vineyard.*

PARKS

Arnold Arboretum. The sumptuously landscaped Arnold Arboretum is open all year to joggers and in-line skaters. Volunteer docents give free walking tours in spring, summer, and fall. ⊠ *125 Arborway, Jamaica Plain* ☎ *617/524–1718* ⊕ *www.arboretum.harvard.edu* Ⓜ *Forest Hills.*

Ⓒ
Fodor'sChoice
★
Boston Harbor Islands National Park Area. Comprising 34 islands and peninsulas, the Boston Harbor Islands National Park Area is somewhat of a hidden gem for nature lovers and history buffs, with miles of lightly traveled trails and shoreline and several little-visited historic sites to explore. The focal point of the national park is 39-acre Georges Island, where you'll find the partially restored pre–Civil War Fort Warren that once held Confederate prisoners. Other islands worth visiting include Peddocks Island, which holds the remains of Fort Andrews, and Lovells Island, a popular destination for campers. Lovells, Peddocks, Grape, and Bumpkin islands allow camping with a permit from late June through Labor Day. There are swimming areas at the four camping-friendly islands as well, but only Lovells has lifeguards. Pets and alcohol are not allowed on the Harbor Islands. **National Park Service.** The National Park Service is a good source for information about camping, transportation, and the like. ☎ *617/223–8666* ⊕ *www.bostonislands.com.*

Charles River Reservation. Runners, bikers, and in-line skaters crowd the Charles River Reservation at the Esplanade along Storrow Drive, the Memorial Drive Embankment in Cambridge, or any of the smaller and less-busy parks farther upriver. Here you can cheer a crew race, rent a canoe or a kayak, or simply sit on the grass, sharing the shore with packs of hard-jogging university athletes, in-line skaters, moms with strollers, dreamily entwined couples, and intense academics, often talking to themselves as they sort out their intellectual—or perhaps personal—dilemmas. **Hatch Memorial Shell.** The Hatch Memorial Shell

on the Esplanade holds free concerts and outdoor events all summer. ☎ *617/626–4970* ⊕ *www.mass.gov/dcr/hatch_events.htm* Ⓜ *Charles/ MGH* ☎ *617/626–1250* ⊕ *www.mass.gov/dcr/parks/charlesRiver.*

ⓒ **Emerald Necklace.** The six large public parks known as Boston's Emerald
Fodor's Choice Necklace stretch 5 mi from the Back Bay Fens through Franklin Park,
★ in Dorchester; the natural treasure also includes Arnold Arboretum, Jamaica Pond, Olmstead Park, and the Riverway. Frederick Law Olmsted's design heightened the beauty of the Emerald Necklace, which remains a well-groomed urban masterpiece. Locals take pride in and happily make use of its open spaces and its pathways and bridges connecting rivers and ponds. **Emerald Necklace Conservancy.** The Emerald Necklace Conservancy maintains a regular calendar of nature walks and other events in the parks. (☎ *617/522–2700* ⊕ *www.emeraldnecklace. org*) **Boston Parks & Recreation Department.** Rangers with the Boston Parks & Recreation Department lead tours highlighting the area's historic sites and surprising ecological diversity. ✉ *1010 Massachusetts Ave.* ☎ *617/635–4505* ⊕ *www.cityofboston.gov/parks/parkrangers*

Harbor Express. To reach the Harbor Islands, take the Harbor Express from Long Wharf (Downtown) or the Hingham Shipyard to Georges Island or Spectacle Island. High-speed catamarans run daily from May through mid-October and cost $14. Other islands can be reached by the free interisland water shuttles that depart from Georges Island. ☎ *617/223–8666* ⊕ *www.harborexpress.com.*

Mt. Auburn Cemetery. Cambridge's historic Mt. Auburn Cemetery is known as one of the best birding spots in the area, and also has walking paths, gardens, and unique architecture. You can also see the graves of such distinguished New Englanders as Oliver Wendell Holmes, Henry Wadsworth Longfellow, and Mary Baker Eddy. ✉ *580 Mt. Auburn St., Mt. AuburnCambridge* ☎ *617/547–7105* ⊕ *www.mountauburn. org* Ⓜ *Harvard, then Bus 71 or 73 to Mount Auburn St. at Aberdeen Ave. stop.*

Rose Fitzgerald Kennedy Greenway. After Boston's Central Artery (I–93) was moved underground as part of the Big Dig project, the city transformed the footprint of the former highway into the Rose Fitzgerald Kennedy Greenway, a gorgeous mile-long oasis filled with plazas, parks, gardens, fountains, and even a merry-go-round. The tranquil greenway stretches from the North End (New Sudbury and Cross streets) to Chinatown (Kneeland and Hudson streets), curving through the heart of downtown, just a few blocks from the harbor in most places. Though most of the Greenway has been completed, it's still a work in progress. Several installations are scheduled to open in the coming years: the new Boston Museum is slated to be completed in 2013, and the New Center for Arts and Culture expects to break ground on its Daniel Libeskind-designed home in the next few years. ☎ *617/292–0020* ⊕ *www. rosekennedygreenway.org.*

13

SPORTS

⇨ *See the Fenway Park spotlight for information on the Boston Red Sox.*

BASKETBALL

★ **Boston Celtics.** The Boston Celtics, one of the most storied franchises in the National Basketball Association, have won the NBA championship 17 times since 1957, more than any other team in the league. The last title came in 2008, after a solid defeat of longtime rivals the LA Lakers ended an 18-year championship dry spell. Basketball season runs from late October to April, and play-offs last until mid-June. ⊠ *TD Garden, Old West End* ☎ *866/423–5849, 617/931–2222 Ticketmaster* ⊕ *www.celtics.com.*

BICYCLING

★ It's common to see suited-up doctors, lawyers, and businesspeople commuting on two wheels through Downtown; unfortunately, bike lanes are few and far between. Boston's dedicated bike paths are well used, as much by joggers and in-line skaters as by bicyclists.

Department of Conservation & Recreation (*DCR*). For other path locations, consult the Department of Conservation & Recreation Web site. ⊕ *www.mass.gov/dcr.*

Dr. Paul Dudley White Bike Path. The Dr. Paul Dudley White Bike Path, about 17 mi long, follows both banks of the Charles River as it winds from Watertown Square to the Museum of Science.

Massachusetts Bicycle Coalition (*MassBike*). The Massachusetts Bicycle Coalition, an advocacy group working to improve conditions for area cyclists, has information on organized rides and sells good bike maps of Boston and the state. Thanks to MassBike's lobbying efforts, the MBTA now allows bicycles on subway and commuter-rail trains during nonpeak hours. ⊠ *171 Milk St., Suite 33, Downtown* ☎ *617/542–2453* ⊕ *www.massbike.org.*

Minuteman Bikeway. The tranquil Minuteman Bikeway courses 11 mi from the Alewife Red Line T station in Cambridge through Arlington, Lexington, and Bedford. The trail, on the bed of an old rail line, cuts through a few busy intersections—be particularly careful in Arlington Center. ⊕ *www.minutemanbikeway.org.*

Pierre Lallement Bike Path. The Pierre Lallement Bike Path winds 4 mi through the South End and Roxbury, from Copley Place to Franklin Park.

BICYCLE RENTALS **Back Bay Bicycles.** Back Bay Bicycles has city cruiser bike rentals for $35 per day, road bikes for $55 per day, and full-suspension mountain bikes for $100 per day (weekly rates are also available). Staff members also lead group mountain-bike rides on nearby trails. ⊠ *366 Commonwealth Ave., Back Bay* ☎ *617/247–2336* ⊕ *www.backbaybicycles.com.*

ON YER BIKE!

Boston may be dubbed America's Walking City, but it's a fine place for pedal-pushing, too.

Boston Bike Tours. Boston Bike Tours offers a variety of themed excursions on weekends from spring through fall. Most outings cover about 10–12 mi. The main tours cost $35 per person (special tours, including a beach and brewery tour, are offered several times a month and cost around $45). No reservations are needed: just show up at the Visitor Information Center on the Boston Common at 10 am for the morning option, or at 2 pm for the afternoon outing. Tours are offered daily from July through August, and weekends and holidays from mid-April through June and September through October. You bring the adrenaline, they bring the bikes, helmets, and water. ☎ 617/670–0637 ⊕ www. bostonbiketours.com.

Community Bicycle Supply. Community Bicycle Supply rents cycles from April through October, at rates of $25 for 24 hours. ✉ 496 Tremont St., at E. Berkeley St., South End ☎ 617/542–8623 ⊕ www. communitybicycle.com.

BOATING

Except when frozen over, the waterways coursing through the city serve as a playground for boaters of all stripes. All types of pleasure craft, with the exception of inflatables, are allowed from the Charles River and Inner Harbor to North Washington Street on the waters of Boston Harbor, Dorchester inner and outer bays, and the Neponset River from the Granite Avenue Bridge to Dorchester Bay.

Boat drop sites. There are several boat drop sites along the Charles. **Clarendon Street** ✉ Back Bay. **Hatch Shell** ✉ Embankment Rd., Back Bay. **Pinckney Street Landing** ✉ Back Bay. **Brooks Street** ✉ Nonantum Rd., Brighton. **Richard T. Artesani Playground** ✉ Off Soldiers Field Rd., Brighton. **Charles River Dam, Museum of Science** ✉ Cambridge. **Watertown Square** ✉ Charles River Rd. Watertown

Charles River Watershed Association. The Charles River Watershed Association publishes detailed boating information on its Web site. ☎ 781/788–0057 ⊕ www.charlesriver.org.

Christopher Columbus Waterfront Park. Sailboats can be rented from one of the many boathouses or docks along the Charles. Downtown, public landings and float docks are available at the Christopher Columbus Waterfront Park with a permit from the Boston harbormaster. ✉ Commercial St., Boston Harbor, North End ☎ 617/635–4505.

LESSONS AND EQUIPMENT

★ **Boston University.** From May to October Boston University offers beginner to advanced rowing and sailing programs. ✉ Soldier's Field Rd. ☎ 617/353–9307 boathouse ⊕ www.bu.edu/fitrec.

Charles River Canoe & Kayak Center. From May through mid-November you can rent a canoe, kayak, paddleboat, rowboat, or rowing shell from

Charles River Canoe & Kayak Center. There are a variety of canoeing and kayaking classes for all skill levels, as well as organized group outings and tours. **Canoe & Kayak Center's kiosk**. The Canoe & Kayak Center's kiosk rents canoes and kayaks and is open Thursday evening, Friday afternoon, and weekends early May through mid-October. It's open weekdays only for group appointments. ⊠ *Soldiers' Field Rd. near Eliot Bridge, AllstonNewton* ⊠ *2401 Commonwealth Ave.* ☎ *617/965– 5110* ⊕ *www.paddleboston.com.*

Community Boating. Community Boating, near the Charles Street footbridge on the Esplanade, is the host of America's oldest public sailing program. From April through October $99 nets you a 30-day introductory membership, beginner-level classes, and use of sailboats and kayaks. Full memberships grant unlimited use of all facilities; splash around for 60 days for $179 or all season long for $249. Experienced sailors short on time can opt for a one-day sailboat rental for $75. ⊠ *21 David Mugar Way, Beacon Hill* ☎ *617/523–1038* ⊕ *www.community-boating.org.*

Community Rowing. Community Rowing teaches introductory to competitive adult and youth rowing courses. Private lessons are also available. ⊠ *Daly Memorial Skating Rink, 20 Nonantum Rd., Brighton* ☎ *617/779–8267* ⊕ *www.communityrowing.org.*

Jamaica Pond Boat House. From April to October the Jamaica Pond Boat House provides lessons and equipment for rowing and sailing on its namesake pond. ⊠ *Jamaica Way and Pond St., Jamaica Plain* ☎ *617/522–5061.*

EVENTS

★ **Head of the Charles Regatta.** In mid-October about 300,000 spectators turn out to cheer the more than 7,500 male and female athletes who come from all over the world to compete in the annual Head of the Charles Regatta. Crowds line the banks of the Charles River with blankets and beer (although the police disapprove of the latter), cheering on their favorite teams and generally using the weekend as an excuse to party. Limited free parking is available, but the chances of finding an open space close to the race route are slim; take public transportation if you can. During the event, free shuttles run between the start and end point of the race route on both sides of the river. ☎ *617/868–6200* ⊕ *www.hocr.org.*

FISHING

Efforts to clean up the city's waterways have heightened the popularity of recreational fishing in and around Boston. For saltwater fishing, locals cast their lines from the **John J. McCorkle Fishing Pier** on Castle Island off Day Boulevard in South Boston and **Tenean Beach** and **Victory Road Park** off Morrissey Boulevard in Dorchester.

Blue Hills Reservation. Houghton's Pond in Blue Hills Reservation is an excellent place to freshwater fish. ⊠ *Off Rte. 128, Milton.*

Rowers ready for races during the Head of the Charles Regatta.

Boston Harbor Islands National Park Area. The Boston Harbor Islands National Park Area is also known for great fishing, although no public piers are available. ☎ 617/223–8666 ⊕ *www.bostonislands.com.*

Jamaica Pond. You can freshwater fish in Jamaica Pond. ⊠ *Jamaica Way and Pond St., Jamaica Plain* ⊕ *www.jamaicapond.com.*

MassWildlife Boston Office. Nonresidents can purchase a three-day Massachusetts fishing license for $23.50 at the MassWildlife Boston Office, Brookline Town Hall, and some sporting-goods stores around the city. No license is required for recreational ocean angling. ⊠ *251 Causeway St., North End* ⊕ *www.mass.gov/dfwele.*

Middlesex Fells Reservation. You can fish at Quarter Mile Pond and Dark Hollow Pond in Middlesex Fells Reservation. ⊠ *Off Rte. 93, Stoneham.*

Stony Brook Reservation. Turtle Pond in Stony Brook Reservation has excellent fishing. ⊠ *Turtle Pond Pkwy., Hyde Park.*

FOOTBALL

Boston College Eagles. With the only Division 1A football program in town, the Boston College Eagles play against some of the top teams in the country. ⊠ *Alumni Stadium, Chestnut Hill* ☎ 617/552–4622 ⊕ *bce-agles.cstv.com/sports/m-footbl/bc-m-footbl-body.html.*

Harvard University Crimson. Built in 1903, Harvard Stadium is the oldest concrete stadium in the country and the home of the Harvard University Crimson. The tongue-in-cheek halftime shows of the Harvard Band make any game worth the trip. ⊠ *Harvard Stadium, N. Harvard St. and Soldiers Field Rd., Allston* ☎ 617/495–2211 ⊕ *www.gocrimson.com.*

New England Patriots. Boston has been building a football dynasty over the past decade, starting with the New England Patriots come-from-behind victory against the favored St. Louis Rams in the 2002 Super Bowl. Coach Bill Belichick and heartthrob quarterback Tom Brady then brought the team two more championship rings in 2004 and 2005, and have made Patriots fans as zealous as their baseball counterparts. Exhibition football games begin in August, and the season runs through the play-offs in January. The state-of-the-art Gillette Stadium is in Foxborough, 30 mi southwest of Boston. ⊠ *Gillette Stadium, Rte. 1, off I–95 Exit 9, Foxborough* ☎ *800/745–3000 Ticketmaster* ⊕ *www.patriots.com.*

GOLF

Although you'll need to know someone who knows someone who *is* someone to play at Chestnut Hill's Country Club, one of the nation's top-rated private courses, anyone can use the public courses in Boston, which are among the best in the country.

George Wright Golf Course. The hilly George Wright Golf Course is more challenging than the other Donald Ross–designed course at Franklin Park. The par-70, 6,096-yard course is open for the season starting in April each year. Weekend 18-hole greens fees are $45 ($37 for residents); weekday fees are $38 ($33 for residents). Tee times are necessary on weekends. ⊠ *420 West St., Hyde Park* ☎ *617/364–2300.*

William J. Devine Golf Course at Franklin Park. Donald Ross crafted the 6,009-yard, par-70 William J. Devine Golf Course at Franklin Park in the early 1896. It's open year-round, weather permitting. Greens fees without a cart are $23 for 9 holes and $38 for 18 holes on weekdays, and $27 and $45, respectively, on weekends. (You can play 9 holes only after 1 pm on weekends.) Charges for a golf cart tend to run about $11 to $20 more. Club rentals run $11 for 9 holes and $20 for 18 holes. The course is part of delightful Franklin Park, which also has picnic facilities and jogging courses. Festivals and other outdoor activities take place all year. ⊠ *1 Circuit Dr., Dorchester* ☎ *617/265–4084.*

Massachusetts Golf Association. The Massachusetts Golf Association represents 400 clubs in the state, and has information on courses that are open to the public. ⊠ *300 Arnold Palmer Blvd., Norton* ☎ *774/430–9100* ⊕ *www.mgalinks.org.*

HIKING

With the Appalachian Trail just two hours' drive from Downtown and thousands of acres of parkland and trails encircling the city, hikers will not lack for options in and around Boston.

☾
★ **Blue Hills Reservation.** A 20-minute drive south of Boston, the Blue Hills Reservation encompasses 7,000 acres of woodland with about 125 mi of trails, some ideal for cross-country skiing in winter, some designated for mountain biking the rest of the year. Although only 635 feet high, Great Blue Hill, the tallest hill in the reservation, has a spectacular view of the entire Boston metro area. It's open daily, and maps are available for purchase at the reservation headquarters or the Blue Hills Trailside

Museum. To get there, take Route 93 South to Exit 3, Houghton's Pond. ✉ *695 Hillside St., Milton* ☎ *617/698–1802* ⊕ *www.mass.gov/dcr/parks/metroboston/blue.htm.*

Blue Hills Trailside Museum. The Blue Hills Trailside Museum, which is managed by the Massachusetts Audubon Society, organizes hikes and nature walks. Open Thursday through Sunday and Monday holidays 10–5, the museum has natural-history exhibits and live animals. Admission is $3. Take Route 93 South to Exit 2B and Route 138 North. ✉ *1904 Canton Ave., Milton* ☎ *617/333–0690* ⊕ *www.massaudubon.org.*

Boston Harbor Islands National Park Area. Easily accessible from downtown Boston, the Boston Harbor Islands National Park Area is seldom crowded. The park maintains walking trails through diverse terrain and ecosystems *(⇨ Parks, above).*

Boston Parks & Recreation Department. Rangers with the Boston Parks & Recreation Department lead walks through the Emerald Necklace parks. ✉ *1010 Massachusetts Ave.* ☎ *617/635–4505* ⊕ *www.cityofboston.gov/parks/parkrangers.*

Middlesex Fells Reservation. Just a few miles north of Boston, the 2,575-acre Middlesex Fells Reservation has well-maintained hiking trails that pass over rocky hills, across meadows, and through wetland areas. Trails range from the quarter-mile Bear Hill Trail to the 6.9-mi Skyline Trail. Mountain bikers can ride along the reservation's fire roads and on a designated loop trail. This sprawling reservation covers area in Malden, Medford, Stoneham, Melrose, and Winchester. To get to the western side of the reservation from Boston, take Route 93 North to Exit 33, and then take South Border Road off the rotary. ☎ *617/727–5380* ⊕ *www.mass.gov/dcr/parks/metroboston/fells.htm.*

Stony Brook Reservation. Excellent hiking footpaths crisscross the 475-acre Stony Brook Reservation, which spans Hyde Park and West Roxbury. ✉ *Turtle Pond Pkwy.* ☎ *617/333–7404* ⊕ *www.mass.gov/dcr/parks/metroboston/stony.htm.*

HOCKEY

Boston hockey fans are informed, vocal, and extremely loyal. Despite frequent trades of star players, disappointing losses, and high ticket prices, the stands are still packed at Bruins games (especially after a playoff run in 2009). That said, local college hockey teams tend to give spectators plenty to celebrate at a much more reasonable price.

Beanpot Hockey Tournament. Boston College, Boston University, Harvard, and Northeastern teams face off every February in the Beanpot Hockey Tournament at the TD Garden. The colleges in this fiercely contested tournament traditionally yield some of the finest squads in the country. ⊕ *www.beanpothockey.com.*

Boston Bruins. The Boston Bruins are on the ice from September until April, frequently on Thursday and Saturday evenings. Play-offs last through early June. ✉ *TD Garden, 100 Legends Way, Old West End* ☎ *617/624–2327* ⊕ *www.bostonbruins.com.*

Boston Common becomes an icy wonderland in winter.

ICE SKATING

Boston Common Frog Pond. Thanks to a refrigerated surface, the Boston Common Frog Pond transforms into a skating park from November to mid-March, complete with a warming hut and concession stand. Admission is $4 for adults; kids 13 and under skate free. Skate rentals cost $8, and lockers are $1. Frog Pond hours are Monday 10–4, Tuesday through Thursday and Sunday 10–9, and Friday and Saturday 10–10. ☎ 617/635–2120 ⊕ *www.bostonfrogpond.com.*

Boston Public Garden. Skaters flock to the frozen waters of the lagoon at Boston Public Garden. Ice on one side of the bridge is theoretically reserved for figure skating and the other for faster-paced ice hockey, though most ignore the rule during slow times.

Larz Anderson Park. Outside the city, try the skating rink in Larz Anderson Park, at the top of a wooded hill. Admission for Brookline residents is $5; nonresidents pay $8. Skate rentals are $5. The rink is open from December through early March. ✉ *23 Newton St. Brookline* ☎ 617/739–7518.

Public Ice-skating Rinks. The Department of Conservation & Recreation operates more than 20 public ice-skating rinks; hours and season vary by location. Call for a complete list of rinks and their hours of operation. ☎ 617/626–1250 ⊕ *www.mass.gov/dcr.*

SKATE RENTALS

Beacon Hill Skate Shop. Beacon Hill Skate Shop rents skates for use in the Frog Pond and Public Garden for $10 per hour or $20 per day. A credit card is required; call in advance and they'll have the skates sharpened and ready for you. ⊠ *135 Charles St., off Tremont St., near Citi Performing Arts Center, South End* ☎ *617/482–7400.*

RUNNING AND JOGGING

Boston's parks and riverside pathways almost never lack for joggers, even in the worst weather. Paths on both sides of the Charles River are the most crowded and best maintained, particularly along the **Esplanade.** Watch out for in-line skaters and bikers. At **Castle Island** in South Boston, skaters and joggers zip past strolling lovebirds and parents pushing jogging strollers. The tranquil, wooded 1½-mi-long loop around idyllic **Jamaica Pond** is a slightly less crowded option.

Bill Rodgers Running Center. For equipment and information on local running routes, contact the Bill Rodgers Running Center. ⊠ *Faneuil Hall Marketplace, Government Center* ☎ *617/723–5612* ⊕ *www. billrodgers.com.*

EVENTS

Fodor'sChoice **Boston Marathon.** Every Patriots' Day (the third Monday in April), fans
★ gather along the Hopkinton–to–Boston route of the Boston Marathon (⇨ *Close-Up box in this chapter)* to cheer on more than 25,000 runners from all over the world. The race ends near Copley Square in the Back Bay. **Boston Athletic Association.** For information, call the Boston Athletic Association ☎ *617/236–1652* ⊕ *www.bostonmarathon.org.*

Tufts Health Plan 10K for Women. In October women runners take the spotlight on Columbus Day for the Tufts Health Plan 10K for Women, which attracts 7,000 participants and 20,000 spectators. Four American records have been set at this race since it began in 1977. ☎ *888/767–7223 registration* ⊕ *www.tufts-healthplan.com/tufts10k.*

SKIING

CROSS-COUNTRY

Weston Ski Track. From mid-December to March, the Weston Ski Track provides cross-country skiers and snowshoers with 15 mi of groomed, natural trails and a snowmaking area with a lighted 2-mi ski track. Rentals and basic instruction are available. ⊠ *200 Park Rd., Weston* ☎ *781/891–6575* ⊕ *www.skiboston.com.*

DOWNHILL

Berkshires. The Berkshires region in western Massachusetts offers a little bit of Aspen on the East Coast, with tony ski resorts, fine dining, and an upscale atmosphere for those able to take a daylong or weekend ski trip. For details on the various resorts in the Berkshires, go to www. berkshireskiing.com. ⊠ *135 mi west of Boston along I–90 and Rte. 2,* ⊕ *www.berkshires.org.*

Blue Hills Ski Area. The closest downhill skiing to Boston is at the Blue Hills Ski Area. It has 60 acres of skiing terrain and 9 trails to choose from. There's a snow sports school, equipment rentals, and a restaurant. Off-peak and group rates are available. Take Route 93 South to Exit

The Boston Marathon

Though it missed being the first U.S. marathon by one year (the first, in 1896, went from Stamford, Connecticut, to New York City), the Boston Marathon is arguably the nation's most prestigious. Why? It's the only marathon in the world for which runners have to qualify; it's the world's oldest continuously run marathon; it's been run on the same course since it began. Only the New York Marathon compares with it for community involvement. Spectators have returned to the same spot for generations, bringing their lawn chairs and barbecues.

Held every Patriots' Day (the third Monday in April), the marathon passes through Hopkinton, Ashland, Framingham, Natick, Wellesley, Newton, Brookline, and Boston; only the last few miles are run in the city proper. The first marathon was organized by members of the Boston Athletic Association (BAA), who in 1896 had attended the first modern Olympic games in Athens. When they saw that the Olympics ended with a marathon, they decided the same would be a fitting end to their own Spring Sports Festival, begun in the late 1880s.

The first race was run on April 19, 1897, when Olympian Tom Burke drew a line in the dirt in Ashland and began a 24.5-mi dash (increased to its current 26.2 mi in 1924) to Boston with 15 men. For most of its history, the race concluded on Exeter Street outside the BAA's clubhouse. In 1965 the finish was moved to the front of the Prudential Center, and in 1986 it was moved to its current location, Copley Square. The race's guardian spirit is the indefatigable John A. Kelley, who ran his first marathon shortly after Warren G. Harding was sworn

in as president. Kelley won twice—in 1935 and 1945—took the second-place spot seven times, and continued to run well into his eighties, finishing 58 Boston Marathons in all. Until his retirement in 1992, his arrival at the finish signaled the official end of the race. A double statue of an older Kelley greeting his younger self stands at the route's most strenuous incline—dubbed "Heartbreak Hill"—on Commonwealth Avenue in Newton.

Women weren't allowed to race until 1972, but in 1966 Roberta Gibb slipped into the throngs under a hooded sweatshirt; she was the first known female participant. In 1967 cameras captured BAA organizer Jock Semple screaming, "Get out of my race," as he tried to rip off the number of Kathrine Switzer, who had registered as K. Switzer. But the marathon's most infamous moment was when 26-year-old Rosie Ruiz came out of nowhere to be the first woman to cross the finish line in the 1980 race. Ruiz apparently started running less than 1 mi from the end of the course, and her title was stripped eight days later. Bostonians still quip about her taking the T to the finish.

Traveler's at Fodors.com have enjoyed the race, both as spectators and runners:

"The town was hopping! . . . Coolidge Corner was between 23 and 24. It was a blast."   —ilana25841

"I don't remember much of mile 24–25 other than pain. The last mile we round the corner and on the home stretch I see the big blue finish line . . . Shortly I feel better and celebrate with a cheeseburger, fries, and two Sam Adams beers. Life is sweet; I love Boston."   —Queenie

2B and Route 138 North. ⊠ *Blue Hills Reservation, 4001 Washington St.Canton* ☎ *781/828–5070* ⊕ *www.ski-bluehills.com.*

On weekends and holidays serious skiers and snowboarders head north to the mountain resorts along I–93 in New Hampshire.

Cannon Mountain Resort. Farther north in Franconia Notch, the historic Cannon Mountain Resort is the site of North America's first aerial tramway and home to the New England Ski Museum. There are 72 trails and 9 lifts. ⊠ *Off I–93 N Exit 34B or -C,* ☎ *603/823–8800* ⊕ *www. cannonmt.com.*

Loon Mountain Resort. Near Waterville Valley Resort, Loon Mountain Resort has 52 trails spanning more than 2,100 vertical feet and six terrain parks. ⊠ *Off I–93 Exit 32,* ☎ *603/745–8111, 800/229–5666* ⊕ *www.loonmtn.com.*

Ski NH. Ski NH is a good source for local ski information. ☎ *603/745– 9396, 800/887–5464* ⊕ *www.skinh.com.*

Waterville Valley Resort. The first big resort off I–93, Waterville Valley Resort, is one of the state's most popular ski destinations, with 52 trails and a terrain park with a 400-foot half pipe. ⊠ *Rte. 49, off I–93 Exit 28,* ☎ *800/468–2553, 603/236-8311* ⊕ *www.waterville.com.*

SOCCER

☾ **New England Revolution.** New England's major-league soccer team, New England Revolution, plays from late March to late October. ⊠ *Gillette Stadium, 1 Patriot Pl.Foxborough* ☎ *877/438–7387, 617/931–2222 Ticketmaster* ⊕ *www.revolutionsoccer.net.*

On any clear weekend morning, pickup games at most of Boston's parks, especially the fields at the western end of **Back Bay Fens Park** and at **Mayor Thomas W. Danehy Park** near the Alewife transit center in Cambridge, become meeting places for amateur soccer players and fans.

TENNIS

Department of Conservation & Recreation. The Department of Conservation & Recreation maintains more than 25 public tennis courts throughout the greater Boston area. These operate on a first-come, first-served basis. Lighted courts are open from dawn to 10 pm; other courts are open from dawn to dusk. **Charlesbank Park**. Some of Boston's most popular lighted courts are those at Charlesbank Park ⊠ *Storrow Dr. opposite Charles St., Beacon Hill.* **Marine Park**. A popular place to play tennis, Marine Park has lighted courts. ⊠ *Day Blvd., South Boston.* **Weider Playground**. Weider Playground also has lighted courts. ⊠ *Dale St., Hyde Park* ☎ *617/626–1250* ⊕ *www.mass.gov/dcr.*

Shopping

WORD OF MOUTH

"Newbury St. is fun for shopping and strolling, I also agree that
Cambridge, and more specifically Harvard Square, are musts."
—Kwoo

SHOPPING PLANNER

Hours

Boston's shops are generally open Monday through Saturday from 10 or 11 until 6 or 7 and Sunday noon to 5. Many stay open until 8 pm one night a week, usually Thursday. Malls are open Monday through Saturday from 9 or 10 until 8 or 9 and Sunday noon to 6.

Top Experiences

■ Head to **Louis Boston** for exquisitely made clothing and personalized attention.

■ Pick up a Red Sox hat at the T-shirt stand outside **Fenway Park** on a game day.

■ Make an appointment with designer **Daniela Corte** to buy one of her signature custom-made wrap dresses.

■ Pick up a slew of Danish-designed tableware and home decor (that no one else will have!) at **Lekker** in the South End.

■ Hit **Charles Street** to troll through the dozens of antiques shops.

Getting Around

Study the T map *(⇨ On the Go map)* before plunging into a shopping tour of Boston or Cambridge. You're almost always better off leaving your car behind than trying to navigate congested city streets and puzzle out parking arcana. Most major shopping neighborhoods are easily accessible on the T: Boston's Charles Street and Downtown Crossing and Cambridge's Harvard, Central, and Porter squares are on the Red Line; Copley Place, Faneuil Hall, and Newbury Street are on the Green Line; the South End is an easy trip on the Orange Line.

Blitz Tours

Beantown Bahgains. Thriftiness is considered one of the highest moral virtues in New England—even when buying luxury items. At **DSW** you can always find high-end designer shoes for both sexes at decent prices. Several shops full of watches and jewelry at reduced prices (some barely above wholesale) are found along Washington Street. If vintage is your thing, Newbury Street is dotted with consignment shops lined with gently worn Prada, Gucci, Burberry, and their ilk. Look first in **Second Time Around,** or try across the river in Harvard Square at **Oona's.** Both are also known to carry more daring labels such as Chloé and Catherine Malandrino for women, and Ermenegildo Zegna for men.

Books. Boston is a bibliophile's dream. For rare, antique, or just plain unusual books, start at **Ars Libri Ltd.** in the South End, a few blocks away from the Back Bay T stop. From here, head to Newbury Street (turn right on Waltham Street, walk three blocks, and cross Tremont Street, then pick up Clarendon Street to Newbury Street) for a break at the **Trident Booksellers & Café,** one of the city's first bookstore-cafés, almost directly across the street. Alternatively, from Ars Libri follow Waltham to Tremont Street, make a right, and head over the turnpike to reach West Street and the **Brattle Bookshop.** From here, catch the Red Line T into Harvard Square to browse through the **Harvard Book Store** and, just around the corner, **Grolier Poetry Bookshop.**

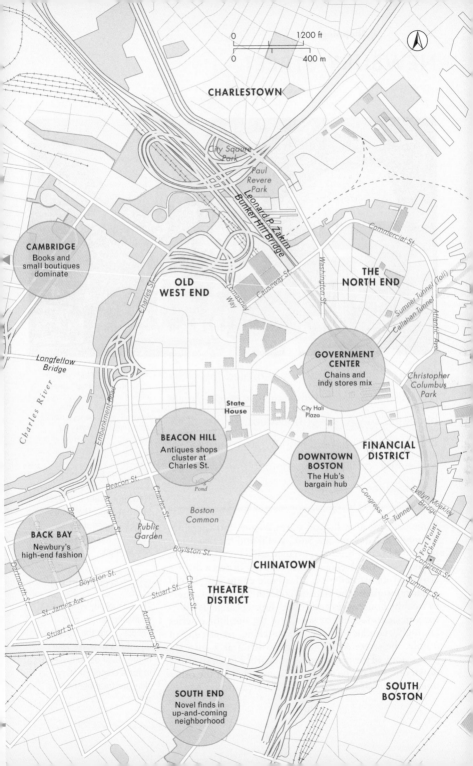

CHARLESTOWN

City Square Park

Paul Revere Park

Leonard P. Zakim Bunker Hill Bridge

THE NORTH END

Commercial St.

Sumner Tunnel (Toll)

Callahan Tunnel

Atlantic Ave.

CAMBRIDGE
Books and small boutiques dominate

OLD WEST END

Charles St.

Lomasney Way

Causeway St.

Washington St.

GOVERNMENT CENTER
Chains and indy stores mix

Christopher Columbus Park

Longfellow Bridge

Charles River

Embankment Rd.

State House

City Hall Plaza

BEACON HILL
Antiques shops cluster at Charles St.

DOWNTOWN BOSTON
The Hub's bargain hub

FINANCIAL DISTRICT

Evelyn Moakley Bridge

Beacon St.

Charles St.

Pond

Boston Common

Congress St. Tunnel

Fort Point Channel

Congress St.

BACK BAY
Newbury's high-end fashion

Public Garden

Arlington St.

Boylston St.

CHINATOWN

Summer St.

Dartmouth St.

Boylston St.

Stuart St.

THEATER DISTRICT

St. James Ave.

Stuart St.

Charles St.

Arlington St.

Stuart St.

SOUTH BOSTON

SOUTH END
Novel finds in up-and-coming neighborhood

0   1200 ft
0   400 m

NEWBURY STREET

Newbury Street is Boston's unrivaled top shopping spot. The eight-block strip is packed with big-name shops, novel boutiques, and a plethora of salons. Spend money, save money, or just enjoy a nice walk among the beautiful brownstones.

(above) Shoppers of every ilk amble down Newbury Street looking for bargains, splurges, and the perfect accessory. (lower right) Boutiques mingle with chains and cafés on Newbury.

Some call this area Boston's 5th Avenue, but there are definitely key differences. Sure, you'll find the usual suspects like Brooks Brothers, Chanel, and Giorgio Armani. Unlike New York's elite street, Newbury draws a diverse crowd to its art galleries, affordable chain stores, and small boutiques. The eclectic collection of shops caters to wealthy housewives and college hipsters alike. It's Boston's place to see and be seen, and the outdoor eateries are highly conducive to people-watching. At just shy of a mile, the street isn't too long, so stroll at a leisurely pace. Many of the best shops are at garden level, so cruise down one side of the street and come back on the other to ensure you don't miss any hidden treasures.

BEST TIME TO GO

Newbury Street is a weekend hot spot. The stores here are open daily, so come on a quieter weekday instead.

BEST HOME FIND

The beautifully wrapped soaps, perfumes, and candles from the Boston-based **Fresh** make your home smell delicious. Pop in for a complimentary skincare treatment or for gifts.

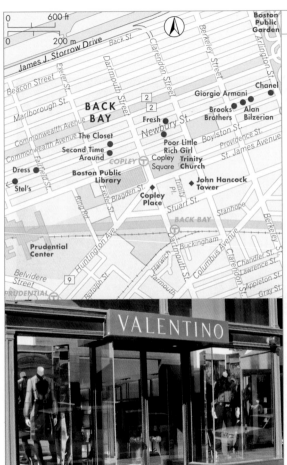

REFUELING

The locally owned and operated **J.P. Licks** (✉ *352 Newbury St.* ☏ *617/236–1666*) scoops homemade ice cream, frozen yogurts, sherbet, and sorbet in all the basic varieties plus seasonal flavors like Apple Crisp and Wild Turkey Bourbon. Grab reading materials and order off the extensive menu at **Trident Booksellers & Cafe** (✉ *338 Newbury St.* ☏ *617/267–8688*), a charming eatery in a great "mom and pop" book shop. **The Upper Crust** (✉ *222 Newbury St.* ☏ *617/262–0090*) serves up ultra-thin-crust slices on the go.

BEST FOR

BIG NAMES
Brooks Brothers: The place to stock up on business and casual classics from cardigans to bow ties.

Chanel: Home to the timeless quilted purses, costume jewelry, and feminine suits that women lust after.

Giorgio Armani: Luxurious men and women's attire from the famed Italian designer.

UPSCALE BOUTIQUES
Alan Bilzerian: Hard-to-find clothing and accessories for men and women.

Dress: Mostly dresses, with a side of skirts, tops, and accessories.

Stel's: An exclusive high-end shop with standout pieces and wardrobe staples.

VINTAGE
The Closet: A pricier vintage spot with well-kept designer clothing and accessories.

Poor Little Rich Girl: From big brands to no-names, this store sells them all.

Second Time Around: A large consignment shop with great finds and great prices.

CHARLES STREET

Welcome to John Kerry's neck of the woods. Charles Street is in beautiful Beacon Hill, one of Boston's priciest neighborhoods. The scenic area, strewn with apartments and brick-lined sidewalks, has a warm, residential feel. The tiny street is walkable and filled with great finds.

(above) Holiday decorations and gas streetlamps warm Charles Street during the chilly winter. (lower right) Some of the best antiques finds in Boston are hidden away on Charles Street.

Charles Street is at the "flat of the hill." Named after the neighboring Charles River, it was one of the first roads to be included in Boston's expansion in the early 1800s. The entire street divides the Boston Common and the Public Garden, but the shopping area is sectioned off between Beacon and Cambridge streets. There are no major chain stores anywhere in sight, and even the 7-11 has classy signage. The whole area has a grown-up, sophisticated vibe, without being overly ritzy. Students and tourists don't flock to this street as much, so this low-key destination is perfect for a relaxing stroll. Though only five blocks long, Charles Street has enough antiques shops and tiny boutiques to keep any shopaholic occupied for hours.

BEST TIME TO GO

Thursday nights are ideal, since it's quieter and most boutiques are open late.

BEST INNER COWBOY FIND

Helen's Leather Shop has an enormous selection of Western clothing, accessories, and leather goods. Saddle up with a pair of crocodile boots or a turquoise belt buckle.

BEST FOR

WOMEN'S BOUTIQUES
Crush: Everything from office wear to party tops, with a variety of brands and price points.

Holiday: Upscale, sophisticated attire including dresses, sweaters, and skirts.

Moxie: A great selection of shoes from top designers.

Wish: Contemporary clothing and handbags for weekdays and weekends.

ANTIQUING
A Room with a Vieux Antiques: A leading French antiques importer with items from the 18th and 19th centuries.

Devonia: Antiques for Dining: A large selection of heirloom china, stemware, and crystal from the Gilded Age.

Judith Dowling Asian Art: Two floors of Japanese artwork, including paintings, ceramics, and lacquer.

Marika's: A reasonably priced shop, packed wall to wall with great finds.

14

REFUELING

If you're looking for a quick soup and sandwich combo, stop at **Caffé Bella Vita** (⊠ *30 Charles St.* ☎ *617/720–4505*), a spacious spot where locals sip lattes, macchiatos, and tea. Operating since 1937, the **Paramount** (⊠ *44 Charles St.* ☎ *617/720–1152*) serves all the breakfast standards until 4:30 pm. Lunch is also available. If the weather permits, grab a seat on the outdoor patio at **Cafe Vanille** (⊠ *70 Charles St.* ☎ *617/523–9200*), a French café known for its delicious quiches and pastries and Parisian coffee blends.

SOUTH END

The South End isn't what it used to be—and that's a good thing. In the last decade, this section of Boston has rapidly become one of the most sought-after areas for apartments, restaurants, and stores. The spacious streets are now filled with one-of-a-kind gems, making it the city's new shopping mecca.

(above) Funky meets flowy at Flock in the up-and-coming South End. (lower right) Try the SOWA Open Market for unique clothing and art finds.

Forget the Copley Mall. Break away from the chains and get to know an area of Boston that's a treasure trove of unique boutiques and novel finds. Unlike the city's other shopping spots, this isn't a single street, center, or square—it's an entire neighborhood. You'll encounter more people walking their dogs than juggling their Black-Berrys, which is a bonus to being on the outskirts of the city. Getting from spot to spot requires some walking, making it an ideal adults-only outing. Cruise down Tremont, Shawmut, and Washington streets, and weave in and out of their scenic brownstone-lined side streets. Each storefront is cuter than the next, and there are plenty of places to stop and snack along the way.

BEST TIME TO GO

There's some weekend stroller traffic. Avoid Monday, when most of the boutiques are closed.

BEST THRIFTY FIND

SOWA Open Market (⊠ *540 Harrison Ave.* ⊕ *southendopenmarket. com*) features artwork, independent designers, antiques, and local produce every Sunday May–October.

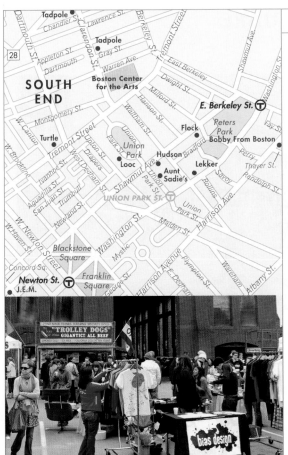

SOUTH END

REFUELING

Recharge with a fresh-baked sticky bun and oversized mug of coffee at neighborhood favorite **Flour Bakery** (✉ 1595 Washington St. ☎ 617/267–4300). Or take a break from bag carrying at **South End Buttery** (✉ 314 Shawmut Ave. ☎ 617/482–1015). Order a bacon, egg, and cheese on a buttermilk biscuit or the homemade turkey chili soup. At the heart of the South End sits **Francesca's Espresso Bar** (✉ 564 Tremont St. ☎ 617/482–9026), a spacious café with sandwiches and a large drink list with everything from lattés to New England's raspberry lime rickys.

BEST FOR

BOUTIQUING:
Flock: Organic cotton T-shirts, flowing dresses, and a great jewelry selection.

Looc: A Zen space with simple, sophisticated clothing.

Turtle: Clothing from up-and-coming local designers.

BABY GEAR
Aunt Sadie's: Onesies, bath toys, and gifts to fit any hipster's household.

Kiwi Baby: Infant fashion and furniture.

Tadpole: Ground zero for strollers, educational toys, and other kiddy needs.

HOME FURNISHINGS
Hudson: One-stop shopping for boho-chic designs from sofas to chairs to wallpaper.

J.E.M.: A hodgepodge of home goods by independent designers.

Lekker: Modern wooden tables and chairs meet contemporary tableware.

HIDDEN GEMS
Bobby from Boston: A consignment shop where the fabulous pieces are hand-selected by the expert owner.

14

HARVARD SQUARE

Cross over the Charles River to Cambridge, where the air is a little fresher and the navigable streets are perfect for a day outdoors. Harvard University's historic campus provides a beautiful backdrop for a unique and charming shopping experience.

(above) Harvard Square offers a mix of book, children's, and clothing stores, and the chance to rub elbows with the neighborhood's scholars. (lower right) Volumes are crammed into every cranny of Grolier Poetry Bookshop.

There's something about Harvard Square that screams sophistication. Maybe it's the area's rich history, with streets and establishments dating back to 1631. Or maybe it's shopping alongside the indigenous brainiacs who attend the surrounding university. Either way, there's nothing pretentious about this fun little plaza. Massachusetts Avenue, Brattle Street, and Mt. Auburn Street shape the area and are adorned with various standout boutiques and a handful of chain stores, including Urban Outfitters, Lush, and Gap. Naturally, a collegiate crowd is drawn to the area, but the stores don't cater to one individual, and the old-meets-new atmosphere makes it a destination for your whole family. On weekends the square holds many festivals, fairs, and events, making it more than your average shopping destination.

BEST TIME TO GO

Crowds gather on weekends, but for good reason—stores are open late, the area is well lit, and there's usually a special event taking place. For a more low-key experience, weekday afternoons are ideal. If possible, avoid early September, when college co-eds instinctively flock to the region in need of back-to-school everything.

14

WHAT TO WEAR

Concepts: A sneaker collector's dream, with highly sought-after, limited-edition footwear.

Mint Julep: The place for an adorable dress for any occasion.

Passport: Clothes, accessories, journals, and other fashionable, yet affordable jet-setting items.

The Tannery: One location has shoes, the other high-end clothing brands and a great boot selection.

READING MATERIAL

Grolier Poetry Book Shop: An institution among poetry buffs.

Harvard Book Store: A landmark independent bookstore offering new and used works.

Raven Used Books: A selection of scholarly used books spanning philosophy, art, architecture, history, and more.

Schoenhof's: 100% foreign literature.

FOR KIDS

Curious George & Friends: A wonderland of children's books, games, toys, and George merchandise (of course).

REFUELING

Step into **Hi Rise** (⌧ *56 Brattle St.* ☎ *617/492–3003*) for sweets or a gourmet sandwich made on freshly baked breads. Try the El Presidente: grilled chicken breast, spicy harissa, black-olive spread, tomato, and onion. For a jolt of caffeine, **Crema Café** (⌧ *27 Brattle St.* ☎ *617/876–2700*) is unrivaled, and known for its delicious blends and cozy atmosphere. Stop by **Cardullo's Gourmet Shoppe** (⌧ *6 Brattle St.* ☎ *617/491–8888*), a deli and upscale convenience store where you can get a hearty sub to eat at an outdoor bench or in the Cambridge Common nearby.

Updated by
Amanda Knorr

Shopping in Boston is a lot like the city itself: a mix of classic and cutting-edge, the high-end and the handmade, and international and local sensibilities. Though many Bostonians think too many chain stores have begun to clog their distinctive avenues, there remains a strong network of idiosyncratic gift stores, handicrafts shops, galleries, and a growing number of savvy, independent fashion boutiques. For the well-heeled, there are also plenty of glossy international designer shops.

Most stores accept major credit cards and traveler's checks. There's no state sales tax on clothing. However, there's a 5% luxury tax on clothes priced higher than $175 per item; the tax is levied on the amount in excess of $175.

MAJOR SHOPPING DISTRICTS

Boston's shops and department stores are concentrated in the area bounded by Quincy Market, the Back Bay, and Downtown. There are plenty of bargains in the Downtown Crossing area. The South End's gentrification creates its own kind of consumerist milieus, from houseware shops to avant-garde art galleries. In Cambridge you can find lots of shopping around Harvard and Central squares, with independent boutiques migrating west along Massachusetts Avenue (or Mass Ave., as the locals and almost everyone else calls it) toward Porter Square and beyond.

BOSTON

Pretty **Charles Street** is crammed beginning to end with top-notch antiques stores such as Judith Dowling Asian Art, Eugene Galleries, and Devonia, as well as a handful of independently owned fashion boutiques whose prices reflect their high Beacon Hill rents. River Street, parallel to Charles Street, is also an excellent source for antiques. Both are easy walks from the Charles Street T stop on the Red Line.

Copley Place (✉ *100 Huntington Ave., Back Bay* ☎ *617/369–5000* Ⓜ *Copley*), an indoor shopping mall in the Back Bay, includes such high-end shops as Christian Dior, Louis Vuitton, and Gucci, anchored by the pricey but dependable Neiman Marcus and the flashy, overpriced Barneys. A skywalk connects Copley Place to the **Prudential Center** (✉ *800 Boylston St., Back Bay* ☎ *800/746–7778* Ⓜ *Hynes*). The Pru, as it's often called, contains moderately priced chain stores such as Ann Taylor and the Body Shop.

Downtown Crossing (✉ *Washington St. from Amory St. to about Milk St., Downtown* Ⓜ *Downtown Crossing, Park St.*) is a pedestrian mall with a Macy's, H&M, and TJ Maxx. Millennium Place, a 1.8-million-square-foot complex with a Ritz-Carlton Hotel, condos, a massive sports club, a 19-screen Loews Cineplex, and the brand new W Hotel turned this once seedy hangout into a happening spot.

Faneuil Hall Marketplace (✉ *Bounded by Congress St., Atlantic Ave., the Waterfront, and Government Center, Downtown* ☎ *617/523–1300* Ⓜ *Government Center*) is a huge complex that's also hugely popular, even though most of its independent shops have given way to Banana Republic, Crate & Barrel, and other chains. The place has plenty of history, one of the area's great à la carte casual dining experiences (Quincy Market), and carnival-like trappings: pushcarts sell everything from silver jewelry to Peruvian sweaters, and buskers perform crowd-pleasing feats such as break dancing.

★ **Newbury Street** (Ⓜ *Arlington, Copley, Hynes*) is Boston's version of New York's 5th Avenue. The entire street is a shoppers' paradise, from high-end names such as Brooks Brothers to tiny specialty shops such as the Fish and Bone. Upscale clothing stores, up-to-the-minute art galleries, and dazzling jewelers line the street near the Public Garden. As you head toward Mass Ave., Newbury gets funkier and the cacophony builds, with skateboarders zipping through traffic and garbage-pail drummers burning licks outside the hip boutiques. The big-name stores run from Arlington Street to the Prudential Center. Parallel to Newbury Street is **Boylston Street,** where a few standouts, such as Shreve, Crump & Low, are scattered among the other chains and restaurants.

South End (Ⓜ *Back Bay/South End*) merchants are benefiting from the ongoing gentrification that has brought high real-estate prices and trendy restaurants to the area. Explore the chic home-furnishings and gift shops that line Tremont Street, starting at Berkeley Street. The MBTA's Silver Line bus runs through the South End.

CAMBRIDGE

CambridgeSide Galleria (✉ *100 CambridgeSide Pl., Kendall Sq.* ☎ *617/621–8666* Ⓜ *Lechmere, Kendall/MIT via shuttle*) is a basic three-story mall with a food court. Macy's makes it a good stop for appliances and other basics; it's a big draw for local high-school kids.

Central Square (⊠ *East of Harvard Sq.* Ⓜ *Central*) has an eclectic mix of furniture stores, used-record shops, ethnic restaurants, and small, hip performance venues.

Harvard Square (Ⓜ *Harvard*) takes up just a few blocks but holds more than 150 stores selling clothes, books, records, furnishings, and specialty items. (⇨ *Harvard Square Spotlight for more information.*)

The **Galleria** (⊠ *57 JFK St.* Ⓜ *Harvard*) has various boutiques and a few decent, independently owned restaurants. A handful of chains and independent boutiques are clustered on **Brattle St.** (⊠ *Behind Harvard Sq.* Ⓜ *Harvard*).

Porter Square (⊠ *West on Mass Ave. from Harvard Sq.* Ⓜ *Porter*) has distinctive clothing stores, as well as crafts shops, coffee shops, natural-food stores, restaurants, and bars with live music.

DEPARTMENT STORES

★ **Barneys New York.** The hoopla (not to mention the party) generated by this store's arrival was surprising in a city where everything new is viewed with trepidation. But clearly Boston's denizens have embraced the lofty, two-story space because it's filled with cutting-edge lines like Comme des Garçons and Nina Ricci, as well as a few bargains in the second-level Co-op section. ⊠ *100 Huntington Ave., Back Bay* ☎ *617/385–3300* Ⓜ *Copley*.

Filene's Basement. Though habitués bemoan the loss of the original Filene's and its historic building, the Basement is still the place for deals on designer labels—if you're willing to dig. Automatic markdowns are taken according to the number of days an item has been on the rack, so don't be surprised to find that perfect little black dress hidden for safekeeping among the men's sport jackets. ⊠ *497 Boylston St., Back Bay* ☎ *617/424–5520* Ⓜ *Arlington*.

Lord & Taylor. This is a reliable, if somewhat overstuffed with merchandise, stop for classic clothing by such designers as Anne Klein and Ralph Lauren, along with accessories, cosmetics, and jewelry. ⊠ *760 Boylston St., Back Bay* ☎ *617/262–6000* Ⓜ *Prudential Center*.

Macy's. Three floors offer men's and women's clothing and shoes, housewares, and cosmetics. Although top designers and a fur salon are part of the mix, Macy's doesn't feel exclusive; instead, it's a popular source for family basics. ⊠ *450 Washington St., Downtown* ☎ *617/357–3000* Ⓜ *Downtown Crossing*.

Neiman Marcus. The flashy Texas-based retailer known to many as "Needless Markup" has three levels of swank designers and a jaw-dropping shoe section, as well as cosmetics and housewares. ⊠ *5 Copley Pl., Back Bay* ☎ *617/536–3660* Ⓜ *Back Bay/South End*.

Saks Fifth Avenue. The clothing and accessories at Saks run from the traditional to the flamboyant. It's a little pricey, but an excellent place to find high-quality merchandise, including shoes and cosmetics. ⊠ *Prudential Center, 1 Ring Rd., Back Bay* ☎ *617/262–8500* Ⓜ *Prudential Center*.

SPECIALTY STORES

ANTIQUES

Newbury Street and the South End have some excellent (and expensive) antiques stores, but Charles Street—coincidentally, one of the city's oldest streets—is the place to go for a concentrated selection.

A Room With a Vieux Antiques. There's an abundant collection of French antiques from the 19th and 20th centuries here. A restoration department in the back alters furniture to your individual needs. ✉ *20 Charles St., Beacon Hill* ☎ *617/973–6600* ⊕ *aroomwithavieux.com* ☉ *Mon.– Sat. 10–5; closed Sun.*

14

Autrefois Antiques. Come here to find French country and Italian 18th-, 19th-, and 20th-century furniture, mirrors, and lighting. ✉ *130 Harvard St., Brookline* ☎ *617/566–0113* Ⓜ *Coolidge Corner.*

Boston Antique Co-op. This flea market–style collection of dealers occupies two floors, containing everything from vintage photos and paintings to porcelain, silver, bronzes, and furniture. ✉ *119 Charles St., Beacon Hill* ☎ *617/227–9810 or 617/227–9811* Ⓜ *Charles/MGH.*

Brodney Gallery. In addition to plenty of porcelain and silver, Brodney claims to have the biggest selection of estate jewelry in New England. ✉ *145 Newbury St., Back Bay* ☎ *617/536–0500* Ⓜ *Copley.*

Cambridge Antique Market. Off the beaten track this may be, but it has a selection bordering on overwhelming: five floors of goods ranging from 19th-century furniture to vintage clothing, much of it reasonably priced. There are two parking lots next to the building. ✉ *201 Monsignor O'Brien Hwy., Cambridge* ☎ *617/868–9655* Ⓜ *Lechmere.*

★ **Eugene Galleries**. This store is chockablock with prints, etchings, old maps, and books; a 19th-century print of a Boston landmark, for instance, makes for a unique and lasting souvenir. ✉ *76 Charles St., Beacon Hill* ☎ *617/227–3062* Ⓜ *Charles/MGH.*

Judith Dowling Asian Art. Judith Dowling's sophistication results from spareness and restraint. High-end Asian artifacts range from Japanese pottery to scrolls, Buddha figures, painted screens, cabinets, and other furnishings. ✉ *133 Charles St., Beacon Hill* ☎ *617/523–5211.*

Marika's. Every available inch of space in this jam-packed store, including the walls, is used to display wares. That silver chafing dish might need a polish, and the telephone table may be slightly scratched, but such imperfections keep the prices reasonable. ✉ *130 Charles St., Beacon Hill* ☎ *617/523–4520* Ⓜ *Charles/MGH.*

Reruns Antiques. Don't let its low prices and jumble-shop aspect fool you. Poke around Reruns and you may come up with a Hiroshige print, a 19th-century Moroccan lamp, or an Asmat ancestral figure. If you're in the mood for a history or an anthropology lesson, owner Tom Armstrong is glad to oblige. ✉ *125 Charles St., Beacon Hill* ☎ *No phone* Ⓜ *Charles/MGH.*

ART GALLERIES

Although Newbury Street has the highest concentration of galleries in the city, a neighborhood in the South End, discordantly dubbed SoWa (for South of Washington), has emerged as a hot spot for contemporary artists.

★ **Alpha Gallery**. This gallery specializes in 20th-century and contemporary American and European painting, sculpture, and master prints. ⊠ *38 Newbury St., Back Bay* ☎ *617/536–4465* Ⓜ *Arlington.*

Barbara Krakow Gallery. Krakow shows contemporary paintings, photographs, drawings, prints, and sculptures by emerging and established regional and international artists. ⊠ *10 Newbury St., 5th fl., Back Bay* ☎ *617/262–4490* Ⓜ *Arlington.*

Bernard Toale Gallery. Toale's contemporary tastes tend toward more experimental pieces, including sculpture, paintings, photographs, and works on paper. ⊠ *450 Harrison Ave., South End* ☎ *617/482–2477* Ⓜ *Tufts Medical Center.*

Bromfield Art Gallery. A small, cooperative operation, Bromfield mounts monthlong shows of its members' work, including oil and acrylic paintings, charcoals, and pastels. ⊠ *450 Harrison Ave., South End* ☎ *617/451–3605* Ⓜ *Tufts Medical Center.*

Childs Gallery. Childs carries paintings, prints, drawings, watercolors, and sculpture from the 1500s to the present. ⊠ *169 Newbury St., Back Bay* ☎ *617/266–1108* Ⓜ *Copley.*

Copley Society of Boston. After more than a century, this nonprofit membership organization continues to present the works of well-known and aspiring New England artists. ⊠ *158 Newbury St., Back Bay* ☎ *617/536–5049* Ⓜ *Copley.*

Gallery NAGA. Here are contemporary paintings, sculpture, and furniture displayed in a striking space: the Church of the Covenant. ⊠ *67 Newbury St., Back Bay* ☎ *617/267–9060* Ⓜ *Arlington.*

Nielsen Gallery. Both established and aspiring artists show their representational and abstract paintings and prints. ⊠ *179 Newbury St., Back Bay* ☎ *617/266–4835* Ⓜ *Copley.*

Rolly-Michaux. You'll find only the highest quality works here, from the likes of Moore, Calder, Picasso, Chagall, Miró, and Matisse. ⊠ *290 Dartmouth St., Back Bay* ☎ *617/536–9898* Ⓜ *Copley.*

Samson Projects. A truly cross-cultural blend of exhibits, this gallery shows the experimental works of young contemporary artists. ⊠ *450 Harrison Ave., South End* ☎ *617/357–7177* Ⓜ *Tufts Medical Center.*

Vose Galleries. Established in 1841, Vose specializes in 19th- and 20th-century American art, including the Hudson River School, Boston School, and American impressionists. The addition of works of contemporary American realism recognizes an area that is often overlooked by the trendier set. ⊠ *238 Newbury St., Back Bay* ☎ *617/536–6176* Ⓜ *Copley, Hynes.*

14

BEAUTY

A Matter of Face. Bliss cosmetics and Paula Dorf tools put this spot on any makeup maven's hit list. ✉ *425 Hanover St., North End* ☎ *617/742–5874* ⊕ *amatterofface.com* ⊘ *Tues., Wed., and Fri. 11–7, Sat. 10:30–7, Sun. noon–5. Closed Mon. and Thurs.*

The Beauty Mark. The tiny cosmetics boutique has everything to make you look gorgeous including DuWop lip gloss, Julie Hewitt eye shadow, and St. Tropez self tanner. Manicures, pedicures, and eyelash extensions are available on-site. ✉ *33 Charles St., Beacon Hill* ☎ *617/720–1555* ⊕ *thebeautymark.com* ⊘ *Weekdays 11–7, Sat. 10–6, Sun. noon–5.*

Bella Sante. As pristine as it is serene, the beautifully designed Bella Sante is well stocked with high-end products and staffed by a well-trained crew. The locker room is stocked with thoughtful amenities such as body creams and just about any hair product you might need. ✉ *38 Newbury St., Back Bay* ☎ *617/424–9930* Ⓜ *Arlington.*

Exhale. This Zen-like sanctuary is deceptively large. The subterranean lower level houses a first-rate spa and yoga studio. Upstairs, you'll find holistic body and skin-care products. ✉ *28 Arlington St., Back Bay* ☎ *617/532–7095* Ⓜ *Arlington.*

James Joseph Salon. Sleek and modern, yet utterly free of pretense, James Joseph has a fun, talented staff that gives customers exactly the cuts, color, and treatments they ask for. ✉ *30 Newbury St., Back Bay* ☎ *617/266–7222* Ⓜ *Arlington.*

The Loft Salon + Day Spa. Stylist Michael Albor is the master of hair color. He'll also sculpt your do into a work of art for events. ✉ *253 Newbury St., Back Bay* ☎ *617/536–5638* ⊕ *theloftsalonanddayspa.com* ⊘ *Tues. 9:30–6, Wed.–Fri. 9:30–7, Sat. 9–4:30; closed Sun. and Mon.*

Michaud Cosmedix. Makeup artist Julie Michaud and her staff have worked hard to become Boston's go-to studio for natural-looking makeup application, brow grooming, waxing, and facials. ✉ *69 Newbury St., Back Bay* ☎ *617/262–1607* Ⓜ *Arlington, Copley.*

Mizu. Renowned hair stylist Charles Maksou calls this place home. The futuristic salon offers all the usual treatments, plus a pair of Myvu glasses to watch TV through. ✉ *776 Boylston St., Back Bay* ☎ *617/585–6498* ⊕ *mizuboston.com* ⊘ *Weekdays 9–8, Sat. 8–7, Sun. 10–7.*

Salon Mario Russo. It may be the most coveted cut in town, but Mario Russo and his expert staff retain a down-to-earth attitude as they provide excellent styling and color services. The manicures are equally good. ✉ *60 Northern Ave., South Boston* ☎ *857/350–3139* Ⓜ *South Station.*

BOOKS

If Boston and Cambridge have bragging rights to anything, it's their independent bookstores, many of which stay open late and sponsor author readings and literary programs.

Barnes & Noble. Inside the Prudential Center is a large branch of the popular chain selling a variety of books. The company now runs

The Harvard Coop has peddled books to university students since 1882.

the Harvard Coop. ✉ *800 Boylston St., Back Bay* ☎ *617/247–6959* Ⓜ *Prudential Center* ✉ *660 Beacon St., Kenmore Sq.* ☎ *617/267–8484* Ⓜ *Kenmore.*

SPECIALTY

Ars Libri Ltd. It's easy to be drawn into the rare and wonderful books on display here. The airy space is filled with books on photography and architecture, out-of-print art books, monographs, and exhibition catalogs. ✉ *500 Harrison Ave., South End* ☎ *617/357–5212* Ⓜ *Tufts Medical Center.*

Brattle Bookshop. The late George Gloss built this into Boston's best used- and rare-book shop. Today his son Kenneth fields queries from passionate book lovers. If the book you want is out of print, Brattle has it or can probably find it. ✉ *9 West St., Downtown* ☎ *617/542–0210 or 800/447–9595* Ⓜ *Downtown Crossing.*

Calamus Bookstore. This friendly, informal store carries not only books, but also videos, music, and gifts for the gay, lesbian, bisexual, or transgender shopper. ✉ *92B South St., Leather District* ☎ *617/338–1931* ⊘ *Mon.–Sat. 9–7, Sun. noon–6* Ⓜ *South Station.*

Globe Corner Bookstore. Hands down, this is the best source for domestic and international travel books and maps. The store also has very good selections of books about New England and by New England authors. ✉ *90 Mt. Auburn St., Cambridge* ☎ *617/497–6277 or 800/358–6013* Ⓜ *Harvard.*

Grolier Poetry Bookshop. Proprietor Louisa Solano is an outspoken proponent of all things poetic—and her dog, Jessie, is one of the friendliest shopkeepers in Harvard Square. The store, founded in 1927, carries in-print poetry from all eras and from all over the world. ⊠ *6 Plympton St., Cambridge* ☎ *617/547–4648* ⊗ *Tues. And Wed. 11–7, Thurs.–Sat. 11–6. Closed Sun. and Mon.* Ⓜ *Harvard.*

Fodor'sChoice ★
Harvard Book Store. The intellectual community is well served here, with a slew of new titles upstairs and used and remaindered books down-stairs. The collection's diversity has made the store a favored destination for academics. ⊠ *1256 Massachusetts Ave., Cambridge* ☎ *617/661–1515* Ⓜ *Harvard.*

Harvard Coop Society. Begun in 1882 as a nonprofit service for students and faculty, the Coop is now managed by Barnes & Noble. In addition to books and textbooks (many discounted), school supplies, clothes, and accessories plastered with the Harvard emblem are sold here, as well as basic housewares geared toward dorm dwellers. ⊠ *1400 Massachusetts Ave., Cambridge* ☎ *617/499–2000* Ⓜ *Harvard.*

Kate's Mystery Books. A favorite Cambridge haunt, Kate's is a good place to track down mysteries by local writers; look for authors in the flesh at the shop's frequent readings and events. ⊠ *2211 Massachusetts Ave., Cambridge* ☎ *617/491–2660* Ⓜ *Porter.*

Raven Used Books. Find a selection of scholarly used books. It's a popular place for local grad students to unload their read and unread texts. ⊠ *52 JFK St., Cambridge* ☎ *617/441–6999* ⊕ *ravencambridge.com* ⊗ *Mon.– Sat. 10–9, Sun. 11–8.*

Schoenhof's. The friendly staff will help you navigate through thousands of foreign books, including ones in French, German, Italian and Span-ish. ⊠ *76 Mount Auburn St., Harvard Sq.* ☎ *617/547–8855* ⊕ *www. schoenhofs.com* ⊗ *Mon.–Wed., Fri. and Sat. 10–6, Thurs. 10–8, Sun. noon–5.*

Trident Booksellers & Café. Browse through an eclectic collection of books, tapes, and magazines; then settle in with a snack. It's open until mid-night daily, making it a favorite with students. ⊠ *338 Newbury St., Back Bay* ☎ *617/267–8688* ⊗ *Daily 8 am–midnight* Ⓜ *Hynes.*

CLOTHING AND SHOES

The terminally chic shops are on Newbury Street, and the hip hang in Harvard Square—but everyone goes Downtown for the real bargains.

★ **Alan Bilzerian.** Satisfying the Euro crowd, this store sells luxe men's and women's clothing by such fashion darlings as Yohji Yamamoto and Ann Demeulemeester. ⊠ *34 Newbury St., Back Bay* ☎ *617/536–1001* ⊗ *Mon.–Sat. 10–6. Closed Sun.* Ⓜ *Arlington.*

Anne Fontaine. You can never have too many white shirts—especially if they're designed by this Parisienne. The simple, sophisticated designs are mostly executed in cotton and priced around $160. ⊠ *318 Boylston St., Back Bay* ☎ *617/423–0366* Ⓜ *Arlington, Boylston.*

Betsy Jenney. Ms. Jenney herself is likely to wait on you in this small, per-sonal store, where the well-made, comfortable lines are for women who cannot walk into a fitted size-4 suit—in other words, most of the female population. The designers found here, such as Philippe Adec, Teenflo, and Nicole Miller, are fashionable yet forgiving. ⊠ *114 Newbury St., Back Bay* ☎*617/536–2610* Ⓜ *Copley.*

Brooks Brothers. Founded in 1818, Brooks still carries the classically modern styles that made it famous—old faithfuls for men such as navy blazers, summertime seersucker, and crisp oxford shirts. Its Newbury Street store offers a similar vibe for women as well. ⊠ *46 Newbury St., Back Bay* ☎*617/267–2600* Ⓜ *Arlington* ⊠ *75 State St., Government Center* ☎*617/261–9990* Ⓜ *Government Center.*

14

Calypso. The women's clothing here bursts with bright colors, beautiful fabrics, and styles so fresh you might need a fashion editor to help you choose. ⊠ *114 Newbury St., Back Bay* ☎*617/421–1887* Ⓜ *Copley.*

Chanel. Located at No. 5 in honor of its famous perfume, this branch of the Parisian couture house carries suits, separates, bags, shoes, cosmetics, and, of course, a selection of little black dresses. ⊠ *5 Newbury St., Back Bay* ☎*617/859–0055* Ⓜ *Arlington.*

Cibeline. Local designer Cibeline Sariano handcrafts and designs all of her garments, including wrap dresses, blazers, and skirts. ⊠ *120 Charles St., Beacon Hill* ☎*617/742–0244* ⊕ *cibelinesariano.com* ☉ *Weekdays 10–7, Sat. 10–6, Sun. 11–5.*

Fodor'sChoice ★ **Concepts.** Sneaker collectors love having what other people can't find. At Concepts, fanatics will line up around the block when a limited-edition shoe debuts. Their store features exclusives by Nike, Jordan, Clarks, Adidas, and more. ⊠ *37 Brattle St., Cambridge* ☎*617/868–2001* ⊕ *cncpts.com* ☉ *Daily 10–7.*

Crush Boutique. This garden-level shop is perfect for everyday work essentials, weekend casual outfits, and even party-girl attire. You'll also find affordable jewelry and handbags to dress up any ensemble. ⊠ *131 Charles St., Beacon Hill* ☎*617/720–0010* ⊕ *shopcrushboutique.com* ☉ *Mon.–Sat. 10–7, Sun. noon–6.*

Daniela Corte. Local designer Corte cuts women's clothes that flatter from her sunny Back Bay studio. Look for gorgeous suiting, flirty halter dresses, and sophisticated formal frocks that can be bought off the rack or custom tailored. ⊠ *211 Newbury St., Back Bay* ☎*617/262–2100* Ⓜ *Copley.*

Dress. True to its name, this shop owned by two young local women carries a number of great party dresses as well as flattering tees, pretty tops, and shoes from emerging designers. ⊠ *221 Newbury St., Back Bay* ☎*617/424–7125* ☉ *Mon.–Thurs. 11–7, Fri. and Sat. 11–6, Sun. noon–5* Ⓜ *Copley, Hynes.*

DSW. Major discounts on high-quality (and big-name) shoes for men and women are what draw much of Boston to DSW, also known as Designer Shoe Warehouse. Everything from Nike to Prada can be found at varying discounts—sometimes up to 90% off. ⊠ *385 Washington St., Downtown* ☎ *617/556–0052* Ⓜ *Downtown Crossing.*

Flock. Browse the collection of organic cotton T-shirts, everyday dresses, and vintage-inspired jewelry at this whimsical, boho-chic boutique. ⊠ *274 Shawmut Ave., South End* ☎ *617/391–0222* ⊙ *Tues.–Sat. 11–7, Sun. noon–5. Closed Mon.*

French Dressing. This tucked-away lingerie shop is a local favorite. Stop in for everyday undergarments by Cosabella, sexier numbers by Elle Macpherson, or to stock up on more Hanky Panky colors. ⊠ *49 River St., Beacon Hill* ☎ *617/723–4968* ⊕ *frenchdressinglingerie.com* ⊙ *Tues., Wed., and Fri. 11–7, Sat. 11–6, Sun. noon–5. Closed Mon.*

Giorgio Armani. This top-of-the-line Italian couturier is known for his carefully shaped jackets, soft suits, and mostly neutral palette. ⊠ *22 Newbury St., Back Bay* ☎ *617/267–3200* Ⓜ *Arlington.*

Grettaluxe. Drop by Copley's sassy little boutique and pick up the latest "it" pieces—from velour hoodies by Juicy Couture to the must-have Stella McCartney design du moment. There are also jewelry, handbags, and other accessories. ⊠ *Westin Hotel, 10 Huntington Ave., Back Bay* ☎ *617/266–6166* Ⓜ *Copley.*

Helen's Leather Shop. Choose from half a dozen brands of boots (Lucchese, Nocona, Dan Post, Tony Lama, Justin, and Frye); then browse through the leather sandals, jackets, briefcases, luggage, and accessories. ⊠ *110 Charles St., Beacon Hill* ☎ *617/742–2077* Ⓜ *Charles/MGH.*

Holiday. A stockpile of flirty and feminine getups are the rage here. Cult lines such as Mint, Eberjey, and Tracy Reese are in regular rotation among the fashionable racks. Keep your eye out for the occasional vintage clutch. ⊠ *53 Charles St., Beacon Hill* ☎ *617/973–9730* Ⓜ *Charles/MGH.*

In-Jean-Ius. The name says it all. Citizens of Humanity, Rock & Republic, Paige, and more denim cult favorites reside here. ⊠ *441 Hanover St., North End* ☎ *617/523–5326* ⊕ *injeanius.com* ⊙ *Mon. and Tues. 11–7, Wed.–Sat. 11–8, Sun. noon–6.*

In the Pink. Don't be caught dead at the Vineyard this year without your Lilly Pulitzer resort wear, available here along with shoes, home decor, and children's clothing. ⊠ *133 Newbury St., Back Bay* ☎ *617/536–6423* Ⓜ *Copley.*

John Fluevog Shoes. Many clubgoers have at least one pair of these oh-so-hip shoes in their closets, perhaps because of the company's claim that their Angel soles repel all kinds of nasty liquids "and Satan." ⊠ *302 Newbury St., Back Bay* ☎ *617/266–1079* ⊙ *Mon.–Sat. 11–7, Sun. noon–6* Ⓜ *Copley.*

Jos. A. Bank Clothiers. Like Brooks Brothers, Joseph Bank is well known to the conservatively well dressed everywhere. ⊠ *399 Boylston St., Back Bay* ☎ *617/536–5050* Ⓜ *Arlington.*

Looc. The pristine, all-white atmosphere directs your focus to the clothing. Parisian designers share racks with lesser-knowns, providing a classy, yet edgy selection. ⊠ *12 Union Park St., South End* ☎ *617/357–5333* ⊕ *loocboutique.com* ⊗ *Tues.–Fri. 11–7, Sat. 11–6, Sun. noon–5; closed Mon.*

Fodor'sChoice
★
Louis Boston. Impeccably tailored designs, subtly updated classics, and the latest Italian styles highlight a wide selection of imported clothing and accessories. Visiting celebrities might be trolling the racks along with you as jazz spills out into the street from the adjoining Restaurant L. ⊠ *60 Northern Ave., South Boston* ☎ *617/262–6100* ⊗ *Mon.–Wed. 11–6, Thurs.–Sat. 11–7, Sun. 11:30–5* Ⓜ *South Station.*

Marc by Marc Jacobs. The two-floor boutique carries his younger, casual line with menswear on the first floor and women's on the second. Look, too, for cheap accessories. ⊠ *81 Newbury St., Back Bay* ☎ *617/425–0707* Ⓜ *Copley.*

Matsu. This shop trends toward the funkier, with edgy pieces from designers like Lilith and Comme des Garçons. Look for a well-edited jewelry selection as well as high-end handbags and accessories. ⊠ *259 Newbury St., Back Bay* ☎ *617/266–9707* Ⓜ *Copley, Hynes.*

Mint Julep. Cute dresses, playful skirts, and form-fitting tops make up the selection here. The Cambridge location is a little larger and easier to navigate, but Brookline houses the original. ⊠ *6 Church St., Cambridge* ☎ *617/576–6468* Ⓜ *Harvard* ⊠ *1302 Beacon St., Brookline* ☎ *617/232–3600* Ⓜ *Coolidge Corner.*

Moxie. The selection is always fashion-forward and sophisticated at this home to the season's hottest shoes. ⊠ *51 Charles St., Beacon Hill* ☎ *617/557–9991* ⊕ *moxieboston.com* ⊗ *Weekdays 10–7, Sat. 10–6, Sun. 11–6.*

North River Outfitters. A preppy New Englander's heaven, with walls of Tory Burch tunics, Nantucket red pants, and needlepoint belts. ⊠ *126 Charles St., Beacon Hill* ☎ *617/742–0089* ⊕ *northriveroutfitters.com* ⊗ *Mon.–Thurs. 10–7, Fri. and Sat. 10–6, Sun. 11–5.*

Passport. You don't need to be a celebrity to get jet-setting style. Passport offers wrinkle-free clothing, foldable ballet flats, headphones, luggage, and everything you need to be a chic traveler. ⊠ *43 Brattle St., Cambridge* ☎ *617/576–0900* ⊕ *passportboutique.com* ⊗ *Mon.–Sat. 10:30–6, Sun. noon–5.*

Fodor'sChoice
★
Shake the Tree. This one-stop shop has an eclectic array of contemporary clothing, bags, jewelry, gifts, and home items. ⊠ *67 Salem St., North End* ☎ *617/742–0484* ⊕ *shakethetreeboston.com* ⊗ *Mon. 11–6, Tues. and Wed. 11–7, Thurs. and Fri. 11–8, Sat. 10–8, Sun. noon–5.*

Fodor'sChoice
★
Stel's. At this cozy boutique with casual and dressy options for men and women, top designer brands mean the prices are steep, but the cost-per-wear should counter that. ⊠ *334 Newbury St., Back Bay* ☎ *617/262–3368* ⊕ *shopstels.com* ⊗ *Mon.–Sat. 11–7, Sun. noon–6.*

Stil. Local designers such as Daniela Corte and Elaine Perlov share rack space with cutting-edge Scandinavian labels such as Rutzou and Bruun's

14

Bazaar—all of it at surprisingly earthly prices. ✉ *The Mall at Chestnut Hill, 199 Boylston St., Chestnut Hill* ☎ *617/527–7845.*

The Tannery. One of the three stores carries a bountiful selection of foot-wear from Frye to Converse. The 39 Brattle Street and 711 Boylston Street locations add in high-end accessories and clothing brands like Helmut Lang and Vena Cava. ✉ *39 Brattle St., Cambridge* ☎ *617/491–0810* ⊕ *thetannery.com* ☾ *Mon.–Sat. 9–8, Sun. 10–7* ✉ *11A Brattle St., Cambridge* ☎ *617/491–0810* ☾ *Weekdays 9–9, Sat. 9–8, Sun. 10–7* ✉ *711 Boylston St., Back Bay* ☎ *617/267–5500* ☾ *Mon.–Sat. 9–8, Sun. 10–7.*

Toppers. There's nothing old hat about this place, where you can cover your head in anything from a tam-o'-shanter to a 10-gallon. ✉ *151 Tremont St., Back Bay* ☎ *617/859–1430* Ⓜ *Back Bay.*

Turtle. Prove you're no slave to labels and shop where local, up-and-coming designers showcase their merchandise. ✉ *619A Tremont St., South End* ☎ *617/266–2610* ⊕ *turtleboston.com* ☾ *Mon. 11–7, Tues. 10–6, Wed.–Fri. 11–7, Sat. 10–6, Sun. noon–5.*

Twilight. This neatly organized boutique is where you'll find the perfect dress for a date, cocktail party, or wedding. Save on cash with their affordable costume jewelry. ✉ *12 Fleet St., North End* ☎ *617/523–8008* ☾ *Mon. and Tues. 11–7, Wed.–Sat. 11–8, Sun. noon–6.*

Uniform. A casual menswear shop with an urban, classic feel. You'll find everything from jackets to socks to shaving needs. ✉ *511 Tremont St., South End* ☎ *617/247–2360* ⊕ *uniformboston.com* ☾ *Tues. and Wed. 11–7, Thurs.–Sat. 11–8, Sun. noon–5; closed Mon.*

Wish. The contemporary women's boutique is home to beloved brands including Diane von Furstenberg, Theory, and Joie. Be sure to stop by in the cooler months—their cashmere selection is otherwordly. ✉ *49 Charles St., Beacon Hill* ☎ *617/227–4441* ☾ *Mon. and Tues. 10–6, Wed.–Fri. 10–7, Sat. 10–6, Sun. noon–5* Ⓜ *Charles/MGH.*

CRAFTS

Beadworks. Find beads of every color, texture, size, and material in the tiny bins in Back Bay's do-it-yourself jewelry store. The prices are reasonable, the staff is helpful and friendly, and there's a worktable where you can assemble your masterpiece in the center of the shop. ✉ *167 Newbury St., Back Bay* ☎ *617/247–7227.*

Cambridge Artists' Cooperative. The ceramics, weavings, jewelry, and leatherwork here can be pricier than most, but they're all one-of-a-kind or limited edition. ✉ *59A Church St., Cambridge* ☎ *617/868–4434* Ⓜ *Harvard.*

Society of Arts & Crafts. More than a century old, this is the country's oldest nonprofit crafts organization. It displays a fine assortment of ceramics, jewelry, glass, woodwork, and furniture by some of the country's finest craftspeople. ✉ *175 Newbury St., Back Bay* ☎ *617/266–1810* Ⓜ *Copley.*

GIFTS

Aunt Sadie's. Baby items, delicious-smelling candles, and home decor mingle here. It's the perfect place to grab a party gift. ✉ *18 Union Park St., South End* ☎ *617/357–7117* ⊕ *auntsadiesinc.com* ⊗ *Mon. 10–5, Tues.–Sat. 10–6; closed Sun.*

Black Ink. A wall full of rubber stamps stretches above unusual candles, cookie jars, and other home accessories and gift items. ✉ *101 Charles St., Beacon Hill* ☎ *617/723–3883* Ⓜ *Charles/MGH* ✉ *5 Brattle St., Cambridge* ☎ *617/497–1221* Ⓜ *Harvard.*

Buckaroo's Mercantile. It's Howdy Doody time at Buckaroo's—a great destination for the kitsch inclined. Find pink poodle skirts, lunch-box clocks, Barbie lamps, *Front Page Detective* posters, and everything Elvis. ✉ *5 Brookline St., Cambridge* ☎ *617/492–4792* Ⓜ *Central.*

14

The Flat of the Hill. There's nothing flat about this fun collection of seasonal items, toiletries, toys, pillows, and whatever else catches the fancy of the shop's young owner. Her passion for pets is evident—pick up a Fetch & Glow ball and your dog will never again have to wait until daytime to play in the park. ✉ *60 Charles St., Beacon Hill* ☎ *617/619–9977* Ⓜ *Charles/MGH.*

★ **Fresh.** You won't know whether to wash with these soaps or nibble on them. The shea butter–rich bars come in such scents as clove-hazelnut and orange-cranberry. They cost $6 to $7 each, but they carry the scent to the end. ✉ *121 Newbury St., Back Bay* ☎ *617/421–1212* Ⓜ *Copley.*

Kiwi Baby. From rugs to nightlights to car seats, this store has every baby need covered. Pick up a fun toy or an entire bedroom set. ✉ *1636 Washington St., South End* ☎ *617/247–2229* ⊕ *kiwibabyboston.com* ⊗ *Weekdays 10–7, Sat., 10–6, Sun. 10–5.*

★ **Nomad.** Low prices and an enthusiastic staff are just the beginning at this imports store; it carries clothing as well as Indian good-luck *torans* (wall hangings), Mexican *milagros* (charms), mirrors to keep away the evil eye, silver jewelry, and curtains made from sari silk. In the basement you'll find kilims, hand-painted tiles, and sale items. ✉ *1741 Massachusetts Ave., Cambridge* ☎ *617/497–6677* ⊗ *Weekdays 10–7, Sat. 10–6, Sun. noon–6* Ⓜ *Porter.*

Tibet Emporium. More upscale than your average imports store, Tibet Emporium goes beyond the usual masks and quilted wall hangings to offer beautifully delicate beaded silk pillowcases, pashmina wraps in every color imaginable, appliquéd and silk clothing, and finely wrought but affordable silver jewelry. ✉ *103 Charles St., Beacon Hill* ☎ *617/723–8035* Ⓜ *Charles/MGH.*

Tokai Japanese Gifts. Chopstick rests, origami paper, Yukata cotton robes, and high-end kimonos are among the wares here. ✉ *1815 Massachusetts Ave., Cambridge* ☎ *617/864–5922* Ⓜ *Porter.*

SHOP SOUTHIE

You may recognize South Boston or "Southie," from movies like *Good Will Hunting* and *The Departed*. Not to be confused with the South End, this area over the bridge is where you'll hear that thick Boston accent à la Matt Damon and Ben Affleck. The location is primarily known for two things: its large Irish-America population and its beaches. Since 2004, however, it has become one of the city's up-and-coming neighborhoods for great boutiques and top-notch salons. The shift took place under an ambitious redevelopment plan by the mayor. Shops cluster around Summer and East Broadway streets, but there aren't many pit stop places to snack. For great eateries and bars, try Channel Café, Sportello, and Drink on the Fort Point Channel side, also known as South Boston's waterfront and terminal area. The not-to-be missed Institute of Contemporary Art (and its killer gift shop) is over there, too. In addition to elegant Louis Boston (⇨ *Clothing and Shoes*), here are some of our top picks in the neighborhood.

Habit. Find a great denim selection including James Jeans, Tag Jeans, Citizens, and Hudson along with men and women's casual chic attire and a few home items here.

✉ *703 E. Broadway, South Boston* ☎ *617/269–1998* ⊕ *habitshop.com* ✆ *Mon.–Wed. 11:30–7:30, Thurs. and Fri. 11:30–8, Sat. 11–6, Sun. noon–5.*

Ku de Ta. Name brands and new designers unite in this store, which offers affordable handbag and jewelry options as well. ✉ *663 E. Broadway, South Boston* ☎ *617/269–0008* ⊕ *kudetaboston.com* ✆ *Weekdays 10:30–7, Sat. 11–7, Sun. noon–6.*

Sarra. By far the best place to get your brows done, this large studio has a talented staff who takes its time to teach you all the necessary steps to look fabulous. All of the products are available for purchase. ✉ *840 Summer St., South Boston* ☎ *617/269–8999* ⊕ *sarraboston.com* ✆ *Tues.–Sat. 11–6 and evenings by appointment* ✉ *104A North St., Hingham* ☎ *781/749–5599* ✆ *Tues.–Sat. 10–5 and evenings by appointment.*

Shag. This much hyped salon delivers with an extremely talented crew that will have you feeling like a rock star by the time you leave. ✉ *840 Summer St., Suite 3, South Boston* ☎ *617/268–2500* ⊕ *shagboston.com* ✆ *Tues. and Wed. noon–8, Thurs. 1–10, Fri. noon–8, Sat. 10–6. Closed Sun. and Mon.*

GROCERS

Cardullo's. This 50-year-old shop in Harvard Square purveys exotic imports, sandwiches to go, chocolates, breads, olive oils, cheeses, wines, and beer amid impressive clutter. ✉ *6 Brattle St., Cambridge* ☎ *617/491–8888 or 800/491–8288* Ⓜ *Harvard.*

Deluca's Market. Here's one neighborhood grocer that delivers the gourmet goods: an international cheese counter, homemade pâtés, fresh produce, and a snacks section that includes a dream team of cookies. ✉ *11 Charles St.* ✉ *239 Newbury St., Back Bay* ☎ *617/262–5990* Ⓜ *Copley.*

Savenor's. If you're looking for exotic game meats, you've come to the right place. Savenor's food market, once Julia Child's favorite butcher,

Boston-area specialty markets nod to its rich cultural heritage.

carries buffalo rump, alligator tail, even iguana. There are plenty of
tamer choices, too, as well as outstanding cheeses, breads, and treats
such as foie gras and smoked salmon. ⊠ *160 Charles St., Beacon Hill*
☎ *617/723–6328* Ⓜ *Charles/MGH* ⊠ *92 Kirkland St., Cambridge*
☎ *617/576–6328* Ⓜ *Central.*

HOME FURNISHINGS

A home-furnishings hot spot has emerged in the South End, as well as
some options on Massachusetts Avenue in Cambridge.

Abodeon. New York decorators come to town just to shop this incredible
collection of 20th-century modern housewares, both newly produced
classic designs and pristine-condition vintage. You might come across a
mint 1963 stove, a complete set of Jetson-esque dinnerware, or a Lucite
dining set from the early 1970s. As a bonus, the back room contains
more than 10,000 hard-to-find records. ⊠ *E. 1731 Massachusetts Ave.,
Cambridge* ☎ *617/497–0137* ◷ *Mon.–Sat. 10–6, Sun. noon–5* Ⓜ *Porter.*

Acquire. The bright space boasts the perfect mix of modern and vintage
furnishings, including lamps, pillows, pictures, and chairs. ⊠ *61 Salem
St., North End* ☎ *857/362–7380* @ *acquireboutique.com* ◷ *Mon. 11–6,
Tues.–Fri. 11–7, Sat. 10–7, Sun. noon–5.*

Hudson. Find carpeting, lighting, seating, vintage items, and everything
you'll need for a casual, yet chic home. ⊠ *312 Shawmut Ave., South
End* ☎ *617/292–0900* ⊕ *hudsonboston.com* ◷ *Mon.–Wed., Fri., and
Sat., 10–6, Thurs. 10–7, Sun. 11–5.*

J.E.M. What looks like an artist's workshop is actually a tiny corner boutique showcasing independent designers and their creative home accents. ✉ *470 Shawmut Ave., South End* ☎ *617/391–0490* ⊕ *jem-home.com* ⊗ *Tues.–Sat. 11–6, Sun. noon–5. Closed Mon.*

Koo de Kir. Break out of the blond-wood school with this offbeat selection of furniture, lamps, candles, wine racks, table settings, and other urban necessities. ✉ *65 Chestnut St., Beacon Hill* ☎ *617/723–8111* ⊗ *Tues.–Fri. 11–7, Sat. 10–6, Sun. noon–6. Closed Mon.* Ⓜ *Charles/ MGH.*

★ **Lekker.** Dutch design with contemporary panache pervades South Washington Street's coolest home store—the best place to pick up bright oversize pillows, china, tables, Asian cabinets, and sleek, contemporary flatware. ✉ *1317 Washington St., South End* ☎ *617/542–6464* Ⓜ *Back Bay/South End.*

14

Mohr & McPherson. These stores are an exotic visual feast; cabinets, tables, chairs, and lamps from Japan, India, China, and Indonesia, as well as new and antique Oriental rugs, make up the impressive array. Also impressive are the high prices. ✉ *460 Harrison Ave., Back Bay* ☎ *617/210–7900* Ⓜ *Arlington* ✉ *75 Moulton St., Cambridge* ☎ *617/520–2000* Ⓜ *Alewife* ✉ *151 Alewife Brook Pkwy., Cambridge* ☎ *617/520–2112* Ⓜ *Alewife.*

Posh on Tremont. "Where do you get this stuff?" is something the owners hear often at Posh, a shop that somehow manages to be all things to all South End nesters. A pair of sleek silver candlesticks would be perfect for a contemporary loft, for instance, and a brownstone buyer could snap up vintage end tables. ✉ *557 Tremont Ave., South End* ☎ *617/437–1970* Ⓜ *Back Bay/South End.*

Showroom. This industrial-looking shop has some of the finest modern furniture in town. Collections from Italian lines Flexform and Cappellini are set up in roomlike designs on the floor to give shoppers an accurate visual of their future interior design. ✉ *240 Stuart St., Back Bay* ☎ *617/482–4805* Ⓜ *Arlington.*

JEWELRY

Brodney Gallery. Brodney sells the most estate jewelry in New England, and its wide selection of platinum filigree diamond rings ensures a steady stream of nervous male customers about to pop the question. ✉ *145 Newbury St., Back Bay* ☎ *617/536–0500* Ⓜ *Copley.*

Dorfman Jewels. This elegant shop glows with first-class watches, pearls, and precious stones. ✉ *24 Newbury St., Back Bay* ☎ *617/536–2022* Ⓜ *Arlington.*

★ **Shreve, Crump & Low.** Since 1796, Shreve has specialized in high-end treasures, including gems and handcrafted platinum rings, as well as high-quality antiques. But don't get the impression that you can't afford anything here: one of the store's best-selling items is a $95 ceramic pitcher called "The Gurgling Cod," in honor of the state fish. ✉ *440 Boylston St., Back Bay* ☎ *617/267–9100* Ⓜ *Arlington.*

Small Pleasures. The antique and estate jewelry—from Victorian-era tourmaline cocktail rings to mint-condition pocket watches—that fills these cases should not be missed by vintage lovers. The staff is notably helpful and informed. ⊠ *Copley Pl., 142 Newbury St., Back Bay* ☎ *617/267–7371* Ⓜ *Copley.*

Tiffany & Co. Fine service complements the finest in gems and precious metals, as well as crystal, china, stationery, and fragrances. ⊠ *100 Huntington Ave., Copley Pl., Back Bay* ☎ *617/353–0222* Ⓜ *Copley.*

Twentieth Century Limited. Every kind of rhinestone concoction imaginable for the bauble babe in your life is here, as well as gently used 20th-century ladies' hats and pocketbooks. ⊠ *73 Charles St., Beacon Hill* ☎ *617/742–1031* Ⓜ *Charles/MGH.*

MUSIC STORES

As befitting a town with so many colleges and universities, live music of all kinds is never far away. Unfortunately, the market for recorded music has diminished over the years, and CD and record stores are disappearing along with it.

★ **Newbury Comics**. These local outposts for new rock and roll carry especially good lineups of independent pressings. Frequent sales keep prices down. ⊠ *332 Newbury St., Back Bay* ☎ *617/236–4930* Ⓜ *Hynes* ⊠ *36 JFK St., Cambridge* ☎ *617/491–0337* Ⓜ *Harvard* ⊠ *Faneuil Hall Marketplace, North Bldg.* ☎ *617/248–9992* Ⓜ *Government Center.*

ODDS AND ENDS

The Fish and Bone. This boutique is dedicated to all things cat and dog. Choose from the enormous selection of collars, toys, and food. ⊠ *217 Newbury St., Back Bay* ☎ *857/753–4176* ☉ *Mon.–Sat. 9–7, Sun. 10–6.*

Grasshopper Shops. The souvenirs in this little collection of independently owned shops in historic Faneuil Hall are Boston-centric but not cheesy. The **Bostonian Society Museum Shop** (☎ *617/720–3284*) has history books for children and adults. At **Explore Boston** (☎ *617/725–1055*) you can buy saltwater taffy or a Boston-in-a-Box board game. **Out of Left Field** (☎ *617/722–9401*) sells Red Sox gear. ⊠ *Faneuil Hall Sq., Government Center* Ⓜ *Government Center.*

Kate Spade. Trendsetters go wild for Kate's colorful and classically whimsical handbags, as well as her shoes, PJs, accessories, and travel and cosmetics cases. ⊠ *117 Newbury St., Back Bay* ☎ *617/262–2632* Ⓜ *Copley.*

Lannan Ship Model Gallery. Though a sign on the door says it's open by appointment only, a simple knock almost always gains you admission to this water rat's dream store—but call ahead to be sure. The 6,000-square-foot space looks like the attic of a merchant seaman: in addition to finished 18th- and 19th-century ship models ($200 to $100,000-plus) and vintage pond yachts, you can find lanterns, navigational instruments, and marine charts, prints, and oils. ⊠ *99 High St., Downtown* ☎ *617/451–2650* Ⓜ *South Station.*

Out-of-Town News. Smack in the middle of Harvard Square is a staggering selection of the world's newspapers and magazines. The stand is open daily 6 am–10:30 pm. ⊠ *0 Harvard Sq., Cambridge* ☎ *617/354–1441* Ⓜ *Harvard.*

RUNNING GEAR

★ **Marathon Sports.** Marathon is known for its personalized service and advice for choosing the perfect shoe, whether you're a beginning walker or a serious runner. Many marathon runners find their way here before the Boston race each spring. ⊠ *1654 Massachusetts Ave., Cambridge* ☎ *617/354–4161* Ⓜ *Harvard.*

THRIFT SHOPS

Fodor's Choice
★
Bobby from Boston. For years this hidden gem was kept on the down low—but the word's out. Owner Bobby Garnett's been in the vintage game for decades, and his one-of-a-kind finds are unmatched. The two-room space is mostly menswear, but there are plenty of finds for females, too. ⊠ *19 Thayer St., South End* ☎ *617/423–9299* 🕘 *Tues.– Sun. noon–6. Closed Mon.*

The Closet. Chanel purses, Rick Owens jackets, and Hermés bracelets have all graced this jam-packed consignment shop. Their picky choices are your gain. ⊠ *175 Newbury St., Back Bay* ☎ *617/536–1919* ⊕ *closet-boston.com/blog/* 🕘 *Tues.–Sat. 10–6, Sun. noon–5; closed Mon.*

Garment District. This warehouselike building is crammed with vintage, used, and new clothing and accessories. Students crowd the store year-round, and everyone comes at Halloween for that perfect costume. ⊠ *200 Broadway, Cambridge* ☎ *617/876–5230* Ⓜ *Kendall/MIT.*

Keezer's. Since 1895 this shop has been many a man's secret weapon for formal wear at an informal price. Pick up new or used suits, tuxedos, ties, shirts, and pants. ⊠ *140 River St., Cambridge* ☎ *617/547–2455* Ⓜ *Central.*

Oona's. Crowded racks of cared-for, secondhand clothing for women and men are reason enough to browse through the multiple rooms of reasonably priced stock. A helpful staff and fun, eclectic vibe just make doing so that much more fun. ⊠ *1210 Massachusetts Ave., Cambridge* ☎ *617/491–2654* Ⓜ *Harvard.*

Poor Little Rich Girl. A museum of carefully selected vintage designer duds, the top floor here is dedicated to big-name brands and trends, while the bottom is a mishmash of clothing and accessories. ⊠ *166 Newbury St., Back Bay* ☎ *617/425–4874* ⊕ *shoppoorlittlerichgirl.com* 🕘 *Tues.–Sat. 12–7. Closed Sun. and Mon.*

Second Time Around. OK, so $700 isn't all that cheap for a used suit—but what if it's Chanel? Many of the items here, from jeans to fur coats, are new merchandise; the rest is on consignment. The staff takes periodic markdowns, ranging from 20% to 50% over a 90-day period. ⊠ *176 Newbury St., Back Bay* ☎ *617/247–3504* Ⓜ *Copley* ⊠ *8 Eliot St., Cambridge* ☎ *617/491–7185* Ⓜ *Harvard.*

14

Vintage Revenge. You won't find a single ripped seem, tear, or hole in this vintage shop. Owner Denise Goldhagen stocks flawless, iconic pieces, steams garments, and gives her honest opinion on fit. ⊠ *1105 Mass. Ave., Cambridge* ☎ *617/498–0999* ☾ *Daily noon–7.*

TOYS

☺ **Curious George & Friends**. Time can really slip away from you in this jungle of kids' books and gifts. Decorated with tropical plants, a fake hut, and tot-size chairs, and equipped with puzzles, toys, activity sets, and books of all kinds for all ages, this store is a wonderland for kids and a parent's salvation on a rainy day. ⊠ *1 JFK St., Harvard Sq., Cambridge* ☎ *617/498–0062* Ⓜ *Harvard.*

☺ **Henry Bear's Park**. The specialty at this charming neighborhood store is huggable bears and collectible dolls, although it also sells books, toys, and games. ⊠ *361 Huron St., Cambridge* ☎ *617/547–8424* Ⓜ *Porter* ⊠ *19 Harvard St., Brookline* ☎ *617/264–2422* Ⓜ *Brookline Village.*

☺ **Stellabella**. Creative toys are the draw here—books and games to stimulate kids' imaginations and get their brains going without relying on TV or violence. No gun or weapon toys are sold. ⊠ *1360 Cambridge St., Cambridge* ☎ *617/491–6290* Ⓜ *Central.*

Tadpole. This is a treasure trove of educational games, dolls, trucks, blocks, and every other necessity for a kid's toy chest. Toddler items are stored at the main location (37 Clarendon Street), while infant gear is in their smaller space just up the street. ⊠ *37 Clarendon St., South End* ☎ *617/778–1788 Ext. 1* ⊕ *shoptadpole.com* ☾ *Tues.–Fri. 10–7, Sat. 10–6, Sun. noon–5. Closed Mon.* ⊠ *58 Clarendon St., South End* ☎ *617/778–1788 Ext. 2* ⊕ *shoptadpole.com* ☾ *Tues.–Fri. 10–7, Sat. 10–6, Sun. noon–5. Closed Mon.*

Side Trips

WORD OF MOUTH

"The Gloucester/Rockport area might be a nice overnight destination with several nice beaches in either town. Rockport has some nice artist studios and galleries, as well as Bearskin Neck which has some nice non-chain shops; downtown has some decent restaurants."

—gail

SIDE TRIPS FROM BOSTON

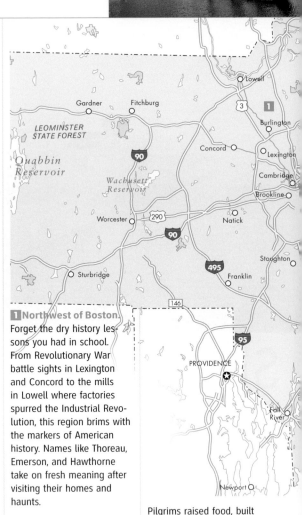

TOP REASONS TO GO

★ **Early American History:** From Plimoth Plantation to Salem, Deerfield, Sturbridge Village, and Hancock Shaker Village, you can visit Colonial reenactment museums, preserved villages, homes, and inns.

★ **Seafaring Communities:** Set off on a whale watch from Gloucester, warm yourself after a windy coastal walk in Rockport with clam chowder, and admire the dedicated routine of local fishermen.

★ **Revisit your Reading:** Nathaniel Hawthorne's *House of Seven Gables* still stands in Salem. Liberate yourself with a swim in Thoreau's Walden Pond. In Concord, see where both Louisa May Alcott and Ralph Waldo Emerson penned their works.

★ **Cranberry Bogs:** The bogs' red, green, gold, and blue colors dot Cape Cod and the Plymouth area.

★ **The** *Mayflower II:* The story of the Pilgrims' Atlantic crossing comes alive in Plymouth.

1 Northwest of Boston. Forget the dry history lessons you had in school. From Revolutionary War battle sights in Lexington and Concord to the mills in Lowell where factories spurred the Industrial Revolution, this region brims with the markers of American history. Names like Thoreau, Emerson, and Hawthorne take on fresh meaning after visiting their homes and haunts.

2 South of Boston. Equally historic, the area south of Boston offers insights into what the earliest American settlers experienced. In Plymouth and Plimoth Plantation, learn how the Pilgrims raised food, built their homes, and survived under the harshest conditions. New Bedford's whaling culture and Portuguese heritage come alive on the cobblestone streets along the docks.

3 **Cape Cod.** An easy ferry ride from Boston, Provincetown, on Cape Cod's outer tip, is a wonderfully diverse, offbeat village of galleries, crafts, and good restaurants. Refuel with pastry or coffee, then walk around this culturally rich, free-spirited haven. The Cape Cod National Seashore is close by, with good beaches and spectacular sand dunes.

GETTING ORIENTED

Visit Concord and Lexington, to the northwest of Boston, and that history class from high school may suddenly come rushing back to you. The state's coast from Boston to Cape Ann is called the North Shore, visited for its beautiful beaches, quintessential New England seaside communities, and the bewitching Salem. South of Boston lies more history in Quincy and Plymouth, and more seaside scenery at Cape Cod.

15

SIDE TRIPS PLANNER

Air Travel

Boston's Logan International Airport is the state's major airport. Trains, ferries, and small commuter flights take you to points around the state. If you're driving to Cape Cod, avoid the Friday late-afternoon-to-early-evening summer rush.

Boat Travel

High-speed ferries provide transportation to Martha's Vineyard and Nantucket. The Bay State Cruise Co. and Boston Harbor Cruises run 90-minute ferry rides between Boston and Provincetown on Cape Cod from May through October. Reservations are strongly recommended.

Bay State Cruise Co. ☎ 877/ 783-3779.

Boston Harbor Cruises ☎ 617/ 227-4321, 877/733-9425.

Train Travel

The MBTA's commuter rail offers service to Newburyport, Ipswich, Rockport, Salemm, and Gloucester. Travel times are usually 70 minutes or less.

Massachusetts Bay Transportation Authority ☎ 800/392-6100 ⊕ www.mbta.com.

Car Travel

Outside of Boston you need a car to explore the state. Expect heavy traffic heading in and out of the city at rush hour, generally from 6 am to 9 am and 4 pm to 7 pm.

From Boston to Lexington, pick up Route 2 West in Cambridge. Exit at Routes 4/225. Turn left on Mass Ave for the National Heritage Museum. For Lexington's town center, take the Waltham Street–Lexington exit from Route 2. Follow Waltham Street just under 2 mi to Mass Ave.; you'll be just east of the Battle Green. The drive takes about 30 minutes. To continue to Concord, head farther west on Route 2. Or take Interstate 90 (the Massachusetts Turnpike) to Interstate 95 North, and then exit at Route 2, heading west. Driving time is 40–45 minutes from Boston.

The primary link between Boston and the North Shore is Route 128, which follows the coast northeast to Gloucester. To pick up Route 128 from Boston, take Interstate 93 North to Interstate 95 North to Route 128. If you stay on Interstate 95, you'll reach Newburyport. From Boston to Salem or Marblehead, follow Route 128 to Route 114 into Salem or continue to Marblehead. Driving from Boston to Salem takes about 35–40 minutes; to Gloucester or to Newburyport, about 50–60 minutes.

To get to Plymouth, take the Southeast Expressway Interstate 93 South to Route 3 (toward Cape Cod); Exits 6 and 4 lead to downtown Plymouth and Plimoth Plantation, respectively. Allow about one hour.

For access to Cape Cod and Provincetown, take Interstate 93 south from Boston to Route 3. Continue over the Sagamore Bridge to Route 6. Provincetown is about two hours' drive.

When to Go

The dazzling foliage and cool temperatures make fall the best time to visit Massachusetts. Summer, especially late in the season when the water is a bit warmer, is ideal for beach vacations. Many towns save their best for winter—inns open their doors to carolers, shops serve eggnog, and lobster boats parade around Gloucester Harbor.

Restaurants

Massachusetts invented the fried clam, and it's served in many North Shore and Cape Cod restaurants. Creamy clam chowder is another specialty. Eating seafood "in the rough"—from paper plates in seaside shacks—is a revered local custom. On the Cape, specialties from the Portuguese community like kale soup and linguiça sausage appear on some menus. At country inns you'll find traditional New England dinners: double-cut pork chops, rack of lamb, game, Boston baked beans, Indian pudding, and the dubiously glorified New England boiled dinner (corned beef and cabbage with potatoes, carrots, turnips, and other vegetables).

Hotels

While Boston has everything from luxury hotels to charming bed-and-breakfasts, the signature accommodation outside Boston is the country inn; less extravagant and less expensive are B&B establishments, many of them in private homes. On Cape Cod inns are plentiful, and rental homes and condominiums are available for long-term stays. You'll want to make reservations for inns well in advance during peak periods: summer on the Cape and islands, and summer through winter in the Berkshires. Smoking has been banned in all Massachusetts hotels.

WHAT IT COSTS					
	¢	$	$$	$$$	$$$$
Restaurants	under $8	$8–$14	$15–$24	$25–$32	over $32
Hotels	under $75	$75–$150	$151–$225	$226–$325	over $325

For restaurants, prices are per person, for a main course at dinner. For hotels, prices are for two people in a standard double room in high season, excluding 11.95% in hotel and sales tax and service charges. Local taxes may also apply.

Tours

Brush Hill Tours. Brush Hill Tours offers daily motor-coach tours from Boston to Lexington's Battle Green and Concord's Old North Bridge area on weekends in May and June and then daily until November. Seasonal trips to Salem, Marblehead, and Plymouth are also available. ☎ 781/986–6100, 617/720–6342, 800/343–1328 ⊕ www.brushhilltours.com.

Walking tours run April through October. Concord Chamber of Commerce runs walking tours April through October. They last about 1½ hours and depart from the Concord Visitor Center at 11 am Friday through Monday, with additional tours on weekends at 1 pm. ☎ 978/369–3120 ⊕ www.concordchamberofcommerce.org.

Essex River Cruises & Charters. Essex River Cruises & Charters organizes narrated cruises of nearby salt marshes and rivers. Call ahead for schedules and reservations. ☎ 978/768–6981, 800/748–3706 ⊕ www.essexcruises.com.

Budgeting Your Time

Though Massachusetts is small, you can easily spend several weeks exploring it. If you have a few days, head to a town or two north and south of Boston, such as Concord, Plymouth, and Salem. With a week you may want to add on the Berkshires or spend the entire time relaxing on Cape Cod.

15

Updated
by Bethany
Cassin
Beckerlegge

History lies thick on the ground in the towns surrounding Boston—from Pilgrims to pirates, witches to whalers, the American Revolution to the Industrial Revolution. The sights outside the city are at least as interesting as those on Boston's Freedom Trail.

Rich in more than history, the areas surrounding Boston also allow visitors to retrace the steps of famous writers, bask in the outdoors, and browse shops in funky artist communities. The haunts of literary luminaries of every generation lurk throughout Massachusetts. Head to Concord to visit the place where Henry David Thoreau wrote his prophetic *Walden* and where Louisa May Alcott's *Little Women* brightened a grim time during the Civil War. Relive Nathaniel Hawthorne's vision of Puritan-era Salem. Stop in Lowell to see where Jack Kerouac lived before going *On the Road*.

The seaside towns of Massachusetts were built before the Revolution, during the heyday of American shipping. Ipswich's First Period homes (there are more here than anywhere else in the nation) and Newburyport's majestic Federal Style mansions, grand old houses, and bustling waterfronts evoke a bygone world of clipper ships, robust fisherman, and sturdy sailors.

In a more contemporary vein, Boston and its suburbs have become a major destination for food and wine lovers. Internationally acclaimed chefs, including Barbara Lynch, Frank McClelland, and Ming Tsai, draw thousands of devoted, discerning foodies to their restaurants each year. The state's extensive system of parks, protected forests, beaches, and nature preserves satisfies everyone from the avid hiker to the beach bum.

NORTHWEST OF BOSTON

Northwest of the city, Lexington and Concord embody the spirit of the American Revolution. Sites of the first skirmishes of the Revolutionary War, these two quintessential New England towns were also cradles of American literature; several historic homes and small museums here

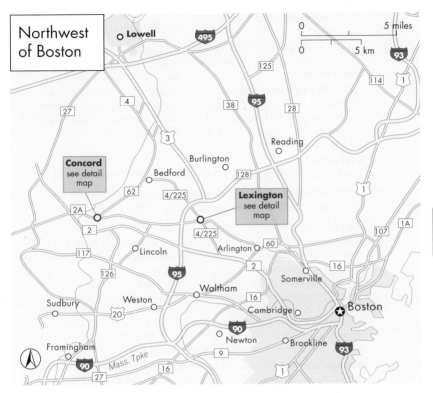

are dedicated to some of the country's first substantial writers—Ralph Waldo Emerson, Nathaniel Hawthorne, Louisa May Alcott, and Henry David Thoreau.

LEXINGTON

16 mi northwest of Boston.

Discontent with the British, American colonials burst into action in Lexington in April 1775. On April 18, patriot leader Paul Revere alerted the town that British soldiers were approaching. The next day, as the British advance troops arrived in Lexington on their march toward Concord, the Minutemen were waiting to confront the Redcoats in what became the first skirmish of the Revolutionary War.

These first military encounters of the American Revolution are very much a part of present-day Lexington, a modern suburban town that sprawls out from the historic sites near its center. Although the downtown area is generally lively, with ice-cream and coffee shops, boutiques, and a great little movie theater, the town becomes especially animated each Patriots' Day (April 19 but celebrated on the third Monday in April), when costume-clad groups re-create the Minutemen's battle maneuvers and Paul Revere rides again.

To learn more about the city and the 1775 clash, stop by the **Lexington Visitor Center.**

GETTING HERE AND AROUND
Massachusetts Bay Transportation Authority (MBTA) operates bus service in the greater Boston area and serves Lexington.

TAKE A TOUR

Liberty Ride. Liberty Ride offers guided trolley tours that visit many of the historic sites in Lexington and Concord. Tickets are good for 24 hours and allow on-off privileges ☎ 781/862–0500 ⊕ www.libertyride.us ▭ $25.

ESSENTIALS
Bus Contacts MBTA ☎ 617/222–3200, 800/392–6100 ⊕ www.mbta.com.

Visitor Information Lexington Visitor Center ✉ 1875 Massachusetts Ave. ☎ 781/862–2480 ⊕ www.lexingtonchamber.org ⊗ Daily 9–5.

EXPLORING

Battle Green. It was on this 2-acre triangle of land, on April 19, 1775, that the first confrontation between British soldiers, who were marching from Boston toward Concord, and the colonial militia known as the Minutemen took place. The Minutemen—so called because they were able to prepare themselves at a moment's notice—were led by Captain John Parker, whose role in the American Revolution is commemorated in Henry Hudson Kitson's renowned 1900 *Minuteman* statue. Facing downtown Lexington at the tip of Battle Green, the statue's in a traffic island, and therefore makes for a difficult photo op.

Buckman Tavern. While waiting for the arrival of the British on the morning of April 19, 1775, the Minutemen gathered at this 1690 tavern. A half-hour tour takes in the tavern's seven rooms, which have been restored to the way they looked in the 1770s. Among the items on display is an old front door with a hole made by a British musket ball. ✉ 1 Bedford St. ☎ 781/862–1703 ⊕ www.lexingtonhistory.org ▭ $6; $10 combination ticket includes Hancock-Clarke House and Munroe Tavern ⊗ Apr.–Oct., daily 10–4.

Hancock-Clarke House. On April 18, 1775, Paul Revere came here to warn patriots John Hancock and Sam Adams, who were staying at the house while attending the Provincial Congress in nearby Concord, of the advance of British troops. Hancock and Adams, on whose heads the British king had put a price, fled to avoid capture. The house, a parsonage built in 1698, is a 10-minute walk from Lexington Common. Inside are the pistols of the British major John Pitcairn, as well as period furnishings and portraits. ✉ 36 Hancock St. ☎ 781/862–1703 ⊕ www. lexingtonhistory.org ▭ $6; $10 combination ticket includes Buckman Tavern and Munroe Tavern ⊗ Apr.–mid-June, weekends 10–4; mid-June–Oct., daily 10–4.

Minute Man National Historical Park. West of Lexington's center stretches this 1,000-acre, three-parcel park that also extends into nearby Lincoln and Concord (⇨ Concord, Exploring). Begin your park visit at Lexington's **Minute Man Visitor Center** to see its free multimedia presentation, "The Road to Revolution," a captivating introduction to the events of

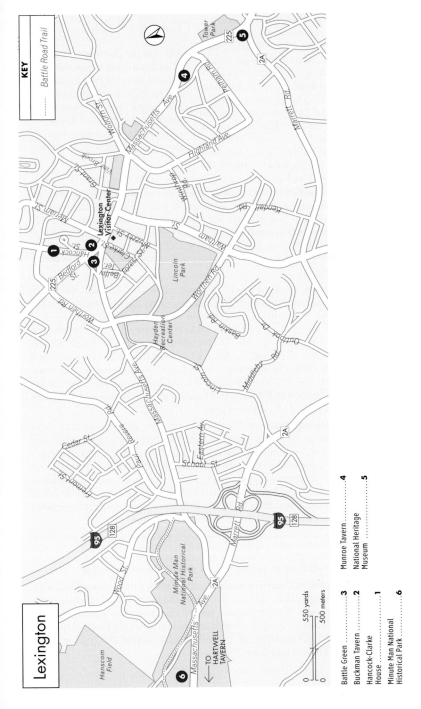

Lexington

TO HARTWELL TAVERN

KEY

······· Battle Road Trail

15

Battle Green **3**	Munroe Tavern **4**
Buckman Tavern **2**	National Heritage
Hancock-Clarke	Museum **5**
House **1**	
	Minute Man National
	Historical Park **6**

0   550 yards

0   500 meters

April 1775. Then, continuing along Highway 2A toward Concord, you pass the point where Revere's midnight ride ended with his capture by the British; it's marked with a boulder and plaque, as well as an enclosure where rangers sometimes give educational presentations. You can also visit the 1732 **Hartwell Tavern** (open mid-April through late May, weekends 9:30–5:30, and late May through late October, daily 9:30–

5:30), a restored drover's (driver's) tavern staffed by park employees in period costume; they frequently demonstrate musket firing or open-hearth cooking, and children are likely to enjoy the reproduction colonial toys. ☒ *250 North Great Rd., (Hwy. 2A), ¼ mi west of Hwy. 128* ☎ *978/369–6993 ⊕ www.nps.gov/mima ☉ North Bridge Visitor Center, Apr.–Oct., daily 9–5; Nov., daily 9–4; Dec.–Mar., call for hrs. Minute Man Visitor Center, Apr.–Oct., daily 9–5; Nov., daily 9–4; Dec.–Mar., call for hrs.*

Munroe Tavern. As April 19, 1775, dragged on, British forces met fierce resistance in Concord. Dazed and demoralized after the battle at Concord's Old North Bridge, the British backtracked and regrouped at this 1695 tavern 1 mi east of Lexington Common, while the Munroe family hid in nearby woods. The troops then retreated through what is now the town of Arlington. After a bloody battle there, they returned to Boston. Tours of the tavern last about 30 minutes. ☒ *1332 Massachusetts Ave.* ☎ *781/862–1703 ⊕ www.lexingtonhistory.org ☒ $6; $10 combination ticket includes Hancock-Clarke House and Buckman Tavern ☉ June–Oct., noon–4 pm.*

National Heritage Museum. View artifacts from all facets of American life, put in social and political context. An ongoing exhibit, "Lexington Alarm'd," outlines events leading up to April 1775 and illustrates Revolutionary-era life through everyday objects such as blacksmithing tools, bloodletting paraphernalia, and dental instruments, including a "tooth key" used to extract teeth. ☒ *33 Marrett Rd., Hwy. 2A at Massachusetts Ave.* ☎ *781/861–6559 ⊕ www.monh.org ☒ Donations accepted ☉ Wed.–Sat. 10–4:30. Closed Sun.–Tues.*

CONCORD

About 10 mi west of Lexington, 21 mi northwest of Boston.

The Concord of today is a modern suburb with a busy center filled with arty shops, places to eat, and (recalling the literary history made here) old bookstores. Autumn lovers, take note: Concord is a great place to start a fall foliage tour. From Boston, head west along Route 2 to Concord, and then continue on to find harvest stands and apple-picking around Harvard and Stow.

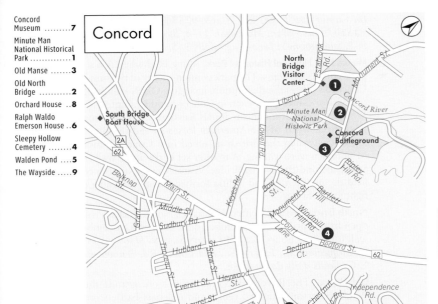

15

GETTING HERE AND AROUND

The MBTA runs buses to Concord. On the MBTA Commuter Rail Concord is a 40-minute ride on the Fitchburg Line, which departs from Boston's North Station.

ESSENTIALS

Bus and Train Contact MBTA ☎ *617/222–3200, 800/392–6100* ⊕ *www.mbta. com.*

Visitor Information Concord Visitor Center ⊠ *58 Main St.* ☎ *978/369–3120* ⊕ *www.concordchamberofcommerce.org* ⊘ *Apr.–Oct., daily 10–4.*

EXPLORING

☺ **Concord Museum.** The original contents of Emerson's private study, as well as the world's largest collection of Thoreau artifacts, reside in this 1930 Colonial Revival building just east of the town center. The museum provides a good overview of the town's history, from its original American Indian settlement to the present. Highlights include American Indian artifacts, furnishings from Thoreau's Walden Pond cabin (there's a replica of the cabin itself on the museum's lawn), and one of the two lanterns hung at Boston's Old North Church to signal that the British were coming by sea. If you've brought the children, ask for a free family activity pack. ⊠ *200 Lexington Rd., entrance* *on Cambridge Tpke.* ☎ *978/369–9763* ⊕ *www.concordmuseum.org* ⊑ *$10* ⊙ *Jan.–Mar., Mon.–Sat. 11–4, Sun. 1–4; Apr.–Dec, Mon.–Sat. 9–5, Sun. noon–5; June–Aug., daily 9–5.*

🕐 **Minute Man National Historical Park.** Along Highway 2A is a three-parcel
★ park with 1,000 acres. The park contains many of the sites important to Concord's role in the Revolution, including Old North Bridge, as well as two visitor centers, one each in Concord and Lexington (⇨ *Lexington, What to See*). Although the initial Revolutionary War sorties were in Lexington, word of the American losses spread rapidly to surrounding towns: when the British marched into Concord, more than 400 Minutemen were waiting. A marker set in the stone wall along Liberty Street, behind the North Bridge Visitor Center, announces, "On this field the minutemen and militia formed before marching down to the fight at the bridge."

North Bridge Visitor Center. The park's North Bridge Visitor Center is open from April through October, daily 9–5, and November, daily 9–4 (call for winter hours). ⊠ *174 Liberty St.* ☎ *978/369–6993* ⊠ *Bounded by Monument St., Liberty St., and Lowell Rd.* ⊕ *www.nps.gov/mima* ⊙ *Grounds daily dawn–dusk.*

Old Manse. The Reverend William Emerson, grandfather of Ralph Waldo Emerson, watched rebels and redcoats battle from behind his home, which was within sight of the Old North Bridge. The house, built in 1770, was occupied continuously by the Emerson family for almost two centuries, except for a 3½-year period during which Nathaniel Hawthorne rented it. Furnishings date from the late 18th century. Tours run throughout the day and last 45 minutes, with a new tour starting within 15 minutes of when the first person signs up. ⊠ *269 Monument St.* ☎ *978/369–3909* ⊕ *www.thetrustees.org/places-to-visit/greater-boston/old-manse.html* ⊑ *$8* ⊙ *Mid-Apr.–Oct., Mon.–Sat. 10–5, Sun. noon–5; Nov.–Mar. Tours Thurs. and Fri. 2, 3, and 4 pm and weekends noon–4:30 (weather permitting).*

Old North Bridge. A half-mile from Concord center, at this bridge the Concord Minutemen turned the tables on the British on the morning of April 19, 1775. The Americans didn't fire first, but when two of their own fell dead from a Redcoat volley, Major John Buttrick of Concord roared, "Fire, fellow soldiers, for God's sake, fire." The Minutemen released volley after volley, and the Redcoats fled. Daniel Chester French's famous statue *The Minuteman* (1875) honors the country's first freedom fighters. Inscribed at the foot of the statue are words Ralph Waldo Emerson wrote in 1837 describing the confrontation: "By the rude bridge that arched the flood / Their flag to April's breeze unfurled / Here once the embattled farmers stood / And fired the shot heard round the world. The lovely wooded surroundings give a sense of what the landscape was like in more rural times."

Orchard House. The dark brown exterior of Louisa May Alcott's family home sharply contrasts with the light, wit, and energy so much in evidence inside. Named for the apple orchard that once surrounded it, Orchard House was the Alcott family home from 1857 to 1877. Here Louisa wrote *Little Women*, based on her life with her three sisters; and

Retrace Henry David Thoreau's steps at Walden Pond.

her father, Bronson, founded his school of philosophy—the building remains behind the house. Because Orchard House had just one owner after the Alcotts left, and because it became a museum in 1911, many of the original furnishings remain, including the semicircular shelf-desk where Louisa wrote *Little Women.* ⊠ *399 Lexington Rd.* ☎ *978/369–4118* ⊕ *www.louisamayalcott.org* ✉ *$9, tours free* ⊙ *Apr.–Oct., Mon.–Sat. 10–4:30, Sun. 1–4:30; Nov. and Dec. and Jan. 3–Mar., weekdays 11–3, Sat. 10–4:30, Sun. 1–4:30. Half-hour tours begin every 30 mins Apr.–Oct.; call for off-season schedule.*

Ralph Waldo Emerson House. The 19th-century essayist and poet Ralph Waldo Emerson lived briefly in the Old Manse in 1834–35, then moved to this home, where he lived until his death in 1882. Here he wrote the *Essays.* Except for artifacts from Emerson's study, now at the nearby Concord Museum, the Emerson House furnishings have been preserved as the writer left them, down to his hat resting on the newel post. You must join one of the half-hour-long tours to see the interior. ⊠ *28 Cambridge Tpke., at Lexington Rd.* ☎ *978/369–2236* ⊕ *www.rwe.org/ emersonhouse* ✉ *$8* ⊙ *Mid-Apr.–mid-Oct., Thurs.–Sat. 10–4:30, Sun. 1–4:30; call for tour schedule.*

Sleepy Hollow Cemetery. In the Author's Ridge section of this cemetery are the graves of American literary greats Louisa May Alcott, Ralph Waldo Emerson, Henry David Thoreau, and Nathaniel Hawthorne. Each Memorial Day Alcott's grave is decorated in commemoration of her death. ⊠ *Bedford St. (Hwy. 62),* ☎ *978/318–3233* ⊙ *Daily dawn–dusk.*

Fodor's Choice ★ **Walden Pond.** For lovers of early American literature, a trip to Concord isn't complete without a pilgrimage to Henry David Thoreau's most

Literary Concord

The first wholly American literary movement was born in Concord, the tiny town west of Boston that, quite coincidentally, also witnessed the beginning of the American Revolution.

Under the influence of essayist and poet Ralph Waldo Emerson, a group eventually known as the Transcendental Club (but called the Hedges Club at the time) assembled regularly in Emerson's Concord home. Henry David Thoreau, a fellow townsman and famous proponent of self-reliance, was an integral club member, along with such others as pioneering feminist Margaret Fuller and poet Ellery Channing, both drawn to Concord simply because of Emerson's presence.

These are the names that have become indelible bylines in high school anthologies and college syllabi, but Concord also produced beloved authors outside the Transcendentalist movement. These writers include Louisa May Alcott of *Little Women* fame and children's book author Harriet Lothrop, pseudonymously known as Margaret Sydney. Even Nathaniel Hawthorne, whose various temporary homes around Massachusetts constitute a literary trail all their own, resided in Concord during the early and later portions of his career.

The cumulative inkwells of these authors have bestowed upon Concord a literary legacy unique in the United States, both for its influence on literature in general and for the quantity of related sights packed within such a small radius. From Alcott's Orchard House to Hawthorne's Old Manse, nearly all their houses remain standing, well preserved and open for tours.

The Thoreau Institute, within walking distance of a reconstruction of

Thoreau's famous cabin in the woods at Walden Pond, is a repository of his papers and original editions. Emerson's study sits in the Concord Museum, across the street from his house. Even their final resting places are here, on Authors Ridge in Sleepy Hollow Cemetery, a few short blocks from the town common. **Concord Bike Tours** (☎ 978/697–1897 ⊕ *www. concordbiketours.com*) will guide you through the sites on two wheels, usually April through November (weather permitting).

famous residence. Here, in 1845, at age 28, Thoreau moved into a one-room cabin—built for $28.12—on the shore of this 100-foot-deep kettle hole formed by the retreat of an ancient glacier. Living alone for the next two years, Thoreau discovered the benefits of solitude and the beauties of nature. The essays in *Walden*, published in 1854, are a mixture of philosophy, nature writing, and proto-ecology. The site of the first cabin is staked out in stone. A full-size, authentically furnished replica of the cabin stands about ½ mi from the original site, near the Walden Pond State Reservation parking lot. Even when it's closed, you can peek through its windows. Now, as in Thoreau's time, the pond is a delightful summertime spot for swimming, fishing, and rowing, and there's hiking in the nearby woods. To get to Walden Pond State Reservation from the center of Concord—a trip of only 1½ mi—take Concord's Main Street a block west from Monument Square, turn left onto Walden Street, and head for the intersection of Highways 2 and 126. Cross over Highway 2 onto Highway 126, heading south for ½ mi. ⊠ *915 Walden St.(Hwy. 126)* ☎ *978/369–3254* ⊕ *www.mass.gov/ dcr/parks/walden* ⌕ *Free, parking $5* ⊙ *Daily 8 am–sunset, weather permitting.*

The Wayside. Nathaniel Hawthorne lived at the Old Manse in 1842–45, working on stories and sketches; he then moved to Salem (where he wrote *The Scarlet Letter*) and later to Lenox (*The House of the Seven Gables*). In 1852 he returned to Concord, bought this rambling structure called The Wayside, and lived here until his death in 1864. The subsequent owner, Margaret Sidney, wrote the children's book *Five Little Peppers and How They Grew* (1881). Before Hawthorne moved in, the Alcotts lived here, from 1845 to 1848. An exhibit center, in the former barn, provides information about the Wayside authors and links them to major events in American history. Hawthorne's tower-study, with his stand-up writing desk, is substantially as he left it. ⊠ *455 Lexington Rd.* ☎ *978/318–7863* ⊕ *www.nps.gov/archive/mima/wayside* ⌕ *$5* ⊙ *Open by guided tour only, May–Oct.; call for reservations.*

SPORTS AND THE OUTDOORS

BOATING **South Bridge Boat House.** You can reach the North Bridge section of the Minute Man National Historical Park by water if you rent a canoe or kayak at the South Bridge Boat House and paddle along the Sudbury and Concord rivers. You can even paddle all the way to Sudbury or up to Billerica. ⊠ *496 Main St.* ☎ *978/369–9438* ⊕ *www.canoeconcord. com* ⌕ *Canoes $13.50/hr weekdays, $15.50/hr weekends; kayaks $15/ hr single, $17/hr double* ⊙ *Apr.–Nov. weekdays 10–1 hr before dusk, weekends and holidays 9–1 hr before dusk.*

WHERE TO EAT

$$ ✕ **Main Streets Cafe.** Cyclists, families, and sightseers pack into this brick
AMERICAN building, which was used to store munitions during the Revolutionary
★ War. Wood floors and blackboard menus add a touch of nostalgia, but the extensive menu includes many modern hits. Breakfast offerings include a quiche and breakfast sandwich of the day. At lunch, the grilled panini are excellent; they also serve flatbread pizza and pub fare. At night heartier offerings dominate the menu, including baked lobster

mac and cheese, scallop and shrimp risotto, and a Yankee pot roast dinner. There's a full bar, and in summer the small alley outside leads to a counter that serves ice cream. ⊠ *42 Main St.* ☎ *866/413–3981* ⊕ *www.mainstreetsmarketandcafe.com.*

$$
AMERICAN

× **Walden Grille.** Chowders, salads, and sandwiches are typical fare at this old brick firehouse-turned-dining room. Start with the Philly spring rolls or crispy fried oysters. Sandwiches include burgers and BLTs, plus more creative options like the chicken curry roll-up or croque monsieur. Entrées run the gamut from braised short ribs to rock shrimp risotto. ⊠ *24 Walden St.* ☎ *978/371–2233* ⊕ *www.waldengrille.com.*

THE NORTH SHORE

The slice of Massachusetts's Atlantic Coast known as the North Shore extends past Boston to the picturesque Cape Ann region just shy of the New Hampshire border. In addition to miles of woods and beaches, the North Shore's highlights include Marblehead, a stunningly classic New England sea town; Salem, which thrives on a history of witches, writers, and maritime trades; Gloucester, the oldest seaport in America; Rockport, rich with crafts shops and artists' studios; and Newburyport, with its redbrick center and clapboard mansions, and a handful of typical New England towns in between. Bustling during the short summer season and breathtaking during the autumn foliage, the North Shore is calmer (and colder) between November and June. Since many restaurants, inns, and attractions operate on reduced hours, it's worth calling ahead off-season.

MARBLEHEAD

17 mi north of Boston.

Marblehead, with its narrow and winding streets, beautifully preserved clapboard homes, sea captains' mansions, and harbor, looks much as it must have when it was founded in 1629 by fishermen from Cornwall and the Channel Islands. One of New England's premier sailing capitals, Marblehead continues to attract boats from along the Eastern seaboard each July during Race Week—first held in 1889. Parking in town can be difficult; lots at the end of Front Street or on State Street by the Landing restaurant are the best options.

ESSENTIALS

Visitor Information **Marblehead Chamber of Commerce Information Booth** ⊠ *62 Pleasant St.* ☎ *781/631–2868* ⊕ *www.visitmarblehead.com.*

EXPLORING

The 1768 Jeremiah Lee Mansion. Marblehead's 18th-century high society is exemplified in this mansion run by the town's museum and historical society. Colonel Lee was the wealthiest merchant and ship owner in Massachusetts in 1768, and although few original furnishings remain, the unique hand-painted wallpaper and fine collection of traditional North Shore furniture provide clues to the life of an American gentleman. ⊠ *161 Washington St.* ☎ *781/631–1768* ⊕ *www.marbleheadmuseum.org/LeeMansion.htm* ⊡ *$5* ⊙ *June–Oct., Tues.–Sat. 10–4.*

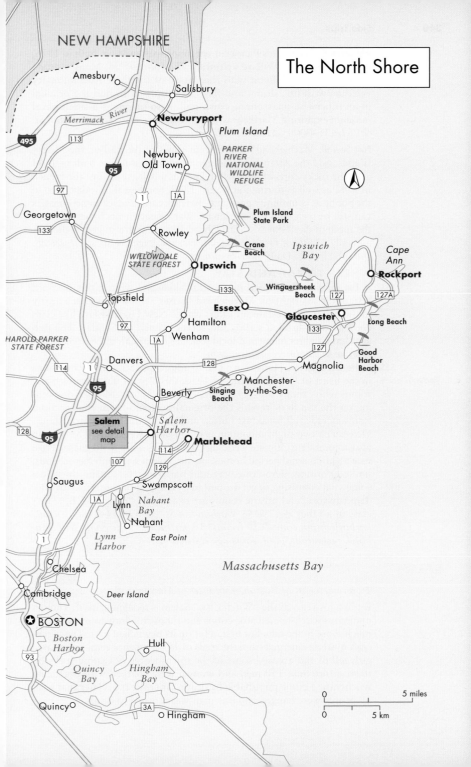

The North Shore

NEW HAMPSHIRE

Amesbury
Salisbury
Merrimack River
Newburyport
Plum Island
495
113
Newbury
Old Town
95
PARKER
RIVER
NATIONAL
WILDLIFE
REFUGE
97
1
1A
Georgetown
Plum Island
State Park
133
Rowley
Crane
Beach
Ipswich
Bay
Cape
Ann
WILLOWDALE
STATE FOREST
Ipswich
Rockport
133
Wingaersheek
Beach
127
127A
Essex
Topsfield
127
Long Beach
Gloucester
Hamilton
133
97
1A
Wenham
HAROLD PARKER
STATE FOREST
127
Good
Harbor
Beach
Danvers
128
Magnolia
114
1
95
Beverly
Manchester-
by-the-Sea
Singing
Beach
128
Salem
see detail
map
*Salem
Harbor*
95
Marblehead
107
114
Saugus
129
Swampscott
1A
Lynn
*Nahant
Bay*
Nahant
*Lynn
Harbor*
East Point
1
Massachusetts Bay
Chelsea
Cambridge
Deer Island
⊛ BOSTON
*Boston
Harbor*
Hull
93
*Quincy
Bay*
*Hingham
Bay*
Quincy
3A
Hingham

0   5 miles
0   5 km

Abbott Hall. The town's Victorian-era municipal building, built in 1876, displays Archibald Willard's painting *The Spirit of '76*. Many visitors, familiar since childhood with this image of the three Revolutionary veterans with fife, drum, and flag, are surprised to find the original in an otherwise unassuming town hall. Also on site is a small naval museum exploring Marblehead's maritime past. ⌂ *188 Washington St.* ☎ *781/631–0000* 🏷 *Free* ⊙ *Call for hrs.*

Fort Sewall. Marblehead's magnificent views of the harbor, the Misery Islands, and the Atlantic are best enjoyed from this fort built in 1644 atop the rocky cliffs of the harbor. Used as a defense against the French in 1742 as well as during the War of 1812, Fort Sewall is today open to the public as community parkland. Barracks and underground quarters can still be seen, and Revolutionary War reenactments by members of the modern-day Glover's Marblehead Regiment are staged at the fort annually. ⌂ *End of Front St.* ⊕ *www.essexheritage.org/sites/fort_sewall. shtml* 🏷 *Free* ⊙ *Daily sunrise–sunset.*

WHERE TO EAT AND STAY

$$$

SEAFOOD

✕ **The Landing.** Decorated in nautical blues and whites, this pleasant restaurant sits right on Marblehead harbor, with a deck that's nearly in the water. The restaurant offers classic New England fare like clam chowder and broiled scrod, and serves brunch on Sunday. The pub area has a lighter menu and local feel. ⌂ *81 Front St.* ☎ *781/639–1266* ⊕ *www.thelandingrestaurant.com.*

$$$

Fodor's Choice

★

🛏 **Harbor Light Inn.** Housed in a pair of adjoining 18th-century mansions in the heart of Old Town Marblehead, this elegant inn features many rooms with canopy beds, brick fireplaces, and Jacuzzis. A soaring ceiling on the top floor reveals the original post-and-beam construction. Rates include full breakfast buffet, and during the high season (June–October) a two-night minimum is required on weekends. The inn can also accomodate intimate weddings and parties of up to 40 guests. **Pros:** nice location amid period homes; on-site tavern with pub menu. **Cons:** limited parking; many one-way and narrow streets make this town somewhat confusing to get around in by car, and the inn tricky to find. **TripAdvisor:** "and private rooms are exquisite," "classic B&B," "first class in all they do." ⌂ *58 Washington St.* ☎ *781/631–2186* ⊕ *www. harborlightinn.com* 🛏 *20 rooms; 3 apartments* ⚹ *In-room: Wi-Fi. In-hotel: restaurant, pool, some age restrictions.*

SALEM

16 mi northeast of Boston, 4 mi west of Marblehead.

Known for years as the "Witch City," Salem is redefining itself. Though numerous witch-related attractions and shops still draw tourists, there's much more to the city. But first, a bit on its bewitched past. The witchcraft hysteria emerged from the trials of 1692, when several Salem-area girls fell ill and accused some of the townspeople of casting spells on them. More than 150 men and women were charged with practicing witchcraft, a crime punishable by death. After the trials later that year, 19 people were hanged and one man was crushed to death.

The House of the Seven Gables inspired Nathaniel Hawthorne's book of the same name.

Though the witch trials might have built Salem's infamy, it'd be a mistake to ignore the town's rich maritime and creative traditions, which played integral roles in the country's evolution. Frigates out of Salem opened the Far East trade routes and generated the wealth that created America's first millionaires. Among its native talents are writer Nathaniel Hawthorne, the intellectual Peabody Sisters, navigator Nathaniel Bowditch, and architect Samuel McIntire. This creative spirit is today celebrated in Salem's internationally recognized museums, waterfront shops and restaurants, galleries, and wide common.

To learn more on the area, stop by the **Regional Visitor's Center**. Innovatively designed in the Old Salem Armory, the center has exhibits, a 27-minute film, maps, and a gift shop.

ESSENTIALS
Visitor Information Destination Salem ⊠ *54 Turner St.* ☎ *978/744–3663, 877/725–3662* ⊕ *www.salem.org.* **Regional Visitor's Center** ⊠ *2 New Liberty St.* ☎ *978/740–1650* ⊕ *www.nps.gov/ner/sama/* ⊙ *Daily 9–5.*

EXPLORING

★ **House of the Seven Gables.** Immortalized in Nathaniel Hawthorne's classic novel, this site itself is a literary treasure. Built in 1668 and also known as the Turner-Ingersoll Mansion, the house includes a secret staircase, a garret containing an antique scale model of the house, and some of the finest Georgian interiors in the country. Also on the property is the small house where Hawthorne was born in 1804; built in 1750, it was moved from its original location a few blocks away. ⊠ *115 Derby St.* ☎ *978/744–0991* ⊕ *www.7gables.org* ⊠ *$12.50* ⊙ *Nov., Dec., and mid-Jan.–June, daily 10–5; July–Oct., daily 10–7.*

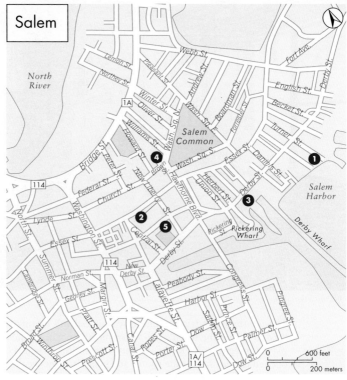

Fodor's Choice
★

Peabody Essex Museum. Salem's world-class museum celebrates maritime art, history, and the spoils of the Asian export trade. Its 30 galleries, housed in a contemplative blend of modern design, represent a diverse range of styles; ranging from American decorative and seamen's art to idea studios and photography. ⊠ *East India Sq.* ☎ *978/745–9500, 866/745–1876* ⊕ *www.pem.org* 💲 *$15* ⊙ *Tues.–Sun. 10–5; holiday Mondays 10–5.*

Salem Maritime National Historic Site. Near Derby Wharf, this 9¼-acre site focuses on Salem's heritage as a major seaport with a thriving overseas trade. It includes an orientation center with an 18-minute film; the 1762 home of Elias Derby, America's first millionaire; the 1819 Customs House, made famous in Nathaniel Hawthorne's *The Scarlet Letter*; and a replica of the *Friendship,* a 171-foot, three-masted 1797 merchant vessel. There's also an active lighthouse dating from 1871, as well as the nation's last surviving 18th-century wharves. The West India Goods Store, across the street, is still a working 19th-century store, with glass jars of spices, teas, and coffees. ⊠ *193 Derby St.* ☎ *978/740–1650* ⊕ *www.nps.gov/sama* 💲 *Site free, tours $5* ⊙ *Hrs vary; check Web site or call ahead.*

Salem Witch Museum. An informative, if somewhat hokey, introduction to the 1692 witchcraft hysteria, this museum has a short walk-through

Landlubbers can go to sea at Salem's Peabody Essex Museum.

exhibit, "Witches: Evolving Perceptions," that describes witch hunts through the years. ✉ *Washington Sq. N* ☎ *978/744–1692* ⊕ *www.salemwitchmuseum.com* ✉ *$8.50* ☉ *Sept.–June, daily 10–5; July and Aug., daily 10–7.*

Salem Witch Trials Memorial. Dedicated by Nobel Laureate Elie Wiesel in 1992, this melancholy space—an antidote to the relentless marketing of the merry-witches motif—honors those who died because they refused to confess that they were witches. A stone wall is studded with 20 stone benches, each inscribed with a victim's name, and sits next to Salem's oldest burying ground. ✉ *Off Liberty St. near Charter St.,* ⊕ *www.salemweb.com/memorial/memorial.shtml.*

ARTS AND ENTERTAINMENT

THEATER **Cry Innocent: The People versus Bridget Bishop.** This show, the longest continuously running play north of Boston, transports audience members to Bridget Bishop's trial of 1692. After hearing historical testimonies, the audience cross-examines the witnesses and must then decide the verdict. Actors respond in character revealing much about the Puritan frame of mind. Each show is different and allows audience members to play their "part" in history. ✉ *Old Town Hall, 32 Derby Sq.* ☎ *978/867–4767* ⊕ *www.gordon.edu/historyalive* ✉ *$10* ☉ *June–Oct., showtimes vary.*

WHERE TO EAT AND STAY

$$ ✕ **The Lyceum Bar & Grill.** Always a hit for classy fare, the restaurant
SEAFOOD takes advantage of its historic building, where Alexander Graham Bell
Fodor's Choice made the first long-distance phone call. The "local ingredients, global
★ flavors" philosophy is seen best in the panko-crusted fish-and-chips, oysters, and lobster cannelloni. Jazz is played most weekends. ✉ *43*

The First Witch Trial

It was in Danvers, not Salem, that the first witch trial was held, originating with the family of Samuel Parris, a minister who moved to the area in 1680 from Barbados, bringing with him two slaves, including one named Tituba. In 1691 Samuel's daughter, Betty, and niece, Abigail, began having "fits." Tituba, who had told Betty and Abigail stories of magic and witchcraft from her homeland, baked a "witch cake" to identify the witches who were harming the girls. The girls in turn accused Tituba of witchcraft. After three days of "questioning," which included beatings from Samuel and a promise from him to free her if she cooperated, Tituba confessed to meeting the devil (in the form of a black hog or dog). She also claimed there were other witches in the village, confirming the girls' accusations against Sarah Good and Sarah Osborne, but she refused to name any others. Tituba's trial prompted the frenzy that led to the deaths of 20 accused "witches."

Church St. ☎ *978/745–7665* ⊕ *www.thelyceum.com* ☯ *No dinner Sun. (brunch only).*

$ ⊡ **Amelia Payson House.** Built in 1845, this Greek Revival house is a comfortable bed-and-breakfast near all the historic attractions. With high ceilings, floral-print wallpaper, and marble fireplaces, the three guest rooms are delicate and feminine. **Pros:** spotless; cozy; decorated in period furniture. **Cons:** no children under 14. **TripAdvisor:** "absolutely gorgeous," "superb breakfast," "great place to stay in Salem." ⊠ *16 Winter St.* ☎ *978/744–8304* ⊕ *www.ameliapaysonhouse.com* ⟳ *3 rooms* ᗚ *In-room: Wi-Fi. In-hotel: parking* ☯ *Closed Nov.–Mar.* ⦿ *Breakfast.*

$ ⊡ **The Hawthorne Hotel.** Elegantly restored, this full-service landmark hotel celebrates the town's most famous writer. The historic hotel and tavern is within walking distance from the town common, all museums, and the waterfront. Across the street is Nathaniel's statue and a fine gift shop named after his wife Sophia (Peabody) in the couple's former home. Rooms are outfitted with iPod docking stations and flat screens, and in 2010–11 the hotel will be remodeling all the guest baths and updating rooms with new beds and linens. **Pros:** lovely, historic lobby; parking available behind hotel; easy walking access to all the town's features. **Cons:** many rooms are small. **TripAdvisor:** "are always clean," "tiny rooms," "staff was amazing and very helpful." ⊠ *18 Washington Sq. W* ☎ *978/744–4080* ⊕ *www.hawthornehotel.com* ⟳ *93 rooms* ᗚ *In-room: Wi-Fi. In-hotel: restaurant, some pets allowed.*

GLOUCESTER

37 mi northeast of Boston, 8 mi northeast of Manchester-by-the-Sea.

On Gloucester's fine seaside promenade is a famous statue of a man steering a ship's wheel, his eyes searching the horizon. The statue, which honors those "who go down to the sea in ships" was commissioned by the town citizens in celebration of Gloucester's 300th anniversary in 1923. The oldest seaport in the nation (with some of the North Shore's best beaches) is still a major fishing port. Sebastian Junger's 1997 book *A Perfect Storm* was an account of the fate of the *Andrea Gail*, a Gloucester fishing boat caught in "the storm of the century" in October 1991. In 2000 the book was made into a movie, filmed on location in Gloucester.

ESSENTIALS

Visitor Information Cape Ann Chamber of Commerce ⊠ *33 Commercial St.* ☎ *978/283–1601* ⊕ *www.capeannchamber.com/.* **Rockport Chamber of Commerce** ⊠ *33 Commercial St.* ☎ *978/546–6575* ⊕ *www.rockportusa.com.*

EXPLORING

The Cape Ann Historical Association. Downtown in the Captain Elias Davis 1804 house, this is Gloucester's surprising museum and gallery. It reflects the town's commitment to artists, and has the world's largest collection by maritime luminist Fitz Henry (Hugh) Lane. There's also an excellent exhibit on Gloucester's maritime history. ⊠ *27 Pleasant St.* ☎ *978/283–0455* ⊕ *www.capeannmuseum.org* 🖃 *$8* ☉ *Tues.–Sat. 10–5, Sun. 1–4.*

Hammond Castle Museum. Inventor John Hays Hammond Jr. built this structure in 1926 to resemble a "medieval" stone castle. Hammond is credited with more than 500 patents, including inventions associated with the organ that bears his name. The museum contains medieval-style furnishings and paintings, and the Great Hall houses an impressive 8,200-pipe organ. From the castle you can see Norman's Woe Rock, made famous by Longfellow in his poem "The Wreck of the Hesperus." ⊠ *80 Hesperus Ave., south side of Gloucester off Rte. 127* ☎ *978/283–2080, 978/283–7673* ⊕ *www.hammondcastle.org* 🖃 *$9* ☉ *May–early June, weekends and mid-June–Oct., daily. Call for hrs.*

Rocky Neck. The town's creative side thrives in this neighborhood, the first-settled artists' colony in the United States. Its alumni include Winslow Homer, Maurice Prendergast, Jane Peter, and Cecilia Beaux. ⊠ *53 Rocky Neck Ave.* ☎ *978/282–0917* ⊕ *www.rockyneckartcolony. org* ☉ *Galleries 10–10, May 15–Oct. 15. Call or check Web site for winter hrs.*

SPORTS AND THE OUTDOORS

BEACHES   Gloucester has the best beaches on the North Shore. From Memorial Day through mid-September parking costs $20 on weekdays and $25 on weekends, when the lots often fill by 10 am.

Good Harbor Beach. Good Harbor Beach is a huge, sandy, dune-backed beach, with showers and snack bar, and a rocky islet just offshore. ⊠ *Easily signposted from Rte. 127A* 🖃 *Parking $20 per car; $25 on weekends and holidays.*

Long Beach. For excellent sunbathing, visit Long Beach. ⊠ *Off Rte. 127A on Gloucester-Rockport town line.*

Wingaersheek Beach. Wingaersheek Beach is a well-protected cove of white sand and dunes, with the white Annisquam lighthouse in the bay.

Kids enjoy the white sands of Wingaersheek Beach in Gloucester.

✉ *Exit 13 off Rte. 128* 🚗 *Limited parking, $20/car; $25 on weekends and holidays.*

BOATING **Thomas E. Lannon.** Consider a sail along the harbor and coast aboard the 65-foot schooner Thomas E. Lannon, crafted in Essex in 1996 and modeled after the great boats built a century before. From mid-May through mid-October there are several two-hour sails, including trips that let you enjoy the sunset or participate in a lobster bake. Tickets are $37.50. ✉ *63 Rear Rogers St., Seven Seas Wharf* ☎ *978/281–6634* ⊕ *www.schooner.org.*

WHERE TO EAT AND STAY

$$ ✕ **Franklin Cape Ann.** This contemporary nightspot offers bistro-style
AMERICAN chicken, roast cod, and steak frites, perfect for the late-night crowd (it's open until midnight). Live jazz is on tap most Tuesday evenings. Look for the signature martini glass over the door. ✉ *118 Main St.* ☎ *978/283–7888* ⊗ *No lunch.*

$$ ✕ **Passports.** With an eclectic lunch and dinner menu—hence the name—
SEAFOOD Passports is a bright and airy café with French, Spanish, and Thai dishes, as well as lobster sandwiches. The fried calamari and house haddock are favorites here, and there's always local art hanging on the walls for patrons to buy. Occasionally there are wine tastings. ✉ *110 Main St.* ☎ *978/281–3680.*

$$ 🏨 **Cape Ann's Marina Resort.** This year-round hotel and spa less than a mile from Gloucester comes alive in summer. A restaurant, whale-watch boat, and deep-sea fishing excursions are available from the premises. The rooms all have balconies and water views. Be sure to confirm that you're getting one of the renovated rooms when you book—the rooms

that didn't get refreshed are in dire need of updating.**Pros:** guests get a free river cruise during summer. **Cons:** "resort" is a bit of a misnomer, as the hotel is surrounded by parking lots; expect motel quality. **TripAdvisor:** "lights were dim," "watch the boats come and go," "enjoyed the pool." ⊠ *75 Essex Ave.* ☎ *978/283–2116, 800/626–7660* ⊕ *www.capeannmarina.com* ⥱ *31 rooms* ⚇ *In-room: kitchen. In-hotel: restaurant, pool.*

$$ 🏨 **Cape Ann Motor Inn.** On the sands of Long Beach, this three-story, shingled motel has no-frills rooms except for the balconies and ocean views. Half of them have well-furnished kitchenettes. The Honeymoon Suite is pricier but has a full kitchen, fireplace, whirlpool bath, king-size bed, and private balcony. **Pros:** exceptional view from every room; kids under 5 stay free. **Cons:** thin walls; motel quality; summer season can be loud and crowded. **TripAdvisor:** "beds are comfortable," "outdated beach motel," "rooms have a beautiful view." ⊠ *33 Rockport Rd.* ☎ *978/281–2900, 800/464–8439* ⊕ *www.capeannmotorinn.com* ⥱ *30 rooms, 1 suite* ⚇ *In-room: no a/c, kitchen. In-hotel: some pets allowed* ⑩ *Breakfast.*

15

ROCKPORT

41 mi northeast of Boston, 4 mi northeast of Gloucester on Rte. 127.

Rockport, at the very tip of Cape Ann, derives its name from the local granite formations. Many Boston-area structures are made of stone cut from its long-gone quarries. Today the town is a tourist center with a well-marked, centralized downtown that is easy to navigate and access on foot. Unlike typical tourist-trap landmarks, Rockport's shops sell quality arts, clothing, and gifts, and its restaurants serve seafood or home-baked cookies rather than fast food. Walk past shops and colorful clapboard houses to the end of Bearskin Neck for an impressive view of the Atlantic Ocean and the old, weather-beaten lobster shack known as "Motif No. 1" because of its popularity as a subject for amateur painters and photographers.

ESSENTIALS

Visitor Information Rockport Chamber of Commerce ⊠ *33 Commercial St., Gloucester* ☎ *978/546–6575* ⊕ *www.rockportusa.com.*

WHERE TO EAT AND STAY

$$ ✕ **Brackett's Ocean View.** A big bay window in this quiet, homey restaurant provides an excellent view across Sandy Bay. The menu includes chowders, fish cakes, and other seafood dishes. ⊠ *25 Main St.* ☎ *978/546–2797* ⊙ *Closed Mon. and Tues. and Nov.–mid-Apr.*

SEAFOOD

$$ ✕ **The Greenery Restaurant and Café.** This spot has become a local institution because it is one of Rockport's only restaurants open year-round. In-season, the second floor opens to accommodate the boom of tourists. Stop in for a sandwich or pastry from the bakery or dine in the back room surrounded by bay windows overlooking the harbor. Breakfast is served daily until 4 pm. ⊠ *15 Dock Sq.* ☎ *978/546–9593.*

AMERICAN

$$ 🏨 **Addison Choate Inn and Periwinkle Cottage.** Just a minute's walk from

★ both the center of Rockport and the train station, this 1851 inn sits in a prime location. The sizable and beautifully decorated rooms have their share of antiques and local seascape paintings, as well as pine floors and large bathrooms; the Captain's Room contains a canopy bed, handmade quilts, and Oriental rugs. In the third-floor suite huge windows look out over the rooftops to the sea. Two spacious stable-house apartments have skylights, cathedral ceilings, and exposed wood beams. Rates include afternoon tea. **Pros:** proximity to the ocean, shopping, and train station. **Cons:** only one bedroom on the first floor. **TripAdvisor:** "cozy, friendly, and accomodating," "rooms are spacious and immaculate," "welcoming host." ⊠ *49 Broadway* ☎ *978/546–7543, 800/245–7543* ⊕ *www. addisonchoateinn.com* ↴ *7 rooms, 2 suites apartments* ⌂ *In-room: no TV, Wi-Fi. In-hotel: restaurant* ¶○¶ *Breakfast.*

$ | ⊞ **Sally Webster Inn.** This inn was named for a member of Hannah Jump-
Fodor's Choice | er's "Hatchet Gang," teetotalers who smashed up the town's liquor
★ | stores in 1856 and turned Rockport into the dry town it remains today. Sally lived in this house for much of her life, and the poshly decorated guest rooms are named for members of her family. Caleb's Room is a romantic retreat with a four-poster bed and floral quilts, and William's Room has a crisply nautical theme. Other rooms have wide-board pine floors, nonworking brick fireplaces, rocking chairs, and four-poster, brass, or canopy beds. **Pros:** homey atmosphere in an excellent location with attentive staff. **Cons:** only two rooms have fireplaces. **TripAdvisor:** "great service and friendly staff," "innkeepers were very hospitable," "great homemade breakfasts." ⊠ *34 Mt. Pleasant St.* ☎ *978/546–9251, 877/546–9251* ⊕ *www.sallywebster.com* ↴ *7 rooms* ⌂ *In-room: Wi-Fi. In-hotel: business center* ⊙ *Closed Jan.* ¶○¶ *Breakfast.*

ESSEX

35 mi northeast of Boston, 12 mi west of Rockport.

The small seafaring town of Essex, once an important shipbuilding center, is surrounded by salt marshes and is filled with antiques stores and seafood restaurants.

GETTING HERE AND AROUND

Head west out of Cape Ann on Route 128, turning north on Route 133.

ESSENTIALS

Visitor Information **Escape to Essex** ⊕ *www.visitessexma.com.*

EXPLORING

Ⓒ **Essex Shipbuilding Museum.** At what is still an active shipyard, this museum traces the evolution of the American schooner, which was first created in Essex. The museum sometimes offers shipbuilding demonstrations. One-hour tours take in the museum's many buildings and boats, especially the *Evelina M. Goulart*—one of only seven remaining Essex-built schooners. ⊠ *66 Main St.(Rte. 133)* ☎ *978/768–7541* ⊕ *www.essexshipbuildingmuseum.org* ⊠ *$7* ⊙ *June–Oct., Wed.–Sun. 10–5; Nov.–May, weekends 10–5.*

SHOPPING

Chebacco Antiques. Open every weekend, this shop concentrates on lighting and country furniture, as well as Staffordshire plates and sterling silver. ⊠ *38 Main St.* ☎ *978/768–7371.*

Head to Woodsman's of Essex for classic New England seafood.

Howard's Flying Dragon Antiques. On weekends come here for antique statuary and glass. ✉ *136 Main St.* ☎ *978/768–7282.*

WHERE TO EAT

$$
SEAFOOD
Fodor'sChoice
★

✕**Woodman's of Essex.** According to local legend, this is where Lawrence "Chubby" Woodman invented the first fried clam back in 1916. Today this sprawling wooden shack with indoor booths and outdoor picnic tables is *the* place for seafood in the rough. Besides fried clams, you can tuck into clam chowder, lobster rolls, or the popular "down-river" lobster combo. ✉ *121 Main St.(Rte. 133)* ☎ *978/768–2559, 800/649–1773* ⊕ *www.woodmans.com.*

IPSWICH

30 mi north of Boston, 6 mi northwest of Essex.

Quiet little Ipswich, settled in 1633 and famous for its clams, is said to have more 17th-century houses standing and occupied than any other place in America; more than 40 were built before 1725. Information and a booklet with a suggested walking tour are available at the **Ipswich Visitor Information Center.**

ESSENTIALS

Visitor Information Ipswich Visitor Information Center ✉ 36 S. Main St. ☎ 978/356–8540 ⊕ www.ipswichma.com.

EXPLORING

Great House at Castle Hill. This 59-room Stuart-style mansion, built in 1927 for Richard Crane—of the Crane plumbing company—and his family, is part of the Crane Estate, a stretch of more than 2,100 acres along the Essex and Ipswich rivers, encompassing Castle Hill, Crane Beach, and the Crane Wildlife Refuge. Although the original furnishings were sold at auction, the mansion has been elaborately refurnished in period style; photographs in most of the rooms show their original appearance. The Great House is open for one-hour tours and also hosts concerts and other events. ⊠ *Argilla Rd.* ☎ *978/356–4351* ⊕ *www.thetrustees.org* ✉ *$8 per car weekends, Monday holidays, and Memorial Day to Labor Day; $5 per car at other times; 50% discount after 3 pm. Tours $10* ☉ *Memorial Day–Oct., Wed.–Sat.; call for hrs.*

SPORTS AND THE OUTDOORS

★ **Crane Beach.** Crane Beach, one of New England's most beautiful beaches, is a sandy, 4-mi-long stretch backed by dunes and a nature trail. Public parking is available, but on a nice summer weekend it's usually full before lunch. There are lifeguards and changing rooms. Check ahead before visiting mid-July to early August, when greenhead flies terrorize sunbathers. ■TIP→ **The Ipswich Essex Explorer bus runs between the Ipswich train station and Crane Beach weekends and holidays from June to September; the $5 pass includes round-trip bus fare and beach admission. Contact the Ipswich Visitor Information Center for information.** ⊠ *Argilla Rd.* ☎ *978/356–4354* ⊕ *www.thetrustees.org* ✉ *$2 on foot; additional charges apply if you arrive by car. Check Web site for details. Parking $15 weekdays, $25 weekends mid-May–early Sept.; $7 early Sept.–mid-May* ☉ *Daily 8–sunset.*

HIKING   **Ipswich River Wildlife Sanctuary.** The Massachusetts Audubon Society's Ipswich River Wildlife Sanctuary has trails through marshland hills, where there are remains of early colonial settlements as well as abundant wildlife. Make sure to grab some birdseed and get a trail map from the office. Enjoy bridges, man-made rock structures, and other surprises on the Rockery Trail. ⊠ *87 Perkins Row, southwest of Ipswich, 1 mi off Rte. 97, Topsfield* ☎ *978/887–9264* ⊕ *www.massaudubon.org* ✉ *$4* ☉ *Office May–Oct., Tues.–Fri. 9–4, weekends 9–5; Nov.–Apr., Tues.–Sun. 9–4. Trails Tues.–Sun. dawn–dusk.*

WHERE TO EAT

$$ ✕ **Clam Box.** Shaped like a giant fried clam box, this small roadside stand
SEAFOOD   is the best place to sample Ipswich's famous bivalves. Since 1938 locals
Fodor'sChoice   and tourists have been lining up for clams, oysters, scallops, and onion
★   rings. ⊠ *246 High St.(Rte. 1A)* ☎ *978/356–9707* ⊕ *www.ipswichma.com/clambox* ♠ *Reservations not accepted* ▬ *No credit cards* ☉ *Closed mid-Dec.–Feb.*

¢   ✕ **Stone Soup Café.** This cheery café provides consistently good food.
SEAFOOD   Excellent breakfasts include omelets, French toast and assorted pancakes; lunch features chowders, pot roast, or delicious Cuban sandwiches. Dinner can include lobster bisque, porcini ravioli, or whatever contemporary fare the chef is inspired to cook from the day's farm-stand finds. ⊠ *141 High St., off Rte. 1A* ☎ *978/356–4222* ▬ *No credit cards* ☉ *No dinner Mon.–Wed., breakfast but no lunch Sun.*

NEWBURYPORT

38 mi north of Boston, 12 mi north of Ipswich on Rte. 1A.

Newburyport's High Street is lined with some of the finest examples of Federal-period (roughly, 1790–1810) mansions in New England. The city was once a leading port and shipbuilding center; the houses were built for prosperous sea captains. Although Newburyport's maritime significance ended with the decline of the clipper ships, the town was revived in the 1970s. Today the town bustles with shops, restaurants, galleries, and a waterfront park and boardwalk. The civic improvements have been matched by private restorations of the town's housing stock, much of which dates from the 18th century, with a scattering of 17th-century homes in some neighborhoods.

Newburyport is walker-friendly, with well-marked restrooms and free parking all day down by the water.

A stroll through the **Waterfront Park & Promenade** offers a view of the harbor as well as the fishing and pleasure boats that moor here. A causeway leads from Newburyport to a narrow piece of land known as Plum Island, which harbors a summer colony (rapidly becoming year-round) at one end.

15

EXPLORING

Custom House Maritime Museum. Built in 1835 in Greek Revival style, this museum contains exhibits on maritime history, ship models, tools, and paintings. ✉ *25 Water St.* ☎ *978/462–8681* ⊕ *www.customhousemaritimemuseum.org* 🗐 *$7* ⊙ *Mid-May–mid-Dec., Tues.–Sat. 10–4, Sun. noon–4.*

SPORTS AND THE OUTDOORS

Parker River National Wildlife Refuge. On Plum Island, this 4,662-acre refuge of salt marsh, freshwater marsh, beaches, and dunes is one of the few natural barrier beach–dune–salt marsh complexes left on the Northeast coast. Here you can bird-watch, fish, swim, and pick plums and cranberries. The refuge is a popular place in summer, especially on weekends; cars begin to line up at the gate before 7 am. There's no restriction on the number of people using the beach, but only a limited number of cars are let in; no pets are allowed in the refuge. ✉ *6 Plum Island Tpke.* ☎ *978/465–5753* ⊕ *www.fws.gov/northeast/parkerriver* 🗐 *$5 per car, bicycles and walk-ins $2* ⊙ *Daily dawn–dusk. Beach usually closed during nesting season in spring and early summer.*

Fodor's Choice ★ **Salisbury Beach State Reservation.** Relax at the long sandy beach, or play at the amusement area and nearby arcades. From Newburyport center, follow Bridge Road north, take a right on Beach Road, and follow it until you reach State Reservation Road. ✉ *Rte. 1A, 5 mi northeast of Newburyport, Salisbury* ☎ *978/462–4481* ⊕ *www.mass.gov/dcr/parks/northeast/salb.htm* 🗐 *Beach free, parking $7.*

NIGHTLIFE

Grog. The Grog hosts blues, rock bands, and salsa lessons several nights weekly. ✉ *13 Middle St.* ☎ *978/465–8008* ⊕ *www.thegrog.com.*

Dip a toe in the ocean at Salisbury Beach.

SHOPPING

Todd Farm Flea Market. A New England tradition since 1971, the Todd Farm Flea Market features up to 240 vendors from all over New England and New York. It's open every Sunday from mid-April through late November, though its busiest months are May, September, and October. Merchandise varies from antique furniture, clocks, jewelry, recordings, and tools to fishing rods, golf accessories, honey products, cedar fencing, vintage toys, and seasonal plants and flowers. Antiques hunters often arrive before the sun comes up for the best deals. ⊠ *285 Main St., Rt. 1A, Rowley* ☎ *978/948–3300* ⊕ *www.toddfarm.com* ◷ *Apr.–Nov., Sun. 5 am–3 pm.*

WHERE TO EAT AND STAY

$$$
SEAFOOD
✕ **Glenn's Restaurant & Cool Bar.** A block from the waterfront parking lot, Glenn's offers creative combinations from around the world, with the occasional New England twist. The ever-changing menu might include sesame-crusted yellowfin tuna or house-smoked baby-back ribs. There's live jazz or blues on Sunday. ⊠ *44 Merrimac St.* ☎ *978/465–3811* ⊕ *www.glennsrestaurant.com* ◷ *Closed Mon. No lunch.*

$$
★
▣ **Clark Currier Inn.** Once the home of the 19th-century sea captain Thomas March Clark, this 1803 Federal mansion has been beautifully restored. Guest rooms are spacious and furnished with antiques. Rates include continental breakfast and afternoon tea. **Pros:** easy to find, it is close to shopping and the oceanfront; good for couples looking for a peaceful and quiet experience. **Cons:** children under 10 not allowed; rooms can get hot in summer. **TripAdvisor:** "great place to stay," "well maintained historic home," "cute and quiet but small and stuffy." ⊠ *45*

Green St. ☎ *978/465–8363* ⊕ *www.clarkcurrierinn.com* ↩ *8 rooms* ⌂ *In-room: no TV. In-hotel: some age restrictions* |◎| *Breakfast.*

SOUTH OF BOSTON

People from all over the world travel south of Boston to visit Plymouth for a glimpse into the country's earliest beginnings. The two main stops are the Plimoth Plantation, which re-creates the everyday life of the Pilgrims; and the *Mayflower II,* which gives you an idea of how frightening the journey across the Atlantic must have been. As you may guess, November in Plymouth brings special events focused on Thanksgiving. Farther south, New Bedford recalls the world of whaling.

EN ROUTE

While driving from Boston to Plymouth, you can easily make a stop at **Quincy,** where sites pay tribute to the nation's second and sixth presidents.

15

Adams National Historic Park. The Adams National Historic Park contains the birthplaces, homes, and graves of both John Adams and his son John Quincy Adams. You can stop by for a guided visit or see it as part of a trolley tour of the property and family church. ⊠ *Carriage house, 135 Adams St., ; visitor center and bookstore, 1250 Hancock St., Quincy* ☎ *617/770–1175* ⊕ *www.nps.gov/adam* 🖂 *$5* ⊙ *Tours 9:15–3:15 daily mid-Apr.–mid-Nov.*

PLYMOUTH

40 mi south of Boston.

On December 26, 1620, 102 weary men, women, and children disembarked from the *Mayflower* to found the first permanent European settlement north of Virginia. Today Plymouth is characterized by narrow streets, clapboard mansions, shops, antiques stores, and a scenic waterfront. To mark Thanksgiving, the town holds a parade, historic-house tours, and other activities. Historic statues dot the town, including depictions of William Bradford, Pilgrim leader and governor of Plymouth Colony for more than 30 years, on Water Street; a Pilgrim maiden in Brewster Gardens; and Massasoit, the Wampanoag chief who helped the Pilgrims survive, on Carver Street.

ESSENTIALS

Visitor Information Plymouth Visitor Information Center ⊠ *170 Water St., at Hwy. 44* ☎ *508/747–7533, 800/872–1620* ⊕ *www.visit-plymouth.com.*

EXPLORING

★ **Mayflower II.** This seaworthy replica of the 1620 *Mayflower* was built in England through research and a bit of guesswork, then sailed across the Atlantic in 1957. As you explore the interior and exterior of the ship, sailors in modern dress answer your questions about both the reproduction and the original ship, while costumed guides provide a 17th-century perspective. Plymouth Rock is nearby. ⊠ *State Pier* ☎ *508/746–1622* ⊕ *www.plimoth.org/features/mayflower-2* 🖂 *$10, $28 with admission to Plimoth Plantation* ⊙ *Late Mar.–Nov., daily 9–5.*

National Monument to the Forefathers. The largest freestanding granite statue in the United States, this allegorical monument stands high on a grassy hill. Designed by Hammet Billings of Boston in 1854 and dedicated in 1889, it depicts Faith, surrounded by Liberty, Morality, Justice, Law, and Education, and includes scenes from the Pilgrims' early days in Plymouth. ⊠ *Allerton St.*

Pilgrim Hall Museum. From the waterfront sights it's a short walk to one of the country's oldest public museums. Established in 1824, Pilgrim Hall Museum transports you back to the time of the Pilgrims' landing with objects carried by those weary travelers to the New World. Included are a carved chest, a remarkably well-preserved wicker cradle, Myles Standish's sword, John Alden's Bible, American Indian artifacts, and the remains of the *Sparrow Hawk*, a sailing ship that was wrecked in 1626. ⊠ *75 Court St.(Hwy. 3A)* ☎ *508/746–1620* ⊕ *www.pilgrimhall. org* ✉ *$8* ☉ *Feb.–Dec., daily 9:30–4:30.*

☾
Fodor's Choice
★

Plimoth Plantation. Over the entrance to this popular attraction is the caution: You are now entering 1627. Believe it. Against the backdrop of the Atlantic Ocean, and 3 mi south of downtown Plymouth, this Pilgrim village has been carefully re-created, from the thatch roofs, cramped quarters, and open fireplaces to the long-horned livestock. Throw away your preconception of white collars and funny hats; through ongoing research, the Plimoth staff has developed a portrait of the Pilgrims that's more complex than the dour folk in school textbooks. Listen to the accents of the "residents," who never break out of character. You might see them plucking ducks, cooking rabbit stew, or tending gardens. Feel free to engage them in conversation about their life, but expect only curious looks if you ask about anything that happened after 1627. "Thanksgiving: Memory, Myth & Meaning," an exhibit in the visitor center, offers a fresh perspective on the 1621 harvest celebration that is now known as "the first Thanksgiving." Note that there's not a lot of shade here in summer. ⊠ *137 Warren Ave.(Hwy. 3A)* ☎ *508/746–1622* ⊕ *www.plimoth.org* ✉ *$24, $28 with Mayflower II* ☉ *Late Mar.–Nov., daily 9–5.*

★   **Plymouth Rock.** This landmark rock, just a few dozen yards from the *Mayflower II*, is popularly believed to have been the Pilgrims' stepping-stone when they left the ship. Given the stone's unimpressive appearance—it's little more than a boulder—and dubious authenticity (as explained on a nearby plaque), the grand canopy overhead seems a trifle ostentatious.

Sparrow House. Built in 1640, this is Plymouth's oldest structure. It is among several historic houses in town that are open for visits. You can peek into a pair of rooms furnished in the spartan style of the Pilgrims' era. The contemporary crafts gallery also on the premises seems somewhat incongruous, but the works on view are of high quality. ⊠ *42 Summer St.* ☎ *508/747–1240* ⊕ *www.sparrowhouse.com* ✉ *House $2, gallery free* ☉ *Open daily 10–5.*

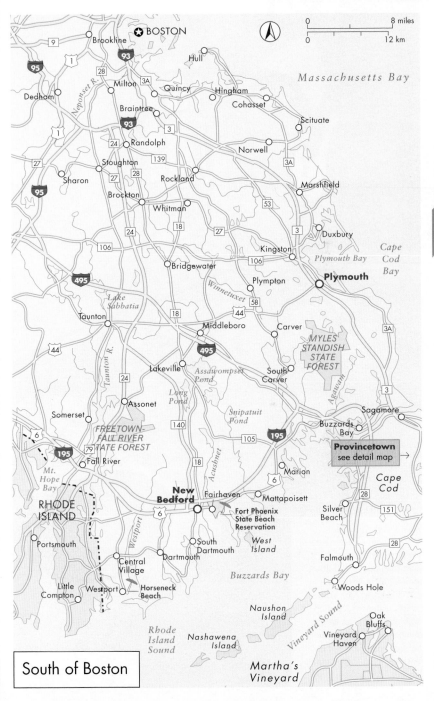

South of Boston

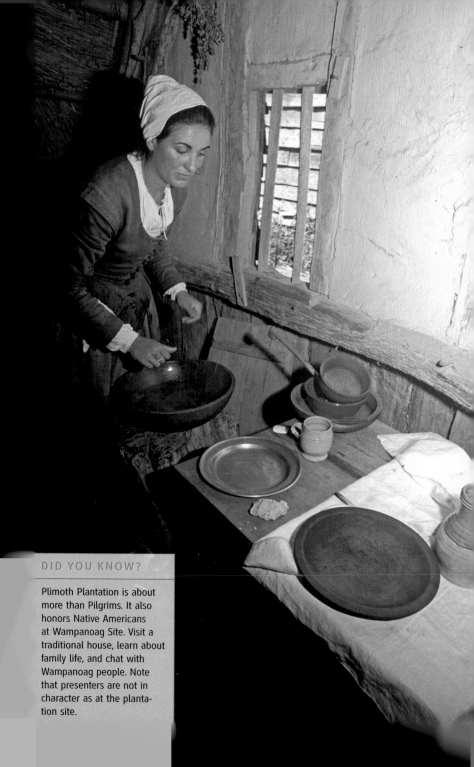

WHERE TO EAT AND STAY

$$ ✕ **Blue-eyed Crab Grille & Raw Bar.** Grab a seat on the outside deck over-
SEAFOOD looking the water at this friendly, somewhat funky (plastic fish dan-
gling from the ceiling), fresh-fish shack. If the local Island Creek raw
oysters are on the menu, go for them! Otherwise start with thick crab
bisque full of hunks of floating crabmeat or the steamed mussels. Din-
ner entrées include seafood stew with chorizo and sweet potatoes and
the classic fish-and-chips. Locals come for the brunch specials, too,
like grilled shrimp and poached eggs over red-pepper grits, the lobster
omelet, and banana-ginger pancakes. ⊠ *170 Water St.* ☎ *508/747–6776*
⊕ *www.blueeyedcrab.com.*

$ 🏨 **Best Western Cold Spring.** Walk to the waterfront and downtown Plym-
outh from this clean, family-friendly, two-story motel. Rooms, some
with balconies and ocean views, are minimalist, with white walls, dark
carpeted floors, and contemporary furniture. **Pros:** half-mile from Plym-
outh Rock and *Mayflower II;* some of the best wallet-pleasing rates in
the area; friendly owners. **Cons:** basic rooms without much character.
TripAdvisor: "comfy hotel with a welcoming vibe," "just a few min-
utes from the waterfront," "room was very clean." ⊠ *188 Court St.*
☎ *508/746–2222, 800/678–8667* ⊕ *www.bestwesternmassachusetts.*
com ⥱ *56 rooms* ⚭ *In-room: Internet. In-hotel: pool, laundry facilities,*
business center, parking.

$$ 🏨 **John Carver Inn & Spa.** This three-story colonial-style redbrick building is steps from Plymouth's main attractions. The public rooms are
lavish, with period furnishings and stylish drapes. The guest rooms
include six "environmentally sensitive" options with filtered air and
water and four-poster beds; others are a bit dark and drab. The suites
have fireplaces and whirlpool baths. There's also an indoor pool with a
Mayflower ship model and a waterslide. **Pros:** waterfront setting. **Cons:**
pool is noisy and often overcrowded; some rooms need updating. **Trip-**
Advisor: "wonderful breakfast," "close to the center of Plymouth,"
"would definitely stay here again." ⊠ *25 Summer St.* ☎ *508/746–7100,*
800/274–1620 ⊕ *www.johncarverinn.com* ⥱ *74 rooms, 6 suites* ⚭ *In-*
room: Wi-Fi. In-hotel: restaurant, bar, pool, gym, spa, laundry facili-
ties, parking.

NEW BEDFORD

45 mi southwest of Plymouth, 50 mi south of Boston.

In 1652 colonists from Plymouth settled in the area that now includes
the city of New Bedford. The city has a long maritime tradition, beginning as a shipbuilding center and small whaling port in the late 1700s.
By the mid-1800s it had developed into a center of North American
whaling. Today New Bedford has the largest fishing fleet on the East
Coast. Although much of the town is industrial, the restored historic
district near the water is a delight. It was here that Herman Melville set
his masterpiece, *Moby-Dick,* a novel about whaling.

ESSENTIALS

Visitor Information New Bedford Office of Tourism ✉ *Waterfront Visitor Center, Pier 3* ☎ *800/508–5353* ⊕ *www.newbedford-ma.gov/Tourism/ DestinationNB/visitorcenter.html.*

EXPLORING

☺ **New Bedford Whaling Museum.** Established in 1903, this is the world's largest museum of its kind. A highlight is the skeleton of a 66-foot blue whale, one of only three on view anywhere. An interactive exhibit lets you listen to the underwater sounds of whales, dolphins, and other sea life—plus the sounds of a thunderstorm and a whale-watching boat—as a whale might hear them. You can also peruse the collection of scrimshaw, visit exhibits on regional history, and climb aboard an 89-foot, half-scale model of the 1826 whaling ship *Lagoda*—the world's largest ship model. A small chapel across the street from the museum is the one described in *Moby-Dick.* ✉ *18 Johnny Cake Hill* ☎ *508/997–0046* ⊕ *www.whalingmuseum.org* ☜ *$10* ☾ *Jan.–May, Mon.–Sat. 9–4, Sun. noon–4; June–Dec., daily 9–5.*

New Bedford Whaling National Historical Park. The city's whaling tradition is commemorated at this park that takes up 13 blocks of the waterfront historic district. The park visitor center, housed in an 1853 Greek Revival building that was once a bank, provides maps and information about whaling-related sites. Free walking tours of the park leave from the visitor center at 10:30, 12:30, and 2:30 in July and August. ✉ *33 William St.* ☎ *508/996–4095* ⊕ *www.nps.gov/nebe* ☜ *Free* ☾ *Daily 9–5.*

Rotch-Jones-Duff House & Garden Museum. For a glimpse of upper-class life during New Bedford's whaling heyday, head one-half mile south of downtown to this 1834 Greek Revival mansion. Amid a full city block of gardens, it housed three prominent families in the 1800s and is filled with elegant furnishings from the era, including a mahogany piano, a massive marble-top sideboard, and portraits of the house's occupants. A free self-guided audio tour is available. ✉ *396 County St.* ☎ *508/997– 1401* ⊕ *www.rjdmuseum.org* ☜ *$5* ☾ *Mon.–Sat. 10–4, Sun. noon–4.*

WHERE TO EAT

$$ ✕ **Antonio's.** Expect the wait to be long and the dining room to be loud, but it's worth the hassle to sample the traditional fare of New Bedford's large Portuguese population at this friendly, unadorned restaurant. Dishes include hearty portions of pork and shellfish stew, *bacalau* (salt cod), and grilled sardines, often on plates piled high with crispy fried potatoes and rice. ✉ *267 Coggeshall St., near intersection of I–195 and Hwy. 18* ☎ *508/990–3636* ▭ *No credit cards.*

PORTUGUESE

$$ ✕ **Davy's Locker.** A huge seafood menu is the main draw at this spot overlooking Buzzards Bay. Choose from more than a dozen shrimp preparations, or a choice of healthful entrées—dishes prepared with olive oil, vegetables, garlic, and herbs. For landlubbers, chicken, steak, ribs, and the like are also available. ✉ *1480 E. Rodney French Blvd.* ☎ *508/992–7359* ⊕ *www.davyslockerrestaurant.com.*

SEAFOOD

PROVINCETOWN, CAPE COD

★ *9 mi northwest of Wellfleet, 62 mi from Sagamore Bridge.*

Incorporated as a town in 1727, Provincetown was for many decades a bustling seaport, with fishing and whaling as its major industries. Fishing is still an important source of income for many Provincetown locals, but now the town ranks among the world's leading whale-watching—rather than whale-hunting—outposts.

Artists began coming here in the late 1890s to take advantage of the unusual Cape Cod light—in fact, Provincetown is the nation's oldest continuous art colony. This bohemian community attracted young writers as well, including Eugene O'Neill (his *Bound East for Cardiff* premiered in a tiny wharf-side East End fish house). Today the town draws artists and gay and lesbian—as well as straight—tourists. You can make a quick day trip to Provincetown from Boston during the summer by traveling there on high-speed ferries from Boston (⇨ *Getting Here and Around, below*).

GETTING HERE AND AROUND

Bay State Cruise Company offers both standard and high-speed ferry service between Commonwealth Pier in Boston and MacMillan Wharf in Provincetown on Cape Cod. High-speed service runs a few times daily from mid-May through September (with a few additional weekend runs through mid-October) and costs $72 round-trip; the ride takes 90 minutes. Standard service runs weekends from late June through early September and costs $33 round-trip; the ride takes three hours. Boston Harbor Cruises runs a fast ferry from Long Wharf in Boston mid-May to mid-October for $79 round-trip. From the State Pier in Plymouth, Capt. John Boats operates a 90-minute ferry daily from late June to Labor Day for $40 round-trip. Year-round flight service by Cape Air connects Provincetown with Boston's Logan Airport.

Driving the 3 mi of Provincetown's main downtown thoroughfare, Commercial Street, in season could take forever, and parking is not widely available. Many visitors opt to walk or bike the downtown area. Shuttles are available to out-oaf-town beaches and the National Seashore. The Shuttle, run by the Cape Cod Regional Transit Authority, provides a seasonal (mid-June–mid-Sept.) route from Truro, heading into town, with trips to Herring Cove Beach, Race Point Beach, and the Provincetown Airport. Bikes are accommodated.

ESSENTIALS

Airline Contacts Cape Air ☎ 866/227–3247, 508/771–6944 ⊕ www.flycapeair. com.

Ferry Contacts Bay State Cruise Company ☎ 617/748–1428, 877/783–3779 ⊕ www.baystatecruisecompany.com. **Boston Harbor Cruises** ☎ 617/227–4321, 877/733–9425 ⊕ www.bostonharborcruises.com. **Capt. John Boats** ☎ 508/747–2400, 800/225–4000 ⊕ www.provincetownferry.com. **Plymouth to Provincetown Express Ferry** ☎ 508/747–2400, 800/225–4000 ⊕ www.provincetownferry.com.

Visitor Info Provincetown Chamber of Commerce ⊠ *Information booth, 307 Commercial St., Box 1017, Downtown Center* ☎ 508/487–3424 ⊕ www. ptownchamber.com. **Provincetown Business Guild (gay and lesbian)** ⊠ 3

15

A WHALE OF A TALE

by Steve Larese

WHALING IN NEW ENGLAND TIMELINE

mid-1600s	America enters whaling industry
1690	Nantucket enters whaling industry
1820	*Essex* ship sunk by sperm whale
1840s	American whaling peaked
1851	*Moby-Dick* published
1927	The last U.S. whaler sails from New Bedford
1970s	Cape Cod whale-watching trips begin
1986	Ban on whaling by the International Whaling Commission
1992	Stellwagen Bank National Marine Sanctuary established

Cameras have replaced harpoons in the waters north of Cape Cod. While you can learn about New England's whaling history and perhaps see whales in the distance from shore, a whale-watching excursion is the best way to connect with these magnificent creatures—who may be just as curious about you as you are about them.

Once relentlessly hunted around the world by New Englanders, whales today are celebrated as intelligent, friendly, and curious creatures. Whales are still important to the region's economy and culture, but now in the form of ecotourism. Easily accessible from several ports in Massachusetts, the 842-square-mi Stellwagen Bank National Marine Sanctuary attracts finback, humpback, minke, and right whales who feed and frolic here twice a year during their migration. The same conditions that made the Stellwagen Bank area of the mouth of Massachusetts Bay a good hunting ground make it a good viewing area. Temperature, currents, and nutrients combine to produce plankton, krill, and fish to feed marine mammals.

(opposite) Whaling museum custodian and a sperm whale jaw in the 1930s. (top) Hunted to near extinction, humpbacks today number about 80,000, and are found in oceans worldwide.

ON LAND: MARINE AND MARITIME MUSEUMS

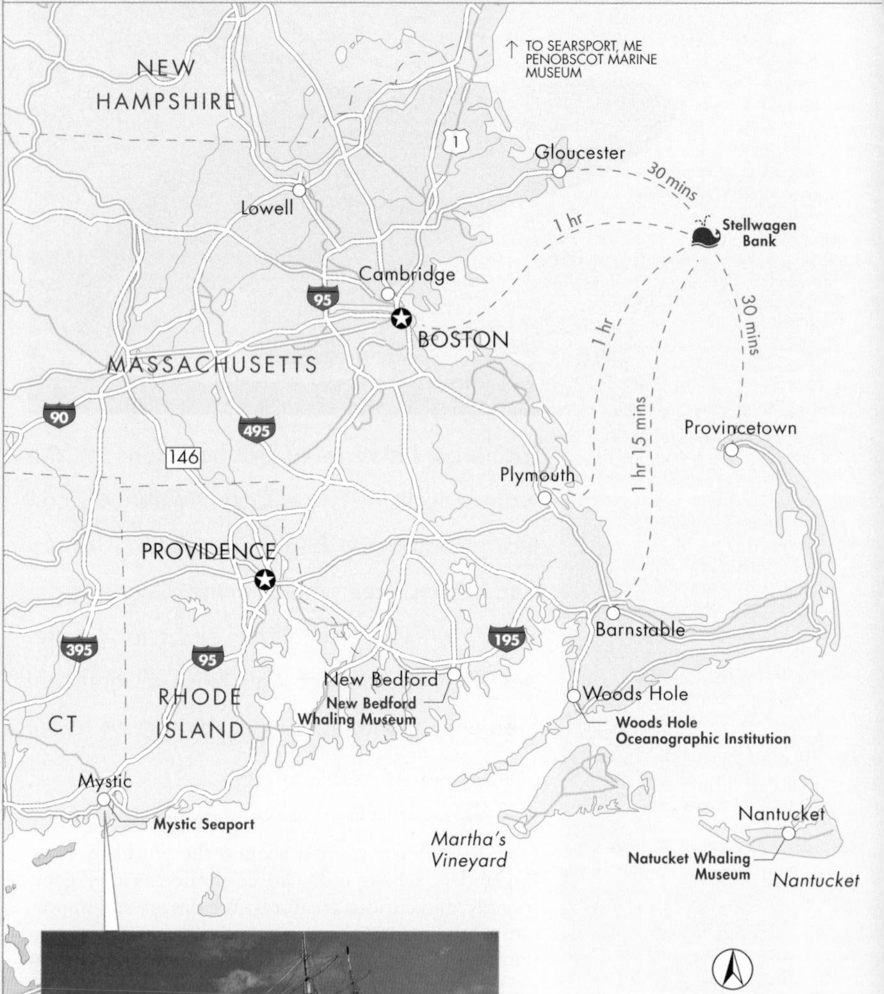

NEW HAMPSHIRE

↑ TO SEARSPORT, ME
PENOBSCOT MARINE
MUSEUM

1

Lowell

Gloucester

30 mins

1 hr

Stellwagen
Bank

Cambridge

95

BOSTON

MASSACHUSETTS

1 hr

30 mins

90

495

Provincetown

146

Plymouth

1 hr 15 mins

PROVIDENCE

Barnstable

395

95

195

RHODE
ISLAND

New Bedford
New Bedford
Whaling Museum

Woods Hole
Woods Hole
Oceanographic Institution

CT

Mystic

Nantucket

Mystic Seaport

Martha's
Vineyard

Natucket Whaling
Museum

Nantucket

0 ————————— 20 miles

0 ————————— 20 km

Whaling ships, like the *Charles W. Morgan* at Mystic Seaport, hunted whales for their baleen and oil.

Even landlubbers can learn about whales and whaling at these top New England institutions.

Nantucket Whaling Museum. This former whale-processing center and candle factory was converted into a museum in 1929. See art made by sailors, including masterful scrimshaw—intricate nautical scenes carved into whale bone or teeth and filled in with ink (⊠ *Nantucket, Massachusetts* ⊕ *www.nha.org*).

★ **New Bedford Whaling Museum.** More than 200,000 artifacts are collected here, from ships' logbooks to harpoons. A must-see is the 89-foot, half-scale model of the 1826 whaling ship *Lagoda* (⊠ *New Bedford, Massachusetts* ⊕ *www.whalingmuseum.org*).

Woods Hole Oceanographic Institution. The Ocean Science Exhibit Center at this famous Cape Cod research facility highlights deep-sea exploration. An interactive exhibit examines the importance of sound to cetaceans, or marine mammals (⊠ *Woods Hole, Massachusetts* ⊕ *www.whoi. edu*).

★ **Mystic Seaport.** Actors portray life in a 19th-century seafaring village at this 37-acre living-history museum. Don't miss the 1841 *Charles W. Morgan*, the world's only surviving wooden whaling ship (⊠ *Mystic, Connecticut* ⊕ *www. mysticseaport.org*).

Penobscot Marine Museum. Maine's seafaring history and mostly shore-whaling industry is detailed inside seven historic buildings (⊠ *Searsport, Maine* ⊕ *www.penobscotbayhistory.org*).

Nantucket Whaling Museum

New Bedford Whaling Museum

THE GREAT WHITE WHALE

Herman Melville based his 1851 classic *Moby-Dick: or, The Whale* on the true story of the *Essex*, which was sunk in 1821 by huge whale; an albino sperm whale called Mocha Dick; and his time aboard the whaling ship *Acushnet*.

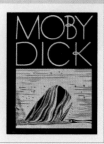

Mystic Seaport

★ = **Fodor's** Choice

AT SEA: WHALE-WATCHING TOURS

COMMON NORTH ATLANTIC SPECIES

0	10	20	30	40	50	60	70 (ft)

Atlantic white-sided dolphin. These playful marine mammals can grow to 7 feet. Note the distinct yellow-to-white patches on their sides. Highly social, dolphins group in pods of up to 60 and hunt fish and squid.

Minke whale. Named for a Norwegian whaler, this smallest of baleen whales grows to 30 feet and 10 tons. It is a solitary creature, streamlined compared to other whales, and has a curved dorsal fin on its back.

Humpback whale. These 40-ton baleen whales are known for their acrobatics and communicative songs. Curious animals, they often approach boats. By blowing bubbles, humpbacks entrap krill and fish for food.

North Atlantic right whale. Called the "right" whales to hunt, this species travels close to shore and is the rarest of all whales—there are only around 300. Note the callosities (rough skin) on their large heads.

Finback whale. The second-largest animal on Earth (after the blue whale, which is rarely seen here), these baleen whales can weigh 50 tons and eat 4,000 lbs of food a day. Look for the distinctive dorsal fin near their fluke (tail).

SEAWORTHY TRIP TIPS

When to Go: Tours operate April through October; May through September are the most active months in the Stellwagen Bank area.

Ports of Departure: Boats leave from Barnstable and Provincetown on Cape Cod, and Plymouth, Boston, and Gloucester, cutting across the Cape Cod bay to the Stellwagen area. Book tours at least a day ahead. Hyannis Whale Watcher in Barnstable, the Dolphin Fleet, Alpha Whale Watch and Captain John's Whale Watch in Provincetown, and the New England Aquarium, Beantown Whale Watch and Boston Harbor Cruises in Boston are just a few of your options. *For more specifics, see Thar She Blows box in this chapter for more information.*

Cost: Around $40. Check company Web sites for coupons.

What to Expect: All companies abide by guidelines so as not to harass whales. Tours last 3 to 4 hours and almost always encounter whales; if not, vouchers are often given for another tour. Passengers are encouraged to watch the horizon for water spouts, which indicate a surfaced whale clearing its blowhole to breathe air. Upon spotting an animal, the boat slows and approaches the whale to a safe distance; often, whales will approach an idling boat and even swim underneath it.

What to Bring: Plastic bags protect binoculars and cameras from damp spray. Most boats have a concession stand, but pack bottled water and snacks. ■ TIP→ Kids (and adults) will appreciate games or other items to pass the time in between whale sightings.

What to Wear: Wear rubber-soled footwear for slick decks. A waterproof outer layer and layers of clothing will help in

Hyannis Whale Watcher Cruises, Cape Cod Bay

varied conditions, as will sunscreen, sunglasses, and a hat that can be secured. Most boats have cabins where you can warm up and get out of the wind.

Comforting Advice: Small seat cushions like those used at sporting events may be appreciated. Consider taking motion-sickness medication before setting out. Ginger candy and acupressure wristbands can also help. If you feel queasy, get some fresh air and focus your eyes on a stable feature on the shore or horizon.

Photo Hints: Use a fast shutter speed, or sport mode, to avoid blurry photographs. Most whales will be a distance from the boat; have a telephoto lens ready. To avoid shutter delay on your point-and-shoot camera, lock the focus at infinity so you don't miss that breaching whale shot.

DID YOU KNOW?

Most boats have a naturalist aboard to discuss the whales and their environment. Many companies contribute to population studies by reporting the individual whales they spot. Whale tails, called flukes, are distinct and used like fingerprints for identification.

CLOSE UP

Thar She Blows

Ships depart regularly for whale-watching excursions from April or May through October, from coastal towns all along the bay. Humpbacks, fin-backs, and minkes feed locally in season, so you're sure to see a few—and on a good day you may see dozens. Bring warm clothing, as the ocean breezes can be brisk; rubber-soled shoes are also a good idea.

Boston Harbor Cruises. The high-speed catamarans of Boston Harbor Cruises glide to the whaling banks in half the time of some other cruises, allowing nearly as much whale time in only a three-hour tour. ⊠ *1 Long Wharf, next to aquarium, Downtown* ☎ *617/227–4321, 877/733–9425* ⊕ *www.bostonharborcruises.com.*

Cape Ann Whale Watch. Cape Ann Whale Watch has run whale-watch tours since 1979. ⊠ *Rose's Wharf, 415 Main St., Gloucester* ☎ *800/877–5110* ⊕ *www.caww.com.*

Captain Bill's Deep Sea Fishing/ Whale Watch. Tours with Captain Bill's Deep Sea Fishing/Whale Watch make use of knowledgeable natural-ists from the Whale Center of New England. ⊠ *24 Harbor Loop, Glouces-ter* ☎ *978/283–6995, 800/339–4253* ⊕ *www.captbillandsons.com.*

Capt. John Boats. Capt. John Boats sends out several daily whale-watch cruises from Plymouth Town Wharf. ⊠ *10 Town Wharf, Plymouth* ☎ *508/746–2643, 800/242–2469* ⊕ *www.captjohn.com.*

New England Aquarium. The New England Aquarium runs daily whale-watching cruises from Central Wharf. The trip, with an aquarium staff whale expert on board, lasts three to four hours. ⊠ *Central Wharf at end of Cen-tral St., Downtown* ☎ *617/973–5206* ⊕ *www.neaq.org.*

Freeman St., Box 421–94, Downtown Center ☎ *508/487–2313, 800/637–8696* ⊕ *www.ptown.org.*

EXPLORING

★ **Commercial Street.** Take a casual stroll by the many architectural styles (Greek Revival, Victorian, Second Empire, and Gothic, to name a few) used in the design of the impressive houses for wealthy sea captains and merchants. The Provincetown Historical Society puts out a series of walking-tour pamphlets available for about $1 each at many shops in town. The center of town is where the crowds and most of the tour-isty shops are. The East End is mostly residential, with an increasing number of nationally renowned galleries; the similarly quiet West End has a number of small inns with neat lawns and elaborate gardens.

QUICK BITES

Spiritus. The local bars close at 1 am, at which point the pizza joint/coffee stand Spiritus becomes the town's epicenter. It's the ultimate place to see and be seen, slice in hand and witty banter at the ready. In the morning, the same counter serves restorative coffee and croissants as well as Häagen-Dazs ice cream. ⊠ *190 Commercial St., Downtown Center* ☎ *508/487–2808* ⊕ *www.spirituspizza.com* ▭ *No credit cards* ⊙ *Closed Nov.–Apr.).*

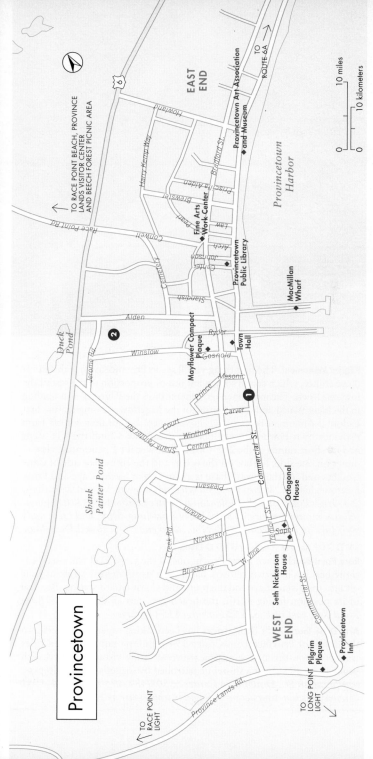

Provincetown

EAST END

WEST END

Provincetown Art Association and Museum

Fine Arts Work Center

Provincetown Public Library

MacMillan Wharf

Mayflower Compact Plaque

Town Hall

Octagonal House

Seth Nickerson House

Pilgrim Plaque

Provincetown Inn

Provincetown Harbor

Duck Pond

Shank Painter Pond

Howland

Harry Kemp Way

Priscilla Alden

Bradford St.

Brewster

Pearl

Law

Conwell

Arch

Center

Johnson

Standish

Alden

Ryder

Winslow

Gosnold

Masonic

Prince

Carver

Court

Winthrop

Central

Pleasant

Franklin

Nickerson

Blueberry

W. Vine

Tremont St.

Soper

Commercial St.

Race Point Rd.

Cemetery

Jerome Rd.

Shank Painter Rd.

Creek Rd.

Commercial St.

TO ROUTE 6A

TO RACE POINT BEACH, PROVINCE LANDS VISITOR CENTER AND BEECH FOREST PICNIC AREA

TO RACE POINT LIGHT

TO LONG POINT LIGHT

Province Lands Rd.

0   10 miles
0   10 kilometers

Commercial Street 1
Pilgrim Monument 2

The neon lights of the Lobster Pot light up Provincetown's Commercial Street.

★ **Pilgrim Monument.** The first thing you'll see in Provincetown is this grandiose edifice, which seems somewhat out of proportion to the rest of the low-rise town. The monument commemorates the Pilgrims' first landing in the New World and their signing of the Mayflower Compact (the first Colonial-American rules of self-governance) before they set off from Provincetown Harbor to explore the mainland. Climb the 116 steps and 60 short ramps of the 252-foot-high tower for a panoramic view—dunes on one side, harbor on the other, and the entire bay side of Cape Cod beyond. At the tower's base is a museum of Lower Cape and Provincetown history, with exhibits on whaling, shipwrecks, and scrimshaw. ⊠ *1, High Pole Hill Rd., Downtown Center* ☏ *508/487–1310* ⊕ *www. pilgrim-monument.org* ✉ *$7* ⊙ *Early Apr.–June, Sept., and Oct., daily 9–5; July and Aug., daily 9–7; Nov., weekends 9–5; closed Dec.–Mar.*

SPORTS AND THE OUTDOORS

Fodor's Choice
★ **Race Point Beach.** Race Point Beach, one of the Cape Cod National Seashore beaches in Provincetown, has a wide swath of sand stretching far off into the distance around the point and Coast Guard station. Because of its position facing north, the beach gets sun all day long. ⊠ *Race Point Rd., east of U.S. 6* ✉ *Parking: $15 per day.*

Fodor's Choice
★ **Art's Dune Tours.** Art's Dune Tours has been taking eager passengers into the dunes of Province Lands since 1946. Bumpy but controlled rides transport you through sometimes surreal sandy vistas peppered with beach grass and along a shoreline patrolled by seagulls and sandpipers. ⊠ *4 Standish St., Downtown Center* ☏ *508/487–1950, 800/894–1951* ⊕ *www.artsdunetours.com* ✉ *Regular tours start at $26.*

WHALE-
WATCHING

Dolphin Fleet. Tours are accompanied by scientists from the Center for Coastal Studies in Provincetown, who provide commentary while collecting data on the whales they've been monitoring for years. They know many of them by name and will tell you about their habits and histories. ⊠ *Ticket office: Chamber of Commerce building at MacMillan Wharf, Downtown Center* ☎ *508/240–3636, 800/826–9300* ⊕ *www. whalewatch.com* ☛ *$39* ☼ *Tours mid-Apr.–Oct.*

NIGHTLIFE

Atlantic House. Atlantic House is the grandfather of the gay nightlife scene. ⊠ *4 Masonic Pl., Downtown Center* ☎ *508/487–3821* ⊕ *www. ahouse.com.*

WHERE TO EAT

$$

AMERICAN

Fodor'sChoice

★

✕ **Devon's.** This unassuming tiny white cottage—with a dining room that seats just 42 lucky patrons—serves up some of the best food in town, judging by the continual crowds that wait for seats. Specialties from the oft-changing menu include brown butter and herb roasted Atlantic halibut or grilled Provincetown day-boat scallops. Be sure to save some room for knockout dessert selections like blackberry mousse over ginger-lemon polenta cake with wild-berry coulis. It's also a good spot for breakfast. ⊠ *401½ Commercial St., Downtown Center* ☎ *508/487–4773* ⊕ *www.devons.org* ☚ *Reservations essential* ☼ *Closed Wed. and Nov.–Apr. No lunch.*

$

SEAFOOD

✕ **Lobster Pot.** Provincetown's Lobster Pot is fit to do battle with all the lobster shanties anywhere (and everywhere) else on the Cape—it's often jammed with tourists, but the crowds reflect the generally high quality. The hardworking kitchen turns out classic New England cooking: lobsters, generous and filling seafood platters, and some of the best chowder around. Eat like a local and try the barbeque pepper shrimp. ⊠ *321 Commercial St., Downtown Center* ☎ *508/487–0842* ⊕ *www. ptownlobsterpot.com* ☚ *Reservations not accepted* ☼ *Closed Jan.*

$$

AMERICAN

Fodor'sChoice

★

✕ **The Mews.** This perennial favorite with magnificent harbor views focuses on seafood and grilled meats with a cross-cultural flair. Sit upstairs at the café and choose from a lighter bistro menu or the regular fine-dining fare. Some popular entrées include roasted vegetable and polenta lasagna with a tomato-olive sauce and Shaking Beef, a Vietnamese-inspired dish with beef tenderloin sautéed with scallions and red onions and a lime–black pepper sauce. The view of the bay from the bar is nearly perfect, and the gentle lighting makes this a romantic spot to have a drink. The restaurant claims its vodka bar is New England's largest, with more than 275 varieties. Sunday brunch is served from Mother's Day to Columbus Day; fall and winter Monday nights get lively with the very popular open-mike coffeehouse. ⊠ *429 Commercial St., East End* ☎ *508/487–1500* ⊕ *www.mews.com* ☼ *No lunch.*

WHERE TO STAY

$$$

Fodor'sChoice

★

🏠 **Brass Key.** One of the Cape's most luxurious small resorts, this meticulously kept year-round getaway comprises a beautifully restored main house—originally a sea captain's home built in 1828—and several other carefully groomed buildings and cottages. Rooms mix antiques with such modern amenities as Bose stereos and DVD players (loaner laptops

15

and iPod docks are also available). A widow's-walk sundeck has a panoramic view of Cape Cod Bay. **Pros:** ultraposh rooms; beautiful and secluded grounds; pool on-site. **Cons:** among the highest rates in town; rooms close to Bradford Street can get a bit of noise; significant minimum-stay requirements in summer. **TripAdvisor:** "staff was very friendly," "room was very spacious," "location was good." ⊠ *67 Bradford St., Downtown Center* ☎ *508/487–9005, 800/842–9858* ⊕ *www.brasskey.com* ⤴ *43 rooms* ⚘ *In-room: safe, Wi-Fi. In-hotel: pool, spa, some age restrictions* ⦿ *Breakfast.*

$$ 🛏 **Snug Cottage.** Noted for its extensive flower gardens and enviable perch atop one of the larger bluffs in town, this convivial Arts and Crafts–style inn dates to 1825 and is decked in smashing English country antiques and fabrics. The oversize accommodations have distinctly British names (Victoria Suite, Royal Scott); most are full suites with sitting areas, and many have wood-burning fireplaces and private outdoor entrances. **Pros:** steps from East End dining and shopping; stunning grounds and gardens; most units are extremely spacious. **Cons:** rooms close to Bradford Street can get some noise; a bit of a walk to West End businesses; top suites aren't cheap. **TripAdvisor:** "charming getaway," "hosts were friendly," "elegant yet cozy and warm." ⊠ *178 Bradford St., east of Downtown Center* ☎ *508/487–1616, 800/432–2334* ⊕ *www.snugcottage.com* ⤴ *3 rooms, 5 suites* ⚘ *In-room: kitchen, Wi-Fi.*

Travel Smart Boston

GETTING HERE AND AROUND

Boston is a mix of old and new that comes together in a seemingly endless array of narrow and twisting one-way streets that radiate away from Boston Harbor in the east. As you travel north, Downtown gives way to the concrete jungle of Government Center, and then to the bustling streets of the Italian-flavored North End. Head generally southwest from here and you'll encounter the Old West End—home of the "Gah-den"—and Beacon Hill. The Back Bay's grid of streets runs southwest from the base of Beacon Hill, and to the south of the Back Bay is the eclectic and historic South End. Head west from here and you'll encounter the retail wonderland of Prudential Center, and then the Fenway, home to many of Boston's art museums, and, of course, the city's beloved Red Sox.

The Charles River serves as a natural dividing line between Boston and its northern neighborhoods and suburbs, including Charlestown and the cities of Cambridge and Somerville. The Four Point Channel separates South Boston—which is, you guessed it, to the south of Boston—and the Dorchester neighborhood from the city proper.

The best form of transportation within Boston or Cambridge/Somerville is the MBTA system, or the T, as it's known locally. Five subway lines—which are actually composed of underground trains, above-ground trolleys/light rail, and buses—run through the entire city and to the outlying suburbs. A series of buses fills in the gaps, and you can ride the T to every major point of interest in the city. A car is only necessary for getting out of town.

■TIP→ Ask the local tourist board about hotel and local transportation packages that include tickets to major museum exhibits or other special events.

■ AIR TRAVEL

Flying to Boston takes about 1 hour from New York, 1½ hours from Washington, D.C., 2¼ hours from Chicago, 3¾ hours from Dallas, 5½ hours from Los Angeles, 7½ hours from London, and 21–22 hours from Sydney (including connection time). Delta, US Airways, and jetBlue have many daily shuttle flights from New York and Washington.

■TIP→ The Boston Convention and Visitor Bureau's Web site, ⊕ *www.bostonusa.com*, has direct links to 19 airlines that service the city. You can book flights here, too.

Airlines and Airports Airline and Airport Links.com (⊕ *www.airlineandairportlinks.com*) has links to many of the world's airlines and airports.

Airline Security Issues Transportation Security Administration (⊕ *www.tsa.gov*) has answers to almost every question that might come up.

AIRPORTS

Boston's major airport, Logan International (BOS), is across the harbor from Downtown, about 2 mi outside the city center, and can be easily reached by taxi, water taxi, or bus/subway via MBTA's Silver or Blue lines. Logan has four passenger terminals, identified by letters A, B, C, and E. A free airport shuttle runs between the terminals and airport hotels. Some airlines use different terminals for international and domestic flights; most international flights arrive at Terminal E. A visitor center in Terminal C offers tourist information. T.F. Green Airport, in Providence, Rhode Island, and the

Manchester Boston Regional Airport in Manchester, New Hampshire, are both about an hour from Boston.

Airport Information Logan International Airport (Boston) (✉ *I–90 east to Ted Williams Tunnel* ☎ *800/235-6426* ⊕ *www.massport. com/logan* Ⓣ *Airport*). **Manchester Boston Regional Airport** (✉ *Off I–293/Rte. 101, Exit 2, Manchester, NH* ☎ *603/624-6556* ⊕ *www. flymanchester.com*). **T.F. Green Airport** (✉ *Off I–95, Exit 13, Providence, RI* ☎ *888/268-7222 or 401/691-2471* ⊕ *www.pvdairport.com*).

FLIGHTS

Airline Contacts Alaska Airlines/Horizon Air (☎ *800/252-7522* ⊕ *www.alaskaair.com*). **American Airlines** (☎ *800/433-7300* ⊕ *www. aa.com*). **Continental Airlines** (☎ *800/523-3273* ⊕ *www.continental.com*). **Delta Airlines** (☎ *800/221-1212* ⊕ *www.delta.com*). **JetBlue** (☎ *800/538-2583* ⊕ *www.jetblue.com*). **Southwest Airlines** (☎ *800/435-9792* ⊕ *www. southwest.com*). **Spirit Airlines** (☎ *800/772-7117* ⊕ *www.spiritair.com*). **United Airlines** (☎ *800/864-8331* ⊕ *www.united.com*). **US Airways** (☎ *800/428-4322* ⊕ *www.usairways. com*).

GROUND TRANSPORTATION
RENTAL CARS AND TAXIS

For recorded information about traveling to and from Logan Airport, as well as details about parking, contact the airport's ground-transportation hotline. Traffic in the city can be maddening; it's a good idea to take public transportation to and from the airport.

When driving from Logan to downtown Boston, the most direct route is by way of the Sumner Tunnel ($3.50 toll inbound; no toll outbound). On weekends, holidays, and after 10 PM weekdays, you can get around Sumner Tunnel backups by using the Ted Williams Tunnel ($3.50 toll inbound; no toll outbound), which will steer you onto the Southeast Expressway south of downtown Boston. Follow the signs to I–93 northbound to head back into the downtown area.

NAVIGATING BOSTON

■ Boston is a walkable city, but since its streets were originally laid out as cow paths leading from the waterfront to spots around the city, they are sometimes tricky to navigate. Be sure to bring a map when you explore.

■ In most cases, address numbers are listed in even numbers on one side of the street and odd number on the opposite side.

■ Boston Common and the Public Garden (which are next to each other) are central spots in the city, and there are maps posted around the park to help direct you around the city. Or, if you're near the waterfront, head toward Quincy Market, where there are also maps to help you navigate.

■ The Financial District and Downtown Crossing are part of Downtown. The streets here have no rhyme or reason and often run only one-way.

■ In general, signage in Boston is hard to come by, especially on roadways. But the city has done a great job of posting street maps at major visitor points throughout the city. If you find yourself wandering around lost, your best bet is to ask for directions. Most residents will take pity on you and help you get your bearings.

■ The public transportation system, the T, offers easy-to-read navigation guides and maps in every station. It stops at all major points of interest throughout the city and just beyond the city limits, too.

■ If you decide to drive in the city (or the greater Boston area), we cannot stress how helpful it is to have a GPS unit in your car. Most rental agencies offer GPS as an option, and this is one place in the country where this upgrade is money well spent.

Taxis can be hired outside each terminal. Fares to and from Downtown should be about $20, including tip. Taxis must pay an extra toll of $5.25 and a $2.75 airport fee when leaving the airport, which will be tacked onto your bill at the end of the trip. (On the way back to the airport, you'll pay the $2.75 fee again, but not the $5.25 toll.) Major traffic jams or taking a longer route to avoid traffic will add to the fare.

Contacts Logan Airport Customer Information Hotline (☎ 800/235–6426). **Metro Cab** (☎ 617/782–5500). **Town Taxi** (☎ 617/536–5000).

SUBWAY

The Blue and Silver lines on the subway, commonly called "the T" (and operated by the MBTA), run from the airport to downtown Boston in about 20 minutes. The Blue Line is best if you're heading to North Station, Faneuil Hall, North End/Waterfront, or Back Bay (Hynes Convention Center, Prudential Center area). Take the Silver Line (which is actually a bus with a dedicated lane) to South Station, Boston Convention and Exhibition Center, Seaport World Trade Center, Chinatown, Theater District, and South End areas. From North and South stations you can reach the Red, Green, or Orange lines, or commuter rail. The T costs $2 for in-town travel if you're paying in cash or $1.70 if you purchase a CharlieCard (a prepaid stored-value card). ⇨ *See Subway, Train, and Trolley Travel below for more information.* Free 24-hour shuttle buses connect the subway station with all airline terminals. Shuttle Bus 22 runs between the subway and Terminals A and B, and Shuttle Bus 33 runs between the subway and Terminals C and E.

Contact MBTA (☎ 800/392–6100, 617/222–3200, 617/222–5146 TTY ⊕ www.mbta.com).

BUSES OR SHUTTLE VANS

Several companies offer shared-van service to many Boston-area destinations. Ace American provides door-to-door service to several major Back Bay and Downtown hotels. (Check their Web sites for a listing of hotels.) Reservations are not required, because vans swing by all terminals every 15 minutes. One-way fares are and $14.50 per person. Easy Transportation is also a shared-van service, which runs from the airport to the Back Bay Hilton, Radisson, and Lenox hotels from 7 AM to 10 PM. Star Shuttle operates shared vans from the airport to the Marriott Copley Place and Sheraton Copley, every hour on the half hour, from 5:30 AM to 11:30 PM. Logan Express buses travel from the airport to the suburbs of Braintree, Framingham, Peabody, and Woburn. One-way fares are $12.

Contacts Ace American (☎ 800/517–2281 ⊕ www.aceamericancoach.com). **Easy Transportation** (☎ 617/869–7760 ⊕ www.easytransportationinc.com). **Logan Express** (☎ 800/235–6426 ⊕ www.massport.com/logan/getti.html). **Star Shuttle** (☎ 617/230–6005 ⊕ www.starshuttleboston.com).

▌ BOAT TRAVEL

ARRIVING BY BOAT

Several boat companies make runs between the airport and downtown destinations. Take the free Shuttle Bus 66 from any terminal to the airport's ferry dock to catch Boston's water taxis.

Rowes Wharf Water Taxi shuttles from Logan Airport to Rowes Wharf, Downtown, for $10 per person ($17 round-trip). It operates daily year-round between 7 AM and 7 PM, and from April through October, 7 AM to 10 PM Monday through Saturday and 7 AM to 8 PM on Sunday.

Harbor Express water taxis (part of the MBTA system) take passengers from Logan Airport to Long Wharf, Downtown ($10), and to Quincy and Hull on the South Shore ($12). Boats leave approximately every 40–45 minutes 6:20 AM–10:30 PM weekdays, and 8:20 AM–10:30 PM weekends.

City Water Taxi has an on-call boat service between the airport and several Downtown locations that operates from

7 AM to 10 PM Monday through Saturday and 7 AM to 8 PM on Sunday year-round. One-way fares to or from the airport are $10, and round-trip tickets are $17. Service to Charlestown, North Station, and the Black Falcon Cruise Ship Terminal is also available for $20 (one-way); if two or more people are traveling together the price drops to $15 per passenger (one-way).

GETTING AROUND BY BOAT

MBTA commuter boat service operates weekdays between several Downtown harbor destinations, Charlestown, and quite a few locations on the South Shore. One-way fares range from $1.70 to $12 depending on destination. Schedules change seasonally, so call ahead.

Information City Water Taxi (☎ 617/422–0392 ⊕ www.citywatertaxi.com). **Harbor Express** (☎ 617/222–6999 ⊕ www.harborexpress.com). **MBTA** (☎ 617/222–3200 ⊕ www.mbta.com). **Rowes Wharf Water Taxi** (☎ 617/406–8584 ⊕ www.roweswharfwatertaxi.com).

▌BUS TRAVEL

ARRIVING BY BUS

Greyhound has buses to Boston from all major cities in North America. Besides its main location at South Station, Greyhound has suburban terminals in Newton and Framingham. Peter Pan Bus Lines connects Boston with cities elsewhere in Massachusetts, Connecticut, New Jersey, New York, and Maryland; their buses now have Wi-Fi.

Concord Coach runs buses between Boston and Concord, New Hampshire; Portland, Maine; and Bangor, Maine. C&J sends Wi-Fi–equipped buses up the New Hampshire coast to Newburyport, Massachusetts; Dover, New Hampshire; Durham, New Hampshire; and Portsmouth, New Hampshire. Concord and C&J both leave from South Station (which is connected to the Amtrak station) and Logan Airport.

COMMUTING WITH A VIEW

The Rowes Wharf Water Taxi offers a stunning glimpse of the city's skyline as it makes seven-minute trips across Boston Harbor between Logan Airport and Rowes Wharf in downtown Boston.

BoltBus offers cheap fares in shiny, new, Wi-Fi-and-electrical-outlet–equipped buses between Boston, New York, Philadelphia, and Washington D.C. (express service between Boston and New York is also offered), starting at just $1 (if you reserve early enough). Megabus also offers low fares, and its Wi-Fi–equipped buses serve New York City (and many other points on the East Coast via New York). BoltBus and Megabus leave from South Station.

If you want to travel in style, the Limo-Liner provides luxury bus service (with television, movies, high-speed Internet, and food-and-drink service) between Boston's Hilton Back Bay and Manhattan's Hilton New York for $89 each way. This service is open to the general public, not just guests of the Hilton. Reservations are a good idea.

Fares and schedules for all buses except LimoLiner are posted at South Station, at many of the tourist kiosks, and online.

Major credit cards are accepted for all buses. You can usually purchase your tickets online.

Bus Information BoltBus (☎ 877/265–8287 ⊕ www.boltbus.com). **C&J** (☎ 800/258–7111 ⊕ www.ridecj.com). **Concord Coach** (☎ 800/639–3317 ⊕ www.concordcoachlines.com). **Greyhound** (☎ 800/231–2222 ⊕ www.greyhound.com). **LimoLiner** (☎ 888/546–5469 or 508/436–7425 ⊕ www.limoliner.com). **Megabus** (☎ 877/462–6342 ⊕ www.megabus.com). **Peter Pan** (☎ 800/343–9999 ⊕ www.peterpanbus.com).

Station Information South Station (⊠ 2 South Station, Atlantic Ave. and Summer St., Downtown Ⓣ South Station).

GETTING AROUND BY BUS

Buses of the Massachusetts Bay Transportation Authority (MBTA) crisscross the metropolitan area and travel farther into suburbia than subway and trolley lines. Buses run roughly from 5:30 AM to 12:30 AM.

At this writing, fares are $1.50 if paying in cash, $1.25 if paying with a prepurchased CharlieCard for trips within the city; you often pay an extra fare for longer lines that run to the suburbs. The SmarTraveler information line provides service updates.

CharlieCards (prepaid stored-value fare cards), sold at all subway terminals, can be purchased with cash or with debit or credit cards. To pay the bus fare, either tap your pass on the fare plate or pay in cash when you enter. Drivers accept dollar bills but don't have change.

Bus Information MBTA (☎ *617/222–3200, 617/222–5146 TTY ⊕ www.mbta.com*). **SmarTraveler** (⊕ *www.smartraveler.com*).

▌ CAR TRAVEL

While having a car can be convenient in Boston if you're planning day trips outside the city limits, driving in the city can be stressful. Roads are confusing and difficult to maneuver on, signage is confusing (or nonexistent), and parking can be hard to come by (especially during major events like the Boston Marathon and Red Sox games).

It's important to plan out a route in advance if you're unfamiliar with the city. There's a profusion of one-way streets, so always keep a detailed map handy. Traveling with a GPS unit (or renting one from your car rental agency) is an even better idea.

Boston motorists are notorious for driving aggressively. Pay extra attention to other drivers, and watch out for those using the emergency breakdown lanes (illegal unless posted otherwise), passing on the right, failing to yield, or turning from the wrong lane.

Unlike the rest of the country, the Boston area has many, many traffic circles. Follow one simple rule, and you'll be fine: cars entering traffic circles must yield to cars that are already in the circle.

GASOLINE

Gas stations are not plentiful in downtown Boston. Try Cambridge Street (behind Beacon Hill, near Massachusetts General Hospital), near the airport in East Boston, along Commonwealth Avenue or Cambridge Street in Allston/Brighton, or off the Southeast Expressway just south of downtown Boston.

Cambridge service stations can be found along Memorial Drive, Massachusetts Avenue, and Broadway. In Brookline, try Commonwealth Avenue or Boylston Street. Gas stations with 24-hour service can be found at many exits off Route 3 to Cape Cod, suburban Route 128 and Interstate 95, and at service plazas on the Massachusetts Turnpike (Interstate 90). Many offer both full- and self-service.

PARKING

Parking on Boston streets is tricky. Some neighborhoods have strictly enforced residents-only rules, with just a handful of two-hour visitors' spaces; others have meters, which usually cost 25¢ for 15 minutes, with a one- or two-hour maximum. Keep a few quarters handy, as most city meters take nothing else.

Parking-police officers are ruthless—it's not unusual to find a ticket on your windshield five minutes after your meter expires. However, most on-street parking is free after 8 PM in the city and on Sunday. Repeat offenders who don't pay fines may find the "boot" (an immovable steel clamp) secured to one of their wheels.

Major public lots are at Government Center and Quincy Market, beneath Boston Common (entrance on Charles Street), beneath Post Office Square, at the Prudential Center, at Copley Place, and off Clarendon Street near the John Hancock Tower. Smaller lots and garages are scattered throughout Downtown, especially around the Theater District and off Atlantic Avenue in the North End. Most are expensive; expect to pay up to $8 an hour or $24 to park all day. The few city garages are a bargain at about $7–$11 per day. Theaters, restaurants, stores, and tourist attractions often provide customers with one or two hours of free parking (always ask if the establishment validates). Most downtown restaurants offer valet parking.

ROAD CONDITIONS

Bostonians tend to drive erratically (to say the least). These habits, coupled with inconsistent street and traffic signs, one-way streets, and heavy congestion, make it a nerve-wracking city to navigate. Many roadways in the city are under construction or in need of repairs. Potholes and manhole covers sticking up above the street are the most common hazards. In general, err on the side of caution, and give yourself a few extra minutes travel time whenever you're driving anywhere in the city.

ROADSIDE EMERGENCIES

Dial 911 in an emergency to reach police, fire, or ambulance services. If you're a member of the AAA auto club, call their 24-hour help bureau.

Emergency Services AAA (☎ 800/222–4357).

RENTING

Rates in Boston begin at about $40 a day and $200 or more a week for an economy car with air-conditioning, automatic transmission, and unlimited mileage. This doesn't include gas, insurance charges, or the 5% tax. All major agencies listed *below* have branches at Logan International Airport.

Major Agencies

Alamo (☎ 877/222–9075 ⊕ www.alamo.com). **Avis** (☎ 800/331–1212 ⊕ www.avis.com). **Budget** (☎ 800/527–0700 ⊕ www.budget. com). **Hertz** (☎ 800/654–3131 ⊕ www.hertz. com). **National Car Rental** (☎ 877/222–9058 ⊕ www.nationalcar.com).

■ SUBWAY, TRAIN, AND TROLLEY TRAVEL

The Massachusetts Bay Transportation Authority (MBTA)—or T when referring to the subway line—operates subways, elevated trains, and trolleys along five connecting lines (as well as commuter rail lines and myriad bus lines that reach other areas of the city and surrounding areas). Trains operate from about 5:30 AM to about 12:30 AM. A 24-hour hotline and the MBTA Web site offer specific information on routes, schedules, fares, wheelchair access, and other matters. Free maps are available at the MBTA's Park Street Station information stand, open daily from 7 AM to 10 PM. They're also available online at ⊕ *www.mbta.com*, which also has a useful trip planner tool.

GETTING AROUND ON THE SUBWAY

"Inbound" trains head into the city center and "outbound" trains head away from downtown Boston. If you get on the Red Line at South Station, the train heading toward Cambridge is inbound. But once you pass the Park Street station, the train becomes an outbound train. The best way to figure out which way to go is to know the last stop on the train, which is usually listed on the front of the train. So from Downtown the Red Line to Cambridge would be the Alewife train and the Green Line to Fenway would be the Boston College or Cleveland Circle train. Each station has a large, useful map posted on the wall that shows the routes that serve that station (with each stop marked).

The Red Line originates at Braintree and Mattapan to the south; the routes join near South Boston and continue to Alewife, the northern portion of Cambridge (near the border with suburban Arlington). The Green Line operates elevated trolleys that dip underground in the city center. The line originates at Cambridge's Lechmere, heads south, and divides into four routes that end at Boston College (Commonwealth Avenue), Cleveland

Circle (Beacon Street, in Brighton), Riverside (in Newton), and Heath Street (Huntington Avenue). Buses connect Heath Street to the old Arborway terminus.

The Blue Line runs weekdays from Bowdoin Square and weeknights and weekends from Government Center to the Wonderland Racetrack in Revere, north of Boston. The Orange Line runs from Oak Grove in north suburban Malden to Forest Hills near the Arnold Arboretum. The Silver Line (a bus line with its own lane) consists of four transit lines. SL1 connects South Station to Logan Airport; SL2 runs between South Station and the Design Center; SL4 connects Dudey Square and South Station, and SL5 runs between Downtown Crossing and Dudley Square, also stopping in Boylston (SL4 and SL5 are actually officially part of the bus system, so the fare on these lines is only $1.50). Park Street Station (on the Common) and State Street are the major downtown transfer points.

FARES AND PASSES

T fares are $2 for adults paying in cash or $1.70 with a prepurchased Charlie-Card. There are CharlieCard dispensing machines at almost every subway stop. Children under age 11 ride free and senior citizens pay 60¢. Fares on the commuter rail—the Purple Line—vary widely; check with the MBTA.

One-day ($9) and seven-day ($15) passes are available for unlimited travel on subways, city buses, and inner-harbor ferries. Buy passes at any full-service MBTA stations. Passes are also sold at the Boston Common Visitor Information Center (⇨ *Visitor Information*) and at some hotels.

TICKET/PASS	PRICE
Single Fare	$2
Day Pass	$9
Weekly Pass	$15
Monthly Unlimited Pass	$59

Contact **MBTA** (☎ *800/392–6100, 617/222–3200, 617/222–5854 TTY ⊕ www.mbta.com*).

■ TAXI TRAVEL

Cabs are available around the clock. You can also call for a cab or find them outside most hotels and at designated cab stands around the city that are marked by signs. Taxis generally line up in Harvard Square, around South Station, near Faneuil Hall Marketplace, at Long Wharf, near Massachusetts General Hospital, and in the Theater District.

A taxi ride within the city of Boston starts at $2.60, and costs 40¢ for each 1/7 mi thereafter. Licensed cabs have meters and provide receipts. An illuminated rooftop sign indicates an available cab. If you're going to or from the airport or to the suburbs, ask about flat rates. (Be aware that you'll also need to pay a $5.25 toll and a $2.75 airport fee when leaving the airport, and a $2.75 airport fee when traveling to the airport in a cab.) Cabdrivers sometimes charge extra for multiple stops. One-way streets often make circuitous routes necessary and increase your cost.

Note that if you're in need of a cab at around 2 AM, when most bars close, hailing one can prove difficult and there will often be a 20- to 30-minute wait if you call for one. Heading to a cab stand is the most efficient late-night choice.

Taxi Companies Independent Taxi Operators Association (ITOA) (☎ *617/338–8294*). **Metro Cab** (☎ *617/782–5500*). **Town Taxi** (☎ *617/536–5000*).

■ TRAIN TRAVEL

Boston is served by Amtrak at North Station, South Station, and Back Bay Station. North Station is the terminus for Amtrak's *Downeaster* service from Boston to New Hampshire and Maine. South Station and Back Bay Station accommodate frequent Northeast Corridor departures to and arrivals from New York, Philadelphia, and Washington, D.C.; Amtrak's pricey high-speed Acela train cuts the travel time between Boston and New York from 4½ hours to 3½ hours. Boston is also the eastern terminus of Amtrak's *Lake Shore Limited,* which travels daily between Boston and Chicago by way of Albany, Rochester, Buffalo, and Cleveland (trains travel to South Station and Back Bay Station). The MBTA runs commuter trains to points south, west, and north. Those bound for Worcester, Needham, Forge Park, Providence, Rhode Island, and Stoughton leave from South Station and Back Bay Station; those to Fitchburg, Lowell, Haverhill, Newburyport, and Rockport operate out of North Station; those to Middleborough/Lakeville, Kingston/Route 3, Plymouth, and Greenbush depart from South Station.

Amtrak tickets, schedules, and reservations are available at Amtrak stations, by telephone, through travel agents, or online. Free maps are available at the MBTA's Park Street Station information stand.

Amtrak ticket offices accept all major credit cards, cash, traveler's checks, and personal checks when accompanied by a valid photo ID and a major credit card. You may pay on board with cash or a major credit card, but a surcharge may apply. MBTA commuter-rail stations generally accept only cash. You may also pay in cash on board commuter trains, but there may be a $1–$2 surcharge.

Amtrak has both reserved and unreserved trains. During peak times, such as a Friday night, get a reservation and a ticket in advance. Trains at nonpeak times are unreserved, with seats assigned on a first-come, first-served basis.

Train Information Amtrak (☎ *800/872–7245* ⊕ *www.amtrak.com*). **Back Bay Station** (✉ *145 Dartmouth St., Back Bay*). **North Station** (✉ *100 Legends Way, Causeway and Friend Sts., North End*). **South Station** (✉ *2 South Station, Atlantic Ave. and Summer St., Downtown* Ⓣ *South Station*).

ESSENTIALS

■ COMMUNICATIONS

INTERNET

Most downtown hotels have started offering either free or fee-based wireless in their rooms and common areas. Call your hotel before arriving to confirm.

There are also a small number of Internet cafés on Newbury Street and scattered Downtown that charge a small fee ($2 and up) depending on how many minutes you use. Most Starbucks locations and locally based coffee shops, such as Espresso Royale, have Wi-Fi service.

Contacts Cybercafes (⊕ www.cybercafes. com) lists more than 4,200 Internet cafés worldwide. **Wi-Fi Free Spot** (⊕ www. wififreespot.com/mass.html) lists hundreds of spots where you can connect to free Wi-Fi around Boston and the state of Massachusetts.

■ DAY TOURS AND GUIDES

Traveling to Boston on a package tour makes it quite convenient for those interested only in hitting the highlights or major historic sites such as the Freedom Trail, Faneuil Hall, the Bunker Hill Memorial, Quincy Market, and Harvard Square. If you're interested in exploring more neighborhoods, a tour will likely not give you access to these.

BOAT TOURS

Boston has many waterways that offer stunning views of the city skyline. Narrated sightseeing water tours generally run from spring through early fall, daily in summer, and on weekends in the shoulder seasons. (Labor Day weekend is often the cutoff point.) These trips normally last ¾–1½ hours and cost about $20. Many companies also offer sunset or evening cruises with music and other entertainment.

The Boston Duck Tours, which give narrated land-water tours on a World War II amphibious vehicle, are particularly popular. After driving past several historic sights, the vehicle dips into the Charles River to offer a view of the Boston skyline. These tours, costing $32 per person, run later than most, through late November (they also offer a handful of weekend tours in December).

June through September, you can relive the golden age of sail aboard the *Liberty Clipper,* a replica two-masted gaff-rigged schooner that operates midday harbor tours and romantic sunset cruises from Long Wharf.

Boston Harbor Cruises and Massachusetts Bay Lines have tours around the harbor. Trips with Boston Duck Tours and the Charles Riverboat Company are along the Charles River Basin.

Fees and Schedules Boston Duck Tours (✉ *Departures from Prudential Center, Huntington Ave., in front of Shaw's supermarket; from New England Aquarium; and from Museum of Science* ☎ 617/267–3825 ⊕ www.bostonducktours.com). **Boston Harbor Cruises** (✉ *1 Long Wharf* ☎ 877/733–9425 or 617/227–4321 ⊕ www.bostonharborcruises. com). **Charles Riverboat Company** (✉ *100 Cambridge Pl., Suite 320, Cambridge* ☎ *617/621–3001* ⊕ www.charlesriverboat.com). *Liberty Clipper* (✉ *67 Long Wharf* ☎ *617/742– 0333* ⊕ www.libertyfleet.com). **Massachusetts Bay Lines** (✉ *60 Rowes Wharf* ☎ *617/542– 8000* ⊕ www.massbaylines.com).

BUS TOURS

Bus tours, which cost around $25 and run daily from mid-March to early November, traverse the main historic neighborhoods in less than four hours. Reserve bus tours at least a day in advance. Boston Private Tours has customized tours in vans or limousines. Brush Hill has more traditional charter bus tours as well as smaller tours, with lots of prepackaged options and add-ons; the 1½-hour narrated tour is popular.

Fees and Schedules Boston Private Tours (✉ *707 Main St.* ☎ *800/620–1136* ⊕ www.

bostonprivatetours.com). **Brush Hill Tours** (✉ *Transportation Bldg., 16 Charles St. S* ☎ *800/343–1328 or 781/986–6100* ⊕ *www. brushhilltours.com*).

THEME TOURS

See how a brewery operates at the Boston Beer Museum & Samuel Adams Brewery; hear spine-tingling tales about Boston's famous cemeteries; or tour (for free) the offices and printing plant of the *Boston Globe*. These tours (and others) are often given a few days a week. Some organizations have special restrictions, such as an age limit for children. Many tours are free, but you'll often need to make a reservation at least a few days in advance (and it's always a good idea to call ahead to confirm schedules).

Beer Tours **Boston Beer Museum & Samuel Adams Brewery** (✉ *Boston Beer Company, 30 Germania St., Jamaica Plain* ☎ *617/368–5080* ⊕ *www.samueladams.com*).

Bike Tours **Boston Bike Tours** (✉ *Meet at Boston Common near Visitor Information Center* ☎ *617/670–0637* ⊕ *www.bostonbiketours. com*).

Children's Tours **Boston by Little Feet** (✉ *Meet at Samuel Adams statue in front of Faneuil Hall* ☎ *617/367– 2345* ⊕ *www.bostonbyfoot.com/tours/ Boston_By_Little_Feet*).

Gardens and Parks Tours **Beacon Hill Garden Club Tours** (✉ *Charles and Beacon Sts., Beacon Hill* ☎ *617/227–4392* ⊕ *www. beaconhillgardenclub.org*). **Boston Park Rangers** (✉ *Parks and Recreation Dept. kiosk in Boston Common* ☎ *617/635–4505* ⊕ *www. cityofboston.gov/parks*).

Movie Tours **Boston Movie Tours** (✉ *Meet at the Boston Common Visitor Center, 147 Tremont St.* ☎ *866/668–4345, option 1* ⊕ *www. bostonmovietours.net*).

TROLLEY TOURS

Narrated trolley tours, which usually cost $36 or so, don't require reservations and are more flexible than bus tours; you can get on and off as you wish. A full trip normally lasts 1½–2 hours. All trolleys run daily, though less frequently off-season. Because they're open vehicles, be sure to dress appropriately for the weather.

Old Town Trolley tours, which usually focuses on history, includes a tour that's 1½-hours and narrated.

Old Town Trolley (✉ *380 Dorchester Ave., South Boston* ☎ *800/868–7482 or 617/269– 7010* ⊕ *www.historictours.com/boston*).

WALKING TOURS

Boston is the perfect city for walking tours, to explore topics ranging from history and literature to ethnic neighborhoods. Most tours cost about $20 and last one to two hours. Guides prefer to keep groups at fewer than 20 people, so always reserve ahead. Several organizations give tours once or twice a day spring through fall and by appointment (if at all) in winter. Others run tours a few days a week, spring through fall.

The Women's Heritage Trail, the Freedom Trail, and the Black Heritage Trail can be completed as self-guided tours. Maps for the Women's Heritage Trail are available online and at the Old State House and the National Park Service Visitor Center. The Boston Common Visitor Information Center has maps of the Freedom Trail, which is indicated with a red line painted on the ground. The Freedom Trail and the Black Heritage Trail can also be completed with a ranger-led group. The Boston and Cambridge Centers for Adult Education lead in-depth educational tours on many topics, most of them centered around art, architecture, and literature.

Harvard Square is the starting point for free student-led campus tours.

Fees and Schedules **Black Heritage Trail** (☎ *617/725–0022* ⊕ *www.afroammuseum. org*). **Boston by Foot** (✉ *77 N. Washington St.* ☎ *617/367–2345* ⊕ *www.bostonbyfoot. com*). **Boston Center for Adult Education** (✉ *122 Arlington St.* ☎ *617/267–4430* ⊕ *www. bcae.org*). **Boston Common Visitor Information Center** (☎ *888/733–2678* ⊕ *www. bostonusa.com*). **Cambridge Center for**

Adult Education (✉ *42 Brattle St., Cambridge* ☎ *617/547–6789* ⊕ *www.ccae.org*). **Freedom Trail** (☎ *617/357–8300* ⊕ *www. thefreedomtrail.org*). **Harvard Campus Tours** (☎ *617/495–1573* ⊕ *www.harvard.edu/visitors*). **Historic New England** (✉ *141 Cambridge St.* ☎ *617/227–3957* ⊕ *www.historicnewengland. org*). **North End Market Tour** (✉ *6 Charter St.* ☎ *617/523–6032* ⊕ *www.northendmarkettours. com*). **National Parks Service Visitor Center** (☎ *617/242–5642* ⊕ *www.nps.gov/bost*). **Women's Heritage Trail** (⊕ *www.bwht.org*).

▌ GEAR

The principal rule on Boston weather is that there are no rules. A cold, overcast morning can become a sunny, warm afternoon—and vice versa. Thus, the best advice on how to dress is to layer your clothing so that you can remove or add garments as needed for comfort. Rain often appears with little warning, so remember to pack a raincoat and umbrella. Because Boston is a great walking city—with some picturesque but uneven cobblestone streets—be sure to bring comfortable shoes. In all seasons, remember it's often breezier (and colder) along the coast; always carry a windbreaker and fleece jacket or sweatshirt to the beach or harbor area.

▌ HOURS OF OPERATION

Banks are generally open weekdays 9–4 or 5, plus Saturday 9 AM–noon or 1 PM at some branches. Public buildings are open weekdays 9–5.

Although hours vary quite a bit, most museums are open Monday through Saturday 9 or 10 AM–5 or 6 PM and Sunday noon–5 PM. Some are closed one day a week, usually Monday.

The major pharmacy chains—Brooks, CVS, and Walgreens—are generally open daily between 7 or 9:30 AM and 8 or 10 PM; independently owned pharmacies usually close earlier. Several pharmacies are open 24 hours a day.

Boston stores are generally open Monday through Saturday 10 or 11 AM–6 or 7 PM, closing later during the holiday-shopping season. Mall shops often stay open until 9 or 10 PM; malls and some tourist areas may also be open Sunday noon–5 or 6 PM.

▌ MONEY

Prices are generally higher in Beacon Hill, the Back Bay, and Harvard Square than elsewhere. You're more likely to find bargains in the North End, Kenmore Square, Downtown Crossing, and Cambridge's Central Square. Many museums have one evening of free admission each week. There are no "happy hours" at any Boston bars due to a state regulation (part of the blue laws) that forbids promotions of discounted liquor.

ITEM	AVERAGE COST
Cup of Coffee	$2
Glass of Wine	$6 and up
Glass of Beer	$3.50 and up
Slice of Pizza	$1.50–$2.50
One-Mile Taxi Ride	$6
Museum Admission	$9–$21

Prices throughout this guide are given for adults. Substantially reduced fees are almost always available for children, students, and senior citizens.

CREDIT CARDS

Throughout this guide, the following abbreviations are used: **AE**, American Express; **D**, Discover; **DC**, Diners Club; **MC**, MasterCard; and **V**, Visa.

Reporting Lost Cards American Express (☎ *800/528–4800* ⊕ *www.americanexpress. com*). **Discover** (☎ *800/347–2683* ⊕ *www. discovercard.com*). **Diners Club** (☎ *800/234–6377* ⊕ *www.dinersclub.com*). **MasterCard** (☎ *800/627–8372* ⊕ *www.mastercard.com*). **Visa** (☎ *800/847–2911* ⊕ *www.visa.com*).

▌RESTROOMS

Public restrooms outside of restaurants, hotel lobbies, and tourist attractions are rare in Boston, but you'll find clean, well-lighted facilities at South Station, Faneuil Hall Marketplace, and the Visitor Information Center on Boston Common.

Find a Loo The Bathroom Diaries (⊕ *www. thebathroomdiaries.com*) is flush with unsanitized info on restrooms the world over—each one located, reviewed, and rated.

▌SAFETY

With their many charming neighborhoods, Boston and Cambridge often feel like small towns. But they're both cities, subject to the same problems plaguing other urban communities nationwide. Although violent crime is rare, residents and tourists alike sometimes fall victim to pickpockets, scam artists, and car thieves. As in any large city, use common sense, especially after dark. Stay with the crowds and walk on well-lighted, busy streets. Look alert and aware; a purposeful pace helps deter trouble wherever you go. Take cabs or park in well-lighted lots or garages.

Store valuables in a hotel safe or, better yet, leave them at home. Keep an eye (and hand) on handbags and backpacks; do not hang them from a chair in restaurants. Carry wallets in inside or front pockets rather than back pockets. Use ATMs in daylight, preferably in a hotel, bank, or another indoor location with security guards.

Subways and trolleys tend to be safe, but it's wise to stay on your guard. Stick to routes in the main Boston and Cambridge tourist areas—generally, the downtown stops on all lines, on the Red Line in Cambridge, on the Green Line through the Back Bay, and on the Blue Line around the New England Aquarium. Know your itinerary, and make sure you get on the right bus or train going in the right direction. Avoid empty subway and trolley cars and lonely station hallways and platforms, especially after 9 PM on weeknights. The MBTA has its own police officers (who patrol stations and monitor them via video); don't hesitate to ask them for help.

▌**TIP→ Distribute your cash, credit cards, IDs, and other valuables between a deep front pocket, an inside jacket or vest pocket, and a hidden money pouch. Don't reach for the money pouch once you're in public.**

▌TAXES

Hotel room charges in Boston and Cambridge are subject to state and local taxes of up to 14.95%.

A sales tax of 7% is added to restaurant and take-out meals, and a sales tax of 6.25% is added to all other goods except nonrestaurant food and clothing valued at less than $175.

▌TIME

Boston is in the Eastern time zone, 3 hours ahead of Los Angeles, 1 hour ahead of Chicago, 5 hours behind London, and 15 hours behind Sydney. Daylight Savings Time is observed. (Clocks are set ahead one hour on the second Sunday in March, when Daylight Savings Time begins; they are set back an hour when Daylight Savings Time ends on the first Sunday in November).

▌TIPPING

In restaurants the standard gratuity is 15%–20% of your bill. Many restaurants automatically add a 15%–20% gratuity for groups of six or more.

Tip taxi drivers 15% of the fare, and airport and hotel porters at least $1 per bag. It's also usual to tip chambermaids $1–$3 daily. Hotel room-service tips vary and may be included in the meal charge. Masseuses and masseurs, hairstylists, manicurists, and others performing personal services generally get a 15%

FOR INTERNATIONAL TRAVELERS

CURRENCY

The dollar is the basic unit of U.S. currency. It has 100 cents. Coins are the penny (1¢), the nickel (5¢), dime (10¢), quarter (25¢), half-dollar (50¢), and the rare golden $1 coin and rarer silver $1. Bills are denominated $1, $5, $10, $20, $50, and $100, all mostly green and identical in size; designs and background tints vary. There is a $2 bill, but it is extremely rare.

CUSTOMS

Information U.S. Customs and Border Protection (⊕ www.cbp.gov).

DRIVING

Driving in the United States is on the right. Speed limits are posted in miles per hour (usually between 55 mph and 75 mph). In small towns and on back roads limits are usually 25 mph to 40 mph. Most states require front-seat passengers to wear seat belts (though back seat passengers should do so as well); children should be in the back seat and buckled up. In major cities rush hours are 7 to 10 AM and 4 to 7 PM. Some freeways have high-occupancy vehicle (HOV) lanes, ordinarily marked with a diamond, for cars carrying two people or more.

Highways are well paved. Interstates—limited-access, multilane highways designated with an "I–" before the number—are fastest. Interstates with three-digit numbers circle urban areas, which may also have other expressways, freeways, and parkways. Limited-access highways sometimes have tolls.

Gas stations are plentiful, except in rural areas and city centers. Most stay open late (some 24 hours). Along larger highways roadside stops with restrooms, fast-food restaurants, and sundries stores are well spaced. State police and tow trucks patrol major highways. If your car breaks down, pull onto the shoulder and wait, or have passengers wait while you walk to a roadside emergency phone (most states). On a cell phone, dial *55.

ELECTRICITY

The U.S. standard is AC, 110 volts/60 cycles. Plugs have two flat pins set parallel to each other.

EMBASSIES

Contacts Australia (☎ 202/558–2216 ⊕ www.austemb.org). Canada (☎ 202/682–1740 ⊕ www.canadianembassy.org). UK (☎ 202/588–7800 ⊕ ukinusa.fco.gov.uk/en).

EMERGENCIES

For police, fire, or ambulance, dial 911 (0 in rural areas).

HOLIDAYS

New Year's Day (Jan. 1); Martin Luther King Day (3rd Mon. in Jan.); Presidents' Day (3rd Mon. in Feb.); Memorial Day (last Mon. in May); Independence Day (July 4); Labor Day (1st Mon. in Sept.); Columbus Day (2nd Mon. in Oct.); Thanksgiving Day (4th Thurs. in Nov.); Christmas Eve and Christmas Day (Dec. 24 and 25); and New Year's Eve (Dec. 31).

MAIL

You can buy stamps and send letters and parcels in post offices. Stamp-dispensing machines can occasionally be found in airports, bus and train stations, office buildings, drugstores, convenience stores, and in ATMs. U.S. mailboxes are stout, dark-blue steel bins; pickup schedules are posted inside the bin (pull the handle). Mail parcels over a pound at a post office.

A first-class letter weighing 1 ounce or less costs 44¢; each additional ounce costs 17¢. Postcards cost 28¢. Postcards or 1-ounce airmail letters to most countries cost 98¢; postcards or 1-ounce letters to Canada or Mexico cost 79¢.

To receive mail on the road, have it sent c/o General Delivery to your destination's main post office. You must pick up mail in person within 30 days with a driver's license or passport for identification.

FOR INTERNATIONAL TRAVELERS CONT'D

Contacts **DHL** (☎ *800/225–5345* ⊕ *www. dhl.com*). **FedEx** (☎ *800/463–3339* ⊕ *www. fedex.com*). **UPS (United Parcel Service)** (☎ *800/742–5877* ⊕ *www.ups.com*). **USPS (United States Postal Service)** (⊕ *www. usps.com*).

PASSPORTS AND VISAS

Visitor visas aren't necessary for citizens of Australia, Canada, the United Kingdom, or most citizens of EU countries coming for tourism and staying for under 90 days. A visa is $100, and waiting time can be substantial. Apply for a visa at the U.S. consulate in your place of residence.

Visa Information **U.S. Department of State** (⊕ *travel.state.gov/visa*).

PHONES

Numbers consist of a three-digit area code and a seven-digit local number. In Boston the area code is 617; surrounding areas use 781, 508, or 978. Within many local calling areas, dial just seven digits. In others, dial "1" first and all 10 digits; this is true for calling toll-free numbers—prefixed by "800," "888," "866," and "877." Dial "1" before "900" numbers, too, but know they're very expensive.

For international calls, dial "011," the country code, and the number. For help, dial "0" and ask for an overseas operator. Most phone books list country codes and U.S. area codes. The country code for Australia is 61, for New Zealand 64, for the United Kingdom 44. Calling Canada is the same as calling within the United States (country code: 1).

For operator assistance, dial "0." For directory assistance, call 555–1212 or 411 (free at many public phones). To call "collect" (reverse charges), dial "0" instead of "1" before the 10-digit number.

Instructions are generally posted on pay phones. Usually you insert coins in a slot (usually 25¢–50¢ for local calls) and wait for a steady tone before dialing. On long-distance calls the operator tells you how much to insert; prepaid phone cards, widely available, can be used from any phone. Follow the directions to activate the card, then dial your number.

CELL PHONES

The United States has several GSM (Global System for Mobile Communications) networks, so multiband mobiles from most countries (except for Japan) work here. It's almost impossible to buy just a pay-as-you-go mobile SIM card in the U.S.—needed to avoid roaming charges—but cell phones with pay-as-you-go plans are available for well under $100. AT&T (GoPhone) and Virgin Mobile have the cheapest with national coverage.

Contacts **AT&T** (☎ *888/333–6651* ⊕ *www. att.com*). **Virgin Mobile** (☎ *888/322–1122* ⊕ *www.virginmobileusa.com*).

tip. Theater ushers, museum guides, and gas-station attendants generally do not receive tips. Tour guides may be tipped a few dollars for good service. Concierges may be tipped anywhere from $5 to $20 for exceptional service, such as securing a difficult dinner reservation or helping plan a personal sightseeing itinerary.

TIPPING GUIDELINES FOR BOSTON	
Bartender	$1–$2 per drink
Bellhop	$1 to $5 per bag, depending on the level of the hotel
Hotel Concierge	$5 or more, if he or she performs a service for you
Hotel Doorman	$1–$2 if he helps you get a cab
Hotel Maid	1$–$3 a day (either daily or at the end of your stay, in cash)
Hotel Room-Service Waiter	$1 to $2 per delivery, even if a service charge has been added
Porter at Airport or Train Station	$1 per bag
Skycap at Airport	$1 to $3 per bag checked (in addition to any airline-imposed fees)
Taxi Driver	15%–20%, but round up the fare to the next dollar amount
Tour Guide	10% of the cost of the tour
Valet Parking Attendant	$1–$2, but only when you get your car
Waiter	15%–20%, with 20% being the norm at high-end restaurants; nothing additional if a service charge is added to the bill
Other	Restroom attendants in more-expensive restaurants expect some small change or $1. Tip coat-check personnel at least $1–$2 per item checked unless there is a fee, then nothing.

▌ VISITOR INFORMATION

Contact the city and state tourism offices for general information, details about seasonal events, discount passes, trip planning, and attraction information. The National Park Service has a Boston office where you can watch an eight-minute slide show on Boston's historic sites and get maps and directions. The Welcome Center and Boston Common Visitor Information Center offer general information. The Cambridge Tourism Office's information booth is in Harvard Square, near the main entrance to the Harvard T stop.

Contacts Boston Common Visitor Information Center (✉ *148 Tremont St. where Freedom Trail begins, Downtown* ☎ *888/733–2678* ⊕ *www.thefreedomtrail.org/visitor/boston-common.html*). **Boston National Historical Park Visitor Center** (✉ *15 State St., Downtown* ☎ *617/242–5642* ⊕ *www.nps.gov/bost*). **Cambridge Tourism Office** (✉ *4 Brattle St., Harvard Sq., Cambridge* ☎ *800/862–5678 or 617/441–2884* ⊕ *www.cambridge-usa.org*). **Greater Boston Convention and Visitors Bureau** (✉ *2 Copley Pl., Suite 105, Back Bay* ☎ *888/733–2678 or 617/536–4100* ⊕ *www.bostonusa.com*). **Massachusetts Office of Travel and Tourism** (✉ *State Transportation Bldg., 10 Park Plaza, Suite 4510, Back Bay* ☎ *800/227–6277 or 617/973–8500* ⊕ *www.massvacation.com*).

ONLINE RESOURCES

Boston.com, home of the *Boston Globe* online, has news and feature articles, ample travel information, and links to towns throughout Massachusetts. The site for Boston's arts and entertainment weekly, the *Boston Phoenix* has nightlife, movie, restaurant, and arts listings. The Bostonian Society answers some frequently asked questions about Beantown history on their Web site. The iBoston page has some wonderful photographs of buildings that are architecturally and historically important. *Bostonist, The Improper Bostonian*, and *WickedLocal* provide a more relaxed (and somewhat irreverent) take on Boston news and information.

All About Boston Boston.com (⊕ *www. boston.com*). **Boston Phoenix** (⊕ *www. bostonphoenix.com*). **Bostonian Society** (⊕ *bostonhistory.org*). **Bostonist** (⊕ *www. bostonist.com*). **iBoston** (⊕ *www.iboston.org*). **The Improper Bostonian** (⊕ *www.improper. com*). **Wicked Local** (⊕ *www.wickedlocal.com*).

Safety **Transportation Security Administration** (*TSA* ⊕ *www.tsa.gov*).

INDEX

PHOTO CREDITS

1, Kindra Clineff. 2-3, Chee-Onn Leong/Shutterstock. 5, Tony the Misfit/Flickr. 8-9, Kindra Clineff. 10, Kindra Clineff. 11 (left), Kindra Clineff. 11 (right), ojbyrne/Flickr. 12, Kindra Clineff. 13 (left), Kindra Clineff. 13 (right), Kindra Clineff. 14, joyosity/Flickr. 15 (left), Jorge Salcedo/iStockphoto. 15 (right), Iwan Baan. 18 (top left), Kindra Clineff. 18 (bottom left), Kindra Clineff. 18 (top right), Copyright Tony Rinaldo images. 18 (bottom right), Kindra Clineff. 19 (top left), Kindra Clineff. 19 (bottom left), Kindra Clineff. 19 (top right), Chee-Onn Leong/Shutterstock. 19 (bottom right), Kindra Clineff. 20, Kindra Clineff. 21 (left), Kindra Clineff. 21 (right), Kindra Clineff. 22, Kindra Clineff. 23, NikiSublime/Flickr. 24, Kindra Clineff. 25, Kindra Clineff. 26, Kindra Clineff. 27 (top left), MCS@flickr/Flickr. 27 (bottom left), Classic Vision / age fotostock. 27 (center), A. H. C. / age fotostock. 27 (top right), cliff1066ô/Flickr. 27 (center right), Classic Vision / age fotostock. 27 (bottom), Kindra Clineff. 28, Kindra Clineff. 29 (top left), Kindra Clineff. 29 (center left), Tony the Misfit/Flickr. 29 (bottom left), Tim Grafft/MOTT. 29 (center bottom), Scott Orr/iStockphoto. 29 (top right), Freedom Trail Foundation. 29 (center right), Kindra Clineff. 29 (bottom right), Kindra Clineff. 30 (top), Kindra Clineff. 30 (bottom), Jim Reynolds/Wikimedia Commons. 31 (top), revjim5000/Flickr. 31 (bottom), Kindra Clineff. 32, Kindra Clineff. Chapter 2: Beacon Hill, Boston Common, and the Old West End: 33, Kindra Clineff. 35, Chee-Onn Leong/Shutterstock. 36, David Eby/Shutterstock. 39, Kindra Clineff. 48, Raymond Forbes / age fotostock. Chapter 3: Government Center and the North End: 51, Kindra Clineff. 53, Biruitorul/ Wikimedia Commons. 54, Kindra Clineff. 57, Jorge Salcedo/iStockphoto. 58, Kindra Clineff. 63, Jorge Salcedo/Shutterstock. Chapter 4: Charlestown: 67, Kindra Clineff. 69, Kindra Clineff. 70, Jorge Salcedo/Shutterstock. 72, Kindra Clineff. Chapter 5: Downtown Boston: 75, Stuart Pearce / age fotostock. 77, Kindra Clineff. 78, Stephen Orsillo/Shutterstock. 79, Danita Delimont / Alamy. 81, Kindra Clineff. 83, Hannu J.A. Aaltonen/Shutterstock. 85, Konstantin L/Shutterstock. Chapter 6: Back Bay and the South End: 89, Kindra Clineff. 91, Kindra Clineff. 92, Kindra Clineff. 95, Kindra Clineff. 96, Chee-Onn Leong/Shutterstock. 98, Kindra Clineff. 104, Kindra Clineff. Chapter 7: The Fenway: 107, Israel Pabon/Shutterstock. 109, Kindra Clineff. 110, Museum of Fine Arts, Boston. 111, Museum of Fine Arts, Boston. 112, Isabella Stewart Gardner Museum, Boston. 113, Kindra Clineff. 114, Allie_Caulfield/Flickr. 115, Museum of Fine Arts, Boston. Chapter 8: Boston Outskirts: 117, Frank Siteman / age fotostock. 119, Kindra Clineff. 120, Iwan Baan. 122, Kindra Clineff.Chapter 9: Cambridge: 125, Steve Dunwell / age fotostock. 127, Kindra Clineff. 128, Ming Vandenberg, www.hmnh.harvard.edu. 130, Harvard Crimson. 133, Kindra Clineff. 142, Jorge Salcedo/Shutterstock. Chapter 10: Where to Eat: 145, Kindra Clineff. 146, Stephi's on Tremont. 154, Kindra Clineff. 155 (top), davidburn/Flickr. 155 (bottom), psd/Flickr. 163, StarChefs.com. 168, Kindra Clineff. 169 (top), Kindra Clineff. 169 (bottom), MASA 24 by Oscar Rohena; http://www.flickr.com/photos/oscalito/643766437/; Attribution License. 170, Izzy Berdan. 172, Adam Gesuero. 177, Annie Libby / Alamy. 178, Kindra Clineff. Chapter 11: Where to Stay: 197, The Charles Hotel. 198, Fairmont Hotels & Resorts. 203 (top), Michael Weschler Photography. 203 (bottom), Boston Harbor Hotel. 216 (top), Charlesmark Hotel. 216 (bottom), Warren Jagger. 219 (top), Fairmont Hotels & Resorts. 219 (bottom), Michael J Lee Photography LLC. 226 (top), Hotel Commonwealth. 226 (bottom), The Charles Hotel. Chapter 12: Nightlife and the Arts: 233, John Coletti / age fotostock. 236, James Cridland/Flickr. 249, John Coletti / age fotostock. 257, gkristo/Flickr. 264, MCC Dave Kaylor/Wikimedia Commons. 267, Clive Grainger. Chapter 12: Sports and the Outdoors: 271, Kindra Clineff. 272, ChrisDag/Flickr. 273 (top), Kindra Clineff. 273 (bottom), Kindra Clineff. 274, Kindra Clineff. 276, Kindra Clineff. 278, Kindra Clineff. 283, Kindra Clineff. 285, Kindra Clineff. 287, Kindra Clineff. Chapter 13: Shopping: 291, dk / Alamy. 294, Kim Karpeles / Alamy. 295, nicholas bird / Alamy. 296, Steve Dunwell / age fotostock. 297, Kindra Clineff. 298, Flock. 299, AndWat/Flickr. 300, chensiyuan/Wikimedia Commons, 301, Vespasian / Alamy. 302, Kindra Clineff. 306, Kindra Clineff. 309, Megapress / Alamy. 317, Kindra Clineff. 318, Danita Delimont / Alamy. Chapter 14: Side Trips: 323, Kindra Clineff. 324, Kindra Clineff. 325 (top), Kindra Clineff. 325 (bottom), Kindra Clineff. 328, Kindra Clineff. 335, Kindra Clineff. 336, Public Domain. 341, Kindra Clineff. 343, Raymond Forbes / age fotostock. 346, Kindra Clineff. 349, Kindra Clineff, 352, Kindra Clineff. 356, Kindra Clineff. 360, Nantucket Historical Association. 361, Michael S. Nolan / age fotostock. 362, Kindra Clineff. 363 (left), Random House, Inc. 363 (top right), Kindra Clineff, 363 (center right), Penobscot Marine Museum. 363 (bottom right), Kindra Clineff. 365, Jeff Greenberg / age fotostock. 368, Kindra Clineff.

NOTES

NOTES

ABOUT OUR WRITERS

Former Fodor's production editor, Bethany Beckerlegge, enjoyed getting back to her roots for this project. A native of Massachusetts, this Connecticut-based writer and editor rediscovered her favorite Beantown haunts while updating *Boston 2012*. When not on assignment, Bethany and her husband Robb travel the coasts of Maine, New Hampshire, and Connecticut with their son, Andy.

Amanda Knorr is the founder of Spreedia, an online boutique guide for Boston and Cambridge. Knorr also serves as style and beauty editor for the *Improper Bostonian*. Raised in New York, she received her B.A. in Journalism from Boston University and has lived in Boston for 7 years now. She updated the Shopping chapter and wrote the shopping spotlights.

When she's not traveling on assignment for Fodor's and assorted other publications, freelancer Susan MacCallum-Whitcomb makes her home in Halifax, Nova Scotia. But she remains proud of her New England roots. Susan's family has been bouncing back and forth across the Canada/U.S. border since 1662, and she returns to Boston as often as possible to visit two of her relatives—Anne Hutchinson and Mary Dyer—both of whom are immortalized in bronze outside the State House. Susan updated the Experience chapter for *Boston 2012*.

Lisa Oppenheimer updated Where to Eat for *Boston 2012*.